# Marketing Channel Strategy

Eighth Edition

Global Edition

# Marketing Channel Strategy

## Robert W. Palmatier
*University of Washington's Foster School of Business*

## Louis W. Stern
*Northwestern University's Kellogg School of Management*

## Adel I. El-Ansary
*University of North Florida's Coggin College of Business*

Boston   Columbus   Indianapolis   New York   San Francisco   Upper Saddle River
Amsterdam   Cape Town   Dubai   London   Madrid   Milan   Munich   Paris   Montréal   Toronto
Delhi   Mexico City   São Paulo   Sydney   Hong Kong   Seoul   Singapore   Taipei   Tokyo

**Editor in Chief:** Stephanie Wall
**Acquisitions Editor:** Mark Gaffney
**Senior Acquisitions Editor, Global Editions:**
Steven Jackson
**Project Editor, Global Editions:**
Suchismita Ukil
**Program Manager Team Lead:** Ashley Santora
**Program Manager:** Jennifer M. Collins
**Director of Marketing:** Maggie Moylen
**Executive Marketing Manager:**
Anne Fahlgren
**Project Manager Team Lead:** Judy Leale
**Project Manager:** Thomas Benfatti

**Head of Learning Asset Acquisition, Global Editions:** Laura Dent
**Media Producer, Global Editions:** M. Vikram Kumar
**Senior Manufacturing Controller, Production, Global Editions:** Trudy Kimber
**Operations Specialist:** Nancy Maneri
**Cover Photo:** © Karyna Che/Shutterstock
**Creative Director:** Jayne Conte
**Digital Production Project Manager:**
Lisa Rinaldi
**Full-Service Project Vendor:** Anandakrishnan Natarajan/Integra Software Services

Credits and acknowledgments borrowed from other sources and reproduced, with permission, in this textbook appear on appropriate page within text (or on page 19).

Pearson Education Limited
Edinburgh Gate
Harlow
Essex CM20 2JE
England

and Associated Companies throughout the world

Visit us on the World Wide Web at:
www.pearsonglobaleditions.com

© Pearson Education Limited 2015

The rights of Robert W. Palmatier, Louis W. Stern, and Adel El-Ansary to be identified as the authors of this work have been asserted by them in accordance with the Copyright, Designs and Patents Act 1988.

Authorized adaptation from the United States edition, entitled Marketing Channel Strategy, 8th edition, ISBN 978-0-13-335708-0, by Robert W. Palmatier, Louis W. Stern, and Adel El-Ansary, published by Pearson Education © 2015.

ISBN 10: 1-292-06046-8
ISBN 13: 978-1-292-06046-0

British Library Cataloguing-in-Publication Data
A catalogue record for this book is available from the British Library

10 9 8 7 6 5 4 3 2 1
14

Typeset in 10/12 ITC Garamond by Integra Software Services

Printed and bound by Courier/Westford in The United States of America

*This book is dedicated to my wife Kimberley and
my daughter Alexandra, with much love and thanks.*

*Robert W. Palmatier*

*To the love of my life, Rhona, with whom life has been
exciting, challenging, surprising, and, above all, loving.*

*Louis W. Stern*

*To my family, the guiding lights of my life, wife Stephana,
sons Waleed and Tarik, stepdaughters Johanna and Stephanie,
and grandchildren Noor, Boody, Haya, and Isabelle.*

*Adel I. El-Ansary*

# BRIEF CONTENTS

**PART I    Introduction**

Chapter 1      Understanding Channel Strategies    31

**PART II   Designing Channel Strategies**

Chapter 2      End-User Analysis: Segmenting and Targeting    64

Chapter 3      Channel Analysis: Auditing Marketing Channels    83

Chapter 4      Make-or-Buy Channel Analysis    125

Chapter 5      Designing Channel Structures and Strategies    155

**PART III  Channel Structures and Strategies**

Chapter 6      Retailing Structures and Strategies    193

Chapter 7      Wholesaling Structures and Strategies    236

Chapter 8      Franchising Structures and Strategies    262

Chapter 9      Emerging Channel Structures and Strategies    294

**PART IV  Implementing Channel Strategies**

Chapter 10     Managing Channel Power    320

Chapter 11     Managing Channel Conflict    350

Chapter 12     Managing Channel Relationships    381

Chapter 13     Managing Channel Policies and Legalities    412

Chapter 14     Managing Channel Logistics    448

# CONTENTS

*Preface   19*
*About the Author   25*

## PART I   Introduction

Chapter 1   **Understanding Channel Strategies   31**

The Importance of Marketing Channel Strategies   31

What Is a Marketing Channel Strategy?   33

Who Participates in Marketing Channels?   33

Manufacturers: Upstream Channel Members   34

Intermediaries: Middle Channel Members   35

End-Users: Downstream Channel Members   36

Combinations of Channel Members   36

Why Do Marketing Channels Exist?   36

Benefits for Downstream Channel Members   36

Benefits to Upstream Channel Members   38

■ SIDEBAR 1-1  Tea selling in Taiwan: The key roles of tea intermediaries   41

What Are the Key Functions Marketing Channels Perform?   42

Channel Strategy Framework   44

End-User Analysis: Segmentation and Targeting   46

Channel Analysis: Auditing Marketing Channels   48

Make-or-Buy Channel Analysis   49

Designing Channel Structures and Strategies   49

Benchmarking Traditional and Emerging Channel Systems   51

Implementing Channel Strategies   52

▶ Take-Aways   **54**

*Endnotes   55*

*Appendix   56*

## PART II   Designing Channel Strategies

Chapter 2   **End-User Analysis: Segmenting and Targeting   64**

Understanding the Importance of Segmentation   65

■ SIDEBAR 2-1  CDW and PC purchases by small to medium-sized business buyers   65

End-User Segmentation Criteria: Service Outputs   67

Bulk Breaking   67

Spatial Convenience   68

Waiting Time   68

Product Variety and Assortment   69

Customer Service   70

Information Sharing   71

Segmenting End-Users by Service Outputs   72

Targeting End-User Segments   75

▶ Take-Aways   **77**

*Endnotes   77*

*Appendix   79*

**Chapter 3   Channel Analysis: Auditing Marketing Channels   83**

Channel Audit Criteria: Channel Functions   84

■ **SIDEBAR 3-1**   CDW and PC purchases by small and medium-sized business buyers: Channel functions and equity principle insights   86

■ **SIDEBAR 3-2**   Reverse logistics: Channel functions for returned merchandise   90

Auditing Channels Using the Efficiency Template   96

Evaluating Channels: The Equity Principle   100

Evaluating Channels: Zero-Based Channel Concept   101

Auditing Channels Using Gap Analysis   103

Sources of Channel Gaps   103

Service Gaps   105

Cost Gaps   106

Combining Channel Gaps   108

Evaluating Channels: Gap Analysis Template   111

▶ Take-Aways   **115**

*Endnotes   117*

*Appendix   119*

**Chapter 4   Make-or-Buy Channel Analysis   125**

Trade-Offs of Vertical Integration   127

Degrees of Vertical Integration   127

Costs and Benefits of Make-or-Buy Channels   128

Payment Options for Buying Marketing Channels   129

■ **SIDEBAR 4-1**   Vertical integration forward: Harder than it looks   130

Make-or-Buy Channel Options: The Buying Perspective   131

Return on Investment: The Primary Criterion   132

Buying or Outsourcing Channels as the Base Case   132

Six Reasons to Outsource Distribution   133

Make-or-Buy Channel Options: The Making Perspective   136

The Role of Company-Specific Capabilities   137

Six Company-Specific Distribution Capabilities   140

■ **SIDEBAR 4-2** Battle of the Greek yoghurts   142

Vertically Integrating to Deal with Thin Markets   144

Vertically Integrating to Cope with Environmental Uncertainty   145

Vertically Integrating to Reduce Performance Ambiguity   147

Vertically Integrating to Learn from Customers   148

Channel Members Integrating Upstream   149

■ **SIDEBAR 4-3** A retailer loses focus by integrating backward   149

Summary: Make-or-Buy Decision Framework   150

▶ Take-Aways   **151**

Endnotes   153

Chapter 5   **Designing Channel Structures and Strategies   155**

Channel Intensity Decisions   157

Downstream Channel Members' Perspective on Intensive
Distribution   157

■ **SIDEBAR 5-1** Big Boys Toys   160

Upstream Channel Members' Perspective on Intensive
Distribution   161

Channel Competition to Prevent Complacency (Factor 1)   164

Product Category (Factor 2)   165

Brand Strategy: Premium and Niche Positioning (Factor 3)   167

■ **SIDEBAR 5-2** A unique art of expansion   168

Channel Influence (Factor 4)   170

Dependence Balancing (Factor 5)   173

Opportunity Cost (Factor 6)   175

Transaction Costs (Factor 7)   176

Other Manufacturers' Strategies (Factor 8)   177

Channel Type Decisions   179

■ **SIDEBAR 5-3** Tupperware's retail channels cannibalize the party   180

Dual Distribution Decisions   181

The Demonstration Argument   182

Carrier-Rider Relationships   183

Closing Channel Gaps   184

Closing Service Gaps   184

Closing Cost Gaps   185

Closing Gaps Produced by Environmental or Managerial
Bounds   186

Summary: Designing Effective Channel Structures
and Strategies   187

▶ Take-Aways   **189**

Endnotes   190

# PART III   Channel Structures and Strategies

Chapter 6   **Retailing Structures and Strategies   193**
Retail Structures   194
Retail Positioning Strategies   204
  Cost-Side Positioning Strategies   204
    ■ **SIDEBAR 6-1** Zara: A European retailer using the low-margin, high-turnover model of retailing   205
    ■ **SIDEBAR 6-2** H&M: Another low-margin, high-turnover European retailer, with a different channel strategy   207
  Demand-Side Positioning Strategies   209
  Taxonomy of Retail Positioning Strategies   212
Multichannel Retail Strategies   215
  Internet Retail Channel   215
  Direct Selling Channel   216
  Hybrid Retail Channels   219
Adapting to the Increasing Power of Major Retailers   220
  Effects of Forward Buying   223
  Effects of Slotting Allowances   223
  Effects of Failure Fees   224
  Effects of Private Branding   224
  Effects of Globalization of Retailing   225
Summary: Retailing Structures and Strategies   227
  ▶ Take-Aways   **227**
    *Endnotes   228*
    *Appendix   230*

Chapter 7   **Wholesaling Structures and Strategies   236**
Wholesaling Structures   236
  Wholesaler-Distributors   237
  Master Distributors   238
  Other Supply Chain Participants   240
Wholesaling Strategies   241
  An Historical Perspective on Wholesaling Strategy   242
  Wholesaling Value-Added Strategies   243
  Wholesaling Strategies in Foreign Markets   244
    ■ **SIDEBAR 7-1** Export trading companies   245
  Wholesaling Strategies in Emerging Economies   245
  Alliance-Based Wholesaling Strategies   248
    ■ **SIDEBAR 7-2** Co-operative Group   250
    ■ **SIDEBAR 7-3** Egypt's first female cooperative   252

Consolidation Strategies in Wholesaling    253

Adapting to Trends in Wholesaling    255

International Expansion    255

Electronic Commerce    255

B2B Online Exchanges    256

Online Reverse Auctions    257

Fee for Services    257

Vertical Integration of Manufactures into Wholesaling    258

Summary: Wholesaling Structures and Strategies    259

▶ Take-Aways    259

*Endnotes    260*

Chapter 8  **Franchising Structures and Strategies    262**

Franchising Structures    264

Benefits to Franchisees    264

■ **SIDEBAR 8-1**  McDonald's    265

Benefits to Franchisor    269

Another View: Reasons Not to Franchise    274

Franchising Strategies    275

Product and Trade Name Franchising Strategies    275

■ **SIDEBAR 8-2**  ADA discovers the benefits of franchisees    275

Business Format Franchising Strategy    276

Franchise Contracting Strategies    276

Company Store Strategies    282

Adapting to Trends in Franchising    286

Survival Trends    286

Multiunit Franchising    288

Summary: Franchising Structures and Strategies    289

▶ Take-Aways    **291**

*Endnotes    291*

Chapter 9  **Emerging Channel Structures and Strategies    294**

Trends Influencing Marketing Channels    294

Channel Strategies for Services    295

Drivers of the Shift to Services    295

Effect of Key Service Characteristics on Channel Strategies    297

Effects of Product Aspects on Channel Strategies    300

Effects of Acquiring Service Capabilities, Infrastructure, and
Knowledge    301

■ **SIDEBAR 9-1**  Fujitsu and Federal Express build a close relationship    302

Channel Members' Responses to Service Transition
Strategies    303

Channel Strategies for Globalization    303
Drivers of Globalization    304
Effects of Globalization on Channel Strategies    305
Channel Strategies for E-Commerce    309
Drivers of Increased E-Commerce    309
■ **SIDEBAR 9-2** Souq.com, the Arabian e-commerce dream    310
Effects of E-Commerce on Channel Strategies    313
■ **SIDEBAR 9-3** Channel conflict and Internet Commerce    314
Hierarchical Multichannel Strategies    314
Summary: Emerging Channel Structures and Strategies    316
▶ Take-Aways    **317**
*Endnotes*    *318*

## PART IV    Implementing Channel Strategies

Chapter 10    **Managing Channel Power    320**
The Nature of Power    320
Power Defined    321
Power as a Tool    322
The Need to Manage Channel Power    323
The Five Sources of Channel Power    324
Reward Power    325
Coercive Power    325
Expert Power    326
■ **SIDEBAR 10-1** Retailers build expertise power over suppliers    327
■ **SIDEBAR 10-2** The mystery shopper    328
Legitimate Power    329
Referent Power    331
■ **SIDEBAR 10-3** Patent wars    332
Grouping the Five Power Sources    333
Summary of Power Sources    334
Dependence as the Mirror Image of Power    334
Defining Dependence    334
■ **SIDEBAR 10-4** New market channels for Malaysian retailers    335
Measuring Dependence    336
Balancing Power: A Net Dependence Perspective    338
Imbalanced Dependence    339
Power-Based Influence Strategies    341
Effectiveness of Six Influence Strategies    342
Framing Influence Strategies    344

Summary: Managing Channel Power    335
▶ Take-Aways    **346**
*Endnotes    347*

**Chapter 11    Managing Channel Conflict    350**

The Nature of Channel Conflict    350
Types of Conflict    351
Measuring Conflict    352
Consequences of Conflict    353
Functional Conflict: Improving Channel Performance    353
■ **SIDEBAR 11-1**  Functional conflict in plumbing and heating supplies    354
Manifest Conflict: Reducing Channel Performance    355
Major Sources of Conflict in Channels    356
Competing Goals    356
Differing Perceptions of Reality    357
Intrachannel Competition    359
Multiple Channels    359
Unwanted Channels: Gray Markets    363
Minimizing the (Negative) Effects of Channel Conflict    365
Reducing the Use of Threats    366
Intolerance of Conflict in Balanced Relationships    366
■ **SIDEBAR 11-2**  Apple, Hong Kong, and parallel imports    367
Mitigating the Effects of Conflict in Balanced Relationships    368
Perceived Unfairness: Aggravating the Effects
of Conflicts    369
Conflict Resolution Strategies    370
Forestalling Conflict Through Institutionalization    370
Ongoing Conflict Resolution Styles    372
Using Incentives to Resolve Conflict    374
Summary: Managing Channel Conflict    375
▶ Take-Aways    **376**
*Endnotes    377*

**Chapter 12    Managing Channel Relationships    381**

The Nature of Channel Relationships    381
Upstream Motives for Building a Strong Channel
Relationship    383
■ **SIDEBAR 12-1**  South Africa's MWEB goes Spanish    384
Downstream Motives for Building a Strong Channel
Relationship    386
Effectiveness of Strong Channel Relationships    387

Building Channel Commitment   389
  Need for Expectations of Continuity   389
  Need for Reciprocation: Mutual Commitment   390
  Strategies for Building Commitment   392
Building Channel Trust   394
  Need for Economic Satisfaction   395
  ■ **SIDEBAR 12-2**  Philip Morris substitutes channels for advertising   396
  Strategies for Building Channel Partners' Trust   396
The Channel Relationship Life cycle   400
  The Five Stages of a Channel Relationships   400
  Managing the Stages   403
  Managing Troubled Relationships   404
  Relationship Portfolios   405
Summary: Managing Channel Relationships   406
  ▶ Take-Aways   407
Endnotes   408

Chapter 13  **Managing Channel Policies and Legalities   412**
Market Coverage Policies   413
  ■ **SIDEBAR 13-1**  Continental TV v. GTE Sylvania   414
Customer Coverage Policies   416
Pricing Policies   418
  Price Maintenance   418
  ■ **SIDEBAR 13-2**  Monsanto v. Spray-Rite   419
  ■ **SIDEBAR 13-3**  Business Electronics Corp. v. Sharp Electronics   420
  ■ **SIDEBAR 13-4**  Albrecht v. Herald and State Oil Co. v. Khan   421
  Price Discrimination   422
  ■ **SIDEBAR 13-5**  Liggett & Myers v. Brown & Williamson   424
  ■ **SIDEBAR 13-6**  Texaco v. Hasbrouck   429
Product Line Policies   429
  Exclusive Dealing   429
  ■ **SIDEBAR 13-7**  Tampa Electric Co. v. Nashville Coal Co.   431
  Tying   432
  ■ **SIDEBAR 13-8**  Jefferson Parish Hospital District No. 2 v. Hyde   433
  ■ **SIDEBAR 13-9**  Eastman Kodak Co. v. Image Technical Service, Inc.   435
  Full-Line Forcing   435
  Designated Product Policies   436
  ■ **SIDEBAR 13-10**  U.S. Federal Trade Commission v. Toys 'R US   436
Selection and Termination Policies   437
Ownership Policies   439
  Vertical Integration by Merger   439

Vertical Integration by Internal Expansion   440

Dual Distribution   440

Summary: Managing Channel Policies and Legalities   441

▶ Take-Aways   **442**

Endnotes   444

Chapter 14   **Managing Channel Logistics   448**

Impact of Channel Logistics and Supply Chain Management   448

■ **SIDEBAR 14-1** Reverse logistics   449

Efficient Channel Logistics   450

Efficient Consumer Response   451

Barriers to Efficient Consumer Response   452

Quick Response Logistics   453

Barriers to Quick Response   454

■ **SIDEBAR 14-2** Zara, the quick response master   455

Supply Chain Strategies   457

Physical Efficiency Versus Market Responsiveness   457

Effective Supply Chain Management   458

■ **SIDEBAR 14-3** How to build triple-A supply chains   460

Summary: Managing Channel Logistics   460

▶ Take-Aways   461

Endnotes   462

Name Index   465

Subject Index   472

Company Index   491

# PREFACE

## NEW TO THIS EDITION

The primary goal for this Eighth Edition, as reflected in the change in the title—from Marketing Channels to Marketing Channel Strategy—has been to create a comprehensive, research-based, action-oriented guide for practicing managers and managers-in-training with an interest in how to adopt and apply real-world channel strategies. This edition of the book is structured to provide background knowledge and process steps for understanding, designing, and implementing high-performing channel strategies.

Other significant changes to this edition include the following:

- A new channel strategy framework, introduced in Chapter 1, defines the structure of the rest of this book, providing a structured approach that guides managers through the steps necessary for evaluating an existing marketing channel strategy or for developing and implementing a new one. A new figure offers a visual representation of this approach (see Figure 1-3).
- To provide a foundation for developing channel strategies, three newly formulated chapters each support a specific stand-alone analysis that is critical for designing an effective channel strategy:
  - End-user analysis in Chapter 2
  - Channel analysis and audits in Chapter 3
  - Make-or-buy analysis in Chapter 4
- A completely revised Chapter 5, on designing channel structures and strategies, integrates material from multiple chapters in the previous edition together with new material, to walk readers through three key channel design decisions. The revised chapter also offers a new perspective on the eight factors that influence the intensity versus selectivity trade-off and its effects on channel strategy.
- Chapter 9 is completely new. It focuses on the emerging channel structures and strategies that result from dramatic changes in the business environment, such as the shift from products to services, the globalization of firms and industries, and increases in e-commerce. These changes are causing new channel systems to emerge, with the potential of disrupting many tradition channel institutions.
- Chapter 12, now titled "Managing Channel Relationships," offers an increased emphasis on the role of strong relationships in successful channel management. Recent academic research added to this chapter cites the key influence of relationship velocity on future channel performance and the detrimental effect of perceived unfairness in channels.
- Noting the increasing importance of information and knowledge sharing for channel success, we have integrated information-sharing notions and applications throughout the book as a key channel function. Thus, information sharing appears within the efficiency templates in Chapter 3, demonstrated with new examples related to CDW and building materials.
- Some of the most dramatic changes in retail structures and strategies for the top 250 global retailers, due to globalization and consolidation, are outlined in

Chapter 6. The fundamental shift to e-commerce in many product categories is also highlighted throughout the book (e.g., music, books), along with the necessary shifts in strategy.

Overall, *Marketing Channel Strategy* is designed for an international audience of managers and managers-in-training. The focus is firmly on marketing channel strategy, that is, the set of activities focused on designing and managing a marketing channel to enhance the firm's sustainable competitive advantage and financial performance. More simply, companies and processes come together to bring products and services from their point of origin to their point of consumption. Through marketing channels, the originator of the products or services gains access to markets and end-users. Channel structures and strategies thus are critical to any firm's long-term success.

The book features examples taken from around the world and from a range of industries and markets. However, the ideas and processes generalize to virtually any context and channel situations. Sidebars appear in every chapter to highlight key channel issues and strategies and provide concrete examples of the theories, processes, and ideas presented in the text.

Each chapter is also designed to stand on its own. The chapters are modular, so they can be combined with other material and used in various classes for which channels play an important role (e.g., service marketing, marketing strategy, sales management, business-to-business marketing). The content of each chapter reflects leading academic research and practice in distinct disciplines (e.g., marketing, strategy, economics, sociology, political science).

Beyond this modular design, the four major parts of this book reflect some overriding themes. Part I consists of just one chapter, which introduces the basic ideas and concepts underlying channel strategy. To help channel managers design a strategy and then manage it over time, Chapter 1 addresses some central channel questions:

- Why are marketing channels important?
- What is a marketing channel strategy?
- Who participates in a marketing channel?
- Why do marketing channels exist?
- What are the key functions performed by marketing channels?

The answers suggest that a marketing channel strategy entails three stages: (1) analyzing and designing, (2) benchmarking, and (3) implementation or management. Parts II–IV address each of these stages in turn.

In particular, Part II, Designing Channel Strategies, comprises four chapters that describe how to align the needs of upstream and downstream members of the channel to enable all the parties to work together to meet target end-users' demands, at minimum cost. We start with a detailed discussion of how to employ an end-user analysis to segment markets, in accordance with end-users' needs, and then select certain segment(s) to target (Chapter 2). In Chapter 3, we outline methods for evaluating existing channels by auditing their efficiency and potential service or cost gaps. These two analysis steps lead into the task of determining whether to perform channel functions in-house or outsourced, so Chapter 4 describes the make-or-buy channel analysis. Finally, we summarize the design phase, as it appears with regard to three design questions: the degree of channel intensity, the mix of channel types, and the use of dual distribution (Chapter 5).

With Part III, Channel Structure and Strategies, we provide the means for channel managers to understand some of the most common channel structures and strategies: retailing (Chapter 6), wholesaling (Chapter 7), and franchising (Chapter 8). With such an understanding, managers can identify best practices to integrate into their new or revised channel systems, as well as compare their own channel structure and strategy with previously developed channel systems. This section thus provides lessons learned by previous channel managers, helps today's readers avoid the same common mistakes, and allows them to take advantage of known channel efficiencies. Finally, Chapter 9 offers guidelines to help managers address and design creative, emerging channel structures and strategies, in accordance with constantly changing business environments.

Finally, Part IV, Implementing Channel Strategies, focuses on the five factors that lead to optimal channel management and help ensure ongoing channel success. Specifically, channel managers need to identify and work with the source of each channel member's power and dependence (Chapter 10), as well as recognize and avoid potential channel conflict (Chapter 11), so that they can build and maintain good working relationships among channel partners (Chapter 12). The last two chapters detail how to manage channel policies and legalities (Chapter 13) and logistics (Chapter 14), and thus maintain the effectiveness and efficiency of the channel system.

The framework presented in this book is thus useful for creating a new channel strategy in a previously untapped market, as well as for critically analyzing and refining a preexisting channel strategy. Supporting materials for this textbook are available to adopting instructors through our instructors' resource center (IRC) online at www.pearsonglobaleditions.com/Palmatier.

# ACKNOWLEDGMENTS

The authors express their appreciation to Erin Anderson for her past efforts on this book and the deep insights into channel strategy she provided. Her passing was a loss to her family, to us, and to the academic discipline.

Rob Palmatier thanks the authors of previous editions of this book, including the founding authors, Lou Stern and Adel El-Ansary, whose efforts made this book possible, as well as Anne Coughlan for her extraordinary efforts and contributions to the core knowledge offered by this text. He is also very grateful to Charles and Gwen Lillis for their generous support of the Foster School of Business and his research activities, which helped make this edition possible. In addition, he also appreciates his colleagues and doctoral students, whose ongoing insights into channel research have helped inform this revision in multiple ways: Todd Arnold, Inigo Arroniz, Joshua T. Beck, Kevin Bradford, Steven Brown, Robert Carter, Fred C. Ciao, Daniel Claro, Rajiv P. Dant, Kenneth R. Evans, Eric Fang, Shankar Ganesan, Gabriel Gonzalez, Morris George, Srinath Gopalakrishna, Dhruv Grewal, Rajiv Grewal, Sujan Harish, Colleen Harmeling, Conor Henderson, Mark B. Houston, Gary Hunter, Sandy Jap, Cheryl Jarvis, Frank R. Kardes, Irina V. Kozlenkova, Ju-Yeon Lee, Vincent Onyemah, Dominique Rouzies, Stephen Samaha, Lisa K. Scheer, Arun Sharma, Shrihari Sridhar, Rosann Spiro, Jan-Benedict E.M. Steenkamp, Lena Steinhoff, George F. Watson IV, Bart Weitz, and Jonathan Zhang.

Lou Stern would like to acknowledge the support, encouragement, and friendship of his Northwestern University marketing department colleagues over a long period of time who have never waivered in their enthusiasm for his work. He is especially grateful to Anne Coughlan who shouldered a number of revisions of the text along with his dear, late friend, Erin Anderson of Insead. His greatest debt is, however, owed to his doctoral students at Northwestern and Ohio State (one of whom, Adel El-Ansary, has been his coauthor on this text for more than 40 years) who kept him current, intellectually stimulated, and enthusiastic throughout his career. And his appreciation of Rob Palmatier is unbounded. Rob agreed to take the leadership on this edition and, by doing so, to keep the text alive for future generations of students who find the study of marketing channels fascinating, challenging, and rewarding. Lou's gratitude for what he has done is infinite.

Adel El-Ansary would like to acknowledge the intellectual exchange and friendship of faculty colleagues of the Inter-organizational and Relationship Marketing Special Interest Groups, Academic Division of the American Marketing Association and the Board of Governance, Distinguished Fellows, and Leadership Group of the Academy of Marketing Science. His greatest debt is, however, owed to his mentors at the Ohio State University. William R. Davidson and the late Robert Bartels fueled his interest in the study of marketing. Lou Stern sparked his interest in marketing channels, leading to a lifetime of intellectual inquiry and partnership on the text for over 40 years. Rob Palmatier is a leader of the field. His taking charge, commencing with this edition of *Marketing Channel Strategy*, extends the life of the brand and ensures that future generations of students will be informed of the importance of the role of channels in marketing and society.

Finally, we are indebted to the vast number of authors whose work we cite throughout this text. Without their efforts, we could not have written this book.

***Robert W. Palmatier***
*Seattle, Washington*

***Louis W. Stern***
*Evanston, Illinois*

***Adel I. El-Ansary***
*Jacksonville, Florida*

Pearson would like to thank and acknowledge the following people for their work on the Global Edition:

Contributors
Hamed Shamma, The American University in Cairo, Egypt
Jon and Diane Sutherland, Writers, U.K.

Reviewers
David Brown, Northumbria University, U.K.
Gabriella Kereszturi, Regent's University, U.K.
Varat Kamolchotiros, Assumption University, Thailand

# ABOUT THE AUTHORS

Robert W. Palmatier is Professor of Marketing, and he holds the John C. Narver Chair of Business Administration at the University of Washington's Foster School of Business. He earned his bachelor's and master's degrees in Electrical Engineering from Georgia Institute of Technology, as well as an MBA from Georgia State University and his doctoral degree from the University of Missouri. He did a one year post doctoral study at Northwestern University's Kellogg School of Management. Prior to entering academia, Professor Palmatier held various industry positions, including President and Chief Operating Officer of C&K Components and European General Manager and Sales & Marketing Manager at Tyco-Raychem Corporation. He also served as a U.S. Navy Lieutenant onboard nuclear submarines.

Professor Palmatier's research interests focus on relationship marketing, channels, and marketing strategy. His research has appeared in *Journal of Marketing, Journal of Marketing Research, Marketing Science, Journal of Retailing, Journal of Consumer Psychology, Journal of Academy of Marketing Science, Marketing Letters, International Journal of Research in Marketing,* and *Industrial Marketing Management.* He has also published a monograph entitled *Relationship Marketing* and chapters in various texts, including *Channel Relationships, Relationship Marketing, Anti-Relationship Marketing: Understanding Relationship Destroying Behaviors,* and *Understanding the Relational Ecosystem in a Connected World.* His research has also been featured in *The New York Times* Magazine, *Electrical Wholesaling, Agency Sales,* and *The Representor,* as well as on *NPR* and *MSNBC.*

In addition to serving as an area editor for *Journal of Marketing,* Professor Palmatier sits on the editorial review boards for *Journal of the Academy of Marketing Science, Journal of Retailing,* and *Journal of Business-to-Business Marketing.* His publications have received multiple awards, including the Harold H. Maynard, Louis W. Stern, and the American Marketing Association Best Services Article awards. He also received the Varadarajan Award for Early Contribution to Marketing Strategy Research. He teaches marketing strategy in the doctoral, EMBA, and MBA programs at the University of Washington. He has received numerous teaching awards including the Robert M. Bowen EMBA Excellence in Teaching Awards, MBA Professor of the Year Award, and PhD Student Mentoring Awards.

Among the numerous industry and governmental committees on which Professor Palmatier has served, he chaired proposal selection committees for the National Research Council (NRC), National Academy of Sciences (NAS), and the Wright Centers of Innovation, which awarded grants of $20 million for the development of a new Wright Center of Innovation based on joint academic–industry proposals. He has served on NASA's Computing, Information, and Communications Advisory Group, with the AMES Research Center. This advisory group assesses the current state of technology development within academia, governmental agencies, and industry related to NASA's information technology activities and space exploration requirements; recommends future investment areas; and outlines a sustainable process to ensure optimal investment strategies and technology portfolios for NASA's Space Exploration Enterprise. He has also consulted for numerous firms including Microsoft, Emerson, Telstra, Fifth Third Bank, Littelfuse, Cisco, Wells Fargo, Premera, and Manufacturers' Representative Educational Research Foundation.

Professor Palmatier lives in Seattle, Washington, with his wife Kimberley and daughter Alexandra.

Louis W. Stern is the John D. Gray Distinguished Professor Emeritus of Marketing at the Kellogg School of Management of Northwestern University. Professor Stern joined the Northwestern faculty in 1973. Prior to that, he was Professor of Marketing at the Ohio State University. He was appointed to the Ohio State faculty in 1963 after having spent two years at the industrial research firm Arthur D. Little, Inc., Cambridge, Massachusetts. From January 1965 until June 1966, he served as a principal economist for the National Commission on Food Marketing in Washington, D.C., and during the 1969–1970 academic year, he was a visiting associate professor of business administration at the University of California, Berkeley. From 1977 to 1980, he served as chairman of the Department of Marketing at Northwestern, and from 1983 to 1985, he was Executive Director of the Marketing Science Institute, Cambridge, Massachusetts. During the 1984–1985 academic year, he was the Thomas Henry Carroll Ford Foundation Visiting Professor at Harvard Business School. From 1998 to 2001, concurrent with his position at Northwestern, he was appointed a visiting scholar at the Haas School of Business at the University of California, Berkeley. From 2004 to 2006, he was designated the Dorinda and Mark Winkelman Distinguished Scholar at The Wharton School of the University of Pennsylvania, a Senior Fellow of the Wharton School, and codirector of Wharton's Jay H. Baker Retailing Initiative, positions he held in addition to the John D. Gray professorship at Kellogg.

Professor Stern's research efforts have focused on issues related to designing and managing marketing channels and on antitrust issues. His articles have appeared in a wide variety of marketing, legal, and behavioral science journals. Among the books he has coauthored are *Marketing Channels* (Prentice-Hall, 7th Ed., 2006), *Management in Marketing Channels* (Prentice-Hall, 1989), and *Legal Aspects of Marketing Strategy: Antitrust and Consumer Protection Issues* (Prentice-Hall, 1984). His article "Distribution Channels as Political Economics: A Framework for Comparative Analysis" (with Torger Reve) was named the best article on marketing theory to appear in the *Journal of Marketing* during 1980. In 1986, he received the Paul D. Converse Award from the American Marketing Association for "outstanding contribution to theory and science in marketing." In 1989, he was named "Marketing Educator of the Year" by Sales and Marketing Executives-International, and in 1990, he received the same honor from the Sales & Marketing Executives of Chicago. In 1992, he was voted "Outstanding Professor of the Year" by the students at Kellogg. He has received six times the "Outstanding Professor Award for Electives" from Kellogg's Executive Masters Program. In 1994, he was selected as the recipient of the American Marketing Association/Irwin Distinguished Marketing Educator Award, which is designed to be "the highest honor a marketing educator can receive." Also in 1994, he was named as one of the 12 best teachers in U.S. business schools by *Business Week* magazine. In 1999, his Kellogg classroom was purchased and named in his honor by his former students, friends, clients, and family. And, in June 1999, he was the first recipient of Kellogg's newly created Special Lifetime Achievement Award for Teaching Excellence.

Professor Stern has participated in distinguished lecturer/visitor series at numerous universities. He has taught at the Hernstein Institute in Vienna and at the Norwegian School of Economics and Business Administration in Bergen, and has been a faculty associate at the Management Centre Europe in Brussels. Professor Stern has served on the editorial boards of *the Journal of Marketing, the Journal of Marketing Research*, and *Marketing Letters*. He was on the Board of Directors of the Council of Better Business Bureaus, Inc., from 1978 to 1983. He was a member of the Board of Trustees of the Williston Northampton School in Easthampton, Massachusetts. He is a member of the Board of Directors of the Academy for Urban School Leadership, a non-profit organization dedicated to improving student achievement in Chicago's chronically failing schools. In addition, he is a member of the Executive Directors Council of the Marketing Science Institute.

Among the numerous business firms for which he has consulted are IBM, Ford, Hewlett-Packard, S.C. Johnson, Brunswick, Roche Laboratories, Steelcase, ExxonMobil, Xerox, Boise Cascade, Johnson & Johnson, and Motorola. He has also served as a consultant to the Federal Trade Commission and as an academic trustee of the Marketing Science Institute. Professor Stern is a member of the American Marketing Association.

Adel I. El-Ansary is the Donna L. Harper Professor of Marketing at the Coggin College of Business, University of North Florida, and Distinguished Fellow of the Academy of Marketing Science. He received the State of Florida University System Professional Excellence Award in 1999 and was named Prime Osborne, III Distinguished Professor in 2001. Prior to joining the faculty at the University of North Florida as the First Holder of the Paper and Plastics Educational Research Foundation Eminent Scholar Chair in Wholesaling, he served as professor and chairman of Business Administration at the George Washington University, Washington, D.C.

El-Ansary is a Fulbright scholar. He is coauthor of the leading text-reference book on *Marketing Channels,* first[t] through eighth[h] edition, Prentice-Hall, 1977–2015 and *E-Marketing*, third and fourth editions, Prentice-Hall, 2003 and 2006. He is a contributor to the *Encyclopedia of Marketing, Encyclopedia of Economics, American Marketing Association Marketing Encyclopedia*, and *The Logistics Handbook*. Also, he has contributed over 35 papers and articles to books and conference proceedings.

El-Ansary's research and writing contributed 18 key articles published in major journal including the *Journal of Marketing, Journal of Marketing Research, Journal of Marketing Channels, Journal of Retailing, Journal of the Academy of Marketing Science, Journal of Relationship Marketing, Journal of Macro Marketing, European Business Review, Journal of Personal Selling and Sales Management*, and *International Marketing Review.*

El-Ansary's scholarly interests are diverse but revolve around marketing systems reform to improve distribution effectiveness, efficiency, and equity with particular reference to food distribution in developing countries. He served on a sub-Presidential Mission for President Reagan's Caribbean Initiatives on improving food distribution in Central America. His teaching interest includes Marketing Channels, Marketing Strategy, Marketing on the Internet, and Global Branding Strategy and Management.

El-Ansary was on leave from the University of North Florida 1995–1996 to serve as Chief of Party of International Business and Technical consultants, Inc. in Cairo, Egypt. He was in charge of all aspects of project management for the monitoring and evaluation of the Privatization Program of the Government of Egypt funded through technical assistance provided by the U.S. Agency for International Development (U.S. AID). El-Ansary served as team leader and project coordinator, implemented, or participated in, over 20 government and international organization contracts and assignments including U.S. AID, the World Bank, and the Governments of Egypt, Saudi Arabia, Tunisia, Kuwait, and Qatar. He served on Presidents' Nixon and Ford national Advisory Council for the U.S. Small Business Administration.

El-Ansary served on the Global Council of the American Marketing Association. He is the founding chairman of the Special Interest Group in Wholesale Distribution and served as cochairman of the Relationship Marketing Interest Group of the Academic Council of the American Marketing Association. He is chartered member of the Academy of Marketing Science since its foundation in 1972 and was elected member of its Board of Governors, 1994–1998.

# Marketing Channel Strategy

CHAPTER **1**

# Understanding Channel Strategies

**LEARNING OBJECTIVES**

**After reading this chapter, you will be able to:**

- Define a marketing channel.
- Explain why manufacturers choose to use intermediaries.
- Define the marketing functions that constitute the work of the channel.
- Identify the members of marketing channels and the functions in which they specialize.
- Outline the elements of a framework for marketing channel design and implementation.

## THE IMPORTANCE OF MARKETING CHANNEL STRATEGIES

Nearly every product and service goes through multiple marketing channels before a consumer can actually purchase it. Raw materials and component products are sold by distributors and manufacturer representatives to original equipment manufacturers (OEMs); the OEMs assemble these components into finished products and services, which they sell to wholesalers and retailers; the retailers then make the products available to consumers. A marketing channel strategy thus deals specifically with how to design and manage a channel structure to ensure that the overall channel system operates efficiently and effectively. Well then, what are the reasons you should be interested in marketing channel strategies?

1. Marketing channels represent a significant portion of the world's business. *Total sales* through sales channels (e.g., retailers, wholesalers) represent approximately one-third of worldwide annual gross domestic product (GDP), which makes understanding and managing sales channels critical to most businesses.[1]
2. The channel is a *gatekeeper* between the manufacturer and the end-user. Channel partners control customer access to manufacturers' products and

services, so without an effective channel strategy, the manufacturer's products or services suffer from limited reach and a lack of attractiveness to buyers. Perhaps the largest driver of a movie's success is the number of theater screens on which it is shown; it is therefore in the interest of a movie producer to understand how theaters decide to screen movies, for how long, and on how many screens.

3. The channel *experience* determines people's perceptions of the manufacturer's brand image and thus end-user satisfaction. For example, in the automotive market, consumers who take better care of their cars actually perceive their quality to be higher, and purchasers of higher-quality cars tend to have them serviced at dealerships. These findings imply that the dealer's postsales service inputs are crucial to the brand's long-term quality image (and hence its resale price, repurchase intentions, and future consumer quality perceptions).[2]

4. As an important asset in the company's overall *marketing and positioning* strategy, the channel often serves to differentiate the company's market offering from those of its competitors. Differentiation is fundamental to building and maintaining a competitive advantage. But differentiation of what? It might be *product* or *feature differentiation*, both of which require manufacturers to focus on research, development, and innovation as keys to success. But what if the firm is selling a commodity or mature product line (i.e., products that were innovative technology leaders yesterday)? The product is just one part of the total purchase bundle for the end-user, and the services rendered by channel members are not only part of the total bundle but also often the determinant of purchases. Effective differentiation does not just depend on product features but also can occur through innovative channel offerings.

5. Finally, channels often are underutilized sources of *sustainable competitive advantage*. In many industries, the distribution process gets (erroneously) depicted as a necessary and costly evil to move products into the hands of eager end-users. But in any sort of competitive environment, a CEO or manager who recognizes the value of positioning through effective channel design, and investing in related cost efficiencies, is likely to beat the company's rivals handily.

In short, a strong channel system is a competitive asset, not easily replicated by other firms, which makes it a source of a sustainable competitive advantage. Furthermore, building or modifying the channel system involves costly, hard-to-reverse investments. Taking the effort to do it right the first time has great value; conversely, making a mistake may put the company at a long-term disadvantage.

This book examines how to design, modify, and maintain efficient, effective channel strategies and structures, in both consumer goods markets and business-to-business markets, for both physical products and services, and within nations and across country borders. In this first chapter, we define the concept of a marketing channel and discuss its purposes, including using these channels to reach the marketplace, together with the functions and activities that exist in marketing channels. We also note who participates in marketing channels and how a framework for analysis can improve channel decisions made by an executive acting as a channel manager or designer.

## WHAT IS A MARKETING CHANNEL STRATEGY?

A firm's overall marketing strategy traditionally focuses on four marketing mix elements: product, price, promotion, and channel (or "place," in the popular 4P designation). Each firm makes a series of strategic decisions to determine how to distribute its products and service to the firm's end customers. The total firm-to-end-user links make up a **marketing channel** or **marketing channel system**, defined as a set of interdependent organizations involved in the process of making a product or service available for use or consumption.

This definition bears some explication. It first highlights that a marketing channel is a *set of interdependent organizations*. That is, it cannot be limited to one firm doing its best in the market—whatever that firm's position in the channel (i.e., manufacturer, wholesaler, or retailer). Many entities generally are involved in the business, and each channel member depends on the others to do their jobs.

What are their jobs? The definition makes clear that running a marketing channel is a *process*, not an event. Distribution frequently takes time to accomplish, and even when a sale finally occurs, the relationship with the end-user is not over (consider our discussion of postsales service at a car dealership, or think about a hospital purchasing a piece of medical equipment and its perpetual demands for postsales service).

Finally, the definition suggests that the purpose of this process is to *make a product or service available for use or consumption*. That is, it is to satisfy end-users in the market, whether they are consumers or final business buyers, whose goal is the use or consumption of the product or service being sold. A manufacturer that sells through distributors to retailers, which serve final consumers, may be tempted to think that it has generated "sales" and developed "happy customers" when its sales force successfully places product in the distributors' warehouses. The definition we use in this book argues otherwise. All channel members, whatever their roles, must focus their attention on the end-user.

Business managers want to make their products and services available to customers through channels, but they also want to use marketing channels to enhance the firm's sustainable competitive advantage and financial performance. Thus, managers invest their inherently limited resources to turn their marketing channels into strategic assets that can increase customer satisfaction, reduce distribution costs, minimize competitor rivalry, and ultimately result in superior financial performance. In turn, we establish our definition of **marketing channel strategy**:

> The set of activities focused on designing and managing a marketing channel to enhance the firm's sustainable competitive advantage and financial performance.

## WHO PARTICIPATES IN MARKETING CHANNELS?

Not only can marketing channels be viewed from various perspectives, but they also often involve many different entities organized in a complex network or system. To avoid too much confusion for this book though, we identify and define three key entities involved in every marketing channel: *manufacturers*, *intermediaries* (wholesale, retail, and specialized), and *end-users* (business customers or consumers). The presence or absence of a particular type of channel member is dictated by its ability to perform the necessary channel functions in such a way that it adds value. Often there is one channel member who serves as the **channel captain**, taking the keenest interest in the workings of the channel for this product or service and acting as the prime mover in establishing and maintaining channel links. The channel captain is often the manufacturer, particularly in the case of branded products. Thus, we frequently take the manufacturer's perspective when describing a firm's marketing channel strategy. But we also acknowledge that manufacturers are not the only channel captains that can appear.

### Manufacturers: Upstream Channel Members

When we refer to **manufacturers**, we mean the producer or originator of the product or service being sold. A common distinction separates branded from private-label manufacturing:

- Manufacturers that brand their products are known by name to end-users, even if they use intermediaries to reach them, such as Coca-Cola, Budweiser beer (Anheuser-Busch), Mercedes-Benz, and Sony.
- Manufacturers that make products but do not invest in a branded name for them produce **private-label products**, and the downstream buyer (manufacturer or retailer) puts its own brand name on them. For example, Multibar Foods Inc. focuses on making private-label products for the neutraceuticals marketplace (health, diet, and snack bars); its branded clients include Dr. Atkins' Nutritionals and Quaker Oats Co. The company prides itself on its research and development, which make it valuable to brand companies that hire it to make their products.[3] Branded manufacturers sometimes choose to allocate part of their production capacity to private-label goods even though they do so at the risk of building a future competitor; in the U.K. market, private labels account for over half the goods sold in many leading supermarkets.[4]

In the modern retail marketplace, ownership of the "brand" can belong to the manufacturer (Mercedes-Benz) or the retailer (e.g., "Arizona" clothing at JCPenney). The retailer also may *be* the brand (e.g., The Gap).

A manufacturer can be the originator of a service too, such as tax preparation services offered by H&R Block (a franchisor) or insurance policies provided by State Farm or Allstate. These brands sell no physical products to end-users; rather, the manufacturers create families of services to sell, which constitutes its "manufacturing" function. In turn, their marketing channel functions typically focus on promotional or risk-oriented activities: H&R Block promotes its services on behalf of itself and its franchisees by guaranteeing to find the maximum tax refund allowed by law. The insurance companies similarly tend to ignore physical product handling and focus instead on promotion (on behalf of independent agents in the marketplace) and risk (risk management is the very heart of the insurance business). That is, the lack of a physical product to move through the channel does not mean that channel design or management issues disappear.

The examples also suggest that the manufacturer need not be the channel captain. For branded, produced goods, such as Mercedes-Benz automobiles, the manufacturer serves this role; its ability and desire to proactively manage channel efforts for its products relates intimately to its investment in the brand equity of its products. But a private-label apparel or neutraceutical manufacturer is not evidently the owner of the brand name, at least from end-users' perspectives, who instead see another channel member (in these cases, the retailer) as the owner.

The manufacturer's ability to manage production does not mean it excels in other marketing channel activities. An apparel manufacturer is not necessarily a retailing or logistics expert. But there are some activities that nearly every manufacturer must undertake. Physical product manufacturers must hold on to the product and maintain ownership of it, until the product leaves their manufacturing sites and travels to the next channel member. Manufacturers also must engage in negotiations with buyers, to set the terms of sale and merchandising of the product. The manufacturer of a branded good also participates significantly in promoting its products. Yet various intermediaries in the channel still add value through their superior performance of other functions that manufacturers cannot, so manufacturers voluntarily seek out these intermediaries to increase their reach and appeal to the end-user market.

## Intermediaries: Middle Channel Members

The term **intermediary** refers to any channel member *other* than the manufacturer or the end-user. We differentiate three general types: wholesale, retail, and specialized. **Wholesalers** include merchant wholesalers or distributors, manufacturers' representatives, agents, and brokers. A wholesaler sells to other channel intermediaries, such as retailers, or to business end-users, but not to individual consumer end-users. Chapter 7 discusses wholesaling in depth. Briefly though, we note that merchant wholesalers take title to and physical possession of inventory, store inventory (frequently from many manufacturers), promote products in their line, and arrange for financing, ordering, and payment by customers. They earn profits by buying at a wholesale price and selling at a marked-up price to downstream customers, then pocketing the difference (net of any distribution costs they bear). Manufacturers' representatives, agents, and brokers rarely take title to or physical possession of the goods they sell; rather, they engage in promotion and negotiation to sell the products of the manufacturers they represent and negotiate terms of trade for them. Some intermediaries (e.g., trading companies, import/export agents) specialize in international selling, regardless of whether they take title or physical possession.

**Retail intermediaries** come in many forms: department stores, mass merchandisers, hypermarkets, specialty stores, category killers, convenience stores, franchises, buying clubs, warehouse clubs, cataloguers, and online retailers, to name just a few. Unlike purely wholesale intermediaries, they sell directly to individual consumer end-users. Their role historically entailed amassing an assortment of goods that would appeal to consumers, but today that role has greatly expanded. Retailers might contract to produce private-label goods, such that they achieve effective vertical integration upstream in the supply chain. They also may sell to buyers other than consumers; Office Depot earns significant sales by selling to businesses rather than consumers (i.e., about one-third of its total sales), even though its storefronts nominally identify the chain as a retailer. In particular, Office Depot's Business Solutions Group sells services to businesses through various routes, including direct sales, catalogs, call centers, and Internet sites, and it makes these business-to-business sales services available in the United Kingdom, the Netherlands, Japan, France, Ireland, Germany, Italy, and Belgium as well.[5] Chapter 6 discusses retailing in depth.

**Specialized intermediaries** enter the channel to perform a specific function; typically, they are not heavily involved in the core business represented by the products being sold. For example, insurance, financing, and credit card companies are all involved in financing; advertising agencies participate in the channel's promotion function; logistics and shipping firms engage in physical possession; information technology firms may participate in ordering or payment functions; and marketing research firms generate marketing intelligence that can support the performance of many functions.

### End-Users: Downstream Channel Members

**End-users** (either business or individual consumers) are themselves channel members as well, because they can and frequently do perform channel functions, just as other channel members do. Consumers who shop at a hypermarket like Costco, Sam's Club, or Carrefour and stock up on paper towels are performing physical possession, ownership, and financing functions, because they are buying a much larger volume of product than they will use in the near future. They pay for the paper towels before they use them, thus injecting cash into the channel. They store the paper towels in their house, lessening the need for warehouse space maintained by the retailer, thus taking on part of the physical possession function. They bear all the costs of ownership as well, including pilferage, spoilage, and so forth. Naturally, consumers expect a price cut when they shop at such a store, because they are bearing so many more channel function costs, relative to buying a single package of paper towels at the local grocer.

### Combinations of Channel Members

This variety of channel participants can be combined in many ways to create an effective marketing channel strategy. The range and number of channel members is affected by the needs of the end-users and manufacturers. In addition, the identity of the channel captain can vary from situation to situation. Appendix 1-1 summarizes different possible channel formats for manufacturers, retailers, service providers, as well as other, channel structures.

## WHY DO MARKETING CHANNELS EXIST?

Why don't manufacturers just sell their products and services directly to all end-users? That is, why do marketing channels exist? Once it is in place, why should a marketing channel ever change shape or emerge in new forms? To understand optimal channel structures and strategies, it is critical to understand what benefits the intermediaries in the channel provide to both upstream and downstream channel members.

### Benefits for Downstream Channel Members

**SEARCH FACILITATION**   Marketing channels containing intermediaries arise partly because they facilitate searches. The **search** process is characterized by uncertainty for both end-users and sellers. End-users are uncertain about where to find the products or services they want; sellers do not know exactly how to reach target end-users. If intermediaries did not exist, sellers without an already established brand name would be unable to generate many sales. End-users would not know whether to believe the claims made by manufacturers about the nature and quality of their products. Nor could manufacturers be certain that they were reaching the right kinds of end-user through their promotional efforts.

Intermediaries thus facilitate search on both ends of the channel. Cobweb Designs is a top-quality needlework design firm headquartered in Scotland. It is the sole licensee for needlework kits relating to the Royal Family, The National Trust for Scotland, the architect Charles Rennie Mackintosh, and the great socialist writer and designer William Morris. Cobweb's needlework kits are available at all retail outlets of the National Trust for Scotland, as well as on the company's website (www.cobweb-needlework.com), but its proprietor Sally Scott Aiton also recognized the potentially untapped market for her kits outside the United Kingdom. The challenge was finding a way to reach the large, dispersed market of potential buyers in markets such as the United States. Ultimately, Scott Aiton sought more retail placements in gift shops at major art museums and botanical gardens throughout Europe and the United States. Gaining shelf space in a gift shop of a museum like the Smithsonian Institution in Washington, DC, or the Art Institute of Chicago could greatly enhance the company's sales reach, because U.S. consumers who do not frequently travel to the United Kingdom still could find the company's designs (or become aware of the company's designs for the first time). Such retailers, which offer compelling brand images on their own, thus facilitate the search process on the demand side: A consumer seeking museum reproduction needlework kits knows that she can find them at museum shops, along with other museum reproduction products. Similarly, from Cobweb's point of view, museum shops have images that are consistent with the high quality of Cobweb Designs' kits, such that they are likely to attract visitors who tend to represent Cobweb's target market. Such access to a broad base of viable buyers again facilitates search, this time from the manufacturing end of the channel. In short, the intermediary (retail museum shop) becomes the "matchmaker" that brings the buyer and seller together.

**SORTING**    Independent intermediaries in a marketing channel perform the valuable function of *sorting goods* and thus resolving the natural discrepancy between the assortment of goods and services produced by a manufacturer and the assortment demanded by the end-user. This discrepancy arises because manufacturers typically produce a large quantity of a limited variety of goods, whereas consumers demand only a limited quantity, but of a wide variety of goods. The sorting functions performed by intermediaries include the following:

1. *Sorting out.* This task involves breaking down heterogeneous supply into separate stocks that are relatively homogeneous (e.g., a citrus packing house sorts oranges by size and grade).
2. *Accumulation.* The intermediary combines similar stocks from multiple sources to provide a broader, homogeneous supply (e.g., wholesalers accumulate varied goods for retailers, and retailers accumulate goods for their consumers).
3. *Allocation.* Breaking homogeneous supply down into smaller and smaller lots helps other channel members handle the supply more easily; at the wholesale level, allocation is referred to as *breaking bulk*. For example, goods received in

carloads might be sold in case lots, and the buyer of the case lots in turn might sell individual units.

4. *Assorting*. This function entails building up an assortment of products for resale in association, such that wholesalers build assortments for retailers, and retailers build assortments for their consumers.

In short, intermediaries help end-users consume a combination of product and channel services that are attractive to them. In this sense, intermediaries *create utility* for end-users. In particular, they provide *possession*, *place*, and *time* utilities, such that they ensure a product is available in the assortments and at the places that are most valuable to target end-users, at the right time.

## Benefits to Upstream Channel Members

**ROUTINIZATION OF TRANSACTIONS**  Each purchase transaction involves ordering, determining the valuation of, and paying for goods and services. The buyer and seller must agree on the amount, mode, and timing of payment. These costs of distribution can be minimized if the transactions are routinized; otherwise, every transaction would be subject to bargaining, with an accompanying loss of efficiency.

Routinization also leads to the standardization of goods and services whose performance characteristics can be easily compared and assessed. It encourages the production of items with greater value. In short, routinization leads to efficiencies in the execution of channel activities. *Continuous replenishment programs (CRP)* remain an important element of efficient channel inventory management. First created by Procter & Gamble in 1980, to automatically ship Pampers diapers to a retailer's warehouses without requiring the retail managers to place orders, this CRP came to Wal-Mart in 1988—and the rest is retailing history. In CRPs, manufacturing and retailing partners share inventory and stocking information to ensure that no products are under- or overstocked on retail shelves. These systems typically increase the frequency of shipments but lower the size per shipment, producing lower inventories held in the system and higher turnaround, both sources of increased channel profitability. However, a CRP demands a routinized, strong relationship between channel partners. *Trust*, or the confidence in the reliability and integrity of a channel partner, is required in order to have the high degree of cooperation among channel partners necessary for managing CRP over time.[6]

**FEWER CONTACTS**  Without channel intermediaries, every producer would have to interact with every potential buyer to create all possible market exchanges. As the importance of exchange in a society increases, so does the difficulty of maintaining all of these interactions. Consider a simple example: In a small village of only ten households trading themselves, 45 transactions would be necessary to conduct decentralized exchanges at each production point (i.e., [10 × 9]/2). But if the village added a central market with one intermediary, it could reduce the complexity of this exchange system and facilitate transactions, such that only 20 transactions would be required to carry out the centralized exchange (10 + 10).

Implicit in this example is the notion that a decentralized system of exchange is less efficient than a centralized network that uses intermediaries. The same rationale applies to direct selling from manufacturers to retailers, relative to selling through wholesalers. Consider Figure 1-1. Assuming four manufacturers and ten retailers that

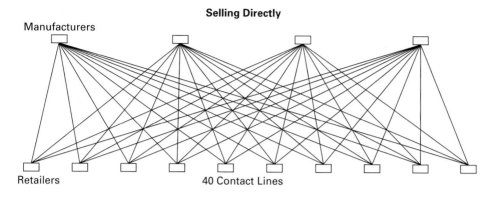

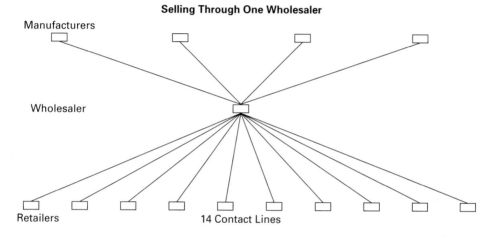

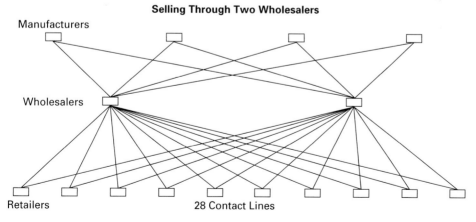

**FIGURE 1-1**   Contact costs to reach the market with and without intermediaries

buy goods from each manufacturer, the number of contact lines amounts to 40. If the manufacturers sold to these retailers through one wholesaler, the number of necessary contacts would fall to 14.

The number of necessary contacts instead increases with more wholesalers. For example, if the four manufacturers in Figure 1-1 used two wholesalers instead of one, the number of contacts would rise from 14 to 28; with four wholesalers, the number of contacts grows to 56. Thus, employing more and more intermediaries creates diminishing returns, viewed solely from the point of view of the number and cost of contacts in the market. Of course, we have assumed that each retailer contacts each of the wholesalers used by manufacturers. But if a retailer prefers a certain wholesaler, restricting the number of wholesalers, such that the preferred wholesaler is excluded from the channel, could leave the manufacturer unable to reach the market served by that retailer.

In this simplistic example, we also have assumed that the cost and effectiveness of each contact—manufacturer to wholesaler, wholesaler to retailer, manufacturer to retailer—are equivalent. Such an assumption clearly does not hold in the real world, where selling through one type of intermediary generally entails very different costs from those accrued by selling through another intermediary. Not all intermediaries are equally skilled at selling or are motivated to sell a particular manufacturer's product offering, which certainly affects the choice of which and how many intermediaries to use.

Thus, we assert that it is the *judicious* use of intermediaries that reduces the number of contacts necessary to cover a market. This principle guides many manufacturers that seek to enter new markets but want to avoid high-cost direct distribution through their own employee sales force. The trend toward rationalizing supply chains by reducing the number of suppliers also appears consistent with reducing the number of contacts in the distribution channel.

In this context, it becomes increasingly interesting to ponder how manufacturers sell their wares efficiently and directly online. Internet selling implies **disintermediation**, or shedding, rather than using intermediaries. What we often find though is companies such as Levi-Strauss, which try selling their products directly online but then discontinue this practice and rely on third-party retailers, such as Target and Wal-Mart, to enhance their channel efficiency but reduce channel conflict (i.e., by no longer competing with retailer partners for end-user sales). The benefits of interacting directly with end-users through direct selling (e.g., information on consumer demand and sources of dissatisfaction) must be counterbalanced against the incremental costs of doing so (e.g., breaking bulk early in the distribution process, shipping many small packages to many different locations rather than large shipments to few locations).

These upstream and downstream benefits, supporting the use of intermediaries in a channel, are detailed in Sidebar 1-1, which describes the Taiwanese tea trade in the early 1900s. In this example, intermediaries facilitated search, performed various sorting functions, and significantly reduced the number of contacts required in the channel. Their success even killed a government-supported direct-sale auction house as an alternative route to market.

## Sidebar 1-1

### Tea selling in Taiwan: The key roles of tea intermediaries[7]

The Taiwanese tea industry got its start when tea trees imported from China got planted in the Taiwanese hills in the mid-1800s. By the late 1920s, there were about 20,000 tea farmers in Taiwan, who sold their product (so-called *crude tea*) to one of about 60 tea intermediaries, who in turn sold it to 280 tea refineries located in Ta-tao-cheng, on the ocean, to ready for commercial sale and exportation. The tea intermediaries traversed the hills of Taiwan to search for and buy tea and then bring it down to the dock to sell to refineries.

But they also suffered a poor reputation among both farmers and refineries. Intermediaries were accused of exploiting the market by buying low and selling high; critics suggested that a simple direct trading system could be instituted to bypass them completely. Thus in 1923, the Governor-General of Taiwan set up a tea auction house in Ta-tao-cheng. Farmers could ship their tea directly to the auction house, where a first-price, sealed-bid auction would determine the price refineries would pay to obtain their products. The auction house's operating costs were covered by farmers' membership fees, trading charges, and subsidies by the Governor-General, so the tea intermediaries suddenly had to compete with the auction house. Despite this new and well-supported form of competition, the intermediaries not only survived, they ultimately forced the closing of the auction house. But how could this outcome arise if they were just "exploiters" of the buy–sell situation?

The answer is that they weren't. They served key functions. First, the intermediaries *facilitated search* in the marketplace. An intermediary would visit many farms, finding tea to sell, which constituted an upstream search for product supply. With the product supply in hand, the intermediary would take samples to a series of refineries and ask for purchase orders. Visiting multiple refineries was necessary because the same variety and quality of tea could fetch very different prices from different refineries, depending on the uses to which they would put the tea. This search process repeated every season, because each refinery's offer changed from season to season. The

intermediaries thus found buyers for the farmers' harvest and tea supplies for the refineries.

Second, tea intermediaries performed various *sorting* functions. Crude tea was highly heterogeneous; even the same species of tea tree, cultivated on different farms, exhibited wide quality variations. Furthermore, 28 different species of tea trees grew in the Taiwanese hills! The appraisal process, at both intermediary and refinery levels, therefore demanded considerable skill. Refineries hired specialists to appraise the tea they received; intermediaries facilitated this process by *accumulating* the tea harvests of multiple farmers into homogeneous lots for sale.

Third, tea intermediaries *minimized the number of contacts* in the channel system. With 20,000 tea farmers and 60 refineries, up to 1,200,000 contacts would be necessary for each farmer to market the product to get the best refinery price (even if each farmer cultivated only one variety of tea tree). Instead, each farmer tended to sell to just one intermediary, such that about 20,000 contacts existed at this first level of the channel. If the average intermediary collected $n$ varieties of tea, and we assume that each of the 280 intermediaries negotiated, on behalf of the farmers, with all 60 refineries, we find $[60 \times 280 \times n]$ negotiations between intermediaries and refineries. The total number of negotiations, throughout the channel, in the presence of intermediaries thus was $[20{,}000 + 16{,}800 \times n]$, a value that exceeds 1,200,000 negotiations only if the number of tea varieties exceeded 70. But because there were only about 25 tea varieties in Taiwan at the time, intermediaries reduced the number of contacts from more than 1 million to about 440,000.

Such value-added activities had been completely ignored in the attacks made on the tea intermediaries as "exploiters." The resulting failure of the government-sanctioned and government-subsidized auction house suggests that, far from merely exploiting the market, tea intermediaries were efficiency-enhancing market makers. In this situation, the intermediation of the channel added value and reduced costs at the same time.

In summary, intermediaries participate in the work of the marketing channel because they both *add value* and *help reduce costs*. These roles raise another key question then, namely, What types of work do channels actually perform?

## WHAT ARE THE KEY FUNCTIONS MARKETING CHANNELS PERFORM?

The marketing channel performs a range of **channel functions** that constitute a process, flowing through the channel system that is performed at different points in time by different channel members. In business settings, we might note the need to carry or hold inventory, generate demand through selling activities, physically distribute products, engage in after-sales service, and extend credit to other channel members. We formalize this list of nine universal channel functions in Figure 1-2, as they might be performed in a hypothetical channel that consists of producers, wholesalers, retailers, and consumers. Some functions move forward through the channel (physical possession, ownership, and promotion); others move up the channel from the end-user (ordering and payment); and still other channel functions can move in either direction or reflect activities by pairs of channel members (negotiation, financing, risk, information sharing).

We discuss channel functions in much more detail in Chapter 3, but a few remarks are in order here. First, the channel functions in Figure 1-2 may occur in different ways at different points of the channel. It is very common for spare parts distribution to be handled by a separate third-party distributor, uninvolved in the distribution of original products, for example. Three competing manufacturers—Ingersoll-Rand International

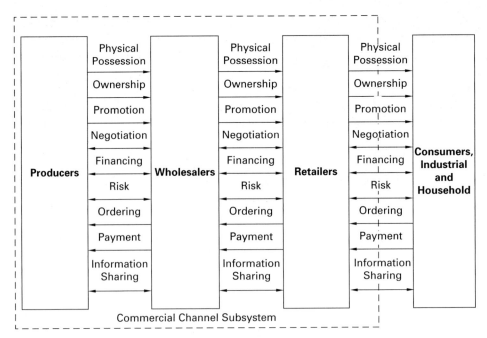

**FIGURE 1-2** Marketing functions in channels

Bobcat, Clark Material Handling, and the Spicer Division of Dana Corporation—all use the same German third-party logistics (3PL) firm Feige to handle all non-U.S. distributions of spare parts. Feige simplifies the otherwise difficult job of managing spare parts inventories that must be shipped quickly to multiple countries that speak different languages. Feige not only receives, stores, and ships spare parts, but it also provides debt, credit, and cash management services for its manufacturer clients. Dealers in turn can order from Feige online and track their orders, after first checking to verify that the desired parts are in stock. Feige's sophisticated information technology systems produce a remarkable 95 percent in-stock rate for these dealer customers. Customers' constant demands for quick delivery of spare parts make the use of this intermediary a superior strategy, from both cost-control and demand-satisfaction perspectives.[8] In such situations, a channel designer even might depict its two physical possession activities (original equipment vs. spare parts) separately, because they represent important and unique functions in the movement of products to the market.

Second, not every channel member need participate in every channel function. Specialization is a hallmark of an efficient channel. Figure 1-2 depicts a channel in which physical possession of the product moves from the manufacturer to wholesalers to retailers and finally to end-users; an alternate channel might eliminate wholesalers and rely instead on manufacturers' representatives, who never take physical possession or ownership. Thus, the physical possession function would still be performed by the manufacturer and retailer, but not by other intermediaries, on its way to the end-user. In general, channel functions get shared only by channel members that can add value or reduce costs by bearing them. However, specialization also increases interdependencies in channels, creating a need for close cooperation and coordination in channel operations.

Third, the performance of certain channel functions is correlated with that of other functions. Any time inventories are held and owned by one member of the channel system, a financing operation is occurring. That is, when the wholesaler or retailer takes title and assumes physical possession of some portion of a manufacturer's output, this intermediary is financing the manufacturer, because the greatest component of any carrying costs is the capital tied up by inventories held in a dormant state (i.e., not moving toward final sale). Other carrying costs include obsolescence, depreciation, pilferage, breakage, storage, insurance, and taxes. If the intermediary did not have to invest its funds to pay inventory holding costs, it could invest instead in other profitable opportunities. Capital costs thus equal the opportunity costs of holding inventory.

This discussion suggests that, given a set of functions to be undertaken in a channel, a manufacturer must assume responsibility for it, shift some of it to various intermediaries populating its channel, or shift all of it to others. Accordingly, we note one more important truth about channel design and management: It is possible to eliminate or substitute for the *members* of the channel but not for the *functions* they perform. When channel members leave the channel, their functions shift, either forward or backward, to be assumed by other channel members. Thus, a channel should eliminate a member only if the function it performs could be done more effectively or less inexpensively by other channel members. In this sense, any cost savings achieved by eliminating a channel member result not because that member's profit margin gets shared by the rest of the channel but rather because the functions performed by that channel member get completed more efficiently through another channel design.

Finally, we highlight an important channel function that permeates all value-added activities of a channel: information sharing. Manufacturers share product and sales information with their distributors, independent sales representatives, and retailers, which helps them perform the promotion function better. Consumers provide their preference information to the channel, which improves its ability to supply valued services. Producing and managing this information effectively then is central to developing distribution channel excellence.

## CHANNEL STRATEGY FRAMEWORK

Now that we have established what marketing channels are, who participates in them, the benefits they provide to upstream and downstream channel members, and the key functions performed by their various members, we need to consider how we might use these insights to design and implement better marketing channel strategies and structures. We offer a comprehensive channel strategy framework to guide channel managers through both the design of the channel strategy and its ongoing management over time.

Our proposed marketing channel strategy framework involves three major stages: (1) analyzing and designing, to develop the most effective channel structures and strategies; (2) benchmarking, to compare the new or revised channel structures and strategies against traditional and emerging channel systems to identify best practices; and (3) implementation or management, to address the five key success factors for channel management. The **analyzing and designing stage** begins with an *end-user analysis* to segment the market on the basis of end-users' needs and choose which segment(s) to target (Chapter 2). Then the *channel analysis* focuses on evaluating existing channels by auditing them according to efficiency and gap templates to identify any service or cost gaps (Chapter 3). The final analysis step determines if channel functions should be performed in-house or outsourced according to a *make-or-buy channel analysis* (Chapter 4). These analysis steps will inform the design phase by supporting decisions with regard to three key design questions: the degree of channel intensity, mix of channel types, and use of dual distribution (Chapter 5). In addition, any channel service or cost gaps these analysis steps have identified need to be closed by the new channel structure and strategy design. Overall, the analyzing and designing stage requires matching the needs of the upstream and downstream sides of the channel in such a way that it meets target end-users' demands, with minimum possible costs.

The **benchmarking** stage focuses on comparing a newly designed or revised channel structure and strategy against the most common channel structures and strategies, including *retailing* (Chapter 6), *wholesaling* (Chapter 7), and *franchising* (Chapter 8), to identify best practices that might be integrated into the new channel system. Managers also develop creative, *emerging channel structures and strategies* (Channel 9) to address constantly changing business environments. Channel managers should compare and contrast their channel structure and strategy with well-developed and emerging channel systems to learn from previous channel managers, prevent repeating common mistakes, and take advantage of known efficiencies in channel functions.

The **implementing** stage focuses on the five key success factors of channel management. Specifically, channel managers must understand the source of each channel member's *power and dependence* (Chapter 10) and potential for *channel conflict* (Chapter 11) to develop a plan for building and maintaining *relationships* among channel partners (Chapter 12). With such an understanding, the firm can create an environment for effectively executing the optimal channel strategy on an ongoing basis. Finally, two chapters focused on managing the channel's *policies and legalities* (Chapter 13) and *logistics* (Chapter 14) describe how to maintain the health and effectiveness of the channel system.

Figure 1-3 depicts the proposed channel strategy design and implementation framework, which mirrors the organization we use in this book. The framework is

**Analysis Phase**

- End-user Analysis: segmenting and targeting end-user groups (Chapter 2)
- Channel Analysis: auditing channels and identifying channel gaps (Chapter 3)
- Make Versus Make-or-Buy Analysis: determining if channel functions should be done in-house or outsourced to channel partners (Chapter 4)

**Decision Phase**

- Design Channel Structure & Strategy: focuses on making three key design decisions (degree of channel intensity, mix/identity of channel types, and use of dual distribution) and closing service and cost gaps (Chapter 5)

**Benchmarking Traditional and Emerging Channel Systems**

Compare and contrast "new" channel structure and strategy to traditional and emerging channel systems to identify best practices and opportunities for improvement

- Retailing Channel Structures and Strategies (Chapter 6)
- Wholesaling Channel Structures and Strategies (Chapter 7)
- Franchising Channel Structures and Strategies (Chapter 8)
- Emerging Channel Structures and Strategies (Chapter 9)

**Implementing Channel Strategies**

Implement channel structures and strategies by addressing five key success factors for effective channel management

- Managing Channel Power (Chapter 10)
- Managing Channel Conflict (Chapter 11)
- Managing Channel Relationships (Chapter 12)
- Managing Channel Policies and Legalities (Chapter 13)
- Managing Channel Logistics (Chapter 14)

**FIGURE 1-3** Framework for designing and implementing channel strategy

useful for creating a new channel strategy in a previously untapped market, as well as for critically analyzing and refining a preexisting channel strategy. We provide an overview by describing each major step in the process, and we expand on each step in the subsequent chapters in this book

## End-User Analysis: Segmentation and Targeting

A fundamental principle of marketing is the segmentation of the market. **Segmentation** means splitting a market into groups of end-users who are (1) maximally similar to one another and (2) maximally different from other groups of end-users. But how do we define similarity or difference, that is, according to what criterion? For channel managers, *segments can be best defined on the basis of the service outputs that the end-user needs to obtain from the marketing channel.* A marketing channel is more than just a conduit for product; it is also a means to add value to products and services marketed through it. In this sense, the marketing channel represents another "production line," engaged in producing not the product (or service) being sold but rather the ancillary services that define *how* the product will be sold. Value-added services created by channel members and consumed by end-users, together with the product purchased, represent service outputs.[9] **Service outputs** include (but are not limited to) *bulk breaking, spatial convenience, waiting and delivery time, assortment and variety, customer service*, and *product/market/usage information sharing.*

End-users (whether ultimate consumers or business buyers) express varying demands for these service outputs. Consider two different book buyers: a consumer browsing for some entertaining best sellers to take on an upcoming vacation and a student buying textbooks for school. Table 1-1 outlines the differences in their service output demands. For example, the vacationer values a broad assortment of books to choose from, in-store amenities such as a coffee bar, and advice from well-informed salespeople. But she likely cares less about bulk breaking, because she intends to buy several books; spatial convenience, because she could easily shop several bookstores; or delivery time, because she has some time before her vacation starts, so she can wait to find just the right books. The student textbook buyer has almost the opposite demands: She wants just one textbook per class, cannot travel far to get it, and needs it virtually immediately, before the start of the course. Yet the student does not need to browse the store, because the assigned text has already been dictated by the professor, nor does she need to solicit advice about what book to buy. Although she might appreciate a jolt of caffeine, she likely cares little about the attractiveness of in-store amenities such as a coffee bar to enjoy while shopping.

Thus, different marketing channels exist to meet the needs of these two segments of shoppers. The vacationer likely is satisfied shopping at a large, well-stocked bookstore somewhere in town, such as a Barnes and Noble bookstore. The student instead should favor a university bookstore close to campus that caters to students. Of course, subsegments of both groups increasingly turn to the Internet for their purchases. A student who plans ahead or knows her reading list in advance has less intense delivery needs and thus can order textbooks from an online bookseller, receive delivery to her home or college residence (i.e., extremely high level of spatial convenience) in less than a week's time (i.e., moderate level of quick delivery), and obtain the exact number and titles of books she needs (i.e., bulk breaking, assortment, and

**TABLE 1-1    Service output demand differences: Book-buying example**

| | Vacationer Buying Best Sellers | | Student Buying Textbooks for Fall Semester | |
|---|---|---|---|---|
| | Descriptor | Service Output Demand Level | Descriptor | Service Output Demand Level |
| *Bulk-breaking* | "I'm looking for some 'good read' paperbacks to enjoy." | Medium | "I only need one copy of my Marketing textbook!" | High |
| *Spatial convenience* | "I have lots of errands to run before leaving town, so I'll be going past several bookstores." | Medium | "I don't have a car, so I can't travel far to buy." | High |
| *Waiting and delivery time* | "I'm not worried about getting the books now … I can even pick up a few when I'm out of town if need be." | Low | "I just got to campus, but classes are starting tomorrow, and I'll need my books by then." | High |
| *Assortment and variety* | "I want the best choice available, so that I can pick what looks good." | High | "I'm just buying what's on my course reading list." | Low |
| *Customer service* | "I like to stop for a coffee when book browsing." | High | "I can find books myself, and don't need any special help." | Low |
| *Information sharing* | "I value the opinions of a well-read bookstore employee; I can't always tell a good book from a bad one before I buy." | High | "My professors have already decided what I'll read this semester." | Low |

variety). Customer service and information sharing might diminish, but because these are not intensely demanded by the college student, their absence is not missed. The vacationer might just browse the Kindle site to download books to her e-reader, such that she receives immediate delivery, enjoys great spatial convenience, and chooses only those specific titles she prefers. Although she cannot solicit a salesperson for advice, recommendations from other readers and online rankings provide much of the information sharing function in this channel. Yet this buyer still might miss the in-store experience and information obtained through physical browsing, as provided by a brick-and-mortar bookstore.

Thus, the same product can be demanded by consumers whose demanded service outputs vary widely, resulting in very different demands for the ultimate offering bundle, which comprises the product plus service output. An analysis of service output demands by segment offers important inputs into channel strategy designs, which can help increase the reach and marketability of a product to multiple market segments.

After identifying end-user segments, channel managers should determine which of these segments to target. Usually the end-user segments targeted are those that are attractive in terms of their size, predicted growth, or price sensitivity and that match up with the competitive strengths of the manufacturer (e.g., brand awareness, image, product offering). A manufacturer's overall channel strategy often involves targeting multiple end-user segments with different channel partners, types, and structures. Chapter 2 describes in detail the process for segmenting and targeting on the basis of the service outputs needed by end-users from marketing channels.

## Channel Analysis: Auditing Marketing Channels

To design an optimal channel strategy for a targeted end-user market, the designer needs to audit existing marketing channels serving this segment. This audit should evaluate the capabilities of each potential channel, in terms of the nine key channel functions, to determine how well it is suited to meet the segment's service output demands. Channel functions pertain to all channel activities that add value to the end-user, such that we move beyond merely handling or moving the product along the channel to include promotion, negotiation, financing, ordering, payment, and so forth (see Figure 1-2). Our college student looking for textbooks (see Table 1-1) has a high demand for spatial convenience and a minimal tolerance for out-of-stock product, so the channel function of physical possession (i.e., holding inventory, especially at the college retail bookstore) takes on great importance. Each end-user segment has its own set of service output demands, so the importance of channel functions depends on the segment being targeted.

Channel structure decisions related to intensity, type/identity of channel members, and dual distribution all must be made while keeping the minimization of channel function costs in mind. That is, each channel member has a set of channel functions to perform; ideally, the allocation of activities results in their reliable performance at a minimum total cost. This task is not trivial, particularly because it involves comparing activities across different members of the channel. Therefore, channel managers should rely on **efficiency and gap analysis templates** to perform their evaluations. The efficiency template codifies information about the importance of each channel function, in both cost and value terms, as well as about the proportion of each function performed by each channel member. In turn, it produces a metric, the **normative profit share** for each channel member, that indicates the proportional value added to the total channel's performance by each channel member. If there are no intervening adverse competitive conditions, the normative profit shares should at least approximate the actual shares of total channel profits enjoyed by each channel member, following the **equity principle**.

Next, managers should complete the gap analysis template to identify both **service gaps** (i.e., service levels provided by the channel do not match the levels desired by end-users) and **cost gaps** (i.e., prices in the channel are higher than desired by end-users). Matching the service outputs demanded by targeted end-users to the offerings provided give channel managers a good idea of discrepancies from ideal channel structures required to meet target segments' needs.

Auditing the specific channel functions performed by each channel member in the existing channel system, by whom, at what levels, and at what cost also is helpful in several important ways. First, detailed knowledge of the capabilities of each channel member enables the channel manager to diagnose and remedy shortcomings in the provision or price of service outputs. Second, the audit may identify service outputs that are desired by targeted end-user segments but are not being provided, which can suggest new or revisions to existing channels. Third, knowing which channel members have incurred the costs of performing specific channel functions facilitates the more equitable allocation of profits throughout the channel, preserving a sense of fairness and cooperation and thus averting channel conflicts. Chapter 3 describes in detail the processes for conducting channel audits using the efficiency and gap analysis templates.

## Make-or-Buy Channel Analysis

A fundamental question to ask when designing a channel strategy: Should the firm integrate vertically by performing both upstream (e.g., manufacturing) and downstream (e.g., distribution) functions? Should a single organization perform all channel functions (i.e., manufacturer, agent, distributor, retailer—all rolled into one)? Or should outsourcing apply to either distribution (upstream looking down) or production (downstream looking up), or both, such that the identities of manufacturers and downstream channel members are separate?

When a manufacturer integrates a distribution function (e.g., selling, fulfilling orders, offering credit), its employees do downstream work, and the manufacturer has integrated forward from the point of production. Vertical integration also occurs in the other direction: A distributor or retailer might produce its own branded products and thereby integrate backward. Whether the manufacturer integrates forward or the downstream channel member integrates backward, the result is that one organization does all the work in a vertically integrated channel.

Vertical integration decisions are not necessarily aggregate; rather, the decision can and should be made specifically, channel function by channel function. Given sufficient power and investment, a channel member can decide to vertically integrate some subset of the channel functions, in a way that exhibits the best combination of make and buy, together in one channel structure. But managers need a structured way to analyze these issues; frame a coherent, comprehensive rationale; and reach a decision (make or buy, function by function) that can be communicated convincingly. Make-or-buy analyses offer such a structured approach. In the base case, the manufacturer rarely should vertically integrate a downstream function, because it is typically inefficient to do so. However, a manufacturer should take responsibility for a wider set of functions in the channel if it has sufficient resources and could increase its returns on investment over time through integration. Similarly, though downstream channel members typically suffer from integrating backward, they should do so if they have the resources and would increase their long-run returns on investment. The framework outlined in Chapter 4 specifies these conditions in which vertical integration (i.e., making) versus outsourcing (i.e., buying) channel functions raise the long-run returns for different channel participants.

## Designing Channel Structures and Strategies

A channel manager employs the preceding analyses to inform decisions about the degree of channel intensity, mix of channel types/identities, and use of dual distribution, as well as to close any service or costs gaps. By identifying demands for service outputs among different segments in the market, the channel analyst can find an optimal channel structure to satisfy these demands efficiently and effectively.

For each segment, the level of **intensity**, or the number of channel partners competing for customers, must be determined. A channel might include many retail outlets (intensive distribution), just a few (selective distribution), or only one (exclusive distribution) for a given market area; determining which option to choose depends on both efficiency and implementation factors. More intensive distribution makes the product more easily available to all target end-users, but it could create conflict among the retailers competing to sell it. Chapter 5 notes factors that a manager should consider when making this key design decision.

In turn, if the channel manager decides to sell a line of fine watches in retail stores, the next question pertains to the type and exact identity of channel partners to use: upscale outlets, such as Tiffany's, or family-owned local jewelers? This choice has implications for both channel efficiency and brand image. Furthermore, if the company seeks distribution for its products in a foreign market, it likely needs to choose a distributor to sell and distribute the product line in the overseas market. The right distributor should have better relationships with local channel partners in the target market, such that this choice significantly affects the potential success of the foreign market entry. Finally, the channel type decision refers to multiple levels of the channel structure. For example, an ethnic food manufacturer could sell its grocery products through small independent retailers with urban locations or through large chain stores that operate discount warehouse stores, as well as on EthnicGrocer.com, an online seller of ethnic foods and products from various countries that operates no retail stores. Moving up the channel, additional decisions pertain to whether to use independent distributors, independent sales representative companies (called "reps" or "rep firms"), independent trucking companies, financing companies, export management companies, or any of a host of other possible independent distribution channel members that could be incorporated into the channel design.

The channel decision revolving around make-or-buy analyses—namely, whether to vertically integrate or outsource—is another critical strategic choice, because the firm's decision to own a part of or its entire marketing channel has an enduring influence on its ability to distribute and produce. The manufacturer becomes identified with its marketing channels, which influence its end-users and determine their image of the manufacturer. In addition, the manufacturer gains some of its market and competitive intelligence from its channels: What the manufacturer knows (or can learn) about its markets is heavily conditioned by how it goes to market. Among downstream channel members, decisions to integrate backward put them in conflict with other suppliers and eat up resources, which may jeopardize their ability to offer unbiased advice to their customers, yet for many, moving up the value chain seems irresistible (why let the producer take all the margins when the downstream channel member better understands demand?).

An understanding of the optimal channel structure and strategy to reach each targeted segment gives the channel manager the freedom to establish the best possible channel design—as long as no other channel currently exists in the market for this segment. If a preexisting channel already is in place, the channel manager needs to undertake a gap analysis to identify differences between the optimal and actual current channels. For example, the service output could be undersupplied or oversupplied. This problem is obvious in the case of undersupply, in that the target segment is dissatisfied by the low level of service they are receiving. The problem is more subtle in the case of oversupply though, because target end-users are getting all the service they desire—and then some—but because that service is costly to supply, an oversupply implies higher prices than target end-users are willing to pay.

Similarly, a cost gap arises when at least one function in the distribution channel requires too high a cost, leading to wasted channel profit margins, prices that are higher than the target market is willing to pay, and reduced sales and market shares. Such gaps might result from a lack of up-to-date expertise in channel function management or simply waste in the channel. The challenge is to reduce costs without dangerously reducing service outputs.

The process of channel strategy and structure design requires matching the needs of the upstream and downstream sides of the channel in such a way as to meet target end-users' demands at a minimum possible cost. We cover the three key design decisions to achieve the most appropriate goals and strategies in detail in Chapter 5.

## Benchmarking Traditional and Emerging Channel Systems

This channel structure design process also unites the activities and efficiencies of multiple companies and entities holistically, to satisfy end-users' demands for not just the products they buy but also key channel services. In this sense, it may be valuable to use existing channel systems as benchmarks, comparing them against "new" channel designs, which play important roles in their own right. Other channel systems can offer important insights that new designs need to leverage. Among existing channel systems, the three most notable or well known are retailing, wholesaling, and franchising. As we noted previously, retailing connects the channel to the end-user, and the multiplicity of retailing models today offers testimony of the vast range of end-user segments seeking different concatenations of service outputs. Wholesaling is distribution's "back room," moving and holding product both efficiently (i.e., to minimize cost) and effectively (i.e., to create spatial convenience and quick delivery). Logistics firms specialize in coordinating the activities of the marketing channel (and frequently participate in key activities themselves, such as FedEx does for package shipping). Resolving supply chain issues requires looking upstream toward vendors, not just downstream toward end-users, in an effort to improve service and efficiency throughout the entire chain, from raw material to end-user consumption. Finally, **franchising** is an important method of selling that allows small businesspeople to operate retail product and service outlets, with the benefits of a large-scale parent company's (the franchisor's) knowledge, strategy, and tactical guidance.

Dramatic changes in the business environment—the shift from products to services, increases in e-commerce, globalization—are leading to the emergence of new channel systems, with the potential to disrupt many tradition approaches. For example, the shift to online purchases of books and music has dramatically transformed the channel system for these products. We discuss the three tradition channel institutions in Chapters 6, 7, and 8; emerging channel structures and strategies are covered in Chapter 9.

## Implementing Channel Strategies

If a good channel design already is in place in the market, the channel manager still needs to stick around to ensure the implementation of the optimal channel design, then continue to assess and implement the optimal design over time. The value of doing so might seem self-evident, but a channel is made up of multiple, interdependent entities (companies, agents, individuals) that may not have the same incentives to implement the optimal channel design. Channel managers must manage five key channel elements to ensure that the channel system runs smoothly and all participants cooperate to optimize it: power, conflict, relationships, policies and legalities, and logistics.

Incompatible incentives among channel members would not be problematic if they were not dependent on one another. But the very nature of the distribution channel structure and design ensures that specific channel members *specialize* in particular activities and functions. If any one of them performs poorly, the entire channel system effort suffers. For example, even with everything else in place, a poorly performing transportation system results in late (or no) deliveries of product to retail stores, which prevents the channel from selling the product. Because similar statements could refer to the performance of any channel member performing any of the necessary functions in the channel, inducing *all* of channel members to implement a channel design appropriately is critical.

How can a channel captain implement the optimal channel design, in the face of interdependence among channel partners, not all of whom have incentives to cooperate? The answer lies in the possession and use of **channel power**. A channel member's power "is its ability to control the decision variables in the marketing strategy of another member in a given channel at a different level of distribution."[10] These sources could be used to further the member's individual ends. Instead, if it uses its channel power to influence channel members to perform the jobs that the optimal channel design specifies are their responsibility, the result will be a channel that delivers demanded service outputs at a lower cost, as we detail in Chapter 10.

Alternatively, incompatible incentives can lead to **channel conflict**, generated when one channel member's actions prevent the channel from achieving its goals. Such conflict is both common and dangerous. Because of the interdependence of all channel members, any one member's actions exert an influence on the success of the channel effort and thus can harm overall channel performance.[11] Channel conflict might stem from differences between channel members' goals and objectives (*goal conflict*); disagreements over the domain of action and responsibility in the channel (*domain conflict*); or varying perceptions of the marketplace (*perceptual conflict*). These conflicts cause channel members' failure to perform the functions assigned to them by the optimal channel design, thus inhibiting total channel performance. The management problem accordingly is twofold. First, the channel manager must *identify* the sources of channel conflict and, in particular, differentiate between poor channel design and poor performance due to channel conflict. Second, the channel manager must decide on which actions to take (if any) to manage and reduce these identified channel conflicts.

In general, reducing channel conflict requires applying one or more sources of channel power. Imagine, for example, that a manufacturer identifies a conflict in its independent distributor channel, such that the distributor is exerting too little sales effort on behalf of the manufacturer's product line, so product sales are suffering. A good analysis can show why the effort level is so low, namely, because the distributor earns more profit from selling a competitor's product rather than the focal manufacturer's. In this *goal* conflict, the manufacturer's goal is to maximize profits earned from its own product line, whereas the distributor's goal is to maximize profits earned over *all* of the products it sells, only some of which come from this particular manufacturer. To resolve such goal conflict, the manufacturer could use some power to reward the distributor by increasing its discount, thus increasing the profit margin it can make on the manufacturer's product line. Or it might invest in developing brand equity and thus pull the product through the channel, such that its brand power induces the distributor to sell the product more aggressively because its sales potential has risen. In both cases, some leverage or power exerted by the manufacturer is necessary to change the distributor's behavior and reduce channel conflict. Considering the various sources of conflict, channel managers also should ensure generally equitable profit sharing across channel partners, because perceptions of unfairness dramatically undermine channel performance and aggravate minor conflicts,[12] as we discuss in Chapter 11.

The next step is determining how deeply committed channel members should be to a particular channel of distribution. In other words, how important are **channel relationships** to a functioning cooperative channel? At one end of the spectrum, channel members might engage in distribution-related transactions without any commitment. Such relationships are inherently transactional, with no guarantee that a supplier (or buyer) in a transactional channel will continue to do business with the company in the future; it is similarly easy for the company in question to find a different source of supply or downstream market for its goods or services.

Alternatively, channel members can build a strong, committed relationship, such that the channel members maintain an enduring set of connections, spanning multiple functions and personnel throughout the firms. This effective relationship is characterized by partners that act according to a single, overarching interest, rather than merely following their own individualized goals. Such committed partners may make seemingly irrational, short-term sacrifices to improve the long-term viability and success of the channel system. As we outline in Chapter 12, the relationships among channel partners thus are critical determinants of long-term financial performance.[13]

Managing **channel polices and legalities** provides the "formal" backdrop to a channel system. Channel managers use specific policies to administer distribution systems, which is especially critical when employees and channel partners change over time or disagreements arise. However, some policies restrain or redirect the activities of various channel members and affect the competitiveness of the overall market, which may bring them under legal antitrust scrutiny. Chapter 13 outlines the variety of policies available for managing channels and offers several business reasons for their adoption. In addition, details of when and how such policies might run afoul of U.S. federal antitrust laws appear in this chapter.

Finally, managing **channel logistics** involves processing and tracking factory goods throughout the channel, during warehousing, inventory control, transport, customs documentation, and delivery. Since the 1980s, channel managers have invested more significant time and money into *supply chain management* to coordinate routes to market (downstream) with manufacturing processes (upstream). Over time, the flow and storage of goods and services (i.e., logistics) has grown far more efficient, largely through coordination across not just functional silos within the firm but also the many firms in a value-added chain. Supply chain management requires that every player in the channel send information or place orders that trigger behavior by *any and every other player*, including downstream members. These decisions involve marketing and channel management. That logistics should influence marketing may be a revolutionary idea to many managers, and we cover it and its implications in Chapter 14.

## TAKE-AWAYS

- A marketing channel is a set of interdependent organizations involved in the process of making a product or service available for use or consumption.
- Both upstream and downstream factors affect the development of channels and provide reasons to adjust channels over time. Upstream factors include the following:
  - Routinization of transactions
  - Reduction in the number of contacts

  Downstream factors include the following:
  - Search facilitation
  - Sorting
- Marketing functions are elements of work, performed by members of the marketing channel. There are nine universal channel functions:
  - Physical possession
  - Ownership
  - Promotion
  - Negotiation
  - Financing
  - Risk
  - Ordering
  - Payment
  - Information sharing
- A channel member can be eliminated from a channel, but the functions performed by that member cannot be. Before eliminating a channel member, the channel manager should consider the cost of replacing the performance of that member's channel functions.
- The key members of marketing channels are manufacturers, intermediaries (wholesale, retail, and specialized), and end-users (business customers or consumers).
- A framework for analyzing channel design and implementation is crucial for creating create effective (i.e., demand satisfying) and efficient (i.e., cost effective) routes to market, in which members continue to be willing to perform the channel functions assigned to them (Figure 1-3).

# Endnotes

1. See "2011 Top 250 Global Retailers," *Stores*, January 2012, http://www.stores.org; http://www.naw.org, http://data.world-bank.org, and http://www.commerce.gov.

2. Conlon, Edward, Sarv Devaraj, and Khalil F. Matta (2001), "The Relationship Between Initial Quality Perceptions and Maintenance Behavior: The Case of the Automotive Industry," *Management Science* 47 (September), pp. 1191–1202.

3. Fuhrman, Elizabeth (2003), "Multibar Multi-Tasking," *Candy Industry* 168 (June), pp. 28–32.

4. Kumar, Nirmalya and Jan-Benedict E.M. Steenkamp (2007), *Private Label Strategy: How to Meet the Store Brand Challenge* (Boston, MA: Harvard School Publishing).

5. See http://www.officedepot.com and the company's 2011 Annual Report.

6. Fang, Eric, Robert W. Palmatier, Lisa Scheer, and Ning Li (2008), "Trust at Different Organizational Levels," *Journal of Marketing* 72 (March), pp. 80–98.

7. See Koo, Hui-Wen and Pei-yu Lo (2004), "Sorting: The Function of Tea Middlemen in Taiwan during the Japanese Colonial Era," *Journal of Institutional and Theoretical Economics* 160 (December), pp. 607–626.

8. See "Outsourcing: A Global Success Story," *Logistics Management* 42, no. 2 (February 2003), pp. 60–63.

9. Louis P. Bucklin defines service outputs in *A Theory of Distribution Channel Structure* (Berkeley, CA: IBER Special Publications, 1966); and *Competition and Evolution in the Distributive Trades* (Englewood Cliffs, NJ: Prentice-Hall, 1972), pp. 18–31.

10. El-Ansary, Adel I. and Louis W. Stern (1972), "Power Measurement in the Distribution Channel," *Journal of Marketing Research* 9 (February), p. 47.

11. See Stern, Louis W. and J. L. Heskett (1969), "Conflict Management in Interorganization Relations: A Conceptual Framework," in Louis W. Stern (ed.), *Distribution Channels: Behavioral Dimensions* (Boston, MA: Houghton Mifflin Co.), pp. 288–305; Rosenberg, Larry J. and Louis W. Stern (1971), "Conflict Measurement in the Distribution Channel," *Journal of Marketing Research* 8 (November), pp. 437–442; Etgar, Michael (1979), "Sources and Types of Intrachannel Conflict," *Journal of Retailing* 55 (Spring), pp. 61–78.

12. Samaha, Stephen, Robert W. Palmatier, and Rajiv P. Dant (2011), "Poisoning Relationships: Perceive Unfairness in Channels of Distribution," *Journal of Marketing* 75 (May), pp. 99–117.

13. Palmatier, Robert W., Rajiv P. Dant, Dhruv Grewal, and Kenneth R. Evans (2006), "Factors Influencing the Effectiveness of Relationship Marketing: A Meta-Analysis," *Journal of Marketing* 70 (October), pp. 136–153.

# APPENDIX 1-1

## Alternate Channel Formats: Definitions and Examples

Alternate channel formats may stem from any of the three sections of the traditional distribution channel, that is, manufacturer, distributor, or customer. But they also could have other bases. This appendix summarizes the variety of channel formats and the characteristics on which they rely for gaining strategic advantages, as well as some examples of specific companies, types of companies, or product categories that use the specific channel format. By comparing each market against this information, channel managers can identify opportunities and vulnerabilities.

### MANUFACTURER-BASED CHANNEL FORMATS

1. **Manufacturer Direct.** Product shipped and serviced from manufacturer's warehouse. Sold by company sales force or agents. Many manufacturer-direct companies also sell through wholesaler-distributors.

   *Examples:* Wide variety of products for customers with few service needs and large orders, Firms such Hewlett Packard, IBM, and GE all sell using a direct sales forces to their largest customers

2. **Manufacturer-Owned Full Service Wholesaler Distributor.** An acquired wholesale distribution company serving the parent's and other manufacturers' markets. Typically, diverse product lines in an industry support synergies between a company's manufacturing and distribution operations. Due to customer demand, some companies also distribute other manufacturers' products.

   *Examples:* Revlon, Levi-Strauss, Kraft Foodservice, GESCO, clothing and apparel products

3. **Company Store/Manufacturer Outlets.** Retail product outlets in high-density markets; often used to liquidate seconds or excess inventory of branded consumer products.

   *Examples:* Outlet malls, Hostess bakery outlets

4. **License.** Contracting distribution and marketing functions through licensing agreements, which usually grant exclusivity for some period of time. Often used for products in the development stage of the life cycle.

   *Examples:* Mattel, Walt Disney, importers

5. **Consignment/Locker Stock.** Manufacturer ships the product to the point of consumption, but title does not pass until consumed. Risk of obsolescence and ownership remains with manufacturer. Focus on with high-priced/high margin items and emergency items.

   *Examples:* Diamonds, fine art galleries, machine repair parts

6. **Broker.** Specialized sales force contracted by manufacturer that also carries comparable product lines and focuses on a narrow customer segment; product is

shipped through another format, such as the preceding options. Typically used by small manufacturers attempting to attain broad coverage.

*Examples:* Schwan's frozen foods, paper goods, lumber, newer product lines

## RETAILER-BASED CHANNEL FORMATS

1. **Franchise.** Product and merchandising concept is packaged and formatted. Territory rights are sold to franchisees. Various distribution and other services are provided by contract to franchisees for a fee.

   *Examples:* KFC, McDonald's

2. **Dealer Direct.** Franchised retailers carry a limited number of product lines supplied by a limited number of vendors. Often these big-ticket items need high after-sales service support.

   *Examples:* Heavy equipment dealers, auto dealers

3. **Buying Club.** Buying services requiring membership. Good opportunity for vendors to penetrate certain niche markets or experiment with product variations. They also provide buyers with a variety of consumer services; today, they are largely consumer-oriented.

   *Examples:* Compact disc/tape clubs, book clubs

4. **Warehouse Clubs/Wholesale Clubs.** Appeal is to price-conscious shopper. Size is 60,000 square feet or more. Product selection is limited, and products are usually sold in bulk in a "no-frills" environment.

   *Examples:* Pace, Sam's Club, Price Club, Costco

5. **Mail Order/ Catalog.** Nonstore selling through literature sent to potential customers. Usually has a central distribution center for receiving and shipping direct to the customer.

   *Examples:* Lands' End, Spiegel, Fingerhut

6. **Food Retailers.** Will buy canned and boxed goods in truckloads to take advantage of pricing and manufacturing rebates. Distribution centers act as consolidators to reduce the number of trucks received at the store. Pricing is not required, because manufacturer bar codes are available. Includes full lines of groceries, health and beauty aids, and general merchandise items. Some food retailers have expanded into other areas, such as prescription and over-the-counter drugs, delicatessens, and bakeries.

   *Examples:* Publix, Safeway

7. **Department Stores.** These stores offer a wide variety of merchandise with moderate depth. The product mix usually includes soft goods (clothing, linens) and hard goods (appliances, hardware, sporting equipment). Distribution centers act as consolidators of both soft goods and hard goods. Quick response for apparel goods demands a direct link with manufacturer. A national basis motivates retailers to handle their own distribution.

   *Examples:* JCPenney, Mervins, Dayton Hudson Corp., Federated Stores

8.  **Mass Merchandisers.** Similar to department stores, except product selection is broader and prices are usually lower.

    *Examples:* Wal-Mart, Kmart, Target

9.  **Specialty Stores.** Offer merchandise in one line (e.g., women's apparel, electronics) with great depth of selection at prices comparable to those of department stores. Due to the seasonal nature of fashion goods, partnership with the manufacturer is essential. Manufacturer ships predetermined store assortments and usually prices the goods. Retailers might have joint ownership with the manufacturer.

    *Examples:* The Limited, The Gap, Kinney shoes, Musicland, Zale

10. **Specialty Discounters/Category Killers.** Offer merchandise in one line (e.g., sporting goods, office supplies, children's merchandise) with great depth of selection at discounted prices. Stores usually range in size from 50,000 to 75,000 square feet. Buys direct in truckloads. Manufacturer will ship direct to the store. Most products do not need to be priced. National chains have created their own distribution centers to act as consolidators.

    *Examples:* Toys "R" Us. Office Max, Drug Emporium, F&M Distributors

11. **Convenience Store.** A small, higher-margin grocery store that offers a limited selection of staple groceries, nonfoods, and other convenience items; for example, ready-to-heat and ready-to-eat foods. The traditional format includes stores that started out as strictly convenience stores, but they may also sell gasoline.

    *Examples:* 7-Eleven, White Hen Pantry

12. **Hypermarket.** A very large food and general merchandise store with at least 100,000 square feet of space. Although these stores typically devote as much as 75 percent of their selling area to general merchandise, the food-to-general merchandise sales ratio typically is 60/40.

    *Examples:* Auchan, Carrefour, Super Kmart Centers, Hypermarket USA

## SERVICE PROVIDER-BASED CHANNEL FORMATS

1.  **Contract Warehousing.** Public warehousing services provided for a fee, typically with guaranteed serviced levels.

    *Examples:* Caterpillar Logistics Services, Dry Storage

2.  **Subprocessor.** Outsourcing of assembly or subprocessing. Usually performed with labor-intensive process or high fixed-asset investment when small orders are needed for customer. These channel players are also beginning to take on traditional wholesale distribution roles.

    *Examples:* Steel processing; kitting of parts in electronics industry

3.  **Cross-Docking.** Trucking companies service high-volume inventory needs by warehousing and backhauling product on a routine basis for customer's narrower inventory needs. Driver picks inventory and delivers to customer after picking up the customer's shipment.

    *Examples:* Industrial repair parts and tools, various supply industries

4. **Integration of Truck and Rail (Intermodal).** Joint ventures between trucking and rail companies to ship large orders door-to-door from supplier to customer, with one way-bill.

    *Examples:* Very economical for large orders, or from manufacturer to customer for a manufacturer with a broad product line.

5. **Roller Freight.** Full truckload is sent from manufacturer to high-density customer markets via a transportation company. Product is sold en route, and drivers are directed to customer delivery by satellite communication.

    *Examples:* Lumber products, large moderately priced items, with commodity-like characteristics that allow for routine orders.

6. **Stack Trains and Road Railers.** Techniques to speed movement and eliminate handling for product to be shipped by multiple formats. The importer might load containers directed to specific customers on a truck body in Hong Kong, ship direct, and unload onto railcars, which can eliminate two to three days' transit time. Large customer orders using multiple transportation techniques.

    *Example:* Importers

7. **Scheduled Trains.** High-speed trains leave daily at prescribed times from high-density areas to high-density destinations. Manufacturer "buys a ticket" and hooks up its railcar, then product is picked up at the other end by the customer.

    *Example:* High density recurring orders to large customers with limited after-sales service needs

8. **Outsourcing.** Service providers sign a contract to provide total management of a company's activities in an area in which the provider has particular expertise (computer operations, janitorial services, print shop, cafeteria, repair parts, tool crib). The outsourcer then takes over the channel product function for products associated with the outsourced activity (janitorial supplies). Outsourcing has spread to virtually every area of the business (repair part stockroom, legal, accounting) and may not use merchant wholesaler-distributors. Wide variety of applications and growing.

    *Examples:* ServiceMaster, ARA, R.R. Donnelly

9. **Direct Mailer.** Direct mail advertising companies expanding services in conjunction with market research database services to directly market narrower line products. Product logistics and support performed by either the manufacturer or outsourced to a third party.

    *Examples:* Big ticket consumer products, high-margin, low-service-requirement industrial and commercial equipment

10. **Bartering.** Service provider, usually an advertising or media company, signs a barter arrangement with a manufacturer to exchange product for media advertising time or space. Bartered product is then rebartered or redistributed through other channels.

    *Example:* Consumer and commercial products that have been discontinued or for which demand has slowed considerably

11. **Value-Added Resellers (VARs).** Designers, engineers, or consultants for a variety of service industries that joint venture or have arrangements with manufacturers

of products used in their designs. The VARs often get a commission or discount to service the product and carry inventory of high-turn items.

*Examples:* Computer software companies that market hardware for turnkey products; security system designers that form joint ventures with electronics manufacturers to sell turnkey products

12. **Influencers/Specifiers.**  Similar to a VAR, but these firms generally design highly complex, large projects (commercial buildings), do not take title to product, and have a group of suppliers whose products can be specified to the design. Selling effort is focused on both the ultimate customer and the specifier. Distribution of product is handled through other channel formats.

*Examples:* Architects, designers, consultants

13. **Financial Service Providers.**  These formats have historically been initiated by joint ventures with financial service companies to finance margin purchases for customers or dealers (e.g., floor planning). They have been expanded to allow manufacturers to initiate distribution in new markets and assess these markets. High-capital, highly controlled distribution channel for one or two suppliers.

*Examples:* Branded chemicals, construction equipment

## OTHER CHANNEL FORMATS

1. **Door-to-Door Formats.**  To some extent these are variations on the channel formats previously listed. These formats have existed in the United States since pioneer days for products with a high personal sales costs and high margins, sold in relatively small orders (encyclopedias, vacuum cleaners). A wide range of variations (e.g., home-party format) attempt to get many small buyers in one location to minimize the sales cost and provide a unique shopping experience. Variations of the format have also spread to industrial and commercial markets to capitalize on similar market needs (e.g., Snap-On Tools uses a variation of the home-party system by driving the product and salespeople to mechanics' garages and selling to them on their lunch hours). Each format is different and needs to be analyzed to understand its unique characteristics. A brief summary of the more identifiable formats follows:

   a. **Individual On-Site.**  Very effective for generating new business for high-margin product requiring a high level of interaction with customers.

   *Examples:* Fuller Brush, Electrolux, bottled water, newspapers

   b. **Route.**  Used to service routine repetitious purchases that do not need to be resold on each call. Sometimes price is negotiated once and only changed on an exception basis. This concept was historically more prevalent in consumer lines (e.g., milk deliveries) but has recently spread to a variety of commercial and industrial segments.

   *Examples:* Office deliveries of copier paper and toner

   c. **Home party.**  Similar to individual on-site sales, this format takes the product to a group of individuals, as outlined in the introduction.

   *Examples:* Tupperware, Snap-On Tools

d. **Multilevel Marketing.** Salesperson not only sells product but recruits other salespeople who become a leveraged sales force that gives the original salesperson a commission on sales. Channel can be used for "high sizzle," high margin, fast-growth opportunities in branded differentiated products.

   *Examples:* Amway, Shaklee, NuSkin, plumbing products, cosmetics, other general merchandise

e. **Service Merchandising/"Rack Jobbing."** Similar to a route but expanded to provide a variety of services with the product. Originally, the rack jobber sold small consumer items to grocery stores, merchandised the product, and owned the inventory, merely paying the retailer a commission for the space. This concept is expanding to the commercial, industrial, and home markets in a variety of niches: maintaining a stockroom of office supplies, maintaining repair parts stock, servicing replenishable items in the home such as chemicals, purified water, salt, and so on.

   *Examples:* Specialty items and gadgets or novelties; paperback books, magazines

2. **Buyer-Initiated Formats.** These formats have been built on the concept of all buyers joining together to buy large quantities at better prices. It has expanded to give these buyers other securities and leverage that they might not be able to obtain on their own (e.g., private labeling, advertising design). As with the door-to-door concepts, variations of this concept are proliferating to meet individual buyers' needs.

   a. **Co-op** Companies, usually in the same industry, create an organization in which each member becomes a shareholder. The organization uses the combined strength of the shareholders to get economies of scale in several business areas, such as purchasing, advertising, or private-label manufacturing. This format is generally designed to allow small companies to compete more effectively with large competitors. Although wholesaler-distributors can form or join co-ops, their use as an alternate channel format may direct buyers from nonwholesalers-distributors.

   *Example:* Topco

   b. **Dealer-Owned-Co-op.** Similar to the co-op format, except the co-op may perform many of the functions rather than contracting for them with third-party suppliers (e.g., own warehouses). Shareholders/members are generally charged a fee for usage, and all profits in the co-op at year-end are refundable to the shareholders on some prorated basis. In many instances, this format has elements of a franchise.

   *Example:* Distribution America

   c. **Buying Group.** Similar to the co-op, except the relationship is usually much less structured. Companies can be members of several buying groups. The loose affiliation usually does not commit the members to performance. This format has taken on a host of roles. A group can buy through the wholesale distribution channel or direct from manufacturers. Often, wholesaler distributors are members of buying groups for low-volume items.

   *Examples:* AMC, May Merchandising

3. **Point-of-Consumption Merchandising Formats.** This concept has grown, from the practice of strategically placing vending machines where demand is predictable and often discretionary and the cost of selling through a full-time salesperson would be too high, to never before imagined commercial, industrial, and home markets for products and services. The increased use of technology and telecommunications has opened this channel to even more products and services.

   a. **Vending/Kiosks.** Kiosks have historically been very small retail locations that carry a very narrow product line. Through interactive video, online ordering technology, and artificial intelligence, this format has been significantly enhanced and can operate unattended. It is also being used for point-of-use dispensing of maintenance supplies and tools. "Purchases" are recorded in a log by the computer to control inventory shrinkage and balance inventory levels.

      *Examples:* Film processing, candy, tobacco, compact discs, and tapes

   b. **Pay-Per-Serving Point of Dispensing.** Product is prepared or dispensed by vending machine at the time of purchase. Vending machines for soup and coffee, soft drinks, and candy or food are usual uses of this format, but it is expanding to include such foods as pizza and pasta.

      *Examples:* Beverages, food

   c. **Computer Access Information.** Many of the computer access information formats have not necessarily altered the product function (products are not available online), but they have significantly altered the service and information function by uncoupling them from the product. This allows the product to pass through cheaper channels.

      *Examples:* Online information services, cable movies, news wire services, shopping services for groceries

4. **Third-Party Influencer Formats.** These formats are designed around the concept that an organization that has a relationship with a large number of people or companies can provide a channel for products and services not traditionally associated with the organization (e.g., a school selling candy to the community, using school children as a sales force). Here again, the concept has broadened across both the commercial and industrial sectors and deepened in terms of the products and services offered.

   a. **Charity** This format typically involves sales of goods and services in which the sponsoring charitable organization receives a commission on the sale. All types of products can be included and can be shipped direct or outsourced. Sales forces may be nonpaid volunteers.

      *Examples:* Market Day, World's Finest Chocolate

   b. **Company-Sponsored Program.** Employers contract with companies for products and services for their employees or segments of employees on an as-needed basis. The provider has access to the employee base.

      *Examples:* Health care and drug services, car maintenance

   c. **Premium and Gift Market.** Companies buy products customized with company logos or names for sale or distribution

      *Examples:* Pens, plaques, awards, T-shirts, novelties

d. **Product Promotion Mailing with Normal Correspondence.** Promotion of products is done by mailing to customers with letters and perhaps phone call follow-up. Typically involves promotional inserts with credit card and other billings. Logistics and order fulfillment activities may be handled by others.

*Examples:* American Express, VISA, MasterCard

e. **Customer List Cross-Selling.** An unusual format in that the customer list is sold by one company to another. In effect, the marketing function is circumvented. Started in the customer industry but migrating to the commercial and industrial segments.

*Examples:* Catalog companies, credit card companies

5. **Catalog and Technology-Aided Formats.** The time-honored catalog marketing channel dates back from their use by department stores to extend merchandising abilities to a predominantly rural U.S. population of the late 1800s. Catalog use has expanded dramatically to follow the buying habits of consumers and institutions. Although it continues to be a threat to traditional merchant wholesaler-distributors through mail order and links to technology, catalogs are have become sales tools for some wholesaler-distributors. The format should be evaluated carefully in all sectors of the market.

a. **Specialty Catalogs.** Uses catalogs to promote a narrow range of special products or services. Mailings are made to potential and repeat customers. Orders come in by mail or phone.

*Examples:* Eddie Bauer, Bass Pro Shops, Williams Sonoma

b. **Business-to-Business Catalogs.** Similar to specialty catalogs except that the product and customer focus is on business.

*Examples:* Moore Business Forms, Global, CompuAdd, Damart

c. **Television Home Shopping and Satellite Networks.** Heavily dependent on technology, these methods offer shopping in the comfort of your own home. Also has business application. Orders are placed by phone.

*Example:* Home Shopping Network

d. **Interactive Merchandising.** Could embody many of the attributes of the three preceding types, but also allows for extensive, interactive, in-store capabilities, as well as online ordering. It may offer inventory checking or physical modeling capabilities and unusually extensive communication linkages.

*Examples:* Florsheim, kitchen planning computers in do-it-yourself home centers

e. **Third-Party Catalog Services.** Catalog selling format in which one or more suppliers provide a combined catalog for a group of customers frequenting a certain place.

*Examples:* Airline in-flight magazines and catalogs, in-room hotel publications

f. **Trade Shows.** A format used in some segments for direct sales order activities. Suppliers sell from booths at major trade shows or conventions. Also used for retail applications.

*Examples:* Boats, cars, hardware/software applications

g. **Database Marketing.** Databases of customer buying habits and demographics are analyzed to enable the company to target customers for future mailing. Also used for retail applications.

*Examples:* Large grocery/consumer products companies, telephone companies

CHAPTER **2**

# End-User Analysis: Segmenting and Targeting

**LEARNING OBJECTIVES**

**After reading this chapter, you will be able to:**

- Understand the central role played by end-users and their demands in the design of marketing channels.
- Define "service outputs" and identify and analyze them.
- Recognize how to divide a market into channel segments for the purposes of marketing channel design or modification.
- Understand how to target channel segments to optimize sales and profits.
- Evaluate when and whether to try to meet all expressed service output demands in the short run in a particular market.
- Describe the relationship between service output demands and solutions to overall channel design problems.

Developing a marketing channel strategy, similar to many other marketing activities, must start with the end-user—even for a manufacturer that does not sell directly to end-users. For example, a manufacturer selling through a distributor may book a sale if the distributor buys some inventory, but ultimately, it is the end-user who holds the "power of the purse." Therefore, the manufacturer's level of demand from the distributor derives only from the ultimate end-users. In turn, a channel manager needs to understand the nature of end-users' demands before he or she can design an effective channel that meets or exceeds such demands. The most useful insights for channel design are not about *what* end-users want to consume but rather *how* they want to buy and use the products or services being purchased. In this chapter, we thus assume, as a given, that there is a viable product for the market, to focus more specifically on understanding *how* to sell this offering, rather than on what to sell.

This chapter also focuses on the **end-user**, or the demand side of marketing channel strategy (i.e., downstream side), by describing end-user behavior. In every market, end-users have varying preferences and demands for **service outputs** that can reduce their search, waiting time, storage, and other costs. Grouping end-users by their service output demands (as opposed to preferences for physical product attributes) helps us define potential target market segments and then design specific marketing channel solutions.

## UNDERSTANDING THE IMPORTANCE OF SEGMENTATION

End-users (whether business-to-business buyers or individual consumers) purchase products and services of every sort. Yet in most cases, they consider more than just the product important. This chapter's sidebar on corporate personal computer (PC) purchases illustrates this idea: A particular product or service can be bought in multiple ways. The product stays the same, but the method of buying and selling the product and the associated services that accompany the product vary. In corporate PC purchases, small to medium-sized corporate buyers can choose between buying PCs directly from the manufacturer or through a corporate supplier, such as CDW. The choice likely depends on the kinds of customer services offered by CDW, which are tailored specifically to this segment of buyer. This and other service outputs offered through the CDW channel create a **product + service output bundle** that this targeted customer really values.

Even when the product can be standardized across global markets, the way the user wants to buy the product often remains unique to each country. Researchers argue that of the four standard marketing mix variables (product, promotion, prices, place), the place, or **channel strategy**, is often the least amenable to global standardization.[1] Channel managers responsible for designing channel strategies to penetrate global markets thus need to segment end-users' needs, even if standardized approaches can work for advertising or product design.

---

### Sidebar 2-1

### CDW and PC purchases by small to medium-sized business buyers[2]

Personal computers have become virtually **commodity products**. The technology is well enough established that buyers know they can purchase a computer with a given combination of characteristics (e.g., memory space, weight, speed, monitor quality) from multiple manufacturers. In such a market, two questions immediately emerge:

1. How can any manufacturer differentiate itself from the competitive crowd to gain disproportionate market share and/or margins higher than purely competitive ones?

2. What role might an intermediary play when the product purchase appears to be a straight commodity one?

CDW (formerly known by its expanded name, Computer Discount Warehouse) has risen to the challenge by adopting an enduring role as a valued intermediary in specific market segments—particularly small and medium-sized business buyers and government/educational markets. In this process, it also has attracted the attention and business of major computer makers.

## Continued

When serving small to medium-sized business buyers, CDW recognizes that it is not just a PC (or a set of PCs) being purchased but rather the products and the *ancillary valued services* accompanying them. The firm argues that it serves as the chief technical officer of small firms. What does this mean in terms of the demand for and supply of service outputs, along with the product purchased?

- CDW is a key provider of *advice and expertise* to buyers, pertaining to everything from the appropriate configuration of products to buy to the set-up of a local area network. CDW is also available after the purchase if any customer service problems arise.
- CDW prides itself on its *speed of delivery*; 99 percent of orders are shipped the day they are received. The company can make this promise because of its investment in a 400,000-square-foot warehouse, which permits it to hold significant speculative inventory and avoid stockouts.
- CDW offers different *customer service* options: A customer can buy online, without a great deal of sales help, but CDW also assigns a salesperson to every account, even small, online purchase accounts. This service output gives the buyer access to a person to talk to if any questions or problems arise, and it increases the buyer's flexibility in terms of how to shop. The salesperson has no incentive to be overly aggressive, because a sale results in the same commission, whether the customer orders online or through the salesperson. A CDW salesperson goes through four months of training before being allowed to serve customers, so his or her level of expertise and professionalism is high enough to serve the customer well.

- CDW offers its customers broad *assortment and variety*. A small business buyer can buy directly from a manufacturer, such as Dell or Hewlett-Packard, but that means restricting him- or herself to one manufacturer's product line. Buying through CDW gives the buyer access to many different brands, which can be useful when putting components together in the optimal computer systems. CDW enhances the effective assortment available by also refiguring products before shipping them out, to customize them to the demands of the business buyer.

How well does CDW compare to the competition? Offering high levels of service outputs is great, but the question always remains: How well did the channel perform against other routes to market through which a customer can buy? When CDW faced a strong challenge from Dell Computer, offering 0 percent financing for the first time, together with free shipping and rebate programs, how did CDW withstand the competitive attack? For an individual buyer, such questions take on a different perspective: How much are CDW's extra service outputs worth to my company? For the buyer that values quick delivery, assortment, and CDW's targeted customer service, the apparent price premium is well worth the money, because it saves the buyer the cost of acquiring those services in another way (or the cost of not getting the desired level of service).

Thus, CDW's strategy of focusing on a particular subset of all computer buyers and providing valued service outputs to them, along with a quality product, has helped the company cement its relationships with these buyers, while also making it a preferred intermediary channel partner to key manufacturers.

These examples suggest a need to identify *how* end-users want to buy, as well as *what* they hope to purchase. Different end-users have different needs; understanding and responding to those demands can create new business opportunities for manufacturers (and failing to understand them can short-circuit such opportunities). We thus turn to a discussion of the types of preferences that are most critical to evaluate when segmenting end-users, by defining the concept of service outputs.

# END-USER SEGMENTATION CRITERIA: SERVICE OUTPUTS

An existing framework codifies and generalizes how end-users want to buy a particular product, as a basis for determining channel structure.[3] We use this approach to discuss how to segment the market for channel design purposes. Specifically, this framework asserts that channel systems exist and remain viable over time because they perform duties that reduce end-users' search, waiting time, storage, or other costs. These benefits are the *service outputs* of the channel. All else being equal (e.g., price, physical product attributes), *end-users prefer a marketing channel that provides more service outputs*. These service outputs in turn can be classified into six general categories:

1. Bulk breaking
2. Spatial convenience
3. Waiting or delivery time
4. Product variety
5. Customer service
6. Information sharing

This list is generic and can be customized to any particular application, but the six service outputs cover the main categories of needs that end-users demand from upstream channel partners.

## Bulk Breaking

**Bulk breaking** refers to the end-user's ability to buy a desired (possibly small) number of units, even if the product or service originally was produced in large, batch-production lot sizes. When the channel system allows end-users to buy in small lots, purchases more easily support consumption, reducing the need for end-users to carry unnecessary inventory. However, if end-users must purchase larger lots (i.e., benefit less from bulk breaking), some disparity emerges between purchasing and consumption patterns, burdening end-users with product handling and storage costs. The more bulk breaking the channel does, the smaller the lot size end-users can buy, and the higher is the channel's service output level, which likely leads the end-user to be more willing to pay a higher price that covers the costs to the channel of providing small lot sizes.

The common practice of charging lower per-unit prices for larger package sizes in frequently purchased consumer packaged goods categories at grocery stores is a well-known example of this phenomenon. Consider how a family might buy laundry detergent at home versus when renting a vacation house. At home, the family likely buys the large, economy size of detergent, perhaps at a supermarket or hypermarket, because it is easy to store in the laundry room at home, and eventually the family will use up that large bottle of detergent. The large bottle is comparatively inexpensive per fluid ounce. But when on vacation for a week at a rental cottage, the family likely prefers a small bottle of detergent—despite its much higher price per fluid ounce—because they do not want to end the week with a large amount left over (which they will probably have to leave at the cottage). Most vacationers are not at all surprised, or even reluctant, to pay a considerably higher price per ounce for the convenience of buying and using a smaller bottle of detergent when on vacation. Indeed, it even is more common for unit prices for such products to be much higher in resort town supermarkets than in supermarkets or hypermarkets serving permanent residents.[4]

With these examples, we assume that the more an end-user consumes, the more utility he or she attains. However, not all goods are "good." Consumers assess the pros and cons of each item they purchase; in the case of vice goods such as cookies or soda, they may want to purchase limited portions to help them stay healthy. Thus, firms can profit more from selling smaller packages when the general consumer finds a small portion more acceptable.[5]

## Spatial Convenience

**Spatial convenience** provided by market decentralization in wholesale and/or retail outlets increases consumers' satisfaction by reducing transportation requirements and search costs. Community shopping centers, neighborhood supermarkets, convenience stores, vending machines, and gas stations are but a few examples of the varied channel forms designed to satisfy consumers' demands for spatial convenience. Business buyers value spatial convenience too: The business PC buyer appreciates that CDW delivers PCs directly to the place of business, as well as coming to pick up computers that need service.

## Waiting Time

**Waiting time** is the time that the end-user must wait between ordering and receiving the goods or postsales service. The longer the waiting time, the more inconvenient it is for the end-user, who must plan or predict consumption levels far in advance. Usually, the longer end-users are willing to wait, the more compensation (i.e., lower prices) they receive, whereas quick delivery is associated with a higher price paid. This trade-off is evident in CDW's positioning for its small and medium business buyers. In response to queries about the threat of lower-priced computers from Dell Computer, the CEO of CDW responded, "We are seldom below Dell's price, but we get it to you faster"—shipping in 1 day versus in the 10–12 days Dell required.[6]

The intensity of demand for quick delivery varies for the purchase of *original equipment* (for which it may be lower) versus the purchase of *postsales service* (for which it is frequently very high). Consider a hospital purchasing an expensive ultrasound machine. Its original machine purchase is easy to plan, and the hospital is unlikely to be willing to pay a higher price for quick delivery of the machine itself. However, if the ultrasound machine breaks down, the demand for quick repair service may be very intense, and the hospital may be willing to pay a price premium for a service contract that promises speedy service. In such cases, a sophisticated channel manager must price the product versus postsales service purchases very differently, to reflect the different concatenation and intensity of demand for these service outputs. Similarly, airline ticket prices change as the departure date approaches, to account for both the number of seats remaining and the lower-price sensitivity of business travelers who need to reach a specific destination and do not want to wait.[7]

Another example combines demands for bulk breaking, spatial convenience, and delivery time. In the beer market in Mexico, understanding market demands requires an understanding of the market's and consumers' environmental characteristics and constraints. A market with limited infrastructural development usually is characterized by consumers with high demands for service outputs, such as spatial convenience (i.e., consumers cannot travel easily to remote retail locations), minimal waiting time for goods, and extensive bulk breaking (consumers lack sufficient disposable income to keep "backup stocks" of goods in their homes in case of retail stock-outs). In the Mexican market, major beer manufacturers sell through grocery stores, liquor stores, and hypermarkets, as well as through restaurants. As an additional channel though, they sell beer through very small local distributors—apartment residents who buy a small keg of beer and resell it by the bottle to neighborhood buyers who cannot afford a six pack. The end-users also usually provide their own (washed, used) beer bottles for the "local" distributor to fill. The manufacturer values this channel, because the other standard retail channels cannot meet the intense service output demands of these lower-end consumers.

## Product Variety and Assortment

When the breadth of the variety or the depth of the product assortment available to end-users is greater, so are the outputs of the marketing channel system, but also so are the overall distribution costs, because offering greater assortment and variety means carrying more inventory. **Variety** describes generically different classes of goods that constitute the product offering, namely, the *breadth* of product lines. The term **assortment** instead refers to the *depth* of product brands or models offered within each generic product category. Discount department stores, such as Kohl's or Wal-Mart, have limited assortments of fast-moving, low-priced items across as wide variety of household goods, ready-to-wears, cosmetics, sporting goods, electric appliances, auto accessories, and so forth. A specialty store dealing primarily in home audiovisual electronic goods instead offers a very large line of receivers, speakers, and high-fidelity equipment, offering the deepest assortment of models, styles, sizes, prices, and so on.

Not only is the extent of the product array important, but also critical is *which* assortment of goods is offered to each target consumer. JCPenney, the U.S. mid-scale department store, has sought to change its image from "your grandmother's store"— and a relatively downscale one at that—to a trendy fashion boutique. It signed an exclusive distribution agreement with Michele Bohbot, the designer of the Bisou Bisou clothing line, previously only sold in boutiques and upscale department stores. It also hired David Hacker, a trend expert who looks for emerging fashion trends to attract the so-called Holy Grail of retail: 25- to 35-year-old women, who account for $15 billion in annual clothing revenue. This target market is a much younger, fashion-forward shopper than JCPenney's traditional, 46-year-old, female buyer. And indeed, at a Bisou Bisou fashion show in the Bronx, New York, JCPenney attracted almost 100 young women. One of them, laden with shopping bags, noted the difference: "I guess I'm going to have to start coming to JCPenney now. Wow!"[8]

The combination of the right assortment and quick delivery is a winning service output combination for Hot Topic too. This chain of more than 600 stores targets teen girls; its CEO and directors often go to concerts to find popular new trends that can be turned into new store merchandise.[9] Hot Topic can roll out a new line (e.g., t-shirts with a popular band's logo) in just eight weeks, whereas its competitor. The

Gap often needs up to nine months to bring new products to store shelves. This speed is critical when the right assortment is fueled by fads, which flame and fade very quickly.

## Customer Service

**Customer service** refers to all aspects of easing the shopping and purchase process for end-users as they interact with commercial suppliers (for business-to-business purchases) or retailers (for business-to-consumer purchases). The CDW sidebar outlines several types of customer service valued by the small to medium-sized business buyers, as encapsulated in the simple statement: "We're the chief technical officer for many smaller firms."

Excellent customer service can translate directly into sales and profit. But a U.S. industry that has long been plagued by poor customer service is cable and other pay television services. In American Customer Satisfaction Index (ACSI) surveys, cable TV operators often earn some of the lowest customer satisfaction scores for any company or industry. Customer service is typically outsourced to third-party providers (another channel partner), which offer low pay and poor training to their employees. In contrast, DirecTV ranks at the top of its industry in customer satisfaction and enjoys a high average monthly revenue from its customers, as well as a very low *churn rate* (i.e., the rate of turnover of end-users buying its service)—even though it uses the same outsourced customer service companies as some of its competitors. How does it accomplish this? It stations an employee at each of its outsourced call centers, to gain more control; it pays the call centers more for customer service, which translates into better service provided; it provides better information to the customer service reps, through its overhauled information system; and it gives the customer service reps various nonmonetary forms of compensation, such as free satellite TV.[10]

The type of customer service offered also must be sensitive to the targeted end-user. Cabela's, a small chain of stores catering to outdoorsy people, recognizes a key feature of its mostly male target market: These men hate to shop. To appeal to them, Cabela's makes its stores showcases of nature scenes, waterfalls, and stuffed animals, then staffs each department liberally with well-trained sales staff who must pass tests to demonstrate their knowledge of the products. Outside its rural stores, it offers kennels (for dogs) and corrals (for horses), to cater to customers who visit in the middle of a hunting trip. Cabela's augments this targeted customer service with a carefully determined product assortment. The depth of its assortment in most categories is six to ten times greater than that of competitors such as Wal-Mart, and it stocks high-end, not just low-priced, low-quality goods. To appeal to other members of the family, it also offers a relatively broad assortment that draws in women and children. Cabela's understands that rural shoppers want more than Wal-Mart can provide, and that they care about service, fashion, and ambiance, not just price, such that it can routinely draw shoppers who travel hours to reach its store (i.e., who are willing to trade off spatial convenience for superior customer service and assortment).[11]

### Information Sharing

Finally, **information sharing** refers to education provided to end-users about product attributes or usage capabilities, as well as pre- and postpurchase services. The business PC buyer values presale information about what products to buy, in what combinations, with what peripheral computer devices attached, and with what service packages, as well as postsales information if and when components or systems fail.

For some manufacturers and retailers, such information sharing has been classified as *solutions retailing*, which appears crucial in generating new and upgrade sales from end-users. Home Depot offers do-it-yourself classes in all sorts of home improvement areas; computer and software companies like Hewlett-Packard (HP) and Microsoft have followed suit, setting up "experience centers" in retail stores to enhance sales of complicated products whose benefits consumers may not understand, such as Media Center PCs, digital cameras that print on computers, personal digital assistants, and the like. A collaboration between Microsoft and HP offered a series of educational programs at various retailers, designed to increase sales of HP Media Center PCs. One section of the display, called "Create," showed consumers how to use the Media Center PC as a digital photography center with Microsoft software. Other displays revealed how to use the PC for home office applications, as part of a home office network, and as a music center. The mini-classes were run by a third-party firm that staffed the retail store booths. Hewlett-Packard found that purchase intentions increased by as much as 15 percent among consumers who saw these product demonstrations, as well as evidence that the programs strengthened products' brand image and brand equity. Such information dissemination is a costly proposition though; Microsoft and HP bear the costs, not the retailers themselves. They also view such efforts as crucial in the short run but redundant in the longer run, because the relevant information eventually diffuses into the broader consumer population.[12] The trend is continuing as Microsoft adds its own retail stores to provide a two-way communication link between Microsoft and end-users.

Note that price has not been listed as a service output. **Price** is what the customer pays to *consume* the bundle of product + service outputs; it is not a service that gets consumed itself. However, it is significant in the sense that end-users routinely make trade-offs among service outputs, product attributes, and price, weighing which product/service bundle (at a specific price) provides the greatest overall utility or satisfaction. Because of this trade-off, marketing researchers often investigate the relative importance of price, together with service outputs and physical product attributes, in statistical investigations (e.g., conjoint analysis, cluster analysis), consistent with our conceptual view of price as something different from a service output, just as a physical product attribute is not a service output yet still affects an end-user's overall utility.

The six service outputs we have discussed here are wide ranging but still may not be exhaustive. That is, it is risky to adopt an inflexible definition of service outputs, because different product and geographic markets naturally may demand different service outputs.[13]

## SEGMENTING END-USERS BY SERVICE OUTPUTS

Service outputs clearly differentiate the offerings of various marketing channels, and the success and persistence of multiple marketing channels at any one time suggests that different groups of end-users value service outputs differently. Thus, we must consider how to group end-users according to their **service output needs**, by segmenting the market into groups of end-users who differ *not in the product(s) they want to buy*, but in *how they want to buy*.

For example, at the very high end of service valuation in any market, there is a (usually small) segment of buyers who are both very service sensitive and very price *in*sensitive and who can be profitably served through a specialized channel. Consider men's clothing. Albert Karoll, a custom tailor in the Chicago area, sells fine custom men's clothing by visiting his customers, rather than making them visit him, as most fine clothiers do. He takes fabric, buttons, and all the makings to the customers, helps them choose the clothing they want, fits them, and then has the clothing made up before personally returning it, to deliver the finished goods and offer any final alterations. His target buyer segment clearly has a very high demand for *spatial convenience*, as stated by one of his loyal suburban customers: "For me to travel downtown is very hard to do. I'd much rather have him come here. It saves me time and money, and I get the same quality that I'd get going downtown to his store." The target customer also values custom clothing made to order—the ultimate in assortment and variety. Karoll provides quick service and delivery, both pre- and postsale; he once flew from Chicago to Birmingham, Alabama, to alter some clothing sent to a client there, just two days after the client received the clothes and found they needed alterations. Ultimately, Karoll's target customer is a man whose most scarce asset is *time*, and who thus has extremely high service output demands with little price sensitivity. Karoll does not seek to serve every man who would like to buy a suit; instead, he has carefully crafted a business centered on the delivery of service, rather than just the sale of a high-end piece of business clothing, and he knows who is in his target segment and who is *not*. In this sense, the targeting decision, when applied to channel design, entails a choice of whom *not* to pursue, just as much as what segment *to* pursue.[14]

From a **process perspective**, there are three general steps to segmenting end-users by service outputs. First, it is essential to generate a comprehensive list of all the potential service outputs desired by each end-user for the products being offered. This list can be derived from qualitative focus groups or exploratory interviews to generate unbiased summaries of all the service outputs that apply to the particular product and market in question.[15] Such research provides a set of service outputs that might be demanded by some or all groups of end-users in the market.

Second, using this list of possible service outputs, the actual segmentation of the market can proceed in multiple ways. The market might be divided into *a priori* segments (e.g., those often used in product or advertising decisions), then analyzed to see whether those segments share common purchasing preferences. Alternatively, research might be designed and conducted to define channel segments that best describe end-users' service output needs and purchasing patterns. This latter path is preferable, because end-users' preferred shopping and buying habits rarely correlate with their preferences for product features, media habits, lifestyles, or other traits that management and advertising agencies usually employ in their segmentation strategies. In general, channel segmentation should be designed to produce groups of buyers who (1) are maximally similar *within* a group; (2) are maximally different *between* groups; and (3) differ on dimensions that *matter* for building a distribution system. Traditional marketing research techniques such as cluster analysis and constant-sum scales can identify groups of end-users with similar service outputs needs. It is not enough to ask respondents their preferences for various service outputs though. With a free choice, most people prefer more of *all* the service outputs. To obtain information that is ultimately useful for designing marketing channels to meet the key needs of target segments, it is essential to understand how end-users actually behave in the marketplace, by asking respondents to trade off one attribute of the channel for another (e.g., locational convenience versus low price; extensive product variety versus expert sales assistance).

Third, when the overall market has been segmented into similar groups of end-users, according to their preferred channel service outputs, price sensitivity, or other product-specific factors, the channel manager should name each segment to capture its identifying characteristics. Naming each segment facilitates internal communication and organizational alignment, which is helpful in executing an effective channel strategy.

Table 2-1 shows how constant-sum scales can be used to segment end-users in the business marketplace for a new high-technology product. The service outputs (references and credentials, financial stability and longevity, product demonstrations and trials), along with price sensitivity, are listed along the left-hand side; the columns represent the segments (lowest total cost, responsive support, full-service, and references and credentials) that emerge according to respondents' strength of preference. The names assigned to the segments were derived from the strength of their preferences for specific service outputs. For example, the lowest total cost segment assigned 32 out of 100 points to the service output "lowest price" but only 8 points to "responsive problem solving after sale" output, whereas the responsive support segment showed flipped allocations (29 points to responsive problem solving after sale, but 8 points to lowest price). Finally, the percentage of respondents in each segment appears at the bottom of each column; the majority of respondents (and thus of the population of customers at large, assuming the sample is representative) are in the full-service segment. This study supports a trade-off between price and service outputs, recognizing that a segment's demand for service outputs really reflects its willingness to pay for them—and highlights the need to include sensitivity to pricing levels in any such analysis.

Some interesting insights arise from Table 2-1. First, marketing channels serving any of the specific segments need to deliver more of some service outputs than others. Thus, it is unlikely that any one-channel strategy can satisfy the needs of all segments. For example, the lowest price is highly valued in only one segment (i.e., the lowest total cost segment, representing only 16 percent of respondents). The majority of the market simply is not driven primarily by price considerations. This information is invaluable for designing channel strategies that respond to the service

**TABLE 2-1**    Business-to-business channel segments for a new high-technology product

| Possible Service Output Priorities | Lowest Total Cost/ Presales Info Segment | Responsive Support/Postsales Segment | Full-Service Relationship Segment | References and Credentials Segment |
|---|---|---|---|---|
| References and credentials | 5 | 4 | 6 | 25 |
| Financial stability and longevity | 4 | 4 | 5 | 16 |
| Product demonstrations and trials | 11 | 10 | 8 | 20 |
| Proactive advice and consulting | 10 | 9 | 8 | 10 |
| Responsive assistance during decision process | 14 | 9 | 10 | 6 |
| One-stop solution | 4 | 1 | 18 | 3 |
| Lowest price | 32 | 8 | 8 | 6 |
| Installation and training support | 10 | 15 | 12 | 10 |
| Responsive problem solving after sale | 8 | 29 | 10 | 3 |
| Ongoing relationship with a supplier | 1 | 11 | 15 | 1 |
| Total | 100 | 100 | 100 | 100 |
| **Percentage of Respondents** | 16% | 13% | 61% | 10% |

*Respondents allocated 100 points among the following supplier-provided service outputs, according to their importance to their company:*

■ = Greatest Discriminating Attributes        ▢ = Additional Important Attributes

Source: Reprinted with permission of Rick Wilson, Chicago Strategy Associates, ©2000.

output needs of customers, even if doing so implies higher prices than a no-frills solution might entail. In contrast, all the segments value installation and training support at least moderately highly; therefore, this support capability must be designed into every single channel solution. Similar insights stem from the rows of Table 2-1, which reveal the contrasts among segments in terms of other specific service output demands.

Appendix 2-1 outlines the process, with prototypical examples, for completing a service output segmentation template, a tool for segmenting end-users to facilitate targeting by specific channel structures. Accompanying Appendix 2-1 is a blank service output segmentation template in Table 2-2 to assist channel managers in conducting an end-user segmentation analysis.

**TABLE 2-2   Service output segmentation template**

| Segment Name/ Descriptor | SERVICE OUTPUT DEMAND: | | | | | |
| | Bulk Breaking | Spatial Convenience | Delivery/ Waiting Time | Assortment/ Variety | Customer Service | Information Sharing |
|---|---|---|---|---|---|---|
| 1. | | | | | | |
| 2. | | | | | | |
| 3. | | | | | | |
| 4. | | | | | | |
| 5. | | | | | | |

*INSTRUCTIONS:* If quantitative market research data are available, enter numerical ratings in each cell. If not, adopt an intuitive ranking system, noting for each segment whether demand for the given service output is *HIGH, MEDIUM,* or *LOW.*

## TARGETING END-USER SEGMENTS

After segmenting the market and identifying each end-user segment's distinct service output needs, the channel manager can integrate these insights into an overall marketing channel design and management plan. In particular, this information should be used to

- assess segment attractiveness,
- target a subset of the segments identified, and
- customize the marketing channel system solution used to sell to each targeted segment.

*Targeting a channel segment* means choosing to focus on that segment, with the goal of achieving significant sales and profits from selling to it, just as Albert Karoll, the custom men's suit seller, has done. He recognizes that his target end-users "are business executives, men who are short on time, who work their brains out."[16] Note that this description *excludes* most buyers, as well as most buyers of business suits. Furthermore, Karoll's segmentation definition hinges not on the product being purchased but rather on the services that accompany it. Therefore, Karoll's high-service (and high-price) offering fails to meet the demands of most suit buyers, but it is ideal for Karoll's identified target buyers.

More generally, if the channel segmentation process has proceeded appropriately, targeting multiple channel segments for channel system design purposes implies the need to build different marketing channels for each segment. Because doing so can be a costly, hard-to-manage activity, channel managers likely choose an "attractive" subset of all the identified segments to target. We thus suggest a corollary to the targeting concept: *Targeting means choosing which segments* not *to target*. Such choices represent difficult challenges for channel management teams, because all segments seemingly offer the potential for revenue dollars (though not always profits). Segmented service output demand information can help the channel manager choose which segments offer the greatest relative growth and profit opportunities for targeting. Even though other segments also offer some potential, only the best should be chosen for targeting. "Best" has different meanings for different companies, but it should include the size and sales potential of the targeted segment, the cost to serve them, the fit with the selling firm's competencies, and the intensity of competition for their business, among other factors.

Information on the targeted segments then can be used to design new marketing channels to meet needs or to modify existing marketing channels to better respond to demands for service outputs. A service output demand analysis can identify a new market opportunity that leads to the development of entirely new ways to sell to a particular segment. For example, fandango.com is a business formed by seven of the ten largest movie exhibitors in the United States, to sell movie tickets online (or by phone).[17] Instead of going to a movie theater the evening one wants to see a particular movie, standing in line, and perhaps finding out that the showing of that movie is sold out, fandango.com allows moviegoers to go online and purchase a ticket for a particular showing of a particular movie at a particular movie theater in advance, for a small fee per ticket. Tickets can be printed at home or picked up at the theater at convenient kiosks, saving time and lessening uncertainty for the consumer. This purchase channel provides consumers with a lower waiting/delivery time (because there is no wait at the theater), higher spatial convenience (because they can search for and buy theater tickets online), and a very broad assortment and variety (fandango.com sells tickets to nearly 70 percent of all theaters in the United States that are enabled for remote ticketing). Clearly, fandango.com is not for every moviegoer though, not least because of the extra charge per ticket it imposes. But fandango.com allows theaters to compete effectively against non-fandango theaters among a target segment of time-constrained moviegoers. It also might expand the total market for in-theater movie watching, because of the greater convenience it offers.

Ideally, the end-user analysis performed on service outputs should support segmenting, targeting, and positioning (channel design). Pursuing a channel strategy without this information is risky, because it is impossible to be sure that it has been executed properly, without knowing what the marketplace wants in its marketing channel. Considering the expense of setting up or modifying a marketing channel, it is prudent to perform the end-user analysis before proceeding to upstream channel decisions, which are also critical to any successful channel strategy. Performed correctly, an analysis of target segments' service output needs can be the foundation for higher profits, due to high-margin sales with intensely loyal end-users.

With this understanding of the end-user side of the marketing channel through a comprehensive segmentation and targeting analysis, we can turn to the upstream side of the channel in Chapter 3, to see how a marketing channel produces service outputs through the concerted efforts of all its members.

## TAKE-AWAYS

- An end-user's decision about where or from whom to purchase a product (or service) depends not just on *what* the end-user is buying but also on *how* the end-user wants to buy.
- The elements that describe *how* the product or service can be bought are called *service outputs*. Formally, service outputs are the productive outputs of the marketing channel, over which end-users exert demand and preference influences.
- A general list of service outputs, customizable to particular marketplace contexts, is as follows:
  - Bulk breaking
  - Spatial convenience
  - Waiting time (or quick delivery)
  - Variety and assortment
  - Customer service
  - Information sharing
- End-users make trade-offs among different combinations of (a) product attributes, (b) price, and (c) service outputs offered by different sellers to make final purchase decisions.
- Segmenting the market by service output demands is a useful tool for channel design, because the resulting groups of end-users are similar (within each group) in terms of the channel that best serves their needs.
- The ultimate purpose of a service output end-user analysis and design is to identify and assess end-user segments, target a subset of the segments identified, and customize the marketing channel system solution used to sell to each targeted segment.

## Endnotes

1. Boryana, Dimitrova and Bert Rosenbloom (2010), "Standardization versus Adaption in Global Markets: Is Channel Strategy Different?" *Journal of Marketing Channels* 17 (2), pp. 157–176.

2. The sources for this Sidebar include Campbell, Scott (2003), "CDW-G Calls on VARs," *Computer Reseller News*, November 17, no. 1071, p. 162; Campbell, Scott (2004), "CDW Snags Companywide Cisco Premier Status: Relationship Advances Reseller's Bid to Build Services Business," *Computer Reseller News* 12 (April 12), p. 2; Gallagher, Kathleen (2002), "CDW Computer Remains Afloat Despite Market's Choppy Waters," *Milwaukee Journal Sentinel*, September 29, p. D4; Jones, Sandra (2004), "Challenges Ahead for CDW: Dell Deals Make Inroads in Already Difficult Market," *Crain's Chicago Business*, June 28, p. 4; Kaiser, Rob (2000), "Vernon Hills, Ill, Computer Products Reseller Has an Approach to Win Business," *Chicago Tribune*, August 16; McCafferty, Dennis (2002), "Growing Like Gangbusters: Sales at Chicago-Area CDW-Government Shot up 63 Percent from 2000 to 2001," *VAR Business*, July 8; Moltzen, Edward (2003), "Looking for SMB Traction, Gateway Inks Reseller Pact with CDW," *CRN*, May 26, p. 55; O'Heir, Jeff (2003), "CDW Teams with Small VARs to Access Government Biz," *Computer Reseller News*, August 25, no. 1059, p. 6; O'Heir, Jeff (2003), "Time to Move On," *Computer Reseller News*, October 20,

no. 1067, p. 98; Schmeltzer, John (2003), "CDW Pulls Out the Stops to Reach Small Business," *Chicago Tribune*, September 8; Zarley, Craig and Jeff O'Heir (2003), "Seeking Solutions—CDW, Gateway and Dell Come Calling on Solution Providers for Services Expertise," *Computer Reseller News*, 16 (September 1).

3. Bucklin, Louis P. (1966), *A Theory of Distribution Channel Structure* (Berkeley, CA: IBER Special Publications); Bucklin, Louis P. (1972), *Competition and Evolution in the Distributive Trades* (Englewood Cliffs, NJ: Prentice Hall); Bucklin, Louis P. (1978), *Productivity in Marketing* (Chicago, IL: American Marketing Association), pp. 90–94.

4. Sailor, Matt (2010), "10 Things You Should Buy in Bulk," *HowStuffWorks,* http://www.money.howstuffworks.com/

5. Jain, Sanjay (2012), "Marketing of Vice Goods: A Strategic Analysis of the Package Size Decision," *Marketing Science* 31 (January), pp. 36–51.

6. Jones, Sandra (2004), "Challenges Ahead for CDW; Dell Deals Make Inroads in Already Difficult Market," *Crain's Chicago Business*, June 28, p.4.

7. "Price of Elasticity of Demand," *Convention Center Task Force*. San Diego County Tax Payer Association, July 31, 2009, http://www.conventioncentertaskforce.org/

8. Daniels, Cora (2003), "J.C. Penney Dresses Up," *Fortune* 147 (11, June 9), pp. 127–130.

9. "Hot Topic, Inc. Reports 1st Quarter Financial Results," *Hot Topic Inc.*, May 18, 2011, http://www.investorrelations.hot-topic.com/

10. Moran, Francis (2012), "Don't Wait until Your Customers Say Goodbye to Tel…," *Francis Moran and Associates,* September 20, http://bx.businessweek.com/

11. Helliker, Kevin (2002), "Retailer Scores by Luring Men Who Hate to Shop," *The Wall Street Journal Online*, December 17.

12. Saranow, Jennifer (2004), "Show, Don't Tell," *The Wall Street Journal Online*, March 22.

13. Kasturi Rangan, V., Melvyn A. J. Menezes, and E. P. Maier (1992), "Channel Selection for New Industrial Products: A Framework, Method, and Application," *Journal of Marketing* 56, pp. 72–73. These authors define five service outputs in their study of industrial goods: product information, product customization, product quality assurance, after-sales service, and logistics. Some outputs are specific examples of the generic service outputs defined by Bucklin (e.g., logistics refers to spatial convenience and waiting/delivery time), yet their work also highlights the value of being aware of the specific application.

14. Stanek, Steve (2003), "Custom Tailor Finds House Calls Often Worth the Trip," *Chicago Tribune Online Edition*, July 13.

15. Such data sometimes already exist. For example, in the computer industry, data on service outputs valued by end-users are collected by firms like IntelliQuest, Inc., and International Data Group.

16. Stanek, op. cit.

17. See http://www.fandango.com for more details.

# APPENDIX 2-1

## Service Output Segmentation Template: Tools for Analysis

Table 2-1 shows a completed end-user segmentation analysis in the market for telecommunications equipment and services. This analysis rests on the collection of sophisticated marketing research data. The marketing channel manager generally is well advised to conduct marketing research to determine what end-users really want in the way of service outputs, because the cost of guessing incorrectly is very high in a channel context.

This appendix describes how to complete the service output segmentation template in Table 2-2 (an empty and generic version of the segmentation in Table 2-1). We assume that the channel manager lacks detailed, quantitative marketing research data and thus seeks to give an intuitive sense of how to perform such an analysis and what to do with the codified information. The segmentation template is designed to help users segment the market, in ways that *matter* for distribution channel design, as well as report on segments' different demands for service outputs.

The first task is to identify the segments in the market being served. Standard segmentation measures may or may not be appropriate in a channel management context though. The key criterion to determine whether the segmentation was appropriate is whether the resulting groups of buyers require different sets of service outputs. For example, we might identify two segments for buyers of laptop computers: men and women. It is likely a valid segmentation criterion for some purposes (e.g., choosing advertising media to send promotional messages) but unlikely to be useful in a channel design and management context, because there is no discernible difference in the service outputs demanded by men and women. A better segmentation thus might be business buyers, personal use buyers, and student buyers.

The next step is to fill in information about the service output demands of each identified segment on the segmentation template. More information is always better, but in the absence of detailed marketing research data, it can be useful to simply identify demands as "Low," "Medium," or "High." It is then often useful to note how service output demands are expressed. Here are a few prototypical examples:

- A business buying laptop computers wants to buy more units than does a personal use or a student buyer. *Breaking bulk* (i.e., providing a smaller lot size) is effortful, so the business segment has a LOW demand for the bulk-breaking service output, whereas the personal use buyer and student have HIGH demands for this output (i.e., they want to buy only one computer at a time).
- *Spatial convenience* may be important to all three segments, but for different reasons. For example, the "sale" of a laptop computer is not over when the unit is purchased; postsales service is a critical factor that affects initial purchase decisions, as well as the subsequent satisfaction of end-users. We then might argue that personal use and student buyers have a relatively LOW demand for spatial convenience at the point of initial purchase, but they might express a HIGH demand for spatial convenience when it comes to getting a faulty unit fixed or getting technical service. Conversely, the business buyer may have a HIGH

demand for spatial convenience at the initial point of purchase (e.g., require a sales rep to visit the company rather than having a company representative go to a retail store); a large enough company also may have in-house computer repair and consulting facilities and thus exhibit LOW demand for spatial convenience for postsales service.

• The demand for *delivery/waiting time* is high if the end-user is unwilling to wait to receive the product or service. Impulse purchases are a classic product category for which almost all segments have HIGH demand for this service output. For our laptop computers, we again can differentiate between initial purchase versus postsales service step demands. At the initial purchase, the personal use buyer probably has a LOW demand for delivery/waiting time, though a student may have a very HIGH demand for quick delivery, particularly if the unit is purchased just in time for the beginning of the school year! Finally, a business buyer may have a very HIGH demand for this service output, if the lack of the laptops means lower sales or affect productivity.

At the postsales service stage, the personal use buyer may have a LOW demand for the delivery/waiting time service output, because he or she likely is willing to wait a few days to receive service or repairs, considering that personal uses of a computer often are not life-or-death concerns. The student instead has a very HIGH demand for the delivery/waiting time service output on the postsales service side, because the cost of downtime for this user is very high (cannot get homework done without the unit). The business buyer also may have a LOW demand for this service output though: Its internal service facilities could make it less dependent on the manufacturer's technical service or repair facilities, and it could have excess units in inventory that can be "swapped out" for a faulty unit until it is fixed.

• *Assortment/variety* demands refer to segments' preferences for a deep assortment in a given category and for a wide variety of product category choices. In our laptop example, we might ask, How intense is each segment's demand for an assortment of computer brands, and how intense are their demands for a variety of computers, peripherals, software, and so forth? The business buyer probably has very precise brand demands (HIGH demand), because it wants conformity across the units in use in the company. This end-user has a LOW demand for assortment. Aggregated across the entire population of business buyers though, our laptop marketer may observe considerable diversity in brand preferences. Thus, we must consider the different types of variety demands when studying markets from a micro (customer-specific) versus a macro (marketwide) perspective. The business buyer may have a moderate to HIGH demand for variety (e.g., software to do word processing, spreadsheets, and database management; printer ports, PC cards as peripherals), depending on the variety of tasks this buyer wants the laptops to perform. Among personal use buyers, the demand for variety is probably very LOW, because they tend to be the least sophisticated users and may demand only the most basic word processing or gaming software. However, their assortment (brand choice) demands may be HIGH; unsophisticated consumers often want to see a broad selection of models and brands before making a purchase decision. Student buyers probably fall in between, at a MEDIUM level, in their demand for assortment/variety: They may have more applications or uses for the laptop, and thus demand more peripherals and software programs, but they may not need to see a wide assortment of brands before making the purchase (the relevant brand set may be small if a school has dictated "acceptable" brands).

- Demands for *customer service* differ widely among the business, personal use, and student buyers in terms of not just levels but also *types* of customer service. The student buyer probably values home delivery very highly, as few students have cars to carry large items back from the store; the personal use buyer may not care about home delivery but value in-home installation services; and the business buyer likely cares little about either of these benefits but demands trade-in options on older machines.

- Finally, *information sharing* demands can be separated into pre- and post-sales information elements. Before purchase, a buyer may need information about differences in physical product attributes, how components fit together in a system, and how to use the new, state-of-the-art features. After purchase, the buyer instead may have questions about which add-on peripheral devices can be used with the computer and how or what software programs versions to install onto the machine. The personal use buyer likely places the highest value on both pre- and postsales information sharing, because she or he is unlikely to have a "support group" in place to provide key information about what, how, and where to buy. A student buyer may have more postpurchase informational needs than prepurchase ones, particularly if the school recommends a certain subset of laptops for use. The business buyer probably has relatively low informational demands, both pre- and postpurchase, particularly if the company is large enough to identify and specify approved laptop models, then support them after purchase. However, a procurement specialist at the company may have significant pre-sale informational needs at the time decisions are made about which laptop models to select and support.

When completed with codified information, the service output segmentation template supports several strategic uses:

1. It can reveal why sales tend to cluster in one segment, to the exclusion of others. If postsales service is poor, it will be difficult to sell to personal use and student buyers.

2. It may suggest a new channel opportunity for building sales among an underserved segment. Perhaps a channel structure can be designed that is ideally suited to the needs of student buyers. Competitors that otherwise fight solely on the basis of price for these sales then would be locked out of the sales channel.

3. Commonalities between and across segments, previously thought to be totally distinct, might emerge. For example, personal use and student buyers may share enough similarities that both can be served with only minor variations on a single channel theme.

4. The template can suggest what channel form would be best suited for serving each segment. Thus, it provides inputs to match segments to channels.

This list of service output demands cannot completely and fully characterize every demand in a specific market. For example, the customer service demand sometimes requires distinctions as pre- and postsales service elements, as does the "information sharing" service output demand. However, this framework provides an initial means to understand the types of service outputs firms must provide to appeal to end-users.

# CHAPTER 3

# Channel Analysis: Auditing Marketing Channels

**LEARNING OBJECTIVES**

**After reading this chapter, you will be able to:**

- Define the generic channel functions that characterize costly and value-added channel activities.
- Understand how the efficiency template helps codify channel function performance according to channel and channel participant.
- Describe the role of channel function allocation in designing a zero-based channel.
- Recognize how channel function performance leads to appropriate allocations of channel profits among channel members, using the equity principle.
- Locate channel function analysis within an overall channel audit process.
- Use the efficiency template even in conditions with little information.
- Define service and cost gaps and describe the sources of these gaps.
- Perform a gap analysis using both service and cost gap analysis templates.

One of the basic precepts in marketing states that sellers must seek to identify and meet the needs of their end-users in the marketplace. In a marketing channel strategy context, this precept means creating and running a marketing channel system that produces the service outputs demanded by targeted end-user segments. Thus, the next step in the process of developing a marketing channel strategy, after identifying targeted segments of end-users, is to *audit existing marketing channels*. Such audits evaluate each available channel member's capability to provide service outputs efficiently (bulk breaking, quick delivery, spatial convenience, assortment, variety, information sharing). This evaluation must include both the level and the cost of the service outputs provided by each channel member, because end-users are sensitive to the overall utility provided by the channel (i.e., benefits at a given price). Manufacturers, wholesalers, and retailers all participate in marketing channels to create the service outputs demanded by their target end-users. Just as the machinery in a production plant produces physical products, the members of a marketing channel are engaged in **productive activity**, even if what they produce is intangible. In this sense, productivity derives from the value that end-users place on the service outputs that result from channel efforts. The activities that produce the service outputs demanded by end-users are the **channel functions**.

Auditing *what* channel functions get performed by each channel member in the existing channel system, *by whom, at what levels,* and *at what cost,* provides several important benefits:

1. Detailed knowledge of the capabilities of each channel member allows them to diagnose and remedy shortcomings in the provision or price of service outputs to targeted segments.
2. An audit may identify gaps in service outputs desired by targeted end-user segments, such that the service providers can add necessary new channels or revise currently existing ones to address any shortcomings.
3. Knowing which channel members have incurred the costs of performing which channel functions helps members allocate channel profits equitably. In turn, channel members can better preserve a sense of fairness and cooperation and thus avert channel conflicts (see Chapter 11).

In this chapter, we continue our discussion of CDW (Sidebar 3-1), which we presented from a service output perspective in Chapter 2. We expand it with a consideration of **reverse logistics**, or the process the channel uses to handle returned merchandise (Sidebar 3-2). Therefore, in this chapter our discussion focuses on identifying and describing channel functions, as well as outline how managers might audit channel systems to identify a zero-based channel and any gaps in services provided and costs incurred.

## CHANNEL AUDIT CRITERIA: CHANNEL FUNCTIONS

As our conceptualization of channel functions in Chapter 1 indicated, specific channel members can specialize in one or more channel functions, even as they are completely excluded from participation in other activities (Figure 3-1). This latter condition may make it tempting to remove a particular member from the channel (i.e., change the channel *structure*). But the specialized functions performed by that channel member cannot simply be eliminated. After a channel member leaves the channel, its functions must shift to some other channel member, to preserve service output provision in the channel. The only exception to this rule arises if the eliminated channel member were performing activities that could be addressed elsewhere in the channel, so its contributions to the service output were redundant. For example, when an employee salesperson and an independent distributor's sales representative call on the same customer, they create wasted effort and cost. The channel may be better off using one or the other, not both, salespeople.

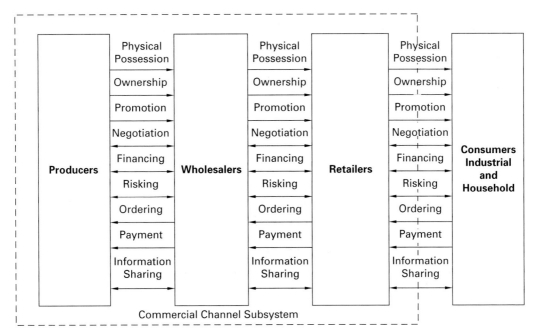

**Notes:** The arrows show how functions move in the channel (e.g., physical possession functions move from producers to wholesalers to retailers to consumers). Each function carries a cost, as the following chart shows:

| Marketing Function | Cost Represented |
|---|---|
| Physical possession | Storage and delivery |
| Ownership | Inventory carrying |
| Promotion | Personal selling, advertising, sales promotion, publicity, public relations costs, trade show |
| Negotiation | Time and legal |
| Financing | Credit terms, terms and conditions of sale |
| Risking | Price guarantees, returns allowances, warranties, insurance, repair, after-sale service |
| Ordering | Order processing |
| Payment | Collections, bad debt |
| Information sharing | Collection and storing |

**FIGURE 3-1   Marketing functions in channels**

Every channel function contributes to the production of valued service outputs and also produces costs. Figure 3-1 offers some examples of channel cost–generating activities associated with each function. **Physical possession** refers to channel activities pertaining to the storage of goods, including transportation between channel members. The costs of running warehouses and transporting products from one location to another are physical possession costs. In the case of commercial personal computer (PC) purchases, as we detail in Sidebar 3-1, CDW's intermediary role creates significant physical possession costs and required investments, including those to maintain its 400,000 square-foot warehouse, where it houses the massive volumes of products it buys from manufacturers.

## Sidebar 3-1

### CDW and PC purchases by small and medium-sized business buyers: Channel functions and equity principle insights[1]

Sidebar 2-1 profiled the computer systems reseller CDW and its success in serving small and medium-sized business buyers through its superior provision of service outputs. Its ability to do so rests on its performance of key channel functions in a more efficient (lower cost) and effective (better at producing service outputs) manner than other channel partners can. The channel functions in which CDW plays a key role are *physical possession, promotion, negotiation, financing*, and *risk*. In addition, CDW offers flexibility to its buyers, so that not all buyers must pay for and consume all of the functions that CDW offers. Through this mechanism, CDW effectively offers differentiated "packages" of function performance to the market, through one umbrella channel structure.

### CDW's Role in Bearing Channel Function Costs

Table 3-1 summarizes CDW's participation in key marketing channel functions. Each has specific implications for channel efficiency (cost management) and/or channel effectiveness (minimizing total channel costs, subject to the maintenance of desired service output levels).

As a channel intermediary, CDW performs *physical possession*. As the entries in Table 3-1 indicate, CDW takes on a significant portion of the costly burden of holding inventory (in its 400,000-square-foot warehouse and through its large-volume purchases). The entries also suggest that CDW's participation in the physical possession function lowers the total channel cost of inventory holding. In particular, CDW ships 99 percent of orders the day they are received, suggesting it has expertise in interpreting demand forecasts, which minimizes its inventory holding costs. Furthermore, CDW's investment in "asset tagging" for its government buyers constitutes a costly channel function investment that aims to reduce subsequent physical possession costs, through its ability to provide quick information to both CDW and its buyers about the location of inventory (e.g., to schedule routine service and maintenance calls, to reduce product theft or loss). CDW's large-volume purchases also reduce

systemwide inventory holding costs, accompanied by reduced wholesale prices from suppliers. The implication here is that taking large volumes of product all at once actually lowers the supplier's cost of selling to the market. Not only does it pass those savings on to CDW, but it also enjoys improved channel efficiency overall.

CDW's *promotional* investments in the channel are also extensive (Table 3-1). It trains its salespeople for several months when they start their jobs, thus providing its channel partners with experienced promotional agents who can sell their products. It devotes a salesperson to every account—even small, new accounts that initially generate low revenues. The company recognizes it cannot afford to have salespeople call on such accounts in person, so it serves them through phone or e-mail contacts, which helps control its promotional channel function costs. But the salesperson remains available to answer customer questions, providing a well-trained sales conduit to each account. A customer with an existing relationship with a CDW salesperson is likely to buy more from CDW, in response to the relatively high-touch relationship (despite initially small purchase levels). Through these investments, CDW reaps reduced promotional costs from the long-tenured sales force it employs and keeps; a salesperson with three or more years of tenure on the job generates approximately $30,000 in sales *per day* on average, twice as much as someone with two years of experience and *ten times* as much as a salesperson with less than six months of experience!

Another interesting example of clever management stems from the *negotiation* function in Table 3-1. CDW's government arm (CDW-G) established a small-business consortium to help small computer services firms compete for U.S. government IT contracts. These small firms benefit from the government directive to award approximately 20 percent of its procurement contracts to small businesses (i.e., small firms already have a *negotiation* advantage with the government as a buyer). Yet they still must offer competitive price bids, which is difficult if they only purchase small product

## Continued

quantities to develop their system solutions. By providing both expertise and more competitive wholesale prices on computer equipment to small firms, CDW enabled them to compete on price. In this sense, CDW offered superior *negotiating* capability

to its small-firm partners, so that they in turn could generate greater sales. For CDW, the benefits are obvious, in that it could not have qualified as a small business in government contracting. This arrangement offers a fine example of complementary

**TABLE 3-1    CDW'S participation in various channel functions**

| Channel Function | CDW's Investments in the Function |
|---|---|
| Physical possession | (a) 400,000 square foot warehouse.<br>(b) Ships 99 percent of orders the day they are received.<br>(c) For government buyers, CDW has instituted an "asset tagging" system that lets buyers track which product is going where; product is scanned into both buyer and CDW databases, for later ease in tracking products (e.g., service calls)<br>(d) Buys product in *large volumes* from manufacturers, receiving approximately eight trailer-loads of product from various suppliers every day, in bulk, with few added services. |
| Promotion | (a) Devotes a salesperson to every account (even small, new ones), so that end-users can always talk to a real person about technology needs, system configurations, postsales service, and so on.<br>(b) Salespeople go through 6½ weeks of basic training, then six months of on-the-job coaching, then a year of monthly training sessions.<br>(c) New hires are assigned to small business accounts to get more opportunities to close sales.<br>(d) Salespeople contact clients *not* through in-person sales calls (too expensive) but through phone/e-mail.<br>(e) Has longer-tenured salespeople than its competitors. |
| Negotiation | CDW-G started a small business consortium to help small firms compete more effectively for federal IT contracts. It gives small business partners lower prices on computers than they could otherwise get, business leads, and access to CDW's help desk and product tools. It also handles shipping and billing, reducing the channel function burden from the small business partner. In return, CDW gains access to contracts it could not otherwise get. |
| Financing | Collects receivables in just 32 days; turns inventories twice per month; and has no debt. |
| Risk | (a) "We're a kind of chief technical officer for many smaller firms"<br>(b) CDW is authorized as a Cisco Systems Premier (CSP) partner, for serving the commercial customer market. |
| Information sharing | (a) Collects information on which manufacturers' computers can best solve specific customers' needs<br>(b) Store warranty information on each customer's product to facilitate servicing |

## Continued

inputs that jointly generate superior *negotiating* power for channel partners.

CDW performs *financing* functions efficiently, as Table 3-1 demonstrates, through its enviable *inventory turn rate* of twice per month (the inventory turn rate measures how frequently a section of shelf space, such as in the CDW warehouse, empties and is replenished with inventory). Furthermore, CDW is efficient in its *payment* collections, with just a 32-day average receivable figure (which helps it minimize the total financing cost borne in the channel), and the company has no debt (which reduces the financing cost of capital).

Finally, CDW's extensive investments in expertise and *information sharing* serve to reduce other channel function costs, as well as reduce *risk* for its buyers. As a manager quoted in Table 3-1 states, "We're kind of chief technical officer for many smaller firms." The small buyer relies on the expertise and knowledge offered by CDW to choose the right systems solutions. Similarly, in serving commercial customers in general, CDW's authorization as a Cisco Systems Premier (CSP) partner signals its expertise with regard to providing full solutions for its commercial customers, not just computer components. A CDW executive explains that this authorization lets CDW act as a "trusted adviser" for the customer, so that CDW can "really talk technical about what a customer is trying to accomplish and really add value to the sale, as opposed to just sending out a box." The channel-level efficiency in managing the cost of risk exists because CDW can learn relevant information and apply it to many customers, rather than each customer having to invest in the knowledge individually. In short, customers benefit from the information gathering economies of scale generated by CDW.

Finally, CDW offers its customers a choice about how much channel function costs they want to transfer to CDW. It routinely performs significant channel functions, but in relationships with end-users that already possess technical service capabilities and with computer manufacturers, CDW lessens its participation. For example, CDW serves the Kellogg School of Management at Northwestern University. The Kellogg School uses CDW to provide laptop and desktop computers for students, faculty, and staff. Once the machines have been purchased (i.e., when CDW passes *physical possession* to the Kellogg buyer), the product *warranty* is with the manufacturer directly, not CDW. The Kellogg School has the technical capability to handle some repairs in-house, and it offers loaner machines to faculty and staff when it must ship their computers back to the manufacturer for service. Yet CDW is not responsible for the postsales services that Kellogg students and faculty enjoy when they buy a Kellogg-sanctioned laptop, because the school installs Kellogg-customized software on the machines and tests them before handing them over to the ultimate buyer. In this example, we find a buyer that can perform certain important channel functions itself, and CDW responds flexibly by offering tiered service levels to let the end-user spin off only those channel functions that the end-user cannot or does not want to perform itself.

### CDW's Use of the Equity Principle in Function Management and Incentive Creation

In two notable ways, CDW acts in accordance with the equity principle in its channel function participation and the rewards it offers to channel partners. First, it compensates employee salespeople with a commission rate that is the same regardless of whether the sale is generated person-to-person through the salesperson or through online ordering (both of which CDW offers). As we discussed in relation to the promotion function, every customer is assigned a CDW salesperson, in the hopes that more promotional (sales force) contacts generate greater customer lifetime value. But imagine that the customer interacts with the CDW salesperson periodically for major purchases but buys replacement components (e.g., printer cartridges) and smaller routine purchases online. Is it "fair" to award sales commissions to the salesperson for these online purchases? CDW believes it is, because the online purchases resulted at least in part from the initial sales efforts of the salesperson to build the customer relationship; without the salesperson, the end-user might have made these routine purchases elsewhere. Moreover, CDW recognizes that it is not just *how costly the inputs were* that matters; it is also

## Continued

*how the customer wants to buy.* If the customer prefers to make certain purchases online, perhaps because it seems easier than contacting a salesperson, CDW's internal incentive system supports the customer's freedom of choice. With this equal commission policy, it avoids creating a pernicious sales incentive to "force" the customer to buy in person rather than online.

Second, CDW offers a different fee to the smaller solution providers with which it partners to serve some ultimate end-users, because it relies on them to perform on-site work for the end-user, such as installation, software or hardware customization, provision of postsales customer service, and so forth. The equity principle suggests that these solution providers would be unwilling to undertake such costly activities unless they knew they would be compensated for doing them. The fee structure offered by CDW gives them an adequate reward for doing so. By "paying them what they're worth," CDW embraces the heart of the equity principle.

For a service, such as online bill payment, physical possession costs seemingly should be lower, but they still apply to channel members who host the data (i.e., own, operate, and maintain the computer hardware and software systems necessary to provide ready access to financial data in the system). This channel function might seem trivial at first glance, but in such a services market, it is both costly and utterly crucial to the channel's success.

When we turn to product returns (whether in consumer or industrial contexts), physical possession and its management drive the channel function's very shape, including who its members are and where the product ultimately will wind up. Figure 3-2 in Sidebar 3-2 shows some probable pathways for a product's physical movement. Controlling physical possession costs—such as by lessening the time the channel holds inventory—is a powerful means to improve overall channel profitability, because of the enormous costs of handling product returns.

The costs of physical possession are distinct from the costs of **ownership**. When a channel member takes title to goods, it bears the cost of carrying the inventory; its capital is tied up in product (whose opportunity cost is the next highest value use of that money). In many distribution systems, such as commercial PC sales, physical possession and ownership move together through the channel, but this pairing is neither necessary nor universal, as three examples show. First, in a *consignment selling*, a retailer physically holds the product (e.g., a painting in an art gallery), but the manufacturer (e.g., painter) retains ownership. In this setting, the manufacturer gives up ownership of the product only by selling it to the end-user. Second, ownership is separate from physical possession when a manufacturer or retailer contracts with a third-party reverse logistics specialist, such as Channel Velocity (www.channelvelocity.com), to handle the reverse logistic function but still retains ownership. The logistics specialist simply receives payment as a fee for service or a percentage split of the ultimate resale revenue earned from returned merchandise. Third, a data hosting company in the online bill payment situation we mentioned previously never actually owns the data it holds.

Despite these examples, we acknowledge that physical possession and ownership move together in many channel systems. The term commonly used to designate

## Sidebar 3-2

### Reverse logistics: Channel functions for returned merchandise[2]

Product returns generate a host of costs that are often ill-understood (or completely ignored) by manufacturers, distributors, and retailers. These costs include freight (for both the outgoing initial sale and the incoming return), handling, disposal or refurbishment, inventory holding costs, and opportunity costs of lost sales. The scope of the problem is very large, as the following table shows:

Furthermore, returns are very significant in many industries. In a survey of more than 300 reverse logistics managers, return percentages varied between 2 and 3 percent for household chemicals, up to 50 percent for magazine publishing. Percentage returns may vary widely by industry, but it is clear that they are often a significant challenge.

### TABLE 3-2    Product returns: A large-scale problem

- The value of returned goods exceeds $100 billion annually in the United States.*
- Some firms charge a large restocking fee (e.g., 15 percent), which can be a large cost to consumers
- Estimates of the cost of *processing* web returns put them at twice as expensive as the merchandise value!
- U.S. companies spend an estimated $35–$40 billion per year on reverse logistics.
- The average company takes 30–70 days to move a returned product back into the market.

*Su, Xuanming (2009), "Consumer Returns Policies and Supply Chain Performance," *Manufacturing & Service Operation Management* 11 (Fall), pp. 595–612.

The high costs of handling returns have led some retailers to put tighter controls on them. Target, Best Buy, and CompUSA all charge "restocking fees" of 10–15 percent on returned electronics products; a consumer who purchases a $500 camera and then returns it receives only $425–$450. Similarly, Baby Mine Store Inc., a baby apparel and accessories store, charges a 10 percent restocking fee. These policies aim to curtail consumer returns and help control the overall cost of returns through the channel. But they also reduce the quality of the experience for the consumer and can lead to poorer brand reputations and lower sales. This potential for negative demand-side effects makes managing returns well even more imperative for firms at all channel levels.

#### What Happens to a Returned Product?

When an end-user returns a product, that unit can end up in one of many places (see Figure 3-2). In one survey, retailers and manufacturers noted disposing of products by

- Sending them to a central processing facility.
- Reselling them as is.
- Repackaging them and selling them as new products.

- Remanufacturing or refurbishing them before selling.
- Selling them to a broker.
- Selling them at an outlet store.
- Recycling them.
- Dumping them in landfills.
- Donating them to charity.

In general, retailers have invested more heavily in reverse logistics management technologies than manufacturers, in terms of their uses of automated handling equipment (31 vs. 16 percent), bar codes (63 vs. 49 percent), computerized return tracking (60 vs. 40 percent), entry (32 vs. 19 percent), electronic data interchanges (31 vs. 29 percent), and radio frequency identification (37 vs. 25 percent).

A perhaps surprising example of refurbishment comes from the greeting card industry: U.S. greeting card companies instruct retailers to box up unsold cards (e.g., the day after Valentine's Day or Mother's Day) and send them to a return center in Mexico, where they are checked for resellability, refurbished if possible (with smoothed-out envelopes and card edges), and readied for the next year's holiday event. Such a process may work well in industries with low inventory holding costs (i.e.,  storing a card for

## Continued

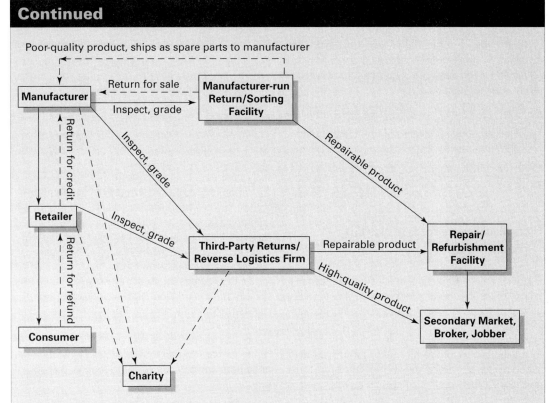

**FIGURE 3-2    Possible pathways for returned products**

Key: Solid lines denote products to be salvaged for subsequent revenue. Dotted lines denote non–revenue-producing product functions.

a year takes up almost no space) but may be too costly otherwise.

Another channel for reselling returned products is eBay, the online auction house. Dell can recover up to 40 percent of a returned computer's value by selling it on eBay, compared with 20 percent when resold through other channels.

Other firms use dedicated third-party reverse logistics firms, such as Channel Velocity (www.channelvelocity.com), which takes over all returns and reverse logistics services, including receiving returned products directly at its dedicated Atlanta warehouse, checking and refurbishing returned products, repackaging products, and running the eBay auction for the product, all for a percentage fee. More generally, a third-party independent specialist in reverse logistics might adopt a "360 degree" management process, combining state-of-the-art function management both for outbound

initial shipments *and* subsequent returns. This offer demands investments in efficient shipping (both ways), expertise in assessing which returned products are salvageable, repairs/refurbishment, repackaging, and returning inventory for resale.

In the pharmaceutical industry, a third-party outsourcer can often manage product returns better than the best drug wholesalers. McKesson Corp., one of the leading drug wholesalers in the United States with annual sales of more than $123 billion, chose to outsource its returns function to the third-party logistics company USF Processors Inc. McKesson encourages its downstream channel partners (e.g., retail pharmacies, hospital pharmacies) to use USF as well, because one of USF's valued capabilities is its evaluation of returned products to allocate credits to the pharmacies that send them back. Each returned item must be checked by lot number and expiration date to verify whether a

## Continued

refund is due or not and to provide for appropriate disposal or recycling of the items. The logistics firm maintains a database of drugs categorized as hazardous or nonhazardous for this purpose, and USF also keeps track of regulations specific to individual states to ensure appropriate treatment of pharmacies in each geographical region. Although product returns in pharmaceuticals are comparatively low— only 1–3 percent of units are returned—the benefits to using a dedicated and efficient third-party outsourcing company can be substantial.

### Poor Management Leads to High Channel Function Costs

Many manufacturers process returns manually, rather than relying on any sort of computerized system, which leads to very high costs. In other cases, the reports of reverse logistics costs are not unified, so it is difficult for manufacturers to recognize how high the costs actually are. Company managers might not prioritize managing returns through state-of-the-art reverse logistics practices, not just because of their minimal interest in reverse logistics

but also due to the poor systems capability for handling them.

Manufacturers and retailers may not *want* to expend much effort managing returns, but in some industries and/or markets, they may be forced to do so. The European Union imposes strict recycling programs on manufacturers of all kinds of products, from glass bottles to computer equipment, and forces their adherence. The United States has yet to back such "green" (i.e., environmentally friendly) proposals nationally, though some states, such as Massachusetts and California, have expressed interest in such policies for computer parts and components. The key issue in implementing such a policy is *paying* for it; various proposals include a fee assessed from the buyer at the point of purchase to cover recycling costs, or the development of a national financing system, jointly funded by manufacturers, retailers, consumers, and government.

The various ways that reverse logistics differ from forward logistics help explain why channel members are not completely adept at managing returns (see Table 3-3).

**TABLE 3-3    Differences between forward and reverse logistics**

| Factor | Difference |
|---|---|
| Volume forecasting | Forward: Difficult for new product sales |
| | Reverse: Even more difficult for their returns |
| Transportation | Forward: Ship in bulk (many of a single product), gaining economies of scale |
| | Reverse: Ship many disparate units in one pallet, with no economies of scale |
| Product quality | Forward: Uniform product quality |
| | Reverse: Variable product quality, requiring costly evaluations of every returned unit |
| Product packaging | Forward: Uniform packaging |
| | Reverse: Packaging varies, with some like new and some damaged, leaving no economies of scale in handling |
| Ultimate destination | Forward: Clear destination to retailer or industrial distributor |
| | Reverse: Many options for ultimate disposition, demanding separate decisions. |
| Accounting cost transparency | Forward: High |
| | Reverse: Low, because activities are not consistently tracked on a unified basis |

## Continued

Thus, many *channel function costs* for handling returns are high and require special decisions by the manufacturer:

- **Physical possession.** The manufacturer must decide where the returned goods should go, that is, from the end-user directly back to the manufacturer; to the retailer or reseller and then back to the manufacturer; or to a third-party reverse logistics specialist. Without a clear decision, the returned product might simply sit in the retailer's back room or get put back on a sales shelf, without proper evaluation. Any decision to ship the returned product back to the manufacturer or a third-party incurs reverse freight charges that the manufacturer likely must bear. Some manufacturers believe that they can use their outbound distribution center to handle inbound returns, but it rarely works well, because forward logistics tend to be large scale and based on economies of scale, whereas returns involve mixed pallets with few or no economies of scale. Warehouse personnel in a combined forward and reverse logistics warehouse likely to prioritize outbound shipments, leaving returns as an afterthought; a dedicated returns warehouse would handle returns more quickly (and efficiently, if the scale is great enough).

- **Ownership.** When the product is returned to a retail store, the consumer no longer owns it. The manufacturer then must set a policy regarding the retailer's right to return the merchandise, and these policies vary widely across firms and industries. In bookselling, for example, retailers return products freely (which gives the retailers encouragement to carry sufficient inventory to meet possibly high demand). If product ownership moves back to the manufacturer, it must plan for this cost; high return rates can wreak havoc with planning.

- **Promotion.** The manufacturer or a third-party returns specialist might *refurbish* the returned product and *repackage* it to look different from new product. The reverse logistics specialist Channel Velocity

differentiates returned, refurbished electric dog fences from new products sold in upscale pet stores by reorganizing the kits, putting the components together in slightly different combinations than are available in the new product market, then repackaging the refurbished products in slightly different boxes and selling them only through eBay. These promotional efforts cost money, but such investments help make the returned product sellable again and differentiate it sufficiently from the new product, which minimizes cannibalization.

- **Negotiation.** The manufacturer may need to negotiate with retailers or distributors over the amount to refund on returned merchandise (net of any *restocking fees*), and even the maximum number of units the retailer is permitted to return.

- **Financing.** These costs rise with product returns, because a given unit of inventory must to be financed twice, rather than just being shipped, sold, and kept by the end-user. One study reports that it takes the average company 30–70 days to move a returned product back into the market—and during that time, the manufacturer must finance this temporarily unsellable inventory.

- **Risk.** Increased channel risk is the heart of the problem. Manufacturers and retailers do not know with certainty the demand they will face, and poor demand forecasting leads to much greater uncertainty about expected return volume. Therefore, poor demand forecasting, which leads to returns, is a risk cost.

- **Payment.** Decisions about the restocking fee to charge the retailer or consumer who returns a product (e.g., cameras often bear a 15 percent fee, and wallpaper companies often assess 30–40 percent fees) then lead to the need to manage and process the fees.

- **Information sharing.** Tracking the cost and actual return rates for different products improves decision making throughout the return process and provides insights into potential opportunities for improving the design, production, and packaging of the

## Continued

product. Recent research suggests that the information content of returns may be more critical than the actual processing cost of the returns, because manufacturers can learn the cause for the returns.[3]

### Tools for Managing Reverse Logistics

Other than contracting with a third-party reverse logistic specialist, the seller might investment in customer service to prescreen customer orders and thus lower subsequent return rates. For example, Lands' End's online store offers web tools to help consumers figure out which size is right for them, which in turn minimizes the practice of ordering of multiple units of one item, in adjacent sizes, and thus lowers the returns per unit sale. W.W. Grainger, the huge industrial products distributor, hires customer service personnel to help buyers choose the right products. In some cases, the cost of handling returns is so high that Grainger simply tells the buyer to keep or dispose of the unwanted product, then sends the right product to the customer. In light of this possibility, bearing the cost of extra employees to avoid returns starts to seem very sensible.

Alternatively, the manufacturer could invest in better demand forecasting and improve customer service. One sure way to get rid of the channel costs of product returns is to undertake other channel investments that eliminate the likelihood of returns!

### Benefits of a Well-Managed Process

A well-managed returns and reverse logistics channel can generate multiple benefits to the firm: the recovery of significant lost sales, better quality across all sales, and control over customer relationships, to name a few. Consider two manufacturers, one that refuses to accept returns and thus leaves unsold products with the retailer or downstream distributor, and another that accepts them and immediately sells them to a broker. In both cases, the manufacturer likely believes it has cleverly minimized return costs. Instead, it simply may have succeeded in creating a "gray market" for its products, because the retailer (in the former case) and the broker (in the latter case) can try to sell those units in another market, as quickly as possible. The firm that instead takes a proactive stance toward managing returns, whether itself or in partnership with an expert third-party reverse logistics provider, reduces both the cost of returns and the possibility of inadvertently creating a cannibalizing competitor.

their combined costs is **inventory holding costs**. Inventories refer to stocks of goods or the components used to make them, and they exist for several reasons:

- *Demand surges* outstrip production capacity. To smooth production, factories anticipate such surges and produce according to the forecast. Inventory results. The demand surge may be natural (e.g., ice cream in summer), or it may be due to marketers' actions, such as short-term promotions. The discipline of supply chain management developed in the grocery industry mainly because retailers stockpile goods to take advantage of manufacturer promotions but then must deal with the high inventory carrying costs, including the cost of obsolescence.
- *Economies of scale* exist in production and transportation. Inventory in this case results because firms batch-process orders to make a long production run or stockpile goods to fill containers, trucks, ships, or planes.
- *Transportation takes time*, especially with greater distances between points of production and points of consumption. Downstream channel members thus keep inventories (pipeline stock) to meet their demands until a shipment arrives and can be unpacked.
- *Supply and demand are uncertain*. Buyers can never be completely sure how long it will take to be resupplied (lead time)—or sometimes if they can get the stock at

all. Thus, they acquire **safety stock** (i.e., excess of inventory, beyond the best estimate of what is needed during an order cycle) as a hedge against uncertainty. That uncertainty often reflects ignorance about what will sell (demand uncertainty).

How much inventory a channel member should hold is a very difficult question. Many operations research models attempt to answer it, and they vary mainly in the assumptions they make to render this inventory problem mathematically tractable. The EOQ (economic order quantity) model is the oldest and likely the best known.[4]

In marketing channels, **promotion** functions take many forms: personal selling by an employee or outside sales force (e.g., brokers and registered investment advisors for mutual funds), media advertising, sales promotions (trade or retail), publicity, and other public relations activities. Promotional activities seek to increase awareness of the product being sold, educate potential buyers about products' features and benefits, and persuade potential buyers to purchase. A third-party reverse logistics specialist helps manufacturers achieve this promotional goal when it refurbishes returned products and sells them through new channels (e.g., eBay); in so doing, it targets new buyer segments and differentiates refurbished units from new products sold through standard channels. Promotional efforts also might increase overall *brand equity*, to increase sales in the future. Of course, any channel member can be involved in promotion, not just the retailer or manufacturer. Even as a distributor, CDW maintains an expensive sales force, which ultimately helps it reduce the total costs of promotion for its computer equipment manufacturers.

The **negotiation** function is present in the channel if the terms of sale or the persistence of certain relationships are open to discussion. The costs of negotiation are measured mainly as personnel's time to conduct the negotiations, and, if necessary, the cost of legal counsel. In its consortium with small businesses to serve the government market (Sidebar 3-1), CDW gives an example of how to use multiple members' capabilities to enhance the channel's joint negotiation power over the buyer: CDW's negotiation abilities allow it to get the product at low prices, and small businesses have a negotiation edge in landing government contracts.

**Financing** costs are inherent to any sale that moves from one level of the channel to another or from the channel to the end-user. Typical financing terms for a business-to-business purchase require payment within 30 days and may offer a discount for early payment. With a 2 percent discount offered for payment within 10 days, for example, the terms of sale would be presented, "2–10 net 30." Regardless of the specifics, the payment terms establish the seller's willingness essentially to finance the buyer's purchase for a period of time (here, 30 days), after the product has been delivered. In so doing, the seller accepts the financial cost of the foregone income that it could have achieved by putting that money to use in an alternative investment activity. Financing costs also may be borne by a manufacturer or intermediary, or even by an outside specialist, such as a bank or credit card company. As a distributor, CDW buys products from computer manufacturers and finances that inventory until customers buy and pay for it; as Sidebar 3-1 notes, it is particularly efficient in this function, according to its good inventory turn rate and the minimal days indicated in its receivables. At the other end of the financing efficiency spectrum is a manufacturer with high product return rates that fails to manage them well. Indeed, the average company finances its returned products for 30–70 days before reinserting them into the market.

There are many sources of **risk**. For example, long-term contracts between a distributor and end-user may specify price guarantees that lock in the distributor to a certain price. If the market price for that product rises while the contract is in force, the distributor loses revenue, because it must continue to sell at the previously determined, lower price. Price guarantees also may be offered to intermediaries who hold inventory, just in case the product's market price falls before the inventory is sold. This practice moves the risk from the intermediary to the manufacturer. Other risk-related costs include warranties, insurance, and after-sales service activities that attempt to mitigate concerns about unforeseeable future events (e.g., parts failures, accidents). The manufacturer or reseller usually bears these risk costs, though in some cases, a specific channel intermediary serves explicitly as a risk manager. When a CDW manager says, "We're kind of chief technical officer for many smaller firms," he is recognizing CDW's greater expertise with computer products and systems. This expertise offers reduced risk to small business customers, who know they can rely on CDW rather than try to identify the best systems on the basis of their own limited knowledge.

**Ordering** and **payment** costs are those incurred during the actual purchase of and payment for the product. They may seem unglamorous, but innovations are radically altering the performance of these functions today. *Automatic replenishment*, an automated reordering system in use by many retailers, uses a computer system to track levels of inventory in the retailer's system and automatically sends a replenishment order to the manufacturer when stocks reach a preset minimum level. This process not only reduces ordering costs but also improves in-stock percentages.

Finally, **information sharing** takes place among and between every channel member, in both routine and specialized ways. Retailers share information with their manufacturers about sales trends and patterns through electronic data interchanges; if used properly, this information can reduce the costs of many other channel functions (e.g., by improving sales forecasts, the channel suffers fewer costs of physical possession due to smaller inventory holdings). Such information content is so important that logistics managers call this function the ability to "transform inventory into information."

The costs associated with performing channel functions demand that channels avoid performing *unnecessarily* well on any of the functions. Knowing which service outputs are demanded by target end-users, at what level of intensity, and at what cost helps the channel manager design a channel system that provides targeted segments of end-users with the exact level of service outputs they demand, at the lowest cost.

## AUDITING CHANNELS USING THE EFFICIENCY TEMPLATE

To audit a channel members' capability to provide each channel function and add value, and at what cost, we use the **efficiency template**. A detailed description of its real-world application appears in Appendix 3-1; here, we discuss its key elements and uses.

The efficiency template describes (1) the types and amounts of work done by each channel member to perform the marketing functions, (2) the importance of each channel function to the provision of end-user service outputs, and (3) the share of total channel profits that each channel member *should* reap. Figure 3-3 contains a blank efficiency template: The rows are the channel functions, and then one set of columns indicates *importance weights* for the functions, while the other lists the *proportional performance of each function* by each channel member.

| | Importance Weights for Functions: | | | Proportional Function Performance of Channel Member | | | | |
|---|---|---|---|---|---|---|---|---|
| | Costs* | Benefit Potential (High, Medium, Low) | Final Weight* | 1 | 2 | 3 | 4 (End-User) | Total |
| Physical possession** | | | | | | | | 100 |
| Ownership | | | | | | | | 100 |
| Promotion | | | | | | | | 100 |
| Negotiation | | | | | | | | 100 |
| Financing | | | | | | | | 100 |
| Risk | | | | | | | | 100 |
| Ordering | | | | | | | | 100 |
| Payment | | | | | | | | 100 |
| Information sharing | | | | | | | | 100 |
| Total | **100** | N/A | **100** | N/A | N/A | N/A | N/A | N/A |
| Normative profit share*** | N/A | N/A | N/A | | | | | **100** |

Notes:
* Entries in each column must add up to 100 points.
** Entries across each row (sum of proportional function performance of channel members 1–4) for each channel member must add up to 100 points.
*** Normative profit share of channel member i is calculated as (final weight, physical possession) × (channel member i's proportional function performance of physical possession) + ... + (final weight, information sharing) × (channel member i's proportional function performance of information sharing). Entries across rows (sum of normative profit shares for channel members 1–4) must add up to 100 points.

**FIGURE 3-3**  The efficiency template

Consider the three columns that refer to the importance weights to be associated with each channel function. The idea is to account for both the *cost* of performing that function and the *value added* by that same performance in the channel. The entries in the "Cost" column should be percentages, totaling 100 percent across all the functions. Thus, if the costs of promotion account for 23 percent of all channel function costs, the analyst enters "23" in the relevant cell and then determines how the other functions account for the remaining 77 percent of the costs. To generate these quantitative cost weights, the **activity-based costing (ABC)** accounting method explains how to measure the cost of performance to one organization.[5] For our purposes, the task is more comprehensive: We need good quantitative measures of the costs of all activities performed by *all* the channel members. If we know the total costs, we still need to ask: What proportion of these total channel costs is accounted for by, say, promotions?

Even without quantitative measures of cost, analysts can use qualitative techniques to estimate the cost weights. A Delphi-type research technique might be applied, such that several highly informed managers in the channel develop their best estimates of the cost weights.[6] The output of this exercise similarly is a set of weights, adding up to 100, that measure the proportion or percentage of total channel costs accounted for by each function.

But costs are not the entire picture. The performance of each function also creates *value*, and determining how much is a more intuitive process, linking the performance of functions to the generation of desired service outputs for a targeted segment of end-users. With this information, we can adjust the "Cost" weight to derive the final set of importance weights for each function in the channel. The adjustment process is judgmental but generally increases the weight for functions that generate "high" added value in the channel, while diminishing the value assigned to functions with "low" value added. Again in this case, the final weights must sum to 100, so if some function weights increase, others *must* decrease. A Delphi analysis can complement this approach and help channel members arrive at a final set of weights to represent both the cost borne and the value created through the performance of a channel function.

To complete the other columns in the efficiency template in Figure 3-3, the channel analyst must allocate the total cost of each function across all channel members. Again, the analyst enters figures adding up to 100, to represent the proportion of the total cost of a function that a particular channel member bears. So if a channel consists of a manufacturer, a distributor, a retailer, and an end-user, the costs of physical possession spread across these four channel members—though not all channel members bear all costs. For example, a manufacturer may use independent sales representatives to help sell its product. These sales reps do not inventory any product or take any title to it; they specialize in promotional and sometimes order-taking activities. Their cost proportion entry in the physical possession row thus would be 0.

Note that the end-user is also a member of the channel. Any time end-users buy a larger lot size than they really need in the short term (i.e., forgoes bulk breaking by stocking up on paper towels at a hypermarket), they are performing some of the physical possession function, because they have to maintain the inventory of the unused product themselves. This consumer therefore bears inventory carrying costs too, which means sharing the costs of ownership in the channel. The costs of financing also might fall on the end-user who pays for the whole lot at the time of purchase. The various ways end-users can participate in channel functions thus produce costs for them and, as for any channel member, these costs should be measured. The resulting information can be particularly useful for contrasting one segment of end-users against another, which sheds light on the fundamental question of why it costs more to serve some end-users than others. The answer is generally because they perform fewer costly channel functions themselves, thrusting this cost back onto other channel members.

After having assigned weights to each function and allocated cost proportions for the performance of each function across all channel members, the channel analyst can calculate a weighted average for each channel member, which reveals its contributions to the costs borne and value created in the channel. This weighted average is calculated as (weight × cost proportion) for each function, then summed across all functions. In our example from Appendix 3-1, the manufacturer's weighted average is 28 percent (= [(.35 × .30) + (.15 × .30) + (.08 × .20) + (.04 × .20) + (.29 × .30) +

$(.02 \times .30) + (.03 \times .20) + (.04 \times .20) + (.00 \times .20)])$. The retailer in the channel contributes 39 percent of the cost/value, and the customer contributes 33 percent.

These percentages have special meaning, especially when we turn to the total profit available to the channel from products sold at full-service list prices. This value equals total revenues (assuming all units sold at their list prices), minus all costs of running the channel. The data from the building materials company in Appendix 3-1 indicate how much each channel member is responsible for generating the channel contribution—28, 39, and 33 percent respectively. These percentages not only measure the proportionate value creation but also suggest the **normative profit shares** that each channel member should receive. Of course, being responsible for a larger proportion of a low value function might not create as much value as performing even a smaller percentage of a highly valued function. Thus, being the "busy" channel member does not always signal that member's high value creation. We return to this notion in our discussion of the equity principle.

In the meantime, what does it imply when an end-user generates channel profits? In the example in Appendix 3-1, the end-users buy large quantities and store them for use, after the time of purchase. That means they pay in advance for product that they will use later, and they are willing to store it. These valued channel functions are costly for the customer, just as they would be for any other channel member, so their performance merits some reward. In general, the reward for end-users who perform valued channel functions is a reduced price.

In addition to taking care about who enters the efficiency template, it is critical to note the need for a separate efficiency template for *each channel* that distributes the product to a targeted segment of end-users. In the Appendix 3-1 case, there might be a separate efficiency template for the retailer, one for the direct channel serving building contractors, and so forth. Such separation is absolutely necessary, because a channel member involved in selling to retail buyers (e.g., retailer) does not bear any channel function costs in the direct sales channel, but it bears plenty of them in the retail channel.

Finally, when completing an efficiency template, the analyst might lack full financial data about the costs borne by each channel member. Without precise ratings—because we do not know precisely how much of a particular function's cost is borne by each particular channel member—do we need to discard the efficiency template? Absolutely not, as long as *some* ranking data are available to calibrate the relative intensity of the performance of each function. Even rough rankings can provide a reasonably good approximation of the relative value created by each channel member. As with any system, the rougher the approximations, the rougher the resulting estimates of value created, but as the example in Appendix 3-1 shows, these approximations are often far more informative than an analysis that completely ignores the relative value added by each channel member.

In summary, the efficiency template is a useful tool for codifying the costs borne and the value added to the channel by each channel member, including end-users. Among its many uses, the efficiency template can reveal how the costs of particular functions get shared among channel members, indicate how much each channel member contributes to overall value creation in the channel, and demonstrate how important each function is to total channel performance. It also can be a powerful explanatory tool and justification for current channel performance or changes to existing operating channels. For products sold through multiple channels, their efficiency templates can be compared to find any differences in the costs of running the different channels, which may help the channel lower costs without compromising desired service output levels.

## Evaluating Channels: The Equity Principle

The normative profit shares calculated from the efficiency template for an operating channel reveal which share of the total channel profits that each channel member is responsible for generating through its efforts. This normative share should relate to the *actual* share of total channel profits each channel member receives, according to our definition of the **equity principle**:

> A member's level of compensation in the channel system should reflect its degree of participation in the marketing functions and the value created by such participation. That is, compensation should mirror the normative profit shares of each channel member.

The equity principle further asserts that it is appropriate to reward each channel member in accordance with the value it creates. Not only is this equivalence fair and equitable, but it also creates strong incentives for channel members to continue generating value. Thus, CDW's equal commission rates for online purchases and salesperson-handled purchases maintain employees' incentives to try to build their client accounts, regardless of how the client wants to buy. But trying to deprive any channel member of its rewards for effort and value created likely will result in its underperformance later. The serious channel conflicts that can result might even lead to the dissolution of the channel.

To live by the equity principle, channel members must identify their actual costs incurred and develop an agreed-upon estimate of the value created in the channel. Otherwise, they likely devolve into disagreements about the value each member actually has added, which represents an unwinnable argument, because it features mostly channel members' individual perceptions of their own contributions, not any facts. If the only member who recognizes the value of a contribution is the member performing it, the channel cannot effectively reinforce this high value activity. The channel members who reward this activity also must perceive it. Although it takes substantial effort to amass the information necessary to complete an efficiency analysis, the payoffs are worthwhile.

Yet in many cases, actual profit shares do not match the normative shares suggested by the efficiency template. In this case, the solution demands further analysis of both the channel situation and the external competitive environment. In certain competitive situations, despite channel members' valiant efforts to contribute to channel performance, one of them earns less profit than the efficiency template suggests, because the availability of competitors makes this member seem easily replaceable. Imagine, for example, a supplier of a commodity product to Wal-Mart. When Wal-Mart announces that its suppliers must adopt RFID (radio frequency identification) technology, the supplier faces significant new costs: buying the equipment to make and insert the tags, purchasing the tags themselves on an ongoing basis, and training employees to handle, affix, and program the tags' contents, to name a few. In addition, the significant cost savings that ultimately should result from RFID technology will be shared by suppliers and Wal-Mart (as well as customers). Thus, the supplier might perceive that it is bearing more than its "fair share" of the cost of implementing this technology, which is a clear violation of the equity principle. Unfortunately for the supplier in this case, it has little recourse: If it refuses to pay the cost of maintaining RFID tags, Wal-Mart can simply drop it as a supplier and replace it with another that provides the commodity and the RFID functionality. Thus, when market power and competitive pressures cause deviations from the equity principle, the channel reward system does not necessarily need to change.

In the long run though, it might not be a bad idea for Wal-Mart to offer some concession to the equity principle. Channel partners who fail to receive rewards commensurate with their perceived contributions cannot remain motivated for long. They might begin looking for ways to exit the channel; at the very least, they are certain to bargain hard for favorable changes in terms. A firm that treats its channel partners poorly develops a bad reputation that will harm its long-term ability to add or manage channels in the future. Finally, violations of the equity principle constitute a primary cause of channel conflict (discussed in more depth in Chapter 11).

Thus, astute channel managers carefully balance long-term relationship risks against the immediate gain of garnering a greater share of immediate channel profits. Thus, we reassert the following: If competitive conditions do not give one channel member leverage over another, profit-based rewards should spread throughout the channel roughly in proportion to the level of performance provided by each channel member. By auditing existing channels using the efficiency template, channel managers learn the suggested relative share of profit; they then should compare those shares with the actual shares of profit enjoyed by each channel member and apply the equity principle to identify any discrepancies. Next, by determining whether these discrepancies reflect an outcome of market power or competitive pressure, the manager can decide whether and how to address them through a channel strategy.

If no marketing channel already exists for a product, such as when a manufacturer seeks to sell its product in a new market or country, it needs to create a new channel. The next section describes how to evaluate and design new marketing channels, using the zero-based channel concept.

## Evaluating Channels: Zero-Based Channel Concept

Imagine being a channel manager with the power and the luxury to design an optimal channel strategy from scratch, without any preexisting channel structure to hamper the design. Where would you start?

Theoretically, you start with a **zero-based channel**, that is, one that meets the target market segment's demands for service outputs by performing necessary channel functions to produce those service outputs at a minimum cost. Unfortunately, you immediately confront an unavoidable tension: You hope to minimize the costs of running the marketing channel, to preserve profit margins, but you have to spend sufficient amounts on performing channel functions to guarantee that your new channel can generate the desired service outputs in such a way that they satisfy end-users. Spending too little (or making poor decisions about where to allocate money) will mean poor provision of service outputs, which competitors can exploit by offering their superior alternative combination of product and service outputs. Yet spending too much will produce more service outputs than the target segment values and unnecessarily increase the costs of running the channel, reducing profitability. Achieving the right balance is a constant and demanding task—and we haven't even considered how changes in the marketplace will alter your new channel.

So next consider the particular task of managing inventory holding costs as an example. Cost control in channels often depends on reducing inventory. But how? Some obvious methods are to avoid items that sell slowly, lengthen the life of goods (e.g., add preservatives to foods), find a vendor who resupplies faster, or locate a cheaper warehouse. Less obvious methods include developing better demand forecasts or altering factory processes to attain scale economies at lower production levels.

Another and undeniably powerful way to cut inventory is to simplify, that is, to reduce *variety*. Of course, that step can be an effective way to cut sales as well. A channel that adopts this approach must find offerings that no one will really miss by rationalizing the product line. Thus, the service output levels pertaining to assortment and variety remain the same, in the target consumer's minds. Some channels have sought the benefits of modular design for products, combined with manufacturing processes that postpone, as late as possible, the point of product differentiation. Thus, Hewlett-Packard's laser printers rely on a standard subassembly process, which is the only element shipped to a distribution center (DC). The DC procures and adds elements to tailor the printer to its destination, such as power supplies, packaging, and manuals that reflect the language and infrastructure of each national market. Because the DC engages in assembly and light manufacturing, its manufacturing costs are slightly higher, yet the total costs (manufacturing, shipping, and inventory) in the channel are significantly percent lower.

These ideas for inventory cost controls may have little effect if your new channel cannot control demand uncertainty, especially in the form of the **bullwhip effect**.[7] The name is clearly evocative: In a supply chain, the end-user constitutes the handle of the whip, because it determines the base of demand throughout the chain. Moving up the whip, we find the retailer who sells the product, the wholesaler who supplies the retailer, and the manufacturer who makes the item. Each party must forecast the end-user's demand, but the farther away the channel member is, the harder that process becomes. That is, the greater and varied the movement in the whip, the farther it is from the base of the handle. Taking production, shipping, and stocking delays into account, each channel member needs to plan how much to obtain to serve its own level of demand, how much safety stock to hold on hand, and how much to procure or manufacture, which ultimately determine how many raw materials to order. Each player focuses on its link in the supply chain, and poor communication often marks their connections. Thus, demand uncertainty arises, inventories of products and ingredients oscillate, and small changes in end-user demands resonate up the supply chain, magnifying into ever-larger changes upstream. The bullwhip effect can be costly, whether in terms of stockouts (unfilled orders, back orders) or excessive inventory.

Aiming for a zero-based channel in the presence of such massive uncertainties is a constant theme, spreading beyond simple product markets. Service providers such as banks also must balance their inventory and investment decisions: Those that save too much money in inventory incur opportunity costs for not investing. Banks that lend out too much money fall below their reserve ratio or even may go bankrupt if their clients start a bank run. Thus, banks must forecast the money supply and money demand not just with respect to themselves but also throughout the (now global) system, to determine if they should invest more or save more.[8]

Establishing a zero-based channel thus entails a recognition of the level of channel functions that must be performed to generate appropriate service outputs in the market. As the preceding pages imply though, zero-based channels may not even exist. What are you to do then, as you structure your brand new, ideal channel system? Consider the following guidelines:

- What less or nonvalued functions (e.g., excessive sales calls) can be eliminated without damaging customer or channel satisfaction?
- Are there any redundant activities? Which could be eliminated and thus lower costs for the entire system?
- Is there a way to eliminate, redefine, or combine certain tasks to minimize the steps for a sale or reduce its cycle time?
- Is it possible to automate certain activities and thereby reduce the unit costs required to get products to market, even though if fixed costs increase?
- Are there opportunities to modify information systems to reduce the costs of prospecting, order entry, quote generation, or similar activities?

For new channel designs, the planner also is likely to face managerial or environmental barriers to establishing a zero-based channel. If a channel already exists, it might not be a zero-based channel.

Understanding the concept of channel functions is critical to any channel manager's ability to design and maintain an effective, efficient channel. Channel functions are both costly to offer and valuable to end-users. If managers can identify and understand the segment(s) of the market that their channel will target, channel managers can use their sophisticated analyses of channel functions to evaluate the cost effectiveness of various channel activities designed to generate service outputs that end-users will appreciate.

## AUDITING CHANNELS USING GAP ANALYSIS

By matching the service outputs demanded by targeted end-users to the offerings (service and price) provided by existing channels, managers gain a good idea of where there might be gaps in the ideal channel structure that is required to meet target segments' needs. By identifying and closing these gaps, managers can build a channel that meets service output demands at a minimum cost, that is, can design a zero-based channel.

### Sources of Channel Gaps

Gaps in channel design might arise simply because management has not thought carefully about target end-users' demands for service outputs or about managing the cost of running their channel. The solution is simple: Pay attention to both service gaps and costs gaps when designing the channel.

Yet the reality often is not quite as simple. **Gaps** can arise because of limitations placed on the best intentioned channel managers. A manager seeking to design a zero-based channel for the company's product likely confronts constraints on his or her actions that prevent the establishment of the best channel design. Before diagnosing the types of gaps, it therefore is useful to discuss the limitations, or bounds, that create them. We concentrate on two: environmental bounds and managerial bounds.

The characteristics of the marketplace in which the channel operates can constrain the establishment of a zero-based channel.[9] Such **environmental bounds** in turn create channel gaps. Two key examples of environmental bounds are local legal constraints and the sophistication of the physical and retailing infrastructure.

Legal conditions in the marketplace shape which channel partners a company may choose—that is, if they do not prevent the company's access to the market altogether. Recall our example of CDW, the computer reseller. Its penetration of the government market is limited by the government's stated goal of using approximately 20 percent small or medium-sized vendors. Through its small and minority business partners program, CDW works with independent companies, whose size meets the governmental preferences. This program thus creates a channel structure for CDW that is mainly the result of the imposition of a legal bound.

The physical and infrastructural environment also could prevent the establishment of certain types of distribution channel structures.[10] Online bill payment systems demand the development of systems that can communicate across different levels of the channel and manage information consistently over time. Not only must the bill be *payable* by the payer electronically, but it also must be able to be *presented* electronically in a common database system. For many bill payers (consumers and businesses), the real value of electronic bill payment is the ability it provides to integrate the payment with the payer's own database of information (e.g., back-office activities, household budgeting information). Limitations on the integration of various electronic data sources limit the possible spread of electronic payments in the market though.

Similarly, companies that want to manage returned products more efficiently may not be able to develop the capacity to do so themselves or to find an appropriate intermediary that can handle its specific needs. For example, in the retail book industry, processing returns represent one of the highest costs for the warehouse. The longstanding legacy of allowing free returns from retailers to publishers appears to be a hard habit to break, and this effective environmental bound persists even for those actors that would prefer to change the system.

Environmental bounds thus occur outside the boundaries of the companies directly involved in the channel and constrain channel members from establishing a zero-based channel, whether because they cannot offer an appropriate level of service outputs or because the constraints impose unduly high costs on channel members. In contrast, though managerial bounds also constrain channel design, they emanate from within the channel structure itself or from the orientation or culture of specific channel members.

**Managerial bounds** refer to constraints on distribution structure arising from the rules within a company. Typically they stem from the company that manufactures the product. Sometimes a desire to control the customer, or simply a lack of trust among channel members, prevents managers from implementing a less bounded channel design.

The bound imposed by management may reflect a lack of knowledge of appropriate levels of investment or activity. One computer company, whose primary route to market was online sales, found that its return rates were very high. In a (misguided) effort to minimize returns, it instituted a new policy: Refunds would be offered on returned products only if the product was broken. The logic was that if the consumer received the product in good condition, it should be kept, but a nonfunctioning product that arrived at the buyer's doorstep should be taken back for a full refund or exchange. After instituting the policy, returns percentages did not fall at all, but a change did occur: *All* of the returned products were now broken, of course! The company had unwittingly created a managerial bound by instituting a policy that led to even worse results than the original problem. Fortunately, management realized the problem quickly and reversed course, but this example suggests that some managerial bounds are obvious enough that they should never be implemented and do not have to cause persistent channel malfunctions.

A lack of focus on managing the costs of returned product may result not from a perverse desire to incur high costs but simply from ignorance about what those costs are and what resources might be available to control them. Here, we find the confluence of a managerial bound ("we don't see the value of focusing on reverse logistics") and a back-up environmental bound ("now that we realize it is worth focusing on, we don't know the solution"). The goal must be to recognize all self-imposed managerial bounds and attack them whenever possible.

Whether channel gaps arise due to managerial bounds, environmental bounds, or a lack of attention to the well-being of the channel, they can profoundly affect either side of a zero-based channel, that is, services or cost gaps. We turn to this taxonomy next.

## Service Gaps

Service gaps can arise in two ways. Think about a single service output. A **service gap** exists if the amount of a service supplied is less than the service demanded (in shorthand, SS < SD) or if the amount of service supplied is greater than the amount demanded (SS > SD). In the first case, insufficient service output is available to satisfy the target market (SS < SD). For example, customers once believed that standard music retailers offered insufficient bulk breaking (few single song formats) and assortment/variety; these gaps helped enhance the success of online alternatives as they came available. In this case, the service supplied by brick-and-mortar music retailers fell below the level demanded by many customers.

In contrast, a service gap may reflect a low service output offering accompanied by a low price; for example, at Dollar Stores, everything is available at a low price, but the assortment and service provision are relatively poor. In this case, despite the very low prices, some end-users do not perceive sufficient *value* (i.e., utility for the price paid). Without sufficient value, they will not purchase the bundle consisting of the product plus its service outputs. Thus, a service gap can arise when the level of service is too low, even controlling for a lower price, and does not generate a reasonable amount of value for the end-user.

We can detail the overly high level of the service output (SS > SD) using the retail music example again. In one target segment (e.g., younger popular music buyers who are well-versed in using the Internet), a standard music retail outlet's provision of customer service is simply too high; they prefer do-it-yourself downloads over sales attention from possibly less well-informed in-store personnel (especially because relevant information about what popular music is "hot" is more readily available on the Internet, not in stores!). Many shoppers are only too familiar with the overly helpful store clerk: At first the attention may seem welcome, but eventually, it becomes irritating and distracting. These overinvestments in service outputs decrease, rather than increase, the end-user's satisfaction, even as they cost more money to provide—a dual penalty.

Businesses have to worry about not just their own service outputs but also the service outputs of other businesses. When one business offers better service, it charges a higher price for the goods it sells; when another business offers poor service, its prices tend to be lower. Some savvy consumers may take advantage of this situation by using the free services one business provides (e.g., in-store demonstrations, test drives), then purchasing the desired product at another business that does not offer these services and thus sells at a lower cost. Interestingly, such *free riding* actually can reduce the intensity of direct price competition among channel members in some cases.[11]

Of course, erring on either side is a mistake by the channel manager. Providing overly high service output levels can be just as bad as providing overly low levels. On the one hand, channel costs (and prices) rise too high for the value created, and on the other hand, the channel "skimps" on service outputs for which the target market would be willing to pay a premium. Profit opportunities get lost on both sides. It also is possible to find service gaps in more than one service output. That is, the level of one service output might be too low, while the level of another is too high, as our traditional music retailing example makes clear (SS < SD for bulk breaking and assortment/variety, but SS > SD for customer service). The channel manager might believe that such combinations balance out, such that the "extra" level of one service output should compensate for a shortfall of another. But service outputs rarely are good substitutes for each other, so no level of excess of one service output can truly compensate for too little of another. Small neighborhood variety stores offer extremely high spatial convenience, but they rarely can match the assortment and variety provided by a hypermarket, and they often charge higher prices. The decline of such stores in many urban and suburban areas in the United States suggests that consumers are not willing to trade off a poor assortment and variety offering for extreme spatial convenience.

Not only is it important to find the right combination of service outputs, but it also is critical to check for service gaps, *service output by service output* and *segment by segment*. Our retail music example shows a shortfall in the provision of some service outputs (bulk breaking, assortment and variety), along with a surfeit of another (customer service). But the output that constitutes a service gap for one target segment (e.g., young digital natives) may represent exactly the right amount for another target segment (e.g., their grandparents, vinyl aficionados). Thus, retail music stores ultimately might not disappear; instead, they may find a smaller segment of target end-users, serve them well, and continue to focus more narrowly on their needs.

Segmentation thus helps identify which service gaps exist for which clusters of potential buyers, rather than suggesting a need for global changes in the channel strategy. Identifying the segment for which a service output offering is appealing can be an enormously useful piece of information when determining how to close service gaps.

## Cost Gaps

A cost gap exists when the total cost of performing all channel functions is too high, generally because one or more relevant channel functions, from physical possession to information sharing, are too expensive. Holding the level of service outputs constant, if a lower cost way to perform the channel function in question exists, a cost gap exists too. It would be meaningless to discuss channel functions performed at too low a cost though—as long as demanded service outputs are being produced, there is no overly low cost!

The cost of training salespeople and managing turnover in the sales force at CDW effectively illustrates a cost gap in the performance of the promotional function. The company puts all its newly hired salespeople through a very rigorous training program to enable them to provide excellent customer education and service—those service outputs most valued by small and medium-sized business customers. But just how costly it is to generate this superior level of service outputs? Furthermore, CDW's annual sales force turnover rate is 25 percent, which means that one-fourth of the newly hired (and expensively trained) salespeople leave the company. Their training costs are wasted investments; even worse, they may have granted one of CDW's competitors a well-trained salesperson (if that competitor engages in *poaching*, or seeking out and hiring employees trained elsewhere). If CDW could identify, before it initiated its costly training efforts, which salespeople were most likely to leave, it could lessen these promotional (sales training) costs without compromising on its delivery of service outputs.

Electronic bill presentment and payment (EBPP) services created cost gaps both before and after the onset of this new technology. Before EBPP technologies spread throughout the United States, the costs of key channel functions, including promotion, negotiation, risk, ordering, and payment, were all higher than necessary to pay bills. Adopting EBPP throughout the system undoubtedly would reduce channel costs significantly, from presentation to final bill payment and reconciliation. Yet the very introduction of this new technology created new cost gaps, because bill payers (who are channel members too) perceived greater risk associated with their new bill payment process. The shift in channel function costs from some channel members to others meant that end-users had to agree to take on the cost (i.e., risk), because otherwise the new technologies could not spread successfully. However, these bill-paying end-users typically received no compensation for the time, effort, or risk associated with adopting the technology; that is, the shift in costs did not coincide with a shift in payments. This example illustrates a general rule: If channel functions are to be shifted (even perceptually), a gap will result unless the channel member to whom the functions are shifted agrees to perform them. If the channel member is not compensated for doing so, the chances of compliance and successful implementation diminish. However, over time even without compensation users and channel members will often adopt the new technology if it is more efficient or becomes the widely accepted norm. Airline self check-in is fairly well accepted, but grocery self check-out still remains somewhat limited.

The criterion for defining a cost gap specifies that the total cost of performing all functions jointly is higher than it needs be. Therefore, a cost gap might not exist, even if one function is performed at an unusually high cost, as long as it minimizes the *total cost* of performing all functions *jointly*.[12] For example, an electrical wire and cable distributor expanded across the United States and internationally, acquiring many other independent distributors and eventually building an international network of warehouses. Some products it stocked and sold were specialty items, rarely demanded but important to include in a full-line inventory (i.e., end-users demanded a broad assortment and variety). But it was very costly to stock these specialty items in every warehouse worldwide. Therefore, the distributor chose to stock them in just one or two warehouses, which minimized the cost of physical possession of inventory. However, sometimes an end-user located far from the warehouse valued quick delivery and demanded a specialty product. To meet that service output demand, the distributor provided air-freight services to get the required product to the end-user, incurring a seemingly inefficiently high transportation cost. Yet this high transportation cost still was lower than the cost of stocking the specialty product in all possible warehouses, awaiting a rare order. Thus, there was not any true cost gap, because the *total cost* of performing all channel functions was minimized.

In this example, it made economic sense to incur high shipping costs, in return for much lower inventory holding costs. Furthermore, both of those costs were borne by the same channel member, namely, the distributor itself. Optimal allocations of channel functions and costs are more difficult when *different* channel members perform the two functions. Say the distributor would bear the inventory holding cost, but another intermediary (e.g., a broker) was responsible for the shipping costs to get the product to the end-user. In this case, without close coordination and cooperation between the channel members, the distributor likely would benefit from lower warehousing costs at the expense of the broker, who would have to bear higher shipping costs. Even though the entire channel might benefit, this optimal solution is unlikely to arise in practice unless the distributor and broker make an explicit arrangement to share the total costs and benefits fairly.

In summary, a cost gap occurs whenever the performance of channel functions is jointly inefficient (costly). Sometimes, one or more functions may seem inefficient, but only because the channel members have purposefully traded off inefficiency in one function for super-efficiency in another, resulting in lower costs overall. More often though, high costs are a strong signal of cost gaps. Furthermore, a cost gap might exist even without any evidence, from the end-user side, of a channel performance problem. That is, end-users may be delighted with the level of service they receive and the products they buy, and they may even consider the price for the product plus service outputs bundle reasonable. But in this scenario, the chances are good that at least some channel members are not receiving a level of profit that adequately compensates them for the functions they are performing. The cost gap inflicts higher costs on channel members than are necessary. Some channel member must pay those costs, whether end-users, paying through higher prices, or upstream channel members, paying through decreased profit margins. A true zero-based channel offers the right level of service outputs at a minimum total cost to the channel.

## Combining Channel Gaps

Our taxonomy of service and cost gaps implies the six possible situations in Figure 3-4, *only one of which is a zero-gap situation*. As this figure reveals, it is critical to identify the *source* of the gap. If the gap arises from the cost side, with the right amount of service outputs, the channel cannot reduce or increase its service output provision in its efforts to reduce costs. Alternatively, if both a service gap involving too much of a particular service output and a cost gap with inefficiently performed functions exist, reducing the level of service outputs offered without also increasing efficiency can never fully close the gap. If a service gap implies insufficient service outputs, combined with a high cost gap, the temptation may be to cut service provision to reduce channel costs. But this result would be doubly disastrous, in that service levels would suffer even more, and efficiency on a function-by-function basis would not improve.

| COST/ SERVICE LEVEL | Service Gap (SD > SS) | No Service Gap (SD = SS) | Service Gap (SS > SD) |
|---|---|---|---|
| No Cost Gap (Efficient Cost) | Price/value proposition are right for a less demanding segment | *Zero-gap* | Price/value proposition are right for a more demanding segment |
| Cost Gap (Inefficiently provided services) | Service levels are too low and costs too high | Service levels are right but costs are too high | Service levels and costs are too high |
| *Note:* Service demanded (SD) and service supplied (SS). | | | |

**FIGURE 3-4  Types of gaps**

Thus, without proper identification of the source of the gap, the channel could easily seek a solution that is worse than the original problem.

To apply Figure 3-4 to a firms channel gaps, the channel manager must specify which service gaps occur for each particular service output that is valued in the marketplace. This specification permits the manager to identify the over- and under-availability of each service output in a single framework. Figure 3-4 also is target segment specific, so it needs to be applied separately for each segment in the market, because a service gap with one segment may not be a gap at all in another (or the gap may differ).

Cost and service gap combinations also might arise from the links between cost decisions and the provision of service outputs. The principles of postponement and speculation offer a good example.[13] **Postponement** refers to the desires, by both firms and end-users, to put off incurring costs as long as possible. For a manufacturing firm, postponement means delaying the start of production until it receives orders, to avoid the differentiation of raw materials into finished goods (e.g., iron ore into carbon steel). Postponement thus minimizes the manufacturer's risk of selling its production and eliminates the costs of holding relatively expensive inventory. But suppose that end-users demand quick delivery; they too want to postpone (i.e., buy at the last minute). In this situation, manufacturers engaging in postponement cannot meet the service output demands of target end-users, and though they may have avoided a cost gap, they almost certainly have created a problematic service gap.

End-users with high demands for quick delivery thus require a successful channel to lessen reliance on postponement and turn instead to greater speculation. **Speculation** involves producing goods in anticipation of orders, rather than in response to them. A lowest total cost channel that employs speculation often relies on a channel intermediary, which specializes in holding finished inventories for the manufacturer (e.g., a retailer holding finished goods for consumers), in anticipation of sales to end-users. Although speculation is risky and creates inventory holding costs, it permits economies of scale in production by allowing the manufacturer to produce in large batch lot sizes (unlike postponement). But as demand for quick delivery increases, total channel costs ultimately must rise, which generally results in a higher total price paid for a product supplied through a speculation-based system.

The modern retail music business faces exactly this trade-off between speculation and postponement. Previously *speculative* sales of CDs required the channel to guess in advance which CDs would sell well, and how well, so that stores could stock the right number of units. Today, more end-users engage in *postponement* sales through instant online downloads of exactly the music tracks they want to hear, at the very moment they decide they want to purchase. The tension between postponement and speculation is also evident in book sales: Many book publishers still favor *speculation*, such that they supply many copies of potential bestsellers to retail bookstores, whereas *postponement* is the predominant form in the electronic book channel, in which a consumer can download books from the Internet on demand to read electronically. Book publishers continue to embrace speculation, out of their belief that consumers still prefer paper books and are not willing to wait to obtain the book they want, if it is not immediately available in a bookstore. That is, publishers assert that even though postponement might minimize channel costs (e.g., physical possession, ownership, financing), it compromises on the delivery of too many service outputs to be profitable overall.

Despite these preferences for postponement across channels, in some conditions, end-users actually are willing to speculate, such as when they find a particularly good price or deal on a product. Thus, grocery shoppers stock up on items on promotion, which also requires them to tie up their capital in household inventory and run the risk of obsolescence, pilferage, breakage, or spoilage. Buying bulk fruit on promotion might not be efficient if the household cannot eat it all before it goes bad. A household that holds a massive inventory of toilet paper might not have to worry about obsolescence or spoilage, but it could confront waste if the teenaged members of the household use up the "excess" toilet paper to decorate the tree branches of friends' houses.

Clearly, the appropriate amount of speculation in inventory holding in the channel depends on the costs of speculation and the intensity of demand for quick delivery by end-users (measured by their willingness to pay a price premium for quicker delivery). A possible solution for minimizing total costs is to offer a particular delivery time to the end-user. This total cost reflects the most efficient level of channel costs and the cost to the end-user of waiting to receive the offering, as Figure 3-5 indicates. The curve ABC depicts the lowest possible cost of delivering the product to end-users, as a function of the required delivery time. With longer delivery times, the manufacturer can seek less expensive delivery methods. Postponement for example is possible only with long delivery times. The curve ABC goes beyond the speculation–postponement continuum though, to include switches to different technologies and channel structures that can facilitate the delivery time service output at the lowest cost.

Curve DE in Figure 3-5 depicts the end-user's cost of holding goods as a function of the offered delivery time. For very short delivery times, inventory holding costs are null. As delivery times increase, the end-user must begin to speculate and buy *safety stocks* of product in advance, so these inventory holding costs increase. Finally, curve AFG is the sum of the channel's and the end-user's costs to acquire the product offered within a particular delivery time. Because the end-user ultimately must pay all channel costs (plus some profit margin for the channel members), it is desirable to seek the lowest total cost method for inventory holding. A cost minimization orientation would direct the channel to seek some combination of postponement and speculation that corresponds to point F in Figure 3-5, because doing so minimizes the total channel costs of providing a particular delivery time.

A similar analysis could be applied to other marketing function costs for availability, bulk breaking, product variety, and information provision. But this more complete set of criteria must include not just total cost minimization but also the utility or benefits accrued by end-users from providing these service outputs. Focusing on

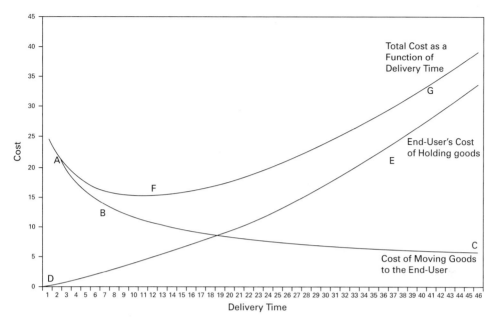

**FIGURE 3-5** Channel costs and the principles of postponement versus speculation

*Source:* Adapted from Louis P. Bucklin, *A Theory of Distribution Channel Structure* (Berkeley, CA: IBER Publications, University of California, 1966), pp. 22–25.

efficiency—that is, cost minimization—within the channel cannot provide a channel solution that minimizes all gaps in the channel, but attention to the relative value of postponement and speculation for all channel members, including end-users, can highlight the sources of some channel gaps.

The multidimensional nature of this gap analysis leaves little question that most selling situations suffer persistent gaps in their channel design. Careful identification of the types of gaps present, and which segments are affected, can help prevent mistakes in gap resolution.

## Evaluating Channels: Gap Analysis Template

This chapter has described the sources of channel gaps, service gaps, and cost gaps, as well as why these two gaps must be considered simultaneously. Figure 3-6, the **Service Gap Analysis Template**, aims to identify service gaps explicitly according to the *targeted end-user segment*. Figure 3-7, the **Cost Gap Analysis Template**, builds on this information and identifies cost gaps, the bounds that give rise to them, and potential actions to close them. It also can denote whether the potential actions create other, unintended gaps.

Figures 3-8 and 3-9 offer an example analysis of the CDW situation using the Gap Analysis Template. The service output demands differ significantly across three key segments: small businesses, large businesses, and government buyers. Spatial convenience and waiting/delivery time demands must be separated, designated as for original equipment or postsales service. Small business buyers need higher levels for postsales service but lower service levels for original equipment purchases (because they have no in-house servicing capabilities), whereas the opposite relationship holds for large business buyers (which have in-house services).

| Service Demanded (SD) Versus Service Supplied (SS) | | | | | | | |
|---|---|---|---|---|---|---|---|
| Segment Name/ Descriptor | Bulk Breaking | Spatial Convenience | Delivery/ Waiting Time | Assortment/ Variety | Customer Service | Information Sharing | Major Channel for this Segment |
| 1. | | | | | | | |
| 2. | | | | | | | |
| 3. | | | | | | | |
| 4. | | | | | | | |
| 5. | | | | | | | |

Notes and directions for using this template:
- Enter names and/or descriptions for each segment.
- Enter whether SS > SD, SS < SD, or SS = SD for each service output and each segment. Add footnotes to explain entries if necessary. If known and relevant, footnote any cost gaps that lead to each service gap.
- Record major channel used by each segment. How does this segment of buyers choose to buy?

**FIGURE 3-6**   Service gap analysis template

Figure 3-8 also highlights that all three segments buy from CDW; that is, CDW is part of the route to market for multiple segments of buyers. The government buyer is bound to use multiple channels though, according to its goal of buying from small business vendors for a significant portion of its purchases. Finally, as Figure 3-8 points out, on several key service outputs, CDW's offerings are either too little (SS < SD) or

| Channel [Targeting Which Segment(s)?] | Channel Members and Functions Performed | Environmental/ Managerial Bounds | Cost Gaps [Affecting Which Function(s)?] | Planned Techniques for Closing Gaps | Do/Did Actions Create Other Gaps? |
|---|---|---|---|---|---|
| 1. | | | | | |
| 2. | | | | | |
| 3. | | | | | |
| 4. | | | | | |
| 5. | | | | | |

Notes:
- Record routes to market in the channel system. Note the segment or segments targeted through each channel.
- Summarize channel members and key functions they perform.
- Note any environmental or managerial bounds facing this channel.
- Note all cost gaps in this channel, by function or functions affected.
- If known, record techniques currently in use or planned to close gaps (or note that no action is planned, and why).
- Analyze whether proposed/actual actions have created or will create other gaps.

**FIGURE 3-7**   Cost gap analysis template

| | | Service Demanded (SD: L/M/H) Versus Service Supplied by CDW (SS) | | | | | |
|---|---|---|---|---|---|---|---|
| Segment Name/ Descriptor | Bulk Breaking | Spatial Convenience | Delivery/Waiting Time | Assortment Variety | Customer Service | Information Sharing | Major Channel for this Segment |
| 1. Small business buyer | H (SS = SD) | Original equipment: M (SS = SD) Postsale service: H (SS = SD) | Original equipment: M (SS > SD) Post-sale service: H (SS = SD) | M (SS > SD) | H (SS = SD) | H (both presale and postsale) (SS = SD) | Value-added reseller such as CDW or retailer |
| 2. Large business buyer | L (SS > SD) | Original equipment: H (SS = SD) Postsale service: L (SS > SD) | Original equipment: M (SS > SD) Postsale service: L (SS > SD) | M/H (SS = SD) | M (SS > SD) | L (SS > SD) | Manufacturer direct or large reseller such as CDW |
| 3. Government/ education | L (SS > SD) | Original equipment: H (SS = SD) Postsale service: H (SS = SD) | Original equipment: M (SS > SD) Postsale service: M (SS > SD) | M/H (SS = SD) | H (SS = SD) | H (both presale and postsale) (SS = SD) | Manufacturer direct or reseller; approx. 20 percent from small business |

*Notes:* L = low, M = medium, H = high.

**FIGURE 3-8** Service gap analysis template: CDW example

| Channel [Targeting Which Segment(s)?] | Channel Members and Functions Performed | Environmental (E)/ Managerial (M) Bounds | Cost Gaps [Affecting Which Function(s)?] | Planned Techniques for Closing Gaps | Do/Did Actions Create Other Gaps? |
|---|---|---|---|---|---|
| 1. CDW direct to buyer (→ small business buyer) | Manufacturer, CDW, small business buyer | (M): no screening of recruits for expected longevity with firm | Promotion [sales force training/turnover] | Better screening of new recruits | No. Buying from CDW closes gaps for customer in *Risk* |
| 2. CDW direct to buyer (→ large business buyer, government) | Manufacturer, CDW, CDW-G, large business or government buyer | (E): government requires 20 percent of purchases from small vendors (M): no screening of recruits for expected longevity with firm | *Promotion* [sales force training/turnover] *Negotiation* [cannot close 2020 percent of deals with government] | Better screening of new recruits. Rely on consortium channel structure | No |
| 3. CDW + small business consortium of value-added resellers (VAR) (→ government) | Manufacturer, CDW-G, small VAR, consortium partner, government buyer | (E): government requires 20 percent of purchases from small vendors (M): VAR's small business size (M): no screening of recruits for expected longevity with firm | *Promotion* [sales force training/turnover] *Negotiation:* small gap for a small VAR not in the CDW alliance | Better screening of new recruits *Negotiation* gap closed through consortium with small VARs | No |

*Notes:* All channel members perform all functions to some extent. Key channel functions of interest are *promotion, negotiation,* and *risk.*

**FIGURE 3-9**  Cost gap analysis template: CDW example

too much (SS > SD) for the target segment. In general, the service gaps appear due to over- rather than underprovision of service, which is common in channel systems with multiple segments of buyers, because the channel seeks to at least *satisfy* every segment. Because segments differ in their demands, it seems inevitable that overprovision to some segments will result.

Noting the gaps in Figure 3-8 and Figure 3-9 reveals the environmental and managerial bounds facing CDW, related to CDW's difficulty in prescreening its sales force for longevity, as well as external governmental dictates about approved vendor sizes. Ensuing cost gaps plague CDW's promotion and negotiation functions in particular. Channel analysts should note any direct links from bounds to service gaps. Finally, for CDW, potential actions to close the gaps do not obviously create new ones, though careful consideration, beyond the obvious, still is required.

In Chapter 5, we focus on integrating information from end-users (e.g., segmentation and targeting) and channel audits (e.g., efficiency, service-gap, and cost-gap templates) to design channel structures and strategies. With such input, channel managers can more effectively close service and cost gaps while still meeting the service output needs of their targeted end-users.

After implementing changes to the channel strategy and structure to close the gaps in service and cost, the channel structure still may just approach a zero-based design, without being *fully* zero-based. That is, some environmental or managerial bounds could remain, continuing to constrain the final channel solution. Nor does the process of gap analysis ever come to a conclusion. Environmental bounds change over time, and end-users' demands for service outputs, as well as the available distribution technology, shift and transform. This propensity for change creates a never-ending opportunity for channel strategy innovations to pursue the moving target of a zero-based channel for each and every targeted segment in the market.

## TAKE-AWAYS

- Just as a production plants produce physical products, the members of a marketing channel engage in *productive activity*. We call the activities of the channel its *functions*.
- Detailed knowledge of function performance in the channel improves service output provision, facilitates channel design or redesign, helps determine rewards for channel members, and can mitigate channel conflicts.
- Every channel function not only contributes to the production of valued service outputs but is also associated with a cost.
- The generic list of channel functions includes *physical possession, ownership, promotion, negotiation, financing, risk, ordering, payment*, and *information sharing*.
- The drive to minimize channel management costs implies that it is important to avoid performing unnecessarily high levels of any of the functions; knowing which service outputs are demanded by target end-users is the key to knowing which service levels to use to create the right level (neither too low nor too high) of service outputs that will be most valued by target end-users.
- The efficiency template describes (a) the types and amounts of work done by each channel member to perform marketing functions, (b) the importance of each channel

function to the provision of consumer service outputs, and (c) the resulting share of total channel profits that each channel member *should* reap.

- A separate efficiency template should be created for *each channel* used to distribute the product and, ideally, for *each market segment* that buys through each channel.

- A zero-based channel design meets the target market segment's demands for service outputs, at the minimum cost of performing the necessary channel functions that produce those service outputs.

- Comparing a zero-based efficiency analysis against the channel's efficiency analysis can inform the channel analyst of situations in which a channel member may be busy (bearing high channel function costs) yet not adding commensurate value to the channel's overall operations.

- The equity principle states that compensation in the channel system should reflect the degree of participation in the marketing functions and the value created by this participation. That is, compensation should mirror the normative profit shares for each channel member.

- Channel gaps arise as a result of *bounds* that prevent the channel captain from optimizing the channel structure.
  - *Environmental* channel bounds are constraints imposed from outside the channel, such as legal restrictions or a lack of adequate infrastructural capabilities in the market that can support an optimal channel structure.
  - *Managerial* channel bounds are constraints imposed from inside the channel, usually due to channel managers' lack of knowledge about the full implications of channel actions or reflecting optimization at a higher level than the channel itself.
  - The channel structure can be optimized *subject to these bounds*, but this solution will not be quite as efficient, nor will it do quite as good a job of satisfying target end-users' service output demands, as would an unconstrained channel.

- *Service gaps* can arise because a particular service output, provided to a particular target segment of end-users, is too *low* and the service outputs demanded exceed the service outputs supplied (SD > SS); or because a particular service output, provided to a particular target segment of end-users, is too *high* and the service outputs supplied exceed the service outputs demanded (SD < SS).
  - When SD < SS, the channel is operating inefficiently, because consumers are not willing to pay for the high level of service offered, due to their low valuation of that service.
  - In general, service gaps may remain if competitors are no better at providing these service outputs than the channel is. However, persistent service gaps provide an ideal opportunity for the channel to build overall market demand and steal market share, by investing in improved service output levels.

- *Cost gaps* arise when one or more channel function(s) are performed at high costs. A superior technology exists to decrease the cost of performing that function, without compromising service output provision.

- The Gap Analysis Templates provide tools for codifying knowledge of both the service and the cost gaps facing the channel in its channel management tasks.

# Endnotes

1. Information for this Sidebar is drawn from Campbell, Scott (2003), "CDW-G Calls on VARs," *Computer Reseller News,* November 17 (no. 1071), p. 162; Campbell, Scott (2004), "CDW Snags Companywide Cisco Premier Status—Relationship Advances Reseller's Bid to Build Services Business," *Computer Reseller News*, April 12; Gallagher, Kathleen (2002), "CDW Computer Remains Afloat Despite Market's Choppy Waters," *Milwaukee Journal Sentinel*, September 29, p. 4D; Jones, Sandra (2004), "Challenges Ahead for CDW; Dell Deals Make Inroads in Already Difficult Market," *Crain's Chicago Business*, June 28, p. 4; Kaiser, Rob (2000), "Vernon Hills, Ill., Computer Products Reseller Has an Approach to Win Business," *Chicago Tribune*, August 16; McCafferty, Dennis (2002), "Growing Like Gangbusters—Sales at Chicago-Area CDW-Government Shot up 63 Percent from 2000 to 2001," *VAR Business*, July 8; Moltzen, Edward (2003), "Looking for SMB Traction, Gateway Inks Reseller Pact with CDW," *Computer Reseller New*, May 26, p. 55; O'Heir, Jeff (2003), "CDW Teams with Small VARs to Access Government Biz," *Computer Reseller News*, August 25 (no. 1059), p. 6; O'Heir, Jeff (2003), "Time to Move On," *Computer Reseller News*, October 20 (no. 1067), p. 98; Rose, Barbara and Mike Highlett (2005), "Balancing Success with High Stress," *Chicago Tribune*, June 5; Schmeltzer, John (2003), "CDW Pulls Out the Stops to Reach Small Business," *Chicago Tribune*, September 8; Zarley, Craig and Jeff O'Heir (2003), "Seeking Solutions— CDW, Gateway and Dell Come Calling on Solution Providers for Services Expertise," *Computer Reseller News*, September 1.

2. Su, Xuanming (2009), "Consumer Returns Policies and Supply Chain Performance," *Manufacturing & Service Operation Management* 11 (Fall), pp. 595–612. Background references for this Sidebar include Andel, Tom (2004), "How to Advance in the Reverse Channel," *Material Handling Management* 59 (February), pp. 24–30; Coia, Anthony (2003), "Channeling e-Tail Resources," *Apparel Magazine* 44 ( August),

pp. 18–20; Cottrill, Ken (2003), "Dumping Debate," *TrafficWORLD*, March; Cottrill, Ken (2003), "Remedying Returns," *Commonwealth Business Media Joint Logistics Special Report 2003*, p. L–19; Enright, Tony (2003), "Post-Holiday Logistics," *TrafficWORLD*, January 6, p. 20; Gooley, Toby B. (2003), "The Who, What and Where of Reverse Logistics," *Logistics Management* (February), pp. 38–44; Hughes, David (2003), "Reverse Thinking in the Supply Chain," *Focus* (September), pp. 30–36; Rogers, Dale S. and Ronald S. Tibben-Lembke (1998), *Going Backwards: Reverse Logistics Trends and Practices* (Reno, NV: Reverse Logistics Executive Council); Spencer, Jane (2002), "The Point of No Return; Stores from Gap to Target Tighten Refund Rules; a 15% 'Restocking Fee,'" *The Wall Street Journal*, May 14, p. D1; Tibben-Lembke, Ronald S. and Dale S. Rogers (2002), "Differences Between Forward and Reverse Logistics in a Retail Environment," *Supply Chain Management* 7 (5), pp. 271–282; Zieger, Anne (2003), "Reverse Logistics: The New Priority?" *Frontline Solutions* 4 (November), pp. 20–24.

3. Shulman, Jeffrey, Anne Coughlan, and R. Savaskan (2010), "Optimal Reverse Channel Structure for Consumer Product Returns," *Journal of Marketing Science* 29 (November–December), pp. 1071–108.

4. For a discussion of EOQ models, see Chopra, Sunil (2012), *Supply Chain Management*, 5th ed. (Englewood Cliffs, NJ: Prentice Hall).

5. We do not develop an in-depth discussion of activity-based costing in this text. However, interested readers should visit the following sources: Horngren, Charles T. (2011), *Cost Accounting*, 14th ed. (Englewood Cliffs, NJ: Prentice Hall); Cooper, Robin and Robert S. Kaplan (1991), "Profit Priorities from Activity-Based Accounting," *Harvard Business Review* 69 (3, May–June), pp. 130–135.

6. See, for example, Forsyth, Donelson R. (1983), *An Introduction to Group Dynamics* (Monterey, CA: Brooks/Cole). The RAND Corporation is credited with developing the Delphi technique in the 1950s to

forecast where the Soviet Union would attack the United States, if it were to launch an attack. It originally put U.S. generals and Kremlinologists into a room to discuss the issue, but they made very little progress. Thus, the RAND Corporation developed the Delphi technique to arrive at an orderly consensus.

7. Lee, Hau L., V. Padmanabhan, and Seungjin Whang (1997), "The Bullwhip Effect in Supply Chains," *Sloan Management Review* 38 (Spring), pp. 93–102.

8. Kaiser, Stefen (2012), "Fears of Bank Runs Mount in Southern Europe," *Speigel Online International*, May 5, http://www.spiegel.de/international

9. See, for example, Achrol, Ravi S., Torger Reve, and Louis W. Stern (1983), "The Environment of Marketing Channel Dyads: A Framework for Comparative Analysis," *Journal of Marketing* 47 (Fall), pp. 55–67; Achrol, Ravi S. and Louis W. Stern (1988), "Environmental Determinants of Decision-Making Uncertainty in Marketing Channels," *Journal of Marketing Research* 25 (February), pp. 36–50; Etgar, Michael (1977), "Channel Environment and Channel Leadership," *Journal of Marketing Research* 15 (February), pp. 69–76; Dwyer, F. Robert and Sejo Oh (1987), "Output Sector Munificence Effects on the Internal Political Economy of Marketing Channels," *Journal of Marketing Research* 24 (November), pp. 347–358; Dwyer, F. Robert and M. Ann Welsh (1985), "Environmental Relationships of the Internal Political Economy of Marketing Channels," *Journal of Marketing Research* 22 (November), pp. 397–414.

10. Achrol and Stern (1988), op cit., refer to the present and projected state of technology, the geographic dispersion of end-users, and the extent of turbulence and diversity in the marketplace as factors that can inhibit optimal channel design. These are all examples of infrastructural dimensions. Achrol and Stern also consider a set of competitive factors, such as industry concentration and competitors' behavior, which constitute different dimensions of the infrastructure facing a firm seeking to manage its channel structure appropriately.

11. Shin, Jiwoong (2007), "How Does Free Riding on Customer Service Affect Competition?" *Marketing Science* 26 (July–August), pp. 488–503.

12. Louis P. Bucklin calls this phenomenon "functional substitutability. See Bucklin, Louis P. (1966), *A Theory of Distribution Channel Structure* (Berkeley, CA: University of California, IBER Special Publications).

13. Bucklin, Louis P. (1967), "Postponement, Speculation and the Structure of Distribution Channels," in Bruce E. Mallen, ed., *The Marketing Channel: A Conceptual Viewpoint* (New York: John Wiley & Sons, Inc.), pp. 67–74.

# APPENDIX 3-1

## The Efficiency Template: Tools for Analysis

This appendix focuses on how to fill out the efficiency template to reflect the current channel structure (including a zero-based channel, if applicable). Figure 3-3 shows a blank efficiency template.

The template is designed to help channel managers understand (1) who is doing what functions in the channel, (2) how much of the combined cost and value each channel member is responsible for, and (3) whether each channel member is being fairly compensated for the performance of these functions. The outputs obtained from a better understanding of these issues are (1) a greater ability to defend the allocation of total channel profits among channel members (based on an in-depth analysis rather than on ad hoc rationales or inertia); (2) a set of recommendations regarding the split of channel profits; and (3) a set of recommendations regarding future emphases on the performance of particular functions in the channel. The template should be filled out separately for each channel used in the market.

The first step is to determine the weights of each channel function. The final assessment of these weights must account not just for the cost of performing this channel function throughout the channel, as a proportion of total channel operation costs, but also the value generated by performing this channel function. If possible, the "Costs" column should reflect financially sound data, collected through a process such as activity-based costing, to determine the proportion of total channel costs allocable to each function. The "Benefit Potential" column should reflect the judgmental inputs of managers knowledgeable about the channel of the likelihood that good performance by that function will create highly valued service outputs. Because these inputs are judgmental, qualitative input can be helpful, such as a ranking by "Low/Medium/High." These rankings then can serve to adjust the purely cost-based weights in the "Costs" column to arrive at final weights for each function. If a function earns a "High" rating for benefit potential, it should receive more weight than its pure cost-based weight suggests, because it also is important on the service output generation side. The sum of the importance weights is 100. If the weight assigned the "Promotion" function needs to increase, the analyst simultaneously must take some points away from some other function, presumably one (or more than one) that received a "Low" benefit potential ranking.

Following the determination of weights, the cost of each function borne by each channel member must be entered into the table. Consider the example of a promotion on laptop computers in a retail channel. Relevant channel members include the manufacturer, the retailer, and the consumer. The consumer probably does not perform any promotional functions (unless word of mouth is influential in this market), so the consumer receives a 0 score in the promotions row. Both the manufacturer and the retailer likely perform promotional functions: The manufacturer conducts national advertising campaigns, and the retailer uses salespeople to promote the product to consumers who walk in the door. Parceling out the costs, we might discover that the manufacturer bears 65 percent of total promotional costs in the channel, while the retailer bears 35 percent. The sum of the three numbers (promotional costs borne by the manufacturer, retailer, and consumer) is 100 percent. This exercise should be repeated for each channel function in the template.

Can consumers perform channel functions and earn entries other than 0 in this template? Of course—consider the example of a consumer shopping for groceries at a hypermarket. This consumer buys in large bulk, including six weeks' worth of paper goods in one visit to the hypermarket. This consumer therefore bears physical possession functions and costs (storing inventory at home instead of going to the store every time the household needs more paper goods), ownership functions (the consumer purchases the paper goods and owns them sooner than she or he needs them), financing functions (the consumer pays for the goods when taking ownership, which improves upstream channel members' cash function positions), and so on. Another shopper, who buys only what he or she needs on a daily or biweekly basis, typically buys smaller lot sizes, does not store much inventory in the home, and therefore does not perform the above-mentioned functions. The former consumer typically pays a lower price than the latter, precisely because the hypermarket shopper is bearing the cost of several channel functions. Thus, we find a direct relationship between bearing channel functions and garnering channel profits (in the consumer's case, a lower price).

Finally, after determining the weights and proportionate shares of function performance in the template, we can calculate a weighted average for each channel member, as described at the bottom of Figure 3-3. The numbers that result can be written in the bottom row of the efficiency template, and they should sum to 100 percent across the bottom row. What do these numbers mean though? Primarily, they indicate which proportion of *total channel profits* each channel member should get, given the current channel structure. We call this value the normative profit share of channel member *i* in the current channel. This normative profit share may or may not equal the *actual* profit share. When these two numbers are not equal, we must ask why; reasons for a divergence between normative and actual profit shares might include the following:

1. Profits are misallocated in the channel and should be reallocated.
2. Competitive conditions force a particular channel member to take a lower profit share than its normative function performance indicates; its economic rents have essentially disappeared in the market due to competition.
3. External constraints, such as government regulations, confer economic rents on a channel member beyond its performance of channel functions. This reason can create particularly thorny issues in international channel management.

Finally, it is relevant to ask what these profit shares actually are. Consider total retail sales, or retail price times total units sold. Now subtract from this total revenue the *total costs* of running the channel and the *cost of goods sold* (to separate out the part of costs accrued in the manufacturing process). What remains are *total channel profits*. To get a really good handle on the allocation of profits among channel members, the channel manager needs to perform an activity-based costing analysis (or some similar analysis) of the channel.

Consider some of the contrasts between a template describing the *current* channel and one describing a *zero-based* channel:

1. There is no reason the weights would necessarily be the same in the two templates. The current channel might underemphasize the importance of promotion,

such that the channel manager decides to increase the proportion of total channel costs spent on promotion. That changes the weights allocated to the other functions accordingly.

2. The ratings in the template can differ. In a zero-based channel, it might make sense to assign the distributor all inventory handling functions, such that the physical possession function costs land much more heavily on the distributor than in the current channel. In this case, the "physical possession" row should show different percentages in the zero-based versus the current template.

3. The column headings themselves may vary. The zero-based channel might be a vertically integrated channel, without a column heading for the currently used distributor, for example.

Managers in particular firms also might think about this list of functions in a different way than enumerated here. For example, managers may clump physical possession and ownership together into an "inventory" function, which is fine—as long as physical possession and ownership *always* go hand in hand. But if they do not (e.g., if some sales are consignment sales), the functions need to be separated.

Consider an efficiency analysis performed for a European building materials company. Data were collected from top managers of the company, who had expertise in the workings of their channels. Table 3-4 shows the efficiency template for the

**TABLE 3-4**  Building materials company efficiency template for channel serving end-users through retailers: Undisguised data

| | Importance Weights for Functions | | | Proportional Function Performance of Channel Member | | | |
|---|---|---|---|---|---|---|---|
| | Costs | Benefit Potential (High, Medium, Low) | Final Weight | Manufacturer | Retailer | End-User | Total |
| Physical possession | 30 | High | 35 | 30 | 30 | 40 | 100 |
| Ownership | 12 | Medium | 15 | 30 | 40 | 30 | 100 |
| Promotion | 10 | Low | 8 | 20 | 80 | 0 | 100 |
| Negotiation | 5 | Low/Medium | 4 | 20 | 60 | 20 | 100 |
| Financing | 22 | Medium | 29 | 30 | 30 | 40 | 100 |
| Risk | 5 | Low | 2 | 30 | 50 | 20 | 100 |
| Ordering | 6 | Low | 3 | 20 | 60 | 20 | 100 |
| Payment | 7 | Low | 4 | 20 | 60 | 20 | 100 |
| Information sharing | 3 | Low | 0 | 20 | 40 | 40 | 100 |
| Total | **100** | N/A | **100** | N/A | N/A | N/A | N/A |
| Normative profit share | N/A | N/A | N/A | **28%** | **39%** | **33%** | **100** |

channel it used to serve small and medium-sized end-users (specifically, contractors), who buy through retailers. Because building materials are bulky and expensive to transport, physical possession costs are the largest proportion of total channel costs, accounting for 30 percent of channel costs in total. Financing is also a significant channel cost, with 22 percent of the total. Other functions have smaller relative costs. In the "Benefit Potential" column, physical possession appears as the main benefit-conferring channel function, because end-users require product provision in a spatially convenient way (to minimize their own transportation costs) and with minimal time delays. Thus, the final weight allocated to the physical possession function for this company in this channel was 35 percent, and ownership and financing increased in importance somewhat. The other functions' final weights should be reduced from their pure cost-based levels.

The channel consists of the manufacturer, who sells directly to retailers, who in turn sell directly to end-users. Small contractors are a major constituency; they buy product in advance and hold small inventories themselves, such that they participate in 40 percent of the physical possession function, and the manufacturer and retailer each take a 30 percent share. Retailers are very active channel members, particularly in their performance of promotional, negotiation, ordering, and payment functions; they also buffer the manufacturer by dealing with the many small customer orders. End-users perform none of the promotional function but participate in a small way in other functions. For their efforts, these end-users deserve one-third of the channel profits, which translates into a price cut, compared with the list price that would be charged to an individual buyer (e.g., do-it-yourself homeowner). The retailer earns a normative channel profit share of 39 percent, and the manufacturer earns a normative channel profit share of 28 percent. Specifically, the manufacturer's normative channel profit share can be calculated as follows:

$$(.35) \times (.3) + (.15) \times (.3) + (.08) \times (.2) + (.04) \times (.2) + (.29) \times (.3) + (.02) \times (.3) + (.03) \times (.2) + (.04) \times (.2) + (.00) \times (.20).$$

This analysis reflects a careful estimation of the total costs of performing all the channel functions in this channel. But suppose that the company did not have exact percentage shares for all the functions but rather had access only to very rough data, such as zero, low, medium, and high ratings. Let's assume that if the true rating was 0, the company would report a "Zero" (=0); a true rating between 1 and 29 percent would produce a "Low" (=1) report; true ratings between 30 and 69 percent lead to a "Medium" (=2) rating, and those between 70 and 100 percent prompt a "High" (=3) score. (This coding scheme is linear, but if there were a strong reason to believe that a nonlinear scheme would be better, it is possible to use one.) We would then generate the efficiency template in Table 3-5.

To translate this information into percentages, we look at the rank-order data for a given function and ask: What proportion of the costs of performing this function is borne by the manufacturer? By the retailer? By the final end-user? For physical possession for example, each entry is 2 (Medium), the point-count total is 6, and each channel member has one-third of the points. We therefore can allocate 33 percent of

**TABLE 3-5    Building materials company efficiency template for channel serving end-users through retailers: Rank-order data**

| | Importance Weights for Functions | | | Proportional Function Performance of Channel Member | | | |
|---|---|---|---|---|---|---|---|
| | Costs | Benefit Potential (High, Medium, Low) | Final Weight | Manufacturer | Retailer | End-User | Total |
| Physical possession | 30 | High | 35 | 2 | 2 | 2 | 100 |
| Ownership | 12 | Medium | 15 | 2 | 2 | 2 | 100 |
| Promotion | 10 | Low | 8 | 1 | 3 | 0 | 100 |
| Negotiation | 5 | Low/Medium | 4 | 1 | 2 | 1 | 100 |
| Financing | 22 | Medium | 29 | 2 | 2 | 2 | 100 |
| Risk | 5 | Low | 2 | 2 | 2 | 1 | 100 |
| Ordering | 6 | Low | 3 | 1 | 2 | 1 | 100 |
| Payment | 7 | Low | 4 | 1 | 2 | 1 | 100 |
| Information sharing | 3 | Low | 0 | 1 | 2 | 2 | 100 |
| Total | **100** | N/A | **100** | N/A | N/A | N/A | N/A |
| Normative profit share | N/A | N/A | N/A | **?** | **?** | **?** | **100** |

the channel function costs to each channel member. The rank-order data for the promotion function instead give the manufacturer a ranking of 1 (Low), the retailer earns a 3 (High), and the end-user gets a ranking of 0. Thus, of the 4 total points in the promotion function, 25 percent of them (i.e., an estimated 25 percent of the channel function costs of promotion) are borne by the manufacturer, and 75 percent are borne by the retailer, with none of them laid on the end-user.

These transformed data produce percentages similar to those in the original efficiency template, but they are based on rougher data inputs (a 4-point scale rather than a 100-point scale, in effect). The transformed efficiency template appears as Table 3-6.

From this analysis, the manufacturer's normative channel profit share is 32 percent, the retailer's is 38 percent, and end-users get 29 percent. These values compare rather well with the 28, 39, and 33 percent proffered according to the "true" data in Table 3-4. Full activity-based costing analysis of the performance of channel functions is not always possible; the rank-order data inputs suggested here may provide reasonable estimates instead.

**TABLE 3-6**    Building materials company efficiency template for channel serving end-users through retailers: Transformed rank-order data

| | Importance Weights for Functions | | | Proportional Function Performance of Channel Member | | | |
| | Costs | Benefit Potential (High, Medium, Low) | Final Weight | Manufacturer | Retailer | End-User | Total |
|---|---|---|---|---|---|---|---|
| Physical possession | 30 | High | 35 | 33 | 33 | 33 | 100 |
| Ownership | 12 | Medium | 15 | 33 | 33 | 33 | 100 |
| Promotion | 10 | Low | 8 | 25 | 75 | 0 | 100 |
| Negotiation | 5 | Low/Medium | 4 | 25 | 50 | 25 | 100 |
| Financing | 22 | Medium | 29 | 33 | 33 | 33 | 100 |
| Risk | 5 | Low | 2 | 40 | 40 | 20 | 100 |
| Ordering | 6 | Low | 3 | 25 | 50 | 25 | 100 |
| Payment | 7 | Low | 4 | 25 | 50 | 25 | 100 |
| Information sharing | 3 | Low | 0 | 20 | 40 | 40 | 100 |
| Total | **100** | N/A | **100** | N/A | N/A | N/A | N/A |
| Normative profit share | N/A | N/A | N/A | **32%** | **38%** | **29%** | **100** |

# CHAPTER 4

# Make-or-Buy
# Channel Analysis

**LEARNING OBJECTIVES**

**After reading this chapter, you will be able to:**

- Understand vertical integration as a continuum from make to buy, rather than as a binary choice.
- Explain why channel players (manufacturers, wholesalers, retailers) often integrate forward or backward with great expectations, only to divest themselves within a few years.
- Frame vertical integration decisions according to whether owning the channel, or some of its functions, improves long-term returns on investment.
- Recognize why outsourcing should be the base case for a market channel, rather than vertical integration.
- Identify three situations in which vertical integration dominates outsourcing in distribution.
- Define six categories of company-specific capabilities.
- Distinguish specificity from rarity.
- Detail the impact of volatile environments on returns from forward integration.
- Identify the sources of performance ambiguity and their relations to returns from forward or backward integration in distribution.
- Recognize the role of vertical integration for learning and creating strategic options—and understand when these rationales do not fit.

In marketing channels, make-or-buy decisions (i.e., vertically integrate or outsource) are critical strategic choices, because the firm's decision to own some or all of its marketing channel exerts an enduring influence on its ability to distribute and produce. Thus, there is a fundamental question to ask when designing a channel strategy: *Should a firm vertically integrate by performing both upstream and downstream functions?* In other words, who should perform different channel functions? Should it be a single organization (manufacturer, agent, distributor, retailer—all rolled into one), or should distribution functions be outsourced (upstream looking down), or should production be outsourced (downstream looking up), or neither, such that manufacturers and downstream channel members remain separate entities?

The vertical integration decision is not an aggregate determination though. Rather, the decision should proceed, channel function by channel function, such that each channel member, assuming it has sufficient power and resources, can decide to integrate some subset of channel functions and achieve the optimal combination of "make" and "buy" options for its unique channel structure. To **integrate** is to combine disparate elements into one, singular entity. When the manufacturer integrates a distribution function (e.g., making sales, fulfilling orders, offering credit), its employees do the work, and the manufacturer has integrated forward or downstream from the point of production. Vertical integration also can begin from a downstream position, such that a distributor or retailer produces its own branded source of product and thereby integrates backward. Whether the manufacturer integrates forward or the downstream channel member integrates backward, the result is that one organization does all the work, and the channel is **vertically integrated**.

Whether it makes or buys, a manufacturer also is closely identified with its marketing channels, which influence its end-user base and determine its image. In addition, the manufacturer gains market and competitive intelligence from its channels: What the manufacturer knows (or can learn) about its markets depends heavily on how it goes to market.[1] Thus, its decision to vertically integrate forward influences what the manufacturer *does*, as well as what it *could learn to do*. The decision also is difficult to reverse, because it entails commitments that are not easy to redeploy. Such enduring, important, structural decisions require great consideration, with an emphasis on their influence on the firm's future performance.

For downstream channel members, the decision to integrate backward may mean the loss of resources, conflicts with other suppliers, and a challenge to their ability to offer unbiased advice to customers. Yet for many firms, moving up the value chain is too appealing to resist, especially when they perceive unmet end-user needs that current manufacturers just don't seem to understand. Why should a distributor leave more of the margins to a manufacturer, if it is the channel member that understands demand better?

As these brief analyses show, all managers need a structured way to analyze their make-or-buy issues that provides them with a coherent, comprehensive, easily communicated rationale for their decisions. The structured framework presented in this chapter centers on the helping manufacturers determine whether they should integrate a given function or a subset of functions in going to market.[2] In the base case, we show that a manufacturer typically should *not* vertically integrate, because doing so tends to be inefficient. However, owning functions (up to and including the entire channel) is appropriate if the manufacturer has sufficient resources *and* can increase its long-term returns on investment by doing so. Similarly, the structured framework reveals that downstream channel members are typically worse off when they integrate backward—unless they have sufficient resources and can increase their long-run returns. In turn, the framework identifies which conditions increase those long-run returns on investment. For clarity, we start with the manufacturer, and then extend the arguments downstream.

## TRADE-OFFS OF VERTICAL INTEGRATION

To appreciate the hidden costs and benefits of vertical integration, imagine a manufacturer, looking downstream at the set of functions that end-users are willing to pay to have performed. For each function, the manufacturer thinks, "Can we make that, or is it better to buy it?" However, the choice is not really binary. The **make-or-buy continuum** instead details how costs, benefits, and responsibilities associated with any particular function can be split among organizations, as Figure 4-1 shows.

### Degrees of Vertical Integration

At the **buy** endpoint of the continuum, manufacturer–distributor arrangements involve no sharing (of risk, of expertise, of image), no distinction, and no continuity. This model outsources every function; it also offers a useful baseline for thinking about distribution. It is not particularly prevalent in the real world though. Most arrangements with third parties exhibit some degree of **relationalism**, such that the manufacturer takes a greater share of both costs and benefits than it would if it is strictly and completely delegated to a third party (i.e., classical market contracting).[3] Thus for our purposes, we consider the buy endpoint as a larger zone of outsourced relationships with third parties, some of which operate in a manner that resembles a single firm. In practice, customers often believe they are dealing with the manufacturer when they really are interacting with a committed third party in the marketing channel.

   **Relational governance** implies a compromise, in which the channels have some properties of *both* owned (make) and independent (buy) channels.[4] Relational governance arises in several ways, such as building and maintaining close, committed relationships (Chapter 12), perhaps through selective distribution (Chapter 5) or franchising (i.e., two organizations attempt to coordinate as though they were one;

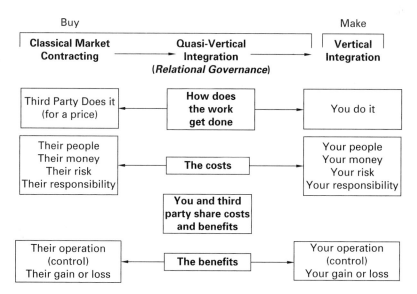

**FIGURE 4-1** Continuum of the degrees of vertical integration

| Function | Classical Market Contracting | Quasi-vertical Integration | Vertical Integration |
|---|---|---|---|
| 1) Selling (only) | Manufacturers' Representatives | "Captive" or Exclusive Sales Agency* | Producer Sales Force (direct sales force) |
| 2) Wholesale Distribution | Independent Wholesaler | Distribution Joint Venture | Distribution Arm of Producer |
| 3) Retail Distribution | Independent (3rd party) | Franchise Store | Company Store |

*Operationally, a sales agency deriving more than 50 percent of its revenues from one principal.

**FIGURE 4-2    Examples of institutions performing channel functions**

Chapter 8). Franchising and close relationships both simulate "quasi-vertical" integration, which is another term for relational governance.[5]

When the argument for integration is strong but not *entirely* compelling, relational governance (i.e., using strong relationships as opposed to contracts or direct ownership to manage an exchange transaction) offers a means to attain some benefits of vertical integration without assuming all its burdens. For example, information sharing in relational partnerships nearly always benefits performance, especially in volatile markets, though contractual agreements may be necessary if information asymmetry is high.[6]

In principle, every distribution arrangement is unique and locates somewhere along the vertical integration continuum, according to the relationship's operating methods and the nature of the contract (if any) between parties. In practice, common institutional arrangements tend to correspond to popular regions on the continuum, as Figure 4-2 shows.

## Costs and Benefits of Make-or-Buy Channels

But what really changes when a channel member chooses the make rather than the buy option? For a manufacturer, the organization assumes all distribution **costs**: personnel, transportation, warehousing, and so on. These substantial costs often get underestimated by a manufacturer before it takes them on, as does the **risk** of the distribution operation and the **responsibility** for all actions in the channel. A frequent result of vertical integration forward thus is that the manufacturer not only fails to improve its market share but actually reduces its return on investment (ROI).[7]

Perhaps the heaviest cost is the opportunity cost of personnel. Manufacturers rarely have staff available to divert from their core activity; without expertise in distribution, they also find it difficult to find the right personnel to meet their service output demands. The existing top management of a vertically integrated firm also tends to find that it lacks sufficient managerial resources to attend to its distribution responsibility sufficiently.

Yet firms keep vertically integrating, and the reason is the substantial benefits that can come along with these costs. Although many firms explain their forward integration by their desire to control the operation, from an economic standpoint, *control has no value per se*. **Control** is beneficial only if the firm's managers exploit it to improve their economic profits. Whereas control may be psychologically appealing to managers (who gain the status of directing a larger enterprise), it conflicts with shareholders' interests unless it also improves profits,[8] which might result simply by appropriating the returns from performing new marketing channel functions. In this sense, vertical integration is a *business opportunity*, like any other. A firm seeking to grow might consider taking on more of its current value chain, if these other elements are attractive as business propositions, in and of themselves.

Consider the choices of some well-known capital equipment manufacturers, such as IBM and General Electric. Both have moved into downstream operations, faced with the diminishing appeal of manufacturing as a business proposition. Tough competition demands ever-increasing production efficiency and more effective marketing; the next logical place to find revenues and cut costs is in the channel, not the factory. Moreover, capital equipment earns most profits not through sales but in maintenance. By integrating downstream, producers tap into a steady stream of maintenance contracts for the products they manufacture, many of which have long life cycles.[9]

From this account, it may seem surprising that vertical integration is not even more common! The idea of applying know-how from one part of the value chain upstream or downstream is undeniably appealing. Yet excitement about the potential for amortization might cloud a basic fact of business: Downstream and upstream activities are very different and conform to distinct financial models. These fundamental differences may drive firms to grow and diversify into other (perhaps related) businesses *at the same level of the value chain* (e.g., production *or* wholesaling *or* logistics *or* retailing), but not all of them—regardless of their expertise and expectations.

To appropriate returns from channel functions, the integrator needs to direct channel function performance with a singular purpose: *to improve sales and margins obtained at the integrator's channel level*. A retailer integrating upstream is more interested in improving returns from retailing than in running a profitable production operation; the manufacturer integrating downstream is more interested in using the channel to improve production results than in running a profitable marketing channel operation. In other words, the integrator must be prepared to sacrifice returns at one level of the value chain to improve returns at another. In theory, the integrated entity benefits financially, when it weighs total returns against total assets employed, adjusting for the risk assumed. In practice, this scenario is distressingly rare. Integrators all too often underestimate the difficulty of assuming new functions and overestimate the benefits of control, as Sidebar 4-1 details.

## Payment Options for Buying Marketing Channels

A manufacturer that prefers to focus solely on production must turn to the marketplace to obtain distribution services. In contracting with a third party, it assigns certain channel functions to this outside organization, in return for some economic consideration, usually a price. This **price** might be expressed as a *margin* (i.e., the difference between the price ultimately paid and the reseller's "cost of goods sold"), a *commission* (fraction of the resale price), or a *royalty* (percentage of the reseller's business).

Although these are the most common ways to determine the price of performing channel functions, many variations are possible. The third party might receive a flat fee or *lump sum*, or else get reimbursed for its *expenses*, such as through a *functional*

## Sidebar 4-1

### Vertical integration forward: Harder than it looks

Allianz, a much admired German insurance giant, paid what in retrospect was a high price to acquire Dresdner, a prominent investment bank. Allianz saw the move as a way to obtain a lucrative distribution channel to sell its insurance products. But the acquisition has proven financially disastrous. Banking is a highly competitive industry, managed differently than insurance, and it appears that Allianz might not have known enough about investment banking to judge whether Dresdner was well run. Furthermore, an investment bank fundamentally might not fit with an insurance company. Rather than enhance Allianz's core business (i.e., insurance), Dresdner has cost the integrated firm heavily.[10]

Manoukian, a French manufacturer of knitwear for women, also discovered that running a downstream channel is harder than it looks. Highly successful when it sold knitwear through franchisees, the firm developed an ambitious growth strategy to transform itself into a full-line clothing maker, with a men's collection as well as several women's collections at different price points and levels of style. Simultaneously, Manoukian became a clothing retailer, replacing its franchisees with company-owned stores. The idea was to benefit from control, because rather than having to convince its franchisees to accept the new product strategy, it could simply tell its own stores to do so.

The results were catastrophic. As a manufacturer venturing outside women's knits, the firm has been unable to differentiate its clothes. But the real ineptitude arises in distribution. Its stock management and logistics capabilities were anarchic.

Stores were too large to be profitable. And special derision was saved for the assortment arrangement. Unlike most clothing retailers, Manoukian presented all its collections, from top to bottom of the price line, in a way that made them easy to compare within the same store. Management believe that the collections, which varied considerably in their price points, would be sufficiently differentiated that each would find its own clientele. But customers failed to appreciate the distinctions and just went for the least expensive line across the board!

These examples reflect a common failing, in which manufacturers focus only on their own perspectives, not those of end-users. Manufacturers tend to be sensitive to the differences in the various items they offer, such that they generate too many product variations, in the belief that end-users must be equally sensitive to fine distinctions. Independent downstream channel members can correct this error by selecting only those variations that their market research tells them will be of interest to end-users. When Manoukian vertically integrated, to ensure its stores would carry the full line (and no other brand),[11] it failed to recognize the **expertise power** of independent retailers.

Both examples show that vertical integration can fail not only because the vertical integrator misestimates the costs of replicating key channel functions but also because it fails to recognize the unique **sources of power** that its independent channel partners possess—which get lost during vertical integration if the integrator does not explicitly seek to replicate them.

*discount.* The third party may also agree to work for some *future consideration*, such as the rights to future business or a percentage of equity in the manufacturer. Such arrangements are more common among entrepreneurial start-ups, which tend to be poorly capitalized and thus cannot make traditional monetary payments. Imagine a new mail-order firm: It might offer a fulfillment house (which take orders, creates a package from warehoused goods, and ships the package) rights to its paying business, after it becomes established, if the fulfillment house will agree to process orders at no charge for a limited time. The fulfillment house thus conducts the ordering function for the manufacturer, along with risk and financing functions, for a greater future consideration.

These special arrangements (i.e., anything other than a commission or gross margin paid at the time of service) are not unusual, but neither are they the norm, because of their greater risk. Paying a reseller a fee or reimbursing expenses creates **moral hazard** risks for the manufacturer, because it is difficult to verify that paid-for activities have been performed or that expenses listed are accurate, so it is temptingly easy for the reseller to cheat after the arrangement has been put into place. In contrast, payments in the form of future business or equity stakes shift the risk to the downstream channel member: The future business may never materialize, or the equity stakes may turn out to be worthless—or even a liability, if the manufacturer cannot cover its obligations. For every success story, in which some entity gets in "on the ground floor" and then enjoys massive returns, there are plenty of failures. Yet the stories we tell are more often about stunning successes, and we prefer to hide our failures, creating the widespread but false impression that a deferred payment strategy isn't all that risky. It is.

Still, channel members continue to operate with deferred payments all the time. For example, French *boulangers* (artisan bakers), having finished their apprenticeships, often start new operations in a small town. Their primary—and often only—resource is their skill, and start-up capital is limited in Europe, so these tiny, artisan bakeries frequently are financed by flour producers. The millers supply flour on extremely generous credit terms, with the understanding that they will remain preferred suppliers, if and when the *boulangerie* builds its clientele. There is no legal obligation to do so; the understanding is based on a norm of reciprocity.[12]

Finally, the option to outsource shifts all costs (accounting, personnel, risk of failure, responsibility) to a third party. In return, the third party gets to control the operation. Recall though that control is not a benefit in economic terms, unless the third party can use it to generate profits that exceed the costs of distribution (which include both accounting and opportunity costs).

## MAKE-OR-BUY CHANNEL OPTIONS: THE BUYING PERSPECTIVE

Even if the decision to vertically integrate is remarkably complex, there must be some way to reach it. These next sections present a decision framework for determining when a greater degree of forward vertical integration is *economically* (not just psychologically or politically) *justifiable*, as a function of the characteristics of the decision maker and its choices. The goal with this framework is to cut through the confusion, in systematic fashion, by prioritizing issues. Subsequent sections of this chapter also cover some rationales that are difficult to justify economically but may be equally legitimate.

For now though, we assume the decision maker begins with the preliminary decision *not* to vertically integrate, which constitutes the base case. By marshaling various supporting arguments, we then investigate if this preliminary buy (i.e., outsource) decision holds up, according to the firm's specific circumstances, or if it should be overturned and replaced with a make (i.e., vertical integration) decision. The decision maker thus serves first as an advocate of the superiority of outsourcing, then as the critic of the outsourcing argument, and finally as an arbitrator, who determines which argument—advocate or critic—is more compelling.

## Return on Investment: The Primary Criterion

The organization's goal is *to maximize the firm's overall return on investment in the long run*. Overall ROI goes beyond any single function or product. In deciding whether to integrate forward into distribution (manufacturer's choice) or backward into production (downstream channel member's choice), the appropriate question is whether the ratio of results obtained (roughly, operating performance, or revenues minus direct costs) to the resources used to obtain them (roughly, overhead, reflecting the amortization of fixed investments) is sustainable. In the short term, the firm could sustain losses or tolerate mediocre results (the numerator). It also might be able to justify dedicating inordinate resources (the denominator) for the results achieved. But the providers of the resources (investors, corporate headquarters) will not accept this situation indefinitely. At some point, the resources invested must produce returns.

For our purposes, three relative terms are relevant: revenues, direct costs, and overhead incurred, for vertical integration (make) versus outsourcing (buy). We use these terms in a *conceptual sense*, because decision makers rarely can create precise accounting estimates of these values in advance. Fortunately, for channel decision making, *it is enough to focus on situational factors that drive revenue up and costs or overhead down*. Thus, conceptually,

$$\frac{\text{Revenues} - \text{Direct Costs}}{\text{Overhead}} = \frac{\text{Net Effectiveness}}{\text{Overhead}} = \text{Efficiency}$$

**Return on investment** is the ratio of net effectiveness to overhead (or results to resources). **Net effectiveness** is the revenues that accrue under vertical integration minus the **direct** (variable) **costs** incurred after integrating. For vertical integration to be efficient, it must increase revenues more than it increases costs. But it is not enough to improve net effectiveness, because vertical integration also encumbers resources, which increase **overhead**. The use of such resources also must be justified by greater net effectiveness.

Two circumstances might bar vertical integration forward, regardless of its ROI effects: (1) The firm lacks and cannot obtain the resources to integrate forward or (2) the firm has other priorities that contribute even more to ROI and exhaust all its capacities. In the latter case, the manufacturer should pursue these other actions, even if vertical integration has a positive payoff.

## Buying or Outsourcing Channels as the Base Case

Substantial research argues that *any* manufacturer should start from the decision to outsource distribution.[13] Why should buying be the default option? The fundamental rationale holds that, under normal circumstances *in developed economies*, markets for distribution services are efficient. Note that we would never claim that markets for distribution services function perfectly—or even well, necessarily. Rather, given current environmental conditions, technology, and know-how, it is difficult for manufacturers to achieve *better* operating results than can be delivered by a third-party service provider. This argument is strictly comparative, not absolute, and it should never be taken to mean that there is no room for improvement. But in the current environment, improvement likely requires a manufacturer to introduce new technology or know-how and challenge prevailing methods, which implies taking on substantial risk.

In China, decades of government dominance of the distribution sector have left it relatively inefficient. But change is happening fast, as exemplified by the auto industry, where leading Chinese (e.g., Legend) and foreign (e.g., Honda) automakers partner with Chinese distributors to create new entities whose purpose is to introduce the best practices, technology, and methods in channel management but adapt them to China's unique market conditions. Within a few years, Chinese distribution is likely to advance dramatically, but in the meantime, the manufacturers continue to bear substantial risk. They cannot shift this risk, because the "normal circumstances of a developed economy" are not in place.[14] In Vietnam as well, many foreign firms are taking the responsibility for distribution, which may give them a first-mover advantage and market share in this growing economy.[15]

The efficient markets argument also does not mean that all manufacturers receive the same downstream services. Superior manufacturers offering superior rewards attract better providers of marketing channel functions and thus the best level of service a given provider can offer; the others gather what is left. In summary, efficient markets for third-party marketing channel services mean the manufacturer would be hard pressed to improve on the results it can buy in the marketplace.

Why should this be so?

## Six Reasons to Outsource Distribution

A firm has six reasons to outsource channel function performance to a third party:

1. Motivation
2. Specialization
3. Survival of the economically fittest
4. Economies of scale
5. Heavier market coverage
6. Independence from any single manufacturer

Let's examine each, one by one.

**MOTIVATION**  External parties have powerful incentives to do their jobs well, because they are independent companies that accept risk in return for the prospect of rewards. Both positive (profit) and negative (fear of loss) motivation spur third parties to perform. In a well-known example, sales agents tend to be more willing to prospect for customers, more persistent, and more inclined to "ask for the sale" (i.e., attempt to close a negotiation successfully) than are company salespeople—which is a large reason that financial services, such as insurance, generally are sold by third parties.[16] An outsider is attracted by entrepreneurial rewards and driven by fear of losses. This motivation also relates to the willingness to operate according to a certain financial model. The detail-oriented downstream operations frequently operate on narrow margins and focus on inventory turnover and cost management. For a manufacturer, such a focus is alien, and the risk-adjusted returns may not appeal.

The motivation rationale also depends on the recognition that outside parties are replaceable and thus subject to **market discipline**. If a distributor underperforms, the manufacturer switches to another. The mere threat of such a move is credible, which gives the distributor an incentive to meet the manufacturer's demands, or at least find an acceptable compromise. Common demands include sharing distribution cost savings with the manufacturer, applying sales efforts to particular products, presenting products in a particular way, advertising, carrying more inventory—but in truth, there is no limit on the possible requests to make of a third party.

Distributors thus also face constant pressure to improve their operating results, by both increasing sales and decreasing costs. In contrast, a manufacturer's distribution division cannot be readily terminated or restructured, and the strength of precedent makes substantial changes to incentive systems difficult. Internal politics shield employees, such that an integrated distribution operation can quickly devolve into an unresponsive, inefficient bureaucracy—particularly if labor laws make it difficult to terminate employees, as in much of Europe. However, even if employment is at the will of the employer, firing a single employee, let alone an entire division, is administratively difficult. Thus, *replaceability is key to making the buy option work.*

**SPECIALIZATION**    For wholesalers, distribution is all they do—they have no distractions. The reverse is true for manufacturers. Specialization engenders and deepens competence. Consider Whirlpool, long a pioneer in terms of outsourcing all its logistics, and Kenco, a large logistics provider that is deeply versed in the intricacies of storage, shipping, and delivery. Outsourcing allows each party to stick to its specialties, and increasing competition has helped Whirlpool and Kenco appreciate the resulting advantages even more over time. Similar generalized efforts to identify and strip down to core competences—and only core competences—are behind many decisions to outsource channel functions.

**SURVIVAL OF THE ECONOMIC FITTEST**    If specialists fail to perform their functions better than their competitors, they do not survive (which also helps reinforce the motivation factor). Distribution in most sectors enjoys low mobility barriers, in the sense that the business is easy to enter and easy to exit. Therefore, this function attracts many entrants, and lesser performers get readily eliminated, who exit swiftly. This argument also relates to specialization, in the sense that an incompetent marketing channel member cannot persist simply by subsidizing its distribution losses with gains in other sectors, such as production. Whirlpool entrusts all its logistics to Kenco, a profitable survivor in a brutally competitive industry that could not offset its logistics losses with gains elsewhere.

**ECONOMIES OF SCALE**    By pooling demands from multiple manufacturers to provide marketing channel functions, the specialized third-party providers achieve **economies of scale**. That is, they do a lot of one thing (a set of distribution functions) for multiple parties and thereby earn volume discounts. The economies of scale also enable outsiders to perform functions that would otherwise be uneconomical. By offering a broad range of brands in a product category, the distributor can amortize its fixed costs for distribution facilities, logistics software, and the like. A retailer that specializes in a single category of merchandise (e.g., appliances) meets the demands issued by many manufacturers for retailing services, as well as the demands of customers for a deep brand assortment in its narrow product category.

**HEAVIER MARKET COVERAGE**   In addition to attracting customers, an external third party can call on many, smaller customers more frequently, because it offers a greater assortment to end-users. For example, manufacturers' representatives (or reps or independent sales agents) create product and service portfolios to meet their customers' related needs. This portfolio justifies the rep's actions, including personalized calls on small accounts, to sell any single brand of any single product within the broader portfolio. By meeting multiple needs for that customer, the rep sells multiple brands and products and converts a small prospect (for the brand) into a large prospect (for the salesperson). The portfolio also supports one-stop shopping, such that time-pressed purchasers are willing to spend a little more time with the individual salesperson.[17] The resulting **deep customer knowledge** gives the rep a means to develop more compelling sales presentations of a greater range of offerings, such that sales of one item might leads into other sales. That is, the rep creates selling synergy within a portfolio of offerings.[18]

Distributors also can draw customers to their locations, websites, or catalogues, all of which offer substantial coverage of the market. A purchaser of standard white paper for the office might remember, while browsing an office supply distributor's website, to order toner, and then recall a particular need for nonstandard paper or colors, and so forth. Astute distributors and their salespeople use such exchanges to learn about the customer, including information about when it might be time to replace the printer itself.

It is difficult for manufacturers to duplicate the thorough coverage afforded by these third parties, for several reasons. First, few manufacturers can match the breadth of related products and services that a third party can assemble. Even if manufacturers have really broad product lines, a distributor still enjoys an advantage, in that it is free to select only the *best* products provided by a variety of manufacturers, bypassing any "weak links." Few broad-line manufacturers are uniformly strong in all elements of their product line. Second, independent distributors can realize potential synergies that a vertically integrated manufacturer cannot reproduce, because even if the manufacturer were to offer to carry products from its competitors (and thus duplicate the independent distributor's assortment), these competitors and sellers of complementary goods likely hesitate out of fear that the manufacturer's sales force will favor its own products at their expense. A manufacturer's acquisition of a distributor often provokes other principals to terminate their contracts and seek another third party for their distribution. (This tendency also explains why downstream channel members might not integrate backward into production.) Third, the degree of substitutability in manufacturers' products influences the equilibrium distribution structure. At low degrees of substitutability, each manufacturer prefers to distribute its product through a company store; for more highly competitive goods, manufacturers are more likely to use a decentralized distribution system.[19]

Ultimately, a third party's ability to amortize the cost of a sale allows it to cover a market much more thoroughly (make calls more often, to more influencers, in smaller accounts, even in pursuit of a low-probability sale) than can most vertically integrated manufacturers, which represents a substantial advantage. The importance of this fundamental point is often understated, but unavoidable, especially when reasonable estimates appear in a spreadsheet analysis of make-or-buy decisions.

**INDEPENDENCE FROM A SINGLE MANUFACTURER** Diversified outside providers of channel functions can serve as a sort of independent counsel or impartial source of advice. Many outside specialists also are local, stable entities, whose personnel serve the same customers, year after year. They thus gain opportunities to learn about their customers and forge strong customer loyalty.[20] Not all providers are quite so independent though; in the Internet travel industry, for example, Travelocity is owned by airlines and hotels, and Orbitz is owned by a group of airlines. These services bill themselves as the best sources for discounted tickets, but seasoned travelers recognize a conflict of interest and do not assume they will get the best offer from these sources. Analysts also were quick to note how the purchase of Orbitz by Cendant—the owner of several hotel chain and car rental agencies, which is motivated to steer travelers to its own brands—may have magnified this lack of independence.

Moreover, some manufacturers disagree that independence is even an advantage. They regard it as obstinacy or a conflict of interest, such that it represents one of the biggest drawbacks of outsourcing. Vertical integration mitigates differences of opinion, because the integrator simply give orders to subordinates—though this may offer a possibly optimistic view of how things get done inside vertically integrated firms. Both distribution divisions and third parties seek to avoid carrying out orders they consider misguided, but in an outsourcing case, it becomes critical to understand *why* they might resist. An independent provider acquires substantial information about the marketplace, so if it has reservations about the manufacturer's ideas, the manufacturer might want to listen and engage with this channel member (recall Sidebar 4-1). The downstream channel member can be analogous to a test market for a new product. If the test market results are poor, the appropriate reaction is not to get angry about the market's obstinate refusal to accept the innovation but rather to make modifications and test it again.

## MAKE-OR-BUY CHANNEL OPTIONS: THE MAKING PERSPECTIVE

We have noted how manufacturers might be too optimistic about their chances; is our preceding sketch of outsourcing similarly idealized? Of course it is—it was the advocate's perspective. Here, we switch gears and take the critic's perspective on the base case, with the preliminary decision to outsource. It is not sufficient to criticize third-party distribution; a compelling critique also must make the case that a vertically integrated firm can do the job *better* (i.e., contribute enough to revenue or reduce direct costs enough to offset other cost increases and justify the higher overhead). Recall a foundational premise for marketing channels: You can eliminate the channel intermediary, but you cannot eliminate the functions it performs.

Two caveats open this discussion. First, vertical integration always entails substantial set-up costs and overhead. Therefore, it is only worth considering if a substantial amount of business potentially is at stake. Second, vertical integration is only worth considering if the firm is prosperous enough to muster the necessary resources—and does not have a better use for them. In this sense, the economic advantages of outsourcing distribution are variations on a familiar theme: Competitive markets are efficient markets. Finding situations that reject outsourcing distribution thus means finding situations in which markets for distribution services are *not* competitive.

## The Role of Company-Specific Capabilities

A frequent noncompetitive scenario arises when small-numbers bargaining arises from company-specific capabilities. Let's explain these terms with a hypothetical, prototypical example:

> Atlas Electronics distributes electronic components; it is one of many distributors in its market area, because electronic components represent a fiercely competitive industry. As salespeople, it hires electrical engineers, well versed in their industry, products, customers, and the applications for which customers use the products. Jupiter Semiconductors, a differentiated manufacturer with unique products, is one of the many manufacturers Atlas represents.
>
> Over the years, Atlas salespeople have learned the myriad idiosyncrasies of the Jupiter product line, including how it functions in conjunction with other component brands. They know how customers apply Jupiter's products. Atlas management estimates that, even with Jupiter's training, salespeople still require two years of on-the-job experience with selling Jupiter products to master this knowledge—even though the salespeople are highly skilled and knowledgeable about the industry in general.

The key here is the idiosyncrasies. Because Jupiter products differ from competing semiconductors, even a salesperson who knows the industry requires substantial training and on-the-job experience to master their sale. That mastery is an asset with considerable value for selling Jupiter products—but *only* for selling Jupiter products. Thus, it is a **company-specific capability**, in this case specific to Jupiter.

*The greater the value of company-specific capabilities, the greater the economic rationale for the manufacturer to vertically integrate forward into distribution.*

The holders of the capabilities (here, salespeople and, by extension, Atlas) become so valuable that they are irreplaceable. If it takes two years to develop sufficient mastery, salespeople with at least two years of Jupiter experience are very expensive to replace. The replacement needs to be trained of course, but we also need to consider the massive opportunity costs of the less effective sales efforts that are available during the recruitment and training periods.

Thus, Jupiter engages in **small-numbers bargaining** with Atlas, because it cannot replace its sales quickly, even if it provides Atlas with the resources to hire very competent salespeople with generalized industry experience. *Such small-numbers bargaining destroys the fundamental premise of competitive markets, namely, market discipline.* Few people possess company-specific capabilities, so even fewer organizations are truly qualified to perform the function (in this case, selling). If the firm cannot find other qualified providers, it cannot credibly threaten to move its business (e.g., terminate the contract with Atlas), even if it is dissatisfied. Note that Jupiter does not start out (*ex ante*) engaging in small-numbers bargaining; small-numbers bargaining emerges *ex post*. That is, the distribution relationship, founded initially on a basis of large-numbers bargaining (choosing from many available distributors), gradually shifts due to the accumulation of distribution relationship-specific investments. Because Jupiter cannot count on *ex ante* competitive markets to ensure efficient outcomes *ex post*, Atlas salespeople have opportunities to shirk their duties, misrepresent the product, exhibit unethical behaviors, falsify expense accounts, or demand more compensation for the same work. Such **opportunism** results from self-interest seeking in a deceitful or dishonest manner.[21]

**JUPITER INTERVENES**    In these circumstances, Jupiter likely needs to step in and replace the market mechanism to prevent opportunism.[22] That is, the invisible hand of the market should be replaced by the visible hand of Jupiter's management. By vertically integrating forward, the manufacturer creates an administrative mechanism (which increases overhead) that it can use to direct activities *for which the market would not otherwise provide the correct incentives.*

This step alone does not quite solve the problem. After all, it is the salespeople who are irreplaceable, whether they are employed by Atlas (outsourcing) or Jupiter (vertical integration). Thus, after it vertically integrates, Jupiter also must exert more direct control over salespeople. As Jupiter employees, they have only Jupiter products to sell. They draw their income from a single principal, rather than from a third party that has gathered revenue from multiple principals, and they report to a Jupiter manager whose sole concern is their performance on behalf of Jupiter, *and no other principal and no other organization.* Finally, as Jupiter employees, salespeople make idiosyncratic investments, which limits the threat to the company, because their company-specific skills and assets have relatively little outside market value.

Beyond these structural controls, Jupiter has the ability to employ negative sanctions and offer positive incentives. (This ability also explains why information collected by mystery shoppers [see Chapter 6] tends to be of more use to employers than to franchisors or third parties, namely, because employers can do more with the data, including tying it to bonuses or penalties and performance evaluations.)[23] The incentives might be monetary (e.g., bonuses, compensation) and nonmonetary. To assess performance, Jupiter further has the right to demand detailed information about what the salespeople do, in the form of audits or monitoring.

In short, Jupiter gains power over the salespeople by eliminating a third party and employing these holders of critical resources directly. It does not necessarily eliminate threats though. These valuable salespeople still may practice opportunism against Jupiter; vertical integration cannot eliminate shirking or dishonesty, for example. However, in comparative, ROI terms, the manufacturer is better off because the vertical integration reduces some forms of opportunism, which should enhance revenues (i.e., salespeople are working more, and more effectively) and minimize direct costs (e.g., lower expense account claims) and thereby increase net effectiveness.

This outcome assumes very valuable company-specific capabilities, in that only valuable idiosyncratic assets offer much room for opportunism. By integrating, the firm greatly increases its overhead and gives up some of the coverage and economies of scale provided by third parties, which simultaneously decreases net effectiveness. That is, firms choosing to integrate vertically run the risk of a lower ROI, unless the potential for opportunism is so substantial that it constitutes a greater threat than the cost of overhead and the lost benefits of dealing with outsiders.

**ATLAS INTERVENES INSTEAD?**    If the problem is opportunism by salespeople, why not shift the responsibility for controlling opportunism to Atlas, rather than seeking to employ Atlas's salespeople directly? Although Jupiter cannot credibly threaten to terminate Atlas, Atlas seemingly should have an interest in satisfying Jupiter by controlling salesperson opportunism itself. After all, if Jupiter vertically integrates, Atlas would lose its own investment in acquiring know-how about Jupiter products and customer applications, which cannot be redeployed to serve another manufacturer. That is, its Jupiter-specific know-how has **zero salvage value** (there is no alternative use for it). Atlas also would lose customer relationships it has built up serving Jupiter customers. Because Jupiter products are unique, Atlas cannot just convince end-users to switch to another principal's products.

Thus, in rational terms, the mere *threat* of vertical integration seems likely to pressure Atlas to simulate the outcome of market forces and control opportunism among its salespeople. There are two counterarguments to this claim though. First, it is not just salespeople who practice opportunism, but Atlas itself. The irreplaceable nature of its salespeople forces Jupiter to enter into small-numbers bargaining with Atlas after the onset of the distribution relationship. Thus, the distributor can use Jupiter's vulnerability to demand more (e.g., better margins) while doing less to earn it (e.g., holding lower inventories). Second, Jupiter cannot justify vertical integration until Atlas's opportunism is substantial. If Atlas stays within a certain latitude of abuse, Jupiter will find it cheaper to remain a victim of opportunism than to vertically integrate. The same rationale explains why insurance companies tolerate some degree of claims fraud: To a point, it is cheaper to pay false claims than to pay the costs of detecting and fighting them.[24]

**A REVISED SCENARIO**    Jump back in time a little, to imagine that Jupiter is just starting to contemplate selling in Atlas's territory, and it has no representation. Should it outsource its distribution to Atlas or should it vertically integrate, setting up a distribution branch to serve the market? Knowing that its products are idiosyncratic, Jupiter may foresee that it will ultimately enter into small-numbers bargaining with Atlas—or any other distributor that sells its products, for that matter. If the idiosyncratic assets involved are sufficiently valuable, Jupiter would be better off, in ROI terms, to start with vertical integration. Field research indicates the likelihood that this is exactly what Jupiter would do.

Vertically integrating, in response to the recognition of the mere prospect of company-specific assets, has two major advantages. First, the manufacturer can confirm that its employees make the necessary investments to acquire the needed capabilities. Second, it can demonstrate its dedication to the market to potential customers and other constituents (e.g., investors). Vertical integration establishes credibility. By investing in its own operations, the firm makes a visible, credible commitment, which can be particularly important when customers regard the purchase as risky and fear the producer will abandon the market if problems arise.[25]

Again, we caution: Finding trends does not imply that a manufacturer cannot work efficiently with a third party when idiosyncratic assets are at stake. Rather, these arguments show that doing so is very difficult and requires careful arrangements to achieve a channel that limits opportunism.

In short, the prospect of accumulating company-specific assets creates an economic rationale to vertically integrate. These assets go by many labels. Economists call them "idiosyncratic" or "transaction-specific" assets or investments: They are customized (specific) to a business relationship (transaction), and they demand investments of effort, time, know-how, and other resources to create.

## Six Company-Specific Distribution Capabilities

The critical, company-specific capabilities for distribution tend to be intangible (unlike vertical integration upstream, which requires physical assets such as customized parts and assemblies). There are six major forms:

1. Idiosyncratic knowledge
2. Relationships
3. Brand equity derived from the channel partner's activities
4. Customized physical facilities
5. Dedicated capacity
6. Site specificity

Let's examine each in turn.

**IDIOSYNCRATIC KNOWLEDGE**    More than knowledge of the manufacturer, its products, its operating methods, or customer applications, **idiosyncratic knowledge** constitutes that part of the overall knowledge base that cannot be readily redeployed to another principal. Even a company that makes standard products, uses generic operating procedures for its industry, and provides products that customers use just as they would use products from another company in the same industry presents features that demand firm knowledge. Downstream channel members make investments to acquire this knowledge, which becomes an asset, though not an idiosyncratic one. Rather, it is a **general-purpose asset**, such that it can be redeployed to benefit another principal, without loss of productive value. The ordinary principals in this situation do not need to vertically integrate downstream, because they can generate efficient distribution outcomes using the market for distribution services, as long as that market is competitive. But if that manufacturer makes unusual products, adopts unique methods of operation, or attracts customers who want to make customized uses of its products, the downstream channel member acquires information that is idiosyncratic and company specific.[26]

**RELATIONSHIPS**    Connections between distributor personnel and the personnel of the manufacturer or the manufacturer's customers imply an ability to get things done quickly and correctly and to communicate effectively. For some transactions, relationships are essential. For example, just-in-time supply arrangements involve exquisite coordination. For a manufacturer to replenish a downstream channel member's supplies at just the time it becomes necessary, there must be very close cooperation between the manufacturer and the channel member. Cooperation demands relationships, and the costs (accounting and opportunity) of failed supply arrangements make such close relationships essential.

**BRAND EQUITY**    This critical idiosyncratic investment applies to the manufacturer's brand name. We distinguish two cases: First, the brand name might enjoy substantial brand equity with consumers, *independent of the downstream channel member's actions*. In this setting, vertical integration downstream is not only unnecessary but wasteful. The manufacturer simply uses its brand equity as a source of power over channel members. Second, brand equity may exist because *downstream channel members* *have exerted influences on it.* That is, brand equity does not arise independent of the channel members' actions, perhaps because of the following:

- A sales force is required to create a credible image for the brand, as is often the case for industrial products.
- The brand's strategy demands that products be stocked, displayed, and presented in a particular manner but provides insufficient downstream margins to appeal to channel members to provide this support. Perfume makers thus sometimes rent dedicated space from department stores and pay salespeople to sell their product.
- The brand strategy demands a level of cooperation that would override any decision-making discretion by a third party.
- Brand-specific support service, such as before or after sales, is required to ensure the branded product is properly installed and used to satisfy the customer and create positive word of mouth.

In all these cases, brand equity stems from customer experiences, driven by marketing channel activities. If the brand name can be made truly valuable, it becomes a substantial asset, specific to the manufacturer of course. The more valuable this asset, the more the firm benefits from vertical integration. If its assets are somewhat valuable but not enough to justify vertical integration, the firm could protect its investments by forging close relationships downstream, franchising, adopting vertical restraints, or seeking other means to influence channel members.

Effective brand equity explains much of the increase in private-label activity by North American and European supermarkets. Rather than putting the retailer's name on products a manufacturer makes, the latest strategy encourages retailers to use their vast knowledge of the product category to design new products, then work with manufacturers to determine how to make it. The Canadian grocery chain Loblaws even maintains an R&D facility expressly for this purpose. Loblaws's market research identified a demand for a much richer cookie than was available, so it worked with a manufacturer to devise solutions to some technical obstacles. Then Loblaws branded the product (Decadent cookies) and invested heavily in promoting it. The brand was so successful that even though Loblaws holds a small portion of the Canadian grocery market, Decadent became the market share leader in the cookie category. Loblaws's backward integration (into product design and development) paid off handsomely, and the chain has repeated its practices in various categories since then.

Similarly, when the value is great enough, the manufacturer is justified in trading influence for more control through forward vertical integration, as the multidecade rivalry between Danone and Yoplait, detailed in Sidebar 4-2, reveals. Know-how, relationships, and brand equity (driven by downstream activities) thus are major categories of company-specific capabilities that justify vertical integration. They also are all intangible, whereas several categories of tangible assets also play roles.

**CUSTOMIZED PHYSICAL FACILITIES**    An important transaction-specific asset can be the actual physical facilities. Amazon has outsourced its warehousing and shipping functions for years, whereas most book wholesalers send many books at a time to one easy-to-find location (bookstore), because sending a single, appropriate book to individual sites would be ruinously costly. Amazon did not become profitable until it

## Sidebar 4-2

### Battle of the Greek yoghurts

In the spring of 2013, after years of intense rivalry in the major consumer markets around the world, Danone captured 27.8 percent of yoghurt sales in the U.S. It had finally overtaken its closest rival, Yoplait who now controlled 25.8 percent of the estimated $7.3 billion U.S. yoghurt market. The success was largely due to the fast-growing Greek yoghurt segment of the market.

Danone was founded back in 1919 as a small Spanish manufacturer of yoghurt. Now based in France, it has seen spectacular growth through strategic reorientation and a wide range of joint ventures. It has been particularly active in the Chinese market. In 2001, it acquired a stake in Bright Dairy, doubling its shareholding by 2005. Bright Dairy had already been manufacturing Danone brands under license. In 2007, Danone sold off its stake in the company. Danone was already in a joint venture with Hangzhou Wahaha Group, setting up deals, joint ventures, and non-joint ventures across China. Danone made several attempts to buy out their Chinese partners. However, this descended into a long-running dispute with the general manager, Zong Qinghou. In 2009, Danone finally exited the joint venture. It sold its 51 percent shareholding in Wahaha back to the Chinese partners for an estimated U.S. $500 million.

Meanwhile, Yoplait, another French-based company founded in 1964, was acquired by the U.S. giant, General Mills in 2011. General Mills announced that it had acquired a 51 percent controlling interest in the company. In China, Bright Foods made a bid for Yoplait, stating that it could generate sales of around U.S. $280 million within five years. In the end, Bright Foods lost out to General Mills, but Gary Chu, the president of General Mills, Greater China confidently stated that with the number of middle-class families in China expected to double by 2020, the growth of the Chinese market was something that the company intended to exploit. The expectation is the General Mills' sales in China would top U.S. $900 million by 2015.

China, it seems will be the latest battleground for the two yoghurt giants. Clearly,

Danone's success in the U.S. has shaken General Mills into action. Just a decade ago, General Mills' U.S. sales accounted for 90 percent of their operations. Now, worldwide sales account for 30 percent of the sales, including its shares in the various joint ventures. Potential areas of rivalry are not just restricted to China or the U.S. In Brazil, for example, the two giants are actively fighting for increased market share. General Mills' latest acquisition was Yoki Alimentos, a leading food company. At a stroke, the acquisition doubled General Mills' sales in Latin America.

The intense global rivalry between the two giants sometimes creates bizarre moments. In New York's Soho, outside a Chobani café, consumers witnessed a face-to-face confrontation between the brands. Chobani has a chain of yoghurt retail outlets across the U.S., and has seen its market share rise from 2 percent in 2007 to 50 percent in 2014. On a bitter, cold January, with the outlet doing a brisk business, Danone and Yoplait both appeared with mobile outlets, and started handing out free samples.

It would seem that Chobani has its own part to play in the global battle for yoghurt supremacy. It was founded in 2007 by Hamdi Ulukaya, a Turkish immigrant to New York. He opened a dairy plant after his move in the early 2000s, and by 2011 Chobani's sales had topped U.S. $700 million. At that time, it became the U.S. best-selling yoghurt with a 18.6 percent market share. Naturally, both Danone and Yoplait moved to regain market share, and combat Chobani in the U.S. market.

Globally, the new battle between the brands is at the very heart of the matter. Just when is Greek yoghurt, Greek yoghurt? The only truly Greek yoghurt is produced in Greece by FAGE Total, and uses traditional production methods. While other manufacturers such as Danone and Yoplait state that the term Greek yoghurt refers to a production process rather than anything else, it is in this respect that the giants are again facing off against one another. Greek yoghurt is created by straining the milk

**Continued**

to remove the whey. The net result is a thicker and creamier product with a higher protein content and a lower fat and lactose content. The major problem is that it uses a huge amount of milk compared to conventional yoghurts. This, of course, drives up the costs.

Yoplait gets around this by using milk concentrate. Other manufacturers strain some of the milk and then add thickeners. Neither approach is strictly speaking, Greek yoghurt. Hence, the fact

is that in many cases, the products are referred to as Greek-style yoghurt. The other accusation being hurled around is that the concentrated milk products that are being used can come from yaks or buffaloes. Chobani has been quick to state that it uses the traditional method of yoghurt production. Danone meanwhile, states that its latest brands use traditional milk and cultures, and that they strain out the whey and do not use thickeners.

invented a radically new way to stock and select books and built its own highly idiosyncratic warehousing and information system.[27]

A similar scenario marks maritime shipping. When a shipping vessel is specific to a narrow use, with very few users (e.g., shipping liquefied nitrogen) or even a single user (e.g., some vessels are fitted to handle a particular brand of car), redeploying the ships to serve a broader group of users, if it is even possible, requires extensive retrofitting. Because the assets (ships) are difficult to redeploy to alternative uses, contracting hazards arise. The carrier hesitates to invoke the manufacturer's opportunism, while the manufacturer worries about the carrier's opportunism. It may appear that this "balance of fear" should make all parties act reasonably, but in reality, neither side wants to enter into small-numbers bargaining with the other. Vertical integration thus is a viable solution.

**DEDICATED CAPACITY** When distribution capability (e.g., warehousing, transportation, selling, billing) is not just customized but even has been created to serve a particular manufacturer, it represents *overcapacity*. If the manufacturer terminates the business, the downstream channel member suffers excess capacity, which it cannot redeploy without sacrificing productive value (i.e., losses). Unlike customized physical facilities, dedicated distribution capacity cannot be put to use to serve another manufacturer—even if there were demand for it, which there is not.

A forward-looking channel member hesitates to incur these obligations, fearing opportunism by the manufacturer once the capacity exists. Some channel members refuse to add such capacity; others require very high compensation to do so. Thus, it may be worthwhile, in ROI terms, for the manufacturer to integrate forward. However, once the capacity is in place, the downstream channel member is vulnerable and may be economically justified in protecting its investment by vertically integrating backward (i.e., acquiring the manufacturer).

**SITE SPECIFICITY** A manufacturer may need its marketing channel functions performed in a specific location, which may be less well suited to the needs of other manufacturers. A channel member that creates a warehouse facility near the manufacturer for example owns a general-purpose asset if the manufacturer is near other manufacturers but an idiosyncratic asset if the manufacturer appears in a remote location. The value of this site thus is specific to the manufacturer (and worth little or nothing to other manufacturers). As an example, we turn to maritime shipping.[28] Raw materials often are mined in remote parts of the world, and then shipped from one relatively obscure port to another, for processing in a refinery that has been built specifically to handle the mine's output. Cargo carriers may refuse to offer service on such routes, because few other customers need to ship in either direction. Thus, manufacturers may be obliged to integrate forward into shipping, or else form alliances with shippers.

The common thread uniting all six factors—idiosyncratic knowledge, relationships, brand equity, customized physical facilities, dedicated capacity, and site specificity—is the production of firm-specific assets that have very low value for any alternative use. The difficulties (and costs) a manufacturer may face before it can convince a high-quality channel partner to take on such investments often are steep enough that the manufacturer needs to vertically integrate and perform the functions itself.

The following topics outline further rationales for vertical integration that rely less on or complement financial arguments, though they may be compelling all the same.

## Vertically Integrating to Deal with Thin Markets

The key to asset specificity is that a resource, tangible or intangible, not only creates substantial value but also loses value if redeployed to a different usage or user. Such assets are customized. In contrast, other assets are *rare* (in short supply) but *not specific*. For example, the combination of selling ability and technical knowledge that makes a good semiconductor salesperson is uncommon, and demand for such services is enormous, so these salespeople are rare and expensive. A semiconductor manufacturer may be tempted to reduce selling costs by employing salespeople directly, rather than going through a representative, but unless the manufacturer's products are unlike other semiconductors, or its methods are highly unusual, the strategy probably will not work. The manufacturer will discover that in lieu of paying high commissions to the reps, it is meeting a high payroll, such that its costs increase because it loses the rep's economies of scale.

Another case of rarity, though not due to specificity, occurs because of industry consolidation. Consolidation among manufacturers, through mergers and acquisitions, command big headlines, but consolidation is also a substantial phenomenon downstream. The effect of **consolidation** (i.e., the concentration of market share in the hands of a few players) is to prune markets so much that they thin out, leaving suppliers hard pressed to find resellers or agents, and downstream channel members unable to find suppliers. The fear of having little real choice pushes organizations to scramble to form alliances with players they estimate will be left standing as the industry continues to consolidate. Because alliances often exclude other parties though, this move thins the market even further! Faced with the prospect of dealing with a monopolist, many firms elect to integrate in response to consolidation. However, this choice is no panacea when the integrating firm lacks competitive competence to perform other channel functions.

## Vertically Integrating to Cope with Environmental Uncertainty

An **uncertain environment** is difficult to forecast, whether because it is very dynamic (fast changing) or very complex. Volatile environments pose special challenges, which manufacturers might integrate forward to meet. Should they? Proponents and critics go back and forth, each offering mixed evidence to support their positions.

To begin, one school of thought holds that a manufacturer should take control, such that it can learn more about the environment and carry out a coherent strategy for dealing with it. But the opposing school of thought likens managing under uncertainty to betting on the winner of an evenly matched horse race: One bet is as good as another, and most bets lose. Therefore, firms should seek to hold their bets until the race is far enough along that it can predict who will win (or at least avoid those that have already gone off track). That is, the manufacturer should *not* to commit to *any* distribution system, including its own, unless and until the uncertainty declines enough that it can ascertain the best way to distribute; in the meantime, it outsources. Thus, uncertainty demands transaction-based third-party distribution, such that the distribution decision can change easily as the situation demands.

Proponents of vertical integration respond with a charge of defeatism: By integrating, the firm can alter the course of the race, rather than simply waiting to see what happens. Critics parry that it would be arrogant of a manufacturer to imagine it possesses sufficient wisdom and power to define the channel. Better to switch from one third party to another and ultimately settle on the best option (whether the best third party or one's own distribution) when it really is possible to ascertain the best option.

Finally, the proponents retort that the best option may be unavailable by the time the manufacturer is ready to settle on it. Critics highlight the frequent ease associated with changing the marketing channel as the environment changes. Proponents of vertical integration often underestimate the difficulty of making real organizational changes, once in-house distribution is in place.

Both sides of the debate thus have valid arguments. How can we incorporate them into one approach? Seemingly counterintuitively, we propose complicating the issue slightly (see Figure 4-3).

With this proposed framework, we start by asking whether there are (or will be) substantial company-specific capabilities involved in distribution. If not, the firm can easily change or find new third parties. Such flexibility is of great value in volatile environments. *Absent significant specificity, uncertainty favors outsourcing.*

But if specificities are substantial, flexibility already has been lost. The firm gets locked in to a channel, and there can be no changing the bet. It thus faces the worst of all worlds: small-numbers bargaining in an environment that requires constant adaptation. The result will be endless bargaining, high levels of opportunism, and high transaction costs. *In the presence of significant specificity, uncertainty favors vertical integration forward.*

There is, of course, a third argument: In the presence of significant specificities, just don't enter the market! To justify the overhead of vertical integration, the business must be very promising, yet the very nature of uncertainty makes it inherently difficult to determine a business's true promise. This conundrum can be solved by avoiding it—a pretty common response to uncertain environments with high specificities. We cannot

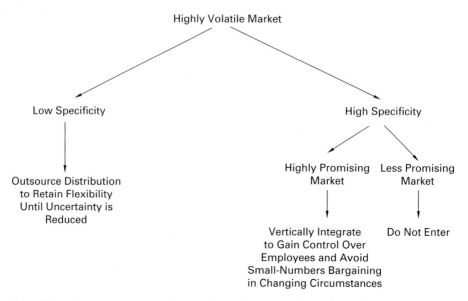

FIGURE 4-3   How environmental uncertainty affects vertical integration

identify which firms decide *not* to enter, so we cannot quantify how often business activities do not take place. Yet despite the difficulty of measuring it, non–market entry is always present (though frequently attributed to other factors).

Consider the example of sub-Saharan Africa, where multinational business activity is minimal, despite the rich potential markets available in a region of more than 700 million people. Explanations often focus on political risk or the lack of economic development, but modern multinationals operate in other, equally risky, just as underdeveloped markets. So why continue to overlook Africa? We propose that not only are many African markets largely unknown and potentially volatile, but that the lack of an existing distribution infrastructure also implies that the manufacturer's distribution decisions and actions will be idiosyncratic to the market. This combination of uncertainty and specificity may better explain the low investments in Africa, especially if we undertake a comparison with some politically risky Asian countries that enjoy better distribution infrastructures, such that multinationals can find qualified third parties already operating in the market. With specificity removed, uncertainty can be handled by outsourcing, which encourages more market entry.

It is also noteworthy that market entry by some firms encourages more entry, because it reduces specificity. When several multinational corporations (MNCs) have entered a market, they create a pool of local personnel, familiar with MNC procedures. Thus, it becomes easier to find qualified third parties that can function in a manner that may be nonstandard to the market but standard for MNCs. After decades of investments by multinationals (and progressive opening of its market by the national government), India is experiencing widespread growth in the number of qualified joint venture partners and distributors. A similar process is well underway in China.[29]

## Vertically Integrating to Reduce Performance Ambiguity

In all these scenarios (specificity, rarity, specificity + uncertainty) in which competition in the market for distribution services fails to yield efficient outcomes, we have made one broad assumption: that few bidders are available to replace a performing poorly firm, and that the manufacturer can tell when outsourcing is not working. But another scenario that favors vertical integration relates not to the failure of the market to provide bidders. Rather, it entails the failure of information.

In a normal market, the contracting firm (principal, which in this chapter has been the manufacturer in most cases) offers to pay an organization (agent) to provide distribution services. If these services are not performed satisfactorily, the principal negotiates for better outcomes or finds another agent. In normal markets, many other agents are qualified, and their bidding for business ultimately improves the ROI for the principal. This process (bid, monitor results, reconsider the arrangement, rebid) works well—*assuming the principal can tell what it is getting.* Herein lies the fundamental problem with market contracting: When **performance ambiguity** exists, the manufacturer cannot discern the level of performance it is receiving. Therefore, the process by which market contracting improves outcomes comes to a halt.[30]

Let's take the selling function, which combines promotion and negotiation functions. It can be outsourced to a manufacturer's representative. The manufacturer knows the rep's performance in terms of sales, so if sales levels are a good indicator of performance, the manufacturer suffers little performance ambiguity. In many cases, this system works, because sales forces are charged primarily with selling, and most manufacturers have some idea of what level of sales is reasonable to expect.

But if the product is radically new, such as a discontinuous innovation (unlike anything that currently exists), current sales may not be a good indicator of performance. Radically new products usually diffuse slowly, and no one knows what the reasonable sales level should be for such a product. If the manufacturer's rep goes for long periods with few or no sales, the manufacturer does not know whether it should be dissatisfied and search for a new rep. Fundamentally, it is impossible to tell how well the rep is doing. There are no baselines, but there are many excuses for failure—both legitimate and not. Such high performance ambiguity makes the assessment process far more complicated.

In general, performance ambiguity occurs when appropriate measures of performance are unknown, as in the case of discontinuous innovation. Therefore, the principal may vertically integrate forward, not to circumvent small-numbers bargaining but rather to gain information and control. By monitoring what salespeople do, the principal can distinguish excuses from genuine reasons for low sales. From these agents, it also can acquire market research to establish a performance baseline. Finally, in perhaps the most powerful advantage of vertical integration for this setting, the principal can control salespeople's behavior. Without good indicators of achievement, the principal can fall back on directing agents to do what it considers best to develop the market. Instead of rewarding for unknowable, unpredictable outputs (achievements), it might reward for inputs (activities). That is, market contracting usually yields indicators of current results, but if current results are not good indicators of performance, performance ambiguity exists. To deal with this ambiguity, the principal may seek to increase its long-term ROI by vertically integrating forward to gain both information and an ability to direct behavior.

## Vertically Integrating to Learn from Customers

According to this rationale, the channel is an observatory. Operations in another part of the value chain provide a window onto the market, therefore a way for the manufacturer to learn. To explain this reasoning, we rely on the example of Luxottica, an eyeglass maker.

The firm's majority owner Leonardo Del Vecchio offers an inspiring rags-to-riches story of seeking work in an eyeglass factory, to find an escape from an orphanage, and ultimately becoming a highly skilled artisan. Del Vecchio founded Luxottica in 1961, but his self-description continues to reflect his production roots: "I am a technician, a producer. It is thanks to our products, our quality, and our productivity that we have made our way." Luxottica's Italian factory's famous productivity enables the firm to compete with lower-cost Asian production.

When Luxottica purchased Lens Crafters, the giant U.S. retailer that offers an enormous selection of frames, eye examinations, and prescription glasses on premises in an hour, Del Vecchio justified the purchase by calling the retailer, "an ideal observatory to know what the market wants." He maintains other "observatories" as well, including a web of exclusive wholesalers that serve European channels of individual opticians. Thus, Luxottica relies on both intermediate and extreme levels of vertical integration to gain information about end-user demand for eyeglasses.

In turn, Luxottica applies this market knowledge to its dealings with designers. Even powerful names must submit their designs for consideration, modification, and approval; the designers tolerate this control, because Luxottica is a proven performer and the world's largest eyeglass producer. Furthermore, it uses its market knowledge to forecast eyewear fashions 18 months in advance, and it makes 500 new models a year. In short, its vertical integration gives Luxottica great power upstream.

Another example also highlights the need for constant reconsideration of the channel and the potential demand to shift the structure. After more than 60 years of selling knives and kitchen tools using a network of sales representative who rang doorbells at individual homes, Cutco Cutlery has started adding retail stores to distribute its goods. Many of its sales reps were college students, such that when they graduated, they often left the firm, taking their accumulated knowledge with them. By adding an owned distribution arm, Cutco gains more control and remains better connected with its end-users.[31]

As both examples show, integration can be justified as a way to learn, such that the decision to integrate rests not just on stand-alone ROI considerations. Rather, the decision is made on the grounds that integration increases effectiveness (profits) for the operation as a whole. Is this a sensible economic rationale, or a rationalization? Unfortunately, here again, the answer is that it depends. Certainly, learning is a lofty objective, easy to invoke to explain any act of vertical integration, no matter how operationally ill-advised. Ultimately though, accountants must assign the inefficiencies that accrue somewhere, such as budgets for R&D or market research, which is likely to spark new debate about the merits of the choice.

This is not to say that learning is not a worthwhile investment. It is no accident that the most large-scale integration among all our examples, Luxottica, pertains to a fashion-sensitive industry, in which massive and frequent change is certain but the direction is unknown. In this setting, learning seems invaluable. But in many other cases, it is difficult to determine if learning is a sufficiently economically justifiable reason to vertically integrate.

## Channel Members Integrating Upstream

For the purposes of exposition, we have presented the principles in this chapter from the standpoint of a manufacturer, looking downstream. Yet each of these principles is general and can be applied to downstream channel members contemplating backward integration into production. As we noted briefly for example, a manufacturer at risk of being held up by a channel member that owns a unique asset interacts with a channel member that is also at risk of being held up by the manufacturer. A manufacturer willing to abandon the channel member inflicts a loss on it, because the channel member is left with an asset that is suddenly worthless. This prospect likely tempts the channel member to integrate backward, just as much as it tempts the manufacturer to integrate forward.

The symmetry of this situation often gets overlooked though. It may feel more "natural" to imagine a manufacturer integrating forward, even though backward integration is far from unusual. It even may be invited by the manufacturers, which welcome the infusion of capital, know-how, and market knowledge.

Fortunately, the issues for the downstream channel member considering vertical integration parallel those we have already discussed for forward integration. In general, vertical integration is a poor idea; outsourcing should be the base case. To make

## Sidebar 4-3

### A retailer loses focus by integrating backward

Intermarché is a large French grocery retailer, organized as an association of independent grocery store owners. It also was among the first French grocers to integrate backward into food production, and aggressively at that. Although the members ("adherents" under French law) are technically independent businesses, Intermarché is tightly managed. Adherents are obliged to follow central initiatives and face restrictive contracts that make it difficult to exit the network. The chain is wrought by internal frictions though, largely because many adherents believe that management sacrifices their interests as retailers to a higher priority: production.

One-third of the average store's sales are of house brands, a fraction that has grown steadily. Some observers (and adherents) question whether consumers abandon Intermarché stores when they cannot find their preferred brands. Perhaps some of the resources devoted to production should be going to matters more immediately relevant to a store owner, such as marketing, merchandising, and store renovation.

As an example, Intermarché owns the largest fishing fleet in Europe and proudly trumpets that distinction—though such tactics are precisely what many adherents resent. As one commented, about backward integration into fishing, it

> gave us a real independence vis-à-vis the multinationals. It also permits us to have our own brands that are comparable to national brands. It's a fabulous tool; we don't want to break it, but rather to put it at the service of stores. We want to move from a situation where the points of sale are outlets for the factories to a situation where they are really at our service. Who cares if we are the #1 European fish producer? What we want to be is the #1 European fish market.

Intermarché's vertical integration backwards consumed management attention at a time when the core business—retailing—clamored for a return to the basics.

an exception, the downstream channel member must determine whether the ongoing transaction involves asset specificities with great value, such as know-how, relationships, brand equity, dedicated capacity, site specificity, or physical facilities. If these specificities have value, a contracting hazard exists. The higher the value, the more appropriate it is to seek protection, perhaps in the form of relational contracting but ultimately in the form of vertical integration.

In Sidebar 4-3 we consider how downstream channel members might falter when they vertically integrate with the goal of ensuring themselves sources of supply or to lock in outlets. Absent specificities, downstream firms will founder in a business they do not know or that might even conflict with their core business.

## SUMMARY: MAKE-OR-BUY DECISION FRAMEWORK

As the preceding sections detail, the vertical integration decision begins with the base case that outsourcing is more attractive (higher ROI) than vertical integration, and with the assumption that the market has many participants (i.e., not thin markets). Then, the first question to ask is, Is the segment of business being evaluated for vertical integration substantial? If not, then outsourcing is preferable. If so, vertical integration potentially is preferable if *either* of two circumstances prevail:

1. Company-specific capabilities are likely to accrue and become substantial. They may be intangible (know-how, relationships, downstream activities brand equity) or tangible (dedicated capacity, site specificity, physical customization). The effects of idiosyncratic assets increase with environmental uncertainty, so firms should learn some important capabilities through vertical integrating that will pay off over time.
2. Performance ambiguity forces the firm to monitor and direct activities, rather than tally up and pay for performance. It is too hard to watch and track channel partners.

If markets work poorly but vertical integration is overly drastic, relational contracting offers an efficient solution. Vertical integration in distribution is never an "all or nothing" decision; it entails decisions whether to make or buy *any* individual channel function or set of functions. Thus, a manufacturer can vertically integrate a subset of channel functions but still use independent intermediaries to perform other functions.

During this analysis, each channel member must respect that the functions performed by every other channel member require certain competences. No party should merely assume that it can take over another party's functions and perform them better and/or more cheaply. Arrogance has no place in a vertical integration decision, which must be undertaken with respect for the competence of other types of organization.

Unfortunately, the decision also must consider opportunism. Such self-interest seeking often prompts negative responses (e.g., "it represents the worst of human nature"). But it is important not to personalize the discussion. Opportunistic behavior is a characteristic of *entities* that interact to conduct business. It is not necessarily a characteristic of interpersonal interactions in private lives, nor does it occur between organizations at all times. But business relations often leave room for opportunism, and it is difficult to forecast in advance which partners will be more or less opportunistic.

The make-or-buy decision rests on anticipating and forestalling opportunism in a pragmatic way.

Being committed to a *system* (e.g., outsourcing) is not the same as being committed to a given *member* of the system. If the only rationale for vertical integration is to avoid unsatisfactory results or relationships with another organization, the firm needs to take a step back and seek ways to improve the workings of the current relationship. Next, it should consider switching to another third-party provider. The drastic step of vertical integration and its high overhead should be invoked only when other options have been explored fully.

The assertion running throughout this chapter, that markets for distribution services are frequently efficient, may seem surprising. But it also should not be taken to imply that a firm can never do better by vertically integrating. Rather, it indicates that to achieve better results, the firm must be prepared to make a substantial commitment and operate in a manner that is unusual for its industry or market. For vertical integration to outpace outsourcing, the firm must accept more risks and substantial commitments.

Although estimating transaction costs, production costs, and ROI precisely is impossible in any scenario, vertically integrated or otherwise, the framework in this chapter suggests how decision makers can forecast the direction of these costs to arrive at a rough approximation of which system will work best in the long term. We present the decision path in steps, beginning with the assumption that outsourcing distribution is superior, and only then questioning this assumption in specific circumstances. If the second step offers sufficiently compelling arguments, such as when vertical integration would lead to critical market insights or create new options for the future, firms are justified to integrate—not necessarily because they can do a better job on the new function but because they can better learn or open the door to a future investment. Integration forward or backward in this case should improve overall performance, not performance *per se.*

## TAKE-AWAYS

- The vertical integration decision, also known as make or buy, applies to each function or set of functions involved in distributing a product or service. Despite its name, the choice is not really binary. Make-or-buy decisions entail a continuum that describes how the costs, benefits, and responsibilities of doing the work get split between organizations.
- Creating a relationship is a way to compromise between making and buying. The closer that relationship, the more it approximates vertical integration. The more distant the relationship, the more it approximates outsourcing.
- Integrating forward or backward is harder than it looks. The firm should not simply assume it can outperform a specialist by taking control of its functions. Rather, it must ask a key question: Will integrating a function improve my long-run economic return on investment? Can I improve my revenues or reduce my costs, and will these gains justify the resources I will need to commit to vertical integration?
- The firm should outsource if
  - Little money is at stake (e.g., it is a minor function).

- The firm cannot afford the resources needed to create an internal operation.
- The firm has better uses for these resources.
- If the market for distribution services also is competitive, outsourcing is the right starting point to benefit from the six fundamental advantages of an outside specialist:
  - Superior motivation
  - Specialization
  - Survival of the economically fittest
  - Economies of scale
  - Heavier market coverage
  - Independence from any single supplier
- If conditions exist that prevent the firm from benefiting from these six advantages, vertical integration (or a close relationship) is called for, as long as there are company-specific capabilities (especially if the environment is volatile), performance ambiguity, and thin markets.
- The potential for substantial company-specific capabilities puts the firm at risk of entering into small-numbers bargaining with a third party, which traps it. Unable to switch to a better supplier, the firm risks being the victim of opportunism.
- The six company-specific capabilities critical for distribution can be split into two categories:
  - Intangible capabilities
    - Idiosyncratic (company-specific) knowledge
    - Relationships among personnel
    - Brand equity that rests on the downstream channel member's actions
  - Tangible capabilities
    - Customized physical facilities
    - Dedicated capacity
    - Site specificity
- The greater the potential for company-specific capabilities to grow and become valuable, the more likely vertical integration is to be more efficient than outsourcing, particularly in volatile, uncertain environments. The combination of uncertainty and specific capabilities is so difficult to manage that firms should demand very high returns to enter such businesses.
- Over time, specific assets may become general purpose assets, such that vertical integration is no longer efficient. Incumbents may be trapped by high switching costs though, unable to switch to outsourcing.
- Necessary capabilities for vertical integration may be rare (low supply relative to demand) but not specific (customized). Securing such capabilities is always costly, even if the firm vertically integrates. As the market grows thin, the firm may vertically integrate simply to ensure a source—but should still expect the function to be expensive to perform.
- Performance ambiguity occurs when it is very difficult to ascertain whether a third party is doing a job well. It arises in two main circumstances:
  - The market is so unfamiliar that the firm has no baseline to judge whether results are good or bad.
  - It is difficult or impossible to gather relevant, timely, accurate result indicators.

- Greater performance ambiguity increases the chances that vertical integration is more efficient than outsourcing.
- Vertical integration may reflect a strategic decision, undertaken to enhance effectiveness speculatively, according to two main rationales:
  - The function serves as a market testing and feedback mechanism (observatory, classroom).
  - The function is an option that the firm plans to exercise later, to enter distribution faster and better if it turns out to be a good idea.
- All these arguments apply to a producer considering integrating forward, as well as to a downstream channel member considering integrating backward.

## Endnotes

1. Bradford, Kevin, Steven Brown, Shankar Ganesan, Gary Hunter, Vincent Onyemah, Robert W, Palmatier, Dominique Rouzies, Rosann Spiro, Sujan Harish, and Barton Weitz (2010), "The Embedded Sales Force: Connecting Buying and Selling Organizations," *Marketing Letters* 21 (September), pp. 239–253.

2. Anderson, Erin and Barton A. Weitz (1986), "Make or Buy Decisions: Vertical Integration and Marketing Productivity," *Sloan Management Review* 27 (Spring), pp. 3–20.

3. Hennart, Jean-Francois (1993), "Explaining the Swollen Middle: Why Most Transactions are a Mix of 'Market' and 'Hierarchy,' " *Organization Science* 4, no. 4, pp. 529–547.

4. Arnold, Todd J. and Robert W. Palmatier (2012), "Channel Relationships," in V. Shankar and G. Carpenter, ed., *Marketing Strategy Handbook* (London: Edward Elgar).

5. Dwyer, F. Robert and Sejo Oh (1988), "A Transaction Cost Perspective on Vertical Contractual Structure and Interchannel Competitive Strategies," *Journal of Marketing* 52 (April), pp. 21–34.

6. He, Chuan, Johan Marklund, and Thomas Vossen (2008), "Vertical Information Sharing in a Volatile Market," *Journal of Marketing Science* 27 (May–June), pp. 513–530.

7. Szymanski, David M., Sundar G. Bharadwaj, and P. Rajan Varadarajan (1993), "Standardization versus Adaptation of International Marketing Strategy: An Empirical Investigation," *Journal of Marketing* 57 (October), 1–17.

8. Bergen, Mark, Shantanu Dutta, and Orville C. Walker Jr. (1992), "Agency Relationships in Marketing: A Review of the Implications and Applications of Agency and Related Theories," *Journal of Marketing* 56, no. 3, pp. 1–24.

9. Fang, Eric, Robert W. Palmatier, and Jan-Benedict E. M. Steenkamp (2008), "Effect of Service Transition Strategies on Firm Value," *Journal of Marketing* 72 (September), pp. 1–15.

10. Tomlinson, Richard (2003), "Insurance for Dummies," *Fortune*, May 26, pp. 31–36.

11. Michel, Caroline (2004), "Manoukian S'Emmêle Dans Sa Maille," *Capital*, July, pp. 36–38.

12. Palmatier, Robert W., Cheryl Jarvis, Jennifer Bechkoff, and Frank R. Kardes (2009), "The Role of Customer Gratitude in Relationship Marketing," *Journal of Marketing* 73 (September), pp. 1–18.

13. Rindfleisch, Aric and Jan B. Heide (1997), "Transaction Cost Analysis: Present, Past, and Future," *Journal of Marketing* 41 (October), pp. 30–54.

14. Bolton, Jamie M., and Yan Wei (2003), "The Supply Chain: Distribution and Logistics in Today's China," *The China Business Review* 10 (September–October), pp. 8–17.

15. "Distribution Market Heats Up," *The Saigon Times*, January 22, 2012.

16. Anderson, Erin and Richard L. Oliver (1987), "Perspectives on Behavior Based Versus Outcome-Based Sales Force Control Systems," *Journal of Marketing* 51 (October), pp. 76–88.

17. Palmatier, Robert W., Fred C. Ciao, and Eric Fang (2007), "Sales Channel Integration after Mergers and Acquisitions: A Methodological Approach for Avoiding Common Pitfalls," *Industrial Marketing Management* 36, no. 5, (July), pp. 589–603.

18. Anderson, Erin and Bob Trinkle (2005), *Outsourcing the Sales Function: The Real Costs of Field Sales* (Cincinnati, OH: Thomson Texere Publishing).

19. McGuire, Timothy W. and Richard Staelin (2008), "An Industry Equilibrium Analysis of Downstream Vertical Integration," *Journal of Marketing Science* 27 (January–February), pp. 115–130.

20. Palmatier, Robert W., Lisa K. Scheer, and Jan-Benedict E.M. Steenkamp (2007), "Customer Loyalty to Whom? Managing the Benefits and Risks of Salesperson-Owned Loyalty," *Journal of Marketing Research* 44, no. 2, May, pp. 185–199.

21. Samaha, Stephen, Robert W. Palmatier, and Rajiv P. Dant (2011), "Poisoning Relationships: Perceive Unfairness in Channels of Distribution," *Journal of Marketing* 75 (May), pp. 99–117.

22. Anderson, Erin (1988), "Determinants of Opportunistic Behavior: An Empirical Comparison of Integrated and Independent Channels," *Journal of Economic Behavior and Organization* 9 (May), pp. 247–264.

23. Rosencher, Anne (2004), "Le Client Mystère, Ou l'Art d'Espionner Ses Points de Vente," *Capital* (November), pp. 124–126.

24. Klein, Benjamin (1996), "Why Hold-Ups Occur: The Self-Enforcing Range of Contractual Relationships," *Economic Inquiry* 34 (July), pp. 444–463.

25. Osegowitsch, Thomas and Anoop Madhok (2003), "Vertical Integration Is Dead, Or Is It?" *Business Horizons* 46, no. 2, pp. 25–34.

26. Coughlan, Anne T. (1985), "Competition and Cooperation in Marketing Channel Choice: Theory and Application," *Marketing Science Spring* 4, no. 2, pp. 110–129.

27. Vogelstein, Fred (2003), "Mighty Amazon," *Fortune*, May 26, 20–28.

28. Pirrong, Stephen Craig (1993), "Contracting Practices in Bulk Shipping Markets: A Transactions Cost Explanation," *Journal of Law, Economics, and Organization* 36 (October), pp. 937–976.

29. Ganesan, Shankar, Morris George, Sandy Jap, Robert W. Palmatier, and Bart Weitz (2009), "Supply Chain Management and Retailer Performance: Emerging Trends, Issues, and Implications for Research and Practice," *Journal of Retailing* 85 (March), pp. 84–94.

30. Bergen, Dutta, and Walker (1992), op. cit.

31. Kumar, Kavita (2012), "Cutco Sharpens Its Business by Adding Retail Stores," *St. Louis Post Dispatch*, April 27.

# Designing Channel Structures and Strategies

**LEARNING OBJECTIVES**

**After reading this chapter, you will be able to:**

- Define selectivity, as the negotiated and often reciprocal limitations on the number of trading partners in a market area.
- Explain why manufacturers prefer more coverage, especially in fast-moving consumer goods industries, combined with a downstream channel member that limits its assortment in their product category.
- Explain why downstream channel members prefer less coverage, combined with a greater assortment in each manufacturer's product category.
- Recognize why limited distribution is preferable to brands with a high-end positioning or a narrow target market.
- Describe the mechanism by which limiting the number of trading partners increases both motivation and power.
- Explain how selectivity reassures trading partners against the threat of opportunism.
- Forecast when either side (upstream, downstream) will concede to a limitation of the number of its trading partners.
- Outline ways to maintain intensive coverage while limiting its destructive effects in the channel.
- Describe the special challenges of multiple formats and dual distribution.
- Summarize how channel managers can close service and cost gaps using data collected in channel audits.

Before *designing* an effective marketing channel strategy, managers must *segment* end-users according to their service needs (bulk breaking, spatial convenience, delivery requirements), as well as determine which end-user segments to *target* (Chapter 2). These segmentation and targeting steps provide a clearer picture of what different groups of end-users want from their channels, as well as which groups the manager should be most interested in reaching.

As we noted in Chapter 3, the next step for channel managers is to *audit* their existing marketing channels. With the efficiency template, they can codify information about the importance of each channel function, in both cost and value terms, and specify the proportion of each function performed by each channel member. The efficiency template also produces the normative profit share metric for each channel member, which *measures* the proportionate value added to the channel by each channel member. Without any intervening, adverse competitive conditions, normative profit shares should approximate the actual shares of total channel profits enjoyed by each channel member, following the equity principle.

Using the gap analysis template, managers next can *identify gaps* in both service (i.e., service provided is different than desired by end-users) and cost (i.e., price provided is more than desired by end-users). Matching up the service outputs demanded by targeted end-users with the offerings (service and price) provided by existing channels gives the manager a good idea of the differences between the actual and the ideal channel structure, which is required to meet target segments' needs most effectively.

Finally, prior to the actual design of a channel structure and strategy, channel managers conduct a make-or-buy channel analysis, as outlined in Chapter 4, to *determine* which channel functions should be performed in-house or outsourced to channel partners. This vertical integration analysis is critical, with long-term cost and strategic implications, including the threats associated with converting channel partners into competitors.

From the three types of analyses—end-user, channel, and make-or-buy—managers gain insights that enable them to make three strategic channel decisions pertaining to (1) channel intensity, (2) channel types, and (3) dual distribution, each of which must align with the firm's overall strategy and competitive positioning plans, demand various design trade-offs, and exert significant influence on the implementation and management of channel strategies. Following these strategic channel decisions, the channel manager is responsible for closing any gaps identified during the channel audit so that the ultimate channel meets service output demands at the minimum cost—that is, represents a *zero-based* channel.

Consider each of these strategic channel decisions. First, the **channel intensity** question entails how much coverage the supplier should have, in various forms. That is, how easy should it be for a potential customer to find and buy the brand or product offering? Most of this chapter focuses on this pivotal issue and its critical influence on a multitude of channel strategy issues. Having determined the intensity level, the firm must choose the **channel types** it will use to go to market and find ways to combine these formats (e.g., stores, kiosks, websites). Finally, should the supplier simultaneously go to market through its own channels and third parties, the **dual distribution** decision, which would involve competing with its own channel members? These three decisions may seem "manufacturer-centric," but they extend far beyond that stage in the channel, because their ramifications depend fully on downstream channel members' perspectives and strategies. In particular, in this chapter, we consider when downstream channel members should demand that suppliers limit their degree and variety of market coverage, and when they should be willing to limit their own brand assortment.

## CHANNEL INTENSITY DECISIONS

**Intensive distribution** means that a brand can be purchased from many possible outlets in a trading area. An extreme version is **saturation**, which implies that it is available in *every* possible outlet. **Exclusive distribution** means in contrast that the brand can be purchased only through one vendor in a trading area, giving that vendor a **local monopoly** on the brand. Both total saturation and monopoly conditions are unusual; typically, brand distribution intensity offers partial coverage in available outlets in a market area. The specific degree in turn largely determines the manufacturer's channel programs.[1] As a general rule:

> The more intensively a manufacturer distributes its brand in a market, the less the manufacturer can influence how channel members perform marketing channel functions.

That is, to control channel functions and their performance, the manufacturer needs to refrain from blanketing or saturating distribution outlets. But limiting coverage may mean the manufacturer gives up some sales and profits to its competitors. Naturally, manufacturers prefer to maximize coverage and actively resist any deliberate restrictions on their brand availability. So *when and why should a manufacturer limit coverage as part of its channel strategy?*

The answer stems from the reflective structure of the channel. Even as the upstream firm (manufacturer) considers how many outlets to pursue (degree of selectivity), the downstream firm (e.g., reseller) considers the flip side, namely, how many competing brands to carry in a product category (category selectivity). Both sides confront trade-offs associated with limiting the number of channel partners they adopt. Although a conventional view of channel intensity decisions uses a bully trope—in which a single strong player imposes restrictions on a weaker channel partner—that view is limited and often misleading. A better framing recognizes the decision as a negotiation outcome, reflecting trade-offs, reciprocity, and each firm's overall positioning.

### Downstream Channel Members' Perspective on Intensive Distribution

For downstream channel members, more intense brand coverage can spell the ruin of their channel advantage, because it eliminates their ability to differentiate themselves by offering unique assortments. When distribution is intensive, all competitors have the same brand, which benefits mainly the manufacturer. Thus, *each downstream channel member prefers exclusivity.* The resulting clash of interests between manufacturers and downstream players builds a permanent source of conflict into any market channel.

In a saturated market in particular, the brand alone cannot attract end-users to the store (though failing to stock the brand could drive them away), and even when buyers choose to visit, the downstream member still has to find some way to get the buyer to purchase on the spot. In many cases, inertia is the best reason: An end-user buys to avoid the nuisance of shopping elsewhere, particularly for a minor purchase like toothpaste or tomato sauce. But for a more important, involved purchase, such as a digital camera, buyers often delay their decisions and continue to shop, unless the channel member can present some reason—such as a price cut—for them to buy immediately. In many markets, the direct conflicts across channel members lead to ferocious **intra-brand price competition**. This price competition takes place among sellers of the same brand, unlike the more standard form of **inter-brand price competition**, among different brands in a product category.

From the manufacturer's perspective, intra-brand price competition at the retail level is desirable—at least in the short term. Channel members sell more by charging lower prices, probably at a cost mainly to their own margins (especially if they already have paid the manufacturer for their inventory). The manufacturer realizes higher volume at the same wholesale price. Coca-Cola may offer a few promotional considerations to its retailers, but many sellers of soft drinks, such as large supermarkets and hypermarkets, carry a massive variety and inventory of each brand that they need to turn over to manage their shelf space effectively. To induce shoppers to buy constantly, the stores themselves offer low promotional prices, though doing so may mean a loss of immediate profits on that product.

But such a situation cannot go on indefinitely. If the brand is never profitable for downstream channel members, they likely demand relief, in the form of lower wholesale prices, from the manufacturer. Even were the manufacturer to provide those lower prices, the profitability problem may persist, because ongoing competition demands that the downstream members give up their newly increased margins to re-attract end-users. Continuing our example of Coca-Cola products, we find the channel in an interesting bind: Stores cannot very well stop selling Coke, nor can they overcome the accounting losses they likely suffer. To avoid any further losses, they may choose to avoid significant additional costs to build end-of-aisle displays or advertise the brand though—an option that may result in lower sales that echo back up the channel.

Coca-Cola also is a remarkably powerful brand. For others, the likely outcome is that some channel members choose to drop a relatively weak brand, through three routes:

1. Overt discontinuation and substitution, in which the downstream member substitutes another, less intensively distributed brand for the saturated brand. This substitution is more likely for weak than for strong brands.
2. Discontinuation of the entire product category, if no satisfactory substitute brand is available and the category is not essential.
3. Covert conversion, such that the downstream channel member appears to carry a brand and offers nominal stock and display but also tries to convert prospective customers to a different brand on site.

If enough downstream channel members drop the brand, it suffers such a low degree of distribution intensity that the intra-brand competition gets resolved, if perhaps not quite to the brand's liking. Thus, it is the channel members in combination, not just the manufacturer, that determine the marketing channel structure. In some cases, regardless of its efforts, the manufacturer may lose its preferred outlets and be forced to rely on inferior outlets, because the best outlets nearly always have the most alternatives.

These channel scenarios and decisions also can create ethical and moral issues for the channel. For example, a flagrant form of substitution behavior is commonly known as the **bait-and-switch**. That is, a downstream channel member advertises one brand, to get customers to visit its site (bait), and then persuades those end-users to buy another brand (switch), on which the seller earns a higher profit. Bait-and-switch concerns are most common for brands with more buyer recognition that serve as attractive bait. Thus, an electronics store might run advertisements promoting a Sony television, and then train its sales personnel to guide consumers to different, perhaps lesser-known brands on which the store earns higher margins.

Another troubling factor is the problem of **free riding**. To understand this channel issue, imagine that you manage a retailer that sells durable consumer entertainment products and pursues a high-quality positioning strategy. Thus, you invest heavily in your channel: Your store is well located and appealing, and you stock full product lines. For a (hypothetical) high-end speaker brand called Johanson, you maintain substantial inventory (even of slow-moving items), devote substantial showroom space to displaying the speakers, advertise on behalf of Johanson, maintain a well-stocked repair facility, offer extended warranties, and so forth. Your large, well-trained sales staff can explain each category of product (speakers, home cinema systems), note the myriad features of each brand and model, explain how features translate into benefits, help end-users discover their own trade-off preferences, and then help them match their preferences to their options.

Your strategy also means that you need to attract an appreciative clientele, who will compensate you for your high costs by paying higher prices and becoming loyal clients. This strategy has worked well for you. Your store has a reputation, which it "lends" to each brand you sell,[2] and your clientele trusts you, as a purchasing agent, to screen products for them.

Recently though, Johanson hired a new distribution manager, who has aggressively pursued distribution through competing outlets to increase the brand's coverage. In the past few weeks, your salespeople have been complaining that all they do is interact with "browsers," who spend hours talking and learning about Johanson speakers, but then end each interaction with an "I'm going to think about it." The salespeople know what that means: They will think about going elsewhere to buy for a lower price. Some customers even get on their smart phones before they leave the store to apply the knowledge they have gained and buy their preferred speakers—on another retailer's website! These lower prices are available from other sellers because they have not invested in offering the same level of support you provide. Nor do they need to, because you are already providing all the assistance end-users need. The other stores are free riding on you: You bear the costs, and they gain the benefits.

As these examples show, manufacturers often fail to ask themselves whether their efforts to benefit their brand are really in the channel's best interest overall. Frequently, they are not. Sidebar 5-1 covers how the Big Boys Toys event makes products appealing to retailers by limiting availability (and targeting a desirable, loyal buyer segment with low price sensitivity), even though its product—pet food—is widely considered a convenience good.

Getting back to our Johanson speaker example though, your first inclination as the store manager may be to discontinue the brand. You need to think before you act,

## Sidebar 5-1

### Big Boys Toys

Branding itself as the "ultimate playground," the Big Boys Toys lifestyle event in Dubai, features some of the most exclusive and luxurious global products. The event takes place at the foot of the world's tallest building, the Burj Khalifa, right beside the world's largest shopping center, the Dubai Mall. Even access to the event is exclusive.

The show opened for the first time in the Middle East in 2013 at the Atlantis Hotel in Dubai, and was deemed the main event of the Dubai Shopping Festival 2013. Exhibiting at the show is not for the fainthearted or the lightweight businesses. Space only (not including any services or utilities) is U.S. $345 per square meter, with shell stands at U.S. $395 per square meter. With exclusive products such as the Confederate limited edition fighter motorcycle at U.S. $110,000—with its carbon fiber, titanium, and aluminum chassis, a 64-inch wheel base, integrated braking system, 1966 cc engine, and a top speed of 190 mph—there might well be a stampede for the 45 of them available.

The show has toured the world during 2009, 2011, and 2012, but it seems to have found its natural home in Dubai. It sells itself as three days of nonstop action and excitement with the world's most exclusive male-orientated products and services showcased under one roof. Visitors can marvel at the range of gadgets and luxury products, all guaranteed to be exclusive and limited editions.

In effect, the event, which is franchised out to various regions, follows the same kind of format. Stunt drivers, comedians, athletes, and a host of other events provide entertainment, while the real business is being done in and around the trade stands. The show pays regular visits to various locations around the U.S., to Mumbai (India), and to New Zealand, among other places.

What sets the event apart from many other exhibitions is the exclusive nature of the products available, and the definite male focus of the show. In many parts of the world, it is the only opportunity to see luxury limited edition products such as these; ones without traditional distribution networks, and certainly those that do not usually offer the opportunity to experience the product before purchasing it.

The exhibition event also provides an opportunity for many luxury product makers to establish contact with some of the individuals with the highest net worth in the world. With one in eighty of Dubai's population a dollar millionaire, the opening day is exclusively reserved for VVIPs only. This select group includes many members of the ruling families, government ministers, diplomats, and well-connected businessmen. In all, the event attracts some 40,000 visitors in Dubai.

In comparison, the New Zealand version of the event attracted just over 35,000 visitors. The core markets for the events are 18- to 45-year-old men, but the events are proving to be increasingly popular with families, with the fastest growing group of visitors being under 12. This has spawned a new feature for the event, Little Boys Toys.

Even economic downturns cannot seem to depress events like this—the combination of exclusivity and showmanship is a heady mix.[3]

because such a choice could be very costly. The parts and merchandise inventory you have on hand already may not be returnable for full credit. The knowledge of Johanson your personnel have spent time and effort to gain will be rendered worthless. Your advertising on behalf of Johanson also will be wasted, while also raising embarrassing questions about why you no longer carry the brand. That is, your Johanson-specific investments are not readily redeployable to another brand.

So you continue to sell Johanson products, but your relationship with the manufacturer is now pretty acrimonious. You are an ethical manager, but really, is it all that dishonorable to give as good as you have gotten, and engage in a little bait and switch, as long as you can switch customers to a brand you feel comfortable endorsing? There are many brands of audio speakers available. You might even start working more closely with these brands' sales reps, leaving Johanson out in the cold.

## For the Downstream Channel Member

Limiting brand assortment is currency
Fever brand = more money
Exclusive dealing =

Downstream Channel Members use the money to "pay" the supplier for:

- limiting the number of competitors who can carry the brand in the Channel Member's trading area
- providing desired brands that fit the Channel Member's strategy
- wording closely to help the Channel Member achieve competitive advantage
- making Channel-Member-specific investments
  - new products
  - new markets
  - differentiated Channel Member strategy requiring supplier cooperation
- accepting the risk of becoming dependent on a strong Channel Member

Downstream Channel Members need to "pay more" when:

- the trading area is important to the supplier
- the trading area is intensely competitive

**FIGURE 5-1**   Category selectivity: The downstream channel member's perspective

The lesson from this hypothetical market channel is clear: *A retailer will not tolerate free riding indefinitely.*

The degree to which the brand assortment gets limited—or the degree of selectivity—offers a bargaining chip for downstream channel members. This role means that managers must account for many factors when making selectivity decisions, as Figure 5-1 summarizes.

## Upstream Channel Members' Perspective on Intensive Distribution

For upstream suppliers of products and services, channel design decisions might seem easier: Get more outlets to carry their offerings, because when more outlets carry a brand, it sells more. Wide coverage makes it easier for buyers to find brands. Furthermore, if prospective buyers encounter vigorous sales efforts for the same brand in every outlet they visit, they eventually must surrender to the combined persuasion, right? Unfortunately, downstream channel partners often lose interest in carrying or pushing a supplier's offering if doing so puts them in competition with many other channels. Intensive distribution thus can lead to lackluster sales support, defection by downstream channel members, and even bait-and-switch tactics. What is a manufacturer to do?

One option is contractual. The contract between the manufacturer and downstream channel member might demand certain standards of conduct (e.g., barring bait and switch) and threaten legal action against offenders. This route is expensive though, requiring documentation of both the agreement and any possible violations, as well as the legal resources needed to design and enforce the contract. This tough implementation approach also may alienate other channel members or generate unfavorable publicity for the brand.[4]

Another solution is to invest in a **pull strategy** that increases brand equity. With greater brand equity, consumers demand that downstream channel members carry the brand, even if they must pay a high wholesale price, charge a low retail price, and suffer low gross margins. Remember our discussion of Coca-Cola? This effective strategy is perhaps most common in fast-moving consumer goods (FMCG) channels.[5] Similarly, in the consumer entertainment sector, Sony's strong brand equity allows it to offer its goods in many channels, because consumers would question the legitimacy of an electronics outlet that failed to carry Sony products. In general, channel members have little choice but to carry intensively distributed brands with high brand equity.

Of course, this strategy also is extremely costly, in that the manufacturer must invest continually and substantially in advertising and promotion. It also suffers several limitations. Manufacturers with sought-after brands often experience an unavoidable temptation to overproduce, and then send downstream channel members more product than they can sell ("channel stuffing"). As these downstream members slash prices to move stock, the product disperses into too many places (including grey, or illegal, channels), making the brand's positioning unclear. Ultimately, the dilution of the brand's equity has shattering effects—including in some famous cases, the end of the careers of the heads of companies:

- The Barbie doll's phenomenal brand equity prompted its maker to expand its 90 Barbie models to 450 in just 15 years and increase production capacity. This avalanche of product provoked market saturation, in terms of both the number and the variety of outlets. Overloaded retailers, seeing that Barbie was available even in supermarkets and on cable television, dumped their stocks, cutting prices by as much as 75 percent. As the brand's price tumbled, so did Mattel's stock price, and the company's president, the architect of the policy, was forced to resign.[6]
- The CEO of Warnaco, a licensor of famous clothing brands such as Calvin Klein and Ralph Lauren, was fired after the apparel company produced so much product that it became available almost anywhere, and nearly always priced to move. Seeking to maximize its coverage, Warnaco sold through many types of retailers, including discount generalist stores (e.g., Wal-Mart), which quickly alienated its traditional department store channel partners. At the same time, the licensors grew angry when they observed the cheapening of their brand images.[7]

In some countries, a third solution is possible: **resale price maintenance (RPM)**. This policy allows the manufacturer to set a price floor, below which no channel members may sell the product. Because RPM permits the manufacturer to limit the normal pricing behavior of its resellers,[8] its legality varies widely. For years, it was illegal in the United States, but now the policy is governed under a rule of reason (see Chapter 13).

Where RPM is allowed, manufacturers can use it to set their minimum resale prices high enough to give all channel members an acceptable margin, even with greater distribution intensity. That is, RPM enables artificially high levels of coverage. For the purchaser, the good news is that the brand is easy to find, and sellers compete on a nonprice basis (e.g., services, amenities). The bad news is that it is difficult to get a discount, because sellers have no choice but to avoid or disguise them and may be subject to legal action for offering them, even if they lack any formal contract with the manufacturer.

Finally, a fourth, widely generally applicable solution for a manufacturer with low sales support is simply to limit its market coverage by carefully establishing some degree of distribution selectivity. With this approach, the manufacturer has an opportunity to target desired channel members, rather than merely settling for those that do not eliminate themselves through intra-brand competition. It also implies the chance for better working relationships. In this case, the manufacturer faces two critical questions:

1. How much coverage should we aim to achieve?
2. In a given product category, how many brands should our downstream channel member carry?

To see how these two seemingly separate questions actually adhere, consider a distributor, say an industrial supply house. It sells consumables (and some durables) to manufacturing plants of all kinds, as well as to a few offices in its trading area. The generality of demand in this market requires the distributor to carry thousands of stock-keeping units in hundreds of product categories. For any given product category, such as metalworking fluids, the industrial supply house must decide how many brands to carry.

It could seek simplicity and prefer to carry just one brand, but that choice is unlikely. It not only wants to benefit from (even limited) competition, but it also needs to meet the assortment demands of its customer base. As an industrial supply house, it promises that whatever the buyer might want will be available, so keeping a broad assortment is required to satisfy customers (though it drives up inventory-related costs).

In each product category, the distributor also must decide how large its brand assortment will be: very broad (all brands) or narrower (down to a single brand, which thus attains **category exclusivity**, or exclusive dealing). A priori, the distributor recognizes the importance of assortment and thus resists category exclusivity for any single manufacturer. Of course, each manufacturer also would prefer *not* to be presented alongside its competitors—another built-in source of permanent channel conflict.

This discussion implies two conflicts: Manufacturers wish to blanket a trading area with outlets; the outlets prefer the reverse. Downstream channel members prefer to have multiple brands to offer in a category, but manufacturers prefer the reverse. But we also need to consider yet another conflict: Manufacturers prefer downstream channel members to support their brands vigorously and take low margins, whereas channel members prefer lower costs and higher margins. In all these cases, the channel members must negotiate their way to a mutually satisfactory arrangement, which often requires a high level of cooperation.

Some degree of selectivity is a bargaining chip for the manufacturer to use to achieve specific goals, based on its assessment of multiple factors that it needs to consider when making its channel intensity decisions. We summarize these factors in Figure 5-2, this time from the manufacturer's perspective.

In the following subsections, we also discuss in more detail eight specific factors that should be considered when making the channel intensity/selectivity decision. The importance of each factor to the overall decision varies dramatically with the circumstances facing the manufacturer and its channel partners.[9]

### For the Manufacturer

Limited coverage is currency
More selectivity = more money
Exclusive distribution =

**Manufacturers use the money to "pay" the Channel Members for :**

- limiting its own coverage of brand in product category
  (gaining exclusive dealing is <u>very</u> expensive)
- supporting premium positioning of the brand
- finding a narrow target market
- coordinating more closely with the manufacturer
- making supplier-specific investments
  - new products
  - new markets
  - differentiated marketing strategy requiring downstream implementation
- accepting limited direct selling by manufacturer
- accepting the risk of becoming dependent on a strong brand

**Manufacturers need to "pay more" when :**

- the product category is important to the Channel Member
- the product category is intensely competitive

**FIGURE 5-2**   Channel intensity: The manufacturer's perspective

## Channel Competition to Prevent Complacency (Factor 1)

Our preceding discussion may have seemed to imply that there was only one real reason to cover a market intensively, namely, to make it easy for end-users to find the brand. But another reason exists as well, attributable not to customer behavior but rather to the channel members. If coverage of a brand is highly selective, the manufacturer faces a difficult situation. That is, if only a small set of channel members carries the brand, intra-brand competition is low, which can grant those selected channel members substantial power. Some manufacturers seek to improve their relative bargaining power with strong retailers by selling to and helping weaker, alternative members, such that they might enter into joint advertising agreements with a local chain but not with Wal-Mart. Such moves attempt to raise the elasticity of demand for the manufacturer's products and prevent complacency by the strong retailer—though the notion of incurring Wal-Mart's wrath is a risky proposition too.[10]

Insufficient competition is problematic even for channel members with the very best intentions. A quasi-monopoly in distribution (as in any other activity) may simply encourage complacency, and thus inadequate performance. Some degree of intra-brand competition thus benefits the channel by encouraging each channel member's best efforts, without putting it into an impossible situation.

In this case, we look at a positive example: Best Buy acquired Future Shop, a Canadian competitor, but rather than simply shutting down Future Shop stores or converting them into Best Buy outlets, the parent company left both names and both stores in place—even when stores appeared literally across the street from each other. In so doing, the two chains could not only cooperate to block a third entrant but also compete constructively to stimulate each chain to perform better.[11] Competing head-to-head with oneself is even more common at a brand/product level, in line with the theory that it is better to be cannibalized by a sibling division than to be bankrupted by another company. Best Buy just elevated this effective logic to the channel level.

## Product Category (Factor 2)

In deciding how much selectivity to grant channel members in a market area, the manufacturer needs to recognize the service output demands common in its product class. For routine, low-involvement purchase categories, buyers generally perceive minor or low risk (i.e., making a significant error is unlikely). Fast-moving consumer goods (FMCG) fall into this category, as do many products (e.g., office supplies) purchased by businesses. These **convenience goods**[12] are the stuff of everyday life. Given an acceptable brand choice, buyers take what is on offer, rather than search for their favorite brand.

Accordingly, FMCG brand market share is disproportionately related to distribution coverage (see Figure 5-3). After a certain threshold of distribution coverage, securing a few more points can prompt a sharp upturn in market share, because for such mundane products, consumers simply will not leave a store to visit another one, as long as they find at least some brands that are acceptable to them. Small retailers, with their space constraints, thus can stock just the top one or two brands, knowing that they will suffice for most customers on most purchase occasions. Collectively, small retailers move large amounts of merchandise, yet they offer consumers very little brand choice. This situation implies that coverage over a threshold level means a boost in coverage in small outlets, which rapidly and disproportionately increase the brand's market share. A positive spiral results: The higher the brand's market share, the greater the likelihood that other small stores adopt that brand, which increases share, and so on (i.e., "the rich get richer").[13]

Consumers of convenience goods, such as milk or copier/printer paper, also demand high spatial convenience and quick delivery (i.e., little tolerance for stock-outs). Therefore, to ensure a fit in the channel between distribution strategy and buyer behavior, *convenience goods should be distributed as intensively as possible.*

In contrast, **shopping goods** (e.g., small appliances) generally prompt some comparisons of brands and prices across outlets, so an intermediate degree of selectivity is likely more desirable. Before they buy **specialty goods** (e.g., home cinema system, production machinery), buyers expend considerable effort to make the best choice, such that they likely seek out outlets they can trust. In this case, highly selective, even exclusive distribution should be acceptable and desirable to the buyer, whether that buyer seeks industrial or consumer products and services.

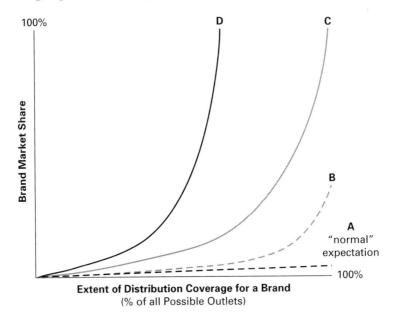

Function A is an example of the type of relationship that would ordinarily be expected between distribution coverage and market share.

Functions B, C, and D are convex and are examples of approximate relationships often found in FMCG markets.

A brand can achieve 100% market share at less than 100% coverage because not every possible outlet will carry the product category. For example, convenience stores sell food but not every category of food.

**FIGURE 5-3   Sample representations of the coverage–market share relationship for fast-moving consumer goods**

*Source:* Based on Reibstein, David J., and Paul W. Farris (1995), "Market Share and Distribution: A Generalization, A Speculation, and Some Implications," *Marketing Science*, Vol. 14, no. 3, pp. G190-G202.

These ideas sound great, but they are often difficult to operationalize, especially when it is less than evident whether and how much buyers are willing to search. Some general rules apply; a new product category often constitutes search goods, because end-users need substantial support before they can be convinced to adopt brand new industrial or consumer products.[14] New-to-the-world categories might be called pre-search goods, because no one even knows to search for them yet.

The distribution of specialty goods and, to some extent, shopping goods puts somewhat less emphasis on the number of outlets than on finding the right outlets. When manufacturers carefully select, cultivate, and support appropriate outlets in a trading area, we call it a policy of **selective distribution**. But we also caution against confusing selective distribution with poor coverage. A brand has poor coverage if few outlets agree to stock it, or those that do are not the best outlets. Merely examining the percentage of outlets carrying a brand in a trading area cannot indicate whether a manufacturer's coverage is selective or merely poor.

## Brand Strategy: Premium and Niche Positioning (Factor 3)

The first two factors referred broadly to product classes and costs applicable to the distribution of any good or service. Another class of factors applies instead to each brand and its unique marketing strategy, as we outline here.

**PREMIUM POSITIONING BRAND STRATEGY**   In any product category, some brands seek to position themselves as high-quality options (e.g., Mercedes-Benz automobiles, Cabasse audio speakers). Operationally, they seek to signal their superior abilities to perform certain functions, which therefore justify a premium price. This **premium positioning** approach remains difficult to achieve, especially because it requires the manufacturer to attend to the image or reputation of each channel member representing its brand. In this case, the manufacturer likely prefers channel members that excel in handling high-end brands.

By definition, excellence is scarce. Finding channel members that match the brand's ideal image demands selective distribution among a specific subset of downstream members that can support a high-quality positioning. This demand is particularly acute when premium pricing is part of the positioning. Thus, higher-priced products are usually limited in their distribution availability,[15] and broadening coverage to other outlets often dilutes the brand's superior-quality positioning. Sidebar 5-2 describes luxury jewelry maker Cartier's experience as a brand of prestige, and how it maintains its position in the market.

Of course, this subset of quality image channel members also are in great demand, with their choice of brands to represent. It can be difficult to induce them to carry any given brand, even one positioned as premium. Even a manufacturer that avoids intensive coverage needs some capable sales force to convince target channel members to carry and support its brand. Because the channel does not end there, it also needs a segment of buyers interested in high quality, convinced the brand is high quality, and willing to exert effort to make a high-quality purchase.

None of this discussion should imply that brands that do not choose a high-quality positioning instead present themselves as low quality. Rather, they promise adequate (not superior) quality. Often these brand focus on other attributes, such as convenience or low price, which tends to be consistent with a more intensive distribution policy.

A specific version of a high-quality positioning relies on **scarcity**. When manufacturers deliberately create product shortages, they recognize that scarcity can be appealing. If not everyone can get the product, the product feels *psychologically* more desirable. Such scarcity may be natural for certain luxury products, such as handcrafted items or original artwork. But an artificial scarcity marketing strategy, coupled with selective distribution, also increases the illusiveness and allure of the product.[16] Thus, Harley-Davidson underproduces its motorcycles, does not quite match supply to demand, and limits distribution to a few outlets (mostly company owned). The long waiting lists for hogs in turn enhance Harley's mystique (and the motorcycles' resale value). Toy manufacturers often use this strategy during the holiday season.

Now imagine: You manage a brand that has managed to position itself as the high-quality offering. You have restricted your distribution coverage, and intra-brand

## Sidebar 5-2

### A unique art of expansion

Founded in 1847, the Cartier brand has maintained an image of elegance, luxury, and exclusivity. Over the years Cartier has developed a range of luxe jewelry, watches, leather goods, and accessories, all the while staying true to the brand's motto—"the art of being unique"—and creating high-end products for its niche and exclusive clientele.

Everything about the Cartier stores screams "prestige." Starting with the store locations, to the ambiance, and the exquisitely displayed jewels, the Cartier store resembles an art gallery more than a retail outlet. Combine that with friendly yet professional sales representatives and you hold the key to your buyer's heart.

Cartier's creations are works of art, with many iconic designs being historicized because of the story behind them. Examples of these are the love collection, that resembles a chastity belt to signify passionate romance and faithfulness, and the trinity collection, that includes three bands in three different shades of gold—signifying love, friendship, and fidelity—intertwined. The brand is also very famous for its panther creations that incorporate color and the nonpareil Cartier panther design. The designs that are produced by Cartier are elegant, sophisticated, and unique to Cartier alone. The designs have become icons that many aspire to own, which gives the brand further value.

Cartier has been known to hold exhibitions in museums and palaces, where it showcases new collections, which validates the extensive and prestigious history of the brand. A glamorous list of clientele is invited to a private viewing of the exhibition, which not only sets them apart from other jewelers, but also ensures publicity through word-of-mouth and press coverage, making it a highly sought-after social event attended by the who's-who of the society. By generating populist curiosity and maintaining an exclusive approach, Cartier holds on to its premium positioning.

Being a luxury-oriented brand, Cartier has actively taken on a strategy of cautious expansion, where it operates a chain of 200 stores in more than 125 countries.[17] In contrast, Damas, the Middle Eastern luxury jeweler, has 300 stored across six countries in the region.

For a deluxe brand, exclusivity has a value. The lesser the number of people who can have access to a brand and afford to buy it, the higher the value of the product. The exclusivity aspect makes people aspire to own the brand more even as the product, on top of being a work of artistic genius, stands for a status symbol.

Moreover, when a brand caters only to the most affluent segment of consumers and the cream of the society, it can really focus on providing high-quality service. This helps to promote and maintain the premium positioning of the brand in the minds of consumers.

competition is low. As you might predict, you are now likely to face a new threat, namely, channel complacency.[18] But you cannot add coverage in weaker quality channels to motivate your best channel members, because doing so would create a conflict with your hard-earned quality positioning (and brand equity). We thus need to ask once again, What can a manufacturer do? Here, the question refers to the need to balance selectivity in distribution with the requirement for channel members to exert extra effort to support the brand.

In this case, a contract might be a more appealing option than it seemed in the more general case. If channel members sign demanding contracts and promise to represent the brand effectively, they might receive competitive protections from the manufacturer, which promises to limit its distribution. Such restrictive contracts curtail the channel member's freedom to manage the brand, such as with clauses detailing its obligations for building displays, offering promotions, and meeting sales goals. Other contractual forms specify conditions in which a manufacturer may terminate the arrangement without further obligation. The French audio speaker maker Cabasse, known for its ultrahigh sound reproduction performance, demands that resellers complete a certification program, obliges store personnel to undertake product training, requires stores to maintain a customized auditorium, and insists that sellers pass consumer opinion back to Cabasse management. In return, Cabasse maintains only 750 points of sale throughout the entire French market.[19]

Another restrictive contract might focus on demanding goals. For example, when J.E. Ekornes, a Norwegian manufacturer of home furniture, first entered the French market, it pursued saturation, such that none of its dealers could earn sufficient profits on the brand. Recognizing its error, Ekornes completely redesigned its channel, reduced the number of dealers it supplied by two-thirds, and asked for the remaining dealers' help in redrawing territories to guarantee exclusive distribution to each. In return, the remaining dealers signed contracts committing them to ambitious sales goals. Ultimately, this drastically reduced sales force of just 150 dealers significantly improved the results achieved by the original glut of dealers, and within three years, Ekornes's sales had tripled.[20]

Why are restrictive contracts effective in this setting? High-quality manufacturers use restrictive contracts to screen out resellers that appear reluctant to support the brand, which know they are unlikely to meet the conditions of a restrictive contract. Thus, high-end brands often combine a selective distribution policy with an insistence on restrictive contracts. In so doing, they can broaden their distribution coverage slightly beyond the level available if they employed lenient or no contracts, confident that the additional resellers will continue to ensure the brand's quality image.

Without contracts, Ekornes might have reduced its intensity to even fewer dealers that it knew (or could closely monitor) would to uphold its brand image. In this case, it would have had to choose those dealers on its own; instead, the 150 dealers willing to commit to a restrictive contract filled with ambitious sales goals self-selected into the channel. Each of them offered a credible signal that it was a dealer in which to invest. That is, the contract provided a way for dealers to communicate a signal to Ekornes, and it gave Ekornes an effective way to screen them.

**NICHE POSITIONING BRAND STRATEGY**    A **niche market positioning strategy** targets a narrow, specialized group of buyers. It may seem as if manufacturers would seek broad coverage, to maximize the probability of finding these specialized customers, but instead brands targeting a narrow spectrum of the market also target a narrow spectrum of outlets. The more restricted the target market, the more selective the distribution.

To some extent, this policy is not by choice: Other channel members are less interested in niche brands than in brands with broad appeal. They also recognize the difficulty of assessing niche markets. Because these target buyers tend to reflect a homogenous group with common shopping patterns, just a few resellers can likely reach all of them.

A prime example of such a specialty group is pregnant women, seeking maternity clothing. They prefer to make relatively minimal investments in a wardrobe that they will wear for only a limited time. Because of their price sensitivity, they likely sacrifice quality (e.g., fabrics, styles, designer labels), even if they typically prioritize such functions in their clothing purchases. Therefore, manufacturers can provide limited coverage and offer women a selection of basic quality clothing at reasonable, or even low, prices, housed in smaller, perhaps less convenient outlets that women will seek out when they need them.

Even within a niche strategy, some brands pursue a concomitant premium position as well. A Pea in the Pod (http://peainthepod.com) maintains boutiques throughout the United States to sell premium-priced maternity clothes to professional women who need high-quality business attire, as well as fashion-conscious women who want maternity clothes that reflect current fashion trends. Yet we can still recognize that a restricted target implies selective distribution by niche brands, regardless of their quality positioning.

## Channel Influence (Factor 4)

Many manufacturers seek inordinate influences over their downstream channel members. Rather than accepting that market outcomes are efficient and channel members know best, they develop strong views about how channel members should handle their brands, perhaps out of fear that market incentives will fail to induce channel members to perform channel functions appropriately for their brands. These interventionist manufacturers want to manage their channels as they manage their subsidiaries.

Such a manufacturer might "purchase" a certain amount of cooperation or at least acquiescence through its skillful exploitation of selective distribution, in such a way that the downstream channel member earns higher margins and higher volume on its brand. Selectivity helps this channel member differentiate its assortment, creating a strategic advantage, and also limits the level of intra-brand competition it faces, offering a cost advantage. Manufacturers that grant exclusivity also tend to exert more effort to influence their channel members' behavior,[21] which may include some forms of assistance. These influence attempts are not inexpensive for the manufacturer, especially considering the considerable opportunity cost associated with low coverage.

But these investment costs tend to be most worthwhile when the brand has a premium quality positioning. To maintain it, manufacturers must be sure the brand is presented and supported in an appropriate fashion, which limits the set of available downstream channel members. The more direction the manufacturer needs to exert, the more it likely restricts its distribution, to ensure the channel member's acquiescence.

**CREATING REWARD POWER**   If manufacturers seek too much influence over downstream decisions and activities, conflict is likely between these channel partners, because the downstream channel member feels pressure to act in ways it might not have done otherwise. For example, a manufacturer that dictates prices, promotional activities, displays, salesperson presentations, stocking levels, and target markets is engaging in outright interference in the reseller's business. The reseller is likely to resist, and the manufacturer needs power to overcome that resistance. The offer of protection from intra-brand competition represents a form of reward power, so in general, a manufacturer that wishes to direct another channel member's activities to align them with the manufacturer's preferences should seek more selective distribution. Consider the following elaborated arguments for this strategic choice:

- Because exclusive or limited market coverage increases reseller margins on average, the manufacturer should be able to attract better resellers, whereas with intensive coverage, each reseller likely anticipates margins that are too low to be worthwhile.
- From this small, dedicated group of resellers, the manufacturer enjoys more vigorous overall market efforts, albeit from a smaller group of channel partners.
  - If each reseller in this smaller group competes vigorously, the manufacturer may reach a greater range of customers, and reach them more effectively.
  - This ability is particularly important for a manufacturer that requires a more motivated selling effort, such as in a new market or for a new product.[22]
  - Motivated resellers also may take on more risk on behalf of the manufacturer, such as by carrying more stock or investing in building the brand name.[23]
    - This motivation in turn encourages market entry.
    - It also raises the overall level of competition across brands at the product category level.

Ultimately, this reasoning may seem perverse; it reduces to the dubious argument that local monopolies are desirable! Clearly, opportunity costs offset these purported benefits in the real world. But we should note that a local monopoly can be desirable in specific circumstances.

This rationale for selective distribution also acknowledges that it not only increases the manufacturer's reward power over a single channel member but also reduces the number and variety of partners. A large, heterogeneous channel makes it difficult for the manufacturer to exert total influence with its inherently limited resources, including time, attention, and support. For example, the manufacturer's brand manager can only visit so many distributors at a time, and hiring more managers creates new coordination challenges and costs. A smaller channel is simpler to manage. Simplicity enhances control.

Fundamentally, intensive distribution instead creates a large but ineffective army of indifferent channel members, each of which carries the brand's banner but only in a desultory fashion. By limiting coverage, the manufacturer creates an elite strike force, composed of its top soldiers. Winning a war likely requires both, though for different purposes.

These arguments also apply in reverse for downstream channel members. If a downstream organization represents only a handful of suppliers, it can offer greater rewards to each and thereby gain more individual influence. With such influence, it can force the manufacturer to provide more support, such as in the form of lower wholesale prices, more promotional materials, or better credit terms. The downstream channel member thus weighs the advantages of an army of potentially indifferent suppliers versus those offered by an elite strike force of more motivated suppliers.

**PROMOTING INVESTMENTS BY DOWNSTREAM CHANNEL MEMBERS**    Recall from our discussion of free riding our hypothetical example of Johanson stereo speakers. The retailer had made Johanson-specific investments—assets that are not readily redeployable to the service of another brand—that would become sunk costs if the relationship were terminated. In contrast, most investments by a downstream channel member in a manufacturer are not specialized but rather can be reused or transferred to another brand. But especially in industrial goods and service settings, some brands demand that a reseller or agent acquire capabilities and commit resources with no alternative uses, such as the following:

- To the extent that a brand's applications and features are unique, the sales staff must learn about them to sell effectively. This is *idiosyncratic knowledge.*
- A brand may require *unusual handling or storage* (e.g., a brand shipped on non-standard pallets requires custom shelving or specialty forklifts).
- *Servicing* the brand after the sale may involve brand-specific *parts and know-how.*
- *Customer training* that is brand specific may be required.
- Joint promotions that *blend the identity of buyer and seller* make it difficult to disentangle the downstream channel member and the brand in end-users' minds.

In consumer goods channels, such investments appear particularly when the end-user buys from a contractor dealer. These dealers assemble and install technical products that may require substantial customization and incorporate a supplier's product into systems that meet each buyer's specific needs. The degree to which these dealers specify, assemble, and install causes consumers to regard them more like a manufacturer than a reseller. Familiar examples include dealers of swimming pools, climate control (heating and cooling), fireplaces, metal buildings, greenhouses, security systems, garage doors, solar energy, and custom doors and windows.[24]

In short, for some brands or product categories, *manufacturer-specific assets are necessary to distribute the brand effectively.* That does not mean downstream channel members want to make them. The investments are expensive on their own, but they also raise the reseller's dependence on the manufacturer.[25] The resulting vulnerability to manufacturer opportunism (recall, defined as the deceptive pursuit of self-interest) is expensive for the reseller as well. A rational reseller thus hesitates to make such investments or incur such dependence.

Instead, the manufacturer needs to induce its downstream channel partners to make the investments. Once more, the answer is offering a degree of selectivity, because it increases the rewards that a reseller can earn from the brand. To prevent the manufacturer from reneging on its agreements once the downstream channel member has made brand-specific investments, the latter likely demands that the former provide some assurance of consistency. Fortunately for the manufacturer, limiting distribution offers such reassurance. Fewer channel partners makes it more difficult for a manufacturer to move resources away from its existing partner; at the limit, an exclusive agent, distributor, or retailer may become nearly impossible to replace. Manufacturers that limit distribution thereby increase their own dependence on their downstream channel members. That is, they counterbalance downstream dependence due to manufacturer-specific investments by making selective distribution choices upstream.

In short, selective distribution in a market area offers a means to balance dependence in a distribution channel. By limiting its coverage, the manufacturer accepts its dependence on the downstream channel—though never lightly. Rather, it demands that the downstream member exhibit its own dependence on the manufacturer, by acquiring brand-specific assets. *One vulnerability offsets the other.* Selective distribution represents the currency the manufacturer uses to purchase the downstream channel member's willingness to make brand-specific investments.

## Dependence Balancing (Factor 5)

**TRADING TERRITORY EXCLUSIVITY FOR CATEGORY EXCLUSIVITY**    The idea of balancing dependence is instrumental to any understanding of how channel members, upstream and downstream, use selectivity strategically to enhance their business interests.[26] No one wants to depend on another channel member, because that scenario gives the other party power and creates vulnerability (as we cover in detail in Chapter 10). However, effective distribution often requires one side (for our illustration, let's say the downstream reseller) to depend on the other side (the manufacturer), despite its unwillingness and resistance to doing so. To overcome reseller resistance, the manufacturer might create offsetting dependence of its own. Such calculated **mutual dependence**, or mutual vulnerability, is designed to establish relationship stability by making it unprofitable for either side to exploit the other.[27] But selective distribution is not the only currency a manufacturer might use to purchase the reseller's willingness to invest in brand-specific assets. In other cases, they engage in the direct exchange of territory exclusivity for category exclusivity. In general, the more the manufacturer limits its coverage of a market area, the more the reseller agrees to limit its coverage in the product category.

At the extreme, each side trades total exclusivity for total exclusivity: The downstream reseller only offers the manufacturer's brand in that product category, and the manufacturer promises that it is the only reseller in the market area to carry the brand. Less extreme examples are somewhat more common though, such that the industrial supply house we considered previously might agree to reduce its line to carry only four of the ten available brands, and in return, the metalworking fluids manufacturer that requested this reduction only authorizes 10 distributors to carry its line in the supply house's territory.

For the manufacturer, trading selectivity for selectivity helps it influence how the downstream channel member composes and displays its brand portfolio, including its presentation relative to its competitive set.[28] This desire to influence downstream assortment and display decisions represents the manufacturer's realization that the end-user's perception of its offering depends mainly on the context in which they encounter it. That context in turn is a function of the other brands available and their display. A retailer that adopts an assortment that contains medium-quality merchandise and then displays that merchandise next to high-quality merchandise likely causes consumers to assimilate these two quality grades, such that the lower-quality offering gets an upgrade, but the higher-quality product suffers a downgrade.[29] **Assortment** and **display** choices are so important that they can even influence a consumers' perception of what the product is.[30] A granola bar might be a breakfast food, a snack food, or an exercise food, depending on the supermarket aisle it occupies.

The need to be embedded in the right assortment, displayed in an appropriate way, led LVMH to sell through a carefully designed combination of company-owned stores and highly selective distribution (as we described in Sidebar 5-2). For example, in France, LVMH stores are nearly all two stories, connected only by a staircase. At the bottom of the stairs appear the shoes; purses get moved to the top. The reasoning is direct: Store browsers will enter the store for shoes, and then climb the stairs to "continue shopping" for purses—but not vice versa.[31] Such shoe-dominant assortment and display decisions likely are not evident to independent retailers, but through the reward of selective distribution, LVMH elicits their cooperation.

For suppliers, assortment and selectivity decisions also are intricately linked. A large assortment instead may hinder brand differentiation. Prior to 1993, Volkswagen obliged its Audi and Volkswagen divisions in Europe to sell through the same dealers, with the reasoning that it could draw in customers with a sufficiently large assortment. But because Audis were built on the same platforms as VWs and looked somewhat similar, their side-by-side display led to massive cannibalization of Audi by the lower priced VW. The dealers created a self-fulfilling prophecy that an Audi prospect would ultimately prefer a VW. After 1993, Audi began allowing separate dealerships, supporting them with territory exclusivity, in return for their close cooperation with management. It turned out that the Audi brand assortment was big enough to attract its own clientele, whom Audi dealers quickly began to recognize, once they no longer needed to sell Volkswagens. These lessons fed back to Audi's top management, such as the notion that female drivers wanted practical, sporty vehicles. The success of the resulting advertising campaign helped Audi reach its current positioning: high quality, highly successful, and increasingly differentiated from VW, even though the brands continue to share some production platforms.[32]

For the downstream channel member, trading selectivity for selectivity entails a different sort of influence. Two venerable Parisian department stores, Galeries Lafayette and Printemps, are located in the same neighborhood and compete vigorously, often by observing what the other is doing and imitating effective practices. But Printemps's unique advantage stems from its relationships with selected clothes designers, which receive extraordinary leeway to determine how their goods will be presented. In return, Printemps negotiates exclusivity, such that of the 47 brands it carries, three-quarters of them are "exclusives" (i.e., no other Parisian department store has them, though some other formats in Paris may carry these same brands).[33] Such negotiations help summarize the unique perceptions of both sides, allowing each to concede some form of "exclusivity" for some return in kind.

These two-party examples are insightful but limited; channel members cannot calculate only the number or value of products they carry but also must recognize the total demand for the product in the marketplace. That is, both the slices kept and the overall size of the pie is important for determining profits.[34] In some situations, even if one channel member's share decreases, overall demand increases enough to compensate, resulting in a net improvement.

The rise of the Internet offers a pertinent example. As the Internet continues to penetrate more product categories, downstream channel members may demand more exclusive rights to differentiated goods—such as wine, a differentiated, confusing product category.[35] Wine stores guide buyers by providing information and composing meaningful, appealing assortments. Online wine stores can perform both these functions, and perhaps even offer a wider assortment to site visitors. Therefore, the traditional wine store may need access to exclusives that differentiate it and its assortment from its online competitors. Widely distributed wines likely induce free riding; the wine stores earn sales from their service provision only if they also offer the cheapest price. But differentiated offerings instead tend to make browsers *less* price sensitive, more attentive to the differences among wines, and more likely to entertain themselves by wine shopping—and purchasing more wine.

It appears that for differentiated categories, only low-cost, low-price sellers do well with intensively distributed brands. Such sellers cannot afford to provide information and other sales support, so if the manufacturer wants a retailer to provide information support, it needs to reciprocate by limiting coverage. By helping the seller differentiate its offering, the manufacturer helps ensure the seller's return on its investment in customer information support—as has always been the case, just accelerated by the Internet.

**REASSURING CHANNEL PARTNERS**   In negotiations between upstream and downstream channel members, both sides are preoccupied with their own concerns about what might happen after they reach an agreement. The more vulnerable party fears the powerful party's misuse of its power.[36] These fears could destabilize the relationship, so it is in the interest of the stronger party to reassure the vulnerable party of its good faith—such as through an offer of selectivity.

In business-to-business (B2B) markets, a brand may have a favorable position, or pull, with the customer base, which causes the distributor to worry that the manufacturer will use this pull to create distributor dependence, and then supplant or exploit the distributor. To reassure the distributor, strong manufacturers voluntarily refrain from maximizing coverage. Alternatively, they might sell some fraction of their products directly, after explicit negotiations with downstream channel members (i.e., to avoid any sense of opportunism) or covertly and accompanied by attempts to disguise it (i.e., opportunism). Regardless of its type, direct selling makes industrial suppliers nervous, so the manufacturer could offer selectivity. In a given trading area, the more direct selling it does, the more it limits the number of channel members in the area, in a sort of tacit understanding: "I reserve the right to sell to your customers, but in return, I will not sell through as many of your competitors as I would otherwise." Channel members that accept this tacit agreement should represent the brand effectively, despite the supplier's direct sales.

As we keep noting, this logic flows both ways. Some downstream channel members enjoy a loyal customer base, whose brand choices depend largely on the distributor.[37] To allay the manufacturer's reasonable fear of the distributor's opportunism, powerful distributors (powerful because they have loyal customers) may limit the brand assortment in a product category. These distributors could represent anyone, but they selectively distribute their trading partners' products, to balance the manufacturers' dependence on them.

## Opportunity Cost (Factor 6)

In bargaining away the right to an unlimited number of trading partners, the manufacturer makes a concession to the downstream channel member, and the price of this concession depends on the **importance** of the market area and the **competitive intensity** of the product category.

Critical markets create higher-opportunity costs of lower coverage, and the manufacturer drives a harder bargain, or perhaps simply refuses to limit coverage. For a minor market area, the manufacturer may concede selectivity more readily. Over time though, a manufacturer may reassess any particular market—especially if a downstream channel member appears to be doing very well with its products. In this case, the conflict inherent to the channel may encourage a manufacturer to try to renege on its implicit or explicit selective distribution agreement.[38]

In intensely competitive categories, manufacturers similarly are more reluctant to limit the number of downstream trading partners, because of the opportunity cost of this concession. If prospective buyers are unlikely to make the effort to seek out limited distribution channels when category-level competition is fierce, lower coverage becomes a very risky proposition for the manufacturer.

The conflict in these cases arises from differing perceptions. A manufacturer in an intensely competitive product category might not be earning great profits, *because of the level of competition*. But it could easily misattribute its disappointing performance to insufficient coverage. Rather than addressing the true reasons for the competitive disadvantage, the manufacturer then could seek a quick remedy: higher sales through more coverage, which requires it to lower its distribution standards and send its products through inferior downstream channels. If this move provokes original downstream channel members to withdraw their support for the brand too, the manufacturer's performance spirals further down, even with its greater coverage.

On the other side, the downstream channel member hesitates to limit the brands it carries in a product category if that category is of great importance in its assortment. The industrial supply house that does little business in metalworking fluids might agree to limit its brand selection; a competitor for whom metalworking fluids are an important category probably will not, because the opportunity cost of limiting this key assortment is too great.

Downstream channel members also hesitate to grant selectivity in categories that are intensely competitive. Doing so would constitute an expensive concession, because prospective buyers lose interest if many brands they like are missing from an assortment. Competitive intensity increases buyers' awareness of alternative brands, their preferences for any one brand, and their insistence on a more complete assortment.

For both sides, selectivity is an expensive concession if the object of the negotiation is important or intensively competitive, whether those features refer to the market area (for the manufacturer) or the product category (for the downstream channel member). The expense stems largely from the opportunity costs of limiting the number of trading partners.

## Transaction Costs (Factor 7)

For a manufacturer, each outlet is an account, and each account requires sales attention and support. Fulfilling each account's orders also creates ordering, shipping, financing, and other costs. Many manufacturers maintain accounts whose orders could not justify even the accounting costs of serving them, let alone the related opportunity costs. (Manufacturers that implement sophisticated, activity-based costing systems often discover that as many as one-quarter or one-third of their accounts are unprofitable.)[39] At some point, the **transaction costs** of serving some accounts may outpace the coverage-based benefits they offer. In response, the manufacturer might seek to achieve greater distribution intensity through master distributors that achieve economies of scope and scale in serving their clientele.[40] Of course, the manufacturer loses control and information, but the additional coverage may be worthwhile. Michelin in Italy thus turns to master distributors rather than try to deal with the multitude of small tire dealers in Italy.

The question in relation to the degree of selectivity pertains to the costs of securing such representation. That is, the rationale for selective distribution no longer centers on reward power; rather, it entails the effort to cut costs by dealing with fewer entities, through the following routes:

- Manufacturers limit the number of trading partners to reduce selling expenses, including fewer salespeople and expenses (travel, entertainment, samples) needed to serve the smaller account base.
- Manufacturers that offer high levels of support to each channel member as a matter of policy tend to distribute more selectively to limit the total costs of their sophisticated channel support.
- To the extent that there are fewer downstream channel members means lower turnover, there is less need to recruit, train, and provide service to new resellers.
- Fewer channel partners tend to engage in fewer but larger transactions, on a regular basis, which reduces inventory holding and other processing costs.
- Fewer but larger orders imply more accurate demand forecasting too, enabling better production planning and thus lower inventories.

From the reseller's standpoint, dealing with fewer brands similarly offers important economies. Consolidating demand may facilitate forecasting and improve inventory practices; dealing with fewer suppliers may economize on the expenses of running the purchasing function.

However, it is also important not to simplify the issue too much. Fewer trading partners may tend to lead to lower transaction costs per partner, but the opportunity costs of fewer partners could dwarf their transaction costs. And though more trading partners are often associated with greater sales, it is not clear whether this outcome represents a cause-and-effect scenario or if other, more influential factors are at work. Fundamentally, the choice of a certain number of trading partners turns on costs and benefits, as well as long-term strategic issues that tend to be both more important and more difficult to estimate.

## Other Manufacturers' Strategies (Factor 8)

The last factor we consider requires the recognition that manufacturers frequently experiment with various ways to gain the most benefits from selective distribution while still maintaining intra-brand competition and making it easy for end-users to buy. We find little systematic evidence about the success of these experiments—manufacturers are unlikely to publicize their failures—but anecdotal evidence suggests that some of the following methods may (or may not) be effective means for gaining the best of both worlds.

**BRAND BUILDING**   If a brand can generate sufficient brand equity (e.g., Coca-Cola), downstream channel members are more likely to tolerate high intra-brand competition and refrain from destructive tactics such as bait-and-switch. This method certainly sounds great, but it is very expensive and perhaps effective mainly for FMCG, because the downstream channel member's ability to change end-users' brand preferences already are limited by the low involvement nature of the product category.

**NEW PRODUCT INTRODUCTIONS**    An innovative firm that offers new products with low failure rates and provides information to downstream partners about these innovations may enjoy an effective position. Perhaps the best-known exemplar of this approach is 3M, famous for its competence in new product development.[41] Channel members maintain unusually close ties with 3M, yet the company distributes intensively. The distribution features a steady stream of well-marketed new products, coupled with information; this welcome, rather scarce combination appears to overwhelm channel members' potential reluctance to coordinate their activities with 3M.

**BRANDED VARIANTS**    By varying the models of branded products,[42] such that specific combinations of the attribute levels are available in each, the manufacturer can provide each (or at least some) downstream channel members with near exclusivity, for that particular variant. Thus, only certain sellers, not the entire channel, might carry a Fossil brand watch that features a certain color of watchband, digital or analogue functionality, and particular face and hand combination (e.g., size, luminosity).

This strategy is effective mainly for strong brand names that sell shopping goods, such that the consumer feels some involvement in the product category. Durables and semi-durables fit this description well, as long as they have not become commodities. In this case, the customer perceives some purchase risk, because of the importance of the category and the sense that the products are not interchangeable. Thus, for consumers seeking to purchase a new mattress and box spring, strong brand names are important, so the retailer must stock them, but it also could achieve differentiation by demanding a specific variant. Sealy manufactures mattresses sold in bedding, furniture, and department stores; in certain cases, while Sealy retains certain product features across the board (e.g., options for durability, firmness, padding, number of springs), it also provides variants (e.g., unique colors, cover styles, "made for" labels) for each set of resellers.

Most evidence, though not definitive, suggests that manufacturers that pursue a branded variants strategy induce more stores to carry the brand and provide more service (e.g., stocking and displaying many models, offering sales assistance) in support of this brand. Why does this strategy work so well? In this specific case, we theorize that busy consumers invest their valuable time to develop preferences across the store's considerable selection of brand names and models. The brand name assures them that it is worthwhile to examine alternatives within that line. Warned by salespeople that other stores lack the same selection (a credible statement, considering the store's large offering), the consumers may refuse to take more time to visit another store and search through a completely new set of variants. Instead, they conclude their purchase with the preferred available variant, without shopping further.

**MITIGATING THE COSTS OF SELECTIVE DISTRIBUTION**    Many durable goods require manufacturer-specific service, which generally gets offered at the point of sale. To induce downstream channel members to invest in appropriate service facilities, manufacturers must be selective in their coverage. But in some cases, the solution may be to decouple sales from service, such as by establishing separate service-only facilities. Relieved of the service burden, more stores become qualified to offer sales.

When General Electric decided to adopt more intensive distribution for its small electrical appliances, it found that it could not obtain adequate service from its expanded retail network. The company therefore developed a nationwide, company-owned chain of service centers to resolve its significant marketing problem. (Eventually, it sold off its appliance business to Black & Decker.) The widespread availability of consumer electronics in superstores and discounters, such as Best Buy and Wal-Mart, even may explain these retailers' virtually limitless return policies: Rather than investing in repair facilities, they merely ship the returned merchandise (defective or not) back to the manufacturer for credit against future purchases.[43]

In short, there appear to be several ways to distribute more intensively while retaining at least some of the benefits of distributing selectively. These expensive, difficult to duplicate methods are, understandably, not very widespread. The question of whether and when their costs outweigh their benefits remains an open question.

## CHANNEL TYPE DECISIONS

Thus far, we have focused on trade-offs involving channel intensity and coverage, regardless of how it may be achieved (first channel decision). But specific channel issues arising from high coverage can be particularly acute depending on the *types* of channels that feature the same merchandise. If merchandise appears in different **channel types**, the likelihood is greater that they provide different service outputs and perform different functions, probably at different price points. Consumers can exploit the service outputs of one channel and then buy in another, which can disrupt channel equity. Thus, the second channel strategy decision still relates to the degree of intensity or coverage in the channel structure but focuses more on the types or mix of types of channel partners, as well as to the specific identities of the channel partners within each type, featured in that structure.

Each channel type uses distinct processes to select, purchase, order, and receive product.[44] The processes vary with channel ownership, with location types (e.g., in-store versus at-home), with technology (e.g., catalog versus Web), and with the type of intermediary included (e.g., mass merchandisers versus drug, grocery, or club stores). In general, different formats appeal to unique clientele and may be strongly associated in buyers' minds with certain product categories, which thus determines the channel type decision.[45]

In developed economies, manufacturers often expand the types of channels they use, to connect with ever more finely segmented customer markets. This move raises coverage **variety** but not necessarily the overall level of coverage, which implies an assumption (or perhaps simply the hope) that the different channels do not collide. This assumption relies on yet another assumption, namely, that customers do not cross-shop channels. For B2B products, this claim is tenuous, because purchasing agents make their living by finding ways to extract value from sellers. Even for business-to-consumer (B2C) products, consumers can refuse to stay in their expected channels, and the result is often cannibalization. Sidebar 5-3 describes the pertinent example of Tupperware.

Yet adding a new channel format also can have positive side effects, especially for consumers. For example, U.S. car buyers have become accustomed to using the

## Sidebar 5-3

### Tupperware's retail channels cannibalize the party

For decades, Tupperware enjoyed fame in North America for its "party" channel. Independent dealers ("Tupperware Ladies") organized social events in private homes, during which they presented and sold the full line of plastic storage goods, offering premium quality and prices and available in a huge assortment of models. This system worked well, partly because the sellers were doing business within their social network, and partly because they ably presented the line, persuading buyers that the varied sizes and types were not only valuable but also well worth the price.

Over time, changing demographics disrupted this sales channel; women entering the labor force had less time, energy, or interest in hosting and attending Tupperware parties. In response, Tupperware added booths in malls and moved online, and yet, rather than cannibalizing the agents still further, these new formats revived interest in the party format. Encouraged, Tupperware extended its coverage to thousands of retail discount stores, hosted within the Target chain. Dealers were invited to demonstrate product in the Target aisles, in the belief that even more new parties would grow from these encounters.

Not so fast. The latter move was disastrous. Tupperware dealers in Target aisles found that few customers were willing to stop and talk. And because Tupperware was easy to find at the local Target, interest in Tupperware parties plummeted, though the Target channel failed to replace these lost party sales. Displayed next to a relatively narrow

assortment of inexpensive plastic storage options made by competitors, Tupperware's broad range of finely distinguished items appeared overpriced and superfluous. And with no one to explain why this impression was wrong, the goods stayed on the shelves. Although Target proclaimed itself "satisfied with the partnership," Tupperware lost customers and dealers and rapidly ended its experiment. But the damage had been done, particularly to its dealer network.

The dealers played a massive role in creating sales, but those dealers needed the right display conditions—a party setting and a friendly atmosphere. In the private parties, the seller can manage virtually everything in the environment: the ambiance, the music, the wine, the cooking demonstrations, and even the target market (i.e., the guest list). The events could become so social that some dealers laughingly reported having to send the buyers home at midnight—right after they wrote up all their sales. The Target format destroyed that ambiance and attracted a clientele in a different kind of mood. Whereas a Tupperware dealer and her friends are willing to hang around an in-home party until midnight, because "when I leave the party, I feel great," the dealers in the aisles leave Target at closing time, along with the last of the customers, feeling mostly tired.

In an ironic postscript, the party format that Tupperware made famous now is being copied by makers of many other products, including candles, cookware, and jewelry, often with great success.[46]

Internet, instead of soliciting information from dealership salespeople, with salutary results. These consumers spend less time (on average, 15 hours total rather than 18 in the pre-Internet era) to gather the information they need to choose their next car. Because they enter the dealership well informed, they also can negotiate better.[47] The online automobile channel thus serves as an "infomediary" that provides information, which the consumer takes to the dealership and uses to bargain—to the detriment of the dealer's margins.

Buyers (both individuals and businesses) also often confound a manufacturer's intentions for its multiple channels. Rather than choosing one, buyers exploit all the multiple routes to market together, **cherry-picking** certain service outputs from one channel and other service outputs from another. Such actions reflect our basic discussion of service outputs and the costly functions that are need to meet them. When different channels specialize in the performance of particular functions, they likely produce service output(s) valued by prospective buyers. If they consume the support offered in one channel but consummate their purchase in another (lower cost) channel, as we have defined it, the prospective customers are free riding in effect. But recall that downstream channel members must be compensated for the functions they perform and will not tolerate free riding indefinitely. If manufacturers want to meet end-users' service output demands throughout the channel, including both services provided and price considerations, they should find a way to compensate the service providers who provide each function (e.g., fees, overrides on business booked with another channel).

Some customers also use the Web to negotiate their purchases. Staying with our example of automotive purchases, this channel may offer both consumer and societal benefits, in that consumer protection groups have long suspected that some demographic groups pay more when they shop for a car in person, regardless of their socioeconomic status or preparedness (previsit information search). If these customers engage a Web agent (e.g., Autobytel.com) to shop and purchase for them, they enjoy anonymity, so disadvantaged groups, such as women, Hispanics, and African Americans, on average find that they pay substantially less than they do if they were to attempt to make the purchase in person.[48] (Note that in the United States, the law requires dealer involvement in the actual sale of a new car, so even if the consumer uses a Web agent to negotiate, he or she literally must buy from an automobile dealer.)

The Internet may tend to be cannibalistic, but adding online distribution actually can create new business (increase the size of the pie), without necessarily taking business from existing channels. Adding Web distribution can work well by increasing long-term growth rates, as long as the channel is reaching new customers or offering differentiated products, which minimizes cannibalization.

Once a channel manager decides on the number of participants in each type of channel format, they need to select the specific channel members. This decision is very idiosyncratic to the specific situation, but typically includes similar process steps. First, a screening process is used to identify the pool of candidates for a certain type of channel format in a specific geography or market segment. Second, a selection process evaluates each candidate based on synergy to the supplier's brand positioning, channel functions and capabilities needed, and relationship desired. Third, a negotiation process facilitates each party's needs and concerns and usually results in a contractual agreement. Finally, an implementation process involves training employees, buying a stocking package, and planning a kickoff promotion in order to increase the partnership's early successes.

## DUAL DISTRIBUTION DECISIONS

On the face of it, **dual distribution** (i.e., going to market through both third parties and one's own distribution divisions) may appear to be just a variation on the theme of multiple formats. But there is a special issue that deserves particular consideration here. When third parties compete, the manufacturer can claim to be neutral, letting the market decide who wins. But when the manufacturer competes against its own channel partners by running employee-staffed channel operations in parallel, the claim of neutrality is no longer credible, leaving the independent channels to suspect the manufacturer is favoring itself. Thus, the third decision channel managers must make when designing a channel strategy and structure is whether the manufacturer will sell directly to consumers, through its own distribution organization, and thus compete directly with its channel partners. This decision should depend on the make-or-buy analyses outlined in Chapter 4.

When AT&T was at the peak of its market position in the 1990s, as a capital equipment manufacturer (it no longer operates under this name), it distributed telecommunications hardware and software through third-party distributors—mostly value-added resellers (VARs)—and its own employees. The VARs regularly complained that AT&T discretely favored its division with better terms of trade, product availability, and service. Although AT&T claimed to be even-handed, its large B2B customers demanded better treatment for the VARs. Why would one downstream channel solicit for another? Because these end-users already had strong relationships with the VARs that, true to their names, added value in the form of a better understanding of the end-users' businesses.[49]

Managing such dual systems is challenging and constantly fraught with the risk of dysfunctional conflict.[50] As AT&T learned, B2B customers are quick to play the "in-house" and "outside" channels against each other—a manipulation made all the easier because the two channels already tend to view each other with some suspicion and rivalry. Thus, CyberGuard, a manufacturer of IT products, adopted a draconian policy, though perhaps not in the expected direction: Any salespeople who booked business that should have gone to an external downstream reseller would not receive any commission on the business.[51]

But the AT&T example also reveals just how much value and variety dual channels can offer customers, such that the manufacturer is better able to match costs and benefits to each segment.[52] In turn, the dual channels offer the manufacturer more information (i.e., one channel serves to benchmark the other) and flexibility (i.e., an ability to shift business from one channel to the other if needed).[53]

## The Demonstration Argument

The **demonstration argument** holds that company outlets show independent channels the brand's potential and how best to sell it. Flagship stores in expensive locations carry exclusive Swatch watches in an unusual depth of assortment; though few downstream channel members are likely to mount such an expensive operation, they should be impressed by the stores' profitability and thus more inclined to stock Swatch's multiple models.[54]

Such moves also can enable manufacturers to mount effective defenses against declining or changing consumption trends. Both the tableware maker Guy Degrenne and the venerable French crystal producer Baccarat have suffered declining demand,[55] especially as consumers embrace more casual lifestyles and forego formal dining décor. Retailers responded by shrinking their displays or moving the high-end merchandise to distant corners; the manufacturers dismissed these notions by opening their own stores. These exemplar stores, stocked and displayed as recommended, showed the downstream operators that the products retained far greater sales potential than they believed.

Finally, the demonstration argument may come into play when the manufacturer has a better understanding of its target market than the downstream channel member.

Sony's market research convinced it that electronics retailers were failing to sell to U.S. women effectively.[56] Therefore, it has opened small Sony stores in upscale malls; these "boutiques" follow a merchandising plan designed to appeal to women, with living room models arranged to display real-world usage situations, rather than row upon row of product. The wide aisles better accommodate strollers, and the television sets on display are rarely tuned to sporting events. Shoppers greeted by the "concierge desk" receive introductions to salespeople. Sony reports that the boutiques perform far better among female shoppers (as well as with high-end customers) than do typical big box electronic retailers or those located in outdoor strip malls (i.e., parking lots enclosed by a "strip" of stores joined by an exterior sidewalk). Sony thus hopes its demonstration can encourage its channels to reconsider their approach.

## Carrier–Rider Relationships

Sometimes the most appropriate channel member to carry products to market is actually *another* manufacturer's owned sales force and distribution abilities, in a relationship called piggybacking. In a **piggybacking channel**, the firm making the product that needs distribution is called the **rider**; another manufacturer with excess capacity in its distribution system to accommodate the rider's product is the **carrier**. In such relationships, the rider gets to avoid the cost of hiring a large employee sales force or finding an independent channel member. The carrier earns a fee from carrying the rider's product; it also may enjoy synergies produced by adding a complementary product to its line.[57] This arrangement is most common among pharmaceutical, consumer packaged goods, and financial service companies.

But in these channels, the issue of coordination is just as important as that of efficiency. Dove International, a maker of superpremium ice cream products, is a part of the M&M/Mars company, which also makes a wide variety of candy products. But M&M/Mars's distribution channel had never included freezer trucks, so Dove signed on with Edy's, another ice cream company, to allow it to physically distribute Dove products to grocery stores.[58] The match worked well, from the perspective of finding the right distribution channel resources, leading Dove to sign a permanent contract with Edy's for distribution. Unfortunately, once Dove invested specific resources in the relationship, Edy's opportunism rose, while its effort declined. With reliable physical distribution, Dove's sales and profits dropped too. Without sufficient balance and coordination in the contracting process, it is difficult to expect a piggybacking partner to maintain effort to support a direct competitor to its own line.

A better alternative as a piggybacking partner, because it is more likely to exert good-faith efforts on behalf of the rider, is a firm that manufacturers complementary, rather than directly competitive, products. Such a partner *wants* to do a good job representing the rider's product, whose sales may improve the sales of its own products. However, if the carrier recognizes just what a good complement the rider's product is, it also could be tempted to introduce its own version. As these developments indicate, carrier–rider relationships are inherently fragile.

To strengthen them, the partners might engage in **reciprocal piggybacking**, such that each firm sells its own products and those of the partner. The rider in one relationship is the carrier in the other, and the level of investment or power in the channel gets better balanced. When the U.S. toymaker Mattel signed a reciprocal piggybacking agreement with the Japanese toymaker Bandai, the latter pledged to sell Mattel toys in Japan, and the former pledged to sell Bandai toys in Latin America (where Bandai had no market presence). In addition, Mattel agreed to buy 5 percent of Bandai's stock, suggesting the notable extensiveness of their relationship.[59] The piggybacking deal represented Mattel's third try to establish distribution in Japan (after a failed partnership with a British marketing firm and a failed attempt to set up its own employee sales network). In such a reciprocal arrangement, neither partner is willing to exert weak selling effort for fear that its own product would suffer the same fate. Each relationship serves as a sort of hostage, protecting the other (see Chapter 12 for more on using mutual hostages to strengthen channel relationships).

## CLOSING CHANNEL GAPS

Finally, after channel managers have made their three strategic channel decisions (channel intensity, channel types, and dual distribution), they have one more job to do to design the ideal channel: Close any gaps they might have identified during their various channel audits. Identifying and closing gaps produces a channel that meets service output demands at a minimum cost (i.e., **zero-based channel**). The changes to the channel structure might seek to close service gaps and cost gaps, but they still must remain consistent with the firm's channel intensity, type, and dual distribution decisions. The best solution depends on the diagnosis of the problem.

### Closing Service Gaps

There are three main methods to close **service gaps**: (1) expand or retract the level of service outputs provided; (2) offer multiple, tiered service output levels to appeal to different segments; or (3) alter the list of segments targeted.

First, recall our discussion in Chapter 3, in which we noted that traditional bricks-and-mortar music retailers suffered from an *undersupply* of bulk breaking and assortment and variety functions, such that the service demanded (SD) was greater than the service supplied (SS), but they also offered an *oversupply* of customer service (SS > SD). To determine which gaps need to be closed, as well as classify them in terms of importance, a determinant factor pertains to the number of alternatives available to consumers. End-users may accept poor assortment or variety offerings in a marketplace that provides few alternatives, but as competing channel forms, such as online music purchases and downloads, emerge, the undersupply of key service outputs becomes a more serious threat to sales, market share, and profits. More generally, providers don't need to worry as much about service gaps if the competition is no better than they are at meeting those service output demands. But when the competition's ability to provide desired service output levels improves, the threat increases too.

It may seem more difficult to determine how *over*supplying customer service is really a problem; isn't more service better? If service provision were costless, that might be true, but providing high levels of service actually is *costly*. Standard wholesale and retail prices for music CDs had reached around $12 and $19, respectively, for a disc with perhaps 12 songs on it. This pricing reflected historical norms, in that the industry had established a particular level of margins and was unlikely to change them just to offer lower retail prices to consumers. But it also reflected the costs of running the bricks-and-mortar stores, including the costs of hiring and training salespeople to supply in-store advice and recommendations. If those services are not highly valued by consumers, *and* consumers have access to an alternative channel that provides good assortment, variety, bulk breaking, and cost functions, then the oversupply of customer service hastens the failure of the brick-and-mortar channel.

To close such service gaps, the channel manager could seek to increase (or decrease) service output provision (depending on the type of gap). Because service outputs result directly from the performance of channel functions, either the intensity of the function performance must change (without changing the identity of the channel members), or there must be some change in responsibilities for function performance, whether by shifting that responsibility across the current set of channel members or by changing the structure of the channel itself.

Second, offering a "menu" of service output levels, from which the end-user can choose, can help close service gaps when the product is targeted at multiple segments with unique service output demands. As you might recall, CDW claims it serves as the "chief technical officer for many smaller firms," which implies a very high level of customer service provision. But it also offers lower service levels to more sophisticated corporate customers that have their own in-house systems integration experts, because it recognizes that not every end-user has the same service output demands, nor the same high willingness to pay for customer service. Some channel conflict (see Chapter 11) can arise if customers who persist in wanting high service levels demand lower prices, such as those paid by customers who consume less service. Ideally, these separate channels would remain self-contained, to avoid any overlap in customer sets; in the real world, some mixing of segments and channels is likely inevitable.

Third, channel managers may decide that rather than trying to change the level of service output provision, it would be easier and more profitable for them to modify or fine-tune the segment targeted. Consider small specialty food retailers in the Chicagoland area and their responses to the entry and success of Trader Joe's (a primarily private-label specialty food retailer that buys in bulk and operates larger stores than the stand-alone specialty retailers against which it competes). Trader Joe's private labels feature many of the same products that appear under the manufacturer's label at other, smaller specialty grocers. Some of these retailers welcome Trader Joe's, because of its ability to raise awareness of specialty and gourmet foods in the market, which increases the size of the pie and benefits all specialty retailers. But others note decreases in their sales volumes since the entry of Trader Joe's, and some claim they suffer from free riding, such that they educate consumers about kale chips or tabouiie, only to see them go to Trader Joe's for the lower prices. Perhaps the best option for existing retailers when Trader Joe's comes to town thus is to "stress what you do well already.... Just keep plugging away at what they do best."[60] That is, the specialty grocers can respond by continuing to differentiate elements of customer service to retain their loyal customers, such as hosting gallery shows and late-night food tastings or simply emphasizing personalized service.

## Closing Cost Gaps

Channel **cost gaps** exist when one or more channel functions are performed at too high a cost, which means that for the same level of service outputs, there is a lower cost way to perform the channel function. Cost gaps similarly can be managed through multiple means, including (1) changing the roles of current channel members, (2) investing in new distribution technologies, or (3) introducing new distribution function specialists to improve channel functioning.

The channel manager may not find it necessary to take drastic action; the first route retains the current roster of channel members but changes their roles and channel function responsibilities to improve cost efficiency. Simply shuffling function responsibilities among the current channel members may not be sufficient to achieve cost efficiencies though, in which case the channel manager could invest in new technologies that enable the channel members to reduce the cost they require to perform their functions.

A third option to reduce cost gaps is to alter the channel structure, to introduce members that specialize in state-of-the-art performance of one or more functions. For example, to improve the efficiency of online bill payment, the channel needs to introduce new channel members that specialize in database management, website design, and software integration, to ensure the system works well, from bill presentment to payment and reconciliation. These newly introduced channel specialists may take a portion of channel profits, but they also increase the size of the channel profit pie sufficiently to more than pay their way.

As a final caution, it is extremely important not to fix the *wrong gaps*. Retailers in our music example initially thought the reason for drooping sales at brick-and-mortar stores was the high price. In response, Vivendi Universal tried to force price cuts at the wholesale and retail levels, which seemed sensible from a cost-focused perspective, because the wholesale margins on CD manufacturing were very high (due to the low marginal cost of producing a CD). But this focus on costs actually ignored the greater significance of the service side—and price cuts could do nothing to address bulk breaking, assortment, and variety gaps. Even worse, closing this insignificant gap exerted not a neutral but a negative effect on channel effectiveness, as retailers rebelled against the forced margin cuts. The resulting channel conflict made the situation worse than if Universal had never taken action! In this case, channel managers should have evaluated the impact of their price discounts on consumer demand before assuming that they would drive demand; as is true in many cases, the low levels of price elasticity likely would have surprised them.[61] In general, channel managers can avoid similar difficulties by carefully diagnosing the actual gaps (service versus cost, for which channels, and affecting which target segments) in their channels and taking actions to close only those they identify as critical.

## Closing Gaps Produced by Environmental or Managerial Bounds

The preceding discussion implicitly assumes that it is in the channel manager's power to first identify channel gaps and then take the necessary steps to close them. Certainly, these assumptions hold if the source of the gaps is managerial oversight or errors in judgment, or if a shifting marketplace makes change in the channel inevitable. But what if the sources of the gaps are environmental or managerial boundaries that remain in place, regardless of channel improvements?

Some boundaries simply cannot be relaxed completely, and in this case, a true, ideal channel design outcome may be impossible. However, many bounds can and routinely should be challenged. Recall CDW's consortium programs with small and minority business partners, which effectively challenged the government's bound on purchasing from large vendors by altering the channel structure. Other possible tactics include the following:

- Organizational buy-in across the board, such that all relevant functions and levels have a say in the channel design process.
- An energetic champion, who can go far in managing the change process. The champion must have power, credibility, political skills, and, perhaps most important, tenacity.
- Assigning clear responsibility for the channel, as soon as possible in the process. Task forces comprising key members of various interest groups might serve such a role, and enhance buy-in, if they are involved in the process from the outset.
- A truly customer-driven approach, which stops counterarguments in their tracks. Opposing the suggested design identifies the critic as opposed to delivering customer satisfaction. Nevertheless, patience and persistence are required, because the transition toward the optimal system will not be immediate, especially when tradition-bound ideas surround existing channel designs.
- A mechanism built into the design process that permits the organization to stay in contact with end-users.[62]

Two major points are worth mentioning here. First, *where you invest your marketing dollars matters.* If you invest them in changing the ground rules for engaging in the market, the channel structure you design is more likely to approximate a zero-based model. Second, *challenging channel bounds and closing associated channel gaps costs money.* Channel managers cannot transform the rules of engagement or the existing channel design without exerting a costly effort to do so. The ultimate gains can be well worth the initial investment, especially because failing to move channel boundaries or close channel gaps can mean significant damage to revenues and market share.

## SUMMARY: DESIGNING EFFECTIVE CHANNEL STRUCTURES AND STRATEGIES

Once a channel manager completes the end-user, channel, and make-or-buy analyses he or she is ready to move onto three strategic channel decisions: (1) channel intensity, (2) channel types, and (3) dual distribution. With these decisions made, the manager also can begin to close the gaps identified during the channel audit, to lead ultimately to a channel that meets service output demands at the minimum cost.

The first strategic channel decision revolves around channel intensity: how thoroughly to cover a market area. For the manufacturer especially, this decision constitutes a critical policy choice, with substantial influences on how well it can implement its channel plans. The intensity of coverage further determines the level of the manufacturer's reward power over downstream channel members, or alternatively, how much it must rely on its downstream counterparts.

At first glance, the issue may seem deceptively simple: open as many channels to end-users as possible. This option appeals to end-users too, who want to find an outlet nearby, especially for convenience goods. Furthermore, it would pressure channel members to sell more (e.g., by cutting prices) to react to competitors' attempts to sell the same brands in their outlets. All these factors suggest that more coverage is better—even the corporate lawyer is likely to approve, because wider coverage eliminates concerns about restricting competition. But a good corporate accountant, adding up the costs of servicing all these outlets, each placing a small order, might have a good reason to object. So might the other channel members themselves. Unable to differentiate themselves from the glut of other downstream channel members that sell the same products, they cannot maintain their margins and ultimately must ask the manufacturer for relief. If intra-brand competition cannot be reduced, they will shift their efforts, perhaps even to improving their bait-and-switch methods. Other entities will refuse to join the manufacturer's channel; those already there might refuse to undertake actions to support the brand unless they can readily redeploy those efforts to other brands. The overall lack of cooperation in the channel rises exponentially when coverage is too high for downstream channel members to earn a reasonable return from the brand.

Thus, a multitude of factors actually influence the distribution intensity decision: creating brand equity to induce pull effects from end-users (effectively obliging the channel to carry the brand), imposing and enforcing restrictive contracts, practicing resale price maintenance (if legal), offering branded variants, decoupling sales and service, and frequently introducing new products that have low failure rates, to name a few. A more direct, and often cheaper and more effective, way to influence the channel also is to limit coverage. Although it increases the manufacturer's dependence on downstream channel members, each of which becomes more important and more difficult to replace, it also grants an important reassurance that the manufacturer is not seeking opportunism when it asks them to make brand-specific investments, gains a strong brand position, or considers undertaking its own direct selling.

Limited distribution also might induce other channel members to make their own concessions—especially to limit the brand assortment they carry. More generally, by limiting coverage, the manufacturer promises greater rewards to each channel member, increasing its ability to attract the best resellers (important for a high-quality positioning) that match a particular customer profile (important for a focused target segment). Manufacturers may also use their reward power to exercise greater influence over how channel members market their brands (important for manufacturers that are reluctant to let market forces dictate outcomes).

The next strategic channel decisions involve determining which channel types to use to go to market and how to combine various formats (e.g., stores, kiosk, and online). A growing trend in both B2B and B2C markets creates multiple routes to market by mixing different formats (combinations of functions and service outputs). Achieving greater coverage by adding more different types of channel members can be a very effective option, as long as different customer segments gravitate to different formats. Otherwise, cannibalization and conflict are more likely. Free riding also becomes a major issue, because downstream channel members will not tolerate being victimized indefinitely.

The third strategic channel decision is whether the supplier should build its own channels to get to customers. Such dual distribution can be effective if the company's own channels meet different service output demands than the independent channels that also sell its products. But it is difficult to prevent perceptions of self-bias toward owned channels, a sense of rivalry among both employee and the third-party channels, or ugly competition between them. Firms must take steps to ensure that each format perceives it is being treated fairly, because when designed and managed well, dual distribution can provide valuable information (benchmarking), demonstration capabilities, and signals of potential underserved demand, such that the manufacturer gains leverage over both channels.

Finally, channel managers must identify and close cost and service gaps to design zero-based channels (or close approximations). Changes to the channel structure must acknowledge the channel intensity, type, and dual distribution decisions already made. However, remaining tactical gaps need to be addressed effectively, once the more "strategic" channel decisions are in place.

## TAKE-AWAYS

- Selective distribution is a purposeful, strategic choice, not to be confused with an inability to attract channel members to carry the brand.
- Manufacturers tend to assume that more coverage is always better. Conflict is therefore inherent, because channel members prefer the manufacturer to offer less coverage.
  - The manufacturer will experience a lack of cooperation when coverage is too high for downstream channel members to earn a good return.
  - Various ways exist to cope with the implementation problems created by intensive distribution, but they are all expensive, and some of them are also difficult to implement.
- A more direct, often cheaper, and perhaps more effective way to influence the channel is to limit coverage. This move raises the manufacturer's dependence on its downstream channel partners, because each becomes more important (and would require more effort to replace). But in return, the manufacturer can reassure channel members that it will not be opportunistic.
- For convenience goods, more coverage is usually better, because buyers purchase impulsively or refuse to expend much effort to find a particular brand. For shopping goods or experience goods, selective distribution is feasible and even desirable.
- The decision to be selective should reflect the brand's marketing strategy, as well as the nature of the product category. Selectivity makes sense
  - to support a premium positioning.
  - to pursue a narrow target market.
  - to pursue a niche strategy (premium positioning in a narrow target market).
- The manufacturer can use limited distribution to induce channel members to make concessions of their own, such as limiting their brand assortment.
- Manufacturers can use the reward power accrued through selective distribution to attract only the best downstream partners or those matching a particular customer profile. Manufacturers with reward power can also exercise greater influence over the way channel members market their brands and save costs by serving a smaller but more active account base.
- The same arguments apply in reverse to a downstream channel member: Representing fewer brands can increase leverage over a manufacturer while reducing costs.
- The customer benefits if these channel choices and control ideas lead to desirable outcomes, such as when vigorous competition leads to lower prices and greater distribution increases convenient availability.

- Achieving greater coverage by adding different types of channel members can be highly effective, if customer segments gravitate to different formats. Otherwise, cannibalization and conflict are highly likely.
- Dual distribution can be highly effective, though firms often appear biased toward their "own" channels.
- Carrier–rider relationships are inherently unstable, which may be remedied by reciprocal piggybacking.
- Closing both service and cost gaps is critical to match the level of services delivered with the level of services demanded by target customers at a minimum cost.

## Endnotes

1. Frazier, Gary L., Kirti Sawhney, and Tasadduq Shervani (1990), "Intensity, Functions, and Integration in Channels of Distribution," in V. A. Zeithaml, ed., *Review of Marketing* (Chicago: American Marketing Association), pp. 263–300.

2. Chu, Wujin and Woosik Chu (1994), "Signaling Quality By Selling Through a Reputable Retailer: An Example of Renting the Reputation of Another Agent," *Marketing Science* 13 (Spring), pp. 177–189.

3. See www.bigboystoysuae.com (accessed 03/03/2014).

4. Samaha, Stephen, Robert W. Palmatier, and Rajiv P. Dant (2011), "Poisoning Relationships: Perceive Unfairness in Channels of Distribution," *Journal of Marketing* 75 (May), pp. 99–117.

5. Steiner, Robert L. (1993), "The Inverse Association Between the Margins of Manufacturers and Retailers," *Review of Industrial Organization* 8, pp. 717–740.

6. Chapdelaine, Sophie (2000), "Les Malheurs de la Famille Barbie," *Capital* 11 (March), pp. 38–40.

7. *The Economist* (2001), "The Wrong Trousers," June 16, p. 74.

8. Breit, William (1991), "Resale Price Maintenance: What Do Economists Know and When Did They Know It?" *Journal of Institutional and Theoretical Economics* 147, pp. 72–90; Fabricant, Ross A. (1990), "Special Retail Services and Resale Price Maintenance: The California Wine Industry," *Journal of Retailing* 66, no. 1, pp. 101–118.

9. The material in this section is based on the following sources: Fein, Adam J. and Erin Anderson (1997), "Patterns of Credible Commitments: Territory and Category Selectivity in Industrial Distribution Channels," *Journal of Marketing* 61 (April), pp. 19–34; Frazier, Gary L. and Walfried M. Lassar (1996), "Determinants of Distribution Intensity," *Journal of Marketing* 60 (October), pp. 39–51.

10. Geylani, Tansev, Anthony J. Dukes, and Kannan Srinivasan (2007), "Strategic Manufacturer Response to a Dominant Retailer," *Marketing Science* 26 (March–April), pp. 164–178.

11. Daniels, Cora (2003), "Canadian Double," *Fortune* 147, no. 5, p. 42.

12. The convenience, shopping, and specialty goods terminology refers to consumer markets and was developed by Copeland, Mervin (1923), "Relation of Consumers' Buying Habits to Marketing Methods," *Harvard Business Review* 1 (March–April), pp. 282–289.

13. Reibstein, David J. and Paul W. Farris (1995), "Market Share and Distribution: A Generalization, A Speculation, and Some Implications," *Marketing Science* 14, no. 3, pp. G190–G202.

14. Rangan, V. Kasturi, Melvyn A. J. Menezes, and E. P. Maier (1992), "Channel Selection for New Industrial Products: A Framework, Method, and Application," *Journal of Marketing* 56 (July), pp. 69–82.

15. Tellis, Gerard J. (1988), "The Price Elasticity of Selective Demand: A Meta-Analysis of Econometric Models of Sales," *Journal of Marketing Research* 25 (November), pp. 331–341.

16. Kalra, Ajay and Shibo Li (2008), "Signaling Quality through Specialization," *Marketing Science* 27 (March–April), pp. 168–184.

17. Marketing Strategy of Cartier Monde, ManagementParadise.com, http://www.managementparadise.com/forums/marketing-management/210549-marketing-strategy-cartier-monde.html (accessed 12/03/14).

18. Fang, Eric, Robert W. Palmatier, and Kenneth R. Evans (2004), "Goal-Setting Paradoxes? Trade-Offs between Working Hard and Working Smart: The United States versus China," *Journal of the Academy of Marketing Science* 32 (Spring), pp. 188–202.

19. Scherrer, Matthieu (2003), "Cabasse Reprend du Volume," *Management* (November), pp. 39–40.

20. Kumar, Nirmalya (1996), "The Power of Trust in Manufacturer-Retailer Relationships," *Harvard Business Review* 60 (November–December), pp. 92–106.

21. Celly, Kirti Sawhney and Gary L. Frazier (1996), "Outcome-Based and Behavior-Based Coordination Efforts in Channel Relationships," *Journal of Marketing Research* 33 (May), pp. 200–210.

22. Rangan, Menezes, and Maier (1992), op. cit.

23. European Commission (1997), *Green Paper on Vertical Restraints in EU Competition Policy*, Brussels, Directorate General for Competition. Available at http://europa.eu.int/en/comm/dg04/dg04home.htm.

24. Magrath, Allan J. and Kenneth G. Hardy (1988), "Working with a Unique Distribution Channel: Contractor-Dealers," *Industrial Marketing Management* 17, no. 1, pp. 325–328.

25. Buchanan, Lauranne (1992), "Vertical Trade Relationships: The Role of Dependence and Symmetry in Attaining Organizational Goals," *Journal of Marketing Research* 29 (February), pp. 65–75.

26. Heide, Jan B. and George John (1988), "The Role of Dependence Balancing in Safeguarding Transaction-Specific Assets in Conventional Channels," *Journal of Marketing* 52 (January), pp. 20–35.

27. Palmatier, Robert W., Rajiv P. Dant, and Dhruv Grewal (2007), "A Comparative Longitudinal Analysis of Theoretical Perspectives of Interorganizational Relationship Performance," *Journal of Marketing* 71 (October), pp. 172–194.

28. Heide, Jan B., Shantanu Dutta, and Mark Bergen (1998), "Exclusive Dealing and Business Efficiency: Evidence from Industry Practice," *Journal of Law and Economics* 41 (October), pp. 387–407.

29. Buchanan, Lauranne, Carolyn J. Simmons, and Barbara A. Bickart (1999), "Brand Equity Dilution: Retailer Display and Context Brand Effects," *Journal of Marketing Research* 36, no. 3, pp. 345–355.

30. Shocker, Allan D., Barry L. Bayus, and Namwoon Kim (2004), "Product Complements and Substitutes in the Real World: The Relevance of 'Other Products,'" *Journal of Marketing*. 68, no. 1, pp. 28–40.

31. Grundahl, Marie-Pierre (2000), "Vuitton: Les Secrets d'une Cash Machine," *Management* (September), pp. 22–26.

32. Chabert, Patrick (2004), "Audi, le Seigneur des Anneaux," *Capital* (November), pp. 38–42.

33. Bialobos, Chantal (2004), "Le Match Galeries Lafayette-Printemps," *Capital* (December), pp. 62–64.

34. Dragnaska, Michla, Daniel Klapper, and Sofia B. Villas-Boas (2010), "A Larger Slice or a Larger Pie? An Empirical Investigation of Bargaining Power in the Distribution Channel," *Marketing Science* 29 (January–February), pp. 57–74.

35. Lynch, John G. and Dan Ariely (2000), "Wine Online: Search Costs Affect Competition on Price, Quality, and Distribution," *Marketing Science* 19 (1), p. 83.

36. This section is based on Fein and Anderson (1997), op. cit.; Frazier and Lassar (1996), op. cit.

37. Butaney, Gul and Lawrence H. Wortzel (1988), "Distributor Power Versus Manufacturer Power: The Customer Role," *Journal of Marketing* 52 (January), pp. 52–63.

38. McAfee, R. Preston and Marius Schwartz (1994), "Opportunism in Multilateral Vertical Contracting: Nondiscrimination, Exclusivity, and Uniformity," *American Economic Review* 84, no. 1, pp. 210–230.

39. Bowman, Douglas and Das Narayandas (2004), "Linking Customer Management Effort to Customer Profitability in Business Markets," *Journal of Marketing Research* 16, no. 4, pp. 433–47.

40. Narayandas, Das and V. Kasturi Rangan (2004), "Building and Sustaining Buyer-Seller Relationships in Mature Industrial Markets," *Journal of Marketing* 68, no. 3, pp. 63–77.

41. Frazier and Lassar (1996), op. cit.

42. Bergen, Mark, Shantanu Dutta, and Steven M. Shugan (1996), "Branded Variants: A Retail Perspective," *Journal of Marketing Research* 33 (February), pp. 9–19.

43. O'Brien, Timothy L. (1994), "Unjustified Returns Plague Electronics Makers," *The Wall Street Journal*, September 26, p. B1.

44. Ganesan, Shankar, Morris George, Sandy Jap, Robert W. Palmatier, and Bart Weitz (2009; authors listed alphabetically), "Supply Chain Management and Retailer Performance: Emerging Trends, Issues, and Implications for Research and Practice," *Journal of Retailing* 85 (March), pp. 84–94.

45. Inman, J. Jeffrey, Venkatesh Shankar, and Rosellina Ferraro (2004), "The Roles of Channel-Category Associations and Geodemographics in Channel Patronage," *Journal of Marketing* 68, no. 2, pp. 51–71.

46. Brooks, Rick (2004), "Sealing Their Fate: A Deal With Target Put Lid on Revival at Tupperware," *The Wall Street Journal*, February 18, pp. 1–2.

47. Ratchford, Brian T., Myung-Soo Lee, and Debabrata Talukdar (2003), "The Impact of the Internet on Information Search for Automobiles," *Journal of Marketing Research* 40, no. 2, pp. 193–209.

48. Morton, Fiona Scott, Florian Zettelmeyer, and Jorge Silva-Risso (2003), "Consumer Information and Discrimination: Does the Internet Affect the Pricing of New Cars to Women and Minorities?" *Quantitative Marketing and Economics* 1, no. 1, pp. 65–92.

49. Torode, Christina (2003), "Partners: AT&T Lives by Channel Playbook," *CRN News*, September 2, pp. 6–7.

50. Vinhas, Alberto Sa (2003), "Dual Distribution Channels in Business-to-Business Marketing: A Transaction Interdependencies View," Ph.D. dissertation, INSEAD, Fontainebleau, France.

51. Neel, Dan (2004), "CyberGuard to Direct-Sales Force: No Commission If You Sell Direct," *CRN*, July 7, p. 15.

52. Moriarty, Rowland T. and Ursula Moran (1990), "Managing Hybrid Marketing Systems," *Harvard Business Review* 68 (November–December), pp. 146–150.

53. Dutta, Shantanu, Mark Bergen, Jan B. Heide, and George John (1995), "Understanding Dual Distribution: The Case of Reps and House Accounts," *Journal of Law, Economics, and Organization* 11, no. 1, pp. 189–204.

54. Aoulou, Yves (2005), "L'Héritier Inattendu de Monsieur Swatch," *Management* (March), pp. 18–22.

55. Gava, Marie-Jose (1999), "Guy Degrenne N'est Pas le Cancre de la Distribution," *Management* (April), p. 16; Bouyssou, Julien (2004), "Le Deuxième Souffle de Baccarat," *Management* (February), pp. 28–30.

56. Spagat, Elliot (2004), "Sony Makes Big Changes With Small Stores," *Marketing News*, November 15, p. 12.

57. Terpstra, Vern and Bernard L. Simonin (1993), "Strategic Alliances in the Triad: An Exploratory Study," *Journal of International Marketing* 5, no. 1, pp. 4–26.

58. Edy's ice cream is marketed by Dreyer's (http://www.dreyers.com/). It is the same ice cream, sold as Dreyer's west of the U.S. Rocky Mountains and as Edy's east of the Rocky Mountains.

59. Bandai, "Execution of a Letter of Intent Regarding an Alliance Between Bandai Co., Ltd. and Mattel, Inc.," http://www.bandai.co.jp/; Mattel, "Mattel, Inc. and Bandai Co., Ltd. Establish Global Marketing Alliance," http://www.mattel.com/.

60. Jersild, Sarah (2004), "Small Specialty Stores Face Fresh Battle," *Chicago Tribune*, February 23.

61. Pauwels, Koen, Shuba Srinivasan, and Philip Hans Franses (2007), "When Do Price Thresholds Matter in Retail Categories?" *Marketing Science* 26 (January–February), pp. 83–100.

62. See Stern, Louis W., Frederick D. Sturdivant, and Gary A Getz (1993), "Accomplishing Marketing Channel Change: Paths and Pitfalls," *European Management Journal* 11 (March), pp. 1–8.

CHAPTER **6**

# Retailing Structures and Strategies

## LEARNING OBJECTIVES

**After reading this chapter, you will be able to:**

- Describe the types of retail structures that exist worldwide.
- Explain how a retail positioning strategy flows from both cost-side and demand-side factors.
- Define the retailer's positioning strategy as a set of service outputs delivered to the market, which helps differentiate a retailer from its competitors, even if the products sold are identical.
- Recognize important trends and developments on the consumer and channel sides that affect retail management.
- Outline the power and coordination issues facing retailers and their suppliers, as well as how suppliers respond to retailers' use of power to influence channel behavior.
- Recognize the increasing globalization of retailing and how it affects not just the retailers that sell outside their national borders but also their suppliers and local competitors.

Modern retailing is fiercely competitive, innovation oriented, populated by an ever-growing variety of institutions, and constantly buffeted by the highly fluid environment. Such a scenario demands careful reactions from the channel members within this environment. This chapter details not just retailers' chosen structures but also some of the more significant competitive developments that have made retailing today so volatile. Furthermore, it offers channel managers suggestions for ways to account for "bottom-up" pressures as they devise strategies and design distribution systems.[1]

To begin, we need to distinguish retail sales from wholesale sales. In turn, we can outline the operational characteristics that define retailers' positions and the nature of retailing competition. Finally, we cover some of the strategic issues currently facing retailers.

## RETAIL STRUCTURES

**Retailing** consists of the activities involved in selling goods and services to ultimate consumers for their personal consumption. A **retail sale** is one in which the buyer is the ultimate consumer, rather than a business or institutional purchaser. A **wholesale sale** instead refers to purchases for resale or for business, industrial, or institutional uses (we address these types of sales in Chapter 7). Thus, the **buying motive** for a retail sale is always personal or family satisfaction, stemming from the consumption of the item being purchased by an end-user.

The distinction between retail and wholesale sales may seem insignificant, but in practice it is critical, because buying motives support market segmentation. Companies that sell personal computers to parents so their high school students can do their homework (or play computer games) make retail sales. Companies that sell personal computers to these same parents so they can run their family business run out of a home office instead are engaged in wholesale sales. Office Depot in the United States makes both retail and wholesale sales, but it also needs to understand which kind of customer it is serving, and how best to serve them, when those parents walk through the door of one of its stores. Businesses, including Office Depot, increasingly sell to other businesses out of what look and feel like retail stores; for this chapter though, we focus specifically on businesses engaged in retail sales.

Such retailers constitute a special category of membership in the downstream segment of the channel. As Table 6-1 shows, retailers represent some of the best known names in the world, as well as a broad range of retail types (supermarkets, hypermarkets, department stores, automobile sellers). That is, retail success comes in many shapes, sizes, and cultural origins, conducted both in stores and outside them (e.g., mail order, online, direct selling).

There are some commonalities too. Notice, for example, that food retailing is a channel component for many of the biggest of the big retailers: 9 of the top 10 sell at least some food (all retailers except Home Depot; Walgreen has some food sales). In this realm, we simply cannot ignore or underestimate the dominance of Wal-Mart on worldwide retailing and its developments. Wal-Mart's sales are more than three times as great as those of the next largest retailer (Carrefour), and its sales account for 11 percent of retail sales of the top 250 global retailers![2]

Partly as a result of this dominance, U.S. retailers as a group account for 41.7 percent of sales by the world's top 250 retailers. In this sense, the United States is the world's biggest retail marketplace, a reputation reaffirmed by the vast number of large retailers that locate there: 30 of the top 100 are headquartered in the United States. European countries host 46 large retailers across them, and Japan follows with 8 of the largest retailers.

Despite such apparent dominance though, increasing **globalization** becomes clear when we perform a more longitudinal (i.e., over time) analysis of the data. In an analogous table in the 6th edition of this book, the top 10 world retailers operated in 9.3 countries on average. In the data in our current Table 6-1, that figure has climbed to 15.6 countries on average for the top 10 retailers. Only one of the top 10 is a single-country retailer (Kroger). The globalization trend of retailers seems well established as the larger retailers grow faster than smaller retailers grow, acquire smaller retailers, and expand into new markets.

**TABLE 6-1** The World's top 100 retailers (2011)

| Retailer by Rank (home country and rank in 2003) | Retail Formats | 2010 Retail Sales (US$ million) | 5-Year Retail Sales Compound Annual Growth Rate | Number of Countries (Continents) |
|---|---|---|---|---|
| 1. Wal-Mart Stores, Inc. (United States) (1) | Apparel/footwear specialty, cash and carry/warehouse club, discount department, discount, hypermarket, supercenter, superstore, supermarket | 418,952 | 6.0% | 16 (N. Am., S. Am., Asia, Eur.) |
| 2. Carrefour S.A (France) (2) | Cash and carry/warehouse club, convenience/forecourt, discount, hypermarket, supercenter, superstore, supermarket | 119,642 | 3.9% | 33 (Af., S. Am., Asia, Eur.) |
| 3. Tesco PLC (United Kingdom) (6) | Cash and carry/warehouse club, convenience/forecourt, department, discount department, discount, hypermarket, supercenter, superstore, supermarket | 92,171 | 9.3% | 13 (N. Am., Asia, Eur.) |
| 4. Metro AG (Germany) (4) | Cash and carry/warehouse club, department, electronics specialty, hypermarket, supercenter, superstore, supermarket, other specialty | 88,931 | 3.8% | 33 (Af., Asia, Eur.) |
| 5. The Kroger Co. (United States) (5) | Convenience/forecourt, hypermarket, supercenter, superstore, supermarket, other specialty | 82,189 | 6.3% | 1 (N. Am.) |
| 6. Schwarz Unternehmens Treuhand (Germany) (16) | Discount, hypermarket, supercenter, superstore | 79,119[e] | 9.8% | 26 (Eur.) |
| 7. Costco Wholesale Corporation (United States) (9) | Cash and carry/warehouse club | 76,255 | 8.0% | 9 (N. Am., C. Am., Asia, Eur., Pac.) |
| 8. The Home Depot, Inc. (United States) (3) | Home improvement | 67,997 | –2.5% | 5 (N. Am., C. Am. Asia.) |
| 9. Walgreen Co. (United States) (17) | Drug/pharmacy | 67,420 | 9.8% | 2 (N. Am., C. Am.) |
| 10. Aldi Einkauf GmbH & Co. oHG (Germany) (10) | Discount, supermarket | 67,112[e] | 5.9% | 18 (N. Am., Eur., Pac.) |

(continued)

**TABLE 6-1** (continued)

| Retailer by Rank (home country and rank in 2003) | Retail Formats | 2010 Retail Sales (US$ million) | 5-Year Retail Sales Compound Annual Growth Rate | Number of Countries (Continents) |
|---|---|---|---|---|
| 11. Target Corp. (United States) (7) | Discount department, hypermarket, supercenter, superstore | 65,786 | 5.1% | 1 (N. Am.) |
| 12. Rewe Group (Germany) (11) | Apparel/footwear specialty, cash and carry/warehouse club, convenience/forecourt, discount, drug/pharmacy, electronics specialty, home improvement, hypermarket, supercenter, superstore, supermarket, other specialty | 61,134 | 5.4% | 13 (Eur.) |
| 13. CVS Caremark Corp. (United States) (26) | Drug/pharmacy | 57,345 | 11.0% | 1 (N. Am.) |
| 14. Seven & i Holdings Co., Ltd. (Japan) (n.l.) | Apparel/footwear specialty, convenience/forecourt, department, hypermarket, supercenter, superstore, supermarket, other specialty | 57,055 | 5.9% | 18 (N. Am., C. Am., Asia, Eur., Pac.) |
| 15. Groupe Auchan SA (France) (18) | Discount, electronics specialty, hypermarket, supercenter, superstore, supermarket, other specialty | 55,212 | 4.7% | 13 (Af., Asia, Eur.) |
| 16. Edeka Zentrale AG & Co. (Germany) (24) | Cash and carry/warehouse club, convenience/ forecourt, discount, electronics specialty, home improvement, hypermarket, supercenter, superstore, supermarket, other specialty | 54,072 | 5.5% | 1 (Eur.) |
| 17. Aeon Co., Ltd. (Japan) (22) | Apparel/footwear specialty, convenience/forecourt, department, discount department, discount, drug/ pharmacy, home improvement, hypermarket, supercenter, superstore, supermarket, other specialty | 53,458 | 2.2% | 8 (Asia) |
| 18. Woolworths Limited (Australia) (31) | Convenience/forecourt, discount department, electronics specialty, home improvement, supermarket, other specialty | 51,771 | 7.3% | 2 (Pac.) |
| 19. Best Buy Co., Inc. (United States) (28) | Electronics specialty, home improvement, nonstore | 50,272 | 10.3% | 15 (N. Am., Asia, Eur.) |

| Company | Format | Revenue | Growth | Countries |
|---|---|---|---|---|
| 20. Lowe's Companies, Inc. (United States) (19) | Home improvement | 48,815 | 2.5% | 3 (N. Am., C. Am.,) |
| 21. Wesfarmers Limited (Australia) (n.l.) | Convenience/forecourt, discount department, home improvement, hypermarket, supercenter, superstore, supermarket, other specialty | 47,631 | 62.3% | 2 (Pac.) |
| 22. Sears Holdings Corp. (United States) (13) | Apparel/footwear specialty, department, discount department, home improvement, hypermarket, supercenter, superstore, nonstore, other specialty | 43,326 | −2.4% | 3 (N. Am. C. Am.) |
| 23. Centres Distributeurs E. Leclerc (France) (25) | Convenience/forecourt, discount, drug/pharmacy, hypermarket, supercenter, superstore, supermarket, other specialty | 41,165[e] | 3.2% | 7 (Eur.) |
| 24. Safeway Inc. (United States) (41) | Supermarket | 40,229 | 1.3% | 3 (N. Am., C. Am.) |
| 25. Koninklijke Ahold N.V (The Netherlands) (8) | Convenience/forecourt, discount, drug/pharmacy, hypermarket, supercenter, superstore, supermarket, other specialty | 39,213 | −0.1% | 10 (N. Am., Eur.) |
| 26. Casino Guichard-Perrachon S.A. (France) (27) | Cash and carry/warehouse club, convenience/forecourt, discount department, discount, electronics specialty, home improvement, hypermarket, supercenter, superstore, supermarket, other specialty | 37,875 | 5.0% | 27 (Af., S. Am., Asia, Eur. ) |
| 27. ITM D (France) (n.l.) | Apparel/footwear specialty, convenience/forecourt, discount, home improvement, hypermarket, supercenter, superstore, supermarket, other specialty | 33,994[e] | 5.1% | 8 (Eur.) |
| 28. Amazon.com, Inc. (United States) (n.l.) | Nonstore | 33,251 | 32.1% | 8 (N. Am., Asia, Eur.) |
| 29. J Sainsbury plc (United Kingdom) (23) | Convenience/forecourt, hypermarket, supercenter, superstore, supermarket | 32,837 | 6.1% | 1 (Eur.) |
| 30. The IKEA Group (INGKA Holding B.V.) (Sweden) (50) | Other specialty | 31,642 | 9.3% | 39 (N. Am., Asia, Eur., Pac.) |
| 31. SuperValu Inc. (United States) (60) | Discount, supermarket | 28,911 | 22.1% | 1 (N. Am.) |

(continued)

**TABLE 6-1** (continued)

| Retailer by Rank (home country and rank in 2003) | Retail Formats | 2010 Retail Sales (US$ million) | 5-Year Retail Sales Compound Annual Growth Rate | Number of Countries (Continents[i]) |
|---|---|---|---|---|
| 32. WM Morrison Supermarkets PLC (United Kingdom) (76) | Supermarket | 25,248 | 6.4% | 1 (Eur.) |
| 33. Rite Aid Corporation (United States) (36) | Drug/pharmacy | 25,215 | 7.9% | 1 (N. Am.) |
| 34. Yamada Denki Co., Ltd. (Japan) (73) | Discount department, electronics specialty | 25,193 | 10.9% | 2 (Asia) |
| 35. Publix Super Markets, Inc. (United States) (35) | Convenience/forecourt, supermarket, other specialty | 25,134 | 4.1% | 1 (N. Am.) |
| 36. Macy's, Inc. (United States) (n.l.) | Apparel/footwear specialty, department, nonstore, other specialty | 25,003 | 2.2% | 3 (N. Am., Asia) |
| 37. Delhaize Group SA (Belgium) (30) | Cash and carry/warehouse club, convenience/forecourt, discount, supermarket, other specialty | 24,918 | 1.8% | 7 (N. Am., Asia, Eur.) |
| 38. The TJX Companies, Inc. (United States) (48) | Apparel/footwear specialty, discount | 21,942 | 6.4% | 7 (N. Am., Eur.) |
| 39. Loblaw Companies Limited (Canada) (46) | Apparel/footwear specialty, cash and carry/warehouse club, discount, hypermarket, supercenter, superstore, supermarket | 21,782 | 1.2% | 1 (N. Am.) |
| 40. Migros-Genossenschafts-Bund (Switzerland) (55) | Apparel/footwear specialty, department, discount, electronics specialty, home improvement, hypermarket, supercenter, superstore, supermarket, other specialty | 20,937 | 8.8% | 3 (Eur.) |
| 41. Systeme U Centrale Nationale SA (France) (74) | Convenience/forecourt, hypermarket, supercenter, superstore, supermarket | 20,423 | 5.1% | 3 (Af., Eur., Pac.) |
| 42. Mercadona, S.A. (Spain) (82) | Supermarket | 20,241 | 9.7% | 1 (Eur.) |
| 43. Alimentation Couche-Tard Inc. (Canada) (n.l.) | Convenience/forecourt | 18,966 | 13.3% | 9 (N. Am., Asia.) |

| Company | Formats | | | |
|---|---|---|---|---|
| 44. Kohl's Corporation (United States) (61) | Department | 18,391 | 6.5% | 1 (N. Am.) |
| 45. Grupo P (Brazil) (n.I.) | Cash and carry/warehouse club, convenience/forecourt, electronics specialty, hypermarket, supercenter, superstore, supermarket, nonstore | 18,318 | 19.1% | 1 (S. Am.) |
| 46. J.C. Penney Company, Inc. (United States) (32) | Department, nonstore | 17,759 | −1.1% | 2 (N. Am.) |
| 47. El Corte Ingles (Spain) (44) | Apparel/footwear specialty, convenience/forecourt, department, electronics specialty, home improvement, hypermarket, supercenter, superstore, supermarket, other specialty | 17,336 | 0.4% | 5 (C. Am., Eur.) |
| 48. Coop Group (Switzerland) (66) | Cash and carry/warehouse club, convenience/forecourt, department, drug/pharmacy, electronics specialty, home improvement, hypermarket, supercenter, superstore, supermarket, other specialty | 16,684 | 6.1% | 5 (Eur.) |
| 49. Inditex S.A. (Spain) (n.I.) | Apparel/footwear specialty, other specialty | 16,343 | 13.2% | 79 (Af., N. Am., C. Am., S. Am., Asia, Eur.) |
| 50. H.E. Butt Grocery Company (United States) (57) | Hypermarket, supercenter, superstore, supermarket | 16,100[e] | 5.2% | 2 (N. Am., C. Am.) |
| 51. AS Watson & Company, Inc. (Hong Kong SAR) (94) | Convenience/forecourt, discount, drug/pharmacy, electronics specialty, hypermarket, supercenter, superstore, supermarket, other specialty | 15,857 | 6.8% | 37 (Asia, Eur.) |
| 52. Coop Italia (Italy) (51) | Discount, hypermarket, supercenter, superstore, supermarket | 15,845[e] | 2.4% | 1 (Eur.) |
| 53. Empire Company Limited/Sobeys (Canada) (75) | Convenience/forecourt, drug/pharmacy, hypermarket, supercenter, superstore, supermarket, other specialty | 15,575 | 4.2% | 1 (N. Am.) |
| 54. Meijer, Inc. (United States) (54) | Convenience/forecourt, hypermarket, supercenter, superstore | 15,323[e] | 3.6% | 1 (N. Am.) |
| 55. Marks & Spencer Group Plc (United Kingdom) (45) | Apparel/footwear specialty, convenience/forecourt, department, supermarket, other specialty, nonstore | 15,157 | 4.6% | 39 (Af., Asia, Eur.) |

(continued)

**TABLE 6-1** (continued)

| Retailer by Rank (home country and rank in 2003) | Retail Formats | 2010 Retail Sales (US$ million) | 5-Year Retail Sales Compound Annual Growth Rate | Number of Countries (Continents[j]) |
|---|---|---|---|---|
| 56. LVMH Mo (France) (n.l.) | Apparel/footwear specialty, department, other specialty | 15,085 | 7.5% | 84 (Af., C. Am., N. Am., S. Am., Asia, Eur., Pac.) |
| 57. H & M Hennes & Mauritz AB (Sweden) (n.l.) | Apparel/footwear specialty, other specialty | 15,051 | 12.1% | 38 (Af., N. Am., Asia, Eur.) |
| 58. Groupe Adeo SA (France) (n.l.) | Home improvement | 15,005[e] | 11.4% | 11 (S. Am., Asia, Eur.) |
| 59. Kingfisher plc (United Kingdom) (43) | Home improvement | 14,846 | 4.5% | 8 (Asia, Eur.) |
| 60. PPR SA (France) (n.l.) | Apparel/footwear specialty, other specialty, nonstore | 14,803 | –4.9% | 91 (Af., C. Am., N. Am., S. Am., Asia, Eur., Pac.) |
| 61. Staples, Inc. (United States) (68) | Nonstore, other specialty | 14,696 | 5.7% | 14 (N. Am., S. Am., Asia, Eur., Pac.) |
| 62. The Gap, Inc. (United States) (38) | Apparel/footwear specialty, nonstore | 14,664 | –1.8% | 32 (N. Am., C. Am., S. Am., Asia, Eur.) |
| 63. Louis Delhaize S.A. (Belgium) (62) | Cash and carry/warehouse club, convenience/forecourt, discount, hypermarket, supercenter, superstore, supermarket, other specialty | 14,100[e] | 1.7% | 8 (C. Am., Eur.) |
| 64. Isetan Mitsukoshi Holdings Ltd. (Japan) (88) | Apparel/footwear specialty, department, supermarket, other specialty | 13,933 | ne | 11 (N. Am., Asia, Eur.) |
| 65. Toys "R" Us, Inc. (United States) (52) | Other specialty | 13,864 | 4.2% | 35 (Af., N. Am., Asia, Eur., Pac.) |

200

| Company | Formats | Revenue | Growth | Countries (Region) |
|---|---|---|---|---|
| 66. Bailian (Brilliance) Group(China) (n.l.) | Convenience/forecourt, department, home improvement, hypermarket, supercenter, superstore, supermarket | 13,344$^e$ | 7.5% | 1 (Asia) |
| 67. Otto (GmbH & Co KG) (formerly Otto Versand) (Germany) (53) | Apparel/footwear specialty, nonstore, other specialty | 13,203 | 1.4% | 32 (N. Am., Asia, Eur., Pac.) |
| 68. Dollar General Corp. (United States) (89) | Discount | 13,035 | 8.7% | 1 (N. Am.) |
| 69. Co-operative Group Ltd. (United Kingdom) (n.l.) | Convenience/forecourt, drug/pharmacy, supermarket | 12,957 | 20.1% | 1 (Eur.) |
| 70. ICA AB (Sweden) (n.l.) | Convenience/forecourt, discount, hypermarket, supercenter, superstore, supermarket | 12,818 | 7.1% | 5 (Eur.) |
| 71. Dixons Retail plc (formerly DSG International plc)(United Kingdom) (56) | Electronics specialty, nonstore | 12,738 | 4.3% | 28 (Eur.) |
| 72. UNY Co., Ltd. (Japan) (63) | Apparel/footwear specialty, convenience/forecourt, department, discount, home improvement, hypermarket, supercenter, superstore, supermarket | 12,635 | −1.7% | 2 (Asia) |
| 73. Dell Inc.(United States) (65) | Nonstore | 12,357 | 0.3% | 180 (Global) |
| 74. Conad Consorzio Nazionale, Dettaglianti Soc. Coop. a.r.l (Italy) (n.l.) | Cash and carry/warehouse, hypermarket, supercenter, superstore, supermarket | 12,170 | 5.8% | 2 (Eur.) |
| 75. Gome Home Appliance Group (China) (n.l.) | Electronics specialty, other specialty | 12,042$^e$ | 21.8% | 2 (Asia) |
| 76. SPAR (Austria) (n.l.) | Convenience/forecourt, hypermarket, supercenter, superstore, supermarket, other specialty | 12,011$^e$ | 6.7% | 7 (Eur.) |
| 77. Alliance Boots GmbH (Switzerland) (n.l.) | Drug/pharmacy, other specialty | 11,859 | 9.0% | 17 (Asia, Eur.) |
| 78. Cencosud S.A. (Chile) (n.l.) | Cash and carry/warehouse, department, drug/ pharmacy, electronics specialty, home improvement, hypermarket, supercenter, superstore, supermarket | 11,791 | 20.2% | 5 (S. Am.) |

(continued)

**TABLE 6-1** (continued)

| Retailer by Rank (home country and rank in 2003) | Retail Formats | 2010 Retail Sales (US$ million) | 5-Year Retail Sales Compound Annual Growth Rate | Number of Countries (Continents[i]) |
|---|---|---|---|---|
| 79. Lotte Shopping Co., Ltd. (S. Korea) (80) | Apparel/footwear specialty, department, hypermarket, supercenter, superstore, supermarket | 11,487 | 9.2% | 5 (Asia, Eur.) |
| 80. John Lewis Partnership plc (United Kingdom) (85) | Convenience/forecourt, department, hypermarket, supercenter, superstore, supermarket, nonstore | 11,359 | 7.4% | 2 (Asia, Eur.) |
| 81. Jer (Portugal) (n.l.) | Cash and carry/warehouse club, discount, drug/pharmacy, hypermarket, supercenter, superstore, supermarket, other specialty | 11,317 | 19.0% | 2 (Eur.) |
| 82. Shinsegae Co., Ltd. (S. Korea) (n.l.) | Cash and carry/warehouse club, department, hypermarket, supercenter, superstore, supermarket | 11,314 | 9.8% | 2 (Asia) |
| 83. X5 Retail Group N.V.(Russia) (n.l.) | Convenience/forecourt, discount, hypermarket, supercenter, superstore, supermarket | 11,264 | ne | 2 (Eur.) |
| 84. Suning Appliance Co. Ltd. (China) (n.l.) | Electronics specialty, other specialty | 11,170 | 36.5% | 3 (Asia) |
| 85. S Group (Finland) (92.) | Apparel/footwear specialty, convenience/forecourt, department, discount, home improvement, hypermarket, supercenter, superstore, supermarket, other specialty | 11,007 | 9.9% | 5 (Eur.) |
| 86. Metro Inc. (Canada) (n.l.) | Convenience/forecourt, drug/pharmacy, hypermarket, supercenter, superstore, supermarket | 10,896 | 11.1% | 1 (N. Am.) |
| 87. BJ's Wholesale Club, Inc. (United States) (n.l.) | Cash and carry/warehouse club | 10,633 | 6.4% | 1 (N. Am.) |
| 88. Tengelmann Warenhandelsgesellschaft KG (Germany) (21) | Apparel/footwear specialty, discount, home improvement, supermarket | 10,599[e] | −18.1% | 14 (Eur.) |
| 89. Dansk Supermarked A/S (Denmark) (n.l.) | Apparel/footwear specialty, department, discount, hypermarket, supercenter, superstore, supermarket | 10,563 | 3.2% | 5 (Eur.) |

| Company | Merchandise categories | Revenue | Revenue growth | Countries (continents) |
|---|---|---|---|---|
| 90. The Daiei, Inc. (Japan) (n.l.) | Apparel/footwear specialty, department, discount, hypermarket, supercenter, superstore, supermarket, other specialty | 10,415 | −7.9% | 1 (Asia) |
| 91. Kesko Corporation (Finland) (90) | Apparel/footwear specialty, department, electronics specialty, home improvement, hypermarket, supercenter, superstore, supermarket, other specialty | 10,356 | 4.0% | 8 (Eur.) |
| 92. Shoprite Holdings Ltd. (S. Africa) (84) | Cash and carry/warehouse club, convenience/forecourt, discount, electronics specialty, hypermarket, supercenter, superstore, supermarket, other specialty | 10,279 | 16.7% | 16 (Af.) |
| 93. Shoppers Drug Mart Corporation (Canada) (n.l.) | Drug/pharmacy, other specialty | 10,075 | 7.1% | 1 (N. Am.) |
| 94. J. Front Retailing Co., Ltd. (Japan) (n.l.) | Department, supermarket | 9,866 | ne | 1 (Asia) |
| 95. Apple Inc./Retail (Apple Stores) (United States) (n.l.) | Electronics specialty | 9,798 | 33.1% | 11 (N. Am., Asia, Eur., Pac.) |
| 96. Limited Brands, Inc. (United States) (69) | Apparel/footwear specialty, nonstore, other specialty | 9,613 | −0.2% | 45 (Af., N. Am., C. Am., S. Am., Eur., Asia) |
| 97. GameStop Corp. (United States) (n.l.) | Other specialty | 9,474 | 25.1% | 18 (N. Am., Eur., Pac.) |
| 98. Grupo Eroski (Spain) (n.l.) | Cash and carry/warehouse club, convenience/forecourt, discount, hypermarket, supercenter, superstore, supermarket, other specialty | 9,437[e] | 6.6% | 3 (Eur.) |
| 99. Reitan Group (Norway) (n.l.) | Convenience/forecourt, discount, electronics | 9,420 | 16.2% | 4 (Eur.) |
| 100. Takashimaya Company, Limited (Japan) (72) | Department | 9,398 | −3.6% | 3 (Asia) |

*Source:* "2011 Top 250 Global Retailers," *Stores,* January 2012, available at http://www.stores.org.

*Notes:* Continents are abbreviated as follows: Af. = Africa; N. Am. = North America; C. Am. = Central America; S. Am. = South America; Asia = Asia; Eur. = Europe; Pac. = Pacific (Australia, New Zealand).

n.l. = not listed in top 100 retailers in 2003.

n/a = not available.

ne = not in existence (created by merger or divestiture).

[e] = estimate.

## RETAIL POSITIONING STRATEGIES

When a retailer chooses its positioning strategy, it must do so with a recognition of the significant potential effects on its competitiveness and performance. Having determined these effects, it can select specific cost-side and demand-side characteristics. For example, on the cost side, a retailer might focus on its margin and inventory turnover goals. On the demand side, the retailer needs to determine which service outputs to provide its shoppers. We discuss each of these issues in turn and then summarize our discussion by detailing how these choices helps shape the retailer's overall strategy.

### Cost-Side Positioning Strategies

In a high-service retailing system, **margins** are higher, but **turnover** (i.e., the number of times inventory on the shelf turns over in a specified period, usually a year) is lower. In low-price retailing systems, the opposite holds: low margins, high inventory turnover, and minimal service levels. Although the retail marketplace is filled with both types, most recent excitement and attention has focused on the revolutionary volume efficiencies achieved by the advanced practitioners of low-price retailing systems (e.g., Wal-Mart, Home Depot), which not only attain low margins and high turnover but also add in pretty great service. They are largely able to pay for such expensive service provision because of the high rates of return on their investments they earn by always improving their asset management using sophisticated information systems.

Historically, the low-margin/high-turnover model sought high operational efficiency so that it could pass any savings on to the customer. But as our channel perspective has taught us, passing savings on to the customer actually entails a *transfer* of costs (i.e., opportunity and effort costs), rather than their elimination. A consumer who shops at Costco, Sam's Club, or Carrefour may gain the benefit of a lower price but pays for it by taking on channel functions, such as bulk breaking, transportation from a less convenient location, and higher self-service levels. This operational philosophy, such that the retailer trades off its margin and its turnover, reflects the recognition that certain segments of consumers are willing to absorb certain costs for some of their purchasing behaviors. But if consumers remain unwilling to trade off lower service levels (i.e., take on more channel functions themselves) for lower prices, retailers need to avoid such low-price, low-margin retail operations.

At the same time, lowering operational costs does not always require lowering the levels of *all* service outputs. Fashion-forward clothing retailers such as Zara and H&M offer end-users up-to-date assortments (i.e., excellent assortment and variety) and quick delivery of the hottest new styles but still hold costs down and thus can also provide competitive prices. Sidebars 6-1 and 6-2 highlight the different ways these two retailers have built their channel systems to meet these seemingly contradictory goals: Zara uses a highly vertically integrated path, whereas H&M relies on much more outsourcing. As long as the retailers hold their costs down, either method seems feasible.

Of critical importance in determining whether the retail strategy should emphasize the low margins and high turnover or else seek high margins at low turnover,

## Sidebar 6-1

### Zara: A European retailer using the low-margin, high-turnover model of retailing

Zara was founded in Spain in 1975, and in the three decades of its existence, it has built and fine-tuned a particular model of retailing that appears to balance the need to control costs with the need to meet the demands of its fashion-forward, trendy target market.

Zara's target consumer in Europe is a fashion-conscious, young, female buyer of clothing who values novelty and exclusivity but is also quite price sensitive. The most important service output demands of this consumer are therefore *assortment and variety* (which should be extensive and novel) and *quick delivery* (i.e., extremely fashion forward and available to buy). Providing a quickly changing, market-responsive assortment of reasonably priced, fashion-forward clothing has long been one of the thorniest challenges for retailers. Zara has met this challenge through a combination of strategies:

- It makes 40 percent of its own fabric and owns its own dyeing company, which permits it to buy undyed fabric from outsiders and postpone coloring fabric until it knows what colors are really popular in a given season.
- It owns its own production for more than 50 percent of its clothes, thus retaining control over production from start to finish.
- It concentrates all of its owned production and warehousing in one area, in Galicia in northern Spain.
- It purposely makes small amounts of product at a time, rather than large batch volumes.
- It owns its own logistics and trucking operations, which in some cases may mean sending a half-empty truck through Europe.
- It has invested in significant communications capabilities, from the store manager level back to the designers, from designers to production, from production to warehousing, and from the warehouse back to retail stores.
- It sticks to a rigid reordering, production, and shipping schedule that makes restocking stores extremely predictable to everyone in the system, including consumers.

- It favors introducing new styles over restocking styles it has already shipped once and has invested in an extremely flexible manufacturing operation to permit this approach.

These policies actually contradict many practices throughout retailing today—from the highly vertically integrated set of operations Zara pursues, to the rigid controls it exerts throughout its logistics and ordering systems, to its small-batch production practices, to the constant revamping of product lines in the stores. So how can Zara possibly make money with such a topsy-turvy retailing system?

The answer lies in its apparently high-cost methods of operation, which actually *maximize turnover and save costs* in other parts of its business. Because Zara has invested in significant amounts of communication at all levels of its business (which is also possible because of its investments in vertical integration), designers at headquarters learn about new "hot" styles mid-season, before any of Zara's competitors are able to see the trends and respond to them. With its flexible manufacturing operations, its well-integrated clothing designers can work closely with manufacturing operations to create cutting-edge designs and feed them to manufacturing with no delay. It also is more feasible to respond to this information, because Zara has chosen *not* to make large batch volumes of any styles it innovates; thus, it has the space in the stores to accommodate new styles. Furthermore, it does not suffer from large overstocks and thus does not need to mark down merchandise as heavily as its competitors do. That is, it never produces large volumes of any style, and it only produces styles for which it has market-level indications of demand.

Because Zara actually cultivates slack (i.e., unused) capacity in its factories and warehouse, it can accommodate rush jobs that would cause bottlenecks in standard retail systems. And because Zara's consumers *know* that Zara is constantly coming out with new styles (as well as *exactly when* the stores are restocked), they shop more often (particularly right after a new shipment comes in), to keep up with the new styles. For example, a shopper in London visits a standard clothing store (where she shops routinely)

## Continued

about 4 times per year; the same shopper visits a Zara store 17 times per year! The Zara shopper feels a certain urgency to buy a garment when she sees it at the store, because she may not be able to find it again if she waits to get it. This increases sales rates and merchandise turnover.

So what are the results of Zara's retailing strategy?

1. Zara has almost no inventories in its system:
   - An item sits in its warehouse only a few *hours* on average (not days or weeks!).
   - Store deliveries occur (on schedule) twice per week to each store in the system, worldwide.
   - Most items turn over in less than one week (significantly less than its competitors' inventory turn rates).
2. Zara can create a new design, manufacture it, and have it on its stores' shelves in just *two weeks*, versus 9–12 *months* for other retailers (e.g., The Gap, VF Corporation).
3. Zara's shipments are 98.9 percent accurate, and it enjoys a very low shrinkage rate of 0.5 percent (i.e., loss of inventory due to theft or damage).
4. Its designers bring over 10,000 new designs to market (versus 2,000–4,000 items introduced by The Gap or H&M) each year.

5. Zara maintains net profit margins of about 10 percent annually, as good as the best retailers in the business, even though its prices are fairly low.
6. It does little advertising, spending only 0.3 percent of sales on ads, versus the more typical 3–4 percent of sales for its competitors. It does not need to spend on advertising, because its shoppers are in the stores so many times a year that there is no need for advertising to remind them to come.
7. On average, Zara collects 85 percent of list price on its clothing items, versus an industry average of only 60–70 percent (including markdowns). This rate leads to higher net margins; in one year, Zara's net margin was 10.5 percent, H&M's was 9.5 percent, Benetton's was 7 percent, and The Gap's was 0 percent.

In short, Zara's formula for success rests on its highly centralized control, all the way from its input sourcing (dyes, fabrics), to design, to logistics and shipping, and finally to retailing. Given the high cost of owning all of these resources, Zara has to maximize the value created from them—which it does very well, by excelling at meeting the core service output demands of its target market, namely, novel and extensive variety and assortment, quickly.[3]

management must arrive at its best estimates of the organization's best chance for achieving its financial targets. Such estimates can stem from a **strategic profit model (SPM)**,[4] which states:

$$\frac{\text{net profit}}{\text{net sales}} \times \frac{\text{net sales}}{\text{total assets}} = \frac{\text{net profit}}{\text{total assets}}, \text{ and}$$

$$\frac{\text{net profit}}{\text{total assets}} \times \frac{\text{total assets}}{\text{net worth}} = \frac{\text{net profit}}{\text{net worth}}.$$

Thus:

$$\frac{\text{net profit}}{\text{net sales}} \times \frac{\text{net sales}}{\text{total assets}} \times \frac{\text{total assets}}{\text{net worth}} = \frac{\text{net profit}}{\text{net worth}}.$$

That is, a retailer seeks to manage its margins (net profit/net sales), its asset turnover (net sales/total assets), and/or its financial leverage (total assets/net worth) in its

## Sidebar 6-2

### H&M: Another low-margin, high-turnover European retailer, with a different channel strategy

In contrast to Zara in Sidebar 6-1, consider the strategy of H&M, an international retailer founded in 1947 in Sweden. Like Zara, it sells "cheap chic" clothing, and its core consumer is similar to Zara's (though its stores also offer men's, teens', and children's clothing). The average price of an item in H&M in 2002 was just $18, and shoppers look there for current-season fashions at bargain prices.

H&M's formula for offering this assortment to its consumers at aggressively low prices is somewhat different than Zara's, however. H&M does not own any manufacturing capacity, relying on outsourcing relationships with a network of 900 suppliers located in low-wage countries like Bangladesh, China, and Turkey. It frequently shifts production from one supplier to another, depending on demand in the market for various fabrics, styles, and fashions. All of H&M's merchandise is designed in-house by a cadre of 95 designers in Stockholm (Zara has about 300 designers, all at its headquarters in Spain). The management style is extremely frugal; not only does the company control manufacturing costs, but its managers do not fly business class, and try not to take cabs when traveling.

H&M focuses on minimizing inventory everywhere in its system. It has the ability to create a new

design and get it into stores in as little as three weeks (a bit longer than Zara, but still extremely impressive, given industry norms). It restocks stores on a daily basis, which is not always frequent enough; when it opened its flagship store in New York City, it had to restock on an *hourly* basis. Because its merchandise turns very quickly, it can charge very low prices for it yet maintain good profitability.

H&M has chosen a more aggressive store growth strategy than Zara, which has caused it some problems in recent years. Its entry into the United States was plagued by poor location choices, as well as leases for stores that were too big. It worked on these problems and reached a breakeven point in the United States in 2004.

Whether the H&M-style model—farming out production to third parties and ruthlessly cutting costs everywhere in the system—or the Zara model—purposely cultivating slack capacity and investing in highly flexible but vertically integrated facilities—will dominate is not at all clear. It is entirely possible that both will flourish in the future, as both have well-integrated systems in place that meet the needs of the market, albeit in different ways.[5]

efforts to secure a target return on its net worth (net profit/net worth). (Net sales are gross sales less customer returns and allowances.) If competition or economic conditions exert strong downward pressures on margins, management instead can pursue asset turnover, using more appropriate designs that improve sales per square foot (which reflects space and location productivity), sales per employee (labor productivity), or sales per transaction (merchandising program productivity).

Specific to the retail context, three interrelated performance measures further suggest ways for retailers to improve their profitability (see also Appendix 6-1). First, **gross margin return on inventory investment (GMROI)** is equal to the gross margin percentage, multiplied by the ratio of sales to inventory (at cost). This combination of margin management and inventory management can be calculated for companies, markets, stores, departments, classes of products, or stockkeeping units (SKUs). With the GMROI, the retailer can evaluate its performance according to the return it earns on its investments into inventory. Several tactics in turn have emerged to use this information to improve inventory returns. For example, efficient consumer response (ECR) initiatives in the grocery industry seek to reduce average inventory levels while maintaining sales by relying on just-in-time shipments, electronic data interchange (EDI) linkages between manufacturers and retailers, and the like. Such actions reduce the GMROI denominator without changing the numerator.

However, GMROI suffers a few notable limitations. Items with widely varying gross margin percentages appear equally profitable, as in the following example.

|   | Gross Margin | × | Sales-to-Inventory Ratio | = | GMROI |
|---|---|---|---|---|---|
| A | 50% | × | 3 | = | 150% |
| B | 30% | × | 5 | = | 150% |
| C | 25% | × | 6 | = | 150% |

The gross margin only accounts for the cost of goods sold, not for differences in the variable costs associated with selling different kinds of merchandise. Other measures that include more comprehensive measures tend to be more difficult to derive though.

Second, when it comes to the **gross margin per full-time equivalent employee (GMROL)**, retailers' goals are to *optimize*, not maximize. As sales per square foot rise, some fixed costs (e.g., rent, utilities, advertising) might not increase but rather might even decline as a percentage of sales. Imagine, for example, that a retailer stocks up on inventory before the busy holiday shopping season. By also hiring some additional salespeople to help out in December, it suffers lower average sales per employee, but profitability still jumps, because these additional employees are better able to facilitate sales, by getting the new inventory onto the sales floor faster and leveraging other fixed assets (e.g., opening all the checkout lines, making sure displays are clean and uncluttered) in the store. Of course, during conventional sales periods, comparisons across companies still can reveal that one achieves better GMROL than others.

Third, the **gross margin per square foot (GMROS)** supports an assessment of how well retailers use a unique and powerful asset: the shelf or floor space that they agree to allocate to manufacturers' products.

Retailers' use of such gross margin measures exerts pressure on suppliers, which need to find a way to secure sufficient margins for retailers, earned through their brands. Those margins depend on the sales volume their brands generate, the amount of shelf or floor space consumed by their brands, and the costs incurred to store, handle, and sell their brands.

In response, upstream channel members increasingly seek to speed up inventory replenishment steps, because replenishing stocks more quickly means the retailer can devote less costly shelf space to the frequently replenished items, as well as suffer fewer inventory holding costs. Although related *fixed-cost* investments, such as inventory management systems, eventually reduce marginal costs, they can be difficult to introduce into the channel, because the various channel partners have to bear their substantial costs upfront. For example, Michaels Craft Stores, the leading craft retailer worldwide, tried to start small by educating suppliers about the benefits of incorporating bar coding, common SKU numbers, computerized labels, and electronic invoicing into the channel. Yet suppliers—often small, local, artisanal organizations—resisted the initial costs of incorporating such technologies into their relatively noncomputerized businesses.[6] Such resistance might reflect two key problems. First, the channel partner might not *understand* the marginal cost savings it (and the channel overall) ultimately will accrue by making immediate fixed-cost investments in improved technologies. Second, if various members of the channel do not *trust* the channel manager, they may suspect opportunism, such that their high upfront costs might generate benefits only for one member of the channel. The former problem requires expertise power to educate channel partners about the cost reduction benefits; the latter demands more investments in conflict reduction and trust building.

Finally, we need to consider the effects of one other major retailing cost and its implications for retail strategy choices, namely, the rent that bricks-and-mortar stores pay their landlords. In shopping malls for example, the largest "anchor" stores generate disproportionate benefits for the developer, because they attract shoppers who also patronize other stores in the mall. In return, according to one study, they pay a significantly lower rental rates (up to 72 percent lower per square foot!) than non-anchor stores.[7] Such subsidies even persist despite the generally lower sales per square foot that anchor stores generate, compared with specialty and other smaller stores. Thus, the economics of a retail store, which inform its strategic position choices, depend on internal cost factors but also on the cost factors determined by the retail environment in which the store functions.

## Demand-Side Positioning Strategies

Every retailer would love to earn higher margins and higher merchandise turnover and lower retailing costs. But this ideal combination is likely impossible; instead, retailers combine these variables strategically in their various efforts to attain approximately equitable financial outcomes. Beyond these decisions then, the retailer must consider what service outputs it will supply to make the best use of its combination of characteristics and appeal effectively to its chosen target market.

**BULK BREAKING**   This function is classically the provenance of a retail intermediary. Manufacturers make huge batches of products; consumers want to consume just one unit. Therefore, traditional, service-oriented retailers buy in large quantities and offer the consumer exactly the quantity they want. Some grocery retailers even go beyond conventional bulk breaking. They first separate the pallets of eggs they receive into individual, one-dozen cartons for customers. But they also might allow customers to break the dozen-egg bundle into smaller portions, based on their needs.

Other retailers, such as warehouse stores (e.g., Sam's Club, Costco), offer consumers a lower price but require them to buy larger lot sizes (i.e., break bulk less). Consumers whose transportation, storage, and financing costs already are relatively low may choose to buy a case of paper towels or ten-pound bags of frozen vegetables at lower per unit prices (though they must expend more monetary costs upfront). More traditional grocery retailers also often encourage, but not force, larger lot-size purchases through special pricing, such as "buy one, get one free" deals or bundle pricing (e.g., "three for $1").

On the other end of this trend are the so-called dollar stores, which offer very small quantities of products at very low prices. Thus, a consumer can purchase a small bottle of dishwashing detergent or a package of two or three cookies. The unit price on these items is higher than in other retailers, but consumers enjoy the benefits of massive bulk breaking, which is particularly valuable if the consumer is unable or unwilling to perform financing or inventory holding channel functions.

**SPATIAL CONVENIENCE**    Recall from our discussion in Chapter 5 that products can be classified as convenience, shopping, or specialty goods, and this categorization depends on the extent of search or shopping activity the consumer is willing to undertake. To determine its positioning strategy, a retailer must recall that convenience goods should require little effort to obtain, whereas considerable effort may be required to secure highly regarded, relatively scarce specialty goods. *The retail location decision, and the resulting service output of spatial convenience, thus is inextricable from the type of goods the retailer chooses to offer.* As a general rule, retail locations should be convenient to their target market, a lesson that H&M might have forgotten for its introduction to the United States (see Sidebar 6-2), when it chose suburban locations in New Jersey and Syracuse, New York.

Furthermore, the balance of search/shopping behavior, and thus demand for spatial convenience, varies across consumer segments and with changing demographic and lifestyle trends. Households in which all the adults work face higher opportunity costs for time, such that the effective cost of searches and shopping increases. Thus, one shopper might be impressed with the service offerings of a SuperTarget store (i.e., a format that includes both food and nonfood items) in her area—though not quite impressed enough to overcome the lack of spatial convenience it offers. Because it is farther away than her local grocery store, "It won't replace my weekly grocery store trip."[8] In contrast, Walgreen's drug and convenience store chain purposefully seeks out locations that are conveniently on consumers' usual shopping paths, often finding sites near major grocery stores. By adding service offerings that decrease the average transaction time in the store to 14 minutes, Walgreen's also increases the chances that a shopper will get a parking space close to the store, another form of spatial convenience.[9]

**WAITING AND DELIVERY TIME**    Consumers differ in their willingness to tolerate out-of-stock situations when they shop; even the same consumer exhibits differential willingness across different purchase occasions. Intense demand for this channel function translates into a demand that a product be in stock at all times, which in turn means retailers must take on more of the expensive inventory holding function, by holding extra safety stocks in their stores. To fine-tune its strategy, each retailer must gauge how damaging an out-of-stock occurrence would be. Most grocery retailers make it a high priority to avoid out-of-stock situations for basic products, such as milk or bread, but may feel more confident about running out of an exotic, perishable, specialty fruit. For a furniture retailer, in-store stocks tend to be so low that consumers seeking to purchase likely would not expect to take their desired sofa home with them and instead anticipate waiting (up to 8–12 weeks) to receive delivery (which implies that they trade off long wait times for better delivery service outputs).

Not every combination of waiting and delivery service outputs represents such a clear trade-off though. One furniture manufacturer, England Inc., refigured its manufacturing operations to be able to build 11,000 upholstered sofas and chairs per week, each made to order, for delivery to consumers within three weeks of their order. This speed greatly diminishes the wait time required by its traditional competitors, but it does so without requiring consumers to give up delivery capacity (or assortment and variety services), as they would have to do if they purchased a ready-made sofa from Wal-Mart or another alternative source. By improving both service outputs, England has enjoyed strong sales performance.[10] This provision suggests changing competitive norms in the marketplace as well. When competitors improve their provision of a key service output, the old performance norms may be insufficient to keep consumers loyal, such that constant updates to the retail strategy become necessary. When Lowe's and Home Depot promised quicker delivery of the large appliances on their showroom floors, Sears had little choice but to try to keep pace with next- or same-day delivery offers.[11]

Other retailers continue to deviate purposefully from standard competitive norms, expressly to establish unique retail positions in the market. Zara's planned stock-out policies (see Sidebar 6-1) have served to both minimize inventory holding costs and create consumer excitement and urgency to purchase. Discount club retailers offer no guarantee of in-stock status, so if consumers find their preferred brand of fabric softener on the shelves, they know they had better purchase immediately. Otherwise, they may be forced to wait a long (and perhaps more critically, *unpredictable*) amount of time before finding the product in the store again. A very brand-loyal consumer finds this scenario intolerable, but "treasure hunters" love the prospect of finding a one-of-a-kind item on sale at Costco, never to be seen again on its shelves.

**PRODUCT VARIETY**    **Variety** describes different classes of goods that constitute the product offering, that is, the *breadth* of the product lines. **Assortment** instead refers to the *depth* of product brands or models offered within each generic product category. Discounters such as Target and Wal-Mart offer limited assortments of fast-moving, low-priced items across a wide variety of goods; a specialty store dealing in only, or primarily, home audiovisual electronic goods, such as Tweeter, instead stocks a very large and complete line of a smaller variety of items, offering the deepest assortment of models, styles, sizes, prices, and so on.

Sometimes a retailer's variety and assortment choice is purposefully narrow, to appeal to a particular niche (e.g., pregnant women shopping at maternity clothing stores, as we discussed in Chapter 5). If such a retail concept saturates the market though, further attempts at growth are challenging, as Gymboree learned. The upscale children's clothes stores, located mainly in malls, had to expand into different **store concepts**, rather than trying to extend its own specific assortment or variety. To start, it began opening Janie and Jack stores that could sell a specific assortment of upscale baby gifts. In addition, it plans to advance into an array of related but distinct retail concepts in coming years, allowing the corporate channel to increase both its assortment and its variety, while leaving these factors consistent in each store line.[12] In so doing, it also needs to beware of several pitfalls: avoid cannibalization of the core retail concept while still exploiting its knowledge of the retailing concepts that made it successful to begin.

The variety and assortment dimension clearly demands the careful and strategic attention of top management, because these decisions determine the entire character of the enterprise. After the basic strategy has been established though, the task of choosing *specific* products or brands usually falls to the buyers. **Buyers** play a central role in retailing; some retailers even generate more profits through the trade deals and allowances that their buyers negotiate than they earn through their merchandising efforts. Because buying is such a critical aspect of retailing, it is important to understand the evaluative processes and procedures involved in merchandise and supplier selection. The appendices to this chapter seek to improve such understanding: Appendix 6-1 is a glossary of pricing and buying terms commonly used by retailers, and Appendix 6-2 briefly describes some of their merchandise planning and control procedures.

**CUSTOMER SERVICE**  Virtually all major retail innovations in the past century have relied on manipulating the customer service variable, to greater or lesser degrees. Consider in-store sales help for example. In warehouse clubs that have eliminated expert sales clerks who can help customers locate and compare the various personal computers on offer, the locate–compare–select process becomes the consumer's responsibility. But in Apple stores, the resident Geniuses provide not only detailed, extensive advice about the products for sale but also postsales service, to the extent they will transfer data from the customer's old computer to his or her new Mac while the customer waits.

Retailing is one of the few industries that remains highly labor intensive. **Sales, general, and administrative (SG&A)** expenses for retailers thus must include the cost of keeping salespeople on the floor to help shoppers. As a percentage of net sales, SG&A tends to be higher for specialty stores (e.g., Ann Taylor, The Gap) and department stores (e.g., Nordstrom) than for office supply or drug stores (e.g., Walgreen's). The retailers with the lowest SG&A percentages are general merchandise retailers and hypermarkets (e.g., Costco, Wal-Mart).

Table 6-2 summarizes the net sales, SG&A expenses, and SG&A-to-net sales percentages for several stores in each category. As these data show, providing better service is a costly function for retailers. Lower service retailers such as Costco appear to compensate the consumer for the lack of service provision, with lower costs. On the flip side, a higher SG&A percentage for Ann Taylor or Chico's may be entirely consistent with the very high level of in-store service that its salespeople offer, such that the retailer is able to charge commensurately higher prices. However, it appears somewhat disconcerting when a retailer that adopts a low service strategy also features a high SG&A percentage, as is the case for JCPenney.

These variations reflect the costs of customer service, but also its remarkable benefits. Many retailers continue to invest in customer service because it can bring about these substantial benefits. Consider a seemingly humble example: the provision of shopping carts in retail stores. Carts are common in grocery stores, as well as in mass merchandisers or hypermarkets. But apparel retailers generally resist them as inconsistent with their images, especially for high-end offerings such as Nordstrom offers. At the same time, shoppers in mass market retail outlets buy an average of 7.2 items when using a cart, compared with only 6.1 items without a cart. A department store shopper with a child in the cart's seat, another child hanging onto the cart's handle, and multiple, bulky boxes of children's shoes in the basket seems highly likely to appreciate this service offering! Furthermore, this relatively small investment (each cart costs about $100) generates substantial consumer service benefits for broad segments of shoppers,[13] because it removes the costs of performing a channel function from consumers' shoulders.

In all these demand-based dimensions of retailing strategy, the goal thus is to identify the functions that consumers are (or are not) willing to assume. With that information, the retailer can select its positioning and calculate the cost—in time, money, effort, and convenience—of taking on additional service output functions if doing so might make it more attractive to consumers.

## Taxonomy of Retail Positioning Strategies

The cost-side and demand-side dimensions give retailers a wide variety of possibilities for positioning their retail operations, though the positioning strategy they choose should always be driven primarily by the demands of the target market for their specific

**TABLE 6-2**  Sales, general, & administrative (SG&A) costs as a percentage of net sales for selected retailers

| | Net Sales ($million) | SG&A Expenses ($million) | SG&A as % of Net Sales |
|---|---|---|---|
| **General Merchandise, Hypermarkets, Category Killers** | | | |
| Wal-Mart | 443,854 | 85,265 | 19.2 |
| Costco | 87,048 | 8,682 | 9.9 |
| Home Depot | 67,997 | 15,849 | 22.8 |
| Target | 68,466 | 14,106 | 20.1 |
| Lowe's | 50,208 | 12,593 | 25.1 |
| **Drugs, Home Electronics** | | | |
| Walgreen | 71,633 | 16,878 | 23.6 |
| Best Buy | 50,705 | 10,242 | 20.2 |
| **Department Stores** | | | |
| Kohl's | 18,804 | 4,243 | 22.6 |
| JCPenney | 17,260 | 5,109 | 29.6 |
| Nordstrom | 10,497 | 2,807 | 26.7 |
| Dillard's | 6,264 | 1,630 | 26.0 |
| **Specialty Stores** | | | |
| The Gap | 14,549 | 3,836 | 26.4 |
| Ann Taylor | 2,212 | 1,062 | 48.0 |
| Chico's | 2,196 | 999 | 45.5 |

*Source:* Annual reports for 2011/2012 for each company. Depending on the company's fiscal year end, 2011 or 2012 figures are used.

service outputs. Thus, a high-cost, high-service retail strategy that works perfectly well in an affluent neighborhood could be a grave mistake in an area populated by less wealthy consumers who cannot afford to consume high service levels at high prices. Furthermore, such decisions involve more than just offering generically high service output levels. Within a certain intensity of demand, variations nearly always influence the importance granted to specific service outputs. Thus, as we described previously in this chapter, some furniture retailers can offer broader variety and assortment, at the cost of longer waiting and delivery times, while others offer a somewhat curtailed product line that they can deliver to the consumer more quickly. And price is nearly invariably an arbiter of the system. Higher service output levels can be offered only at higher price levels, because of the costs involved in producing these service outputs. Retailers are thus always constrained by the target consumer's overall willingness to pay, in deciding what services to offer and which to drop.

Table 6-3 characterizes different classes of retailers by their cost- and demand-side positioning strategies. The differences across them allow for the presence of multiple types of retail outlets, selling the same physical merchandise, such as consumer

**TABLE 6-3  A taxonomy of retailer types**

| Retailer Type | Main Focus on Margin or Turnover? | Bulk Breaking | Spatial Convenience | Waiting and Delivery Time | Variety (Breadth) | Assortment (Depth) |
|---|---|---|---|---|---|---|
| Department store (e.g., May Co.) | Margin | Yes | Moderate | Low wait time | Broad | Moderate/Shallow |
| Specialty store (e.g., The Gap) | Margin | Yes | Moderate | Low wait time | Narrow | Deep |
| Mail order/catalog (e.g., Lands' End) | Margin | Yes | Extremely high | Moderate/high wait time | Narrow | Moderate |
| Convenience store (e.g., 7-Eleven) | Both | Yes | Very high | Low wait time | Broad | Shallow |
| Category killer (e.g., Best Buy) | Turnover | Yes | Moderate | Low wait time | Narrow | Deep |
| Mass merchandiser (e.g., Wal-Mart) | Turnover | Yes | Low | Moderate wait time (may be out of stock) | Broad | Shallow |
| Hypermarket (e.g., Carrefour) | Turnover | Yes | Low | Moderate wait time | Broad | Moderate |
| Warehouse club (e.g., Sam's Club) | Turnover | No | Low | Moderate/high wait time (may be out of stock) | Broad | Shallow |

electronics. Tweeter is an electronics **specialty store**, whereas Best Buy is a **category killer**. Both break bulk, reduce consumers' waiting time (i.e., few out-of-stocks), and carry a narrow variety (electronics) together with a deep assortment (many makes and types of products), but few consumers would confuse the two stores. Tweeter focuses on high margin rather than high turnover as a key to its profitability, along with slightly lower spatial convenience on average (because it has fewer stores than Best Buy). Similar comparisons across the rows of Table 6-3 suggest that by making choices on these dimensions, a store creates its position in the marketplace and can survive, even in the face of competition with seemingly similar sets of products and consumers.

## MULTICHANNEL RETAIL STRATEGIES

Consumers are increasingly comfortable with buying through multiple channels and types of outlets, such that their purchase behavior varies not just by segment but also by purchase occasion.[14] Some consumers like to browse through bricks-and-mortar bookstores, because they hope to stumble on a surprise and enjoy a cup of coffee while they review book jackets. Another segment of consumers prefers to order books through Amazon, because their tastes are so unique that they are unlike to find their favorite texts in a regular store. Other consumers have eliminated traditional books from their reading habits altogether, downloading everything they read through Kindle. And yet other consumers practice "hybrid shopping," using online, bricks-and-mortar, and electronic versions of products to complete their shopping process, perhaps by browsing the bookstore on their way home to find a new novel, checking prices on Amazon, and then selecting the Kindle or paperback version, whichever is less expensive, for their final purchase.

This broad array of shopping behaviors means that designing a retail strategy involves careful consideration of the entire process the consumer undergoes, which eventually may culminate in a sale. But the firm needs to be present in many more channel locations before it gets to that point. In this section, we consider some new locations in the retail channel, including current uses of the Internet as a retail outlet and retail facilitator, direct selling as an alternative mode to reach consumers, and hybrid shopping behavior.

### Internet Retail Channel

The dominant "location" consideration for many consumers is convenience, defined in terms of ease and speed of access. The increase in the use of various home shopping technologies (catalogs, online, televised) is a testimony to the importance of spatial convenience in this expanded sense. That is, the critical consideration may still be "location, location, location," but the placement of physical outlets is less of an issue for many firms. In the first quarter of 2012, U.S. retail e-commerce sales reached $53.1 billion, a 15.3 percent increase over second-quarter 2011 sales. E-commerce sales accounted for 4.9 percent of total U.S. retail sales and have shown a steady increase in importance in the overall economy since late 1999 (when data were first collected). We depict this increasing trend in Figure 6-1 for 2006–2012. Not only have e-commerce sales steadily increased, but they have increased at a rate greater than the rate of total

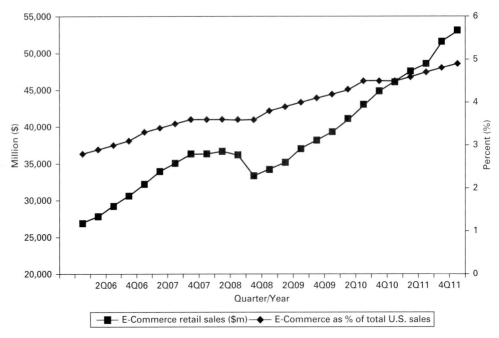

**FIGURE 6-1** **U.S. e-commerce sales ($ million and percentage of total U.S. retail sales)**
*Source:* U.S. Census Bureau, Released August 16, 2012, available at *http://www.census.gov/retail/#ecommerce.*

U.S. retail sales growth, so that the proportion of all retail sales consummated through e-commerce channels keeps increasing as well. It thus appears that the convenience of electronic buying is high and increasing in value over time.

Yet electronic channels also are more important for some product lines than for others, as we show in Figure 6-2. Computer hardware, software, and electronics account for one-fourth of e-commerce sales; clothing and books/magazines account for another one-fourth. Furniture and home furnishings capture 9 percent of e-commerce sales. Among the companies in this U.S. sample of firms that sell at least some product through e-commerce, 48 percent of their sales were electronic. Thus, e-commerce is a significant part of firms' multichannel commitment, but it is not a total commitment.

Using the same database of firms that make at least some e-commerce sales, Figure 6-3 shows the percentage of sales within each product category. For example, 84 percent of all music and videos are sold using e-commerce, but only 8 percent of drug, health, and beauty aids products move through the online channel. These results suggest that electronic buying is very popular, but bricks-and-mortar retailing still captures a significant portion of sales in many categories.

## Direct Selling Channel

**Direct selling** is defined as "the sale of a consumer product or service in a face to face manner away from a fixed retail location."[15] Direct selling organizations, or DSOs, use direct selling techniques to reach final consumers, but unlike catalog sales operations,

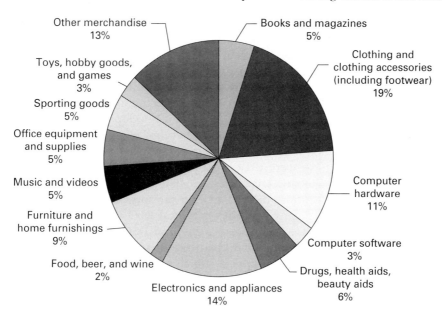

**FIGURE 6-2**   Percentage distribution of e-commerce sales by merchandise line, 2009 (U.S. electronic shopping and mail-order houses), excluding nonmerchandise receipts

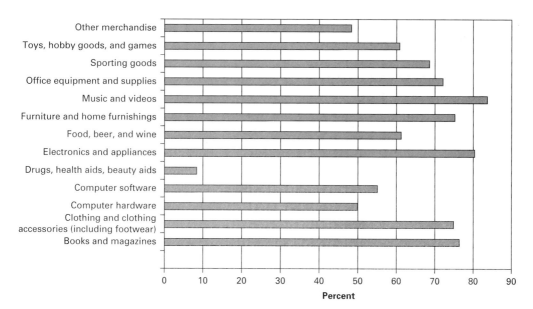

**FIGURE 6-3**   E-commerce as a percentage of sales, 2009 (U.S. electronic shopping and mail-order houses)

they rely on personal selling—the key to their channel structure and their retail positioning. Well-known DSOs include Amway (household cleaning products, personal care products, appliances), Mary Kay (cosmetics), Herbalife (nutritional supplements and vitamins), Avon (cosmetics), and Tupperware (household storage containers)—though various brands sell almost every type of good and service that consumers can buy. The most popular items are consumable products that can be purchased repeatedly, often by the personal network that an independent distributor develops. Direct selling is a very old method of distribution, but it remains viable because of consumers' interest in personal interactions, combined with the low cost of forming and running these channels.

As of August 2011, there were 181 companies listed as members of the U.S. Direct Selling Association. Their global retail sales were almost $154 billion in 2011, achieved through the employment of more than 91 million salespeople worldwide.[16] Although DSO distributors operate in many countries, a typical DSO distributor does not make a living through direct selling. For example, a typical DSO distributor in the United States is female, married, and only works part time. Some DSO distributors certainly make large amounts of money, but it appears much more common for earning levels to supplement the family's main source of income.

Some of these pay discrepancies stem from the unique channel structures of DSOs. Whether the DSO brand manufactures the goods it sells or contracts for their manufacture with other companies, it contracts with downstream intermediaries, variously called "distributors," "consultants," or "salespeople" (we use the term "distributors" here). These **distributors** are independent contractors, rather than employees of the companies, who purchase inventory at a lower price, then resell it at a markup to downstream end-users. They thus bear physical possession and ownership, risking, ordering, and payment flow costs—though perhaps their most important function is promotion, in that standard advertising is very rare among DSOs.

In a multilevel DSO (or MLDSO), distributors earn compensation in three ways. First, they earn the distributor-to-retail markup on the goods they buy wholesale from the DSO. Second, the DSO pays them a commission on every sale. Third, a distributor who recruits other distributors also makes commissions on the sales those recruits make. Compensation plans differ widely in MLDSOs.

The structure of the compensation system in a MLDSO creates different incentives for direct selling versus building a direct selling network, which requires a delicate balance by the DSO. The more time current distributors spend recruiting new distributors, the bigger the DSO's network gets. But recruiting new distributors without spending sufficient time selling products does not generate revenues or profits for the DSO.[17] This balance illustrates the clear distinction between legitimate DSOs and illegitimate pyramid schemes. A **pyramid scheme** is a fraudulent mechanism that demands new recruits pay a nonrefundable fee to become a distributor, and existing distributors earn rewards simply for getting new recruits to sign on and pay this fee. Both the company and the distributor earn money without selling a product or service, which means they do not provide any value and benefits in exchange for customer payments. Many pyramid-scheme victims do not appreciate the risk of this inherent instability, and people who do often try to take opportunistic advantage of the system before it collapses. Although they were not retailers, financiers also have famously exploited pyramid schemes, such as when Bernard Madoff convinced investors to keep adding money to his investment schemes, without ever providing any actual service.[18]

To guard against illegal pyramid schemes, legitimate DSOs have created a code of ethics for their industry. Thus, some positioning choices are made in advance for legitimate DSO: They offer low entry barriers, or costs, of joining (e.g., a reasonable fee for a "starter kit"); accept unsold merchandise for a nearly complete refund (e.g., 90 percent); and provide rewards based primarily on product sales, not the recruitment of downline members of the network. However, this distinction between a legitimate DSO and an illegal pyramid scheme is not always obvious to casual observers, which means that a legitimate DSO has other positioning choices to make. In particular, because it is relatively easy to sign on as a distributor, many people do so without serious consideration of what it takes to run a part-time sales business. Recruits without the right business acumen may make costly mistakes before they quit, and though no DSO can protect its distributors from making some bad decisions, each of them has a vested interest in trying to select and manage new recruits to minimize such problems. Doing so avoids the image problems that continue to plague fraudulent direct selling activities, ensuring a better reputation, and thus stronger sales, for that DSO.

## Hybrid Retail Channels

No single retail form is likely sufficient to reach a market or satisfy a particular target segment's set of service output demands. Some firms are pure online sellers (e.g., Amazon.com), but many others purposely combine bricks-and-mortar with online selling strategies (e.g., Barnes & Noble). Despite Amazon's remarkable successes, the message from Figure 6-3 is that few categories can support a complete focus on online selling. The persistence of mixtures of retail solutions in each product category suggests that on the demand side consumers value having more than one way to access desired products. This value may be a segmentation indication (i.e., some consumers always shop online, others always shop in brick-and-mortar stores, so to attract both segments, a retailer must use both retail outlets) or else an indication that any single consumer routinely can and does use multiple retail outlets to complete a purchase.

The implications of these parallel indications are multiple. First, even if sales appear to be shifting from one type of outlet to another, it may be a bad idea to shut down the former, because its role may have shifted as well, namely, from a place to complete the sale to a place to gather other valued service outputs, such as information provision or customer service. Determining the true economic value added of this type of retail outlet may not be easy, but clearly it offers some economic value by preserving multiple retail routes to market. If these hybrid channels are not vertically integrated, the channel manager's task becomes even more difficult: An information provider likely is not sufficiently compensated for its costly service outputs if another member of the channel earns all the sales. In this case, *free riding* becomes a natural byproduct of hybrid retail channel usage, and the channel manager must decide how to maintain equity.

Second, the question of whether hybrid shopping involves multiple consumers or one consumer using multiple channels is far more critical than it may seem at first. Imagine you are the retail manager for a manufacturer that contracts with both independent bricks-and-mortar retailers and Internet retail outlets (which might be owned by the bricks-and-mortar retailers as part of *own* hybrid retailing strategy). Both outlets are retail outlets, because both can (and do) sell to end-users. However, the bricks-and-mortar store also serves as an infomediary for consumers who like to look in person then buy online.

In this increasingly common type of situation, you really have *three* routes to market: (1) the bricks-and-mortar channel (consumers ignore the online channel), (2) the online channel (consumers ignore the bricks-and-mortar channel), and (3) the **hybrid channel** (consumers obtain some service outputs online and others offline). Only by recognizing the three-part channel structure can the channel manager measure the incremental effectiveness of either outlet accurately. And of course, the measurement grows even more complex if we add in other channels. This way of looking at the channel structure can be useful in negotiations among channel members who worry that their markets are being stolen or that they are not being fairly compensated for the services they render.

Third, manufacturers and retailers that use multiple retail routes to market to create broader brand awareness and market reach still need to find a way to control channel conflict. For bricks-and-mortar retailers, catalog channels are an excellent way to increase their reach; Neiman Marcus, the upscale retailer based in Dallas, Texas, has published a Christmas catalog since 1926 and sends out approximately 90 different catalogs annually to more than 100 million potential consumers who would be hard pressed to find a store in their nearby vicinity.[19] In this case, the additional route to market did not create much conflict, because the retailer owns both the bricks-and-mortar stores and the catalog effort (as well as its recently expanded online channels). For direct sellers, it appears that the hybrid channel challenge has been a bit more stressful, especially as a result of modern demographics. With women just as likely to work out of the home as within, the "stay-at-home mom" model that supported so many companies' direct selling operations suffered a blow. Thus, Avon yielded to the strong temptation to add online selling to its cosmetics channel mix—only to hear from angry "Avon ladies" (its independent distributors) that their newest competitor was also their DSO. Avon's initial hybrid strategy was to sell online directly to end-users, bypassing Avon ladies entirely and not granting them any sales credit for online sales. But after a period of some disarray and the loss of many distributors, Avon modified its model, allowing each distributor to set up her own website, on which she received sales credit for her online sales. In this case, the issue was not *whether* to go online but rather *how* to do so to gain the benefits without incurring the costs of increased channel conflict and cannibalization.[20]

Managing multiple retail routes to market remains a challenge for manufacturers and their retail partners, yet hybrid shopping behavior has penetrated all the combinations of multiple channels. The successful response to its challenges is rarely to shut down an "offending" channel—one with fewer sales, or one that appears to be free riding on the others—because it likely is providing some valued service outputs. Rather, the solution involves offering the right performance rewards for all valued channel functions, to ensure that all the channel members have strong incentives to perform in accordance with the channel design.

## ADAPTING TO THE INCREASING POWER OF MAJOR RETAILERS

At one time, companies such as Procter & Gamble, Colgate, Kraft, and Clorox dominated retailers; now the retailers tend to dominate them. What channel developments have led to such a shift?

First, sales of items normally sold by grocery, drug, and mass merchandise retailers often are approaching saturation, such that they cannot increase at rapid rates. For the retailers to grow, they must steal sales from their competitors, rather than waiting for overall demand to expand. Competition for market share game exerts enormous pressure on retailers to perform; most chains tend to carry similar products, so their competition is largely based on price. Because better prices (coupled with excellent locations, appealing stores, and reasonable service) have become a primary route to survival and success, the chain retailers have had little choice but to pressure suppliers for price concessions of their own. In food retailing in particular, warehouse clubs, general merchandise supercenters, deep-discount drugstores, and mass merchandisers have been growing more rapidly than traditional food stores, allowing them to expand, at the expense of the supermarket, especially among particular niche markets of consumers that value price and a selected set of services.[21] Because supermarket profit ratios (net profits-to-sales) already were low, at about 1 percent, any loss of sales to alternative formats, especially from heavy buyers (e.g., large households), could be disastrous. Even as the power of these traditional retailers has been hemmed in by new entrants, they remain the primary channel for many consumer goods suppliers, which means they can move price pressures immediately back up the channel to manufacturers.

Second, retailers continuously seek to improve their productivity and thereby lower costs, while keeping their prices the same or slightly lower than competitors'. If they can achieve economies of scale, they simultaneously might be better able to provide consumers with the convenience of one-stop shopping in larger store formats. This approach elevates their fixed costs though, forcing supermarket and mass merchandisers to increase their emphasis on generating enormous sales volumes. For example, when Kroger purchased Fred Meyer, it increased its annual sales to $43 billion—or five times the sales of Nestle USA. Such statistics indicate a new type of supplier–retailer negotiation in the grocery arena.[22]

Third, increased pressures on companies mean increased pressures on retail buyers. At one time, buyers focused primarily on purchasing and maintaining balanced inventories. Now, buying centers are also profit centers, responsible for capital management, service levels, turnover, retail margins and pricing, quality control, competitiveness and variety, operating costs, shelf space and position, and vendor float and terms. To help their companies make money, they look to suppliers for price breaks and merchandising support, and those suppliers that fail to provide them may find themselves without a sale.

Fourth, retailers can threaten not to buy most manufacturers' products, because they have so many other alternatives. Approximately 100,000 grocery products exist in the U.S. market, with thousands introduced every year (though most new products do not succeed, with estimated failure rates ranging from 25 to 80 percent[23]). The typical supermarket carries about 40,000 of them. Retailers therefore can choose products that benefit their own, not the manufacturers', profits. Of course, not all product categories are like groceries. Apparel markets, for example, are characterized by a strong preference for new products each season, so total turnover is not uncommon from season to season. However, the fundamental issue, in which many products seek to appear in a fixed amount of shelf space, persists in any brick-and-mortar retail context.

Fifth, suppliers themselves are partly to blame for their weakened position relative to retailers. Not only do they introduce thousands of new products every year, but they also have long engaged in product, price, and promotional allowances to "bribe" their way onto retailers' shelves. These activities have played into the hands of already powerful buyers. Figure 6-4 describes the types and objectives of various trade deals.

Buyers who receive such promotional deals grow to expect and insist on them as a price of doing business. Yet manufacturers and retailers take very different views on the sufficiency of such promotions: Manufacturers generally consider the value they receive for their trade promotions as relatively poor, at the same time that retailers largely report that the share of promotion dollars they receive is "not enough."[24] When asked about the effect of trade promotions on brand loyalty, 21 percent of retailers said trade promotion

1. *Off invoice.* The purpose of an off-invoice promotion is to discount the product to the dealer for a fixed period of time. It consists of a temporary price cut, and when the time period elapses, the price goes back to its normal level. The specific terms of the discount usually require performance, and the discount lasts for a specified period (e.g., one month). Sometimes the trade can buy multiple times and sometimes only once.
2. *Bill-back.* Bill-backs are similar to off-invoice except that the retailer computes the discount per unit for all units bought during the promotional period and then bills the manufacturer for the units sold and any other promotional allowances that are owed after the promotional period is complete. The advantage from the manufacturer's perspective is the control it gives, guaranteeing that the retailer performs as the contract indicates before payment is issued. Generally, retailers do not like bill-backs because of the time and effort required.
3. *Free goods.* Usually free goods take the form of extra cases at the same price. For example, "buy 3 get 1 free" is a free-goods offer.
4. *Cooperative advertising allowances.* Paying for part of the dealers' advertising is called cooperative advertising, which is often abbreviated as co-op advertising. The manufacturer either offers the dealer a fixed dollar amount per unit sold or offers to pay a percentage of the advertising costs. The percentage varies depending on the type of advertising run. If the dealer is prominent in the advertisement, then the manufacturer often pays less, but if the manufacturer is prominent, then it pays more.
5. *Display allowances.* A display allowance is similar to cooperative advertising allowances. The manufacturer wants the retailer to display a given item when a price promotion is being run. To induce the retailer to do this and help defray the costs, a display allowance is offered. Display allowances are usually a fixed amount per case, such as 50 cents.
6. *Sales drives.* For manufacturers selling through brokers or wholesalers, it is necessary to offer incentives. Sales drives are intended to offer the brokers and wholesalers incentives to push the trade deal to the retailer. For every unit sold during the promotional period, the broker and wholesaler receive a percentage or fixed payment per case sold to the retailer. It works as an additional commission for an independent sales organization or additional margin for a wholesaler.
7. *Terms or inventory financing.* The manufacturer may not require payment for 90 days, thus increasing the profitability to the retailer that does not need to borrow to finance inventories.
8. *Count-recount.* Rather than paying retailers on the number of units ordered, the manufacturer does it on the number of units sold, by determining the number of units on hand at the beginning of the promotional period (count) and then determining the number of units on hand at the end of the period (recount). Then, by tracking orders, the manufacturer knows the quantity sold during the promotional period. (This differs from a bill-back because the manufacturer verifies the actual sales in count-recount.)
9. *Slotting allowances.* Manufacturers pay retailers funds known as slotting allowances to receive space for new products. When a new product is introduced the manufacturer pays the retailer X dollars for a "slot" for the new product. Slotting allowances offer a fixed payment to the retailer for accepting and testing a new product.
10. *Street money.* Manufacturers have begun to pay retailers lump sums to run promotions. The lump sum, not per case sold, is based on the amount of support (feature advertising, price reduction, and display space) offered by the retailer. The name comes from the manufacturer's need to offer independent retailers a fixed fund to promote the product because the trade deal goes to the wholesaler.

**FIGURE 6-4**   Trade deals for consumer nondurable goods

*Source:* Robert C. Blattberg and Scott A. Neslin (1990), *Sales Promotion: Concepts, Methods, and Strategies* (Englewood Cliffs, NJ: Prentice-Hall), pp. 318–319.

spending "definitely helps" brand loyalty, but only 12 percent of manufacturers said the same. These attitudes clearly indicate that even as manufacturers spend more on promotion (as demanded by powerful retailers), they perceive its value as lower. In the following sections, we detail several types of deals offered by manufacturers to retailers:

- Forward buying on deals
- Slotting allowances
- Failure fees
- Private labeling
- Globalization

## Effects of Forward Buying

Consumer packaged goods manufacturers can experience wide swings in demand for their products from retailers when they use trade promotions heavily. Temporary wholesale price cuts cause the retailer to engage in **forward buying**, that is, buying significantly more product than it needs, and stockpiling it until stocks run down again. In the past, companies such as Campbell Soup Co. sometimes sold as much as 40 percent of their annual chicken noodle soup production to wholesalers and retailers in just six weeks, due to their trade dealing practices. This strategy increases the quantity sold to the retail trade, and requires the retailer to bear inventory costs, but it also plays havoc with the manufacturer's costs and marketing plans. If a manufacturer marks down a product by 10 percent, retailers commonly might stock up with a 10- to 12-week supply. After the promotion ends, they purchase fewer products at list price, such that the manufacturer might not achieve greater profitability.

To some extent, these problems can be alleviated by technologies such as **continuous replenishment programs (CRP)**. In these cases, the manufacturer and retailer maintain an electronic link that informs the manufacturer when the retailer's stocks are running low, triggering a reorder. If manufacturers and retailers enjoy this level of cooperation, forward buying is less of a problem, though manufacturers' pricing practices still can provoke it.

A related problem is **diverting**. When manufacturers offer a regional trade promotion, perhaps on the West Coast of the United States, some retailers and wholesalers buy large volumes and then distribute some cases to stores in the Midwest, where the discount is not available. This practice upsets manufacturers' efforts to tailor marketing efforts to regions or neighborhoods, but it is fully legal, unlike **gray marketing**, the distribution of authorized, branded goods through unauthorized channels overseas.

## Effects of Slotting Allowances

**Slotting allowances** originated in the 1970s, as a way to compensate the grocery trade for the costs of integrating a new product into its systems, such as creating space in the warehouse, revising computerized inventory systems, resetting the shelves to create space in the store, and stocking and restocking the new item. Because of the scarcity of shelf space, slotting allowances have grown significantly. Slotting allowances reportedly cost manufacturers up to $16 billion in 2001, though the total amount spent is not known for certain.[25]

In 1999, the U.S. Congress held hearings on slotting allowances, in which small manufacturers testified that high slotting allowances prevented their reasonable access to store shelf space, whereas retailers countered that manufacturers should share in the risk of failure of new products. The Federal Trade Commission thus far continues to find no violation of antitrust law, and the continued complaints from manufacturers illustrate that slotting allowances, as an expression of retail power, have not gone anywhere.[26] Studies of slotting allowances continue, but no clear consensus exists about the net effect of these fees on retail performance or prices.

## Effects of Failure Fees

Starting in 1989, J. M. Jones Co., a wholesaling unit of Super Valu Stores Inc., began imposing a fee when it had to pull a failing product from its warehouses. If a new product failed to reach a minimum sales target within three months, Jones withdrew it and charged $2,000 for the effort.[27] **Failure fees**, like slotting allowances, were a focus in a 2000 U.S. Federal Trade Commission conference: Some argued for failure fees, to represent a credible commitment by the manufacturer that its product was good enough to sell. Unlike slotting fees, failure fees are not paid upfront, so even small manufacturers seeking product placement in grocery stores could pay them. But their effectiveness also seems questionable, because a product could fail not due to its inferiority or lack of appeal but as a result of poor retailer support (which creates a so-called moral hazard problem). Collecting failure fees also may be more difficult than collecting slotting allowances upfront.[28] Regardless of their efficacy, the continued use of failure fees is another indication of the degree of retailer control.

## Effects of Private Branding

**Private labels** (or **store brands**) have been, and continue to be, very popular in Europe; their sales account for about 40–50 percent of all supermarket sales in Britain.[29] Yet when a group of U.S. retailers—notably, Sears, JCPenney, Montgomery Ward, and A&P—committed to private labels to generate loyalty to their stores (rather than to manufacturers' brands) and earn extra profits, the generic packaging and varieties they offered failed to give consumers sufficient value. In other words, they were money saving but unexciting alternatives to national, heavily advertised brands. However, grocery retailers in the United States, following European trends, are expanding their private label-branded products (Trader Joe's, Kroger).

More retailers today are upgrading their private-label programs though, to offer an even closer substitute for branded products. There are five basic categories of private brands: (1) store-name identification programs, for which the products bear the retailer's store name or logo (e.g., The Gap, Ace, NAPA, Benetton); (2) retailer's own brand name identity programs, such that the brand image is independent of the store name but the products are available in only that particular company's stores (e.g., Kenmore and Craftsman [Sears], True-Value and Tru-Test [Cotter & Co.]); (3) designer-exclusive programs that feature merchandise designed and sold under a designer's name in an exclusive arrangement with the retailer (e.g., Martha Stewart [Kmart]); (4) other exclusive licensed name programs, usually celebrity-endorsed or signature lines, developed in exclusive arrangements with the retailer (e.g., Michael Graves [Target]); and (5) generic programs with essentially unbranded goods (e.g., Yellow pack no name [Loblaws], Cost Cutter [Kroger]).[30] Many private brands reflecting the first two strategies are positioned as assortment leaders. The Canadian grocery chain Loblaws pioneered its President's

Choice store brand as an upscale offering, selling everything from chocolate chip cookies to olive oil. The brand has been so successful that Loblaws sells it in several chains in the United States as well, where it is positioned as a credible alternative to national brands.

Supermarkets and discount stores in particular have a clear incentive for pushing their own offerings: Private-label goods typically cost consumers 10–30 percent less than other manufacturer brands, but their gross margins are usually higher (approximately 50 percent higher).[31] Private brands also enhance the retailer's channel power by granting the retailer more responsibility for fashion directions, trend setting, innovation, and so forth, as well as for communicating with consumers. Manufacturers thus may start to focus their marketing strategies on important retailers, as opposed to the end-users of their product. Consider that U.S. supermarkets earn 15 percent of their sales from private labels and make an average pretax profit of 2 percent on these sales. European grocery chains, with their heavier focus on store brands, earn 7 percent pretax profits on average. Of course, the European grocery industry also is much more concentrated, leading to less price competition than in the United States (e.g., the top four U.S. supermarket chains accounted for 68 percent of grocery sales in 2009; the top four in the United Kingdom accounted for 79 percent).[32]

In addition, a private-label program might go too far, in the sense that they need strong national brands, for their value comparison to be salient to consumers. When store brands soared to 35 percent of A&P's sales mix in the 1960s, shoppers perceived a lack of choice and defected to competitors. In the late 1980s, Sears added more brand-name goods to appeal to a broader base of customers. Competition from competent, stylish specialty retailers also weakened the position of formerly strong private-goods retailers, such as Marks & Spencer, in the late 1990s.[33]

On balance, retailers can use private-label products to target consumers who seek value for the money they spend in the store. When done well, these private labels are formidable competitors to national (or international) brands. However, when done poorly, or if the environment changes to make a private-label program obsolete, the retailer may suffer. Thus, the threat to name brand manufacturers lies not with private labels *in general* but more specifically with upscale private labels that their retailers manage well.

## Effects of Globalization of Retailing

Retailing has lagged behind other industries in the global race. In 1996, the top retailers earned approximately 12 percent of their sales outside their home markets, but by 2010 sales from foreign markets had increased to about 23 percent of total sales. Table 6-1 makes clear that the internationalization of retailing is a key thrust of most top retailers, but it remains difficult to expand a retail operation across national boundaries, because of the following:

- The need for quality real estate locations on which to build stores.
- The demand for physical logistics operations comparable to those in the home country to source and distribute product.
- The need to develop supplier relationships in new markets, or to internationalize home market suppliers.
- Differences in zoning, pricing, taxation, hours of operation, labor, and hiring and operational choices that must reflect other regulations in each market.
- The need to offer locally attractive products, packaged and positioned in a culturally sensitive manner.

As a result of these difficulties, even well-known retailers such as Marks & Spencer, Tiffany's, and Costco failed to be successful in their initial efforts at international retail operations. These challenges are particularly acute in emerging market economies, where the necessary infrastructure to support a retail effort may be lacking.

Despite these difficulties, retailers have little choice but to globalize (or at least internationalize) their operations, driven by slowing growth in their home markets and the overwhelming attractiveness of developing overseas markets. These developing markets (e.g., the so-called **BRIC nations**: Brazil, Russia, India, and China) offer quickly improving environments and ever-increasing trade liberalization (e.g., free currency convertibility, majority ownership by a foreign business permitted, free repatriation of capital and earnings). Thus, there has been a flurry of expansionary activity by major world retailers, some of it greenfield investment and some of it fueled by acquisitions. Of the top 20 world retailers listed in Table 6-1, only four operate in just one country, whereas Carrefour operates stores in 33 countries, and Wal-Mart operates stores across South America, Asia, and Europe.

What makes for a successful entry into a foreign retail market? There have certainly been well-publicized failures; the key is a sensible balance between exporting the distinctive retail competencies that make the retailer strong in the home market and being sensitive to local preferences. Wal-Mart's initial entry into Argentina failed on these dimensions: It tried to export its U.S. retailing style with no adaptations. The merchandise mix included appliances wired for 110-volt electric power (Argentina operates on 220 volts) and American cuts of beef; the stores themselves had too narrow aisles and carpeting that quickly looked faded and dirty. Not surprisingly, Wal-Mart suffered huge losses in its first two years and only began to turn around when it revised its local strategy to be more in keeping with local norms.[34]

The retailers that successfully expand outside their local borders also can benefit from what is known as a **virtuous cycle**. As they grow, they benefit from greater economies of scale in purchasing and sourcing, as well as advertising and information technology management. Successful products from one market can be easily exported to another. A larger scale also permits efficient investments in common assets, such as marketing research expertise and financing. A successful expansion can funnel the profits into enhancing the brand's equity worldwide. Thus, the big get bigger—a drive motivating the worldwide expansion that characterizes retailing today.

Faced with stronger and stronger transnational competitors, what can a local incumbent retailer do? Some sell to niche segments in their home markets, offering superior service, products, and location, tailored to local tastes. For example, when Carrefour and Wal-Mart arrived in Brazil, rather than try to beat them at their own game, the local retailer Pao de Azucar instead refocused its business to emphasize its convenient locations and provide credit to its customers—a popular local service that the entrants did not provide. But only local competitors that provide the service that specific segments demand likely will survive the onslaught of a multinational retailer.

Finally, an important insight to take away from this description of the globalization of retailing is that international competition is now a given, rather than an exception. Even for local retailers, this trend must be more than a curious development to observe. The entry of multinational retailers into many markets, and not just major, developed ones, requires all channel members to consider how international retail competition is likely to affect them, and how to protect their businesses (or profitably harvest them) in the face of potential and actual competition from outside entrants.

## SUMMARY: RETAILING STRUCTURES AND STRATEGIES

Retailing is an enormously complex and varied enterprise the world over. As the key channel member in direct contact with the end-user, the retailer's actions are critical to the success of the marketing channel. A retailer's position is defined by the demand-side and cost-side characteristics of its operations. These characteristics map into the service outputs provided to consumers who shop with the retailer. Because markets are made up of distinct consumer segments, each of which demands different levels of service outputs, a retailer can successfully differentiate itself from competitors on both demand and cost sides, even if it sells comparable or identical products to those of its competitors. Without a distinct offering on the service output side, or a distinct cost advantage, a retailer of competitive products risks failure in the marketplace. Different types of retailers can be categorized by the levels of service outputs they provide and their cost positions.

One of the most important developments on the consumer side has been the increasing importance of convenience in retail shopping. Consumers in many countries suffer from time poverty; in combination with growing purchasing power, it prompts consumers to demand a broader array of channel services that lower their time cost of shopping. Conversely, if they choose to buy at a lower-service retail outlet, they demand a lower price to compensate for the full cost of shopping there. These trends place increasing pressure on retailers to both control costs and enhance the value they add to the products sold in their stores.

Power and coordination issues still affect retail channel management. Retailers use their leverage to engage in forward buying and to demand concessions from their suppliers. Retailers in grocery and apparel industries have also developed strong private branding programs that pose a competitive threat to nationally branded goods supplied by manufacturers. Manufacturers respond by building and maintaining strong brands and by bearing the cost of more channel flows. They also seek to change the basis for their pricing and use multiple channel strategies to limit their dependence on any one retailer.

The globalization of retailing is an emerging phenomenon that will affect consumers and competing retailers for years to come. Global retailers will likely seek more favorable terms from their suppliers, who will be expected to serve them on a worldwide basis. International product sourcing of the most popular products, combined with greater cost controls, should mean greater choice at lower prices for many consumers. Even local retailers that do not intend to sell in overseas markets cannot escape the competitive effects of global retailers entering their home markets.

## TAKE-AWAYS

- Retailing is the set of activities involved in selling goods and services to end-users for personal consumption.
- A retail positioning strategy involves both cost-side and demand-side decisions.
  - On the cost side, the retailer must decide in general whether to emphasize *high margin* or *high merchandise turnover* more; both are financially beneficial, but it is extremely difficult to achieve both together.
  - On the demand side, the retailer must choose which service outputs to provide to the target consumer segment(s).

- Together, the cost-side and demand-side decisions the retailer makes constitute its *retail position*.
- Retailing strategically involves the following:
  - Managing a multichannel shopping experience that is increasingly demanded by consumers.
    - The Internet is a well-established and growing retail channel, as well as an enabler of shopping through other outlets.
    - Direct selling provides an alternative method of going to market when close interpersonal ties are crucial to building and maintaining consumer relationships.
    - In hybrid shopping, consumers use more than one retail outlet to complete their shopping experience, which requires special skill to avoid channel conflict.
  - Recognition at the manufacturer level of the continued power of retailers in market. Powerful retailers use many tools to further their interests, including:
    - Forward buying on deals
    - Slotting allowances
    - Failure fees
    - Private branding
  - Understanding and leveraging the increased international reach of retailing. Even a retailer that is not present in multiple national markets needs to consider competitors, suppliers, and customers that are focused on global markets. Therefore, it is important to understand the effect of globalization in retailing in various settings.

## Endnotes

1. For a more comprehensive and in-depth discussion of retailing structure, competition, and management than space allows here, see Levy, Michael and Barton A. Weitz (2009), *Retailing Management* 7th ed. (Boston, MA: Irwin/McGraw-Hill).

2. Specifically, the top 250 global retailers' sales in 2010 were about $3.94 trillion. Wal-Mart's 2010 sales were $419 billion. The ratio of Wal-Mart's sales to global sales is therefore 11 percent. "2011 Top 250 Global Retailers," *Stores*, January 2012, available at http://www.stores.org.

3. See http://www.zara.com.

4. For a detailed discussion of financial strategies adopted by retailers, including the strategic profit model, see Levy and Weitz, op. cit.

5. See http://www.hm.com.

6. See Coughlan, Anne T. (2004), *Michaels Craft Stores: Integrated Channel Management and Vendor-Retailer Relations Case*, Kellogg Case Clearing House Number 5-104-010.

7. Pashigian, B. Peter and Eric D. Gould (1998), "Internalizing Externalities: The Pricing of Space in Shopping Malls," *Journal of Law and Economics* 41 (April), pp. 115–142.

8. Berner, Robert (2002), "Has Target's Food Foray Missed the Mark?" *BusinessWeek*, November 25, p. 76.

9. Spurgeon, Devon (2000), "Walgreen Takes Aim at Discount Chains, Supermarkets," *The Wall Street Journal*, June 29, p. B4.

10. Morse, Dan (2002), "Tennessee Producer Tries New Tactic in Sofas: Speed," *The Wall Street Journal*, November 19, p. A1.

11. Berner, Robert (2003), "Dark Days in White Goods for Sears," *BusinessWeek*, March 10, pp. 78–79.

12. See www.janieandjack.com.

13. Cahill, Joseph B. (1999), "The Secret Weapon of Big Discounters: Lowly Shopping Cart," *The Wall Street Journal*, November 24, pp. A1, A10.

14. Ganesan, Shankar, Morris George, Sandy Jap, Robert W. Palmatier, and Bart Weitz, (2009), "Supply Chain Management and Retailer

Performance: Emerging Trends, Issues, and Implications for Research and Practice," *Journal of Retailing*, 85 (March), pp. 84–94.

15. This definition is taken from the Direct Selling Association's website, http://www.dsa.org/. The Direct Selling Association (DSA) is a United States trade association of direct selling organizations, including such well-known, multilevel marketing organizations as Amway, Mary Kay, Tupperware, and Discovery Toys. The DSA serves as the Secretariat for the World Federation of Direct Selling Organizations (WFDSA, http://www.wfdsa.org/), which is the super-organization of all national DSAs around the world. The WFDSA has more than 50 national DSAs as members.

16. See www.dsa.org for more information.

17. See Coughlan, Anne T. and Kent Grayson (1998), "Network Marketing Organizations: Compensation Plans, Retail Network Growth, and Profitability," *International Journal of Research in Marketing* 15, pp. 401–426 for a model showing these effects.

18. Washington, Ruby (2012), "Bernard L. Madoff," *The New York Times*, December 17, 2012.

19. Chandler, Susan (2002), "Retailers Heed Call of Catalogs," *Chicago Tribune*, September 21, Section 2, pp. 1–2.

20. See Godes, David B. (2002), Avon.com *Case*, Harvard Case Clearing House, Case number N9-503-016. For another company's challenge in this realm, see Coughlan, Anne T. (2004), *Mary Kay Corporation: Direct Selling and the Challenge of Online Channels Case*, Kellogg Case Clearing House, Case number 5-104-009.

21. See www.census.gov/retail/ for annual retail sales data.

22. Aufreiter, Nora and Tim McGuire (1999), "Walking Down the Aisles," *Ivey Business Journal* 63 (March/April), pp. 49–54; Peltz, James F. (1998), "Food Companies' Fight Spills into Aisles," *Los Angeles Times*, October 28, Business Section, p. 1; "Loblaw's Continues to Strengthen Position," *MMR/Business and Industry* 16 (October 18, 1999), p. 20.

23. "Slotting Allowances in The Supermarket Industry" (2002), *Food Marketing Institute Backgrounder* http://www.fmi.org.

24. ACNielsen (2002), "Trade Promotion Practices Study," *Consumer Insight*, available at www2.acnielsen.com/pubs/2003_q2_ci_tpp.shtml.

25. Desiraju, Ramarao (2001), "New Product Introductions, Slotting Allowances, and Retailer Discretion," *Journal of Retailing* 77, no. 3, p. 336.

26. Toosi, Nahal (1999), "Congress Looks at the Selling of Shelf Space," *St. Louis Post-Dispatch* September 15, Business Section, p. C1; Superville, Darlene (1999), "Are 'Slotting Fees' Fair? Senate Panel Investigates; Practice Involves Paying Grocers for Shelf Space," *The San Diego Union-Tribune*, September 15, Business Section, p. C-1.

27. Zwiebach, Elliott (1989), "Super Value Division Imposes Failure Fee," *Supermarket News*, May 8, p. 1.

28. Federal Trade Commission (2001), "Report on the Federal Trade Commission Workshop on Slotting Allowances and Other Marketing Practices in the Grocery Industry," February, available at http://www.ftc.gov.

29. Vasquez-Nicholson, Julie (2011), "G.A.I.N. Report: United Kingdom, Retail Foods, 2010," U.S.D.A. Foreign Agricultural Service, February 3, p. 4.

30. Sweeney, Daniel J. (1987), *Product Development and Branding* (Dublin, OH: Management Horizons).

31. Allawadi, Kusum L. and Bari A. Harlam (2004), "An Empirical Analysis of the Determinants of Retail Margins: The Role of Store Brand Shares," *Journal of Marketing* (January), p. 159.

32. The Reinvestment Fund (2011), "Understanding the Grocery Industry," Community Development Financial Institutions Fund, September 30, p. 2; ACNielsen (2005), "The Power of Private Label in Europe: An Insight into Consumer Attitudes," The ACNielsen Global Online Consumer Opinion Survey, p. 2.

33. Beck, Ernest (1999), "Britain's Marks & Spencer Struggles To Revive Its Old Luster in Retailing," *The Wall Street Journal*, November 8, p. A34.

34. Krauss, Clifford (1999), "Selling to Argentina (as Translated From the French)," *The New York Times*, December 5, Business World Section.

# APPENDIX 6-1

## A Glossary of Pricing and Buying Terms Commonly Used by Retailers

**Original Retail**   The first price at which the merchandise is offered for sale.

**Sale Retail**   The final selling price.

**Merchandise Cost**   The billed cost of merchandise less any applicable trade or quantity discounts plus inbound transportation costs, if paid by the buyer. Cash discounts are not deducted to arrive at merchandise cost. Usually, they are either deducted from "aggregate cost of goods sold" at the end of an accounting period or added to net operating profits. If cash discounts are added to net operating profit, the amount added is treated as financial income with no effect on gross margins.

**Markup**   The difference between merchandise cost and the retail price.

**Initial Markup or Mark-on**   The difference between merchandise cost and the original retail value.

**Maintained Markup or Margin**   The difference between the *gross* cost of goods sold and net sales.

**Gross Margin of Profit**   The dollar difference between the *total* cost of goods and net sales.

**Gross Margin Return on Inventory (GMROI)**   Total gross margin dollars divided by average inventory (at cost). GMROI is used most appropriately in measuring the performance of products within a single merchandise category. The measure permits the buyer to look at products with different gross margin percentages and different rates of inventory turnover and make a relatively quick evaluation as to which are the best performers. The components of GMROI are as follows:

| Gross Margin Percentage | Sales-to-Inventory Ratio | GMROI |
|---|---|---|
| (gross margin)/ (net sales) | × (net sales)/(average inventory) (at cost) | = (gross margin)/(average inventory) (at cost) |

**Total Cost**   Total cost of goods sold – gross cost of goods sold + workroom costs – cash discounts.

**Markdown**   A reduction in the original or previous retail price of merchandise. The *markdown percentage* is the ratio of the dollar markdown during a period to the net sales for the same period.

**Off-Retail**   Designates specific reductions off the original retail price. Retailers can express markup in terms of retail price or cost. Large retailers and progressive small retailers express markups in terms of retail for several reasons. First, other operating ratios are expressed in terms of percentage net sales. Second, net sales figures are available more often than cost figures. Finally, most trade statistics are expressed in terms of sales.

Markup on retail can be converted to cost base by using the following formula:

$$\text{markup\% on cost} = (\text{markup\% on retail})/(100\% - \text{markup\% on retail}).$$

On the other hand,

markup% on retail = (markup% on cost)/(100% + markup% on cost).

**FOB**   The seller places the merchandise "free on board" the carrier at the point of shipment or other predesignated place. The buyer assumes title to the merchandise and pays all freight charges from this point.

**Delivered Sale**   The seller pays all freight charges to the buyer's destination and retains title to the goods until they are received by the buyer.

**Freight Allowances**   FOB terms can be used with freight allowances to transfer the title to the buyer at the point of shipping, whereas the seller absorbs the transportation cost. The seller ships FOB and the buyer deducts freight costs from the invoice payment.

**Trade Discount**   Vendors usually quote a list price and offer a trade discount to provide the purchaser a reasonable margin to cover its operating expenses and provide for net profit margin. Trade discounts are sometimes labeled *functional discounts*. They are usually quoted in a series of percentages, such as "list price less 33%, 15%, 5%," for different channel functions performed by different intermediaries. Therefore, if a list price of $100 is assumed, the discount applies as follows for the different channel members:

| | |
|---|---|
| List Price | $100.00 |
| Less 33% | $ 33.00 (retailer-performed functions) |
| | $ 67.00 |
| Less 15% | $ 10.05 (wholesaler-performed functions) |
| | $ 56.95 |
| Less 5% | $  2.85 (manufacturers' representative-performed functions) |
| | $ 54.10 |

**Quantity Discounts**   Vendors offer two types of quantity discounts: noncumulative and cumulative. Although noncumulative discounts are offered on volume of each order, cumulative discounts are offered on total volume for a specified period. Quantity discounts are offered to encourage volume buying. Legally, they should not exceed production and distribution cost savings to the seller because of volume buying.

**Seasonal Discounts**   Discounts offered to buyers of seasonal products who place their order before the season's buying period. This enables the manufacturer to use its equipment more efficiently by spreading production throughout the year.

**Cash Discount**   Vendors selling on credit offer a cash discount for payment within a specified period. The cash discount is usually expressed in the following format: "2/10, net 30." This means that the seller extends credit for 30 days. If payment is made within 10 days, a 2 percent discount is offered to the buyer. The 2 percent interest rate for 10 days is equivalent to a 36 percent effective interest rate per year. Therefore, passing up cash discounts can be very costly. Some middlemen who operate on slim margins simply cannot realize a profit on a merchandise shipment unless they take advantage of the cash discount. Channel intermediaries usually maintain a line of credit at low interest rates to pay their bills within the cash discount period.

**Cash Datings**    Cash datings include cash on delivery (COD), cash with order (CWO), receipt of goods (ROG), sight draft-bill of lading SD-BL). SD-BL means that a sight draft is attached to the bill of lading and must be honored before the buyer takes possession of the shipment.

**Future Datings**    Future datings include the following:

1. Ordinary dating, such as "2/10, net 30."
2. End-of-month dating, such as "2/10, net 30, EOM," where the cash discount and the net credit periods begin on the first day of the following month rather than on the invoice date.
3. Proximo dating, such as "2%, 10th proximo, net 60," which specifies a date in the following month on which payment must be made in order to take the cash discount.
4. Extra dating, such as "2/10-30 days extra," which means that the buyer has 70 days from the invoice date to pay his bill and benefit from the discount.
5. Advance or season dating, such as "2/10, net 30 as of May 1," which means that the discount and net periods are calculated from May 1. Sometimes extra dating is accompanied by an anticipation allowance. For example, if the buyer is quoted "2/10, 60 days extra," and it pays in 10 days, or 60 days ahead, an additional discount is made available.

# APPENDIX 6-2

## Merchandise Planning and Control

Merchandise planning and control start with decisions about merchandise variety and assortment. Variety decisions involve determining the different kinds of goods to be carried or services offered. For example, a department store carries a wide variety of merchandise ranging from men's clothing and women's fashions to sports equipment and appliances. Assortment decisions instead involve determination of the range of choice (e.g., brands, styles or models, colors, sizes, prices) offered to the customer within a variety classification. The more carefully and wisely decisions on variety and assortment are made, the more likely the retailer is to achieve a satisfactory rate of stockturn.

The rate of **stockturn** (stock turnover) is the number of times during a given period in which the average amount of stock on hand is sold. It is most commonly determined by dividing the average inventory at cost into the cost of the merchandise sold. It is also computed by dividing average inventory at retail into the net sales figure or by dividing average inventory in physical units into sales in physical units. To achieve a high rate of stockturn, retailers frequently attempt to limit their investment in inventory, which, in turn, reduces storage space, as well as such expenses as interest, taxes, and insurance on merchandise. "Fresher" merchandise will be on hand, thereby generating more sales. Thus, a rapid stockturn can lead to greater returns on invested capital.

Although the retailing firms with the highest rates of turnover tend to realize the greatest profit-to-sales ratios, significant problems may be encountered by adopting high-turnover goals. For example, higher sales volume can be generated through lower margins, which in turn reduce profitability; lower inventory levels may result in additional ordering (clerical) costs and the loss of quantity discounts; and greater expense may be involved in receiving, checking, and marking merchandise. Merchandise budget planning provides the means by which the appropriate balance can be achieved between retail stock and sales volume.

## MERCHANDISE BUDGETING

The merchandise budget plan is a forecast of specified merchandise-related activities for a definite period. Although the usual period is one season of six months, in practice it is often broken down into monthly or even shorter periods. Merchandise budgeting requires the retail decision maker to make forecasts and plans relative to five basic variables: sales, stock levels, reductions, purchases, and gross margin and operating profit.[35] Each of these variables will be addressed briefly.

### Planned Sales and Stock Levels

The first step in budget determination is the preparation of the *sales forecast* for the season and for each month in the season for which the budget is being prepared. The second step involves the determination of the *beginning-of-the-month* (BOM) *inventory* (stock on hand), which necessitates specification of a desired rate of stock-turn for each month of the season. If, for example, the desired stock-sales ratio for the month of June is 4 and forecasted (planned) sales during June are $10,000, then the planned BOM stock would be $40,000. It is also important, for budgeting purposes, to calculate stock available at the end of the month (EOM) stock. This figure is identical to the BOM stock for the following month. Thus, in our example, May's EOM stock is $40,000 (or June's BOM stock).

## Planned Reductions

This third step in budget preparation involves accounting for markdowns, shortages, and employee discounts. Reduction planning is critical because any amount of reductions has exactly the same effect on the value of stock as an equal amount of sales. Markdowns vary from month to month, depending on special and sales events. In addition, shortages are becoming an increasing problem for retailers. Shortages result from shoplifting, employee pilferage, miscounting, and pricing and checkout mistakes. Generally, merchandise managers can rely on past data in forecasting both shortages and employee discounts.

## Planned Purchases

When figures for sales, opening (BOM) and closing (EOM) stocks, and reductions have been forecast, the fourth step, the *planning of purchases* in dollars, becomes merely a mechanical mathematical operation. Thus, planned purchases are equal to planned stock at the end of the month (EOM) + planned sales + planned reductions – stock at the beginning of the month (BOM). Suppose, for example, that the planned EOM stock for June was $67,500 and that reductions for June were forecast to be $2,500. Then,

| | |
|---|---:|
| Planned EOM stock (June 30) | $67,500 |
| Planned sales (June 1–June 30) | 10,000 |
| Planned reductions | 2,500 |
| **Total:** | $80,000 |
| **Less** | |
| Planned BOM stock (June 1) | 40,000 |
| Planned purchases | $40,000 |

The planned purchases figure is, however, based on *retail prices*. To determine the financial resources needed to acquire the merchandise, it is necessary to determine planned purchases at *cost*. The difference between planned purchases at retail and at cost represents the initial markup goal for the merchandise in question. This goal is established by determining the amount of operating expenses necessary to achieve the forecasted sales volume, as well as the profits desired from the specific operation, and combining this information with the data on reductions. Thus,

initial markup goal = (expenses + profit + reductions)/(net sales + reductions).

A term frequently used in retailing is *open-to-buy*. It refers to the amount, in terms of retail prices or at cost, that a buyer can receive into stock during a certain period on the basis of the plans formulated. Thus, planned purchases and open-to-buy may be synonymous if forecasts coincide with actual results. However, adjustments in inventories, fluctuations in sales volume, unplanned markdowns, and goods ordered but not received all serve to complicate the determination of the amount that a buyer may spend.

## Planned Gross Margin and Operating Profit

The *gross margin* is the initial markup adjusted for price changes, stock shortages, and other reductions. The difference between gross margin and expenses required to generate sales will yield either a contribution to profit or a *net operating profit* (before taxes), depending on the sophistication of a retailer's accounting system and the narrowness of its merchandise budgeting.

# CHAPTER 7

# Wholesaling Structures and Strategies

**LEARNING OBJECTIVES**

**After reading this chapter, you will be able to:**

- Distinguish between three broad categories of institutions that constitute the wholesaling sector.
- Define how an independent wholesaler-distributor adds value and explain why this sector is growing.
- Detail the mechanisms by which channel members join federations or alliances that offer exceptional services while cutting costs.
- Identify the major distinctions between a wholesaler voluntary group and a dealer cooperative, and relate this distinction to the value they provide members.
- Explain why consolidation is common in wholesaling, and explain a manufacturer's possible responses to a consolidation wave.
- Describe how wholesaling is being altered by electronic commerce.
- Compare sales agents with wholesaler-distributors in the ways that matter to a manufacturer.
- Explain why the future for wholesaler-distributor is optimistic.

## WHOLESALING STRUCTURES

**Wholesaling** (wholesale trade, wholesale distribution) refers to business establishments that do *not* sell many products to ultimate households or end-users. Instead, they sell products primarily to other businesses: retailers, merchants, contractors, industrial users, institutional users, and commercial users. *Wholesale businesses sell physical inputs and products to other businesses.* Thus, wholesaling is closely associated with tangible goods, yet the value created by wholesale entities stems from the value they add by providing services—or in the terms we use in this book, by performing channel functions. Although that value added is quite real, very little about wholesaling is tangible. In this sense, it is the epitome of a service industry. In a channel stretching from the manufacturer to the end-user, wholesaling is an intermediate step. This chapter pertains to the institutions that wholesale, that is, that provide physical goods as inputs to other businesses. We investigate not just the nature of these institutions but also the strategies they employ.[1]

## Wholesaler-Distributors

Many different institutions perform channel functions in business-to-business (B2B) marketing channels. Wholesaler-distributors are the largest and most significant of these institutions.

**Wholesaler-distributors** are independently owned and operated firms that buy and sell products over which they claim **ownership**. Generally, they operate through one or more warehouses, in which they receive their purchased goods, which they hold in inventory for later reshipping. In the United States, this industry exerts a large, influential role; consider figures reported by the National Association of Wholesale-Distributors (NAW, a federation of 86 national wholesale line-of-trade associations and individual firms, totaling more than 40,000 companies; www.naw.org/):

- Total wholesale distribution trade represented $4.8 trillion dollars of sales in the United States in 2011—that is, about 28 percent of U.S. gross domestic product (GDP).
- Distributors account for $1 out of every $5 spent on computer hardware and software. Wholesale distribution spends more on information technology (IT) on a per-employee basis than almost any other U.S. industry.

There is a distinction between wholesalers and distributors. But we *ignore* it for the purposes of this chapter. Instead, we simply note that the terms have different roots and at one time represented distinct sectors. Traditionally, the term "wholesaler" referred to a company that resold products to another intermediary, whereas a "distributor" implied that the company resold products to a customer that would use the product. Formally then, a pharmaceutical *wholesaler* resells prescription drugs to a retail pharmacy, which resells the product to a household consumer. An industrial maintenance *distributor* instead sells cutting tools to an industrial customer that uses those tools in its manufacturing facilities.

But this terminology also varies from industry to industry. For example, distributors of printing paper are called "merchants," and distributors of automotive aftermarket products are "jobbers." This terminology even might vary from market to market within an industry. Because our critical point is that wholesaler-distributors have the **title** to the goods they resell—that is, they have the authority to set prices—we override these terminology distinctions. This chapter instead highlights the key functions and traits of wholesaler-distributors: They know the identity of the next buyer in the channel, which they may or may not share with the manufacturer. They are defined primarily by their performance of an ownership channel function.[2]

The importance of wholesaler-distributors also is striking in two main ways: in itself and because it is not particularly evident in the business press. Yet the latest reports seemingly always predict the doom and death of the sector. Oddly enough, this pessimism may prevail because the sector is generally well organized in active trade associations. These effective bodies commission regular reports that suggest ways their members can improve operations and caution against complacency. But as we have already learned, such efforts to adjust, improve, and increase efficiency likely signal the *health* of this channel function, not its demise.

A more fundamental reason for the misplaced pessimism is that the wholesale sector has been subject to a massive, decades-long wave of **consolidation**, industry by industry (which we examine later in this chapter). For now, suffice it to say that, understandably, the disappearance of two-thirds of the companies in an industry (as has happened in some sectors) creates an atmosphere of panic and dread. But the fear is unfounded. Most firms in a consolidation wave actually exit by being acquired, not by going bankrupt or shutting down. The acquirers are large, healthy businesses that have supported steady increases in the wholesale sector's share of the channel in recent decades. Consolidation strengthens wholesaler-distributors even as it reduces their number—and some inefficiencies in the industry.

Consolidation was largely sparked by IT. That is, actors performing the distribution function experience intense pressures to invest in IT. The customer-facing elements of the business in particular are increasingly expected to be Internet enabled and sophisticated. Concurrently, operations benefit from IT system investments that allow the distributors to participate in the supply chain management revolution (see Chapter 14; briefly, **supply chain management** refers to the strategic coordination of traditional business functions systematically across the channel, with the goal of enhancing long-term performance for the channel, or supply chain, overall). Then these new systems must interface seamlessly. Such competitive demands encourage wholesaler-distributors to consolidate so that they can achieve the scale economies that justify massive investments in automation.

Despite these consolidation trends though, traditional measures of industry **concentration** remain low in comparison with manufacturing sectors. To some extent, low concentration reflects the geographically distinct markets that mark most competition among wholesaler-distributors. A single wholesaler-distributor might totally dominate one region of a country but account for a miniscule proportion of national sales. Thus, the apparent fragmentation of wholesale distribution does not reflect the true nature of concentration, as measured in any single region.

This discussion sets up an issue we address in Chapter 10: *Power is a property of a relationship, not of a business.* A very large and reputable manufacturer, such as Monsanto or DuPont, may not be any more powerful than a single wholesaler-distributor, *in a given market.* This supplier even may be less powerful, if customer loyalty prevents the big supplier from bypassing a downstream channel member to access a territory. Distributors of pesticides, herbicides, and farm equipment often enjoy excellent relations with the farmers in their markets, many of whom simply will not do business without going through their favored distributor.

## Master Distributors

Observers often find themselves puzzled by **master distributors**, a sort of super wholesaler, as represented in Figure 7-1.

Consider RCI, a master distributor of electrical motors for the refrigeration industry. (Recall that we make no distinction between "wholesaler" and "distributor"

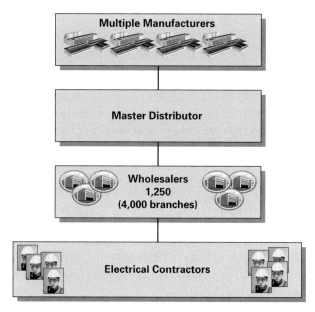

**FIGURE 7-1**   Representative master distributor channel
*Source:* Based on Das Narayandas and V. Kasturi Rangan (2004),
"Building and Sustaining Buyer-Seller Relationships in Mature
Industrial Markets," *Journal of Marketing*, Vol. 68, no. 3, pp. 63–77.

in this chapter, so we use these terms interchangeably.) The customer, such as an air conditioning contractor, makes purchases from one of its 4,000 conveniently located branches, run by 1,250 independent wholesalers (i.e., distributors to B2B customers). These wholesalers do not deal with the manufacturer though but with another, single point of contact, namely, the master distributor, which only distributes to other distributors. In other words, Figure 7-1 really features 1,251 wholesalers: 1 master distributor + its 1,250 wholesaler customers, all of which sell to other businesses rather than to consumers. However, for a given manufacturer's products, this master distributor does not compete with other wholesalers for contractors' business. Although on paper, it looks like an extra layer (hence, observers' widespread confusion at its existence), the master distributor actually creates a stable, prosperous system that suits all parties. To understand its value, we have to ask: What functions would be pushed onto some other player in the channel if the master distributor were eliminated?

Distributors rely on many services provided by manufacturers. But master distributors also can provide those services, so they thrive when they can do so more effectively and/or efficiently than the manufacturer does. Contractors, which represent the end-user in a B2B channel, demand enormous assortments (e.g., each specific replacement motor) and fast delivery (e.g., of refrigerated goods that spoil quickly). In Figure 7-1, the 4,000 branches of 1,250 wholesalers each would need to rush to provide one of the thousands of parts demanded, making the goal of keeping adequate stock close to the customer totally infeasible. Instead, distributors want to buy products as needed, using the master distributor as their "invisible warehouse." (Not surprisingly, the master distributor spends a lot on express delivery services!)

Master distributors also consolidate orders from all their manufacturers, so their customers avoid minimum order requirements established by the manufacturer. Rather, these individual distributors can buy a variety of products from a multitude of vendors, but still enjoy the quantity discount and lower transportation costs obtained by the master distributor.

Finally, master distributors' roles sometimes mirror those of a franchisor (see Chapter 8). They help their customers (i.e., other distributors) improve their business processes, demonstrate best practices, and shoulder some of their channel functions, such as advertising.

Essentially, master distributors give distributors economies of scope and scale and help them resolve their logistic and support problems. Competitive pressures have driven their B2B customers to seek out such benefits, even as manufacturers rediscover that it often does not pay to provide individualized, direct services to all their distributors. In the United States in particular, master distributors have gained a lot of ground, often because manufacturers have adopted **balanced scorecard methods** to evaluate their performance.[3] That is, rather than looking just at volume, manufacturers increasingly consider other performance criteria, such as marketing support, service levels, and next-day delivery. Master distributors fare well on such balanced scorecards, especially when they help manufacturers expand into new channels. Georgia-Pacific sells paper products and dispensing systems, but most distributors view these bulky, inexpensive products as a minor market. Thus, master distributors solve the problem by helping the distributors meet their customers' needs without requiring them to devote warehouse space to products that offer them low value per cubic meter.

Many manufacturers in turn have grown far more sophisticated in their pricing for distributors, such that they offer functional discounts for:

- No minimum order size.
- Willingness to break case quantities down to small lots.
- Same-day shipping.
- Marketing support (e.g., customized catalogues, flyers, Internet ordering).
- Holding inventory.
- Taking responsibility for logistics.

This fine-grained approach favors master distributors because it offers more ways for them to get paid for what they already do. Why did this new flexibility arise? Because manufacturers increasingly focus on supply chain management (Chapter 14) and thus are interested in anything that can increase their coordination with downstream channel members.

## Other Supply Chain Participants

Supply chains are complex and involve multiple participants, intermediaries, and service providers, all of which seek to facilitate the movement of goods and services from their source to their consumption location. Thus, in a supply chain, the channel functions and activities that traditionally are the focus of wholesaler-distributors often get performed by other participants. For example, **manufacturers' sales branches** are captive wholesaling operations, owned and operated by manufacturers. Many manufacturers also maintain sales offices to perform specific selling and marketing functions. These locations rarely take physical possession of inventory though, so they may continue to work with independent wholesaler-distributors. **Customers**, particularly large, multiestablishment retail firms, perform wholesale distribution functions, especially in vertically integrated channels, whether forward integrated by the manufacturer or backward integrated by the end-customer in a B2B sector.

**Agents, brokers, and commission agents** buy or sell products and earn commissions or fees, without ever taking ownership of the products they represent. These channels are critical in service industries, which have nothing to inventory and thus nothing to own. By convention, agents in service industries are not considered part of the wholesale trade, because there are no tangible goods involved. However, ignoring them would limit our view of wholesaling in practice.

The other examples of companies that perform supply chain activities in a B2B marketing channel are nearly innumerable. The transportation and warehousing industry provides logistics functions; increasingly, third-party logistics providers and value-added warehousing companies view to perform some functions too. Unlike wholesaler-distributors, **third-party logistics providers (3PL)** do not take title to the products that they handle. Rather, they charge their customers an activity-based fee for services rendered, which replace traditional sell-side markup pricing by wholesaler-distributors. The emergence of large, sophisticated, end-to-end logistics providers remains a key challenge to wholesaler-distributors. Without sounding too pessimistic, we note that the number of manufacturer-owned distribution centers has declined sharply in the past decade or so, in part as manufacturers increasing outsource their work to 3PLs.[4]

## WHOLESALING STRATEGIES

Wholesalers add value as they perform nine generic channel functions (from Chapter 3): They take physical possession of the goods, take title (ownership), promote the product to prospective customers, negotiate transactions, finance their operations, risk their capital (often by granting credit to both suppliers and customers), process orders, handle payments, and manage information. In general, they manage the flow of information both ways: upstream to the supplier and downstream to other channel members and prospective customers. In so doing, they provide utility upstream and downstream. Wholesaler-distributors survive and thrive if they perform these functions more effectively and efficiently than either manufacturers or customers.

This generalization varies from one economy to another of course. Japan has long been noted for its very long channels, in which multiple wholesalers touched the goods several times between their emergence from the manufacturer and their final point of consumption. Many wholesalers added margin but little value; thus in the 1990s, Japan's wholesale sector began to shrink steadily. Channels grew shorter; wholesalers were excluded, starting with secondary and tertiary wholesalers. But as Japanese consumers continued to express increasing price consciousness, retailers sought to purchase directly from manufacturers, which led to still shorter channels—and even greater pressures on wholesalers.[5]

## An Historical Perspective on Wholesaling Strategy

The wholesaling sector is a funny scenario. It is critical and massive, and yet it remains largely invisible to the buyer, who takes the functions is performs for granted. Both manufacturers and customers have a troubling tendency to underestimate the three great challenges of wholesaling:

1. Doing the job **correctly** (no errors).
2. Doing the job **effectively** (maximum service).
3. Doing the job **efficiently** (low costs).

The history of the U.S. pharmaceutical wholesaling industry offers a good example.[6] The wholesale drug trade can be traced back to the mid-1700s. Europe already had retail pharmacies, but the American colonies did not. Instead, medical practitioners prescribed and dispensed medicine on their own. But wholesalers arose to meet demands for medicines imported from Europe. These wholesalers then integrated forward (e.g., opening retail apothecaries) and backward (e.g., manufacturing drugs from indigenous plants).

In the nineteenth century, new pharmacies arose, independent of physicians. These channel members grew in parallel with the growth of the hospital industry, which needed wholesalers to support its burgeoning demands. Drug wholesalers operated locally, and in stiff competition with the vast numbers that operated in the same area. But instead of integrating forward or backward, these manifestations of the concept remained largely independent.

In the mid-twentieth century, the industry entered a new phase: Larger wholesalers offered regional, or even national, coverage of pharmaceuticals but also expanded their product lines to include health and beauty aids. Two large national firms dominated in terms of name recognition, but most of these wholesalers were smaller, regional firms, operated by a founding family out of a single location. From 1978 to 1996, this long-standing industry went through a period of dramatic consolidation. Drug wholesalers dropped from 147 firms down to 53, mostly through acquisitions. At the end of this period, just 6 firms accounted for 77 percent of the national market.

Why did it take so long to discover such enormous economies of scale in the industry? The answer is the difficulty of doing the simple job of wholesaling drugs correctly, effectively, and efficiently. The heart of drug wholesaling (and actually, much of wholesaling in general) is the relatively banal task of **picking**—taking from a shelf the items that the customer needs and assembling them for shipment. Pharmacies typically order frequently, requesting a few units of many different items. The variety of the units is substantial, with many stock-keeping units (SKUs). Because the products are medicinal, doing the job correctly (i.e., picking exactly the right item in the right quantity, with no room for error) is critical. For generations, this job was done by people, picking from warehouse shelves. And there are simply few economies of scale to find in picking millions of items to move from a pallet to a warehouse loading dock to a storage shelf, and then picking those items from the shelves to put into a bottle for individual customers.

Beginning in the 1950s though, firms began experimenting with different ways to do the picking better, faster, and accurately. But it was not until the task could be wholly restructured, using IT and automation, that the fundamentals of the industry shifted—and not in just one way. Many firms have experimented with IT and automation, and multiple methods continue to be in use, with no standard, best practice in place. Instead, a few tactics turned out to be clearly inappropriate, and firms that bet all their resources on one poor approach or another have since left the market.

But the winners changed so many operational aspects that they became nearly unrecognizable. On the operations side, they changed their picking technology, together with their order processing, billing, inventory control, delivery route scheduling, and inventory tracking through newly enormous warehouses. Electronic links with suppliers have replaced hundreds of clerks. On the demand side, wholesalers also profited from IT by turning to bar coding, scanning, and electronic order systems with direct data entry (which replaced salespeople who took handwritten notes about each pharmacist's order and clerks who entered in these orders into the system). The wholesale systems allow customers (i.e., pharmacies) to benefit from computerized accounts receivable and credit accounts, which they in turn offer to *their* customers. The pharmacies never could have been able to afford to provide such services otherwise. Then using the information obtained through these systems, wholesalers offered detailed advice about which inventory to hold and how to display it (planograms), while also updating their prices quickly.

In short, technology made it possible to change *everything*, and very rapidly. Acquiring firms rushed to achieve the size needed to amortize their huge investments. Firms being acquired sought to avoid making such investments. Through the free use of such mutually beneficial mergers and acquisitions, a few big firms emerged that had instituted an astonishing degree of organizational change. That is, the winners used technology to do the job right (fewer picking errors), effectively (swift and complete service to pharmacies), and efficiently (lower cost). This story recounts how it might take an industry 200 years to grow large—and then 20 years to consolidate.

Subsequently in this chapter, we also cover the profiles of wholesalers that tend to dominate after the shakeout phase. We also suggest strategies for manufacturers that need to cope with a shrinking downstream (wholesale) channel.

## Wholesaling Value-Added Strategies

Let's have a pop quiz: As quickly as you can, make a list of all the functions that wholesalers perform.[7] You might refer back to our generic channel functions. But often the first thing that pops to mind is that wholesalers gather, process, and use **information** about buyers, suppliers, and products to facilitate transactions. Although this traditionally has earned them substantial compensation, modern communication methods are likely to erode their information advantage for all forms except the most complex, idiosyncratic transactions that demand substantial tacit knowledge.

In addition, as we noted briefly already, wholesalers add value by creating an **efficient infrastructure** to exploit economies of scope (i.e., operating across brands and product categories) and scale (high volume). This advantage, which they can share with suppliers (upstream) and customers (downstream), reflects their specialization in channel functions and enables wholesalers to compete with manufacturers on price. Manufacturers frequently underestimate the magnitude of the wholesaler's efficiencies in terms of providing market coverage. Some of this advantage also stems from the wholesalers' ability to provide **time and place utility** by putting the right product in the right place at the time the customer wants it.

Many customers also value the wholesaler's ability to **absorb risk**, in the sense that they guarantee everything they sell in some form. Risk declines further when the wholesalers **filter** the product offering, suggesting appropriate choices for each customer and reducing the customer's information overload. Thus, the future for wholesalers might lie in *collaborative filtering* software, which uses information the wholesaler gathers about the preferences and choices of all its customers to suggest the best solutions for a prospect with particular characteristics or needs. Collaborative filtering likely is the key reason for Amazon's success: Its early-introduced, proprietary, collaborative filtering algorithms have for years steered customers to the books and music considered or purchased by "other people who bought" the same product the focal customer is buying.

For B2B buyers, wholesalers also engage in many functions that traditionally constitute manufacturing functions, in the sense that they **transform the goods** they sell. Some wholesalers receive components and subassemblies and put them together at the last minute (*assemble to order*). In general, they support *customization* through *postponement* of the final manufacturing step; *kitting* combines various components into sets, often with instructions for finalizing their manufacture. They also might *add on proprietary complements*, such as hardware and software. Wholesalers even *design* new products from unique combinations of components, or *program* semiconductors, or perform other actions in which they treat various elements as input to their channel functions. In this context, wholesalers enjoy an advantage because they can **unite knowledge** of the supplier base with information about the customer base and their specialized knowledge of customers' needs.

Consider Wesco, a distributor of electrical equipment and supplies. By distributing such products, Wesco enters everywhere in the B2B customer's facility; electricity touches all functions. Wesco then uses the knowledge it gains to help key accounts manage their facilities better. This management can have various, unexpected effects. When a hurricane destroyed a customer's oil refinery, Wesco's knowledge of how the electricity flowed through the facility helped the owner reconstruct its refinery in just six months.[8]

## Wholesaling Strategies in Foreign Markets

When a manufacturer exports to a foreign market, new complications easily arise. The manufacturer may be poorly versed in the market's situation. The product may be badly suited, or the proper marketing strategy to make it fit might not be evident. The strategy that worked in the home market could be a disastrous misfit, even if the product appeals to the foreign market. And of course, there are inevitable issues involved with foreign currency, customs regulations, and language. Faced with these complexities, many manufacturers enter foreign markets with little ambition—and equally little investment. Particularly among small and medium-sized manufacturers (which make up the bulk of exporting firms), exporting seems almost like a throwaway tactic. If it works, the incremental business is welcome. If it doesn't, little is lost.

Studies of the drivers of export performance demonstrate the folly of this attitude though. Profitable sales and strategic advantages emerge when the strategy supports the channel members responsible for the exported good, because manufacturers enable channel members to make arguments other than those focused on sheer price competition, so they in turn can achieve a sustainable differentiated position. Sidebar 7-1 profiles one type of intermediary that can be of particular assistance to such manufacturers.

## Sidebar 7-1

### Export trading companies

One type of channel member for exports is the **export intermediary**,[9] an independent firm located in the *exporter's* country, not the host country. These intermediaries perform channel functions (and forge marketing strategies) for multiple manufacturers in noncompeting product categories. In effect, they function as outsourced export departments for multiple manufacturers, searching for markets, negotiating contracts, and monitoring contracts for performance. In the United States, they generally are known as export management or export trading companies. Many manufacturers bypass them, but these intermediaries can help a manufacturer make a quantum leap in its level of international sophistication—and therefore its export performance.

The best performers in this category have two characteristics. First, they master the products they sell, by taking training from manufacturers, and then training foreign customers and giving them after-sales service. Second, they are deeply knowledgeable about foreign markets and export processes. Visible indicators usually identify these firms, such as their multilingual and foreign-born personnel. They also tend to be smaller firms, such that another good indicator of their knowledge level is the makeup of the top three managers. In more knowledgeable firms, the top three

- travel frequently,
- have extensive export experience, and
- have considerable industry experience.

Overall, the firm possesses extensive foreign connections, as well as strong industry experience.

In particular, exporters must be ready to adapt their distribution strategy to the market situation they face. A blind insistence that "this is our global distribution policy" dampens export performance. Rather, it matters little what type of intermediary the manufacturer uses (i.e., merchants, agents, distributors, direct buying offices), as long as the choice reflects local conditions, and the channel member receives support. For example, manufacturer must deliver exported goods to the channel member in a timely, reliable way, because such reliability often determines export performance. Channel intermediaries even tend to screen suppliers mainly on the basis of their ability to meet delivery commitments.

Relationships between manufacturers and their export distribution channels pay off particularly when the two parties can forge solid working relationships. Such relationships are flexible, with both parties willing to make modifications as the need arises. They also are open: The parties exchange information freely, frequently, and informally. And they are cooperative, with each party interested in sharing gains and seeing the relationship pay off for both sides. These relationships have strong internal working norms, which in turn reflect the time, effort, and resources the manufacturer devotes to its export efforts. Firms that view export as a side activity create a self-fulfilling prophecy of poor performance.

### Wholesaling Strategies in Emerging Economies

Previously we noted that customers tend to take the services provided by a wholesaler for granted, blissfully unaware of the costs that wholesalers incur. These blinders are particularly strong in emerging economies. In emerging markets, the low level of institutional trust further undermines business trade, leaving wholesalers without the trust and credibility that are their main tools for promoting business transactions and ensuring business performance.[10] Yet effective and efficient wholesaling is a vital prerequisite of nearly any industry. *In developing economies, the need for good distribution is both particularly acute and badly met.*[11] The reasons may have to do with societal attitudes.

Consider Niger, a desperately poor nation in West Africa.[12] Its harsh natural climate prevents most value-added agricultural commodities from growing well there—with the exception of onions. A superior onion variety, the Violet de Galmi, is appealing enough to offer a viable export crop, and since the 1960s, onion growing practices have taken off in Niger. Yet onions have not been nearly as successful as they should be, considering the agricultural situation and market demand. That is, farmers produce onions, and consumers want them. So what was blocking the channel? According to a team of aid agency analysts, it was the lack of a wholesaling sector.

In agriculture, wholesaling usually consists of brokers and wholesalers. Brokers move the crop from the field to the wholesaler, which involves the considerable physical operations of sorting, sacking, and moving. Wholesalers then transfer the onions to the distributors, which sell to retailers (in Niger, either street merchants or fixed stores). Some 50–75 percent of the retail price of each onion goes to the wholesaler (even after farmer co-ops use their countervailing power to reduce that level). On the surface, their profits appear to be **exploitation**, according to farmers, retailers, and government officials. Wholesalers thus are reviled by other members of the distribution channel, including end-users who believe the price they pay is too high. But all these members are ignoring the costs that the wholesalers incur. These onion wholesalers also are not getting rich. As one put it, "It's a lot like playing the national lottery." Consider the costs involved in the following functions that account for so much of the onion's final market value:

- Locating, assembling, and sorting produce from different farmers in many locations. Sorting is particularly important, because it provides a bulk breaking function. Many consumers can afford only one onion. Bulk breaking can even mean buying a smaller onion.
- Assuming credit risks for all actors in the channel, including farmers and retailers. These actors regularly pay late, if at all, or want to use another currency, or ask if they may provide goods or future considerations (offsets) rather than currency.
- Absorbing opportunism by retailers, who systematically make false claims, after taking delivery, that some percentage of the merchandise arrived spoiled, and simply switch wholesalers that challenge these claims.
- Building and maintaining expensive storage facilities.
- Absorbing the risk of improper pricing, which is considerable. Information about prices, supply, and demand is difficult to obtain in a timely way, due to Niger's poor national infrastructure.
- Meeting transportation costs, both traditional and illicit. That is, the greatest element of this cost is not the truck, though Niger suffers from poor roads that increase shipping costs. Rather, it is illicit rent seeking by government officials (e.g., customs, police), who erect multiple unnecessary checkpoints, even within Niger's borders, extort bribes, and hand out fictitious traffic tickets. Wholesalers who protest find their trucks held up until the onions spoil. Wholesalers who take their grievances to the government might find their entire truck fleet vandalized in the night.

- Absorbing the risk of crop loss—not only the onion crop but also any merchandise they might have taken as payment in lieu of cash.
- Absorbing the costs required to meet official regulations and observe informal arrangements of all kinds.

These broadly ranging costs are difficult to estimate. When the aid analysts attempted it, they were unpleasantly surprised by their vast magnitude. By far the greatest cost was illicit rent seeking; beyond its direct costs, this effect has indirect implications too. For example, onion production is subject to sharp seasonal swings, which could be smoothed out by holding onions in storage facilities. But wholesalers hesitate to build them because, like trucks, they are easy to see and vandalize. The vandals are likely to be disgruntled government employees who feel entitled to more bribe money than they are getting.

Why do officials behave this way? And why doesn't public pressure stop them? The single greatest reason is the wholesalers' poor reputation everywhere in Niger. They are viewed as greedy parasites who exploit hapless farmers and consumers without adding value. The public believes wholesalers are getting rich by engaging in speculative hoarding or oligopolistic, collusive behavior. Extorting them and vandalizing their property thus seems fair or justified. Officials even offer a positive spin, arguing that bribe money saves the taxpayer higher civil servant wages!

Risk thus is pervasive in onion wholesaling onions, and contracts are no solution, considering Niger's institutional infrastructure. Therefore, wholesalers tend to work with relatives, friends, and other in-group members, as a way to coordinate their responses and mobilize unsecured credit on short notice. (Relying on informal ties is a standard way to hedge high risks in any economy, including highly developed ones.[13]) Furthermore, women in Niger are limited in many sectors but flourish in wholesaling, though their low literacy rates demand that they employ literate people to read and write for them. The collection of illiterate women hiring relatives looks, on the surface, like strong evidence of nepotism and favoritism, rather than merit-based considerations (particularly among observers who do not see the wholesalers' costs from the start). Consumers simply take for granted the time and place utility these wholesalers create and assume they are making supernormal profits.

In contrast, wholesalers are not well compensated for their risks. Aid agency analysts concluded that they do a fairly good job under onerous conditions, but they could do more, particularly if they were willing to invest more. The Niger onions would be perfect sources for a Nestlé factory *in Niger* that makes dried onions. But the factory does not source locally, because the multinational requires its onions be certified to meet strict standards. Certification requires wholesaler investment.

Ultimately, analysts concluded that the best way to help the Niger farmer would be to help the Niger wholesaler.[14] They recommended a program of public education to change attitudes and create social pressure to stop illicit rent seeking. But this example is not an isolated situation: Recall our discussion in Chapter 1 (Sidebar 1-1) about tea middlemen. Negative public attitudes (again based on the mistaken impression that exploitative wholesalers added no value) encouraged Japanese colonial administrators in Taiwan to back farmers' cooperatives to compete with wholesalers. Yet even with a tax subsidy, the cooperatives could not match the wholesalers' efficiency in providing the services most consumers take for granted.[15]

Of course, none of this discussion should be taken as a guarantee that whole-salers are never exploitative. As might any other channel member, they will pursue their own interests to a dysfunctional level, unless checked by countervailing forces. In Niger, those countervailing forces include farmers' co-ops and the preponderance of alternative wholesalers. In Taiwan, many wholesalers also competed vigorously among themselves—as it should be. These examples should not be taken to imply that the problem exists only in emerging economies. In the United States, attitudes toward wholesalers feature widespread skepticism about whether they add any genu-ine value, cover significant costs, or operate efficiently. We return to this theme later in the chapter, when we discuss how wholesalers generate revenue.

## Alliance-Based Wholesaling Strategies

Wholesaler-distributors keep goods on hand that customers need immediately. Such availability often creates a situation in which the wholesaler-distributor backs up and extends the customer's own inventory system. In emergencies, unplanned repairs, or maintenance situations, distributors can supply products and minimize downtime; master distributors are an important provider of this function. Another wholesaling trend seeks other, innovative ways to respond to emergencies *while* cutting costs. The key to this extraordinary feat appears to be **federations** of wholesalers.

In federations, the goal is to enter into progressive, cooperative arrangements with other channel members, in which all elements—the nature of assistance, the procedures for providing it, and the appropriate compensation—have been defined *in advance*.[16] Such arrangements could cut costs substantially (often by 15–20 percent), improve service, and open new business opportunities. By cooperating, the members of the federation eliminate *redundant* inventory or service operations. These adaptive practices are being widely developed; here we describe some prototypes, led by either wholesalers or manufacturers.

**WHOLESALER-LED INITIATIVES**   In new, adaptive channels that depend on alliance (or consortium) relationships, wholesaler-distributors pool their resources to create a new, separate organization for joint action.[17] These **alliances** exist in almost every industry and can grow quite large. For example, Affiliated Distributors is one of the largest distribution alliances in North America, with more than 370 independent wholesaler-distributors and $25 billion in aggregate sales in 2012 (see www.indsupply.com/affiliated-distributors).

Another alliance, Intercore Resources, Inc., sells machine tools. Each of the four distributors that formed this **consortium** had faced difficulty providing timely, high-quality services to large customers with large contracts—the same ones who are most likely to have an emergency and to demand exceptional service. Each distributor in the consortium therefore refers business that it has trouble handling to Intercore Resources, which is administrative operation staffed by personnel sent by each distrib-utor. Intercore Resources draws on the resources of all four distributors (including their inventories, engineers, and other service personnel) to service each customer; it also can call on each distributor to demand the help it needs. Intercore Resources sends invoices and collects payments in its own name, then distributes profits to the owners (the four distributors), in the form of dividends.

Another method for creating an alliance is through a **holding company**. Otra N.V. is a Dutch company that holds 70 wholesalers of electrical products. One of these firms excels in service and training. Therefore, Otra N.V. relies on this expert service firm, BLE, to develop training programs and materials for all the other wholesalers in the group. BLE has become so proficient that it also offers its training to some of the group's suppliers. With its focus on the market, not on the producer, BLE's programs also are more thorough and less biased than the programs that suppliers usually develop themselves.

**MANUFACTURER-LED INITIATIVES**    Adaptive channels need at least one party to take the initiative. Wholesalers might create the preceding consortiums, holding companies, or divisions. Manufacturers that take the initiative instead organize distributors to pool their abilities and increase the efficiency of the supply chains overall, which benefits manufacturers, intermediaries, and end-users.[18] For example, Volvo Trucks North America Incorporated sells commercial trucks and repair parts in the United States, both through truck dealers and in its own regional warehouses. Dealers reported losses of lucrative repair business because they could not provide consistent, timely repairs when they were out of stock of the right parts. Yet the channel overall carried huge inventories. Volvo GM investigated and learned that dealers had trouble predicting the nature of demand for emergency roadside repairs and thus did not know what to stock. Yet truck downtime is so expensive that truck owners shop competing dealers to find substitute parts, rather than wait for an authorized Volvo GM dealer to get the right part.

To address the problem, Volvo GM assumed more of the inventory function and developed a delivery service, for which it bills dealers. Instead of maintaining three midsized supply warehouses, it built a massive new warehouse that stocks every part, locating it near Memphis, Tennessee. This choice of an obscure airport may seem odd, until we recall that Memphis is also the headquarters of FedEx. Thus, Volvo GM made a FedEx-specific investment and took on some risk, which enabled a mechanism by which dealers can call for the precise part they need and get it, via FedEx, the same day. Dealers still have to pay for this service, but they often pass it on to customers, who are price insensitive in the face of roadside emergencies. Furthermore, the result of this centralized solution is more business for the supplier and its dealers and a sharp drop in inventory costs, which offset the sharp rise in express delivery charges.

In contrast, we find a more **decentralized solution** in the warehouses of Okuma, a Japanese machine tool manufacturer. Okuma operates two of its own warehouses, electronically linked to 46 distributors. In addition, it links its distributors to one another, encouraging them to draw on one another's inventories. The Okuma electronic system thus creates 48 possible sources (2 warehouses, 46 distributors) for any tool.

**RETAILER-SPONSORED COOPERATIVES**    A retailer-sponsored co-op may seem similar to wholesalers' voluntary groups, but in this case, a similar idea gets initiated by the retailers. In practice, there is a substantial difference.

To coordinate among themselves, dealers are obliged to create an organization, such as a consortium. When they join, they agree to do a certain amount of business with the consortium and follow some of its procedures—so far, just like a wholesaler voluntary group. But the members also must buy shares in the co-op, such that *they are owners as well as members.* And as owners, they receive shares of the profits generated by their co-op (as stock dividends) and end-of-year rebates on their purchases. Thus, the goals of the co-op and the interests of its members align closely.

Unlike wholesaler voluntary groups, retailer co-ops thus have a more formalized structure, run by dedicated professional managers whose jobs have fairly elaborate role descriptions. They also are better able to influence the marketing efforts of their owner/members, who must adhere to the co-op's advertising, signage, and brands if they hope to stay. In short, their marketing coordination is stronger. Sidebar 7-2 profiles the U.K.'s Co-operative Group, the largest retailer co-op in the U.K. market.

## Sidebar 7-2

### Co-operative Group

The U.K.-based Co-operative Group is run and owned by its 7 million members. Essentially, it is a family of businesses that incorporates food retailing, financial services, pharmacies, funeral services, legal services, and electrical. The group has around 100,000 employees across the U.K., and has an annual turnover of U.S. $22 billion.

The group can trace its roots back to 1844, although it was not until 1863, when 300 individual cooperatives merged to create the North of England Co-operative Wholesale Industrial and Provident Society Limited, that the group became effective. By 1872, this had been renamed as the Co-operative Wholesale Society (CWS). Over the course of the next hundred years, many other smaller cooperatives joined the group.[19]

From its fairly humble beginnings, the group has grown to become one of the leading retailers supporting ethical business practices. In 2002, the group won the Worldaware Shell Award for Sustainable Development for its policies on Fairtrade goods. In 2007, it won the Queen's Award for Enterprise, again for sustainable development practices. The group was on the short list for the Transform Awards (for branding and rebranding) in 2010. In 2012, the group courted controversy when it ended its relationships with its Israeli suppliers that were based around settlements in Palestinian territories.

In the late summer of 2013, the group announced that they were rebranding all of their own-label products. In the U.K. food retail market, own-brand products had become a key battleground. At this point, the Co-op was the fifth largest food retailer in the U.K. It was coming under increasing pressure from the other four retailers.

The move by the Co-op would see 700 own-label lines rebranded to "Loved by Us." The move was timely, as over the next few weeks, the group saw their sales growing at a rate of just over 6 percent. The Co-op had been struggling to match the expansion of its own-brand food lines with that of the biggest market shareholders in the U.K. (Tesco, Sainsbury's, Asda, and Morrisons). Each of these four competitors had made large investments in their food lines, and had been extremely successful in using own-brand products to drive up sales. At the other end of the market, the low-cost food retailers, including Aldi and Lidl had also invested in the own-label ranges, and were gradually taking customers and sales away from the Co-op. Co-op's response to the threats had been to bring in a new management team. Both Euan Sutherland (Group CEO) and Richard Pennycook (finance director) had years of retail experience.[20]

This revamp of the own-label branding is in line with the use of standardized advertising, signage, and branding for all of the retail outlets. As a community-based retailer with 2,800 local, convenience, and medium-sized retail outlets across the U.K., this form of standardization is important.

Recognizing the negative impact of the recent food scandals (such as horse DNA being found in beef products), the Co-op was also keen to emphasize its commitment to British farming. A number of the key products in the own-label range, including foods-to-go, and chilled ready meals, will now only use 100 percent British-sourced meat, fish, and poultry.

Taking advantage of the standardization of labeling and other marketing aspects, the

## Continued

own-label range was supported by a national advertising and marketing campaign. The primary focus was on product quality. The first part of the Loved by Us branding was applied to the breakfast and lunch ranges.

Snacks and convenience food are a vital part of food retailing, and to this end, the Co-op relaunched its snack menu, supported by the new Middle Eastern and Indian-style flatbreads and wraps. The company was also able to steal a march on the competition in certain areas, such as the development of a new prawn sandwich that could boast 50 percent more prawns than the competition.

The bulk of the Loved by Us own-branded products was aimed toward the budget end of the market, but the Co-op also released its own premium range, Truly Irresistible. This range was benchmarked against the competition. The idea was to offer an array of some 50 products that would provide the consumer with restaurant quality meals at a fraction of the cost. They would also provide an affordable alternative to home-cooked meals.

According to Steve Murrells, the Co-op's retail chief executive, the new move was to take their own-brand product range to a new level. The group had invested heavily in new product development. By overhauling the whole range, it was hoped that consumers would re-appraise the Co-op brand. Essentially, it was a back-to-basic approach. The Co-op had refocused on quality, value, and convenience.

Phil Hudson, Head of Food and Farming at the National Farmers Union, endorsed the Co-op's commitment to British sourced meat and poultry for its key ranges. The NFU had recently carried out market research in the aftermath of the horsemeat scandal and discovered that 78 percent of British consumers would prefer British-raised meat products. The Co-op had already signed the NFU's Back British Farming Charter. Hudson saw this as a move by the group to support a more direct, transparent, and fairer supply chain.

The rebranding exercise also aimed to address disparities in consumer perception of the Co-op. Among the over–55-year-olds, some 43 percent viewed the Co-op as the most trusted food retail brand, but for the 16–24 age group, this was at just 12 percent.

Despite a common impression, a co-op is not just for dealers. There can be many types; in principle, the only thing required to define a co-op is that the members set up an organization to serve them and own shares in it. Cooperatives are becoming particularly popular in Japan, as responses to the pressures of shortening marketing channels. Small and medium-sized wholesalers, seeing their roles overtaken by large wholesalers or manufacturers, have been creating their own cooperatives to gain economies of scale.

The Cooperative Association Yokohama Merchandising Center (MDC), for example, is owned by 75 wholesalers, which use the MDC as a vehicle to gain scale. The wholesalers supply MDC, which warehouses the goods in a huge distribution center. By serving from this center, MDC minimizes separate deliveries (and their costs). In addition, MDC's wholesalers have sufficient scale to serve major retailers. They have built a modern, online information center to manage orders.

Another type of cooperative has played a major role in distribution in the United States—the **farm cooperative**. The story of the emergence and growth of farm cooperatives could fill an entire textbook. Suffice it to say that organizations such as Sunkist, Ocean Spray, and Land O'Lakes have become extremely powerful forces, benefiting their members by organizing farm equipment and supply markets, as well as the markets into which farmers sell their produce. Although some farm co-ops have vertically integrated both backward and forward, they remain primarily wholesalers of goods and services, and they administer the channels that they control with the approval of the farmers who own them.

Finally, the **consumer cooperative** also has had impacts on distribution. In the United States, consumer co-ops are not common though; they tend to flourish in small, homogeneous, closed communities, such as college towns or rural communities. But they do better elsewhere, as Sidebar 7-3, regarding the women's agricultural cooperative in Egypt, reveals.

The identities of consumer cooperatives, their characteristics, and the reasons for their success (or lack thereof) are not well understood. They deserve further study, because they have great potential to improve consumer welfare. The Consumer Federation of America, founded in 1968, represents over 100 different consumer cooperatives.[21]

## Sidebar 7-3

### Egypt's first female cooperatives

Nearly 200 miles from Cairo in the village of El-Tod near Luxor, 26 women formed a cooperative. For generations, much of the land in the region was dry and infertile; now there are fields of tomatoes. The women had all been members of the male-dominated El-Tod Agricultural Community Development Farmers' Association. The local land, being owned by men, meant that the women had fewer opportunities to have their views heard.

Today, the 26 women, having left the association, have their own cooperative and are raising their own cattle. The cooperative provides them with secure employment and better working conditions. It also allows them to be shareholders in their own business and retain control over the decision-making processes.

This area of Upper Egypt, according to Egypt's Human Development Report (2008), indicated that some 66 percent of the country's poorest people lived in the region. Upper Egypt also accounted for 95 percent of the poorest villages in the country.

For the women in Upper Egypt, poverty was even more acute. Religious norms restricted their employment opportunities. In short, they felt severely disadvantaged in terms of their ability to earn wages, and they often had to cope with very poor working conditions. Amal Abel Aziz, a graduate architectural engineer, helped to create the cooperative. The process was not without

difficulties but a combination of focus and determination allowed her to succeed.

Traditionally, women in Upper Egypt account for 75 percent, and more, of the agricultural labor force according to the World Food Programme. Hence, it was a natural progression for some of them to consider an alternative. As far as Egypt's Central Agency for Census and Statistics are concerned, the latest report in 2012 suggested that much of the agricultural work carried out by women is informal. In other words, they are unregistered workers. In fact, just 23 percent of the formal workforce in Upper Egypt is female. Clearly, there is a massive disparity in the two sets of figures.

The El-Tod cooperative is part of a much larger project. The global Millennium Development Goal organization funds the Pro-poor Horticulture Value Chains in Upper Egypt (Salasel) Project. This project is charged with improving efficiency in agriculture in Upper Egypt, primarily as a driver to reduce poverty. The overall project is supported by the United Nations Development Programme (UNDP), United Nations Industrial Development Organization (UNIDO), International Labour Organization (ILO), and UN Women. In turn, they work closely with the Egyptian Ministry of Industry and Trade, and the Ministry of Investment. The primary plan is to create income-generating projects in Upper Egypt, with the aim of providing

## Continued

better opportunities for small farmers irrespective of their gender.

The 26 members of the cooperative are now guaranteed an income of U.S. $45–60 per month. In the past, the women did not have a guaranteed income. This was not the only female cooperative to be created in Upper Egypt. Two others have been established in Beni Suef. At the launch of the cooperatives in June 2013, Mohammad Naciri, the UN Women representative for Egypt, stated that this was a move toward empowering women, encouraging female leadership and involvement in the economy, and above all, providing them with a predictable income. The three cooperatives also received the support of the Misr el Kheir Foundation. It was the foundation that provided them with the cattle, business training, and the necessary technical support.

Effectively, the women's cooperatives are examples of micro-starts. The cooperatives will be able to sell their produce directly in the market, principally in the local communities. This will mean that their income will remain in the local area, and generate more jobs and opportunities. Although these cooperatives represent a modest start for the women, and it is clear that they will need long term support and advice, it is the intention to roll out the program to other parts of Upper Egypt. Collectively, as the number of cooperatives increases, the greater the importance the cooperatives will have in the local economies. Ultimately, when the cooperatives have grown to a sufficient size, there will be opportunities for them to export their produce to other parts of Egypt and to the rest of the region.

As for Amal Abel Aziz, her ambitions are even greater than creating and running a successful direct-selling cooperative in El-Tod. She intends, one day, to become the governor of Luxor. She will then have the power and connections to make even more sweeping changes to eradicate poverty in the area.

## Consolidation Strategies in Wholesaling

The popular image of small wholesalers often contrasts with the modern reality, in which wholesalers are large, sophisticated, capital-intensive corporations. This transformation occurred through consolidation, a phenomenon that has swept through many industries in parallel with improvements in IT and changes in the wholesaler's customer base. In the United States, wholesaling remains an active mergers and acquisitions area, often funded by private buyout capital. The pressure to consolidate often comes from the wholesaler-distributor's larger downstream customers, including large manufacturers, multiunit retailers, and sizable purchasing groups. Such buyers value the ability to access multiple suppliers, spread over a vast geography, but pass through only a single source. This preference creates demand for huge wholesalers.

However, as they consolidate through acquisition, wholesalers also use their newfound scale to form partnerships with customers, which limits manufacturers' ability to access these same customers. The newly massive wholesalers thus often prune their supplier list, using their bargaining leverage to wring concessions from a shorter list of vendors. This move in turn sets off a wave of consolidation upstream. That is, large customers provoke wholesaler consolidation, which stimulates manufacturer consolidation. The pace of consolidation can be startlingly fast. For example, the number of U.S. periodical and magazine wholesalers dropped from more than 180 to fewer than 50 firms in just nine years, and the five largest wholesalers quickly gained control of 65 percent of the national market.

What can manufacturers do when they face a wholesale consolidation wave? They have four main solutions to consider. First, they can attempt to predict which wholesalers will be left standing and build partnerships with them. This move is common in Europe, where economic unification has made national boundaries less relevant. But how can they identify likely **winners**? They look for four basic types:

1. "Catalyst firms" that trigger consolidation by moving rapidly to acquire.
2. Wholesalers that enter late, after consolidation has progressed, because such firms would not enter unless they had found defensible niches.
3. Extreme specialists, already attuned to the conditions likely to prevail after consolidation.
4. Their opposite, extreme generalists. These large, full-line firms can serve many environments well, and their versatility is valuable once the market has consolidated.

Second, manufacturers facing wholesale consolidation can invest in **fragmentation**. With this strategy, they bet on and work with smaller, independent firms trying to survive the wave of consolidation. It represents the opposite form of the strategy of betting on a few winners. For example, manufacturers might seek out alliances of smaller, wholesaler-distributors whose members bid for national or multiregional contracts, offering the same geographic reach as a larger company. The alliances also take advantage of volume purchasing opportunities from suppliers, yet each alliance member retains its operational autonomy and thus can continue to provide the same high service levels to local customers. Not only might manufacturers seek to work with these alliances, but they also can create the alliance to offer a credible alternative to consolidators. In South Africa, financial services traditionally were sold through independent brokers. But in the face of changing societal and economic conditions, Old Mutual, a diversified provider of financial services in that country, worried that consolidation would shift the distribution of financial services to banks and vertically integrated competitors. To keep its broker network alive and thriving, Old Mutual launched Masthead Broker Association, a division that sells distribution support services to brokers on highly favorable terms. The highly successful program has given Old Mutual (and its competitors) multiple routes to market that otherwise would have disappeared.

Third, a manufacturer facing wholesale consolidation can build a different, alternative route to market by **vertically integrating forward**. We cover this strategy in Chapter 4.

Fourth, a manufacturer might **increase its own attractiveness** to the remaining channels, usually by increasing its own ability to offer benefits (e.g., a strong brand name). This strategy, namely, of becoming more attractive to channel members, is a theme that permeates this book.

After wholesale consolidation, the balance of power in the channel changes. Industry sales mostly move through a handful of large, publicly traded, professionally managed companies. Entry barriers are high, and entrants must seek niche markets. The large wholesalers achieve lower gross margins than when the industry's wholesalers were fragmented, local, and privately held, but they also engage in more total business and operate more efficiently, such that their net margins are healthy, despite lower gross margins. These wholesalers put great pressures on suppliers, particularly in terms of pricing, and offer improved service to customers. The large surviving wholesalers also redesign supply chain management processes, often revolutionizing their current operating methods.

Wholesaler consolidation thus is a sea change in an industry. Once it begins, it usually progresses rapidly. Manufacturers must react rapidly and be ready to change their marketing channels and methods. Wholesale consolidation is a force that cannot be overlooked.

## ADAPTING TO TRENDS IN WHOLESALING

### International Expansion

A striking feature of wholesaler-distributors is that though they can become quite large, they seldom go global. Is this a historical artifact of the days of family-owned businesses? Will large firms that survive an industry consolidation eventually expand abroad?

Many domestic wholesaler-distributors already *are* expanding internationally (often by acquiring foreign wholesaler-distributors) to meet the needs of their customers and suppliers. Global manufacturers and customers ask their distribution partners to maintain a presence in all their major markets. The reduced costs of cross-border shipping and falling trade barriers also encourage expansion. For the same reasons, foreign wholesaler-distributors are making inroads into domestic markets. This trend of cross-border growth and acquisitions is particularly strong in Europe.

Yet, the very nature of wholesaling suggests that *most wholesalers will never be truly global.* Fundamentally, wholesaling entails meeting the needs of a local market, and these needs are so varied that it is exceedingly difficult to standardize marketing channels. Without standardization, it becomes very difficult for suppliers, customers, or wholesaler-distributors to pursue a truly global supply chain strategy. The few successful examples come from industries in which many participants in the channel are global, such as electronic components or computers.

### Electronic Commerce

Debate rages about the impact of **electronic commerce** on wholesalers. On the one hand, doomsday predictions abound: All intermediaries are doomed to elimination due to the ruthless efficiency of Internet search engines! On the other hand, wholesaling has genuine value added. Eliminating wholesalers will not eliminate their functions. And the Internet cannot provide all channel functions.

A more likely scenario is that e-commerce will change but not replace wholesalers. Wholesalers, and indeed all channel intermediaries, thrive by gaining customer knowledge and combining it with their knowledge of producers to solve the problems of both ends.[22] The Internet creates new problems (e.g., heightened risk of defective goods, fraudulent "merchants," credit card theft, release of private information). It also creates new ways to solve problems (e.g., collaborative filtering to help the customer spend less time while still making better choices). Consequently, the Internet should not eliminate intermediaries—but it does demand a reconsideration of the fundamentals of how they create value and capture a fair share.

Early indications suggest that wholesalers actually are benefiting from e-commerce as they co-opt the Internet for their own uses, to bring in new business and improve how they perform their work. Many distributors are racing to find new ways to use the Internet as a tool to create even more value. In the process, they adopt artificial intelligence to replace salespeople's service roles. Hiring by wholesalers thus has slowed dramatically, but existing salespeople are expected to provide higher levels of service, including consultative selling.

## B2B Online Exchanges

**Independent electronic exchanges** operate as online brokers in a given industry. These exchanges popped up notably in the late 1990s as companies offered aggregation services for online supplier catalogs, enabling buyers of similar products to source and purchase items from multiple suppliers from a single location. To widespread surprise though, these exchanges did not exert devastating impacts on wholesalers, as predicted, but instead have failed themselves at high rates. Where they made inroads, it was often in already commoditized industries, such as personal computers. Why? As you should have guessed by now, the predictions of doom for wholesalers ignored the **basic value added** that wholesalers provide. Arrow Electronics is a large wholesaler of electronic components. In the 1990s, more than 50 Internet exchanges formed that could challenge Arrow's business model,[23] proposing to "cut out the middleman" by handling the information flows and letting the producer handle the product flows. Let's consider how Arrow beat back these exchanges by investigating the three classes of business in which it competed:

- Book and ship: Commodity, standardized products that constitute 25 percent of its business are subject to competition from grey markets. The exchanges expected to win this business.
- Value-added orders: To rationalize the supply chain and lower total ordering costs, Arrow provides services such as kitting, programming, managing the customer's inventory on the customer's site, and guaranteeing inventory buffers. The customer thus benefits from the wholesaler's knowledge of its needs.
- Design wins: Complex sells to customers who are unsure of their requirements means providing brand-neutral advice that customers cannot get from the supplier.

In retrospect, the failure of the exchanges could have been predicted. Strong competition in the book-and-ship business had already dropped its margins drastically. The costs the exchanges proposed to reduce (for a 6 percent fee) were only 4 percent of the purchase price! Furthermore, the exchanges were unknown, whereas Arrow is known and trusted. In the design wins and value-added orders segments, the distributor clearly enjoyed advantages, and because customers benefit from one-stop shopping, the distributor could resist unbundling its book-and-ship business.

A story similar to Arrow's has repeated in various sectors. Wholesaling is brutally competitive. New entrants often have difficulty unseating incumbents, who benefit from their well-established, well-working routines and lean operations.[24] In particular, exchanges could not create new value that the existing wholesalers could not readily match, especially when they exploited the Web as a viable tool.

Nonetheless, exchanges should not be written off completely. They are gaining ground in sectors in which commodities can be separated from other parts of the business. The major obstacle appears to be **codification** of difficult-to-estimate parameters (e.g., quality of customer service). Exchanges founder when customers discover they need something unexpected: emergency or rush service, design know-how, and so forth. Furthermore, just establishing a reliable relationship is costly. Expertise, credit worthiness, and general qualification to bid must be factored in, none of which is easy to do.[25]

## Online Reverse Auctions

Perhaps a greater threat to wholesalers than online exchanges is **online bidding by reverse auction**.[26] In this real-time price competition, prequalified suppliers seek to win a customer's business. Using specialized software, bidders (whether distributors, producers, or both) submit progressively declining bids, and the winner submits the lowest bid before time runs out. Although only a small part of overall transactions, reverse auctions are gaining ground; many buyers perceive them as a fast, easy way to set aside "irrational" considerations (e.g., relationships, "soft" or subjective qualifications) and get straight to a low price.

Wholesalers tend to be suspicious of reverse auctions though, because they seemingly reduce procurement decisions to price, without consideration of capabilities—many of which reflect the wholesalers' supplier-specific investments. Especially when bids are open (revealed to all bidders) rather than sealed (only winning bids are known), wholesalers worry that open bidding may trick them into revealing their positions.

Reverse auctions thus have real dangers: They may destroy excellent relationships, with the potential to generate performance breakthroughs and new ideas. Wholesalers (and other suppliers) hesitate to make investments specific to suppliers that run reverse auctions. And reverse auctions tend to focus on the lowest product prices, rather than the lowest procurement costs or lowest cost of ownership over the product's lifetime. These broader cost concepts involve intangible factors, but considerations of warranties, delivery time, switching costs, and capabilities tend to get lost in bidding wars. Efforts to incorporate such factors into the auction have not been successful, because they are so difficult to codify.

Ultimately, the long-run danger of reverse auctions is that suppliers use them to extract excessive concessions, driving suppliers (wholesalers and manufacturers) right out of business. This forced supply consolidation puts buyers into negotiations with just a few, large wholesalers and producers. In the long run, this scenario may not be the route to sustainable competitive advantages for buyers.

## Fee for Services

It has always been difficult for wholesalers to calculate the true **profitability** of a given product line or customer. Product lines compose a portfolio, and customers demand an assortment. Dropping an unprofitable product line can disrupt the appeal of the package. Dropping an unprofitable customer contradicts the basic notion of spreading costs over a large customer base. Thus, wholesalers carry many customers that cost more than they bring in, usually because they demand multiple services along with their products. Traditionally, wholesalers charge for the product and include the service "for free." This **bundling** is based on the idea that customers will pay more for products from distributors that give them more service.

But over time, many customers have come to violate this convention, relentlessly wearing down distributors on price while training the distributors' personnel not to withhold services. Why do wholesalers tolerate such money-losing customers? Frequently, it is because they cannot identify who they are. It is no simple matter to assign costs to customers nonarbitrarily. One possible method is **activity-based costing (ABC)**, which assigns costs based on approximations of the activities needed to support each customer. An ABC analysis usually suggests that the distributor's portfolio of customers follows the **80/20 rule**: 80 percent of profits are generated by only 20 percent of customers, and the remaining 80 percent of customers actually drain profits away.[27]

A solution to this problem is rapidly gaining ground: **fee for service** models.[28] The idea is to break the traditional connection between the pricing model (gross margin on product) and the value model (providing superior service, which may be worth far more than the product and is more difficult to find elsewhere). By charging a product price and then a fee for each and every service the customer uses, the wholesaler unbundles products and services and makes its value proposition visible. For example, TMI is a cutting tools distributor that has introduced fees for inspecting, kitting, and tracking services associated with cutting tools. These services save the customer time and money in a demonstrable way, which is why TMI can collect fees on them rather than (trying to) charge more for its tools.

At the limit, distributors offer services for a fee *without* supplying the product (which is sourced elsewhere)! The fee for service model represents a revolution in wholesaling, though like most revolutions, it is not easy to introduce, particularly when customers are accustomed to thinking of services as "included" in gross margins. Wholesalers need to demonstrate that their services are valuable. They might do so by accepting more risk, agreeing to be paid only if the customer meets specific targets (e.g., cost savings, labor savings, performance improvements).

## Vertical Integration of Manufactures into Wholesaling

When manufacturers perform wholesaling activities themselves, they operate sales branches and offices, as we discussed in Chapter 4 (make-or-buy analysis). At the retail level, huge "power retailers" also might bypass independent wholesaler-distributors by setting up their own branches to perform channel functions. This trend is gathering momentum in Europe (fueled by the economic union) and Japan (fueled by rising price elasticity among consumers and questions about the length and operating methods of Japanese channels). In the United States, this trend already is well advanced.

That is, wholesaler-distributors are a small part of many traditional (physical) U.S. retail channels, due the influence of **power retailers**[29] that dominate various sectors of retail activity. Power retailers typically buy in large quantities in select product categories (e.g., toys) and take a very prominent position in their channel. Because of this purchase volume, power retailers can often adopt a **buy direct** approach. Retailers such as Wal-Mart squeeze costs out of the channel by creating in-house distribution systems in which wholesaler-distributors play small roles, then further leverage their positions using tactics such as in-store media and advertising. For example, Wal-Mart TV broadcasts on 100,000 screens in more than 2,650 stores, reaching approximately 336 million shoppers every month. In response, many of its suppliers, including Kraft Foods, Gillette, and Frito-Lay, began advertising on Wal-Mart TV, which further strengthened their ties.[30]

Manufacturers must respond to the demands of dominant buyers, often at the expense of wholesaler-distributors. In addition, power retailers trigger industry

---

consolidation among small- and medium-sized retailers—that is, the traditional consumers of wholesale distribution. Thus, the role of wholesaler-distributors in retail channels has diminished or been eliminated in the past 20 years, leaving fewer, larger wholesaler-distributors among the only survivors. This outcome provides another reason e-commerce is unlikely to have a devastating effect on independent wholesalers in most retail sectors: The devastation has already occurred. Power retailers have left few wholesaler-distributors standing for the Internet to affect.

At the same time, the hyperefficient retail distribution systems used by power retailers are not well suited to "unit of one" sales, as required for online buying and shipping to a consumer's home. Thus, many of these retailers partner with wholesaler-distributors or third-party fulfillment companies, such as Fingerhut, to enter e-commerce fields.[31] The Internet, curiously, may prove to be a way to bring independent wholesalers back into retail channels.

## SUMMARY: WHOLESALING STRUCTURES AND STRATEGIES

The wholesaling sector covers the sale of products between businesses, as opposed to sales to ultimate household end-users. It creates value by providing channel functions. Just as the value of these functions is often underappreciated, so too is the value-added and economic importance of the wholesaling sector. The essential tasks that this industry performs may be mundane, but it is no simple matter to carry them out with few errors, bundled with valued services, and at low cost.

Players in the wholesale sector also are experimenting with innovative ways to deliver value while cutting costs, such as assembling federations of channel members to share resources, to eliminate inventory and process redundancies. These efforts may be led by wholesalers or by manufacturers; they can be organized in multiple ways. Channel members further downstream, such as dealers, also might organize to capitalize on economies of scale, such as through cooperatives. Another way to achieve economies of scale is through consolidation, and in wholesaling settings, consolidation is endemic, usually achieved with waves of mergers and acquisitions by a handful of players. As we discussed in this chapter, manufacturers have four main responses to such consolidation and its outcomes.

The future of wholesaler-distributors will be one of changes, due to the pressures and opportunities of international expansion, as well as the new possibilities created by electronic commerce. The idea that electronic commerce will eliminate wholesaler-distributors is overly simplistic. These institutions already are finding ways to benefit from the Internet. But change is certain, and it will continue to affect various wholesaling sectors in different ways.

## TAKE-AWAYS

- Wholesale businesses sell physical inputs and products to other businesses, retailers, merchants, contractors, industrial users, institutional users, and commercial users. Wholesaling is closely associated with tangible goods. However, wholesalers create value added by providing services in channel functions.

- Buyers typically understate the difficulty of the three critical challenges of wholesaling:
  - Doing the job without errors.
  - Doing the job effectively (i.e., with a maximum of service).
  - Doing the job efficiently (i.e., at low costs).
  This tendency is particularly acute in developing economies, in which a healthy wholesaling sector actually can spur considerable development.
- The challenges of wholesaling prompt firms to create economies of scope and scale up and down the channel of distribution. The objective is to offer exceptional service at acceptable costs, such as through:
  - Master distributors, a type of super wholesaler.
  - Federations of wholesalers, which might be led by wholesalers themselves or by manufacturers.
  - Voluntary and cooperative groups of wholesalers, retailers, consumers, or producers.
- Consolidation is a common phenomenon in wholesaling, due in part to the economies of scale available through IT. Yet the wholesaling sector is typically less concentrated than the manufacturing sector.
- Four types of winners emerge when a wholesaling sector consolidates:
  - Catalyst firms (serial acquirers).
  - Late entrants that find defensible niches.
  - Extreme specialists attuned to postconsolidation conditions.
  - Extreme generalists that trade depth for breadth.
- Manufacturers can react to consolidation in wholesaling by:
  - Partnering with one of the four winners.
  - Investing in fragmentation (supporting small independents).
  - Vertically integrating forward.
  - Investing in becoming more attractive to survivors of the consolidation.
- Export distribution channels present special challenges that require the manufacturer to develop cultural sensitivity and alter its normal working arrangements.
- Electronic commerce promises to change the wholesaling sector in many ways, some of which will benefit the sector enormously. Online exchanges and reverse auctions are among these developments. In response, wholesalers are experimenting with new ways to add value and capture a fair share of it.

## Endnotes

1. Fein, Adam J. (2000), "Wholesaling," *U.S. Industry and Trade Outlook 2000* (New York: DRI/McGraw-Hill).

2. Lusch, Robert L. and D. Zizzo (1996), *Foundations of Wholesaling: A Strategic and Financial Chart Book* (Washington, DC: Distribution Research and Education Foundation).

3. Palmatier, Robert W., Fred C. Ciao, and Eric Fang (2007), "Sales Channel Integration after Mergers and Acquisitions: A Methodological Approach for Avoiding Common Pitfalls,"

*Industrial Marketing Management* 36, no. 5 (July), pp. 589–603.

4. Scott, Colin, Henriette Lundgren, and Paul Thompson (2011), *Guide to Supply Chain Management,* (Berlin: Springer).

5. Anonymous (1997), "Ever-Shorter Channels— Wholesale Industry Restructures," *Focus Japan* 24 (July/August), pp. 3–4.

6. Fein, Adam J. (1998), "Understanding Evolutionary Processes in Non-Manufacturing Industries: Empirical Insights From the Shakeout in Pharmaceutical Wholesaling,"

*Journal of Evolutionary Economics* 8, no. 1, pp. 231–270.

7. Anderson, Philip and Erin Anderson (2002), "The New E-Commerce Intermediaries," *Sloan Management Review* 43 (Summer), pp. 53–62. This source provides the primary basis for this section.

8. These services are described on the Wesco corporate website and in the Harvard Business School case #9-598-021, "Wesco Distribution."

9. Peng, Mike W. and Anne S. York (2001), "Behind Intermediary Performance in Export Trade: Transactions, Agents, and Resources," *Journal of International Business Studies* 32, no. 2, pp. 327–346.

10. Zhang, Ran and Zabihollah Rezaee (2009), "Do Credible Firms Perform Better in Emerging Markets? Evidence from China," *Journal of Business Ethics* 90, no. 2, pp. 221–237.

11. Prahalad, C.K. and Allen Hammond (2002), "Serving the World's Poor Profitably," *Harvard Business Review* 9, pp. 49–57.

12. Arnould, Eric J. (2001), "Ethnography, Export Marketing Policy, and Economic Development in Niger," *Journal of Public Policy & Marketing* 20 (Fall), pp. 151–169.

13. Palmatier, Robert W. (2008), *Relationship Marketing* (Cambridge MA: Marketing Science Institute).

14. Bardy, Roland, Stephen Drew, and Tumenta F. Kennedy (2012), "Foreign Investment and Ethics: How to Contribute to Social Responsibility by Doing Business in Less-Developed Countries," *Journal of Business Ethics* 106, no. 3, pp. 267–282.

15. Koo, Hui-wen, and Pei-yu Lo (2004), "Sorting: The Function of Tea Middlemen in Taiwan During the Japanese Colonial Era," *Journal of Institutional and Theoretical Economics* 160 (December), pp. 607–626.

16. Narus, James A. and James C. Anderson (1996), "Rethinking Distribution," *Harvard Business Review* 96 (July–August), pp. 112–120. The section on adaptive contracts and the examples are drawn from this article, which goes into much greater depth on the specifics of such arrangements.

17. Fein, Adam J. (1998), "The Future of Distributor Alliances," *Modern Distribution Management* (September).

18. Granot, Daniel and Shuya Yin (2008), "Competition and Cooperation in Decentralized Push and Pull Assembly Systems," *Management Science* 54 (April), pp. 733–747.

19. See http://www.co-operative.coop/corporate/aboutus/ourhistory/ (accessed 04/03/2014).

20. See http://www.telegraph.co.uk/finance/newsbysector/retailandconsumer/10220840/Co-operative-food-brand-gets-an-overhaul.html (accessed 04/03/2014).

21. Based on 2012 website at http://www.consumerfed.org.

22. Anderson and Anderson (2002), op. cit.

23. Narayendas, Das, Mary Caravella, and John Deighton (2002), "The Impact of Internet Exchanges on Business-to-Business Distribution," *Journal of the Academy of Marketing Sciences* 30 (Fall), pp. 500–505.

24. Day, George S., Adam J. Fein, and Gregg Ruppersberger (2003), "Shakeouts in Digital Markets: Lessons from B2B Exchanges," *California Management Review* 45 (Winter), pp. 131–150.

25. Kleindorfer, Paul R. and D.J. Wu (2003), "Integrating Long- and Short-Term Contracting via Business-to-Business Exchanges for Capital-Intensive Products," *Management Science* 49 (November), pp. 1597–1615.

26. This discussion is based on NAW/DREF and Pembroke Consulting (2004), op. cit.; Jap, Sandy D. (2003), "An Exploratory Study of the Introduction of Online Reverse Auctions," *Journal of Marketing* 67, no. 3, p. 96.

27. Niraj, Rakesh, Mahendra Gupta, and Chakravarthi Narasimhan (2001), "Customer Profitability in a Supply Chain," *Journal of Marketing* 65, no. 3, p. 1.

28. This discussion is based on NAW/DREF and Pembroke Consulting (2004), op. cit.

29. Lusch, Robert F. and D. Zizzo (1995), *Competing for Customers: How Wholesaler-Distributors Can Meet the Power Retailer Challenge* (Washington, DC: Distribution Research and Education Foundation).

30. Dukes, Anthony and Yunchuan Liu (2009), "In-Store Media and Distribution Channel Coordination," *Marketing Science* 29, no. 1, pp. 94–107.

31. See http://www.fingerhut.com.

# CHAPTER 8

# Franchising Structures and Strategies

**LEARNING OBJECTIVES**

**After reading this chapter, you will be able to:**

- Define franchising and distinguish business format franchising from authorized franchise systems.
- Describe why an entrepreneurial person might become a franchisee rather than founding a new business, as well as what might make a candidate hesitate to join a franchise system.
- Explain why a firm with a business model opts for franchising rather than expanding by setting up its own branches run by employee managers.
- Detail the features of businesses that are poorly suited to franchising.
- Describe the essential elements of a franchise contract and why contracts are so important when franchising.
- Compare the positive and negative features of a business that mixes franchisees with company-owned outlets and describe why most franchising systems evolve into this mixed form.
- Explain how multiunit franchising affects the scarcity of good management.
- Evaluate the biggest problems a franchisor faces once a business becomes clearly viable, assuming it survives the founding stage.

**Franchising** is a marketing channel structure intended to convince end-users that they are buying from a vertically integrated manufacturer, even if they really purchase from a separately owned company. **Franchise systems** masquerade as company subsidiaries. In reality, they are a particular type of the classic, two-firm marketing channel structure, in which one supplies and the other performs downstream marketing channel functions.[1] Franchisors[2] are the upstream manufacturers of a product or originators of a service. They write contracts with **franchisees**, which are separate companies that provide the marketing channel functions downstream. End-users (customers of the franchisee) believe they are dealing with the franchisor's subsidiary, because the franchisee *assumes the identity* of the franchisor, projecting itself as though it were part of the franchisor's operation. This **deliberate loss of separate identity** is a hallmark of franchising.

To enable this masquerade, the franchisee awards the franchisor category exclusivity (it does not sell competing brands in the product category). Usually, it does not carry any other product categories either. Thus, franchising goes beyond granting a producer favored status in a single product category.

Franchising is often considered a post–World War II phenomenon. But its roots go back much farther, to ancient times in practice and to the Middle Ages in legal precedent. Its linguistic roots reflect ancient forms of both English and French, drawing from two terms: freedom and privilege. A medieval franchise formally and contractually limited a sovereign's authority in some way (e.g., tax exemption, guarantee of certain rights). Thus, a franchise enlarged the freedom of the franchisee from the sovereign, and it granted the privilege associated with the benefits that should accrue from this advantage.

Franchising as we know it today can be traced to the late nineteenth century, when in the United States, soft drink companies awarded bottling contracts and retailing franchises dominated the sales of gasoline, automobiles, and sewing machines. In business-to-business applications, the franchising concept was largely developed by the McCormick Harvesting Machine Company to sell directly to farmers, bypassing wholesalers. Automobiles, sewing machines, and harvesters each represented relatively new, complex, mass-produced products, which needed to be sold in huge volumes to gain economies of scale in manufacturing. Selling the massive machines at such a large scale required specialized marketing services that were unusual at the time, including the extension of credit, demonstration services, and post-sales repair. Because firms in these industries could not hire and train their own dealers fast enough, they turned to franchisees, as near subsidiaries, as a way to grow quickly. After they achieved the necessary growth, firms often turned their franchising operations into company-owned and managed outlets, in a trend that has repeated itself multiple times in history.

To further the projection of a franchisor-based identity, franchisees purchase the right to use and market the franchisor's brand. The franchisors, or sellers, induce franchisees, or dealers, to acquire some identity of the producer and concentrate on one product line. Fundamentally, dedicated dealers stock a product and resell it, adhering to certain guidelines about what to offer the market. The agreement involves a detailed contract, describing the necessary fees and allowing the franchisee to use the proven methods, trademarks, names, products, know-how, production techniques, and marketing techniques developed by the franchisor. Effectively, the franchisor develops an entire business system, or a **business format**, and licenses it to the franchisee to use in a given market area. In other cases, the agreement stops short of licensing the entire business format. Yet across the board, the producer's aim is to sell its product. The manufacturer seeks to maintain some control the presentation of its brand name, and the franchisee agrees to follow the franchisor's methods. By contract, the franchisee cedes substantial legitimate power to the franchisor. The reasons for both parties entail increasing profits from selling the product.

And yet, the franchisee remains a separate business, with its own balance sheet and income statement. From the standpoint of an accountant or a tax authority, a franchise is a business like any other. Franchisees invest their own capital, run the business, and keep the profits or assume the losses. They own the business; it is theirs to alter, sell, or terminate (though even this fundamental property right can be circumscribed by the franchise contract).

## FRANCHISING STRUCTURES

Franchising is an inherently contradictory marketing channel, yet it functions surprisingly well in many circumstances. Two independent businesses join forces to perform marketing functions to their mutual benefit. But in so doing, they attempt to convince end-users that they are one company, owned and operated under the same brand name. To convince end-users of the cohesiveness of the channel and the brand name, franchisees compromise their independence. They voluntarily cede an astonishing degree of power to the franchisor—and pay the franchisor for the privilege of doing so.

Why would any downstream entrepreneur accept (indeed, seek out and pay for) a franchise? For that matter, why would any manufacturer go to market through independent companies, when its real intention is to control the channel tightly enough that the end-user doesn't know the difference? Why not give customers what they think they are getting, that is, company-owned and -managed outlets?

Such questions make it seem as if franchising is a flawed concept that should be very rare. In contrast, franchising is the fastest growing form of retailing. Chain organizations using franchising, whether in whole or in part, accounted for $740 billion of U.S. sales in 2011, with a growth rate about twice as fast as that of the gross national product (GNP).[3] A broad construal of franchising in the U.S. retailing sector suggests that it accounts for 1.5 million stores in 75 industries, employing nearly 8 million people. In Europe, franchising was once dismissed as an aberrant form of organization, suitable only for North America; instead, it has taken off since it first appeared in Europe in the 1970s. And even as franchising continues to dominate retail sectors, it is growing in B2B markets, particularly in the sale of services to businesses.

As an institution, franchising is so well established globally that it has come full circle. Countries that first experienced franchising as a U.S. import have spawned their own firms that offer business formats they have exported to other countries—including "back" to the United States. The franchising institution is so stable and so pervasive that it offers the single most common way to become an entrepreneur in North America, Europe, and Asia.[4] Sidebar 8-1 describes the world's most admired franchisor, whose operations touch every aspect of the franchising system. Can you name it without looking? We bet you can.

### Benefits to Franchisees

Imagine you are a private entrepreneur with a certain amount of capital, perhaps due to an inheritance, severance pay, accumulated savings, or equity from a previous business. You could invest the money and collect the earnings, but you are more interested in starting a business. Owning your own business sounds great:

- It is intrinsically appealing for psychological reasons (e.g., you feel pride in the idea of ownership).
- Other opportunities in society seem closed off to you, perhaps because of your gender, race, or background.

## Sidebar 8-1

## McDonald's

McDonald's is not only the world's largest retail organization, in terms of the number of outlets (more than 33,000 units located in 119 countries, representing 95 percent of the world's wealth), but it is also its largest and most admired franchisor. The scale of this successful franchising can be difficult to grasp. Consider (www.mcdonalds.com) the following:

- On average, a new outlet opens somewhere in the world every five hours.
- With 1.7 million employees, McDonald's is the world's largest private employer.
- It is also the world's largest holder of real estate.

McDonald's may seem ubiquitous now, but it also made some errors along the way. The format emerged from California, in the aftermath of World War II, when Ray Kroc licensed the hamburger chain concept from its founders (the MacDonald brothers). In 1955, Kroc opened his own McDonald's and began to build his empire. Growth remained steady until 1996, when franchisees suffered declining profitability, mainly because the U.S. market had grown nearly saturated, yet McDonald's continued to add units at a rapid pace, cannibalizing its existing franchises. After an in-house revolt, the chain slowed its growth (in part, by closing one unit for every two it opened) and invested heavily to modernize kitchens and improve both its product and its profitability. This back-to-basics approach, focused on growing same-store sales, to the benefit of franchisees, led the firm back to growth.[5]

Today, of its 33,000 outlets, McDonald's owns 8 percent of those located in the United States. Approximately 4,000 outlets (mostly in Asia and the Middle East) are joint ventures with local shareholders, and the remaining 15,500 outlets are owned by 5,300 franchisees. These franchisees invest heavily to build their outlets, often selling all their possessions to raise the capital. Then they pay McDonald's up to 25 percent of their earned revenue in fees and rent (McDonald's is usually their landlord). In return, they share in the system.

### Provided Format

*Method*

The operating manual weighs two kilograms (over four pounds) and specifies virtually every detail of

how operations must be performed. All servers wear uniforms without pockets, for example, to discourage them from accepting tips or putting their hands in their pockets. Leaving hands free in turn encourages constant action ("if you've got time to lean, you've got time to clean"). Cooking and serving specifications are timed down to the second, and detailed role descriptions mandate the responsibilities of every member of the staff.

*Set-Up Assistance*

Months of on-site training lead to courses at Hamburger University, a literal campus in suburban Chicago that every year teaches approximately 7,000 new franchisees and managers how to run the business. McDonald's also undertakes to secure a site and build the restaurant, which it then rents back to the new franchisee.

*Norm Enforcement*

Once operations are underway, the franchisee receives regular assistance from an army of regional consultants, who also perform frequent and detailed performance checks. McDonald's insists that franchisees abide by its intricate system. Consider the poor French franchisee, who lost his 12 units when he was terminated for noncompliance.

*Worldwide Supply*

McDonald's has a network of favored suppliers that function almost as subsidiaries. When entering a new market, McDonald's seeks out local suppliers and asks them to adapt to its methods. But in most cases, the franchisor finds these local suppliers inadequate and induces its own suppliers to enter the market as replacements. These key suppliers process astonishing quantities of food and supplies, matched precisely to McDonald's exacting specifications. The result is immediate uniformity, combined with economies of scale that allow the franchisor to operate profitably while charging low prices.

*Marketing Strategy and Communications*

McDonald's targets families by providing fast, inexpensive meals that children enjoy. To draw the family into the stores, it focuses on pleasing children with in-store events too (e.g., birthday parties), Happy Meals,

## Continued

and Ronald McDonald. The menu remains extremely similar worldwide, with some limited adaptation to local tastes. This standardization enhances its ability to capture of economies of scale—and not just in food. McDonald's also is one of the world's leading distributors of toys through its Happy Meals.

Furthermore, it assigns massive advertising budgets to marketing campaigns, particularly those backing sporting events. For example, McDonald's spends millions to advertise during international football (for Americans, soccer) events. In contrast with the rest of its strategy, McDonald's advertising is not standardized, such that different countries and regions have their own slogans and campaigns. Communication is partly financed by franchisees, who pay 4.5 percent of their revenue as an advertising fee. They may also run their own local campaigns, for which the franchisor assists them with ready-to-use kits.

### Participation

To enter this system, a prospective franchisee must pass tests of its motivation and capability. Applicants include professionals from a range of fields, including doctors, lawyers, and executives, though these candidates frequently get screened out for their inadequate motivation and lack of customer service orientation. In France, successful candidates invest substantial upfront fees and sunk costs to outfit the interior and kitchen (though the franchisor largely pays to build the restaurant and holds the lease).

Despite such high early costs, most McDonald's locations break even after several years (and often sooner) and become quite profitable. In France, one franchisee draws a salary comparable to an executive paycheck, while also collecting substantial dividends and building wealth in the location (where resale values ran upward of several million Euros). Satisfactory performance also means a franchisee can open more stores, though McDonald's discourages overly large operations, fearing the owner will become too far removed from day-to-day operations.

McDonald's draws criticism as well as admiration though. Social critics charge that the franchisor is too heavy-handed and antiunion in its personnel practices. Suppliers complain of being exploited. The secretive chain is often accused of being a heartless multinational, seeking merely to create an unhealthy, Westernized, fast-food culture wherever it goes by suppressing local businesses and displacing local customs. Yet McDonald's also earns praise for offering employment (and ultimately franchising opportunities) to young people and those who often face discrimination in traditional job markets (e.g., Latinos and African Americans in the United States, people of North African descent in France). The franchisees often operate in struggling neighborhoods, creating jobs and businesses that benefit residents. And the persistent popularity of the product suggests that fast-food culture is not totally unwelcome!

- You have grown tired of working for someone else.
- You are willing to assume some risk to gain independence.
- You are confident that you can earn better returns in the long run if you put your own labor into your own company than if you invest your resources—whether financial or labor—in someone else's.
- By owning a business, you could help support family members or friends who also need employment.

All of these needs and benefits can be fulfilled by starting your own business from scratch or from franchising. But the risks and threats involved with starting a business from the ground up suggest some additional benefits of choosing a franchise arrangement:

- Failure rates for new businesses are high.
- Setting up a business takes months, even years. In particular, it takes time and resources to build a clientele.

- There are literally thousands of decisions, big and small, to be made:
  - Where should the business be located?
  - Should it have a theme?
  - What size should it be?
  - What kind of products should it provide, and how should they be prepared, economically and efficiently?
- There are so many legal, financial, marketing, managerial, and operating decisions to be made that any entrepreneur can be overwhelmed.
- Finally, the business easily could fail, wiping out all your capital.

Contemplating these prospects has made plenty of people too nervous to pursue their entrepreneurial ambitions. You may have met them in the job market, still drawing designs for their great idea on napkins and dreaming of walking into the boss's office to quit. But for those who remain dedicated to the notion of running their own business, while also minimizing some risks, a franchising arrangement offers perhaps the perfect combination. In effect, you sell some portion of your independence to the franchisor, and in return, you obtain the services of a corporate backer, a coach, and a problem solver (as well as another role that we discuss subsequently). Franchisor personnel step in to assist you. They train you, work with you, and share the franchisor's proven formula with you. The business format represents a prepackaged solution to all your startup problems and preset answers to most of the critical decisions you face. By paying a fee (usually in several parts), you buy a license to exploit this format in a particular market area.

**START-UP PACKAGE**    When you buy the license for a business format, you acquire a brand name and an explanation of all the marketing decisions the franchisor already has made about the business. Along with decision-making guidance, you acquire training and assistance to implement those decisions, including the following

- Market survey and site selection
- Facility design and layout (architectural and building services)
- Lease negotiation advice
- Financing advice
- Operating manuals
- Management training programs
- Training for franchisee's employees

All of these initial services are valuable. But **site selection** is particularly important to a retail operation, because market potential is the critical determinant of any store's sales and productivity.[6] The amount of help a franchisor provides varies with the business and contract. For example, McDonald's typically performs all site analysis and most land acquisition and development; Budget Rent-A-Car merely assigns a territory and allows the franchisee to build wherever he or she pleases, subject to franchisor review and advice.

Another critical benefit, available from the very moment the franchisee starts up, is the **brand name** itself. By using the brand equity already associated with this name, the franchisee can quickly build a clientele that is loyal to the brand offering.

These initial services also benefit from **economies of scale**, which the franchisor can capture and share with the franchisee. By providing the same services over and over, the franchisor acquires deep, detailed knowledge of the nuances of every single activity. The franchisor also pools demand for these services, which makes it economical to dedicate specific personnel to the set-up tasks (e.g., statistical specialists to perform site analyses; company lawyers to deal with zoning authorities and draft documents; architects to draw plans and supervise construction; technicians to train, install, and test equipment). Through the franchisor's scale, the franchisee also gains preferred customer status with service providers (e.g., contractors, bankers). All of these benefits suggest better results at lower costs.

**ONGOING BENEFITS**    Were this the end of the story, franchising would only be a system for *launching* a business. But it is primarily a system for *running* a business. Once you have started your franchised business, what services might you expect the franchisor to keep providing?

- Field supervision of operations, including quality inspections
- Management reports feedback
- Merchandising and promotional materials
- Management and employee retraining
- National advertising
- Centralized planning
- Market data and guidance
- Auditing and record keeping
- Group insurance plans

Of this list, the first two items stand out for their potential for conflict. Almost all franchisors have a continuous program of **field supervision**, including monitoring and correcting quality problems. Field representatives (with titles such as "franchise consultant") visit each franchise outlet to aid its everyday operations, check product and service quality, and monitor performance. They serve as coaches and consultants for the franchisee. But they also are employees of the franchisor, such that they serve as inspectors, evaluators, and reporters. These latter policing roles might conflict with the former coaching roles, demanding diplomacy and skill to balance them.

Many franchisees are required to submit management reports, monthly or semimonthly, about key elements of their operations, such as weekly sales, local advertising, employee turnover, profits, and so forth. These regular reports reflect the nearly "subsidiary nature" of franchising but would be highly unusual in other contractual channels. By reporting on operations, the franchisee facilitates various financial, operating, and marketing control procedures throughout the franchise system. It also enables the franchisor to offer feedback to assist the franchisee. But this confidential information constitutes the very heart of the business; to provide feedback, the franchisor might demand that franchisees buy special electronic invoicing and reporting systems that open their books to oversight and review. Such tactics can create resentment, especially if the franchisee's goal was independence from an overseeing boss.

**COMPETITIVE ADVANTAGES OF FRANCHISING**    Look back at the list of services that you, as an entrepreneur, likely are willing to use your capital to obtain from someone else. But why exactly should you buy these services from a franchisor, rather than independent consultants, such as architects, accountants, lawyers, and so forth?

First, franchisors act as **consolidators** in this specific type of channel. They bring together all the necessary services, no more, no less, under one roof and consolidate them, achieving economies of scale (size) and scope (synergy).

Second, franchisors focus on one product line (e.g., fast food restaurants, car repair). They develop benefits from this specialization.

Third, perhaps the most critical and distinguishing benefit of a franchisor is its ability to bring everything together and focus it on a **branded concept**. Everything the franchisor does is dedicated to the needs of the brand and the implementation of its concept. The franchisor develops specialization benefits tied to brand equity, which cannot accrue without a multitude of units. Thus, a major reason to turn to a franchisor is to rent its brand equity and become part of a large network, not just contract for business services.

This discussion brings us to a crucial and often-misunderstood reason for why you would pay for a franchise. *You are hiring an enforcement agency.* The franchisor acts as a police officer, judge, and jury. The business format is a system, and the franchisor makes sure that all players (franchisees) observe its rules, without allowing any opportunism. You, the franchisee, hire the franchisor to police the system, to make sure that everyone else implements the concept too. It is in your interest to have a police officer to protect brand equity—and brand equity is the basis of the franchising concept.

This idea is often labeled the *prevention of free riding.* As we briefly mentioned in Chapter 3, **free riding** occurs when one party reaps benefits while another party bears all the costs. Dunkin' Donuts positions itself as a producer of premium, fresh bakery goods. To sustain this positioning, franchisees agree to throw out unsold product after a few hours and replace them with freshly produced goods. This promise is costly to keep, which creates a temptation to keep selling donuts for a few more hours, hoping that no one will notice they are a bit stale. A franchisee that sells stale donuts benefits from the Dunkin' Donuts image, but this practice hurts the brand's image, which hurts all franchisees. Ultimately, the franchisor's field representatives are likely to find out, and the punishment for the shirking franchisee is likely to be swift and painful.

If franchisees did not have a franchisor, they likely would invent one to provide the channel function of policing the system. Brand equity is utterly critical to franchising. Safeguarding brand equity is a key reason franchising has become associated with the production of all kinds of services. For services such as document handling, building, business aids and services, child care, hospitality, tourism, travel, weight control—even autopsies!—a constant challenge is ensuring consistent outcomes. By branding a service business, the franchisor guarantees consistency, which attracts customers and enhances brand equity, for itself and its franchisees.

## Benefits to Franchisor

Now let's turn the lens around and change our perspective: You head a company with a concept and a brand. You have a business format. You desire tight control over the implementation of your concept. You want that control to uphold the brand's image and ensure the proper sale and servicing of your product. With this directive focus, the logical choice seemingly would be to set up a network of outlets that you can own, operate, and supervise, with the help of managers you hire to supervise the staff at each outlet. Each outlet remains to be set up, after you hire and train the manager and staff.

Such efforts take significant time, effort, and money. You are ultimately responsible for every decision and every staff move. Furthermore, you must remain constantly on guard to avoid agency conflicts, similar to the ones we discussed in Chapter 4. That is, your managers likely have different incentives and goals than you do, so you have to find a way to get them to perform in the way you desire. Such considerations constitute the two main categories of reasons that you might prefer a franchise system rather than an owned network to spread your ideas.

**FINANCIAL AND MANAGERIAL CAPITAL FOR GROWTH** Most people with a great idea want to grow fast, motivated by far more than just entrepreneurial ego or impatience. A unique idea needs to be exploited and established as fast as possible, to gain a first-mover advantage before others have the chance to copy it. If your idea is trendy (e.g., American-style fast food in Southeast Asia), you need to get it going rapidly, before the market becomes saturated. In a business market with fragmented competition and no strong brands, a quickly spreading idea is more likely to build a strong brand name before others. Conversely, if the market hosts a strong competitor, you may need to grow fast, before the competitor really notices or tries to block you. Furthermore, reaching a minimum efficient scale quickly enables you to amortize your costs over a larger operation. For example, to justify national U.S. advertising, you would need to achieve national coverage of a market of several hundred million people.

Such speed to market demands massive amounts of financial capital, which may or may not be available through a public stock offering. The earliest explanations of franchising focused on the idea that franchisees are a cheaper (or perhaps only) source of capital, in that franchisees often are willing to invest for a lower rate of return than passive investors who lack a good understanding of the business or their location. Although appealing, this idea fell into disfavor, because it appeared to contradict financial portfolio theory, which states that investors of any kind prefer less risk. Because the risk of any single location is greater than risk spread across the entire chain, prospective franchisees should prefer to buy a share in the chain, rather than the rights to one location. But the idea also is making a comeback, in part because of the evidence that it persists in practice.[7] Perhaps capital markets remain inefficient for prospective franchisors. And perhaps franchisees do not act as merely rational financial investors, indifferent between owning their own business and owning a piece of a company.[8]

Remember, from the previous perspective, that the franchisees you find to buy into your operations want to be their own boss. They will manage their own outlets, which imply that franchisees who buy in are confident in their ability to influence the risk-to-return ratio of their operations. By buying franchise rights to a location of their choice, they seek to demonstrate their ability to earn high profits at lower risk. Investors in the overall chain instead have minimal influence on day-to-day operations and can earn only returns on their investment; franchisees, after paying suppliers and the franchisor, get to keep all the profits earned from the store. Thus, franchisees are rarely indifferent between owning a franchise and owning a piece of the franchisor, and their willing investments offer the franchise system a ready way to grow quickly and with sufficient financial resources.

The idea that entrepreneurs value the returns from their own wholly controlled operations more than they value equal returns from owning a piece of a larger organization implies that we need to move beyond conventional measures of profit. *Entrepreneurs have other motives.* For example, they may have found what they consider the perfect location for a service provider and just need help getting it up and running. Often entrepreneurs have specific technology innovations that they want to employ, but need help with the peripheral organizational support. Although they may not value the entire chain as highly as they value their location or innovation, you still would have a relatively easy time persuading such a franchisee to invest.[9] By persuading them to invest in your franchise system, rather than another option (note that many would-be franchisors never find any franchisees—or buyers for their stock), you run a successful sort of test run of your idea. By attracting franchisees' investments, you also gain an endorsement of your operations, as well as their own.

Finding franchisees provides another sort of resource, beyond the financial. That is, you address the pressing issue of overcoming a **personnel shortage** of good managers. Even with plenty of capital, an entrepreneur often needs to spend an inordinate amount of time trying to solve the *managerial scarcity problem*.[10] But remember, you're still trying to grow your business quickly, and you have plenty of other issues to occupy your attention. Spending time reviewing resumes, interviewing managerial candidates, and calling references is inefficient, difficult, and often ineffective. Instead, franchising offers a preestablished way to "screen" managerial applicants, *by asking them to become franchisees.* Unmotivated, uninterested, or incapable managers are unlikely to pay a lump-sum entry fee, put up the initial investment, accept payment of an ongoing royalty, or be willing to accept the risk of living off the uncertain profits of their efforts. In contrast, dedicated managers who are confident in their abilities and entrepreneurial in their attitudes likely jump at the chance to prove themselves and their capabilities.

These arguments for starting up through franchising are rationally defensible, but of course, reality is not always quite so rational. Many founders of franchise organizations are focused on an overriding objective to control the enterprise as it grows, and they believe it is easier to influence (or dominate) each franchisee (and thus the entire operation) than to influence a board of directors. In this case, the decision to franchise is driven by a fear of losing control by selling shares, rather than the desire to raise financial capital or resolve a shortage of human capital. Ironically, these founders often find they underestimated the independent spirit of their franchisees.[11] Even more ironically, the founders likely lose control anyway, because they must give up power to professional managers as their organization grows.

**HARNESSING THE ENTREPRENEURIAL SPIRIT**  Instead, an effective and persistent franchise system recognizes that franchisees offer all the benefits and gains of a vast group of entrepreneurs—widely considered the driving force behind successful economies throughout time. Consider a general theory from organizational behavior literature: There are two main ways a firm can motivate the staff who work for it. It can control and monitor them, in which case it seeks to supervise employees, then sanction or reward them as appropriate. Or it can incentivize them to align their own interests with the best interests of the company by making them **residual claimants** of the firm's profits. A residual claimant needs less monitoring, because to earn profits, he or she works hard to make the business succeed. In this sense, franchising encourages work and reduces monitoring costs by transforming managers into owners and residual claimants.

Furthermore, franchisees may gain substantial "psychic income"—not just financial rewards—from owning their own business. They likely feel pride of ownership and a sense of loyalty toward "their" franchise system, and they may appreciate the benefits it offers them, such as the ability to hire relatives and friends who need work. Perhaps most important, running a business offers franchisees a way to maximize the returns on the knowledge and relationships that they bring to the business. Such **human capital** is often so specific that it works only within specific ventures. (This idea of maximizing the returns on specialized human capital reappears in our subsequent discussion of multiunit franchisees.)

The franchisees' more intrinsic (i.e., internal) motivation to exert effort to benefit both the specific outlet and the wider system likely helps explain why franchising is so prominent in retail sectors, for which *effort truly matters for success.* But if the margins earned are too low to pay supervisors well and ensure that all staff members put forth continuous effort, a basic monitoring system will fail. Such concerns are especially problematic in service industries, in which production and distribution are simultaneous, so it would be impossible for an owner to inspect all output before the customer sees it. Table 8-1 lists sectors in which franchising has a strong presence, all of which match these traits and characteristics.

We also need to distinguish between lack of effort and misdirected effort and the influence of franchising on them. A franchising contract is a good way to combat a lack of effort, but it is often unsuccessful in resolving misdirected effort. Instead, franchisees with their entrepreneurial spirits often battle franchisors over exactly how things should be done. A good franchisor takes franchisees seriously and considers their ideas, as if they were consultants, rather than rejecting contradictory ideas out of hand, as difficult as that might be. One franchisor offers a pithy summary of the key challenge[12]: "You see, a manager will do what you want, but he won't work very hard. A franchisee will work hard, but he won't do what you want."

The franchisee as a **consultant** works out implementation problems for the franchise system and generates new ideas, especially on the local level. That is, the franchise system establishes the general vision; to be implemented on a large scale, and even globally, the vision must be *adapted to local circumstances,* as well as to *changes in the marketplace* over time. A franchisor lacks access to local markets and end-users; the franchisee provides it.

Consider the example of Southeast Asia, where U.S.-style fast food has become quite popular. William Heinecke, an American raised in Thailand, approached Pizza Hut with the idea of opening a franchise in Bangkok, but Pizza Hut worried about Asians' well-documented dislike of cheese. Despite corporate misgivings, Heinecke paid the necessary fees and signed a contract to go ahead. Both parties are thrilled he did, because Pizza Hut now enjoys substantial business in Thailand, and Heinecke owns dozens of outlets.

Thus in many situations, the franchisor might not know best; sophisticated franchisees can solve problems that the national office might not even notice. Even in this

| **TABLE 8-1   Sectors with substantial franchise presence** |
|---|
| Amusement |
| Automobiles: |
|     Rental |
|     Service |
|     Equipment |
| Business Services |
| Building Products and Services |
| Children's Products, Including Clothing |
| Cleaning Services and Equipment |
| Educational Services |
| Employment Agencies |
| Health and Beauty (Includes Hair Styling and Cosmetology) |
| Home Furnishings/Equipment |
| Lodging/Hotels |
| Maintenance |
| Miscellaneous Retail |
| Miscellaneous Services, including Training |
| Personal Services and Equipment |
| Pet Services |
| Photography and Video |
| Printing |
| Quick Services |
| Real Estate |
| Restaurants |
|     Fast Food |
|     Traditional |
| Retail Food |
| Shipping and Packing |
| Travel |

*Source:* See 2013 website (www.franchising.com).

seemingly inverted channel though, the franchisor remains a necessary participant. The central corporate office collects the various, diverse ideas provided by all its franchisees, screens out those that appear unworkable, adapts them for application to the entire chain, and then spreads them to other franchisees. Some of the best-known images and product ideas that appear in every modern McDonald's were generated by franchisees but spread by the franchisor.[13] Like the Filet 'O Fish? Thank a franchisee located in a heavily Catholic neighborhood, whose customers avoided meat dishes on Fridays.

A key point to retain from this discussion is an understanding of how franchise systems evolve. The franchisor has the original vision for the business format. Over time though, franchisees develop the vision *collectively*. In general, no single franchisee has a better format. Rather, the franchisor continually *gathers, adapts, and diffuses the best ideas* across the set of franchisees.

In the development of franchise systems, it also turns out that many of the most creative, contributing franchisees come from among managers who once worked for the company. A motivated, capable manager can be rewarded for his or her effort, and also encouraged to remain with the company, by awarding him or her a franchise contract. In France, many large retailers face slow growth in their home market, forcing them to consider secondary locations, such as small towns that cannot support a large, company-owned store. Instead, they give employees the opportunity to transform from managerial employees into self-employed franchisees. Employees get to own their own businesses; franchisors enjoy reduced reduce risk and investment while also growing into new areas. However, employees in this situation often lack the necessary capital, which requires the franchisors to provide additional support and "bet" on their former employees, to preserve their loyalty and know-how. French franchisors might offer these one-time employees additional financial backing, assistance with the transition, and advanced training. As long as this additional assistance does not go so far as to quench their entrepreneurial spirit, it can be a happy outcome for everyone involved.[14]

In a sense, this development brings us full circle. We began by describing franchising as a way to find good managers (without having to hire them) quickly, who were willing to provide the franchisor with ready capital. Now we find franchising used as a way to keep managers already hired, by granting them the necessary capital. This section is thus indicative of the constantly evolving role of franchising. Fast Retailing, a Japanese company that owns the casual clothing retailer Uniglo, operate hundreds of Uniglo outlets by converting proactive employees with at least ten years' experience into franchisees, in line with founder's belief that store managers must be independent and that franchising is a way to establish win–win relationships.[15]

In short, franchising is more than a way to grow fast, obtain capital, or avoid monitoring costs. It offers a versatile, generalized system of management motivation in marketing channels. Yet for many, it remains easy to underestimate the power of franchising and overestimate the value of controlling the operation, as Sidebar 8-2 describes.

## Another View: Reasons Not to Franchise

Not everyone agrees with this rosy view of franchising. By any stretch of the imagination, Starbucks is a highly successful chain.[16] Its fast growth and massive coverage of seemingly every urban corner led many people to assume it was a franchised chain. Instead, every store is a company outlet, managed by all Starbucks employees. Howard Schultz, its founder, remains sharply critical of franchising by arguing that it leads firms to expand too quickly, without stopping to address problems as they arise. The result, he asserts, is that errors (e.g., hiring the wrong people, losing control of operations, compromising on quality, picking bad locations) propagate through the

---

**Sidebar 8-2**

### ADA discovers the benefits of franchisees

ADA rents cars and trucks. Its discount strategy centers on advertising a very low price—though the total price often turns out to be much higher, once the extras get factored in. It also offers minimal service. Initially, the firm kept costs ultralow by sticking to a niche (cars and light trucks in cities) and using franchising to grow fast. But this approach meant that it soon saturated its home market of France. In the belief that it was essential to keep growing, ADA began to open rental counters in airports and train stations, renting a broader assortment of cars and trucks. To run this new operation, management believed it needed to "professionalize" its retail operations, so it staffed these sites with company personnel.

The results were disappointing. City dwellers who went to ADA counters were already well informed and needed little help. Travelers who frequented airports and train stations instead demanded information and assistance. Furthermore, these locations were highly competitive, such that ADA had to add personnel, broaden its vehicle stock, and make its rental terms more flexible. Still, the counters suffered from a lack of referrals from travel agencies, with which ADA has no connections.

As the counters sank to ever lower performance levels, employees deserted, leaving ADA with only its weakest managers. To rectify the situation, ADA added another level of corporate oversight. Ultimately though, it had to concede that it simply could not compensate for poor supervision at the rental site. Its solution? Sell those troubled, "professional" company-run sites—to franchisees.[17]

---

system and become established. Starbucks maintains legendary consistency, in both its operations and its product output, and somehow manages to hire and retain enthusiastic, committed store management. Schultz does it by offering stock options to all full-time employees (a perk that consistently lands Starbucks on lists of the best places to work). Equity stakes in the overall business seemingly allow Starbucks to duplicate the enthusiasm and sense of ownership that franchisees bring to their business. That is, despite strong arguments in favor of a franchising system, Starbucks offers ongoing proof that there is nothing about the industries in Table 8-1 that makes franchising the only viable way to run the channel.

## FRANCHISING STRATEGIES

### Product and Trade Name Franchising Strategies

In a widespread and traditional form of franchising, generally referred to as **product and trade name franchising,** or **authorized franchise systems**, dealers (also known as distributors, resellers, or agents) meet minimum criteria that the manufacturer establishes regarding their participation in different marketing functions. The franchisor thus authorizes distributors (wholesalers or retailers or both) to sell a product or product line while using its trade name for promotional purposes. Examples at the retail level include authorized tire, auto, computer, major appliance, television, and household furniture dealers whose suppliers have established strong brand names. Such authorization can also be granted at the wholesale level—for example, to soft drink bottlers and to distributors or dealers by manufacturers of electrical and electronics equipment. These producers make most of their profits on the margins they obtain by selling to their dealers, rather than on fees and royalties.

Thus, when we refer to franchising today, we usually mean *business-format franchising*, or licensing of an entire way of doing business under a brand name. For a franchisor, the reward for agreeing to this activity is the generation of ongoing fees from its franchisees.

## Business Format Franchising Strategy

Establishing an authorized franchise system helps suppliers increase the probability that channel members provide appropriate types and levels of service outputs to end-users, without assuming financial ownership. For example, organizers of authorized franchise systems might specify or impose restrictions on how channel members can operate. As such, an **authorized franchise system** is a way to exercise power. This term implies that the system is always clearly demarcated, but that implication is misleading. In some areas, legal requirements oblige any so-called franchisor to follow disclosure and reporting rules (and thus pay significant legal costs), but in other arenas, the boundaries between franchising and other methods to exercise power are less clear. Beyond vertical integration, a gray area exists between franchising and other forms of distribution. It thus can be difficult to determine whether a channel is franchised or technically separable but still led or (legally or illegally) dominated by an influential, upstream channel member. Consider a retailer cooperative or wholesaler-sponsored voluntary group. Each of these forms resembles franchising, but regulators have had to intervene to ascertain whether franchising laws apply to these groups.

What "franchising" usually implies today is the licensing of an entire business format. The European Union provides a good definition: A **franchise** is a package of industrial or intellectual property rights, including trade names, trademarks, shop signs, utility models, designs, copyrights, know-how, or patents. The package may be exploited to resell goods or provide services to end-users. The EU definition uses three features to distinguish franchising:

1. The use of a common name or sign, with a uniform presentation of the premises.
2. Communication of know-how from franchisor to franchisee.
3. Continuing provision of commercial or technical assistance by the franchisor to the franchisee.

A careful definition is critical, because the EU exempts franchising from many regulations designed to encourage intra- and international competition within it. This exemption recognizes the need for franchise systems to project a common identity, which in turn requires contracts that may restrict competition. The exemption is justified from a consumer welfare standpoint because, according to the European Commission, franchising should "combine the advantages of a uniform and homogeneous network, which ensures a constant quality of the products and services, with the existence of traders personally interested in the efficient operation of their business."[18]

## Franchise Contracting Strategies

Franchising is tightly governed by elaborate, formal contracts that run on for pages, filled with intricate legal language. It is tempting for both franchisor and franchisee to leave the contracts to the lawyers and simply presume that the working arrangements that arise will govern the relationship anyway. This is a dangerous error. In franchising, the contract really matters. In particular, three sections of a franchise contract determine *who will enter* the arrangement and *how it will function*[19]:

1. The payment system, particularly the lump-sum fee to enter the system, royalty fees, and the initial investment. The calculation of these fees and their potential adjustment over the contract duration are critical.
2. Real estate, including who holds the lease and how it may be transferred. Although this detail appears to entail financing, it is actually distinct and important.
3. Termination. Franchise arrangements anticipate the possible end of the relationship and spell out how it would be conducted.

In the United States, where franchising has a long history, regulators and courts similarly consider its social benefits, out of concern that franchisors (typically regarded as large, powerful, and sophisticated) might exploit franchisees (typically seen as small, weak, and naive). A key reason for this concern is that franchise contracts typically contain clauses that, on their face, outrageously favor the franchisor (probably because franchisors have better lawyers and more bargaining power).

But are the contracts truly unfair?

To explain why they might not be, consider a parallel with international politics, in which, to safeguard an agreement, two parties engage in **hostage exchanges**. The party that is more likely to break its promise offers a hostage to the other side. If it reneges, the other party gets to keep the hostage. If both sides are equally tempted to break their promises, they exchange hostages.

Franchise contracts represent attempts by each side to post hostages to ensure the other side lives up to its promises.[20] Both the franchisor and franchisee are tempted to renege, but the franchisee is in a better position to renege, so it posts more hostages—that is, it accepts contracts that give seemingly greater power to the franchisor.

**PAYMENT SYSTEMS**    The franchisee usually pays a fixed fee, or lump-sum payment, to join the franchise system. If the contract ended there, the franchisor would be sorely tempted to abscond with the fee and do nothing to help the franchisee. This fee is a hostage posted by the franchisee. It also offers its initial investments in acquiring inventory, obtaining and adapting the facility, purchasing tools and equipment, and advertising its store opening. If the store closed quickly, the franchisee would lose much of its investment, especially if its purchases included fixtures and equipment specialized to fit the franchisor's operations or decor (e.g., distinctive colors, patterns, emblazoned logos, and slogans). The part of the initial investment that the franchisee can never recover is called a **sunk cost**. Thus, both the upfront fee and the sunk costs are hostages posted by the franchisee. If it fails to live up to its promises to work in accordance with the franchise system and the businesses fails, it loses its hostages.

Of course, the franchisor must post some hostages of its own. The optimal hostage in this case is a **royalty on sales** (variable fee). If the franchisor refuses to help the franchisee, sales suffer, and the franchisor shares in that suffering by collecting less royalty income. Therefore, royalties motivate the franchisor to assist the franchisee.[21] At this point, we need to explain the appeal of royalties on sales, rather than on profit. That is, the franchisor's function is to help the franchisee make money. So profit seemingly should be the best measure. But in most cases, sales can be readily observed and verified, whereas profit is easy to manipulate and difficult to check.

Thus, franchisors make money from both fees and royalties, and the key question is, *What is the best way to get the most money?* Put differently, what ratio of fixed fees and variable sales royalties should franchisors prefer? One argument holds that fixed and variable payments should correlate negatively.[22] The rationale is that a franchisor charging a high fixed fee sends two signals: My franchise is valuable, but also, I am extracting as much as I can from you upfront so that I can exploit you later (i.e., "take the money and run"). To emphasize the positive signal but mitigate the negative signal, franchisors reduce their upfront fee (sometimes to nothing, even for well-known franchises)[23] and seek to make money later with higher royalty rates. This move also creates a new hostage, in that they share more risk with their franchisees.

The threat at this point is whether they are sharing too much. By forgoing upfront money in favor of potential royalty payments, franchisors take on a risk that franchisees accept their assistance to set up the business, and then try to renegotiate the contract to their advantage. Such **opportunistic holdup** by the franchisee can take various forms, such as negotiating for the deferment or reduction of royalties, extra assistance, rent relief, and so forth. Franchisors might agree to renegotiate to avoid losing the sunk costs they already have invested to set the franchisee up in business. Thus, fear of opportunistic holdup seemingly should drive the franchisor to ask for more upfront money, in lieu of royalties.

In practice though, ultimately we find little relation between the fixed fee and the royalty.[24] In terms of the sheer amount of the fixed fee, franchisors tend to concede and take less upfront money than they would prefer; the franchisees appear to make concessions on other aspects of the contract, which we discuss subsequently. In addition, the franchisee agrees to make heavy initial investments—including sunk costs in things such as franchise-specific decor and equipment or merchandise that is difficult to return or resell—that can run much higher than the franchisor's fixed fee. By incurring this investment, the franchisee offers a valuable hostage to assure the franchisor that it will exert its best efforts to stay in the business, rather than mistreating the franchisor by renegotiating the contract at every opportunity.

Furthermore, franchisors might want to reduce their upfront fixed fees to enlarge the pool of applicants. As we discussed previously, franchising offers a viable method to identify the sort of entrepreneurial profile (i.e., personality, background, management ability, and local knowledge) that makes for an ideal franchisee. If this list included the criterion of substantial personal wealth too, the pool of qualified candidates would shrink dramatically.

But franchisors do not just lower their demands for upfront fees. Real-world evidence indicates they also ask for a lower royalty rate than they might. McDonald's reportedly leaves several hundred thousand dollars on the table (i.e., in the franchisee's bank account) each time it grants a franchise.[25] So we must ask: Why?!

The primary answer is to enhance the value of the business to each franchisee. By being generous, McDonald's ensures that the franchisee has a lot to lose—not least its sense of loyalty to the company that treated it so well. In turn, the franchisee is more motivated to live up to its promises, which constitutes the foundation for effective franchising.

In this vein, consider **tied sales**. Some contracts include a clause obliging franchisees to buy their inputs (products, supplies) from the specific supplier; in the United Kingdom, Avis and Budget require franchisees to purchase the cars they rent from the national franchisor. Such tie-ins appear anticompetitive, in that if franchisees could buy the same car elsewhere for less, they seemingly should be allowed to do so. Regulators make similar arguments to question whether the tie-ins are actually just a disguise for a method to collect more ongoing fees. Furthermore, overcharging franchisees for supplies could prompt retaliation by the franchisee, which looks to compensate for the informal fees by cheating in some other way. A restaurant forced to buy overpriced ingredients from the franchisor might cut portion sizes or reuse food for too long.

For franchisors though, the threats may be worthwhile, because tied sales provide a means to ensure quality. Avis and Budget know the cars being rented are fully equipped (e.g., air conditioning, satellite radio), as promised to end-users. When input quality is difficult to measure continuously, franchisors become more likely to use tied sales clauses. But they also seek to price them fairly, to avoid resentment and allegations of profiteering. Moreover, if any product can serve as input, franchisors rarely write tied sales clauses. Alternatively, if a range of products will do, but not all of them, franchisors might oblige franchisees to buy from approved sources, even if not from the franchisor.

**LEASING**   Regarding rent collection on a franchisee's premises, some franchisors, such as McDonald's, take pains to ensure that they are the landlord, or at least hold the right to lease the property to the franchisee. That is, they might negotiate the lease with the property owner, and then sublet to the franchisee. These leases generally protect the franchisor's rights, at the expense of the franchisee. However, owning land is a capital-intensive practice, and the leasing negotiations absorb much management attention while also creating frequent disputes.

The investments may be worth it for the franchisor though, because retailing depends on **location**, and the best locations are difficult to secure. Owners of prime commercial locations might prefer to deal with franchisors, rather than individual franchisees. The franchisor may also negotiate better than a smaller franchisee.

A clearer explanation for why franchisors might insist on holding the leases for *all* sites (even the lesser ones) instead focuses on the contract with the franchisee, in that lease control makes the franchisor's **termination threats** credible.[26] A noncompliant franchisee that is also a tenant is easy to eject from the system: The franchisor simply terminates the lease, simultaneous with terminating the franchisee. A franchisee tenant agrees to the lease, which favors the landlord, to offer another hostage to the franchisor. This hostage is particularly valuable if the franchisee makes improvements to the property, because such improvements often can be appropriated by the landlord.

Finally, being the landlord provides franchisors with a means to assist franchisees, by reducing their capital requirements. That is, franchisors might defer rents on franchises that are in trouble. But even as they exhibit this flexibility, franchisors that are landlords retain their potent ability to enforce the contract, in that they can evict the franchisee while retaining the site for operations by a new franchisee.

**TERMINATION**   Losing a franchisee is difficult and costly. The franchisor needs to replace it (and in the absence of leasing clauses, it might need to replace the location too), take the time to train the new franchisee, and suffer opportunity costs related to lost business. The franchisee thus faces the temptation of holding up the franchisor by threatening to quit while negotiating a better deal. To a certain point, the franchisor likely concedes to these negotiations, to avoid having to replace the franchisee.

At the same time, franchisors make it expensive and difficult for franchisees to leave. As we noted, they offer lucrative business deals (low royalties, even on a good business) and demand early, franchise-specific investments (e.g., decor). In addition, franchisors have several contract devices at their disposal to make it even more difficult to quit. In the United Kingdom, many contracts require franchisees to find their replacements. Not only must the franchisee find a candidate quickly, but that candidate must be acceptable to the franchisor. If it fails to find a replacement, the franchisor imposes a **transfer fee**, to cover the costs of finding the replacement on its own.

Franchisors also may insert **right of first refusal** clauses, such that they have the right to contract with the franchisee if they can match any offer the franchisee receives, perhaps from a competitor. Although these options protect the franchisor against a franchisee that threatens to sell to an unsuitable buyer, they also create an opportunity for the franchisor to abuse the franchisee, by denying it the right to liquidate its business at a fair value. Thus, many states in the United States regulate termination clauses to prevent such abuse.

**CONTRACT CONSISTENCY**  Despite the various options available, franchise contracts exhibit surprisingly little variance. No two franchisees face the same situation, yet franchisors generally apply a single contract (with perhaps minor variations) and a single price to all franchisees, offered on a take-it-or-leave-it basis.

Contracts also do not vary much over time. Adjustments may occur occasionally, particularly in the price, such that royalties and fixed fees tend to rise as the franchisor becomes better established (McDonald's remains the exception that proves the rule). But in truth, contracts are surprisingly stable.[27] They are often written for fairly long periods, such as 15 years. Furthermore, tailoring contracts too specifically can heighten legal fees, especially in jurisdictions with high disclosure requirements. Finally, franchisors want to be perceived as fair, such that they treat franchisees equitably. By offering the same contract across the board, the franchisor avoids any appearance of discrimination—a threat that seems to loom larger than the possible loss of flexibility or a reputation for arbitrariness.

**CONTRACT ENFORCEMENT**  Beyond contracts, safeguarding a franchise relationship often relies on the influence of reputation. Franchisors that take a long-term view of their businesses worry, rightly, about creating an image of themselves as harsh, oppressive, greedy bullies. Such an image threatens them with the loss of current franchisees, poor cooperation, and an inability to attract new franchisees. More broadly, no franchisor wants to be classed as some fly-by-night operation, out to make money quickly through fees and lucrative tie-in sales and then abandon the franchisees. Thus, franchisors that are not swindlers, that seek to build their business, make a strong effort treat their franchisees correctly. Their reputation is worth far more than any short-term gains they might extract by invoking harsh contract terms to "win" disputes with franchisees.

In turn, franchisors do not always enforce the contracts they have written so carefully. Instead, they weigh the costs and benefits of punishing each act of noncompliance and tolerate those that they can, as Table 8-2 implies.

**TABLE 8-2    When do franchisors enforce the franchise contract?**

**Theoretical Rationales for Enforcing Contracts/Punishing Transgressions**

- Sourcing from a supplier other than those approved by the franchisor.
- Failing to maintain the look and ambiance of the premises.
- Violating the franchisor's standards and procedures.
- Failing to pay advertising fees.
- Failing to pay the franchisor's royalty!

**Costly Enforcement Situations, Making Franchisors More Likely to Overlook Violations**

- Dense, tightly knit network of franchisees, such that the franchisor fears a solidarity reaction because other franchisees would side with the violator.
- A violator is a central player in the franchisee's network.
- Performance ambiguity prevents the franchisor from identifying the situation clearly or monitoring well, so it cannot be sure it has a strong case against the "violator."
- Strong relational governance allows the system to operate on the basis of norms of solidarity, flexibility, and information exchange.

**Benefits of Enforcement Outweigh the Costs, with Punitive Actions More Likely**

- The violation is critical one, such as missing a large royalty payment or operating a very shabby facility in a highly visible location.
- The franchisee is a central player in the network. Rather than avoiding enforcement to reduce system backlash, the franchisor senses the need to send a signal that rules are rules. Tolerating a major violation by a central player instead would signal to other franchisees that the contract is just a piece of paper, with no real weight.
- The violator is a master franchisee with multiple units, such that the violation will propagate across its units and become a large-scale problem.
- The franchisor has invested in the franchise *system* (not the particular franchisee) and thus needs to protect its investment, even if strong relational governance is in place. The franchisor will risk upsetting a given relationship to protect its system investments.
- The franchisor is large.
- High mutual dependence in the franchisee–franchisor relationship suggests it can withstand the conflict that enforcement will create.
- The franchisor is much more powerful than the franchisee and can coerce the franchisee to tolerate enforcement.

*Source:* Antia, Kersi D. and Gary L. Frazier (2001), "The Severity of Contract Enforcement in Interfirm Channel Relationships," *Journal of Marketing* 65, no. 4, pp. 67–81.

**SELF-ENFORCING AGREEMENTS**    Because each side still has incentives to cheat though, a contract seeks to create a **self-enforcing agreement**. In such an arrangement, neither side wants to violate, regardless of monitored or threats, because the contract rearranges their incentives to ensure that cheating is not in their *own* best interest. The trouble is that every clause that stops one side from cheating creates a new way for the *other* side to cheat. *Every effort to balance power creates a new possibility for imbalance.*

This assertion is true of most business arrangements. But if franchisors and franchisees rely only on elaborate contracts to address the problem, they take a great risk. These

| **TABLE 8-3   The franchise contract** |
|---|

The International Franchise Guide of the International Herald Tribune suggests that any franchise contract should address the following topics:

- Definition of terms
- Organizational structure
- Term of initial agreement
- Term of renewal
- Causes for termination or nonrenewal
- Territorial exclusivity
- Intellectual property protection
- Assignment of responsibilities
- Ability to subfranchise
- Mutual agreement of pro forma cash flows
- Development schedule and associated penalties
- Fees: front end, ongoing
- Currency and remittance restrictions
- Remedies in case of disagreement

*Source:* Moulton, Susan L. (ed.) (1996), *International Franchise Guide* (Oakland, CA: Source Books Publications).

two parties are agreeing to tie their fates together for years. The franchisor is providing access to its secrets and trademarks; the franchisee is sacrificing its autonomy. Their arrangement is elaborate and forward looking, and the resulting contracts become highly complex very quickly, as we show in Table 8-3, by listing aspects that need to be covered in some way in any franchise contract. But no contract can fully specify all contingencies and craft proper solutions for all problems in the future.

## Company Store Strategies

Franchisee- and company-owned outlets are usually considered substitutes, such that one or the other seems more apt to fit the situation, but not both. Yet in practice, many franchisors also run company-owned stores.[28] Among U.S. firms that franchise, an average of 30 percent of their outlets are company owned.[29]

**MARKET DIFFERENCES**   The obvious explanation is that some markets differ from others. Therefore, company outlets and franchisee outlets could serve different types of markets. For example, some markets require monitoring by the franchisor because repeat business for any one franchisee is minimal.[30] A fast-food restaurant franchise on a superhighway draws heavily on the market of consumers passing through only once. This franchisee likely is tempted to cheat (e.g., cut costs by serving stale food), because it would not suffer the consequences of its poor quality. Travelers are drawn in by the franchisor's brand name, and their poor experience lessens brand equity. Yet they are unlikely to return to this exact location anyway, so the franchisee does not suffer the usual consequences (i.e., lost future sales). To protect its brand equity, the franchisor likely prefers to own this outlet (and as we noted, other franchisees should welcome this decision).

**TEMPORARY FRANCHISES AND COMPANY OUTLETS**   Another explanation for the simultaneous existence of franchise- and company-owned stores is that some of the stores are **temporary**. Circumstances, at one point in time, create a need for one form of ownership or the other.

Franchisors usually start with one and then a few outlets of their own, which they use to formulate the business format and develop the brand name. If they skip this step and start franchising early, they cannot attract many franchisees, because they have little to offer (e.g., brand equity, proven format). So franchisors start with company stores. Once they have achieved a certain level, they can add franchisees, usually at a high rate.

But once a business is underway, why add any further company stores? Sometimes the cause is accidental: A franchisee has a problem, and the franchisor buys out the location, for system morale (or, in the United States, to avoid lawsuits) or because a profitable franchisee must exit quickly (e.g., for health reasons). For these motives, the company outlet is temporary, and the franchisor seeks to sell it to a new franchisee as soon as possible.

We find a variation on this idea in Italy, where opening a retail store in a particular sector (e.g., food) requires a sector-specific license from local authorities. These licenses are limited in supply and thus valuable, representing a big obstacle for Italian franchisors. If they wish to expand quickly, they may be obliged to accept an undesirable franchisee, simply because it holds one of the licenses to sell that product in the area. They can thus predict conflict with the license holder, so franchisors decline to franchise and use their corporate influence to obtain their own license. In turn, they are required to run a company outlet for some time. Thus, a predominant pattern in Italian franchising reveals *system growth, by divesting of corporate assets*. The franchisor operates the outlet, learns from its experience, and then divests itself of the outlet by selling to a suitable franchisee. This divestment costs the franchisor little, because the newly franchised store cooperates with management, often with better operating results.

Ultimately, the idea of temporary franchisees or company stores cannot explain though why franchisors, as they grow, continue to add new company outlets, at a lower rate than they add franchisees.[31] Systems that grow the fastest do so by favoring franchisees over company units. (And these systems have lower failure rates.)[32] So there must be reasons to maintain both types permanently, in which is known as the plural form.

**PLURAL FORMS AND SYNERGIES**    Simultaneously and deliberately maintaining *both* company and franchised outlets to perform the same functions constitutes a **plural form** strategy.[33] The underlying principle holds that franchisors manage organizational duality (vertically integrated and outsourced) by drawing on the strengths of each system to offset the other's weaknesses. In particular, a plural form enables franchisors to build a control system that creates functional rivalry between the two forms. The rivalry is effective because franchisors monitor their own units very closely, using the following:

1. Elaborate management information systems that generate detailed, daily reports about every aspect of their outlets' operations.
2. Frequent, elaborate, unannounced field audits, covering hundreds of items and requiring hours to complete.
3. Mystery shoppers, or paid professional auditors who pose as customers.

Such heavy, invasive control mechanisms are tolerated by company managers because they have little choice: They are paid a salary to observe the franchisor's rules. Top management tells them what to do, and they do it. They are not separately accountable for earning profits.

Franchisees instead reject such invasive, frequent, thorough monitoring efforts. Rather than telling franchisees what to do, franchisors must attempt to persuade them. The titles that appear in each form thus are telling: Whereas company store managers report to district **managers**, franchisees work with (do not report to) franchise **consultants**. However, the information and experience gained from heavy control mechanisms in company stores help franchisors understand the day-to-day operations of the business it purports to master.

The two forms in plural systems also serve as **benchmarks** for the other. By comparing the performance of company and franchise outlets, the franchisor can encourage each to do better. The company and franchise outlets perform exactly the same roles—which, as we have noted, seems senseless—so direct comparisons are possible. In turn, **competition** within the system increases dramatically.

The connection between the two forms is not solely contested though. In the plural form, each side engages in teaching the other, which can create a **mutual strategy**. That is, the company stores and franchisees both try out ideas and then seek to persuade their counterparts to adopt the ones that work. In this process, strategy emerges from their rigorous debate. Plural forms create more options, which get reviewed more candidly and thoroughly than would unitary forms. Thus, the ideas are well refined, and each side commits more strongly to the new initiatives that arise.

Another advantage of the plural form is that the franchisor can create **career paths** for personnel to move back and forth between the company side and the franchisee side. Not only does this freedom accommodate personnel needs, but it also helps socialize the members of both sides of the franchise "family." One member might prefer a career path through the company side, dealing with company outlets as a manager, then supervisor, and then as a corporate executive. Another might want to focus only on the franchise side, by starting a unit, adding new ones, and growing into a mini-hierarchy. Yet another member of the franchise family might prefer to span both sides, in which case the following three career paths are noteworthy:

1. Company employees become franchisees. This path is common. Company employees like it because they can develop into entrepreneurs, often with less capital than an outsider would need. Franchisors like it because their franchisee community is seeded with people they know and trust.
2. Company unit managers become franchisee consultants. This shift entails moving from running a company store (being on salary, following the rules) to working with franchisees to persuade them. The jobs are very different (similar to a promotion from a factory supervisor to a diplomatic post), so the transition can be difficult, but the ex–company manager likely enjoys credibility with franchisees because of his or her previous hands-on experience.
3. Company managers become franchisee managers. In this move, the member shifts from one organization to another, from the franchisor's hierarchy to managing in a multi-unit franchisor. It offers an important way in which mini-hierarchies mimic the franchisor's organization.

All three spanning career paths solidly **unite** the franchisor and franchisee too. They allow personnel exchanges, regularly and on a large scale.

Beyond trading ideas and human capital, company stores also provide a unique resource: They are good **laboratories**, in which a company can test new ideas while absorbing the risk of failure. Dunkin' Donuts regularly experiments with new products and processes in its own stores, using them as a sort of test market. In this case, the company can confirm that the tests are conducted properly and that the feedback it receives is candid. Once a new product or process has been perfected, Dunkin' Donuts can point to the success in its company-owned stores to encourage franchisees to adopt the change themselves.

Of course, company store managers are less likely to generate the innovative ideas for testing, because they are hired to follow rules. Ideas instead tend to come from the franchisor's central database or the active involvement of motivated entrepreneurs, especially those coping with local circumstances, including competition, labor forces, and customers. The increasing popularity of Indian food in London has led McDonald's to add curry and spice to its British menus.[34] Ideas like this can be tested in company stores, but they likely originate from local franchisees, adapting to local competition and tastes.

In short, plural forms **complement** each other in ways that make the chain stronger, and both franchisors and franchisees benefit—as long as active management is in place. Maintaining company and franchisee units simultaneously is beneficial if all the parties work to make it so and appreciate the benefits of the franchise system's "dual personality."

**EXPLOITING FRANCHISEES WITH COMPANY OUTLETS** Just like any split personality though, there can be a malevolent side, and this explanation for plural forms has attracted substantial attention from regulators and scholars.[35] Franchisors might prefer to run company outlets, to control the operation closely and appropriate all the profits generated by the marketing channel. (Assuming, of course, that the company system would be equally profitable, which is a heroic assumption, as we hope we have shown already.) Given this premise, a trademark owner might franchise merely to build the business. Once established, this franchisor would use its profits to buy back its franchises. If they refuse to sell, the franchisor might attempt to appropriate their property (e.g., by fabricating a reason to invoke a termination clause, ending the lease).

In this sinister scenario, franchisors increase the fraction of company-owned units, especially in the most lucrative locations (e.g., urban commercial districts). That is, franchisors use franchisees to build the system, and then expropriate them, according to this **redirection of ownership** hypothesis. Although existing evidence suggests this development is rare, anecdotal reports and court cases suggest that it does happen.

For example, Zannier, a retailer that covers the children's clothing market in France, uses 13 different brand names and a variety of routes to market (e.g., hypermarkets, single-brand boutiques, multibrand boutiques, company owned and franchisee owned). Zannier seeks to lock up the market by covering every viable position. To do so, it used franchisees to grow quickly. The franchisees later charged that once the franchisor had grown large and successful, it used pricing tactics and restrictive contract terms to squeeze out more than 200 franchisees, in favor of other channels, including its company-owned stores.[36] Zannier simply paid the damages to settle these legal claims.

# ADAPTING TO TRENDS IN FRANCHISING

Franchisors have very high failure rates. Various estimates suggest that three-quarters of the hundreds of franchisors launched in the United States survive less than a decade. In 2012, the Small Business Administration reported that default rate for the 25 worst performing franchise brands ranged between 71 and 37 percent.[37] For every high-profile franchisor such as McDonald's and its wealthy franchisees, there are multiple business formats and brand names that have failed, partially or completely, stripping franchisees of their wealth in the process. Many brands build substantial size over time but then collapse, such as when Krispy Kreme went from a regional treat to a short-lived national phenomenon, before shrinking back again due to the failure of many of its franchisees. Some franchisors fail to spread despite their best efforts; others actually set out to defraud their franchisees, just as they would any other investor. The Malaysian and Thai governments thus have set up departments to help citizens become franchisees, out of concern that their people might be cheated by unscrupulous, would-be franchisors.[38]

## Survival Trends

Most evidence indicates that *success forecasts success*.[39] The older the system and the more units it has, the greater its odds of continuing to exist. For a prospective franchisee, established franchisors may be more expensive, but they also lower the risk of system failure. A period of four years offers an attractive threshold: Franchise systems that are at least four years of age offer a sharply lower probability of failing than do younger systems.[40]

Survival is also more likely if the franchisor can attract a **favorable rating** from a third party. For example, the U.S. magazine *Entrepreneur* surveys franchisors and verifies much of the information it collects, before adding in subjective judgment to compile proprietary ratings of hundreds of franchisors. This rating is a good predictor of franchisor survival for many years, which may actually reflect a sort of bias, in that the ranking creates a self-fulfilling prophesy. The third-party certification of predicted success helps the franchisor gain an image as a **legitimate player** in its operating environment. With this reputation, it can more easily acquire the resources it needs to survive. Yet many entrepreneurs continue to assign relatively a low priority to certification and incomprehensibly refuse to cooperate with certifying bodies.

**MAINTAINING A COOPERATIVE ATMOSPHERE**    To encourage success and survival, the franchisor instead must ensure that franchisees perceive the benefits of opening a new outlet, then that they believe they continue to receive value in exchange for the royalties they pay. Such beliefs generally require a sense of cooperation, but instead, many franchise systems create an inherent conflict between the desire and risk of being one's own boss and being nearly a subsidiary of a central organization. One franchisee summarizes a typical level of ambivalence in this attitude[41]:

> [The franchise name] does not bring in much business, and whatever business it does bring in, I suppose it helps people feel more secure. But right now, I feel it's my business—and that's my name on the front because the numbers would be the same.

But franchisees are likely more cooperative when they sense a solid relationship between themselves and their franchisor. Several conditions encourage business partners to develop feelings of **commitment** and perceive higher levels of **trust** and **fairness**,[42] such as when a partner believes that

1. Their partner encourages them to innovate.
2. A team spirit exists.
3. Good performance is recognized.
4. The partner is fair.
5. Communication is open.
6. The partner is competent and acts reliably.

Although franchising is inherently asymmetric, with franchisees highly dependent on the franchisor, franchisees remain entrepreneurs and feel the entrepreneurial need to be the boss.[43] Accordingly, the franchisor's consultant must exert influence without appearing to threaten the franchisee's autonomy—a difficult balancing act, requiring diplomacy and persuasive skills. Furthermore, franchisors must seek to resolve conflicts by searching for integrative, win–win solutions that allow it to craft a mutually acceptable solution with its franchisees. Moreover, franchisors can motivate partners and increase the size of a franchise system by lowering royalty rates over time, promising low upfront franchise fees that instead increase over time, owning a small and decreasing proportion of stores, keeping franchisees' initial investment low, and helping finance franchisees.[44]

**MANAGING INHERENT GOAL CONFLICT** Every franchise system features a structural source of conflict, in the clash of goals between franchisee and franchisor that arises because of the difference between each side's contribution to the business and each side's outcomes. For franchisors, higher sales are always better, because they lead to higher variable fees and more income. With greater income, they can engage in more promotion and build brand equity, which in turn allows them to increase the (fixed and variable) fees they charge and enlarges the pool of prospective store managers and franchisees. For a franchisee in a specific trading area, more sales means more profit too—up to a point.[45]

In short, franchisors seek to maximize sales; franchisees seek to maximize profits. This **goal incongruity** becomes more vivid as chains expand. In their effort to maximize system sales, franchisors saturate the market area by authorizing many new outlets, to the extent that new stores might encroach on existing outlets and **cannibalize** other franchisees. Even McDonald's has miscalculated the best growth rates; in Brazil, it was at one time the largest (indirect) private employer, because it had added hundreds of franchisees in what McDonald's viewed as a model operation. But franchisees soon began complaining, and even sued, that McDonald's had undermined them by opening too many stores and making it impossible for them to earn profits.[46]

Such events harm the franchisor's reputation with franchisees, though the financial gains from authorizing new outlets may tempt it to encroach anyway. However, even company-owned stores often build too many stores too close to each other, which can undermine long-term profits (e.g., Starbucks). Systematic evidence suggests that few systems can resist this temptation: As the system grows, they locate new outlets close enough to existing outlets to diminish single-store revenues—but the new outlet still adds enough revenue to raise total system royalties. In contrast, vertically integrated firms carefully space out their company-owned outlets to avoid cannibalizing an existing revenue stream, because their focus remains on profits, not just sales.[47]

For franchisors that want to grow, even to the point of encroaching on their existing franchisees, the question is, How can we cover a market densely without alienating our franchisees? One solution is to offer new sites to existing franchisees, or to give them right of first refusal to a new location. If economies of scale arise from operating multiple sites, the franchisee may be in a position to gain from them. This idea leads to the paradox of multiunit franchisees.

## Multiunit Franchising

Does a franchisor prefer a manager (company owned) or an individual entrepreneur (franchisee) in each unit? Curiously, the answer may be, "Neither."[48] Rather than dealing with a multitude of different, individual responsible parties for each location, some franchisors interact with a single company that runs multiple locations, through **multiunit franchising**. Although we note some variations on the idea, it is possible to establish a primary principle: The manager of a unit is not the owner but is employed by the owner, which owns more than one unit and must hire employees to run the various locations. This arrangement is common and growing.

On the face of it, the system is difficult to explain though. If the purpose of franchising is to replace lackluster employee managers with motivated owner-managers, then multiunit franchising should fail, because it just adds a layer of franchisee management, between the franchisor and the person running the outlet. The master franchisee monitors the monitor (i.e., store manager), instead of just controlling the situation itself. Why? The answer is not totally clear, to be honest. Some evidence indicates that franchisors resort to multiunit franchising to grow faster and deal with unfamiliar markets. Thus, U.S. franchisors heavily favor multiunit operators when they need to open operations in Africa and the Middle East.[49] However, doing so may simply postpone problems, such that franchisors that use multiunits franchising appear to fail more frequently than those that insist that franchisees own and manage their stores. This demand slows growth, but it may make the system healthier.

McDonald's prefers (but does not require) single-unit franchising. Perhaps as a result, it has virtually little presence in Africa. In contrast, Burger King embraced multiunit franchising early in its history and used it to grow fast. Eventually, the chain had to confront fundamental flaws in its market strategy and operations, which had been masked by its fast growth. The franchisor also became embroiled in battles with powerful multiunit franchisees, creating a spiral of conflict that hardened into embittered, lasting mediocre relations. Ultimately, the chain suffered severely and continued to remain second fiddle to McDonald's.

Before dismissing multiunit franchising, however, we should examine its positive side. A multiunit franchisee can create an organizational structure that mimics the franchisor's structure and imitates its practices. These "mini-hierarchies" simplify matters enormously for the franchisor, enabling it to deal with one organization, that is, the multiunit franchisee. Because the multiunit operators already replicate the franchisor's management practices and policies, they reduce the enormous job of managing hundreds of relationships into a more tractable management problem. For example, KFC has more than 3,500 U.S. restaurants, more than half of which are owned by just 17 franchisees. If KFC can convince only these largest franchisees of the merits of an idea, it influences almost more than half of the restaurants!

Of course, if mini-hierarchies are to help the franchisor, there needs to be substantial cooperation, such that the mini-hierarchies replicate the franchisor's system. Many large restaurant chains appear to have mastered this process, demonstrating that if prospective franchisees are carefully screened, given a trial period, and observed, multiunit franchising can be a viable and valuable strategy. If a franchisee fails to meet the franchisor's requirements, it simply is not allowed to open more units.

Another benefit of multiunit franchising stems from its ability to preserve knowledge. Again using fast food restaurants as an example, we note that small details (e.g., the fastest way to fold a pizza box) ultimately make a big difference in competitive businesses. Such know-how demands experience and gets transmitted by example, but in this industry, personnel turnover is very high. Thus, personnel enter the learning curve, learn, and then leave, taking their knowledge with them. A new restaurant franchise starts without any such knowledge, and as soon as it gains it, the personnel who possess it are likely to leave. Multiunit franchisees provide a means to preserve and spread such knowledge across their own stores, through holding meetings, making phone calls, and using other means of communication. The resulting personal ties across stores also help spread knowledge. That is, multiunit franchises spread learning curves by actively lobbying to disseminate know-how across their own locations.[50]

They are particularly likely to spread tacit, idiosyncratic knowledge when it refers consistently to a local area. Even in standardized businesses, such as pizza restaurants, local experience matters and can mitigate franchise failure rates. Distant experience, whether gained by the franchisor or the multiunit franchisee, is less helpful than local experience.[51] Therefore, when franchisors use multiunit franchising, they often award new sites to the franchisee that owns the next closest unit to exploit the **power of contiguity** by ensuring units owned by one person are adjacent, without intermingling units owned by different people. This strategy is particularly effective if the new site to be developed is not only contiguous but also offers a demographic profile similar to that served by the rest of the multiunit owner's stores. These franchisors allow franchisees to build up large networks of stores that appear on a map as a single, unbroken mass, uninterrupted by other franchisees or company-owned stores.[52] Owning clusters of stores also makes it easier for franchisees to monitor their monitors (store managers) and amortize human capital connected to an area. Finally, because the local customer base is likely being served by the same owner in various stores, free riding declines.

## SUMMARY: FRANCHISING STRUCTURES AND STRATEGIES

Franchising a business format offers a way to grow quickly while also building brand equity. For the franchisee, it provides a means to gain assistance and reduce risk. In return for paid fees, entrepreneurs receive the services of a corporate backer, a coach, a problem solver, and an enforcement agency, which polices the way the brand is presented across the board. For the franchisor, the system represents access to capital and management resources, as well as a method for harnessing the motivation and capabilities of entrepreneurs. For businesses that can be formatted and transmitted, franchising is an excellent solution to persistent problems of monitoring employee managers.

But codifying the formula also demands writing a complex contract to specify rights and duties. Contracts are crafted to give both sides good reasons to abide by their agreement, in the form of hostages. Many franchisors price their franchises lower than the market will bear to increase the applicant pool and invoke a profit motive for franchisees to stay in business. Lower lump-sum entry fees also denote a signal that the franchisor has no opportunistic intentions of taking the franchisees' money and failing to provide the promised services. But franchisors also frequently bind franchisees with clauses that award control of the property to the franchisor and limit franchisees' ability to terminate, such that the franchisor can punish non-compliance, protect its brand equity, and reinforce the franchisee's dependence on it. Dependence also arises when the franchisee must invest in franchise-specific assets, with low resale value outside the business. Yet franchisors cannot rely entirely on their contracts, which vary surprisingly little across franchisees or over time, to run a franchise system. They must also develop a reputation for fair dealings, by not exploiting franchisees' dependence.

Franchise systems typically mix company-owned outlets in with franchisees, to gain a laboratory and a classroom for training personnel, trying out ideas, and refining their business format. Dual or plural systems also enable the franchisor to achieve synergies between the sides of its business, as well as encourage the franchisor to collect, adapt, and spread new products and practices. Not only do these plural forms spark vigorous debate and build commitment to new initiatives, but the rivalry they invoke also motivates both sides of the operation to improve.

Regardless of such benefits, the failure rates of franchisees are quite high. Survival becomes more likely as a system grows, ages, and acquires certification, but it also depends on cooperation, achieved by building commitment, seeking win–win solutions, offering genuine assistance, and formalizing roles and duties. But conflict is inevitable: Franchisees pursue profit, franchisors pursue sales, and the two goals collide even more as operations grow.

Multiunit franchising, in which one franchisee owns many outlets, is rather difficult to understand but also surprisingly common, often resulting in blocks of contiguous outlets owned by the same mini-hierarchy. It likely provides an effective method to monitor the monitors and capture and spread local knowledge, while obliging multiunit franchisees to bear the cost of free riding. Yet the complexity and risk inherent to franchising also seem to demand that channel managers should consider other solutions, perhaps offering less control but greater cooperation.

We also acknowledge though that by the 1970s, franchising clearly had become a permanent force, not just a fad, in structuring U.S. distribution channels. Today, that trend has repeated itself worldwide. Franchising as an institution is so stable and so pervasive that it represents the single most common way to become an entrepreneur in North America, Europe, and Asia.[53] The dynamism of this channel institution is remarkable. Thus, franchising continues to deserve serious consideration by any manager in any marketing channel.

## TAKE-AWAYS

- Franchising is a marketing channel structure intended to convince end-users that they are buying from a vertically integrated manufacturer, when they may be buying from a separately owned company.
- Franchising a business format is a way to grow quickly while building brand equity.
  - For the franchisor, the system provides quick access to capital and management resources. It also enables the franchisor to harness the motivation and capability of entrepreneurs. For "programmable" businesses (that can be put into a format and transmitted), franchising is an excellent solution to the problems of monitoring employee managers.
  - For the franchisee, the system offers assistance and reduces risk. By paying fees, entrepreneurs purchase a corporate backer, coaching, problem solutions, and brand enforcement.
- The codification of the formula includes writing a complex contract specifying the rights and duties of both sides, to encourage their compliance.
  - Contracts might price franchises lower than the market will bear to increase the applicant pool and give franchisees a profit motive to stay in business.
  - Contracts often bind franchisees with clauses that award control of the property to the franchisor and/or limit the franchisees' ability to terminate their business.
  - Contracts give the franchisor means to punish noncompliance, which protects brand equity but also reinforces the franchisee's dependence on the franchisor.
  - Franchisors cannot exploit the franchisees' dependence opportunistically, so they rarely enforce contracts every time franchisees violate them. Instead, they weigh the costs and benefits and select which battles they want to fight with which franchisees that fail to comply.
- Franchise systems typically mix company-owned and franchised outlets. This plural form gives the franchisor a laboratory and a classroom to train personnel, try out ideas, and refine the business format.
- Failure rates are very high but mitigated by growth, ages, and certification by third parties.
- Conflict is inevitable, in part because of the built-in clash of goals.
- Multiunit franchising is surprisingly common and rather difficult to understand.

## Endnotes

1. We thank Rupinder Jindal and Rozenn Perrigot for helpful discussions during the preparation of this chapter.
2. Spelling note: "Franchisor" is U.S. English, whereas "franchiser" is British English. This textbook adopts the U.S. convention, but many documents, particularly in Europe, use "franchiser."
3. PWC (2011), "Franchise Business Economic Outlook: 2011," January 3.
4. *The Economist* (2000), "The Tiger and the Tech," February 5, pp. 70–72.
5. This information is drawn from multiple sources: Kaufmann and Lafontaine (1994), op. cit., Love, John F. (1986), *McDonald's: Behind the Golden Arches* (New York: Bantam Books);

Wattenz, Eric (1999), "La Machine McDonald's," *Capital* 96 (September), pp. 48–69; Piétralunga, Cédric (2004), "Les Recettes Qui Ont Fait Rebondir McDo," *Capital* (June), pp. 28–32.

6. Reinartz, Werner J. and V. Kumar (1999), "Store-, Market-, and Consumer-Characteristics: The Drivers of Store Performance," *Marketing Letters* 10, no. 1, pp. 5–22.

7. Combs, James G. and David J. Ketchen (1999), "Can Capital Scarcity Help Agency Theory Explain Franchising? Revisiting the Capital Scarcity Hypothesis," *Academy of Management Journal* 42, no. 2, pp. 198–207.

8. Norton, Seth W. (1988), "An Empirical Look at Franchising as an Organizational Form," *Journal of Business* 61, no. 2, pp. 197–218.

9. BarNir, Anat (2012), "Starting Technologically Innovative Ventures: Reasons, Human Capitol and Gender," *Management Decisions* 50, no. 3, pp. 399–419.

10. Shane, Scott A. (1996), "Hybrid Organizational Arrangements and Their Implications for Firm Growth and Survival: A Study of New Franchisors," *Academy of Management Journal* 39, no. 1, pp. 216–234.

11. Dant, Rajiv P. (1995), "Motivation for Franchising: Rhetoric Versus Reality," *International Small Business Journal* 14 (Winter), pp. 10–32.

12. Birkeland, Peter M. (2002), *Franchising Dreams* (Chicago, IL: The University of Chicago Press).

13. Minkler, Alanson P. (1992), "Why Firms Franchise: A Search Cost Theory," *Journal of Institutional and Theoretical Economics* 148, no. 1, pp. 240–249.

14. Aoulou, Yves and Olivia Bassi (1999). "Une Opportunité de Cassière à Saisir," *LSA*, pp. 42–47.

15. Reported with comment in the February 27, 2004, weekly newsletter of IF Consulting (www.i-f.com) and 2012-website content (www.uniqlo.com).

16. See 2013 website (www.starbucks.com).

17. Michel, Caroline (2002), "Ada, le Dernier échec de Papy Rousselet," *Capital* (August), pp. 32–33.

18. European Commission (1997). Green Paper on Vertical Restraints in EU Competition Policy, Brussels, Directorate General for Competition, p. 44. Available at http://europa .eu.int/en/comm/dg04/dg04home.htm.

19. Dnes, Anthony W. (1993), "A Case-Study Analysis of Franchise Contracts," *Journal of Legal Studies* 22 (June), pp. 367–393. This source is the basis for much of this section and the comparative statements about franchising in the United Kingdom.

20. Klein, Benjamin. (1995), "The Economics of Franchise Contracts," *Journal of Corporate Finance* 2, no. 1, pp. 9–37.

21. Agrawal, Deepak and Rajiv Lal (1995), "Contractual Arrangements in Franchising: An Empirical Investigation," *Journal of Marketing Research* 32 (May), pp. 213–221.

22. Lal, Rajiv. (1990), "Improving Channel Coordination through Franchising," *Marketing Science* 9, no. 4, pp. 299–318.

23. The Economist Intelligence Unit (1995), "Retail Franchising in France," *EIU Marketing in Europe* (December), pp. 86–104.

24. Lafontaine, Francine (1992), "Agency Theory and Franchising: Some Empirical Results," *Rand Journal of Economics* 23, no. 2, pp. 263–83.

25. Kaufmann, Patrick J. and Francine Lafontaine. (1994), "Costs of Control: The Source of Economic Rents for McDonald's Franchisees," *Journal of Law and Economics* 36 (October), pp. 417–453.

26. Klein, Benjamin (1980), "Transaction Cost Determinants of 'Unfair' Contractual Arrangements," *Borderlines of Law and Economic Theory* 70, no. 2, pp. 356–362.

27. Lafontaine, Francine and Kathryn L. Shaw. (1998), "Franchising Growth and Franchisor Entry and Exit in the U.S. Market: Myth and Reality," *Journal of Business Venturing* 13, no. 1, pp. 95–112.

28. Ibid.

29. Carney, Mick and Eric Gedajlovic (1991), "Vertical Integration in Franchise Systems: Agency Theory and Resource Explanations," *Strategic Management Journal* 12, no. 1, pp. 607–629.

30. Brickley, James A. and Frederick H. Dark (1987), "The Choice of Organizational Form: The Case of Franchising," *Journal of Financial Economics* 18, pp. 401–420.

31. Lafontaine, Francine and Patrick J. Kaufman (1994), "The Evolution of Ownership Patterns

in Franchise Systems," *Journal of Retailing* 70, no. 2, pp. 97–113.

32. Shane, op. cit.
33. Bradach, Jeffrey L. (1997), "Using the Plural Form in the Management of Restaurant Chains," *Administrative Science Quarterly* 42 (June), pp. 276–303. This source is the basis for this section and is an excellent guide to the working operations of large chain franchisors.
34. See 2013 website (www.mcdonalds.co.uk).
35. This discussion is based on Dant, Rajiv P, Audehesh, K. Paswan, and Patrick J. Kaufman (1996), "What We Know About Ownership Redirection in Franchising: A Meta-Analysis," *Journal of Retailing* 72, no. 4, pp. 429–444.
36. Bouillin, Arnaud (2001), "Comment Zannier Verrouille Son Marche," *Management* (June), pp. 28–30.
37. Small Business Administration. SBA 504 and 7(a) disbursed loans from 2001 to 2011 as reported on www.bluemaumau.org/11665/worst_25_franchises_highest_failure_rates_2012.
38. Reported with comment in the April 2, 2004 weekly newsletter of IF Consulting (www.i-f.com).
39. Shane, Scott and Maw-Der Foo. (1999), "New Firm Survival: Institutional Explanations for New Franchisor Mortality," *Management Science* 45 (February), pp. 142–159.
40. Shane, op. cit.
41. Birkeland, op. cit.
42. Samaha, Stephen, Robert W. Palmatier, and Rajiv P. Dant (2011), "Poisoning Relationships: Perceive Unfairness in Channels of Distribution," *Journal of Marketing* 75 (May), pp. 99–117; and Palmatier, Robert W., Rajiv P. Dant, Dhruv Grewal, and Kenneth R. Evans (2006), "Factors Influencing the Effectiveness of Relationship Marketing: A Meta-Analysis," *Journal of Marketing* 70 (October), pp. 136–153.
43. Dant, Rajiv P. and Gregory T Gundlach (1998), "The Challenge of Autonomy and Dependence in Franchised Channels of

Distribution," *Journal of Business Venturing* 14, no. 1, pp. 35–67.
44. Shane, Scott, Venkatesh Shankar, and Ashwin Aravindakshan (2006), "The Effects of New Franchisor Partnering Strategies on Franchise System Size," *Management Science* 52 (May), pp. 773–787.
45. Carmen, James M. and Thomas A. Klein (1986), "Power, Property, and Performance in Franchising," *Research in Marketing* 8, pp. 71–130.
46. Jordan, Miriam and Shirley Leung (2003), "McDonald's Faces Foreign Franchisees' Revolt," *Dow Jones Business News* (October 21), p. 6.
47. Kalnins, Arturs (2004), "An Empirical Analysis of Territorial Encroachment Within Franchised and Company-Owned Branded Chains," *Marketing Science* 23, no. 4, pp. 476–89.
48. Kaufmann, Patrick J. and Rajiv Dant (1996), "Multi-Unit Franchising: Growth and Management Issues," *Journal of Business Venturing* 11, no. 1, pp. 343–358.
49. Dant, Rajiv P. and Nada I. Nasr (1998), "Control Techniques and Upward Flow of Information in Franchising in Distant Markets: Conceptualization and Preliminary Evidence," *Journal of Business Venturing* 13, no. 1, pp. 3–28.
50. Darr, Eric D., Linda Argote, and Dennis Epple (1995), "The Acquisition, Transfer, and Depreciation of Knowledge in Service Organizations: Productivity in Franchises," *Management Science* 41, no. 11, pp. 1750–1762.
51. Kalnins, Arturs and Kyle J. Mayer (2004), "Franchising, Ownership, and Experience: A Study of Pizza Restaurant Survival," *Management Science* 50, no. 12, pp. 1716–1728.
52. Kalnins, Artur and Francine Lafontaine (2004), "Multi-Unit Ownership in Franchising: Evidence from the Fast-Food Industry in Texas," *Rand Journal of Economics* 35, no. 4, pp. 749–763.
53. *The Economist* (2000), "The Tiger and the Tech," February 5, pp. 70–72.

# CHAPTER 9

# Emerging Channel Structures and Strategies

**LEARNING OBJECTIVES**

**After reading this chapter, you will be able to:**

- Describe the three most significant trends influencing marketing channels' structure and strategy.
- Understand what drives the shift from products to services, for both suppliers and channel members.
- Evaluate the effect of key service characteristics, including the acquisition of service-related capabilities, infrastructure, and knowledge, on channel strategies.
- Understand the drivers and effects of the globalization of both suppliers and downstream channel members on channel strategies.
- Recognize the drivers of increased e-commerce for both suppliers and downstream channel members and explain the effect of increased online sales on channel strategies.

## TRENDS INFLUENCING MARKETING CHANNELS

Dramatic changes in the business environment influence various aspects of marketing channels' structure and strategy. Some trends are well underway in the U.S. market but are just beginning in developing economies:

1. Already 80 percent of all U.S. gross domestic product (GDP) comes from the **service** sector, up from 58 percent in 1970, yet the transition into services is just starting in China.[1] The shift from products to services has important ramifications for a firm's channel strategy.

2. The drive for **globalization** has taken hold across various market and industry segments, with significant channel implications. Of the S&P 500 firms that report foreign sales, 46 percent of total revenue in 2010 came from foreign markets.[2]

3. The shift from bricks-and-mortar retailing to **e-commerce** is transforming channel systems worldwide and in most industries. For example, increasing online sales of music and books have significantly altered the channels for these products, and the extent to which these changes will continue to affect sales remains uncertain.

By their very nature, the impact of market- and technological-based disruptions is difficult to predict. Yet we would be remiss if we were to ignore these three trends that fundamentally influence today's marketing channel structures and strategies. These trends and the resultant business adaptations are leading to **emerging channel structures and strategies**, which is the focus of this chapter.

## CHANNEL STRATEGIES FOR SERVICES

In the shift of world markets from mostly product-based to service-based economies, developed economies are leading the way—while also causing upstream and downstream channel members to look for opportunities to add more services to differentiate their overall offering. For example, manufacturers of consumer electronic products offer service warranties for most products; in many cases, their earnings from these warranties exceed the profits they obtain from their core products. Consumer electronic analysts report that the profit margins on warranties can be up to 18 times greater than the margins on the core products.[3]

In parallel, many retailers are adding competitive warranty plans to jump into this profit stream. But the stream is only so wide, so increasing channel conflict surrounds add-on services. Some retailers also seek to take advantage of the increase of the share of U.S. GNP captured by financial services and health care. For example, Wal-Mart has started offering its Bluebird prepaid debit cards, in conjunction with American Express, which promise no annual fee or minimum balance and expand its traditional product sales (food, apparel, home furnishings) to financial services.[4] In this trend, by which firms shift from services to products, some important questions arise:

- *How does the shift to a service-based economy influence established, product-centric channel ecosystems?*
- *What are the most effective channel structures and strategies for manufacturers that implement service transition strategies?*

### Drivers of the Shift to Services

The shift of sales dollars and employees from product- to service-based enterprises in the United States and other developed economies has been dramatic. The speed of this transition for some emerging markets also has been relatively quick. Over a 30- to 40-year period, Singapore went from an agricultural, to a low-cost manufacturing, and then to a service-based knowledge economy.[5] To understand the impact of such business changes on channel strategy, it is helpful to understand why firms are making this transition. Most firms have added services to their existing product offerings in an attempt to improve their competitiveness and financial performance.[6] Both IBM and General Electric (GE) earned highly publicized financial gains from transitioning from product-centric manufacturers to primarily service providers, which helped draw attention to the attractiveness of this strategy. Alongside these well-publicized successes are some notable failures, including Intel's move to Web-based services and Boeing's offer of financial services. An analysis of U.S. manufacturing firms from 1990 to 2005 reveals that, on average, these firms moved from earning only 9 percent of their sales in services to 42 percent—a nearly fivefold increase over a 15-year period for firms whose primary business focus remains manufacturing![7] But shifting to services has little impact on manufacturing firms' financial performance until those firms earn at least 20–30 percent of their sales from services, at which point performance increases rapidly, as Figure 9-1 shows.

Overall, firms have both **offensive** and **defensive motivations** to shift to a service-based business, as follows:[8]

- Adding services can increase sales and the rate of sales growth, because revenues can be generated from the large installed base of customers that already buy existing products.
- Services increase the level of differentiation with competitive offerings, increasing the firm's profitability.
- Because services demand a higher degree of integration and contact between supplier and customer, they can lock in customers and increase their switching costs, which can lead to stronger, difficult-to-imitate relationships.
- Greater frequency of interaction and depth of customer involvement in service-based businesses leads to more knowledge about customer needs and creates greater opportunities to innovate new products and services.

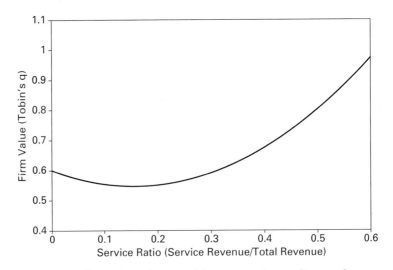

**FIGURE 9-1**  **Effect of service transition strategies on firm performance**

*Source:* Fang, Eric, Robert W. Palmatier, and Jan-Benedict E. M. Steenkamp (2008), "Effect of Service Transition Strategies on Firm Value," *Journal of Marketing* 72 (September), pp. 1–15.

- Services typically generate a steadier flow of revenue than do products, because they better resist economic cycles. Products often represent a onetime purchase that can be postponed if needed; services (e.g., maintenance, repairs, renewals) are necessary and billed on a more regular basis. For example, aircraft engine, railway stock, and elevator manufacturers earn little on their highly competitive product sales, but they do very well in the 10- to 30-year warranty, maintenance, and repair businesses.
- Some firms must add services in response to business declines, due to competition from offshore, "me-too," low-cost product competitors.

Emerson Electric was a large business-to-business firm with one division focused on selling refrigeration products to grocery stores. Its shift to service-based business effectively demonstrates the underlying benefits.[9] The initial impetus for the change occurred when offshore manufacturers reverse-engineered Emerson's refrigeration products and offered significant discounts to U.S. grocery stores for similar products. As Emerson's sales and profits eroded, it began to adopt a service-based business model. Rather than sell refrigeration equipment once every few years, Emerson offered to buy back and then lease the equipment, provided a warranty contract, and included maintenance and calibration service agreements. Refrigeration equipment and service are neither a competency nor a central focus of grocery stores, so they were motivated to shift the risk to Emerson and pay a monthly charge. Although manufacturers often assume risk in offering services, they also might be better suited to understand the costs associated with that risk than are their diverse customers.

This service strategy increased the sales and profits Emerson earned, in that it sold more. But it also erected a higher barrier to offshore equipment suppliers without local service personnel, such that they were unable to build and maintain the relationships required for an ongoing, service-focused business. In addition, it became more critical for Emerson to deal directly with the end-users (grocery and food stores) rather than selling equipment through intermediate channel partners. This **disintermediation** process, in which manufacturers exclude their channel partners so that they can sell directly to end customers, is a common outcome when product-based suppliers shift to service-based businesses. (It also is a common outcome of e-commerce, as we discuss later in this chapter.) By expanding the customer's business to include product leases, warranties, and maintenance, the manufacturer can economically support a direct sale. The service-based transaction also requires more coproduction and relational ties, which might preclude another channel partner's participation. That is, firms shifting into services move down the distribution chain (i.e., downstream vertical integration) to gain multiple benefits and support their service delivery efforts. The **shift-to-services trend** causes product firms to sell directly to customers, which reduces sales going through intermediary channel partners (i.e., disintermediation).

## Effect of Key Service Characteristics on Channel Strategies

Most firms do not sell either a pure product (e.g., salt) or service (e.g., consulting) but rather create an offering with elements of both a product and a service. For example, McDonald's restaurants are classified as services, yet they sell products (hamburgers, fries, drinks), as well as services, including preparation, delivery, and a place to sit and eat. Despite this confluence, every firm is designated either a product or a service business by governmental administrations; in the United States, this designation is based on the firms' primary industry identification classification (North American Industry Classification System, or NAICS).[10] Most retailers and wholesalers are classified as service businesses, but their value proposition involves buying, inventorying, and reselling physical products. In this sense, it is helpful to consider the degree to which a firm's sales come from services, or its **service ratio**, to understand the impact of service characteristics on the firm's channel strategy.[11] Emerson's move to bundle services with its refrigeration products increased the service content of its offering, which affected its channel strategy, even though it continued to offer its core refrigeration products and remained formally classified as a product business.

**Services** are offerings that are not primarily a physical product; are consumed at time they are produced; provide value through convenience, entertainment, timeliness, or health; and are essentially intangible.[12] In many cases, a shift to services involves a gradual transition, such that the service ratio of a particular supplier's offering increases over time. This transition often ends when the "product" supplier no longer manufactures the core product but rather buys it from the same offshore suppliers that initially sparked its service shift. During a service transition period, the product firm's offering takes on more service characteristics, which affects the channel structure and strategies. In discussing the impacts of four key characteristics of services that differentiate them from products, we take the perspective of an upstream manufacturing firm that is implementing a **service transition strategy** in a purposeful attempt to increase its service ratio. Thus, we can clarify how each service characteristic affects a firm's channel strategy.[13]

**Intangibility** is perhaps the most important difference between products and services: A service is "performance in use," and unlike physical objects, it cannot be touched or literally seen. Thus, services cannot be inventoried, patented, or physically displayed, so their marketing channels differ radically. Health services provided by a doctor to a patient (e.g., surgery) and education (e.g., learning) are both hard to see and touch, as well as difficult to evaluate. Several key functions of channel members—taking ownership or title, inventorying, and ultimately selling a physical product to the customer when needed—are simply not viable for intangible services. Continuing the Emerson example, this distributor originally had skills in buying, stocking, and selling refrigeration equipment to grocery stores, but once its sale moved into refrigeration services (**leasing**, warranty, repair, ongoing maintenance), many of its core functions became unnecessary. In addition, buyers sense more anxiety and risk when buying a service, because they cannot easily evaluate the intangible offering, so they prefer stronger relationships and brand reputation to help manage this service-related risk perception.[14] As brands and relationships increase in importance as the offering becomes more intangible, suppliers either need to sell directly to end-users or use channel partners with strong existing brands and/or relationships with targeted end-users.

**Heterogeneity** in service performance is substantial, as well as harder to control than that for products. For example, products might be manufactured in highly controlled factory environments, with precise measurements of attributes and minimal impacts of individual employees on product performance. Services instead are produced at the time of need, in geographically dispersed locations, with high dependence on the employee's deliver, which makes it much harder to standardize performance. In many cases, manufacturers try to alter their channel strategies to control and reduce this heterogeneity.

Johnson Controls, a large multinational firm, is in the temperature control business. Starting with thermostats and moving into heating, ventilating, and air conditioning (HVAC) products, more than half its revenue now comes from maintenance, repair, and consulting services. Many HVAC *products* sell through a network of distributors and dealers to residential customers, but a majority of its *services* sell directly to customers. To deal with each customer group's specific needs, Johnson Controls maintains five service organizations that can effectively deliver highly customized solutions. The service division is more than twice the size of its nearest competitor—and growing faster than product sales. It would be difficult, if not impossible, to offer such services through multiple channel intermediaries.[15]

Similarly, consumers are shifting more weight to the service component of automobile ownership, which has affected automobile manufacturers' channel strategy. When high-end automobile manufacturers first recognized this trend, they realized that service delivery by local car dealerships was highly variable, even though the manufacturers continued to make strides in reducing the variation in product performance (e.g., quality control measures, automated factories). Thus, manufacturers lost repeat business due to poor service levels in heterogeneous retail channels, even though their product performed reliably. To take more control (i.e., increase their power over the retailer) and reduce variability in their offering, manufacturers increased their service standards and bumped up the investment they demanded from their channel partners (increasing the costs of being a dealer), while simultaneously reduced the number of competitive dealers (increasing the benefits of being a dealer). In addition, they increased monitoring, such as by increasing the importance of customer satisfaction surveys and the weights placed on maintenance and service performance. These efforts caused suppliers and channel members to become more interdependent, leading to channel structures with lower channel intensity levels (more selectivity). Thus, suppliers can sell directly to end-users to better control service delivery and/or reduce the level of channel intensity while increasing control and monitoring of channel partners.

**Coproduction** between the provider and end-user and the **perishability of inventory** are both higher for services than for products. Products are typically manufactured, shipped, and held in inventory until the end-user needs the product. In contrast, services are "produced" in conjunction with the end-user at the time of consumption. Thus, services cannot typically be inventoried until needed, and the customer often needs to be present at the point of production, which affects the resulting channel strategy.

Continuing with our automobile example, for a dealer to demonstrate and teach a customer how to use sophisticated new product features (e.g., navigation system, Bluetooth), the dealer needs an employee available, and the customer must be present to participate in the production of this service. Even maintenance requires the car to be brought to the dealership and the specific problem communicated effectively, which then affects the customer's experience. In addition, the customer's experience can be influenced by other customers visiting the dealership at the same time. This cross-customer effect often requires segregating different end-user groups in different locations if one group is likely to have a negative effect on another group's experience. An automobile dealership cannot hold its oil changes in inventory to utilize during slow service periods. Most service capacity also is limited by the number of trained personnel available at any one time, with large differences between slow and peak periods. How do channel managers deal with the complex and interrelated issues involved in the coproduction and perishability of inventory of services?

Similar to responses to increases in intangibility and heterogeneity, a channel manager who wants to control the experience might sell directly to the customer without any intermediary channels. However, with greater coproduction, the relative importance of being geographically and temporally convenient to customers also increases, because the customer needs to be involved. The inability to inventory services also means that every location must have the capacity to "produce" the service at the time and location of the customer's choice. Both these service characteristics require a close match between the offering and the customer's location and time of purchase, so channels provide a critical function that manufacturers transitioning into services often have trouble providing—especially if the offering retains a significant product component. In this case, an e-commerce channel cannot suffice for example. Channel managers want more control over the experience, so channel intensity needs to decrease, even as monitoring and targeting of channel members to specific customer groups or geographical areas has to increase to achieve better control over the coproduction experience. Depending on the offering, temporal and geographic coverage could be improved through a combination of direct selling, traditional retail, and e-commerce or hybrid channels.

In summary, to adjust to higher levels of coproduction and inventory perishability, channel managers in service settings need to build hybrid channel structures, in which distinct channels address specific customer needs, times, segments, or geographies.

## Effects of Product Aspects on Channel Strategies

Many firms shifting into services do so in stages, beginning by bundling services around their core product. Just as Emerson added financing, leasing, maintenance, and warranties to its refrigeration equipment, or IBM initially added software solutions to its hardware products, in the early stages, the product features often overwhelm the service characteristics. However, as the service ratio increases, specific service characteristics become more important for determining a firm's channel strategy. Near the end of IBM's service transformation, it bundled Sun Workstations (a product competitor) into its offerings and sold off its laptop and personal computer divisions, reflecting the decreasing importance of these core products. Today IBM solution offerings (consulting) have little product content and are nearly pure services. This threshold is critical to IBM's channel strategy, because it no longer needs or desires to have intermediaries. Rather its custom solutions reflect close, trusting relationships with end-customers. When a firm transitions to the point of pure services with no physical products, it often has little need for traditional channel structures (e.g., warehousing and inventorying of physical products), and channel strategies are determined mainly by the service offering.

Consider what happened to music retailers when there was no longer any "product" aspect to their offering (i.e., records and CDs were replaced by music downloads). Local music retailers (e.g., Virgin Records, Tower Records) effectively distributed records and CDs to diverse groups of local customers, most of whom would not travel very far to shop for music; these retailers thus could target the specific needs of their local customers. Retailers near universities carried CDs suited to a younger, more hip clientele; those near more affluent suburbs maintained a larger inventory of classical music. Furthermore, they hired knowledgeable personnel to staff their stores. However, once the physical "product" grew less important, the service could be promoted, ordered, delivered, and billed over the Internet at any time and to nearly any location. Thus, the demand for local music retailers diminished. The Internet was an **enabling technology**; the removal of the "product" aspect of the offering in turn enabled the e-commerce channel to perform the majority of the channel functions. Similar disappearances of the "product" aspects from an offering often lead to disintermediation of channel members and a turbulent restructuring of the channel system.

Overall, the higher the service ratio of the offering, the larger the impact on the firm's channel strategy. The impact increases especially dramatically when the supplier no longer offers any physical products. The effect stems from multiple factors:

1. The intermediary performs fewer traditional channel functions for a pure service offering.
2. The supplier needs more control over the overall service experience (e.g., personnel).
3. Bilateral communication with customers is critical to enable problem solving and innovation.

## Effects of Acquiring Service Capabilities, Infrastructure, and Knowledge

When a product supplier adopts a service transition strategy, it quickly recognizes that it must gain access to specialized service capabilities, infrastructure, and knowledge. Suppliers have multiple avenues to do so, each with its own benefits, costs, and channel implications. The three main approaches are in-house development, collaborating with an existing provider, and acquisition. Some firms have developed **in-house service capabilities** successfully; many more have failed in their efforts to do so.[16] For example, GE effectively executes spare parts supply, maintenance, and warranty services for the jet engines it manufactures, because GE already had the knowledge and related service skills to do so, due to the overlap with its product business. However, in-house service development is often slow and expensive, with no guarantee that a product-focused firm can ever develop sufficient capabilities to compete head-to-head with a services-only firm. Furthermore, in-house development often pits a supplier directly against its channel partners, competing for service delivery rights. When service sales are minor, the management team that launched the services often is also responsible for the channel relationship, which can place them in direct competition with channel members, which can lead to channel conflict. This conflict can be aggravated when the in-house development pertains to services related to the core product. Decisions that minimize channel conflict can also undermine the success of the firm's service transition strategy.

For service offerings farther from the core offering, firms may achieve more success if they **collaborate** closely with an existing service provider. These partnerships might be formal joint ventures, contractual agreements, or relationally governed partnerships. The advantage of this approach is that the focal firm can select its partners on the basis of their specific capabilities, the customer groups served, or a lack of conflict. The disadvantages are the same as those that refer to any interfirm partnership: (1) potential loss of proprietary information, (2) management complexities, (3) culture clashes, or (4) loss of control of the relationship with the end-user.[17] Product-focused firms also may have difficulty writing contracts for services, which must be more open ended than a typical product-based contract. Collaborating reduces risk by limiting the level of investments in the service transition strategy, and possibly reducing channel conflict, but it creates its own execution risks.

An obvious alternative would be to collaborate with existing channel members—an option that is viable if the channel member has the necessary service capabilities, though it also generates some additional concerns. First, channel members not included in the service-based partnership may become demotivated. Rarely is it feasible to launch services with all existing channel partners. Second, a supplier could "teach" the channel member to sell services, which would shift the balance of power and make future service efforts by the supplier more difficult. Apple's success in the mobile market has required it to build a strong, enterprise-focused consultant network with downstream channel members to provide necessary support services.[18] As Sidebar 9-1 describes,

## Sidebar 9-1

### Fujitsu and Federal Express build a close relationship

In the 1990s, Fujitsu's personal computer division conducted 70 percent of its business in Japan. Fleeing fierce competition, Fujitsu entered the U.S. laptop market, only to discover the competitive situation was just as bad there. Disappointed with its performance, Fujitsu conducted a thorough review that pinpointed logistics as a major problem. Laptops were manufactured in Tokyo, and then shipped by sea in large batches to two warehouses on the West Coast. The result was that channel partners were served too slowly.

Recognizing that logistics is a channel competence, Fujitsu transferred all warehousing and distribution functions to a third party, Federal Express. Fujitsu also made a FedEx-specific investment by opening a customer support center near Memphis, Tennessee—the FedEx superhub, which is poorly served by other carriers. Fujitsu further increased its reliance on FedEx by closing one of its West Coast warehouses.

Fujitsu's site-specific investment created close physical proximity, which fueled communication. FedEx then came up with a radical idea: Why bring finished laptops from Tokyo? Why not instead expand the Memphis facility to create *customized* laptops? One key hurdle was final assembly: FedEx suggested CTI, a company that did such work for many other FedEx customers. (FedEx got the idea from its work with another customer, Dell Computer. Channel members provide economies of scope!)

Fujitsu implemented the idea. Subassemblies flown from Osaka to Memphis get turned over to

FedEx and CTI. FedEx takes operational responsibility for the entire subassembly and customization process, and then delivers the final product to retailers or end-users.

Within a year, Fujitsu was no longer taking a month to supply mass-produced products to its channel. Instead, it transformed its business into a customized production offering, with delivery guaranteed within *four days* of order placement. The effect on its competitive advantage and profit has been spectacular, leading one analyst to describe the relationship as follows:

> Fujitsu entered the relationship with a spirit of true strategic alliance. The company didn't choose FedEx because it was the cheapest provider. Nor did it reward its purchasing managers for jerking around and lying to FedEx to save a few yen. Nor did it enter the "partnership" with an arm's-length, quasi-adversarial, hyper-legalistic, super-secretive, no-trust, lowest-cost-at-all-cost, dump-them-tomorrow-if-we-get-a-better-deal mind-set.

Instead, it enlisted FedEx as a full, active, intimate partner. Fujitsu and FedEx tackled Fujitsu's operational problems together—openly and cooperatively—and developed a revamped logistics package as a result in order to deliver a new service to customers.[19]

Fujitsu collaborated with FedEx to provide customized laptops to the U.S. market with a guaranteed four-day delivery window.

The last alternative would be to **acquire** a services company that provides the necessary capabilities, which in turn can more easily be partitioned from existing channel members to reduce conflict—at least temporarily. This strategy is the fastest option, and it probably has the most chance of success from a strategic standpoint, even if acquisition costs often undermine the chances of success from a financial standpoint. In many cases, suppliers initially operate the acquisition with a separate management team, so the firm can focus separately on each part of the business. Creating a stand-alone service organization with its own goals, action plans, and financial targets may increase the success rate of service transition strategies.

Research on service transition strategies also highlights other factors that help manufacturers become successful service providers. First, manufacturers need to shift more resources toward the selection, training, and compensation of boundary spanning personnel, who are far more critical in service-oriented businesses. Second, customer assessment and feedback gain importance, because services often deal with intangibles and tend to be more oriented toward customer benefits. Third, manufacturers need deeper relationships with customers, as a critical step in solution selling. Fourth, manufacturers have to change the culture of their organization, to be more customer centric.[20]

## Channel Members' Responses to Service Transition Strategies

Our discussion thus far has adopted the perspective of the upstream supplier or manufacturer. In many cases, the impact of the manufacturer's strategy has negative implications for its downstream channel partners. Thus, these channel members seek to provide services to customers themselves. In response to similar business drivers, downstream channel members adopt service transition strategies; for example, Arrow Electronics has added training, kitting, programming, and assembly to its original electronics distribution functions.[21] These efforts may be performed in partnership with suppliers, or else the channel members might compete in a portion of the business portfolio. Channel members in closer proximity to the customer often enjoy a positional advantage in this competition, especially with regard to relationship building and coproduction.

If channel members anticipate a risk of disintermediation by their supplier, they often withdraw their own effort, investigate ways to counter the potential negative effects by shifting focus and sales to competitive products or services, or launch their own services. Both manufacturers and channel intermediaries must respond to the shift toward service-based economies and its disruption of traditional channel structures and strategies. Thus, shift to services often leads to conflict, but it also can provide opportunities for the firms that can adapt well.

## CHANNEL STRATEGIES FOR GLOBALIZATION

Globalization in many markets and industries is causing changes to channel systems. Today, international trade accounts for 20 percent of global GDP, and as trade quickly expands across borders, firms and foreign customers are becoming increasingly interlinked.[22] Suppliers and their downstream channel partners are expanding globally; both suppliers (e.g., Procter & Gamble) and retailers (e.g., Wal-Mart) see international expansion as a primary source of sales growth in the next decade. The impact on the channel structure and channel relationships depends on who leads the way into international markets and if both parties enter the same new markets. If Procter & Gamble (P&G) wants to sell its products in a new international market, it will try to find the channel with the best access to targeted end-users, which may not be the same as the best channel for the home market. Thus, suppliers often have to build new channel relationships when entering new markets. This situation is ripe for conflict and disruption to existing channel relationships, because the entering supplier builds new relationships with local channels that can undermine existing channel relationships in the new market. In addition, if the home country retailer is entering the same international market as its suppliers, the suppliers need to manage relationships with both home market and local retailers. Alternatively, when retailers enter new international markets, they often continue to offer their existing supplier's products, supplemented with locally sourced products.

Another significant impact of globalization is the one on small, family-owned retailers, which has long been one of the most common retail formats. But global retailers continue to expand internationally; the top 10 retailers have increased the number of countries in which they sell by more than 60 percent in the past decade, such that their combined sales exceeded US$1.1 trillion in 2010.[23] Such growth results from the acquisition of local retailers and direct entry into new markets, which can erode prices and diminish sales by local retailers. The global expansion of both suppliers and channel partners also is an important factor for understanding changes to existing channel ecosystems. Specifically, when both suppliers and downstream channel members (distributors, retailers) expand into international markets, important questions arise:

- *How does globalization influence established channel ecosystems?*
- *What are the most effective channel structures and strategies for entering new markets?*

## Drivers of Globalization

The push for globalization is often intense. To understand the influence of this transition on channel strategies, it is helpful to identify the underlying motivation. Channel participants expand internationally in search of **revenue growth** when domestic markets become saturated. Thus, three of the world's largest retailers—Wal-Mart (the United States), Metro Group (Germany), and Tesco (the United Kingdom)—have grown three times faster in developing markets than in their domestic markets in recent years.[24] The promises of a larger and growing population, expanding consumption, and a fragmented competitive landscape make developing markets especially tempting for large suppliers and retailers. These opportunities become even more appealing when the home market is marked by aging populations, decreasing birthrates, and increasing competitive rivalry (e.g., Japan, Italy, the United States).

Although the overwhelming majority of globalizing activity involves firms from developed markets entering developing markets, some suppliers from emerging markets also are expanding into developed markets. The largest maker and distributor of down clothing in China, Bosideng, has opened retail stores in New York and Milan to increase its brand prestige and better position itself for future growth.[25]

The **opening of international markets** to foreign development, due to expanding trade agreements or a desire to increase foreign investment, further encourages expansion plans. Wal-Mart has cited a relaxation to India's foreign investment rules as the key to the rise of new stores that seek to tap India's $490 billion retail market.[26] In a similar fashion, advances in infrastructure in emerging markets make expansion viable. Beyond roads, legal structures, electrical power, and telecommunication improvements, the increasing availability and use of the Internet as an information and shopping source provides low cost access to new markets. The capability of the Internet to accelerate international expansion cannot be overstated. For example, in 2012, Neiman Marcus shipped luxury goods to more than 100 countries, with a flat shipping rate of $19.95, to increase its exposure, and J. Crew reported sales in 107 different countries through its outsourced, global, e-commerce platform.[27] By entering new markets through online sales, the seller reduces its financial risk, makes it easy for users to evaluate its product assortments, and is able to build a base of customers prior to establishing an expensive brick-and-mortar footprint.

The **focus on globalization** by both upstream and downstream channel members thus is driven primarily by their desire to expand sales by leveraging the relative demographic and competitive advantages in developing versus developed markets, enabled by new enhancements to global infrastructures, changes in regulatory/legal conditions, and the expansion of Internet coverage.

## Effects of Globalization on Channel Strategies

The top management of both upstream and downstream channel members cite global expansion as a top priority, with notable effects on a firm's channel strategy. Most large firms from developed nations have already entered other developed countries; on average, the top 10 retailers sell into 16 countries. Among large U.S. firms for example, nearly 50 percent of sales come from outside the U.S. market. Thus, recent expansion mainly focuses on developing markets. Many leading suppliers and retailers also worry that their competitors will gain an initial foothold in new markets by acquiring or collaborating with the strongest local partners. Later entrants to a new market often lack many strategic alternatives, because early entrants already have acquired or entered into joint ventures with the "best" partners, and their brand-building efforts are well established.

The next decade is likely to be witness to a tough race to expand into the next tier of global markets. Figure 9-2 contains a ranking of the top 30 countries in the developing world, according to their attractiveness on four key criteria: market attractiveness, country risk, market saturation, and time pressure. Brazil, China, and India are in the top five, based on the number of consumers in each country; Chile and Uruguay might seem less obvious. China's score of 100 of 100 on time pressure reflects the criticality of timing, because the channel structure and relationships are already starting to mature in some industry segments.

As new markets open and both upstream and downstream channel partners enter the same high-potential new markets, increased competitive rivalry may disrupt their existing channel relationships. The first entrants into a new market seek to

| 2012 Rank | Country | Region | Market Attractiveness (25%) | Country Risk (25%) | Market Saturation (25%) | Time Pressure (25%) |
|---|---|---|---|---|---|---|
| 1 | Brazil | Latin America | 100.0 | 85.4 | 48.2 | 61.6 |
| 2 | Chile | Latin America | 86.6 | 100.0 | 17.4 | 57.1 |
| 3 | China | Asia | 53.4 | 72.6 | 29.3 | 100.0 |
| 4 | Uruguay | Latin America | 84.1 | 56.1 | 60.0 | 52.3 |
| 5 | India | Asia | 31.0 | 66.7 | 57.6 | 87.9 |
| 6 | Georgia | Central Asia | 27.0 | 68.7 | 92.6 | 54.0 |
| 7 | United Arab Emirates | MENA | 86.1 | 93.9 | 9.4 | 52.9 |
| 8 | Oman | MENA | 69.3 | 98.3 | 17.4 | 50.4 |
| 9 | Mongolia | Asia | 6.4 | 54.4 | 98.2 | 75.1 |
| 10 | Peru | Latin America | 43.8 | 55.5 | 62.9 | 67.2 |
| 11 | Malaysia | Asia | 56.7 | 98.1 | 18.9 | 54.8 |
| 12 | Kuwait | MENA | 81.1 | 88.7 | 36.4 | 20.3 |
| 13 | Turkey | Eastern Europe | 78.8 | 69.3 | 32.3 | 33.1 |
| 14 | Saudi Arabia | MENA | 63.1 | 81.8 | 35.4 | 33.0 |
| 15 | Sri Lanka | Asia | 12.7 | 68.3 | 79.0 | 51.3 |
| 16 | Indonesia | Asia | 39.6 | 61.6 | 47.0 | 62.4 |
| 17 | Azerbaijan | Central Asia | 19.2 | 41.5 | 93.6 | 53.2 |
| 18 | Jordan | MENA | 45.8 | 65.3 | 69.5 | 23.8 |
| 19 | Kazakhstan | Central Asia | 31.5 | 47.5 | 75.5 | 47.5 |
| 20 | Botswana | Sub-Saharan Africa | 44.4 | 88.1 | 42.7 | 23.7 |
| 21 | Macedonia | Eastern Europe | 43.6 | 46.5 | 55.9 | 56.6 |
| 22 | Lebanon | MENA | 60.2 | 30.2 | 48.9 | 54.2 |
| 23 | Colombia | Latin America | 47.8 | 70.1 | 36.7 | 36.6 |
| 24 | Panamas | Latin America | 53.4 | 68.8 | 42.0 | 25.2 |
| 25 | Albania | Eastern Europe | 24.6 | 47.6 | 74.8 | 39.9 |
| 26 | Russia | Eastern Europe | 80.2 | 53.6 | 19.6 | 32.2 |
| 27 | Morocco | MENA | 23.5 | 58.2 | 48.2 | 49.2 |
| 28 | Mexico | Latin America | 71.9 | 70.0 | 15.1 | 20.3 |
| 29 | Philippines | Asia | 28.3 | 54.6 | 52.5 | 38.3 |
| 30 | Tunisia | MENA | 35.7 | 55.4 | 65.0 | 14.4 |

**FIGURE 9-2    Retail opportunities in developing markets**

*Source:* Kearney, A. T. (2012), "Global Retail Development Index Report," www.atkearney.com.

*Notes:* MENA = Middle East, North Africa. Market Attractiveness: 0 = low attractiveness, 100 = high attractiveness. Country risk: 0 = high risk, 100 = low risk. Market Saturation: 0 = saturated, 100 = not saturated. Time Pressure: 0 = no time pressure, 100 = urgency to enter.

acquire and build alliances with the strongest local firms (wholesalers, distributors, retailers) to speed their sales growth, reduce risk, and limit competitors' alternatives. During this initial **shakeout period**, the high level of conflict leads partners to build relationships rapidly, despite the divergent cultural and business norms they might face. Some key initial strategic channel decisions include which end-user segments to target, the level of intensity/selectivity to implement in the network, and the types of channel members to include in the channel system (see Chapter 5 for a review of channel design decisions). If many channel members are added to the network, each firm's motivation can be undermined, and conflict increases. More exclusivity can increase a channel member's willingness to invest in the products, but there might be a corresponding loss of market coverage by the supplier. For example, Apple gave exclusivity to Dixons (a U.K. consumer electronics retailer) to sell iPads ahead of rival retailers; Dixons reciprocated by adding customer service centers to provide specialized technical support for Apple's products.[28]

Perhaps the most difficult decision a firm makes is how much to change its existing channel structure and strategy to adapt to local conditions. This decision determines not only how well the firm fits the local market but also its ultimate ability to compete and exploit its sustainable competitive advantage in the marketplace. When Wal-Mart expands into new markets, it seeks to leverage its economies of scale and exploit its size and scope; this effort assumes that such assets, which have been advantageous in its home market, also are beneficial in new markets. The retailer's failed expansion into Germany offered an example of what happens when such an assumption is incorrect. Wal-Mart's internal resources (logistics, low-cost processes) simply could not be leveraged in Germany, because German consumers prefer specialized grocery stores instead of one-stop shopping.[29]

Firms have several alternatives to accelerate their international expansion. The most common approaches are acquisition, joint ventures, partnerships, franchising, and direct market entry. Each approach has specific strengths and weaknesses. However, most firms find that a combination of market entry strategies is most effective; the exact combination depends on the market, legal, and competitive landscape. Tesco has enjoyed a relatively strong international growth record for more than 20 years, growing from being a local U.K. retailer to one of the largest supermarkets in the work, largely by matching its entry strategy to local market conditions. Tesco started in 1993 with the *acquisition* of Catteau in France. Then it entered South Korea with a *joint venture* with Samsung in 1999, and it expanded in the United States in 2007 by *opening its own stores*. In each case, Tesco evaluated the local market and potential alternatives, and then selected the entry strategy it deemed most effective.

An acquisition approach often helps the entrant quickly reach a meaningful level of sales in a market and integrates local managers with firsthand knowledge of the market. However, acquiring a firm with a different corporate culture and business model can make integration with the overall firm difficult. Firms typically want to integrate all of their acquisitions into one culture, business system, and set of policies, which has the potential to undercut local employees and business success. In an acquisition, the acquirer takes on all the risk; in alliances or joint ventures, the local partner tends to remain more engaged. Another approach is to use a franchising model, such that the business format (brands, processes, offerings) remains the same but local owners and managers operate the channels. Franchising offers the benefits of attracting, retaining, and motivating local managers who are culturally sensitive; it also may allow a firm to expand more quickly, because this approach requires less capital from the firm entering the market.

Firms entering a market should recognize that (other than meeting financial objectives) the greatest barrier, for both suppliers and retailers, is often the ability to gain **local knowledge** and **execution capability**.[30] Navigating local regulatory, governmental, and business conditions can be incredibly difficult for outsiders. A local face to put on the business, local networks of relatives, friends, and business associates, is often necessary to resolve problems and advance the business. This demand is especially acute if the entry strategy requires the acquisition of land or building facilities, to meet local regulatory and political hurdles.

Much of this discussion is equally applicable for upstream suppliers or downstream channel members. However, there is one major difference for downstream channels, in that these channel members often continue to source many of their products from existing suppliers. In essence, the upstream supplier gets introduced into the new market by its channel partners. In contrast, when an upstream supplier wants to enter a new market, it typically seeks to partner with the strongest local channel member, rather than introducing its "home" channel partners into that new market. If the supplier builds a strong business relationship with its local partner, it becomes even more difficult for home channel members to enter. Many of the products to which they have access and with which they are most familiar already are being sold in the new market. Thus, downstream channels may feel more pressure than upstream suppliers to enter new markets early and with a larger initial presence.

Finally, the allure of growth through emerging markets is great, but international expansion also involves significant risk. In 2012 alone, Tesco, Wal-Mart, Carrefour SA, and Home Depot all announced significant changes, pullbacks, or outright exits from the Chinese market, because their business models just were not working.[31] Wal-Mart plans to halve its square footage of floor space; Tesco is closing stores and consolidating those stores still open in an attempt to improve profitability. Home Depot closed the last of its 12 stores in China, after years of attempting to copy its U.S. strategy of cutting out intermediaries by receiving products straight from suppliers and selling them to local consumers. But Home Depot could never quite break the lock on Chinese distribution channels or leverage its global supply base. In addition, Chinese consumers rarely have space to store tools, so they hire local businesses to make home repairs, which undermines Home Depot's very business model (and also implies the chain's lack of local market knowledge). Finally, its fixed price policy caused problems, because haggling is a norm in China and an appealing part of the shopping experience for many consumers. Because its approach did not fit end-users' needs, and few of its competitive advantages offered value in the Chinese market, the example of Home Depot offers a good summary of the barriers and risks that firms face when expanding into new markets.

In summary, most suppliers and their downstream channel partners enter developing markets to access the large, growing opportunities—despite the significant risk associated with introducing their business models into a new culture and economic environment. Firms use various entry approaches, from acquiring or building alliances with local firms to direct market entry, depending on the local circumstances. When a firm enters a new market though, it nearly always faces significant conflict and must build new relationships quickly.

# CHANNEL STRATEGIES FOR E-COMMERCE

The third key trend is the increasing importance of **e-commerce** (i.e., online, Internet-based sales) to global business, which influences channel structures and strategies in a multitude of ways. The technology, logistics, and market reach capabilities of the online channel allow suppliers to sell directly to customers, often without intermediary channel participation. The Internet enables startups and new firms to sell directly to customers, undermining the power of channel intermediaries; it also diminishes the geographic, temporal, and informational constraints that were fundamental to the design of existing channel systems. The shift to online purchases has perhaps most dramatically transformed the channel system for the sales of books and music, such that for books and music retailers with some e-commerce sales more than 70 percent of book and 80 percent of music sales in the United States are via e-commerce.[32] Prior to the Internet, suppliers of music and books built a channel structure of traditional brick-and-mortar retailers to deliver books and music, which entailed shipping, inventorying, and selling to end-users that were geographically dispersed. With e-commerce, suppliers can reach customers anywhere, at any time of day, and provide immediate delivery, without needing to locate inventories in proximity to customers, all of which removes many costly channel layers. Existing book and music retailers instead offer expensive assets (e.g., buildings), high labor and inventory costs, and limited hours, which makes the rapid shift to e-commerce understandable for these offerings.

The shift to services can also be enabled by e-commerce channels, especially when the offering contains limited product content. For example, e-commerce helps local artists distribute their music to consumers directly and cut out large recording studies, as well as music retailers. Accounting for e-commerce trends when designing a channel structure and strategy thus is critical for a multitude of product and service categories, because these trends have the potential to influence a multitude of the key channel functions (e.g., promotion, negotiation, ownership, ordering, payment, information sharing) we outlined in Chapter 1. Internet-based channels are important in their own right but also critical to enabling the shift to services and the globalization of industries. As both suppliers and other channel members (distributors, retailers) add online sales channels, some important questions arise:

- *How does the shift to e-commerce influence established channel ecosystems?*
- *What are the most effective channel structures and strategies for adding e-commerce sales channels?*

## Drivers of Increased E-Commerce

The move to e-commerce in the marketing channel ecosystem has been intense and accelerating. The primary driver is firms' desire to tap the large and growing online market. In 2012, e-commerce sales exceeded $1 trillion for the first time; they are predicted to reach $1.3 trillion in 2013. The United States represents the largest market, with $343 billion in sales, followed by China, the United Kingdom, Japan, and Germany.[33] To understand the rapid growth and ultimate impact of this transition on channel strategies, it is helpful to identify the underlying drivers of this change.

The amazing history of Souq.com, as described in Sidebar 9-2—from its launch online in 2005 to becoming the Arab world's largest online retailer, spread over the

United Arab Emirates, Egypt, Kuwait, and Saudi Arabia—highlights some of the inherent advantages of an online business.[34]

In the previous section, we noted that the motivations for many firms to expand channel structures globally included increased sales growth, though entering new markets also is risky. Similarly, many firms employ e-commerce channels to **enter**

## Sidebar 9-2

### Souq.com, the Arabian e-commerce dream

Launched in 2005, Souq.com is an online marketplace where customers and retailers can interact in a secure fashion. Offering over 200,000 products, it is the largest e-commerce site in the Arab world. Initially, the business model of Souq.com was structured after the U.S. giant eBay, with products being auctioned off to the highest bidder. However, with the realization that the shopping habits of online purchasers was moving away from bidding, Souq.com began to set fixed prices for products, and allowed businesses to ship directly to customers upon purchase.

With the convenience of online shopping and secure payment gateways, the fraud-fearing and security-conscious Arabs could now choose between online payments and cash on delivery, with the added advantages of vendor warranty for a minimum of 30 days and a free returns policy that is enforced by Souq.com. For retailers, the cost of running an online store on Souq.com is approximately U.S. $10 per month, which makes it a very inexpensive platform to connect with the 8 million per month site visitors.

Souq.com offers products across 18 different categories ranging from office supplies to collectible items, books, electronics, clothes and diapers – a reason why it is often referred to as the "Amazon of the Middle East." However, online shopping is not without its pitfalls – sales often decrease due to delays in delivery and slow response from customer service representatives to queries and/or complaints, and can cause skepticism towards the site's service quality. Souq.com, at its inception, was offering a minimum delivery time of 10 days, which was not a competitive estimate by any standards. Additionally, customers would frequently not receive the merchandise within the promised delivery time which caused frustration toward the site. Since then, the site has come a long way and now only takes three to five days to deliver products, with an aim of bringing it down to two days in the future, which is quite good as per the market.

From a retailer's point of view Souq.com is a great way to connect with consumers because there are very few barriers to entry, which can prove beneficial especially to small businesses by allowing them to reach out to a bigger pool of buyers. As more and more consumers become Internet literate and less wary of e-commerce sites in the region, companies like Souq.com are expected to continue growing. This is clearly supported by the exponential growth in sales following the sharp increase in Internet subscribers.

In 2012, the company acquired Sukar.com—the first private online shopping club, exclusive to members only and operating in 9 countries across the region—thereby expanding Souq.com's markets as well as gaining access to select customers. With this acquisition, Souq.com is now the biggest online retail platform in the Middle East.

Recently, and in order to improve their level of customer service, Souq.com has adopted the Amazon model, where it warehouses certain items to slash shipping time and ensure customer satisfaction is maintained. So far they have already opened the Dubai and Riyadh warehouses, and are currently working to open one in Egypt.[35] In this increasingly dynamic world we live in, timing is key, and companies have to ensure they are continuously evolving to meet or exceed the needs of consumers. Especially with the lack of major entrance barriers for setting up online platforms similar to Souq.com, it is essential that its services be consistently competitive at a global standard to ensure the future viability of the business.

**new markets**, such that the online channel becomes a platform to gain initial sales and learn about local customer priorities or else serves as a primary sales strategy in a particular market. An e-commerce entry strategy can be relatively less costly, because it demands little infrastructure or local staff. Many firms even outsource their supply chain and logistics to third parties that have regulatory, legal, or transportation expertise in local markets.

Yet some developing markets simply lack the infrastructure, online awareness, or customer acceptance to support an online market entry strategy. Similar to the ranking of developing countries for overall market entry, A. T. Kearney has ranked the top markets for e-commerce expansion, on the basis of four criteria: online market attractiveness, online infrastructure, digital laws and regulations, and overall retail development.[36] Figure 9-3 provides a ranked list of the top 10 countries for e-commerce expansion for 2012. Unsurprisingly, the top three countries are China, Brazil, and Russia, in terms of the size of their markets and their stage of overall infrastructure development. However, the next group of countries may seem less obvious: three from Latin America (Chile, Mexico, and Uruguay), two in the Middle East (United Arab Emirates, Oman), and one each in Asia (Malaysia) and Eastern Europe (Turkey). This top-ten list makes it clear that e-commerce expansion opportunities are truly global in reach.

The ability of online channels to support search and ordering activities all the time, offer lower prices (due to their lower cost structure), and provide a vast assortment held in central warehouses represent the primary benefits, compared with tradition channels, and thus the drivers of increased online channel share. But these benefits can be offset by the **lack of immediacy** that marks an online shopping experience, in that customers must wait to receive the shipped product—which can take weeks, depending on product locations and shipping methods. Some traditional retailers that also maintain online channels seek to reduce this deterrent and take advantage of their local inventory; for example, Wal-Mart launched same-day delivery in some markets, for a $10 shipping charge, which represents a substantial advantage over online-only channel competitors in terms of speed of delivery.

Because e-commerce provides a means to bypass existing channels and reach end-users directly, it also appeals to relatively small suppliers, which lack traditional channel access, and larger firms that want to launch a new product into a market in which they have no channel coverage. That is, a driver of e-commerce is its ability to remove barriers to new businesses and new product introductions. By eliminating the need for start-up investments or even a proven business model, e-commerce allows firms to get online quickly, with "just a nice looking website" and promotions conducted through social media and search engine targeting.

In summary, e-commerce as a sales channel is undergoing tremendous growth due to a multitude of drivers, including the following:

- Lower startup and operating costs for many products and businesses
- Higher Internet connection rates and capabilities
- Abilities to enable new product, market, and country expansion in an economical and relatively fast manner
- High-quality purchase experiences

These benefits are echoed in a survey of CEOs that asked them to predict future growth: 90 percent stated that they planned to increase their use of e-commerce

| E-Commerce rank | Country | Region | Online market attractiveness (50%) | Online infrastructure establishment (20%) | Digital laws and regulations (15%) | Retail development (15%) |
|---|---|---|---|---|---|---|
| 1 | China | Asia | 100 | 56 | 55 | 58 |
| 2 | Brazil | Latin America | 84 | 56 | 67 | 90 |
| 3 | Russia | Eastern Europe | 83 | 39 | 23 | 48 |
| 4 | Chile | Latin America | 35 | 78 | 100 | 71 |
| 5 | Mexico | Latin America | 53 | 41 | 75 | 26 |
| 6 | United Arab Emirates | Middle East | 22 | 100 | 77 | 49 |
| 7 | Malaysia | Asia | 27 | 78 | 79 | 46 |
| 8 | Uruguay | Latin America | 23 | 40 | 71 | 100 |
| 9 | Turkey | Eastern Europe | 25 | 76 | 65 | 33 |
| 10 | Oman | Middle East | 13 | 61 | 97 | 51 |
| | | | 0 = low attractiveness  100 = high attractiveness | 0 = low infrastructure  100 = high infrastructure | 0 = no digital laws  100 = strong digital laws | 0 = undeveloped retail market  100 = developed retail market |

**FIGURE 9-3   Ranking of top 10 e-commerce opportunities**

*Sources:* Euromonitor, International Telecommunication Union, Planet Retail, World Bank, World Economic Forum, A.T. Kearney analysis.

*Note:* Scores are rounded. Retail development score includes online and brick-and-mortar retail.

channels, and a majority of these CEOs stated that e-commerce was their single biggest growth driver.[37]

## Effects of E-Commerce on Channel Strategies

Adding an e-commerce channel to an existing bricks-and-mortar channel structure often creates issues. It causes conflict with existing channels, which is typical whenever a supplier increases the intensity of its channel coverage. Channel partners start to believe their pie is getting divided among more channel members, so each channel member earns less sales, and the increased competition often leads to lower prices, resulting in an even greater drop in profit. These effects may be intensified with the addition of an e-commerce channel, because e-commerce competitors often can undercut traditional channel members' prices, due to their low-cost structure (e.g., limited land or building costs, fewer employees). In addition, for many e-commerce providers, a low-cost strategy is central, and they purposely target brick-and-mortar channels with price competition, to leverage their lower-cost structures. The resulting inequities in the division of costs and profits across the channel system imply **free riding**: Some channel members provide a local location to observe and test products (adding costs), while others get the business (receiving profits). Recall our detailed discussion of the equity principle and its importance to the health of the channel ecosystem in Chapter 3.

All channel systems have some inequities, but the growth of e-commerce makes this issue ever more pressing, because it is elevating free riding to epidemic levels. To cope, suppliers and downstream channel members must devise new norms for business, such as adding flat payments (i.e., salary), fees for services (i.e., expense accounts), or overrides to compensate more expensive channel members for sales made by another (e.g., group bonuses). Sidebar 9-3 suggests several ways to introduce Web channels, without creating excessive channel conflict, and to resolve the resulting inequities.

Such conflict is not limited to intrachannel competition. Wal-Mart's move to add same-day delivery represented a direct response to Amazon's competitive inroads into its business, based partially on Amazon's ability to offer one-day delivery in some markets. As this example highlights, traditional channel firms often add e-commerce channels mainly because of their desire to respond to online threats to their existing business, while still defending some of their traditional competitive advantages. Yet these effects are constantly shifting, because the online experience is constantly evolving. As Zappos shows, e-commerce firms continually work to enhance the online experience they offer end-users and seek to remove potential barriers to online shopping, which means e-commerce is a constantly moving target.

Increases in e-commerce sales, as well as the growing number of sales channels, also prompt changes in channel pricing. Pure Internet-based companies are much more likely to adopt a **creative pricing** approach that features discounting, bundling, auctions, and other flexible policies.[38] This tendency seems logical: 89 percent of online shoppers report that "best price" is their primary reason for returning to a website after their first purchase. In addition, in many product markets, the prices charged online are lower than in traditional environments.

**Sidebar 9-3**

**Channel conflict and Internet Commerce**

Channel conflict is a major issue for B2B (business-to-business) firms, especially that resulting from the introduction of online e-commerce. Web-based commerce threatens to create divisions within firms, and also threatens third-party vendors with greater competition. Even if a website does not take orders and "merely" provides information, it is replacing, and potentially contradicting, the functions of another channel member. Although something of an issue in B2C (business-to-consumer) marketing, it is particularly menacing in B2B settings, because business customers are strongly motivated to encourage competition among other channel members. These B2B firms also are rushing to embrace the Web as a way to improve their supply chain management.[39] So what are suppliers to do to minimize the conflict sparked by e-commerce in B2B sectors? Eleven options are as follows:

1. Do not offer a lower price on your website than the customer can find from channel members.
2. Divert the fulfillment of website orders to channel partners.
3. Provide information on products and services, but do not take orders.

4. Use your website to promote channel partners.
5. Encourage channel partners to advertise on your website.
6. Limit the online offering to a subset of products that particularly interest online customers, rather than the full line.
7. Use a unique brand name for products on your website.
8. On your website, offer products early in their product life cycle, when demand is growing but the website is less likely to cannibalize partner efforts.
9. Communicate your distribution strategy, internally and externally, to clarify the role your website is expected to play.
10. Work to coordinate the elements of the distribution strategy (in line with suggestion #9), including paying overrides, creating rules of engagement, and assigning roles and responsibilities.
11. Appeal to superordinate goals, such as doing the best possible job to meet customers' needs.

## Hierarchical Multichannel Strategies

Both traditional and online channels thus seek to hit the moving target of effective e-commerce, increasingly by adopting hybrid or multichannel models. Traditional channel members add online capabilities, and dedicated online firms add traditional brick-and-mortar sites (e.g., Amazon's and Google's recent announcements to open retail stores). Both Sony and Apple run storefronts, mail out catalogs, and host online channels, as well as contracting with independent retailers. Across these various levels, an exploding number of channels provide connections among retailers, suppliers, and end-users. This scenario, in which vertical channel partners use multiple routes to their horizontal end-users, implies a **hierarchical multichannel relationship**. In turn, channel managers are focused on building effective multichannel, rather than single-channel, strategies in response to the belief that firms earn more when they are connected to customers through more channels.[40]

Vertical channel partners are sequentially aligned where the upstream supplier supports their downstream partner's interaction with the end-consumer, while horizontal channels function at the same level, often in competition to win the same

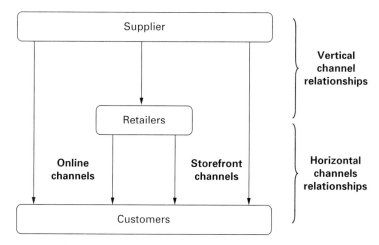

**FIGURE 9-4**   Hierarchical multichannel relationships

end-customer. As Figure 9-4 displays, they engage in simultaneous vertical and horizontal relationships. This shift to hierarchical multichannel relationships is due to the same technologies, global strategies, and emerging customer trends operating across the channel ecosystem.

Due to these similarities, and because both upstream and downstream members of the channel interact with customers, the balance of power shifts in hierarchical multichannel relationships, which can enhance the level of conflict (see Chapters 10 and 11). For example, an end-user who conducts an online search for a particular product likely finds search results that list both the manufacturer of the product and its traditional retail partner. The customer can go to either partner's website to order the desired product, with little differentiation between their offerings. In this case, the retailer likely suffers a decrease in channel power, because it is no longer the only one with a direct connection to the consumer. Furthermore, the manufacturer can use data gathered from its end-user sales to inform its strategies and innovative activities, which means that it depends less on the retailer for such information.

In response, some traditionally powerful retailers are taking rapid action. Home Depot will remove products from shelves if the manufacturer sells the same products through its own website. (See Chapter 12, Sidebar 12-1, for a description of how John Deere has dealt with this apparent restriction.) Other retailers are seeking ways to balance out channel dependence, such as through private-label initiatives, efforts to improve their own e-commerce interfaces, a greater focus on experiential offerings, and even withholding customer data from manufacturers. However, such moves appear destined to increase channel conflict even further, with concomitant reductions in trust and cooperation among vertical supply chain partners. In the long term, such outcomes undermine the effectiveness, and the very purpose, of the sales channel.

Overall, e-commerce offers perhaps the biggest disruption to channel structures and strategies in the global marketplace; most analysts agree that further effects are still to emerge. An online platform offers unique information access, search capabilities, cost benefits, and adaptability, such that suppliers can sell directly to end-users without intermediary channels. The ability of the Internet to level the playing field between large and small sellers also helps remove long-standing barriers to market entry (geographic, temporal, size, informational), causing many markets to fragment into smaller and smaller target segments. As technological capabilities keep increasing, and access to more of the world's population grows, e-commerce channels are likely to continue grabbing a bigger share of sales. In response, suppliers and channel members should develop and launch effective e-commerce channel strategies, which will be critical to the financial and strategic performance of most channel participants for the foreseeable future.[41]

## SUMMARY: EMERGING CHANNEL STRUCTURES AND STRATEGIES

Three modern business trends have dramatic influences on marketing channels, demanding adaptations or the innovation of new channel structures and strategies. First, competitive pressures (e.g., low-cost, offshore suppliers) push sellers to seek a closer degree of integration with their end-users, not only to ensure their current survival but also to erect higher switching barriers to enhance their future survival changes. This pursuit has led to a shift in many developed markets, from mostly product based to mostly service based. The resulting services typically generate steady revenue flows and can resist many economic cycles. However, these benefits require some minimum percentage of sales from services (e.g., 20–30 percent), because the firms need core, service-based capabilities and some economies of scale to generate positive financial outcomes and overcome the costs and organizational turbulence caused by a transition to services.

That is, a service transition strategy implies a demand for access to specialized service capabilities, infrastructure, and knowledge. For example, service-based transactions require coproduction and relationship ties with the end-user, which also may exclude existing channel partners from the sale, in a process known as disintermediation. The transition might occur through in-house development, collaboration with an existing provider, or acquisition. Although all three approaches have risks, they also tend to provide more resources for boundary-spanning personnel, increase customer assessment and feedback efforts, and thus alter the organizational culture to make it more customer-centric. Firms shifting to services thus tend to move further down the distribution chain to gain benefits and support their service delivery efforts.

Second, the saturation of local markets and increasing access to international realms means that international trade currently accounts for one-fifth of global GDP; as foreign customers become increasingly interlinked, accompanying changes appear in newly global channel systems. In their globalization plans, most suppliers and downstream channel partners enter developing markets to access their massive opportunities, regardless of the risk involved in spreading existing business models to different cultures and environments. However, to mitigate this risk, firms adopt different entry approaches, such as acquisitions and alliances, or else take the plunge with a direct market entry. The nearly inevitable conflict associated with entering a new market forces channel members to build new relationships quickly. Perhaps the most difficult decision for a firm in this situation is how much to change its home country channel structure to adapt to local conditions.

Third, e-commerce has created a new, more level playing field, on which existing channels need to recalibrate their strategies. With the remarkable information, search, cost, and adaptability capabilities offered by an online platform, upstream channel members—of varying sizes and located virtually anywhere—can sell directly to end-users, often at a lower cost than traditional sellers can offer. The result is often inequities, in both costs and profits, between full-service providers and free-riding channel members. Therefore, partners throughout a channel need new business norms, to ensure everyone feels fairly treated and to apply a consistent multichannel strategy. Such a strategy is key to financial and strategic success for most channel participants—especially as e-commerce continues to expand the channel options through improved technological capacities and greater international access to the Internet.

## TAKE-AWAYS

- Three modern trends fundamentally influence marketing channel structures and strategies:
  - The shift to service-based economies
  - Globalization of markets
  - Growth of the e-commerce channel
- Services are any offering that is not primarily a physical product; that is consumed at the time it is produced; that provides value through convenience, entertainment, timeliness, or health; and that is essentially intangible.
- Firms shift to service-based businesses because adding services:
  - Can increase sales and sales growth, because they generate revenue from existing customers of their products.
  - Enhances firms' differentiation from competitors.
  - Increases customer interaction frequency and depth, which in turn provide more insights into customer needs and better innovation opportunities.
  - Generates steadier revenue flows than come from products.
  - Allows firms to respond defensively to competition from offshore or low-cost providers.
- The shift to services also induces greater disintermediation, such that upstream firms sell directly to end-users.
- The shift to services increases customer coproduction and inventory perishability, so new service providers often need hybrid channel structures to address specific customer needs, segments, and geographies during the actual purchase process.
- Global expansion results mainly from firms' search for new markets, especially developing ones, that can support their revenue growth, beyond saturated domestic markets. Such expansions occur through direct entry, acquisitions, alliances and joint ventures, and franchising.
- Global channels often erode prices and cause sales losses for local retailers.
- Channels embrace e-commerce to expand into previously inaccessible markets and appeal directly to end-users.
- The technology, logistics, and market reach capabilities of e-commerce channels help suppliers sell directly to customers, which again leads to disintermediation. It also affects the balance of power in existing channels, such that their designs may become unwieldy or unworkable.

- Many e-commerce providers pursue a low-cost strategy and target more expensive brick-and-mortar channel competitors. This situation creates inequities in the division of costs and profits, such as when some channel members provide a local location to observe and test products (adding costs) but another channel member with lower costs makes the sale (receiving profits).

## Endnotes

1. CIA Factbook (2012) www.cia.gov/library/publications/the-world-factbook; U.S. Department of Commerce (1996), "Service Industries and Economic Performance" (March), www.esa.doc.gov.

2. Silverblatt, Howard and Dave Guarino (2011), "S&P 500: 2010 Global Sales," in *S&P Indices* (New York: Standard & Poor's).

3. Bloomberg (2004), "The Warranty Windfall," *Bloomberg Businessweek Online Magazine*, December 19, www.businessweek.com.

4. Townsend, Matt (2012), "Wal-Mart Offers Bank Account Option with American Express," *bloomberg.com*, October 8, www.bloomberg.com.

5. Cahyadi, Gundy, Barbara Kursten, Marc Weiss, and Guang Yang (2004), "Singapore's Economic Transformation," *Singapore Metropolitan Economic Strategy Report*, June, pp. 1–29.

6. Vargo, Stephen L. and Robert F. Lusch (2004), "Evolving to a New Dominant Logic for Marketing," *Journal of Marketing* 68 (January), pp. 1–17.

7. Fang, Eric, Robert W. Palmatier, and Jan-Benedict E. M. Steenkamp (2008), "Effect of Service Transition Strategies on Firm Value," *Journal of Marketing* 72 (September), pp. 1–15.

8. Bolton, Ruth N., Dhruv Grewal, and Michael Levy (2007), "Six Strategies for Competing Through Services: An Agenda for Future Research," *Journal of Retailing* 83, no. 1, pp. 1–4; Lusch, Robert F., Stephen L. Vargo, and Matthew O'Brien (2007), "Competing Through Service: Insights from Service-Dominant Logic," *Journal of Retailing* 83, pp. 5–18; Sawhney, Mohanbir (2006), "Going beyond the Product: Defining, Designing, and Delivering Customer Solutions," in Robert F. Lusch and Stephen L. Vargo, eds.,

*The Service-Dominant Logic of Marketing: Dialog, Debate, and Directions* (New York: M.E. Sharpe), pp. 365–380.

9. See www.emerson.com.

10. U.S. Census Bureau Federal Register Notice-North American Industry Classification System; Revision for 2012; Notice. 76, no. 159.

11. Fang, Palmatier, and Steenkamp, op. cit.

12. Gremler, Dwayne D., Valarie A. Zeithaml, and Mary Jo. Bitner (2012), *Services Marketing: Integrating Customer Focus Across the Firm*, 6th ed. (New York: McGraw-Hill).

13. Fang, Palmatier, and Steenkamp, op. cit.

14. Palmatier, Robert W. (2008), "Interfirm Relational Drivers of Customer Value," *Journal of Marketing* 72 (July), pp. 76–89.

15. Chang, Yu-Sang (2012), "Strategy, Structure, and Channel for Global Leaders of Industrial Service: A Flow Chart Analysis of the Expanded Value Network," *International Journal of Services Technology and Management* 17, no. 2, pp. 138–162.

16. Sawhney, op. cit.

17. Ahlstrom, P. and F. Nordin (2006), "Problems of Establishing Service Supply Relationships: Evidence from a High-tech Manufacturing Company," *Journal of Purchasing & Supply Management* 75, p. 89; Boddy, D., D. Macbeth, and B. Wagner (2000), "Implementing Collaboration Between Organizations: An Empirical Study of Supply Chain Partnering," *Journal of Management Studies* 37, no. 7, pp. 1003–1018.

18. McLaughlin, Kevin (2011), "Apple Channel Strategy Ripens with New Hires, iPad Certification," *CRN*, October 12, www.crn.com.

19. Harari, Oren (1999), "The Logistics of Success," *Management Review* 88, no. 6, pp. 24–26.

20. Sawhney, Mohanbir, Sridhar Balasubramanian, and Vish V. Krishnan (2004), "Creating Growth with Services," *Sloan Management Review* 45 (Winter), pp. 34–43; Zahra, Shaker, R. Duane Ireland, and Michael A. Hitt (2000), "International Expansion by New Venture Firms: International Diversity, Mode of Market Entry, Technological Learning, and Performance," *Academy of Management Journal* 43 no. 5, pp. 925–950.

21. See www.arrow.com.

22. World Trade Organization (2011), *International Trade Statistic* (Geneva, Switzerland: World Trade Organization); Central Intelligence Agency (2010), *The World Factbook* (Washington, DC: Central Intelligence Agency).

23. "2011 Top 250 Global Retailers" (2012), *Stores*, January, www.stores.org.

24. Kearney A. T. (2012), "Global Retail Expansion: Keeps on Moving," 2012 Global Retail Development Index Report, www.atkearney.com.

25. Maidment, Neil (2012), "Chinese Retailer Bosideng Sails Ahead with Overseas Plans," Reuters, October 12, www.reuters.com.

26. Sharma, Amol and Biman Mukherji (2013), "Bad Roads, Red Tape, Burly Thugs Slow Wal-Mart's Passage in India," *The Wall Street Journal*, January 11.

27. Carr, Tricia (2012), "Neiman Marcus Taps Global Desire for Luxury Via Ecommerce Expansion," *Luxury Daily*, November 8, www.luxurydaily.com; Cotterill, Stephen (2012), "'Hello, World,' J. Crew Says, via the Web," *International Marketing*, July 27, www.internationalretailer.com.

28. Satariano, Adam (2012), "Apple Names Browett to Lead Retail Business in Global Expansion," Businessweek.com, February 1, www.businessweek.com.

29. Landler, M. and M. Barbaro (2006), "International Business; No, Not Always," *The New York Times* 8, no. 2, pp. A1–A3.

30. Mattson-Teig, Beth (2012), "Retail Players Overcome Barriers to Entry to Access Emerging Markets," *Retail Traffic*, August 4.

31. Perkowski, Jack (2012), "International Retailers Struggle in China," *Forbes*, October 24.

32. U.S. Census Bureau (2012), August 16, http://www.census.gov/retail/#ecommerce.

33. Reisinger, Don (2013), "E-Commerce Spending Hits $1 Trillion for the First Time," *CNET News*, February 2, news.cnet.com.

34. Attwood, Ed (2014), "Ronaldo Mouchawar: How I created Souq.com," Arabian Business, April 5, http://www.arabianbusiness.com/ronaldo-mouchawar-how-i-created-souq-com-545057.html.

35. Parmar, Neil (2012), "Souq.com accelerates the Amazon way," The National, February 26, http://www.thenational.ae/business/technology/souq-com-accelerates-the-amazon-way.

36. Kearney, A. T. (2012), "E-Commerce Is the Next Frontier in Global Expansion," www.atkearney.com.

37. Karabus, Antony (2011), "Retail CEOs Turn to Global and Digital Expansion Strategies," *BusinessWire*, November 14, www.businesswire.com.

38. Song, Jaeki and Fatemeh Mariam Zahedi, (2006), "Internet Market Strategies: Antecedents and Implications," *Information & Management* 43, pp. 222–238.

39. Webb, Kevin L. (2002), "Managing Channels of Distribution in the Age of Electronic Commerce," *Industrial Marketing Management* 31, no. 1, pp. 95–102.

40. Ganesan, Shankar, Morris George, Sandy Jap, Robert W. Palmatier, and Bart Weitz (2009), "Supply Chain Management and Retailer Performance: Emerging Trends, Issues, and Implications for Research and Practice," *Journal of Retailing* 85 (March), pp. 84–94.

41. Wolk, Agnieszka and Bernd Skiera (2009), "Antecedents and Consequences of Internet Channel Performance," *Journal of Retailing and Consumer Services* 16, pp. 163–173.

# Managing Channel Power

## LEARNING OBJECTIVES

**After reading this chapter, you should be able to:**

- Define power as a critical tool for marketing channels that is not inherently good or bad.
- Describe the relation between power and dependence and when dependence exists.
- Distinguish between five sources of power, as well as the importance and uses of each.
- Describe tactics for building power.
- Explain how to use power as a tool to manage conflict and increase cooperation.
- Recognize the importance of the balance of dependence and describe when a weaker party should exit the relationship or take countermeasures.
- Distinguish between six communication strategies for converting power into influence and their effects on the channel.
- Describe how the framing of an influence attempt drives the target's reaction.

## THE NATURE OF POWER

In marketing channels, getting power, using it correctly, and keeping it are subjects of paramount importance. Virtually every element of marketing channels is permeated by considerations of power, because marketing channels themselves are systems of players who depend on one another. Their interdependence needs to be managed; power is the way to do it. Organizations, or the players in a marketing channel, seek to acquire power and use it wisely for the channel to work together to generate value ("grow the pie") and to enable each player to claim its fair share of that value ("divide the pie").

How players gain and use their power today determines whether they can keep their power tomorrow. The varied sources and uses of power are *not* equivalent. Some tactics for getting and using power are efficacious in the short term but disastrous in the long term. Other means have limited effectiveness in the short run but slowly gain import over time. Therefore, it behooves each member of a channel to understand where the power lies and weigh the best ways to use it—as well as the best ways to react to the power of other channel members.

This chapter begins by considering fundamental questions: *What is the nature of power, and why is it so important in marketing channels?* We then describe two main ways to estimate and index power in a channel relationship: using an inventory of five types of power or estimating the dependence of each organization. We discuss how to deal with not only power imbalances but also the consequences of using one kind of power rather than another. Finally, we cover how to convert power (a latent ability) into day-to-day operating influence.

In the past three decades, substantial resources have gone into studying the dynamics of power in actual distribution channels. This chapter focuses on presenting the major conclusions of this enormous body of research and examining their implications for practicing managers.

## Power Defined

**Power** is the ability of one channel member (A) to get another channel member (B) to do something it otherwise would not have done. Simply put, power is a potential for influence.

Power is rather difficult to diagnose, because false positives are common. That is, power might seem to exist when one firm (the **target** of influence) follows the path that another firm (the **influencer**) desires. This is cooperation—but it isn't power if the target would have done it anyway, regardless of the other firm and its preferences. Consider, for example,[1] how the head of a large IT distributor describes the behavior of one manufacturer:

> It treats me like a slave ... throws my business plan in a bin. It simply slices up its European target, divides it into countries and then allocates an arbitrary figure to me. If I don't hit my target, they get on the phone and ask: "Why don't you buy more?" This company is not interested in my ideas. Anything we suggest is ignored or we are told to put it into next year's business plan.

Ironically, this rude manufacturer may believe it has more power than it really does. For example, imagine it wants the frustrated distributor to cut its prices on the manufacturer's brands, and next month, the distributor lowers those prices. The manufacturer might strut around, thinking the price cut exemplifies its power at work. But the power could lie elsewhere: Maybe customers provoked the price cut, or the distributor's competitors, or even the manufacturer's competitors. In addition to such external forces, the initiative could have come from with the distributor organization, which has chosen to adopt a new, higher-volume, lower-margin strategy. Or maybe the distributor is planning on clearing out old, unwanted inventory. What looks like an exercise of power may be an act of free will, a response to the environment, or an acknowledgment of the power of other players. Here, we need to distinguish between **influence**, which means altering what would have been the course of events, from **exercising power**, which means exerting influence.

Apparent acts of compliance that instead are what another player would have done anyway are common in channels. The resulting misdiagnosis of power (false positive) is hazardous. **False positives** lead the supposedly powerful channel member to overestimate its ability to exert influence and make change happen. Such optimism leads this member to undertake channel initiatives that are doomed to fail. It is important to understand *how* a channel member gains power to be able to tell *whether* it has the potential for influence.

Because power is the ability to change what would have happened, it is hypothetical, speculative, and impossible to verify. Any ability that is unused is easy to overlook. And no one can be sure what would have happened in the normal course of events anyway. Thus, **false negatives** are common in channels too. Channel member B could be acting under A's influence without knowing it, or even while denying it. For example, B may believe it is freely pursuing its economic self-interest—without realizing how effectively A has framed the cost–benefit trade-offs so that B becomes convinced that its self-interest nicely coincides with A's desires.

## Power as a Tool

Power is an emotionally charged term, laden with negative connotations, such as abuse, oppression, exploitation, inequity, and brutality. And properly so: Power can be used to do great damage. As any Spider-Man fan can tell you, "With great power comes great responsibility." In channels especially, power can be used to force a channel member help generate value without receiving compensation for that effort. Used in this way, power is (and should be) condemned.

But this critical view also is one sided. Because power represents the potential for influence, great benefits can be achieved through its judicious use, to drive a channel toward more efficient, more coordinated operations. For example, at one point in its history, Hewlett-Packard (HP) made complete printers in a factory, and then shipped them into the channel, hoping that end-users would buy them. But because different customers demanded many versions of each printer, this policy resulted in high inventories, often of the wrong products. Finally, HP pioneered a strategy to achieve mass customization at low prices. Its printer designs featured standardized, independent modules that could be combined and assembled easily to make many variations of the core product. Thus, channel partners could stock the generic modules and assembly them based on customers' needs.

With its considerable power in the printer channel, HP pushed light manufacturing and assembly out of the factory and down the channel. The move generated conflict, but it also resulted in lower inventories throughout the channel *and* fewer stockouts, an ideal (and often seemingly impossible) combination. End-users enjoyed the benefits of greater choice, at lower prices. Other downstream channel members could appreciate the benefits of increased customer satisfaction, along with lower inventory holding costs. HP thus expanded the market for printers while also taking a greater share of this bigger pie. However, careful to preserve its sterling reputation for fair play, HP never sought to appropriate downstream channel members' share of the new wealth the channel generated.

A tempting alternative would have HP achieve this win–win result without wielding power or pressuring its reluctant channel members. It had strategic alliances in place with its distributors; why not just work with them, instead of exercising power over them? Had the channel recognized how well the modular approach would work, it theoretically would have assumed some of the factory's functions, because the channel members would have adopted postponement of manufacturing of their own free will. But such clarity and certainty exist only with the benefit of hindsight. Mass customization through the postponement of assembly was a radical idea at the time, and even today, it is not widely used. Embracing the idea would have required an act of faith; absent faith, it required HP's exercise of power.

Not all cases of power wielding have such happy endings though. In the newspaper industry in northern Europe in the 1990s, each newspaper faced a choice about whether to add an Internet channel to its existing routes to market. A few newspapers were powerful enough to force their existing channels to accept the increased competition created by the added Internet channel. And for some firms, the addition worked well, particularly if they differentiated their Web content and waited until the pioneers had made costly, first-mover mistakes, and then entered as early followers. But some 30 percent of newspapers lost market value and suffered lower stock prices, mainly because they already had many routes to market, so the new Internet channel simply cannibalized their own sales. For these powerful newspapers, the power to oblige existing channels to accept the Web actually worked against their ultimate interests.[2]

So is power good or bad? Like a hammer, *power is a tool*, and a tool is neutral. We can judge how someone uses the tool, but then we are deciding whether its *usage* is good or bad. Power is merely an implement. It is **value neutral**. Throughout this book, we maintain that "power" should invoke no connotations, either positive or negative.

## The Need to Manage Channel Power

Marketing channel members must work together to serve end-users. But such interdependence does not mean that what is good for one is good for all. Each channel member seeks its own profit. Recall that maximizing the system's profits is not the same as maximizing each member's profits. All else being the same, each member of the system is better off to the extent that it can avoid costs (or push them onto someone else) while garnering revenues (perhaps by taking them from someone else). And one party's costs may generate disproportionate benefits for another party.

For example, imagine a manufacturer that would like to set a high price at wholesale, to gain more revenue from its exclusive retailer. The retailer, to preserve its margins, sets a higher retail price (and exclusivity enables it to uphold this price). As a result, retail demand diminishes, compared with the level that would maximize the total channel's profits. (This problem is called **double marginalization**, because the inefficiency results from two margins, rather than one, in the channel.) If the manufacturer were vertically integrated forward (or the retailer were vertically integrated backward), the single organization, generating one-income statement, would set a lower retail price, following a strategy of lower overall margins but higher volumes.[3] Both the channel (higher profits) and the final customer (lower prices) would benefit. But because the retailer has one-income statement and the manufacturer has another, retail prices will stay higher and unit sales will remain low. In a similar channel, Apple was able to leverage its power when it initially selected an exclusive channel partner for the iPhone, ensuring that the powerful manufacturer would earn significant revenue sharing rate on all sales.[4]

There is usually a "better way" to operate a marketing channel, that is, a way that increases overall system profits. But the organizations in the channel often are unwilling to adopt this approach, because what is best for the system is not necessarily best for each member of it. *Left alone, most channel members will not cooperate to achieve some system-level goal.*

Enter power. It provides a way for one player to convince another to change what it is about to do. This change can be for the good of the system, or for the good of a single member. The tool of power can be used to create value or to destroy it, to appropriate value or to redistribute it. The usage is up to the decision maker, who holds the power. But whether the intent is malevolent or benevolent, channel members *must* engage in the exercise of building, using, and keeping power. They must employ power, to defend themselves and to promote better ways for the channel to generate value. Therefore, we delineate five sources of power and how firms can invest in creating each one.

## THE FIVE SOURCES OF CHANNEL POWER

Power (or the potential for influence) is an ability, and abilities are not easy to assess. An enormous body of research has attempted to catalog all the facets and manifestations of power, in an effort to ascertain who has power and what happens when they use it. Here, we highlight how power gets gathered, used, and maintained in marketing channels.

But how can we take an inventory of an organization's ability to change the behavior of another organization? There actually are many ways; the debate is about which way is best.[5] One way of thinking about indexing power has proven particularly fruitful in marketing channels, though this method, known as the French and Raven approach, comes from psychology.[6] It holds that the best way to **measure power** is to count its genesis from five sources of power: reward, coercion, expertise, reference, and legitimacy. Each of these sources is reasonably observable, so even though power is hidden, it can be approximated by compiling estimates of its sources.

Although the vast and bewildering forms of power may leave many channel members confused, the key message is actually fundamental: Power can be accrued and exerted only by a producer with a viable value proposition that appeals to the end-user. If the producer suffers a serious deficiency in this basic element, no amount of power in the channel can compensate for it. Specifically, the producer must offer[7]

- A product/service whose quality level meets the need of a substantial segment of end-users,
- At a price the end-user considers paying,
- Such that it is saleable enough that the terms of trade offered to other channel members enable them to earn minimum acceptable financial returns at the price the end-user is willing to pay,
- Backed by a minimally acceptable producer reputation, and
- Delivered reliably, such that the producer honors any delays it has negotiated with channel members or their customers.

These five thresholds are fundamental; without them, the downstream channel member has limited ability to create demand and no reason to bother to try to do so, regardless of the power exerted by the upstream member.

## Reward Power

A **reward** is a benefit given in return for a channel member's agreement to alter its behavior. In distribution channels, the emphasis is mainly on financial rewards. Financial returns need not be immediate, nor precisely estimable, but expectations of eventual payoffs, even indirect ones, pervade channel negotiations. Reward power is based on a belief by actor B that actor A has the ability to grant it something valuable. The effective use of reward power rests on A's possession of some resource that B values and believes it can obtain by conforming with A's request. But the *ability* to grant rewards is not sufficient; B must also perceive that A is *willing* to grant rewards. Therefore, B must be convinced that what A desires really will create benefits, and then that B will receive a fair share of those benefits.

Many channel initiatives create reward power in various forms. For example, efforts to boost a reseller's capabilities enable it to increase its profits. Excellent logistics also can increase downstream channel members' rewards indirectly, because their interactions with the producer are more efficient and profitable—which has the added advantage of being difficult to imitate.[8] This chapter cites a lot of examples of reward power, because it is universally effective. Not only do producers gain the ability to alter downstream behavior by increasing rewards, but downstream channel members also can reward producers by more effectively establishing markets for the producers' product or service offers.

Although this dominance of reward power can create the temptation to lump the other four sources of power into this category—coercion, expertise, legitimate appeal, and reference power all generate rewards at some level too—in truth they differ and operate in unique ways.

## Coercive Power

Coercive power stems from B's expectation of *punishment* by A if it fails to conform with A's influence attempt. In the United States, large supermarket chains extract substantial slotting allowances (fees) from branded producers before they will agree to stock new products. Regardless of the potential economic rationale for this practice,[9] empirical evidence suggests that these fees really exist because the retailer has the ability to block market access by a manufacturer that refuses to pay.[10] Other examples of coercive power include margin reductions, a withdrawal of previously granted rewards (e.g., exclusive territorial rights), and slower shipments.

In this sense, **coercion** is synonymous with the potential to threaten another organization, whether implicitly or explicitly. The threat of being dropped from Wal-Mart's approved vendor list has led most of its suppliers to adopt expensive electronic data interchange (EDI) systems and agree to perform bulk breaking to support its various stores. Sock manufacturers might be required to mix different kinds of socks on a pallet to fit a specific Wal-Mart store's requirements, rather than shipping complete pallets and thrusting the costs of recomposing the pallets onto Wal-Mart. This shift is not trivial; the processes required to mix sock types on a pallet costs the manufacturer .15 cents per pair—and the pair sells to Wal-Mart for $2.00.[11]

Coercive power also represents the flip side of reward power. Technically, it is negative reward power (a reward is withheld or does not materialize). So why treat it as a separate category? Why not just consider negative rewards? The main reason is that channel members do not see it this way. They view **negative sanctions** not as the absence of rewards but as an attack on themselves and their business. Coercion thus is synonymous with aggression too and provokes self-defense responses. Channel members that perceive low rewards likely react with indifference or withdrawal, but when they perceive a pathological form of coercion, they react by considering a counterattack. This defensive reaction means that coercive power is less functional over time than other sources of power that produce more positive side effects.[12] Therefore, coercion should be the last tactic used to evoke change, because it is likely to provoke retaliation.

We might make this recommendation, but coercive power often persists, and its users often appear surprised by the intensity of the target's reaction—especially if the reaction is delayed so that the target can marshal its forces and compose its counterattack. Department store chains, such as Saks Fifth Avenue and Bloomingdale's, likely perceive the opening of factory outlet stores as an effort by a manufacturer to coerce them into greater cooperation. Rather than cooperating, they generally **retaliate** in the short run by canceling orders and in the long run by opening their own factory outlet stores, in which they underprice their own suppliers' stores.[13] Other forms of retaliation may be less dramatic, or could even pass unremarked. In general though, when a target perceives the use of threats, it downgrades its estimation of the value of the business of the coercive actor.[14]

In the short term, the relationship suffers three types of damage. First, the target of coercive power is less satisfied with the financial returns it derives (a reaction that tends to be part perception and part reality). Second, the target is less satisfied with the nonfinancial side of the relationship, because a coercive partner seems less concerned, respectful, willing to exchange ideas, fulfilling, gratifying, or easy to work with. Third, the target assumes the relationship has become more conflict-laden.

But so what? A powerful actor seemingly might care little about disillusionment by the target of its coercive power. But in the short run, the target grows less cooperative; in the medium term, the target expresses less trust; and in the long run, the target grows less committed to the relationship.[15] What the powerful member gains from its coercion thus may be lost later; there are always opportunity costs associated with alienating other channel members. Coercion erodes the relationship—even if it does so slowly enough that the influencer fails to realize what it is losing.

And yet, there are times when the benefit of coercion may be worth its cost. Here, we return to our Wal-Mart example, in which it demanded suppliers adopt EDI to automate their purchasing processes. The vast potential of EDI to reduce costs has led many firms to adopt it proactively, but those benefits are far clearer in hindsight. Thus, approximately half of the early EDI adopters actually were forced to buy the related tools by other members of their supply chains—in many cases, by Wal-Mart, which imposed adoption deadlines by threatening to stop its orders.[16] When it became clear that EDI benefitted the entire channel, the coerced targets were willing to forgive their partner; surviving this particular crisis even seems to have strengthened channel relationships. But if the coerced channel member does not benefit, or does not perceive a benefit, the relationship can be seriously and irreparably damaged.[17]

## Expert Power

**Expert (or expertise) power** is based on the target's perception that the influencer has special knowledge or expertise that is useful and that the target does not possess. Of course, such expertise power is at the heart of the division of labor, specialization, and comparative advantages in channel functions. Sidebar 10-1 describes how a retailer leveraged its market access into expertise power that allowed downstream channel members to bypass existing suppliers and bring new sources of supply to its market.

Expertise does not just appear either. It must be built through patient investments of time and resources, as Sidebar 10-2 illustrates.

## Sidebar 10-1

### Retailers build expertise power over suppliers

A traditional view of channels suggests that manufacturers, with their relatively narrow specializations, are primary sources of expertise related to product use. Downstream channel members, whose attention spreads over many product categories, seemingly are less well informed about end-user needs in any given product category.

But downstream channel members also have the twin advantages of "customer touch" (closeness to the purchaser) and assortment (providing a superior view of the family of needs that buyers seek to meet through purchases).[18] Translating this formidable dual advantage into action sometimes requires an extra investment. If resellers become too frustrated with their suppliers' refusals to acknowledge their expertise, they even might go so far as to create new sources of supply that reflect their ideas of market needs. Just such a development has defined the sale of pharmaceutical drugs in Mexico.

The poor often pay more than wealthy people for the same items, because poor neighborhoods are underserved in terms of distribution. In Mumbai, India, the price differentials between a shantytown and a prosperous neighborhood are shocking. Residents of the shantytown—those who can least afford it—pay 1.2 times more for rice, 20 times more for diarrhea medication, 37 times more for safe water, and 53 times more for credit.[19]

Victor Gonzalez noticed similar differentials in Mexico and determined to do something about it.[20] The laboratory Gonzalez owns produced generic, less expensive, legal copies of branded pharmaceuticals. But despite the lack of legal barriers to selling generics, pharmacies chose to stock only expensive, patented foreign drugs, on which they enjoyed a large margin. Gonzalez's sole customer in 1997 was the Mexican government, which negotiated slender margins for generics to stock in public hospitals

and clinics. The less expensive generics in turn were available only to people covered by the public health system—not to the 50 million people living in poverty, who were thus obliged to buy branded drugs at pharmacies. According to Gonzalez, he came to a realization: "I was in the wrong business. I had to sell my generics at the retail level and forget about the government."

So he founded Farmacias Similares, a drugstore chain that sells generic medications (mostly older drugs whose patents have expired). The highly successful chain has opened more than 2,000 stores, most of them located next to clinics that Gonzalez has founded and underwritten through a non-profit group. The clinics handle 800,000 visits a month, at far lower costs than private clinics charge. The independent doctors who staff them are free to prescribe as they see fit, and the visitation fees are low.

In effect, Gonzalez has built an alternative health system. Farmacias Similares prompted a boom in generics, raising their profile and bringing new suppliers into the market. Gonzalez's generic laboratory now provides only one-fifth of the pharmacy chain's stock, with the rest made by local companies. However, the pharmacy chain retains expertise power, due to its vast knowledge of Mexico's drug market and regulations. The firm also is the acknowledged expert at spotting gaps and convincing laboratories to create supply to fill them.

One customer, who earns $4 a day, spent $8 total to bring his sick child in for a clinic visit and to obtain the necessary drug, noting: "This is the only place we can afford to buy our medicines." Gonzalez agrees: "Before we appeared on the scene, poor people in Mexico used to pray to the Virgin to get better because they couldn't afford the medicines. Now they come to us."

## Sidebar 10-2

### The mystery shopper

Gathering marketplace expertise can be a challenge for any manager, particularly when it comes to understanding the experience potential customers have at the point of sale. One tactic relies on mystery shoppers, who are typically employees of specialty research firms. After receiving training to present themselves convincingly as genuine customers, these shoppers sample the service outputs by various firms and rate the point of sale on the basis of their experiences. Mystery shoppers then submit these data, which the independent research firms compile into comprehensive reports.

Who wants these reports? The clients of mystery shopper providers include producers, who want to know how their products fare in their downstream channel partners' locations, as well as downstream channel members (e.g., retail chains) seeking to determine how well a particular store is adhering to company policy. Franchisors often use mystery shoppers to ensure their franchisees' compliance with the mandated business formats. In reality though, this access to expertise power is available to any firm that wants to learn about the performance of another channel member: outlet employees, outlet managers, entire stores, franchisees, even competitors. Thus, the information is often customized to the company that commissions the study. Depending on what the client wants, mystery shoppers might enact an elaborate script, or they may simply rate a list of general measures (how long did they wait in line, was the pizza hot, were the toilets clean, etc.). Shoppers memorize the information, and then leave the premises to transcribe the information, out of sight of the service provider.

The uses of these results are as varied as the types of clients. Specific stores may be complimented, sanctioned, tracked, or paid (typically a bonus or a prize) according to their scores. Other reports support policy decisions: Sharp paid mystery shoppers to find out how its liquid crystal flat screen televisions were being presented by electronics stores. What it discovered was that salespeople regularly advised shoppers to wait for price cuts, a direct result of the manufacturer's own policy of frequently cutting wholesale prices. In response, Sharp changed its pricing policy, constraining itself to two price cuts per year and announcing this policy widely.

Because this sort of research demands its own form of expertise, mystery shoppers need to be good actors, who fit the part, as well as accurate memorizers and note takers. The firms that employ them also need a diverse portfolio of mystery shoppers, who are believable, and eligible, to shop in different situations. For example, Optic 2000, a large French eyeglasses chain, will only contract with a third party that can provide it with a large number of farsighted mystery shoppers who can test how well its salespeople serve this segment.

In addition, these firms provide sensitive, controversial information, gained from "spying on people" and masking their true purpose. It is therefore critical that the mystery shopper and its firm appear neutral, rather than beholden to, say, managers who plan to use the information it provides. This requirement is particularly pertinent if the scenario could be seen as entrapment. For example, BMW sends mystery shoppers to test its dealers' service bays by bringing in motorcycles that are rigged to have certain problems. The service score reflects how well the provider finds and fixes the flaws, and whether it charges fairly for the service. In retail settings, a premium brand might send mystery shoppers into upscale electronics stores with scripts, to determine if they can induce salespeople to recommend less expensive brands, in violation of the stores' partnership agreement with the brand. When confronted with such information, stores and service providers are likely to be less combative if they know the mystery shopper actually is independent of the producer.

Although it takes substantial time and effort to build expert power, this power can dissipate or even disappear in an instant.[21] Expert advice, once given, grants the recipient the ability to operate without further assistance, so the original expert's relationship power drops immediately. A firm that wishes to retain its expert power over the long run thus has three options.

1. It can dole out expertise in small portions, always retaining enough vital data to ensure other channel members' continued dependence. This option implies purposefully keeping other channel members uninformed about some critical aspect of channel performance though. Such a strategy can be self-defeating, because all channel members need to work up to their capacities if the channel as a whole is to succeed.
2. The firm can continually invest in learning, to ensure it always has new, important information to offer channel partners. Its learning might focus on market trends, threats, and opportunities that other channel members would find difficult to generate. Thus, the cost of this option is substantial, but so are the benefits, in terms of achieving channel goals.
3. It might transmit only customized information and encourage channel partners to invest in transaction-specific expertise, which is so specialized that they cannot transfer it easily to other products or services. The specific nature of the expertise, along with the costs involved in acquiring it, thus impedes exit from the channel.

Some writers subdivide expert power into expertise and information sources. The former implies the provision of good judgments (forecasts, analyses); the latter involves the provision of data (e.g., news that a competitor has just dropped prices).[22] Information is not identical to expertise. Supermarkets, for example, receive huge amounts of consumer purchase data from their checkout scanners. To turn this information into insight, they send the data for each product category to selected suppliers ("category captains"), who use their knowledge of the type of product to discern patterns from millions of transactions. Supermarkets have information power over suppliers, who convert the data they receive into expertise power over supermarkets. This exercise is so important that both sides view it as an investment in building a strategic alliance.

Using expert power is not as easy as it may sound, even for an organization that holds considerable amounts of it. First, to exercise expert power, a channel member must be trusted. Otherwise, expert advice looks like an attempt at manipulation. Second, experts are usually accorded very high status, which makes them difficult to identify with and perhaps impedes necessary trust building. Third, independent-minded, entrepreneurial businesspeople don't like to be told what to do. They believe that *they* are the experts (and they are often right!). If an influencer is to employ expert power, the target has to be willing to accept this expert's information and judgments. Such acceptance is far more likely if a good working relationship exists, such that the target believes in the basic competence and trustworthiness of the influencer.[23] It is also easier if the target needs (i.e., is dependent on) the influencer.

## Legitimate Power

To be **legitimate** is to be perceived as right and proper, in accordance with normative or established standards. **Legitimate power** thus stems from the target company's sense that is in some way obligated to comply with the requests of the influencer, because such compliance seems right and proper by normal or established standards. That is, the influencer has legitimate power if the target feels a sense of duty and bound to carry out the influencer's request, due its feeling of being constrained by moral, social, or legal forces to go along with the influencer's recommendation. This sense of responsibility comes from two main sources: the law (legal legitimate power) and norms or values (traditional legitimate power).

**Legal legitimate power** is conferred by governments, stemming from each nation's laws of contracts and commerce. For example, patent and trademark laws give owners some freedom and justification to supervise the distribution of their products. Commercial laws allow firms to maintain agreements, such as franchises and other contracts, that confer on them the legitimate power to demand behavior that is not required in conventional channel arrangements.

In principle, a major source of legitimate power is the contracts that channel members sign. In practice though, contracts rarely carry the force we might expect them to have. In many cultures (particularly outside the Anglo-Saxon sphere of influence), contracts are difficult to enforce. Channel members might not even bother to write them (and merely asking for a contract can signal distrust, which leads to a self-perpetuating, downward cycle). Even in litigious nations such as the United States, channels frequently operate with sketchy, incomplete contracts—or no contract at all! Even when they exist, many channel members remain happily unaware of the terms of their contracts ("the lawyer will look it up if we need it..."), or else pay little attention to contract clauses. Instead, they rely on norms developed within the context of their relationship.[24] This trend is not peculiar to channels: People rely on our working understanding, even when we come from societies with strong legal traditions.[25]

Even when channel members invest in crafting thorough contracts—which still is common, particularly in franchise arrangements—a well-considered contract rarely covers all the power that any channel member might need. Franchisees sign contracts with franchisors, obliging them to maintain their facilities with a certain appearance, honor the standards and procedures set by the franchisor, pay advertising fees or royalties, and buy from approved sources. But as we discussed in Chapter 8, franchisees regularly violate these terms and assume the franchisor will tolerate their breach of contract. And the franchisors often do express just such tolerance, because enforcing a contract is expensive and might prompt backlash against the franchisor. Even with the legitimate right to punish violators, franchisors thus engage in cost–benefit analyses about whether it is worthwhile it to punish a contract violation. It often isn't.[26]

Legal legitimate authority is objective, and any influencer can remind the target of its presence easily. In contrast, **traditional legitimate power** is more ephemeral and cannot exist without the consent of the target. Traditional legitimate authority is based on values that the target already has internalized, such that it believes the influencer "should" or "has a right to" exert influence, which it is largely obliged to accept. When a supervisor gives a directive to a subordinate, the latter feels that the former has this right and therefore generally conforms with the superior's desires. Such legitimized power is synonymous with authority, and it also offers a key reason to vertically integrate forward or backward in a channel. But there is a major difference in most marketing channels, where *no hierarchical authority exists.*

Channel members sometimes forget about this lack of hierarchy. Thus, a frequent and major source of friction between channel members arises when one company seeks to invoke its authority by treating another like a subsidiary. A district sales manager, with a background in managing an employee sales force, might not be the best choice to be the liaison with independent channel members, such as a new sales agency. This manager likely exhibits behavioral norms and patterns learned from a position in which she or he really *did* have authority. But his or her normal, unconscious behavior likely seems imperious and arrogant to independent sales agents, and this perception, even when created unintentionally or innocently, threatens the channel member's autonomy, creating needless resistance.

Of course, legitimate power exists in dealings between organizations; it just does not stem from hierarchical authority. Rather, it comes from **norms**, **values**, and **beliefs**. One firm may believe that a channel member deserves to be accorded certain deference, because of its successful track record or exemplary management. The largest firm could be considered the leader (channel captain) by other channel members. In all these cases, that firm enjoys legitimate power.

Behavioral norms, or expectations of "normal" behavior, arise in a channel to define roles and effectively confer legitimate power on certain channel members. For example, distributors in the information technology (IT) industry work according to norms different than those that mark many other industries: They are far more likely to honor a supplier's request to name their customers and detail their shipments. Norms exist not only within industries but also within certain channels, some of which manage to build norms,[27] such as follows:

- *Solidarity.* Each side expects the other to focus on the relationship in the whole, rather than thinking transaction-by-transaction.
- *Role integrity.* Each side expects the other to perform complex roles that cover not just individual transactions but also a multitude of issues not related to any single transaction.
- *Mutuality.* Each side expects the other to divide up its joint returns in a way that assures adequate returns to each side.

These norms, once created, give one channel member the ability to exert legitimate power over the other, by appealing to the norms as a reason to comply with a request.

Ultimately, the degree of traditional legitimate power is subjective. *It exists in the eye of the beholder.* Channel members build their legitimate power base by investing in partnership building to increase a sense of common norms and values. Traditional legitimate power can also be built by selecting channel partners on the basis of compatibility in their attitudes, values, and operating methods. Some franchisors accordingly screen prospective franchisees on the basis of their attitudes toward legitimate authority, favoring candidates who express respect for the franchisor as an authority figure and for the franchise contract as a binding document. They instead screen out candidates who view the contract as "just a piece of paper," take a skeptical approach to the franchisor, or are "too" independent minded. In a channel, such "troublemakers" are unlikely to attribute legitimate authority to another partner.

## Referent Power

Referent power exists when B views A as a standard of reference and therefore wishes to identify publicly with A. In interpersonal relations, there are many personal, psychological reasons B might sense oneness with A and wish to be associated (identified) with him or her. In a marketing channel, one organization might seek to be publicly identified with another in search of prestige. Downstream channel members seek to carry high-status brands to benefit their own image; upstream channel members "rent the reputation" of prestigious downstream firms.[28]

The existence of referent power is undeniable. It is especially visible when wholesalers or retailers pride themselves on carrying certain brands (e.g., Harley-Davidson motorcycles, Ralph Lauren clothing, Intel semiconductors) and manufacturers pride themselves on having their brands carried by certain outlets (e.g., Neiman Marcus in the United States, Mitsukoshi in Japan, value-added resellers known for exceptional service in business-to-business realms). Creating and preserving **referent power**, defined as the ability to confer prestige, is a key reason manufacturers restrict their distribution coverage to selected outlets, as well as an explanation of why downstream organizations restrict representation to selected brands.

A firm with proprietary know-how might begin with legitimate power, in the form of patent protections, and then use this basis to expand its referent power, as Sidebar 10-3 suggests in the example of Sweden's Ericsson and its 33,000 patents.

## Sidebar 10-3

### Patent wars

In January 2014, it was announced that the South Korean giant, Samsung Electronics Co. would pay the Swedish company Ericsson some U.S. $650 million. In addition, it would pay royalties dating back to several years. This was the conclusion of yet another patent-based technology license argument.

Ericsson is generally regarded as the top mobile network equipment manufacturer in the world. It had sued Samsung in 2012 on the basis of several infringed patents, including network efficiency, touch-screen technology, and voice transmission technology. Samsung had counter-sued.

This action was one of the latest in infringement cases in the telecom industry in the past few years. The main reason behind actions like these is that many of the handsets share the same technology. In effect, it means that businesses have to pay their competitors for licenses to use that technology. At the same time, businesses such as Ericsson, in the face of increasing competition, are keen to maximize their incomes from their patents.

The Ericsson-Samsung dispute came as a result of their inability to agree on a deal in 2011. Back in 2001, Samsung had struck a licensing deal with Ericsson that was subsequently renewed in 2007. When it came up for renewal again in 2011, Ericsson, as far as Samsung was concerned, wanted too high a royalty for using the same patents.

Ericsson is said to hold over 33,000 patents. These cover much of the underlying technology for networks and handsets. It is estimated that it invests upwards of U.S. $4.6 billion per year on research and development. Consequently, it has licensing deals with all of the major telecoms businesses around the world.

Ericsson's chief intellectual property officer, Kasim Alfalahi, declined to say how long the new agreement with Samsung would last. Usually, the agreements are in force for between four to seven years.

The enforcement of the patent power will allow Ericsson to continue developing new technologies and, of course, new patents that can be monetized via licensing agreements in the future.

The exact details of the agreement are confidential, but Ericsson did admit that the initial payment from Samsung would boost sales by around U.S. $650 million. Once the news of the agreement had reached the markets, Ericsson's shares immediately rose by 2.4 percent. The agreement would guarantee a steady income stream for several years. Markets clearly saw this as a key revenue source, and analysts suggested that the annual revenue from this agreement with Samsung alone would be worth some U.S. $320 million. Other analysts set the ongoing annual revenues from Samsung at a more modest U.S. $260 million.

## Continued

Following the agreement, Samsung's shares fell by around 1.2 percent.

In the patent merry-go-round in the mobile technology market, fortunes are still to be won and lost as competitors struggle to apply their patents and monetize their property rights. At the same time, Samsung was deeply involved in a protracted dispute with Apple. The dispute spread across several countries where patents had been taken out.

The market moves on, with licensing and cross-licensing deals taking place at a dizzy pace. It is at the cutting edge of technology where a business can really make its patents count to enable the use of referent power.

### Grouping the Five Power Sources

If we are taking stock of the extent of power in a channel relationship, the five sources of power offer a useful framework. But they also create a risk, namely, that we might double count a particular source when taking a power inventory. Separating sources of power rarely involves a clear-cut distinction, such that many users of the five sources framework do not even try. Instead, they rely on broader groupings, two of which we consider here.

One method is to separate out just **coercive** power and lump all the others together as **noncoercive** power. But even lumping expert, referent, and legitimate power into the broad noncoercive inventory seems a bit arbitrary. For example, is withholding a reward coercive, or is it reward power? To circumvent the problem, we can define **coercion** more specifically as the removal of something a channel member already has. Everything else is noncoercive. For example, a sales agent has coercive power over a supplier if it can credibly threaten to reduce coverage or drop some of the line. A credible offer to increase coverage or take on more of the line is a form of noncoercive power. An auto supplier's power base is coercive if it can slow down deliveries; it is noncoercive if it can speed them up. If it slows down the delivery of popular cars and speeds up the delivery of cars that turn slowly, the power is coercive—and it harms the dealer, which faces both more stockouts *and* more inventory.

Another option would be to consider **mediated** versus **unmediated** power. Power is mediated (by the influencer) when it can be demonstrated; that is, the target is forced to acknowledge these power bases. These mediated forms consist of reward, coercion, and legal legitimate power. Unmediated (by the influencer) bases are ones that would not exist without the target's own perception, namely, expert, referent, and traditional legitimate power. It is much easier to create and wield mediated power, because unmediated power builds more slowly, subtly, and through a process that remains difficult to decipher. Because unmediated power rests on the target's implicit consent, the influencer cannot simply implement a program to guarantee greater unmediated power. Nor can a competitor mimic acquired unmediated power, because even the influencer might not be entirely sure how it acquired this form of power. Such uncertainty and inimitability makes unmediated power a potent competitive advantage.[30] Channel members that enjoy expert, referent, or legitimate power (however acquired) should take great care to avoid endangering this strategic, intangible asset. This sort of asset cannot get entered into a balance sheet, but it is so valuable that it motivates massive changes to marketing channels, even including mergers and acquisitions.

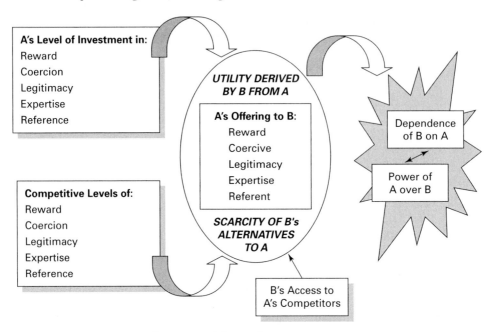

**FIGURE 10-1**    Nature and sources of channel power

## Summary of Power Sources

We thus have come full circle. Power is not merely a descriptive concept, summarizing the current positions of the channel players. It is also a strategic firm choice, made over the medium to long term, in accordance with investments (or lack thereof) in power sources. Figure 10-1 depicts the relations among the nature and sources of channel power. What each party offers can be framed according to the five power bases (reward, coercion, legitimacy, expertise, and reference). The more a channel member invests in being able to provide these five sources, the greater is its utility. Of course, its competitors' power bases determine the scarcity of that utility too.

## DEPENDENCE AS THE MIRROR IMAGE OF POWER

Considering the various elements of power, what we really need is a practical, concrete way to observe and measure the potential for influence. According to sociology, it actually is pretty simple: **A's power over B increases with B's dependence on A.**[31] If it depends on party A, party B also is likely to change its behavior to align with A's desires. Thus, B's dependence gives A greater potential for influence.

### Defining Dependence

That's simple. But then we need to decide just what dependence is. For our purposes, we recognize that B depends more heavily on A when it

1. Obtains greater *utility* (value, benefits, satisfaction) from A and
2. Has access to *fewer alternative* sources of that utility.

Dependence equals utility multiplied by alternative scarcity (in mathematical terms, $D = U \times S$). However, if B derives little value from what A provides (U is null), it is irrelevant whether alternative providers exist: B's dependence is low. If A provides great value but B can readily find other sources to provide just as much value (S is null), it is irrelevant whether A offers benefits: B's dependence again is low. Again, we can apply a mathematical metaphor. Low utility (U) or low alternative scarcity (S) is like multiplying by 0, so the product (D) is 0.

Thinking of one actor's power as the other actor's dependence is useful, because it focuses the analysis on **scarcity**, or how readily B can replace A. This point is easy to overlook. Channel members often consider themselves powerful because they deliver value to their counterparts, but counterparts just don't need them if they are easy to replace, which reduces their power. It also is easy to overestimate scarcity. Sidebar 10-4 describes how a well-established capital equipment company fell into such a trap.

In a common channel scenario, a manufacturer seeks to change a downstream channel member's behavior but then expresses shock when the downstream organization responds by refocusing on competing brands instead. Or a reseller might believe a manufacturer depends on it, because end-users are loyal to the reseller, but a strong manufacturer can retain those same end-users selling through alternative channels, if

## Sidebar 10-4

### New market channels for Malaysian retailers

Malaysia has been slow in recovering from the global economic downturn, but despite that, retailers were able to announce higher than expected sales since 2012. On the one hand, Malaysian consumers were still reluctant to spend on non-grocery products, particularly luxury items, but were keen to take advantage of retailer price reductions and promotions.

For decades, the Malaysian retail market has been somewhat traditional, with an over-reliance on stores and face-to-face sales. Considerable investment in the Internet infrastructure in Malaysia has begun to change the way in which people buy. Major retailers such as Senheng Electric, Parkson, and Isetan have all successfully launched Internet retailing operations. While many retailers were happy to offer Internet retailing as an additional way of making sales, their focus was still very much store-based. These major retailers are at the forefront of what is predicted to be a major shift in the way Malaysians will buy products and services. Simply, other retailers have been forced to move into Internet retailing in order to protect their market share against the Internet-only retailers.

Grocery shopping is also changing, but the changes are not Internet-driven. GCH Retail—that owns the major retailing brands Giant, Cold Storage, and Guardian—has a comprehensive chain of hypermarkets and supermarkets across Malaysia. The retail major's primary focus has always been competitive pricing coupled with the fact that it is perceived as being a local brand. In order to ensure that its market leadership is maintained, the focus of GCH Retail has been further expansion into rural areas. Access has always been a major issue in attracting rural customers. The chain is positioning itself to provide a far more extensive and comprehensive coverage of Malaysia. This brings it into direct competition with a wide variety of new competitors in areas of the country it had not traded in before, and with it challenges in terms of logistics.

This move by the grocery retailer is expected to continue over the next decade, driving consumers to its stores with a mix of promotions and improved convenience, coupled with an unprecedented range of products that rural consumers will have access to for the first time.[32]

its brand equity is strong enough. Either scenario is likely if one party generates benefits but underestimates how easily it can be replaced, such that it overestimates its power (i.e., forgets to multiply by 0).

## Measuring Dependence

A more reasonable estimate of another channel member's dependence on the focal actor comes from assessing both elements (utility and scarcity) separately, combining them only later. To assess **utility**, let's assume you represent the focal actor, and you need to tally up the benefits your firm offers. To do so, you must recognize your channel partner's goals and how your offering helps it meet those pursuits. You might estimate your utility by inventorying your five bases of power, or you could obtain a rough estimate of the profits you generate for your partner, both directly and indirectly. However you choose to assess your worth, you must remember to focus on what is important to the partner (e.g., volume rather than profits).

To assess alternative **scarcity**, or how easily you could be replaced, you need to consider two additional factors. First, who are your (potential) competitors? That is, what other organizations exist (or might enter the market) that can supply what you provide or an acceptable equivalent? When no other options exist, alternative scarcity is very high, so your partner's dependence on you also is high. Second, if alternatives exist (i.e., alternative scarcity is low), you need to determine how easily the channel member can switch from your organization to a competitor. If switching is easy, your partner does not depend on you, and you have essentially no real power. If switching away from your organization is impractical or prohibitively expensive, you enjoy a high alternative scarcity value in the market (even if alternatives exist in principle).

Now return to the benefits you provide, and combine your estimates with your assessment of the difficulty your channel partner would have replacing you. The **combined analysis** reveals the dependence of your channel member on you, and thus your level of power. Try not to be too upset when you realize that you *are* replaceable, despite the value of your offerings. This realization is common and sobering, but also informative and likely accurate.

Let's consider a hypothetical example of a manufacturer P of specialty steel, which supplies distributors X and Y. For both X and Y, manufacturer P's brand attracts end-users, which also helps the distributors' salespeople sell other products in their portfolios. Its utility, both direct and indirect, is thus substantial. But three competitors also offer equivalent products, so P looks easily replaceable. Distributor Y, which is a large, well-known firm, works with whatever manufacturer gives it the best deals at any time, switching readily across the four manufacturers in the market. Thus, P has little power over Y. In contrast, X is a small distributor that continues to struggle to establish itself in its marketplace. Unimpressed by its sales volume, the other three manufacturers in the market refuse to supply X on the same friendly terms that P offers. Because X has no realistic alternative to P (it cannot afford the terms the other manufacturers demand), X depends on P, and P has greater power in this relationship.

Manufacturer P could increase its power over both distributors if it could induce them to make investments that would be difficult to transfer to another manufacturer, such as adopting P's proprietary ordering software, getting training about the unique features of P's products, participating in joint advertising campaigns, or forging close relationships with P's personnel. Any distributor that has invested time and energy in such pursuits likely is reluctant to sacrifice its investments by switching suppliers. The high **switching costs** make P a *de facto* monopolist; even in the face of apparent competition, the distributor's dependence confers power on manufacturer P.

Other methods to approximate dependence seek a rougher proxy indicator, in lieu of a thorough and detailed (also known as slow and costly) assessment of utility and scarcity. Each proxy indicator suffers drawbacks, but these methods are easier to implement and frequently offer a reasonable approximation.

**PERCENTAGE OF SALES OR PROFITS**  A quick method estimates the **percentage of sales or profits** earned by the partner that the focal channel member provides. The higher this percentage, the higher the partner's dependence and thus the more powerful the focal member is. That is, an important (powerful) channel member provides high benefits, and switching threatens the loss of those benefits to partners, which implies higher switching costs. If the benefits also account for a significant proportion of the partner's sales or profits, those switching costs may grow astronomical. This argument has considerable merit. But the percentage of sales/profit method also represents an approximation. It cannot capture all benefits, nor does it assess scarcity directly. Thus, in some situations, the method works poorly. For example, franchisees likely derive 100 percent of their sales and profits from the franchisor, yet some franchisees still are more or less dependent than others.[33]

**ROLE PERFORMANCE**  Dependence approximations can come from assessments of how well the focal actor performs its role compared with competitors. Greater superiority implies higher **role performance**, such that few alternatives can offer a similar level of performance, even if their product offerings appear similar.[34] This direct method comes closer to assessing scarcity, but it cannot address role importance. That is, you may perform a role better than competitors, but your partners depend on you only if they derive utility from the performance of this specific role. Furthermore, your partner likely can access meaningful alternatives if it is willing to accept some diminishment in role performance.

In other circumstances, role performance simply does not capture dependence well. For example, many emerging economies feature sellers' markets, in which demand far outstrips supply, barriers to entry restrict supply, and there are many reseller candidates. In these sectors, every channel member depends on every supplier, regardless of its role performance.[35] Yet role performance remains a reasonable proxy for dependence in many other circumstances. Service excellence confers uniqueness (scarcity), even for commodity products. In this case, superb role performance creates dependence (and power), because excellence is nearly always scarce *and* valuable.

**BOTTOM–UP APPROACH**  The last approach to measuring power that we cover here is based on a different philosophy about how power grows. This **bottom–up approach** takes an inventory of the five ways to amass the potential to change a channel member's behavior—that is, through reward, coercion, expertise, reference, and legitimacy power. In this case, the focal channel member wants a change to occur and thus seeks to influence it partner; the partner is the target of these influence attempts. The extent to which the target makes the change varies with its level of dependence on the influencer, which stems from its power to change the target's behavior.

## Balancing Power: A Net Dependence Perspective

We need to reemphasize a point here: *Power is a property not of an organization but of the relationship.* In reference to a power relationship, it is misleading to say "P is powerful." Rather, P may be powerful only *in relation to* X; it easily could be weak in relation to some other party Y (here, we use the hypothetical identities from our manufacturer–distributor example in the previous section, but these actors could be any combinations of parties). In the P–X relationship, P has some sources of power, as does X, including countervailing power that might offset some of P's power sources. Therefore, any inventory of P's power must focus on one relationship at a time, rather than making general statements. In each assessment, the calculation also must reflect not only just P's ability to exert power (e.g., reward X) but also X's ability to exert power (e.g., bestow rewards) over P. Channel outcomes rest on the **balance of power** in a given relationship.

That is, *dependence is never one way*. Dependence assessments must take both channel partners' perspectives. Just as X depends on P to provide utility, P needs X for a different type of utility. They are interdependent, which blunts P's ability to pressure X to alter its behavior. High mutual dependence, or **interdependence**, is synonymous with high mutual power. High mutual power also gives channel members greater ability to achieve very high levels of value.[36] Each party has leverage over the other, which should drive their coordination and cooperation.[37]

Consider the example of beer brewers. SABMiller Brewing covers a large market (the United States) with relative ease, because 470 wholesalers span the market, though most of them also carry competing brands. Each side needs the other (high utility); both sides have alternatives (low scarcity). East African Breweries Ltd. (EABL) also covers a large market, Kenya, but its ease of access is much lower, because there are only 30 wholesalers in the area. Despite this challenge, EABL achieves 98 percent market coverage, even in rural areas, which enabled it to drive its larger competitor SABMiller right out of Kenya! The key is high mutual dependence: EABL keeps few house accounts and grants exclusive territories, and its wholesalers carry only beer, and often only EABL brands. Thus, the great benefits, and great utility, each side earns through the channel are at stake, so each side chooses to remain exclusive to the other and considers alternatives generally unappealing.

High mutual dependence also is conducive to creating and maintaining **strategic channel alliances**, marked by effective coordination. A channel is coordinated if every channel member acts in the way a single, vertically integrated firm would, namely, by maximizing overall channel profit. Such coordination arises for two reasons, as our beer example showed. First, the two sides encourage each other to design and implement creative, win–win solutions. Second, high, balanced dependence blocks exploitation, because each side has countervailing power, which it can use for self-protection. Without a notably weaker party in the relationship, each side forces the other to share gains, which fosters norms of fairness and solidarity. This level of symmetric dependence promotes bilateral functioning by increasing each side's willingness to adapt in dealing with the other.[38]

Of course, symmetry also might imply low mutual dependence, such that neither side has much need of the other. This low–low combination is so common in marketing channels that it represents a baseline condition for many channel management recommendations. When each side is dispensable, the channel tends to operate in accordance with classic economic relationship predictions.[39]

Finally, to assess countervailing power, as part of the calculation of net dependence, a decision maker might consider the relationship level and calculate net dependence with one other channel member. But in some cases, single channel members (upstream or downstream) can radically and quickly shift the calculation by coming together in a **coalition**. Suddenly, one party faces a bloc—which usually raises both the benefits and alternative scarcity of the other side.

## Imbalanced Dependence

After such sudden shifts, one channel member may become much more dependent than the other. The balance of power favors the less dependent member, whereas the more dependent member suffers exposure to **exploitation**.[40] All too often, that exposure leads to problems. The more dependent party loses out, in both economic terms and noneconomic benefits,[41] even if the more powerful (less dependent) channel member does not actively attempt to appropriate rewards. That is, the weaker member might suffer simply because the fortunes of the stronger member decline. In addition, facing the specter of exploitation, the weaker (more dependent) party senses its own vulnerability and is quick to suspect the stronger party of acting in bad faith. Asymmetric relationships thus tend to be more conflict-laden, less trusting, and less committed than interdependent relations.[42] What are channel members to do then?

**STRATEGIES FOR BALANCING DEPENDENCE**    There are three countermeasures available to the weaker party to reduce its dependence. That is, if B depends more on A than A depends on B, then B can do as follows:

1. Develop alternatives to A.
2. Organize a coalition to attack A.
3. Exit the situation and no longer seek the benefits that A provides.

In channels, the first reaction is the most common. Fear of exploitation drives channel members to develop countervailing power, especially as their dependence increases. For example, some sales agents (e.g., manufacturers' representatives, or reps) tailor their operations to key principals, which creates potentially dangerous dependence imbalances for them. These reps therefore go to great lengths to cultivate their relationships with end-users as well, to build customer loyalty to the reps' agency. With this power relation, the rep can induce customers to change to another brand if necessary. Because the rep can take end-users elsewhere, it achieves countervailing power against the principal. These reps generally earn better profits than those that neglect to balance their dependence after they have tailored their operations to a principal.[43]

This measure also involves the potential ability to add a supplier, if necessary. Many channel members deliberately maintain a diversified portfolio of counterparts, to allow them to react immediately if any one organization exploits their power imbalance. For example, in line with industry norms, U.S. automobile dealers once represented only one brand of car each, making them highly dependent on the manufacturer. After the oil crisis of the early 1970s encouraged dealers to add more fuel-efficient cars, often produced by other brands, it was a short step to broad diversification. Now many auto dealers rely on multiple locations, each of which represents a different brand, or even a single location selling multiple brands. This diversified portfolio reduces the dealer's dependence on any single manufacturer and enables it to resist any given automaker's pressure attempts.

The second countermeasure, organizing a coalition, involves a strategy of bringing in third parties. There are several ways to do so. A common method in Europe is to write contracts that require mandatory arbitration of any disputes. The arbitrators are usually private entities, but the third party also could be a government body. Other coalitions emerge when channel members band together into trade associations. Just as much as they used the first countermeasure, automobile dealers in the United States rely on this tactic. By organizing and lobbying state legislatures, dealers have pushed through "Dealers' Day in Court" laws in many states that limit automakers' ability to coerce or pressure them through lawsuits or penalties. For example, when General Motors vertically integrated forward in selected markets, an organized coalition of dealers demanded it reverse its strategy, leading the CEO to admit: "I learned a lot. Having your key constituents mad at you is not the way to be successful."[44]

The third countermeasure is to withdraw from the business, and therefore from the relationship. Exiting the business and moving resources elsewhere (e.g., selling off an auto dealership) may seem unthinkable, but it also constitutes the most conclusive way to escape dependence. In retail channels, powerful retailers (e.g., Wal-Mart) often use their substantial power to demand reduced prices from dependent manufacturers. Even if manufacturers might prefer to sell through Wal-Mart's extensive distribution system, they also have the option of offsetting the lower prices they offer the retail giant with higher prices charged to weaker retailers and shifting more of their sales focus to these higher-margin channels through advertising and promotion efforts.[45]

Perhaps none of these dependence-reduction strategies is appealing. In that case, to address imbalanced dependence, the weaker member might seek to increase the other party's dependence by offering greater utility and by making itself less replaceable. The best method often is to improve its service levels. If a weaker party begins to offer quicker delivery, for example, its partner may find the service offer nearly irresistible. In our retail channel example, a manufacturer that guarantees on-time deliveries eliminates the threat of stockouts for the retailer, which should lead the retailer to come to rely more on its products. Of course, such a tactic also implies that the manufacturer is devoting substantial resources to its relationship with the retailer, so this strategy might be risky. But ultimately, it could ensure greater mutual dependence between them.

**STRATEGIES FOR TOLERATING IMBALANCED DEPENDENCE**   The most common reaction by weaker parties is no reaction. That is, more often than not, a dependent party simply accepts the situation and tries to make the best of it. It might even deliberately devote a high proportion of its effort or sales to the other party, in the hope that it becomes so important that the stronger party values its contribution and actively avoids taking advantage of its vulnerability. Weaker parties also might rely on internal norms of joint decision making and trust the other party to take its interests into account. Firms are (perhaps surprisingly) willing to be vulnerable in this manner.

Clothing suppliers often make investments in a single powerful retailer and reassure themselves that the retailer will not abuse its position, because they are an important supplier or have a long tradition of joint decision making.[46]

But especially in globally consolidating markets and industries,[47] we need to ask: Are stronger parties always exploitative? Do weaker parties always suffer? Should imbalanced relationships be avoided?

Some imbalanced dependence relationships actually work well. When department store buyers, who select merchandise for each department, rely on manufacturers to supply appealing merchandise with a strong brand name, they willingly grant far greater power to the suppliers, which might not depend on the store as a major outlet. Despite this imbalance, department stores generally benefit from this dominant supplier relationship, especially if the market environment remains stable and *predictable*. That is, if the dominant supplier's product enjoys predictable demand, the department stores minimize their own need to take price reductions. In addition, in this setting, suppliers normatively refrain from exploiting buyers' vulnerability.

In unpredictable settings though, supplier dominance may quickly become a liability. As demand fluctuates, the store cannot oblige the dominant supplier to be more flexible, such as by taking back more unsold merchandise. Thus, in highly *uncertain* market environments, high mutual dependence is preferable, to ensure that both suppliers and buyers are motivated to find common solutions to complex stocking problems. Low mutual dependence is another option, because in that case, the buyer has the option of switching suppliers.

In short, imbalanced dependence is not necessarily detrimental in stable environments and when the less dependent party voluntarily refrains from abusing its power. A channel can function effectively if the stronger party takes care to treat the more vulnerable party equitably.[48] Equitable treatment also improves relationship quality, which enhances the functioning of the channel. Finally, because every channel member's reputation is at stake, unfair treatment creates reputation risks that may make it more difficult for a powerful, exploitative actor to attract, retain, and motivate other channel members in the future.

## POWER-BASED INFLUENCE STRATEGIES

Power is invisible. It is impossible to certify just how much power a single party has in a channel relationship. For example, what happens if a firm has power but chooses not to exercise it? That is, what happens to power that goes unused? Can power be banked or stored for later? These questions sound fascinating, but evidence from the field suggests they also are moot. Parties that have power use it. They don't reserve it for later, nor do they act as they might if they were powerless. **Latent power** rapidly becomes **exercised power**.[49]

This conversion of the potential for influence into demands for real changes in another party's behavior requires communication, and the nature of that communication influences channel relationships.[50] Most channel communications can be grouped into six categories, or *influence strategies*:

1. **Promise.** If you do what we wish, we will reward you.
2. **Threat.** If you don't do what we wish, we will punish you.

3. **Legalistic.** You should do what we wish, because you have agreed to do so (whether in a contract or through an informal working understanding of how we do business).
4. **Request.** Please do what we wish.
5. **Information exchange.** Let's pursue a general discussion about the most profitable way for you to run your business, without mentioning exactly what we want. This oblique strategy seeks to change your perceptions of what is effective, in a way that favors us. We hope this subtle form of persuasion prompts you to draw conclusions about what you should do—and that those conclusions match what we want you to do.
6. **Recommendation.** Similar to an information exchange, let's discuss profitable methods, but we will provide you with the conclusion, namely, you would be more profitable if you would do what we wish. This more overt strategy tends to generate skepticism and counterarguments.

Each influence strategy rests on certain sources of power, as Figure 10-2 maps.

Channel members that have not invested in building corresponding power bases likely find that their influence attempts fail. Again, we caution that power, and thus power bases, are specific to each relationship: Nestlé has far more reward power (and thus can use a promise strategy effectively) with a small retailer than with an international hypermarket chain.

As a general rule, boundary personnel eventually use all six strategies in each relationship they develop. But each relationship also exhibits a particular style that reflects which strategies are most common. The predominant style, or influence strategy used most often, determines how well the firm converts its power into actual behavioral changes by its partner.

## Effectiveness of Six Influence Strategies

The promise, threat, and legalistic influence strategies often provoke a **backlash**, because they are perceived as heavy-handed, high-pressure techniques. Counterparts resent them and tend to respond by using similar strategies too. In particular, the use of threats provokes conflict and damages relationship satisfaction, both economically and psychologically. In the short term, high-pressure techniques can be effective, but they also have damaging longer-term effects on trust and commitment.[51]

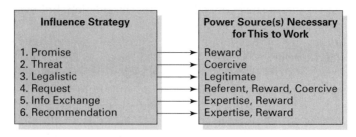

**FIGURE 10-2    Using power to exert influence**

Although a promise strategy may seem like a reward, few targets see it as such. Rather, a promise often looks like a bribe, which is both insulting and unprofessional. Or it might be perceived as a veiled criticism of performance ("If they thought I was doing a good job, they would have given me this benefit already"). Promises also beget more promises, such that each counterpart responds with its own promises, which ultimately can set off a haggling spiral. Over time, a promise strategy's effects likely are mixed. From a process standpoint (i.e., psychological satisfaction based on interpersonal processes), channel members dislike it. But from a strictly economic standpoint, channel members tend to welcome promises, because each actor is likely to deliver on its promises, which improve the channel's financial indicators. If they do so well enough, they can dampen any related conflict. Overall then, though self-perpetuating, a promise strategy offers an effective way to change channel members' behaviors, even while it raises interpersonal tensions.

The latter three influence strategies (request, information exchange, recommendation) are more subtle and nuanced; channel counterparts often welcome these efforts and do not take offense at encountering them. These strategies also increase satisfaction, both economic and interpersonal, because they avoid impressions of high pressure or heavy handedness—even when the influencer's objective is the same. Yet it is difficult to imagine anyone perceiving a pure request as heavy handed. A pure request, without any reason given, is so low pressure that it seems surprising that this strategy is so common! Yet evidence indicates that the two lightest handed strategies, recommendation and request, are the ones used most often (whereas the most heavy-handed strategies, threats and legalisms, are used least often).[52]

Information exchange is risky in a different way: It can be so subtle that the counterpart fails to pick up on the signals, such that it has no effect. This risk disappears with a recommendation strategy, and even though this strategy is overt (i.e., desired behavior is clearly stated) it does not threaten the counterpart's autonomy, because the desired action is presented as being in the other party's business interest. This pattern varies in close, long-term relationships though.[53] These committed parties refrain from threatening each other and spend little time making requests without a reason. But they are candid in their influence attempts, including offering rewards for desired behavior, leaving the other party to draw conclusions (i.e., information exchange), and arguing that the desired behavior benefits the counterpart (i.e., recommendations). Because both parties recognize the importance of win–win solutions, a promises strategy seems less likely to generate resentment, backlash, or pressure, as it often does in more conventional channel relationships.

Most available, systematic evidence thus suggests that more subtle influence strategies improve interpersonal relationship quality, whereas overt influence strategies risk resentment. But a caveat is in order here: This evidence comes mainly from Western business cultures. We must exercise caution before extrapolating this evidence to other settings. Overt efforts to influence distributors by employing threats and citing contracts may damage relationships in North America, but in Japan, such techniques could *improve* the interpersonal quality of working relationships between distributors and suppliers. This is not to say Japanese distributors welcome threats. Rather, what may be perceived as menacing in a Western context instead can represent an appropriate exercise of authority in Japan, based on a supplier's prestige in the channel. This status often confers an inherent right to demand some degree of obedience.[54] In other words, coercive power in one culture may be legitimate power in another. Although perceptions of power bases thus are likely to be culture specific, evidence describing these differences remains regrettably sparse.

## Framing Influence Strategies

What you present may be less important than how you present it. That is, considerable evidence affirms the strong influence of **framing effects** in channels.[55] Imagine a distributor that is already carrying a supplier's line. The supplier decides to launch a major, risky, unproven new product and wants the distributor to agree to carry it. How should the supplier influencer frame this message for its target distributor? Frames can be defined according to two main dimensions: their valence and their contingency.

The **valence** of a frame refers to whether it gets presented as a positive or a negative:

- Positive frame: If you take on our new product, you will get substantial additional marketing support.
- Negative frame: If you don't take on our new product, you won't get substantial additional marketing support.

Both statements say the same thing, namely, that the new product will be accompanied by additional marketing support. But the positive frame is more effective, because the negative frame focuses the target on what sounds like a loss. It is a human tendency to feel threatened by losses (we dread loss far more than we value gains). Thus, negative framing makes decision makers feel pressured, damages their satisfaction and trust, and threatens their autonomy.

In addition to this presentation choice, influencers must decide whether their influence attempt will depend on certain conditions, such that the frame might be **contingent** or **noncontingent**:

- Contingent: If you take on our new product, we will give you our distributor-of-the-year award.
- Noncontingent: Congratulations, you've been named our distributor of the year! Oh and by the way, we also have a new product to propose for you to carry.

Unsurprisingly, targets are more satisfied and trusting, and believe their autonomy is better respected, when the influencer uses noncontingent appeals. More surprisingly, contingent framing also can undermine the force of the appeal. If a target can be persuaded *without* the contingency, the contingent framing leads the target to believe it has complied only because of the contingency. At the extreme, this target might even feel bribed, pressured, or purchased, leading to reduced intrinsic motivation to comply for its own reasons. In contrast, if the framing features no contingency, the target likely explains its compliance by reasoning, "This is what we wanted to do. This choice and this relationship makes sense for us."

For practitioners, the implications are clear: *Train boundary spanners to use positive frames, and don't offer a contingent argument when a noncontingent argument will do.*

These framing effects have the greatest impact when the influencer initially approaches the target. As the performance outcomes of influence attempts become clear, they override initial framing effects. For example, if the distributor finds that the newly introduced line has been performing well for five years, it probably forgets all about any uses of negative frames or contingent appeals. And if the line performs poorly, positive frames and noncontingent appeals cannot stop recriminations.

## SUMMARY: MANAGING CHANNEL POWER

Channel power is the ability to alter another organization's behavior. It is a tool that is not inherently good or bad. And it is necessary. The best choice for the marketing channel is not necessarily in the interest of every channel member, so power enables channels to realize their potential to add value. Like any tool, power must be used judiciously, which means sharing rewards equitably with channel members, even those in weak positions.

One way to think about power is to conceptualize the power of A as equal to the dependence of B. In turn, B's dependence on A is high when B derives great utility from dealing with A and cannot obtain the same utility easily from one of A's competitors, whether because they do not exist or because B would confront high switching costs if it left A. Thinking of power as dependence reemphasizes the issue of replaceability, which is critical to power.

Power can also be conceptualized as a result of five power sources. Reward power is the ability to deliver new benefits in return for specific behaviors. This natural, effective means of exerting power works well because it is frequently unobtrusive. Targets respond to economic incentives, with little awareness that they are altering their behavior to fit the influencer's preferences. Coercive power is the ability to impose punishment. It works well in the short term and can be addictive, such that it escalates through reciprocation. In the long run, in Western business cultures, coercion is corrosive, though it may be justified in the short term to induce a major change to benefit all parties. But unless this benefit is apparent, coercive tactics damage even the most successful relationships. Expert power accrues to a party that holds valuable information. It is an extremely effective mechanism in channels, though it is difficult to implement. Legitimate power comes from laws, contracts, and agreements, as well as from industry norms or norms and values specific to a particular channel relationship. Finally, referent power results from a channel member's desire to identify with another organization, often to borrow its prestige. The five bases of power also can have synergistic effects when used together skillfully.

Power is a two-sided affair; dependence operates in both directions. When B depends on A, A nearly always depends on B, at least to some extent. Mutually dependent relationships can generate exceptional value added, because each side has some leverage to influence the other to develop win–win solutions. This two-sided dependence also can be imbalanced, and the imbalance tends to be uncomfortable, in that the stronger party can readily exploit or ignore the weaker one. The more dependent party thus can take countermeasures, such as diversifying, forming a coalition to pressure the powerful member, or exiting the business. Yet imbalanced relationships are very common and can function quite well, as long as there is some restraint exhibited by the stronger party. It must not only to act equitably but be perceived as a fair player.

Translating power, a latent ability, into influence demands communication—otherwise known as influence strategies. Three communication methods (promises, legalisms, and threats) are fairly obtrusive. In Western cultures, they often provoke resentment and conflict (though they may be less problematic in other business environments). Of these three obtrusive methods, the effective tactic of making promises (offering rewards for desired behavior) is a staple of strong, long-term relationships. Three other communication tactics are less obtrusive: making requests for no stated reason, exchanging information, and making recommendations. These strategies are more subtle (in some cases, too subtle) and do not explicitly invoke the influencer's desires or interests, which may be why they are perceived as less pressuring. Their effectiveness is heightened by their unobtrusive nature.

Finally, in the short term, negative or contingent framing is usually inferior to positive or noncontingent framing. In the long run, performance outcomes override these effects though.

Power permeates all aspects of marketing channels, and its use is critical to effective channel management. The interdependence of channel members makes power a critical feature of their functioning. Channel members must invest to build power. They also must assess power accurately and use it wisely, both to carry out their initiatives and to protect themselves. To ignore considerations of power is to sacrifice opportunities and suffer vulnerabilities.

## TAKE-AWAYS

- Channel power is the ability to alter another organization's behavior. It is a tool, neither good nor bad.
- Power permeates all aspects of marketing channels. The interdependence of channel members makes power a critical feature of their functioning.
- Channel members must invest over time to build power, then assess their power accurately and use it wisely, whether to achieve their own initiatives or to protect themselves from others' influence attempts.
- The power of A is equal to the dependence of B. The dependence of B increases when
  - B derives great utility from dealing with A.
  - B cannot find that utility easily among A's competitors, because there are few competitors, or B faces very high switching costs.
- Power comes from five sources:
  - Reward
  - Coercive
  - Expert
  - Legitimate
  - Referent
- Power is a two-sided affair, specific to each relationship at any given time.
  Any assessment of power must consider the countervailing power of the other side. The best indicator of power is the net dependence of the two sides.
- Mutually dependent relationships often generate exceptional value added, because each side has sufficient leverage to ensure win–win solutions.

- Imbalanced dependence is very common. In these relationships,
  - The stronger party can exploit or ignore the weaker one.
  - The weaker party can take countermeasures, including diversifying, forming a coalition, or exiting the business.
  - Channel success requires the stronger party to exhibit restraint, act equitably, and appear fair.
- Translating power, a latent ability, into influence involves communication (influence strategies).
  - Three communication methods (promises, legalisms, and threats) are obtrusive and can provoke resentment and conflict.
  - Three communication methods are less obtrusive (requests, information exchange, and recommendations).
  - The most common (and effective) methods are making promises, making requests, exchanging information, and making recommendations.
- In the short term, negative frames (losses) and contingent frames (if–then) are usually inferior to positive and noncontingent frames. In the long run, performance outcomes make these effects less significant.

## Endnotes

1. Hotopf, Max (2002), "Tackling the Real Issues," *Routes to Market* (Summer), p. 10.
2. Deleersnyder, Barbara, Inge Geyskens, Katrijn Gielens, and Marnik G. Dekimpe (2002), "How Cannibalistic Is the Internet Channel? A Study of the Newspaper Industry in the United Kingdom and the Netherlands," *International Journal of Research in Marketing* 19, no. 3, pp. 337–348; Geyskens, Inge, Katrijn Gielens, and Marnik G. Dekimpe (2002), "The Market Value of Internet Channel Additions," *Journal of Marketing* 66, no. 2, pp. 102–119.
3. Jeuland, Abel P. and Steven M. Shugan (1983), "Managing Channel Profits," *Marketing Science* 2, no. 3, pp. 239–272.
4. Kai, Gangshu, Yue Dai, and Sean Zhou (2012), "Exclusive Channels and Revenue Sharing in a Complementary Goods Market," *Marketing Science* 31 (January–February), pp. 172–187.
5. Brown, James R., Jean L. Johnson, and Harold F. Koenig (1995), "Measuring the Sources of Marketing Channel Power: A Comparison of Alternative Approaches," *International Journal of Research in Marketing* 12, no. 2, pp. 333–354.
6. French, John R., Jr. and Bertram Raven (1959), "The Bases of Social Power" in Dorwin Cartwright, ed., *Studies in Social Power* (Ann Arbor, MI: University of Michigan), pp. 150–167.
7. Narus, James A. and James C. Anderson (1988), "Strengthen Distributor Performance Through Channel Positioning," *Sloan Management Review* 29, no. 4, pp. 31–40.
8. Mentzer, John T., Daniel J. Flint, G. Tomas, and M. Hult (2001), "Logistics Service Quality as a Segment-Customized Process," *Journal of Marketing* 65, no. 4, pp. 82–104.
9. Chu, Wujin (1992), "Demand Signalling and Screening in Channels of Distribution," *Marketing Science* 11, no. 3, pp. 327–347; Bloom, Paul N., Gregory T. Gundlach, and Joseph P. Cannon (2000), "Slotting Allowances and Fees: School of Thought and the Views of Practicing Managers," *Journal of Marketing* 64, no. 2, pp. 92–108.
10. Rao, Akshay R. and Humaira Mahi (2003), "The Price of Launching a New Product: Empirical Evidence on Factors Affecting the Relative Magnitude of Slotting Allowances," *Marketing Science* 22, no. 2, pp. 246–268.
11. Zimmerman, Ann (2003), "To Sell Goods to Wal-Mart, Get on the Net," *The Wall Street Journal* (November 21), pp. 1–2.
12. Gaski, John F. and John R. Nevin (1985), "The Differential Effects of Exercised and

Unexercised Power Sources in a Marketing Channel," *Journal of Marketing Research* 22 (May), pp. 130–142.

13. Munson, Charles L., Meir J. Rosenblatt, and Zehava Rosenblatt (1999), "The Use and Abuse of Power in Supply Chains," *Business Horizons* 30 (January–February), pp. 55–65. This article gives many examples of channel power in operation.

14. Geyskens, Inge, Jan-Benedict E.M. Steenkamp, and Nirmalya Kumar (1999), "A Meta-Analysis of Satisfaction in Marketing Channel Relationships," *Journal of Marketing Research* 36 (May), pp. 223–238.

15. Geyskens, Inge, Jan-Benedict E.M. Steenkamp, and Nirmalya Kumar (1998), "Generalizations About Trust in Marketing Channel Relationships Using Meta Analysis," *International Journal of Research in Marketing* 15, no. 1, pp. 223–248.

16. Munson, Rosenblatt, and Rosenblatt (1999), op. cit.

17. Hart, Paul and Carol Saunders (1997), "Power and Trust: Critical Factors in the Adoption and Use of Electronic Data Interchange," *Organization Science* 8 (January–February), pp. 23–42.

18. Anderson, Philip, and Erin Anderson (2002), "The New E-Commerce Intermediaries," *Sloan Management Review* 43 (Summer), pp. 53–62.

19. Prahalad, C.K. and Allen Hammond (2002), "Serving the World's Poor Profitably," *Harvard Business Review* 9, pp. 49–57.

20. Luhnow, David (2005), "In Mexico, Maker of Generics Adds Spice to Drug Business," *The Wall Street Journal*, February 22, pp. A1, A6.

21. Rosencher, Anne (2004), "Le Client Mystère, Ou l'Art d'Espionner Ses Point de Vente," *Capital* (November), pp. 124–126.

22. Raven, Bertram H. and Arie W. Kruglanski (1970), "Conflict and Power," in P. Swingle, ed., *The Structure of Conflict* (New York: Academic Press), pp. 69–99.

23. Anderson, Erin and Barton Weitz (1989), "Determinants of Continuity in Conventional Channel Dyads," *Marketing Science* 8 (Fall), pp. 310–323.

24. Anderson, Erin and Barton Weitz (1992), "The Use of Pledges to Build and Sustain Commitment in Distribution Channels," *Journal of Marketing Research* 24 (February), pp. 18–34.

25. Macneil, Ian R. (1980), *The New Social Contract: An Inquiry into Modern Contractual Relations* (New Haven, CT: Yale University Press); Kaufmann, Patrick J. and Louis W. Stern (1988), "Relational Exchange Norms, Perceptions of Unfairness, and Retained Hostility in Commercial Litigation," *Journal of Conflict Resolution* 32 (September), pp. 534–552.

26. Antia, Kersi D. and Gary L. Frazier (2001), "The Severity of Contract Enforcement in Interfirm Channel Relationships," *Journal of Marketing* 65, no. 4, pp. 67–81.

27. Heide, Jan B. and George John (1992), "Do Norms Matter in Marketing Relationships?" *Journal of Marketing* 56 (April), pp. 32–44.

28. Chu, Wujin and Woosik Chu (1994), "Signaling Quality By Selling Through a Reputable Retailer: An Example of Renting the Reputation of Another Agent," *Marketing Science* 13 (Spring), pp. 177–189.

29. Bouillin, Arnaud (2001), "Gore-Tex ou l'Art de se Rendre Indispensable," *Management* (October), pp. 30–32.

30. Lippman, Steven and Richard R. Rumelt (1982), "Uncertain Imitability: An Analysis of Interfirm Differences in Efficiency Under Competition," *Bell Journal of Economics* 13, no. 1, pp. 418–438.

31. Emerson, Richard M. (1962), "Power-Dependence Relations," *American Sociological Review* 27 (February), pp. 31–41.

32. Report on retailing in Malaysia, see www.euromonitor.com/retailing-in-malaysia/report.

33. Kale, Sudhir H. (1986), "Dealer Perceptions of Manufacturer Power and Influence Strategies in a Developing Country," *Journal of Marketing Research* 23 (November), pp. 387–393.

34. Frazier, Gary L. (1983), "On the Measurement of Interfirm Power in Channels of Distribution," *Journal of Marketing Research* 20 (May), pp. 158–166.

35. Frazier, Gary L., James D. Gill, and Sudhir H. Kale (1989), "Dealer Dependence Levels and Reciprocal Actions in a Channel of Distribution in a Developing Country," *Journal of Marketing* 53 (January), pp. 50–69.

36. Lusch, Robert F. and James R. Brown (1996), "Interdependency, Contracting, and Relational Behavior in Marketing Channels," *Journal of Marketing* 60 (October), pp. 19–38.

37. Hallén, Lars, Jan Johanson, and Nazeem Seyed-Mohamed (1991), "Interfirm Adaptation in Business Relationships," *Journal of Marketing* 55 (April), pp. 29–37.

38. Heide, Jan B. (1994), "Interorganizational Governance in Marketing Channels," *Journal of Marketing* 58 (January), pp. 71–85.

39. Palmatier, Robert W., Rajiv P. Dant, and Dhruv Grewal (2007), "A Comparative Longitudinal Analysis of Theoretical Perspectives of Interorganizational Relationship Performance," *Journal of Marketing* 71 (October), pp. 172–194.

40. Provan, Keith G. and Steven J. Skinner (1989), "Interorganizational Dependence and Control as Predictors of Opportunism in Dealer-Supplier Relations," *Academy of Management Journal* 32 (March), pp. 202–212.

41. Ross, William T., Erin Anderson, and Barton Weitz (1997), "Performance in Principal-Agent Dyads: The Causes and Consequences of Perceived Asymmetry of Commitment to the Relationship," *Management Science* 43 (May), pp. 680–704.

42. Kumar, Nirmalya, Lisa K. Scheer, and Jan-Benedict E.M. Steenkamp (1994), "The Effects of Perceived Interdependence on Dealer Attitudes," *Journal of Marketing Research* 32 (August), pp. 348–356.

43. Heide, Jan B. and George John (1988), "The Role of Dependence Balancing in Safeguarding Transaction-Specific Assets in Conventional Channels," *Journal of Marketing* 52 (January), pp. 20–35.

44. Taylor, Alex (2002), "Finally GM Is Looking Good," *Fortune* (April 1), pp. 42–46.

45. Geylani, Tansev, Anthony J. Dukes, and Kannan Srinivasan (2007), "Strategic Manufacturer Response to a Dominant Retailer," *Marketing Science* 26 (March–April), 164–178.

46. Subramani, Mani R. and N. Venkatraman (2003), "Safeguarding Investments in Asymmetric Interorganizational Relationships: Theory and Evidence," *Academy of Management Journal* 46, no. 1, pp. 46–62.

47. An excellent discussion of this trend and its implications appears in Fein, Adam J. and Sandy D. Jap (1999), "Manage Consolidation in the Distribution Channel," *Sloan Management Review* 41 (Fall), pp. 61–72.

48. Kumar, Nirmalya, Lisa K. Scheer, and Jan-Benedict E.M. Steenkamp (1995), "The Effects of Supplier Fairness on Vulnerable Resellers," *Journal of Marketing Research* 32 (February), pp. 54–65.

49. Gaski and Nevin (1985), op. cit.

50. This discussion is based on Frazier, Gary L. and John O. Summers (1986), "Perceptions of Interfirm Power and Its Use Within a Franchise Channel of Distribution," *Journal of Marketing Research* 23 (May), pp. 169–176.

51. Geyskens, Steenkamp, and Kumar (1999), op. cit.

52. Frazier, Gary L. and John O. Summers (1984), "Interfirm Influence Strategies and Their Application within Distribution Channels," *Journal of Marketing* 48 (Summer), pp. 43–55.

53. Boyle, Brett, F. Robert Dwyer, Robert A. Robicheaux, and James T. Simpson (1992), "Influence Strategies in Marketing Channels: Measures and Use in Different Relationship Structures," *Journal of Marketing Research* 29 (November), pp. 462–473.

54. Johnson, Jean L., Tomoaki Sakano, Joseph A. Cote, and Naoto Onzo (1993), "The Exercise of Interfirm Power and its Repercussions in U.S.-Japanese Channel Relationships," *Journal of Marketing* 57 (April), pp. 1–10.

55. This discussion is based on Scheer, Lisa K. and Louis W. Stern (1992), "The Effect of Influence Type and Performance Outcomes on Attitude Toward the Influencer," *Journal of Marketing Research* 29 (February), pp. 128–142.

# CHAPTER 11

# Managing Channel Conflict

**LEARNING OBJECTIVES**

**After reading this chapter, you should be able to:**

- Measure conflict according to whether the relevant issues are frequent, intense, and important.
- Describe the negative effects of high conflict on channel performance but also identify circumstances in which conflict is neutral or even positive.
- Outline inherent sources of conflict in channel relationships and define its three main causes: goals, perceptions, and domains.
- Recognize why multiple channels represent the norm and describe ways to address the conflict they create.
- Explain why many suppliers like gray markets (while protesting the contrary).
- Describe the spiral of coercion and reciprocation to predict outcomes of destructive acts and suggest ways to reduce their impact.
- Understand the institutionalized mechanisms that managers can use to reduce conflict, including those that management can decree and those that naturally arise in a relationship.
- Categorize conflict resolution styles and describe their effects on channel functions.
- Detail the effects of economic incentives on conflict.

## THE NATURE OF CHANNEL CONFLICT

Channel conflict is a state of opposition, or discord, among organizations in a marketing channel. It may seem curious that such conflict is a normal state; in individual, personal relationships, conflict is almost invariably viewed as something to avoid or a sign of trouble. But for the purposes of managing marketing channels, conventional, one-sided interpretations of **conflict** must be set aside, because to maximize channel performance, a certain amount of conflict is desirable.

The word "conflict" derives from the Latin *confligere*, to collide. In this everyday meaning, it offers little that could be considered constructive. Rather, it prompts mostly negative connotations, with emotionally fraught synonyms such as contention, disunity, disharmony, argument, friction, hostility, antagonism, struggle, and battle. But conflict between and among the organizations that comprise a channel should be considered in a more neutral light. Conflict per se is not negative in distribution channels. Rather than disuniting or antagonizing channel members, some conflict, in some forms, actually strengthens and improves the channel—as long as the channel manager deals with it effectively and appropriately.

With this chapter, we therefore specify a definition of **channel conflict** as behavior by a channel member that is in opposition to the wishes or behaviors of its channel counterpart. Through opponent-centered, direct effort, the channel actor seeks a goal or object that its counterpart currently controls. Accordingly, channel conflict arises when one member of a channel views its upstream or downstream partner as an **adversary** or opponent. These interdependent parties, at different levels of the same channel (upstream and downstream) contest each other for control. In contrast, **competition** refers to behavior in which a channel member seeks to attain a goal or object controlled by an external third party, such as regulators or competitors. Whereas competitors struggle against obstacles in their environment, parties in conflict struggle against each other for control.[1]

## Types of Conflict

Conflict implies incompatibility at some level. It frequently exists at such a low level, due mainly to the surrounding conditions, that channel members do not even fully sense it. Such **latent conflict** is a norm in most marketing channels, in which the interests of channel members inevitably collide as the parties pursue their separate goals, strive to retain their autonomy, and compete for limited resources. If each player could ignore the others, latent conflict would disappear. But companies linked in a channel are fundamentally interdependent.[2] Every member needs all other members to meet end-users' service output demands economically.

This fundamental interdependence is taken for granted in marketing channels. Because the organizations in these channels thus face constant conflicts, they lack the time or capacity to deal with each one explicitly. Instead, they focus on a few latent conflicts at any one time,[3] while overlooking others. Although this strategic choice enables the firms to function more efficiently on a day-to-day basis, their failure to account for latent conflict may become a problem if they develop new channel initiatives that transform the latent conflict into active opposition from channel partners.

In contrast with the latent form, **perceived conflict** arises as soon as a channel member senses opposition of any kind: of viewpoints, of perceptions, of sentiments, of interests, or of intentions. Perceived conflict is cognitive, emotionless, and mental, resulting simply from the recognition of a contentious situation. Thus, even if two organizations perceive their disagreement, their individual members likely experience little emotion or frustration. They describe themselves as "businesslike" or "professional" and consider their differences "all in a day's work." This scenario also describes a normal (and often preferable) state in marketing channels, with little cause for alarm. These members might not even describe their dealings as conflict laden, despite their opposition to each other on important issues.

When emotions enter the picture though, the channel experiences **felt (or affective) conflict**. The reasons that this type of conflict arises can vary, but the outcomes are similar: Individual players start mentioning conflict in the channel, as a result of the negative emotions they experience, including tension, anxiety, anger, frustration, and hostility. Organizational members personalize their differences, such that their descriptions of their business interactions begin to sound like interpersonal disputes (i.e., "That company is so rude! It doesn't even care how I feel about things"). Economic considerations fade into the background, and the antagonists impute human features and personal motives to their channel partners. If feelings of outrage and unfairness reach a breaking point, boundary spanners and their managers even might refuse economically sensible choices, harming their own organizations in their efforts to "punish" their channel counterparts.[4]

If left unmanaged, felt conflict thus can escalate quickly into **manifest conflict**. This opposition is expressed visibly through behaviors, such as blocking each other's initiatives or goal achievement and withdrawing support. In the worst cases, one side tries to sabotage the other or take revenge.

Across these types, conflict is often imagined as a state, such that we might assess the level of conflict in a channel relationship, like taking a photograph. But conflict is also a process, like filming a movie: It consists of episodes and incidents, and the interpretation of each episode by each party depends on its experience with previous episodes. When felt and manifest conflict is substantial or frequent in a channel, the "movie" is like a gangster flick: Each new conflict incident gets seen in the worst light, with malevolent motives attributed to the channel counterpart, greater weight attached to each incident, and strong convictions that the channel adversary is incompetent, dishonest, and so forth. Conversely, a positive history is like a lighthearted comedy, creating a positive view that downplays new conflict incidents or laughs at the honest mistakes.

## Measuring Conflict

The true level of conflict in a channel relationship depends on four elements. Here, we present those elements as a hypothetical assessment of how much conflict automobile dealers experience in their relationships with car manufacturers.[5]

**Step 1: Count the issues.**   Which issues are of relevance to the two parties in the channel relationship? For car dealers, there are 15 relevant issues in their relationships with manufacturers, such as inventories (vehicles and parts), allocation and delivery of cars, dealer staff size, advertising, allowances, reimbursement for warranty work, and so forth. It does not matter whether the issues are in dispute at any particular moment; the count must include all major aspects of the channel relationship.

**Step 2: Assess importance.**   For each issue, some measure must exist to ascertain how important it is to the dealer. For example, dealers might indicate, on a 0–10 scale (very unimportant to very important), how important they consider each issue to their profitability.

**Step 3: Determine disagreement frequency.**   How often do the two parties disagree about each issue? Dealers could be asked to recall their discussions with the manufacturer about each issue during the past year and indicate, on a 0–10 scale (never to always), how frequently those discussions involved disagreement.

**Step 4: Measure dispute intensity.** For each issue, how far apart are the two parties' positions? Using another 0–10 scale (not very intense to very intense), dealers can indicate how strongly they disagree during a typical discussion with their dealer about each issue.

These four pieces of information then combine to form an **index of manifest conflict:**

$$\text{Conflict} = \sum_{i=1}^{N} \text{Importance}_i \times \text{Frequency}_i \times \text{Intensity}_i$$

That is, for each issue $i$, we multiply its importance, frequency, and intensity, then add the values for all $N$ issues (for car dealers, $N = 15$), to form an index of conflict. A manufacturer then might compare these estimates across dealers to locate the site of the most serious conflict.

This simple formula also offers a profound insight into channels: No real argument exists over any issue if it

- Is petty (low importance),
- Rarely sparks a difference of opinion (low frequency), and
- Does not create substantial distance between the two parties (low intensity).

If *any* of these elements is low, the issue is *not* a genuine source of conflict (i.e., multiplying by 0 creates a product of 0). Parties to a conflict often can become so emotional that they forget this simple rule. But if allowances are a minor issue, the dealer's and manufacturer's positions about car allowances are not far apart, or allowances seldom come up as topics of discussion, there is little need for concern—even if it might seem so during the height of a heated discussion about allowances.

This conflict formula effectively captures the overall sense of frustration in a channel relationship. Thus, relationship diagnosticians can use it to pinpoint where and why parties have come into opposition, especially when the combatants themselves are unable to identify the sources of their friction. Particularly in conflict-laden channels, the parties involved often become polarized and sense that they disagree more than they really do, because their high running emotions cause them to double count issues, overlook points on which they agree, or exaggerate the importance, intensity, and frequency of their differences. A third party can help them locate the true sources of their disagreement, which is a first step to finding a solution.

## CONSEQUENCES OF CONFLICT

### Functional Conflict: Improving Channel Performance

Despite a widespread (and sometimes accurate) view of conflict as dysfunctional, such that it harms relationship coordination and performance, on some occasions, opposition actually makes a relationship better. **Functional conflict** implies that members recognize each other's contributions and understand that their success depends on others, so they can oppose each other without damaging their arrangement. As a result of their opposition, they

1. Communicate more frequently and effectively.
2. Establish outlets for expressing their grievances.
3. Critically review their past actions.
4. Devise and implement a more equitable split of system resources.
5. Develop a more balanced distribution of power in their relationship.
6. Develop standardized ways to deal with future conflict and keep it within reasonable bounds.[6]

Overall, conflict is functional when it drives channel members to improve their performance. By raising and working through their differences, they push each other to do better and break old habits and assumptions, as Sidebar 11-1 describes.

In principle, all channel conflict should be functional. In practice, it is not. So we must ask: *What makes conflict functional?*[7]

From a downstream channel member's viewpoint, functional conflict is a natural outcome of close cooperation with the supplier. Cooperative relationships are noisy and contentious, because working together to coordinate inevitably generates disputes. But as long as channel members are committed, the resulting conflict should be tolerated, and even welcomed as normal, because it can improve performance in the short term and is unlikely to damage the level of trust in the relationship in the long term, especially if the downstream channel member has considerable influence over the supplier. An influential channel member is a **disputatious** one—willing to give and take to push channel performance.

## Sidebar 11-1

### Functional conflict in plumbing and heating supplies

The use of cooperative (co-op) advertising money has been marked by a long history of conflict. In co-op advertising programs, suppliers share the cost of local advertising by downstream channel members when it features the supplier's products. In principle, co-op advertising is in the interest of both parties and effectively builds partnerships. In practice, it is a source of considerable conflict. Resellers accuse suppliers of exercising too many bureaucratic controls over their ads, delaying payments of co-op funds, and finding pretexts to refuse to pay at all. Suppliers accuse downstream channel members of diverting co-op money to other purposes, running poor ad campaigns, and featuring their products together with those of competitors.

In the plumbing and heating supplies industry, some channel partners thus have sought creative new approaches to joint advertising. Wholesalers have created their own internal advertising staff to increase their promotion competence. Suppliers have revisited their procedures to devise streamlined approval and reimbursement policies, remove hurdles to reimbursement, eliminate bureaucratic rules, and signal their willingness to trust and collaborate with channel partners to run joint campaigns.

Other suppliers copy techniques from other industries, such as building a predefined co-op allowance into their wholesale prices. This sum (e.g., $2 on a $122 faucet) gets tracked and set aside as co-op money. If the distributor runs a sufficiently large campaign by a fixed date, it collects the fund; otherwise, it reverts to the supplier. Proctor & Gamble uses a similar method to sell fast-moving consumer goods. The very existence of the fund pressures distributors to advertise (to avoid "losing" their "advance") and puts pressure on the supplier to be flexible (to avoid appearing as though its has appropriated money for which it is the custodian).[8]

In contrast, suppliers that prefer to find weaker channel members they can domi-nate might enter into relationships that appear harmonious but that never quite real-ize their full potential. Harmonious, peaceful channels also might arise when channel members express little opposition, mostly because of their general **indifference**. The two parties do not bother to disagree about anything. There is no issue about which they have a strong opinion, which is really important to them, and which they care to invest the effort to argue about. These two sides are not in agreement; they simply don't disagree—because they don't care. Consider, for example, a downstream chan-nel member that partners with so many principals that it simply cannot pay atten-tion to all of them. In this case, the harmonious channel signals neglect, and such neglect frequently is mutual. The relationships exist on paper (and may entail some transactions), but the parties never really engage, whether in conflict or in coopera-tion. Regardless of the reason for their existence, these harmonious channels need to increase their activity and communication levels to improve their performance, and such steps will, happily, increase their conflict.

Said in another way, channel performance depends on communication and cooperation among channel members, which means that inevitably they will discover points of opposition and perceive more conflict. Managed properly, these emerging disagreements can be channeled into constructive conflict. Even if perceived conflict becomes felt (i.e., emotions get aroused), channel members may prod their partners to achieve better results, through functional conflict. Only when conflict escalates into substantial manifest conflict does it create tension and frustration, in which case managers must step in to keep it from damaging or ultimately destroying the channel.

## Manifest Conflict: Reducing Channel Performance

If some channel friction is mundane, then we should just accept it as inevitable and dismiss it as normal, right? Not quite. High channel friction still creates costs. Substantial field research documents the outcomes of literally thousands of channel relationships in developed, mostly Western, economies.[9] The distillation of that research indicates that constantly high levels of manifest conflict reduce an organization's satisfaction and damage the channel's long-term ability to function as a close partnership. These findings imply that channel partners cannot focus just on their share of the overall pie; they also need to enhance cooperation while simultaneously seeking to reduce the conflict their cooperation might induce, to increase the size of the overall pie that the parties share.[10]

Consider a focal firm in a channel that encounters higher levels of tension, frus-tration, or disagreement in a channel relationship. Perceived conflict will increase, as will felt (affective) conflict and manifest conflict (blocking behaviors).

With these conflict increases, the focal firm derives less value from the channel, as well as less satisfaction from the business rewards (financial and strategic) that result from this relationship. Some decrease in satisfaction is objective: Profit indicators decline when conflict increases. But there is another element too, because in judging its satis-faction, the focal firm also includes its assessment of what it might expect to gain from alternative uses of its resources. Conflict may increase its anticipated disappointment by inflating the focal firm's belief that there are better alternatives available. Beyond these financial aspects, the focal firm's satisfaction with the psychological and social elements of its relationship declines as well.

It is tempting to disregard these "fuzzier" outcomes of conflict, because they do not translate easily into profit terms. But to the focal firm, interpersonal dissatisfaction is serious. It makes each workday less gratifying to the people involved, and it damages the solidarity of the relationship.

Unsatisfactory social relationships also diminish trust in the channel counterpart. **Trust** is a critical foundation for durable, well-coordinated relationships. A belief that the other party will act with fairness, honesty, and concern for well-being is essential to building committed relationships, in which the parties make sacrifices to build and maintain their channel. Conflict undermines this channel commitment by damaging a focal party's trust in its counterpart, in that not only does conflict directly shake the focal firm's confidence in its counterpart's benevolence and honesty, but it also reduces interpersonal satisfaction, which then delivers another blow to trust.

Intense conflict between two parties even can spill over into other relationships. When they are forced to engage in repeated conflict, parties might organize into coalitions, ready to take action in response to any new threat. We described just such a coalition in Chapter 10, when U.S. automotive dealers organized quickly to prevent General Motors from purchasing some of its own dealerships in the 1990s.[11] Such intense conflicts often lead the combatants to become so focused on their own interests that they forget to pursue improved channel performance.

Finally, conflict is costly, and some costs take years to emerge fully. Therefore, channel managers need to make careful calculations to determine if the costs of conflict are worth the benefits that the conflict might induce. For example, initiatives to change the way things are done in the channel will spark conflict and costs. But the benefits of this initiative might outweigh the costs of the conflict. Conflict does not always need to be minimized; rather, it inherently needs to be managed, such that each member of the channel rationally and realistically chooses to enter into a conflict, rather than being surprised to discover that its initiatives were not worth the costs of the opposition they created.

## MAJOR SOURCES OF CONFLICT IN CHANNELS

Most conflict is rooted in differences in (1) channel members' goals, (2) perceptions of reality, and (3) perceived domains, or areas in which they should be able to operate with autonomy. The last is the most complex of these three sources, because domain conflict comprises many subdimensions. For example, in the product market subdimension, we find that manufacturers today go to market through so many different routes that their channel partners are bound to compete for some of the same business. If the channels are redundant, competition over customers can quickly turn into conflict with the supplier. Other subdimensions include clashes over each party's role and sphere of influence. We therefore build up to this complex discussion and begin instead with one of the most intractable problems: clashing goals.

### Competing Goals

Each channel member has a set of **goals and objectives** that differ from the goals and objectives of other channel members. This built-in difference is fundamental to all businesses, not just channels. A notable theory, called agency theory, highlights the clash between the desires of the principal (who creates work) and the agent (to whom the principal delegates the work). The inherent difference in what they want to achieve and what they value causes principals to seek ways to monitor and motivate agents. **Agency theory** underscores how competing goals create conflict in any principal–agent relationship, regardless of the personalities of the players involved or the history of their relationship. Channel members who personalize conflicts and believe that a change of partner will solve their problems are thus likely to be sorely disappointed, because their fundamental goal conflict remains.[12]

The relationship between the athletic-wear manufacturer Nike and the retailer Foot Locker offers a good example of a generic and perennial form of goal conflict, in this case between suppliers and resellers. Foot Locker carries Nike products because it wants to maximize its own profits, whether by increasing unit sales, achieving higher gross margins per unit (i.e., paying Nike less while charging the customer more), decreasing inventory, reducing expenses, or receiving higher allowances from Nike. In contrast, Nike wants to maximize its own profits, so its preferences are nearly the reverse of the retailer's: It wants Foot Locker to increase unit sales, accept lower gross margins (i.e., pay it more while charging customers less), hold more inventory (to avoid stockouts and maximize selection), spend more to support the product line, and get by without allowances. The two parties' overall profit goals lead them to collide nearly every time they meet, on every objective except one, namely, to raise unit sales.

Figure 11-1 lists some frequent reasons for conflict, inherent to the division of labor upstream and downstream in a marketing channel.[13]

Surprisingly though, much of the tension, anxiety, and frustration in a channel results not from actual goal clashes but from the channel members' *perceptions* of goal divergence. The misperception that their goal incongruity is higher than it actually is continues to fuel conflict and leads to a remarkable practice by supposed channel partners: Salespeople and sales managers express more willingness to deceive distributors than to mislead customers or their own employers.[14]

## Differing Perceptions of Reality

Distinct **perceptions of reality** induce conflict, because they imply the likelihood of divergent responses to the same situation. As a general rule, channel members are confident that they know what's going on, but when they compare their perceptions with that of the others, the results are so different that it is difficult to believe they are members of the same channel. Perceptions differ markedly,[15] even in relation to seemingly basic questions such as follows:

- What are the attributes of the product/service?
- What applications does the product/service support, and for which segments?
- Who is the competition?

With divergence in such basic ideas, it is not surprising that channel members also disagree about more subjective, judgment-laden subjects, such as how readily a product or service can be sold, what added value each channel member offers, or how each side behaves. With inaccurate expectations about what other channel members are likely to do, our focal firm also will choose suboptimal strategies, which can heighten conflict further. Inaccurate expectations spark surprise and opposition when other parties "fail" to react as expected.[16]

| | **Supplier Viewpoint** | **Reseller Viewpoint** | **Expression of Clash** |
|---|---|---|---|
| **Financial Goals** | Maximize own profit by<br>• Higher prices to reseller<br>• Higher sales by reseller<br>• Higher reseller expenses<br>• Higher reseller inventory<br>• Lower allowances to reseller | Maximize own profit by<br>• Higher own-level margins (lower prices from our supplier and higher prices to our customer)<br>• Lower expenses (less support)<br>• Faster inventory turnover (lower reseller stocks)<br>• Higher allowances from manufacturers | *Supplier:* You don't put enough effort behind my brand. Your prices are too high.<br>*Reseller:* You don't support me enough. With your wholesale prices, we can't make money. |
| | **Focus on:** | **Focus on:** | |
| **Desired Target Accounts** | • Multiple segments<br>• Multiple markets<br>• Many accounts (raise volume and share) | • Segment corresponding to resellers' positioning (e.g., discounter)<br>• Our markets only<br>• Selected accounts (those that are profitable to serve) | *Supplier:* We need more coverage and more effort. Our reseller doesn't do enough for us.<br>*Reseller:* You don't respect our marketing strategy. We need to make money too. |
| **Desired Product and Accounts Policy** | • Concentrate on our product category and our brand<br>• Carry our full line (a variation for every conceivable need, plus our efforts to expand our line outside our traditional strengths) | • Achieve economies of scope over product categories<br>• Serve customers by offering brand assortment<br>• Do not carry inferior or slow-moving items (every supplier has some of these) | *Supplier:* You carry too many lines. You don't give us enough attention. You're disloyal.<br>*Reseller:* Our customers come first. If we satisfy our customers, you will benefit. By the way, shouldn't you consider pruning your product line? |

**FIGURE 11-1**    Natural sources of conflict: Inherent differences in viewpoints of suppliers and resellers

*Source:* Magrath, Allan J. and Kenneth G. Hardy (1989), "A Strategic Paradigm for Predicting Manufacturer-Reseller Conflict," *European Journal of Marketing* 23, no. 2, pp. 94–108.

Why are such misperceptions so common—and so serious? A major reason is **focus**. The supplier focuses on its product and its processes. The downstream channel member instead focuses on its functions and customers. These differences expose channel members to very different information and influences, such that they each start to build different segments of the overall puzzle.

Seldom do channel members cooperate enough to assemble the entire puzzle to develop a complete picture. But a lack of communication exacerbates the conflict that results from different perceptions of reality, whereas frequent, timely, and relevant communication at least can align—if not totally match up—perceptions and expectations.[17] When a top manager for Toyota invested the time and effort to visit U.S. dealers regularly and engage in conversations about problems district managers had failed to resolve for example, "I found out that out of ten complaints from each dealer, you could attribute about five or six to simple misunderstandings, another two or three could be solved on the spot, and only one or two needed further work."[18]

In domestic markets, channel members disagree in their views of the situation; the problem is exacerbated in international settings. In the clash of cultures, differences in perception and interpretations of the channel environment are prominent and frequent.[19] Regardless of the product or service sold, channel members experience substantial friction generated by members' culturally divergent ideas of what behavior is appropriate. Resolving this problem still requires communication, but cultural differences make such interactions more challenging. Despite the strong temptation to skip this time-consuming, expensive, and difficult form of communication, in practice, more frequent, thorough, candid, and detailed discussions involving more people who represent multiple cultures and both organizations can go a long way toward rectifying performance issues.

Another solution is to generate greater sensitivity to the business culture of the channel partner. Greater cultural sensitivity demands a foundation of respect for and understanding of the other culture's language, customs, values, attitudes, and beliefs. Channel members who slight another national culture or economize on communication pay a steep price: excessive conflict, with negative impacts on channel performance.

## Intrachannel Competition

From an upstream perspective, suppliers may sense conflict if their downstream partners represent their competitors—as they often do, so that they can provide a large assortment and exploit economies of scale by pooling demand for a class of products. Even though agents and resellers rely on this tactic to provide high coverage and lower prices, such **intrachannel competition** still can spark disputes, especially if the downstream agent appears insufficiently dedicated to meeting its responsibilities to the supplier.

More acrimonious disputes arise if the upstream party believes it has established an understanding to limit competition, on which its downstream partner is reneging. A California medical supply firm won almost $5 million in damages from one of its distributors when an arbitration panel found that the downstream member violated its contract by promoting a competitor's products.[20] However, a more common situation involves an "unspoken understanding" that cannot be proven but still can provoke conflict.

From the downstream perspective, intrachannel competition implies that the supplier relies on various direct competitors to sell its products to the market. We covered this situation, known as intensive distribution, in Chapter 5.

## Multiple Channels

A somewhat related but distinct source of conflict arises when multiple types of channels present the supplier's products to the same geographical market. There are many labels for this situation, including dual distribution (i.e., using both integrated and independent channels), plural distribution (using multiple types of channel members, such as discounters, sales agents, company salespeople, and value-added resellers, which may or may not be owned by the supplier), and hybrid distribution. The most accurate label though is **multiple channels**, which describes the use of more than one route (or channel member, whether integrated or independent) to get to the same market. (Using multiple channels is not the same as distributing intensively, because intensive distribution can be achieved by going through many channel entities, all of the same *type*. However, as we discuss later in this section, they create some similar threats.)

Multiple channels have always been common, but at one time, companies tended to use a single, primary route to market and turn to their other routes only as secondary, downplayed, or even disguised methods, to avert channel conflict and avoid confusing customers. For example, suppliers might quietly open their own sales and distribution organizations, competing directly but not obtrusively, with their own channel customers for end-users (dual distribution). But today, an explosion in the use of multiple channels has made them the norm rather than the exception.[21] Why? Heightened competition has driven many suppliers to change and expand their channels; fragmented markets make it harder to serve customers efficiently through only one channel type. In addition, whereas channels once had to remain simple, to facilitate their administration, technological advances have made it feasible to manage far more complex channel structures.

Moreover, suppliers and customers like multiple channels. For suppliers, they increase market penetration, giving the suppliers a better view of multiple markets, while also raising entry barriers to potential competitors. As their various channels compete, suppliers enjoy the benefits of this "healthy" competition. For customers, multiple channels increase the chances of finding one that meets their service output demands. Multiple-channel types also make it easier for customers to pit one channel against another when they seek more services at lower prices. Thus, multiple channels even make markets: Suppliers and customers can more easily find one another and fulfill their needs by using the most appropriate channel types.[22]

However, the dangers of multiple channels are similar to the dangers of intensive distribution: Downstream channel members may lose motivation and withhold support (a passive response), retaliate, or exit the supplier's channel structure (active responses). Such threats are particularly intense when customers can free-ride, gaining services from one channel but buying from another. By adding channel types, the supplier ironically may reduce, rather than increase, the breadth and vigor of its market representation.

Suppliers fail to anticipate this outcome because they think of their markets as distinct, well-behaved segments, in which a particular type of customer always wants to buy in one manner (e.g., convenient and cheap, with few services), while another type always prefers another manner (e.g., full support, after spending time negotiating and paying a higher price). Each segment calls for different service outputs and thus different channel types (in our examples, a discount catalogue and a value-added reseller, respectively). By offering these multiple channels, suppliers seemingly can better serve multiple segments, without the various channels ever really competing head to head.

That image may hold on a spreadsheet, where buyers can be neatly categorized and served by a single type of channel. But the strategy often collapses when it moves off the page, where customers can move about rather than sticking to their assigned categories. Customers love to free ride (e.g., get advice from the value-added reseller, and then order from the discount catalogue), especially business-to-business (B2B) customers that hire purchasing agents explicitly to find the maximum value at the lowest delivered price. Furthermore, the same customers often behave differently, depending on the *occasions* for their purchase of the same item.

However, four general types of environments usually can support multiple channels without increasing conflict to ruinous levels:[23]

- Growing markets, which offer opportunities to many players
- Markets in which customers perceive the product category as differentiated (so channel members can distinguish their offerings)
- Markets in which buyers' consistent purchasing style involves one type of channel member (so customers are less likely to seek competing channels)
- Markets undominated by buying groups

However, specifying the environment may not be sufficient to clearly establish the presence of multiple-channel conflict. That question demands more in-depth analysis.

**IDENTIFYING MULTIPLE-CHANNEL CONFLICT**   Multiple channels do not automatically compete. Channel members might believe they are serving the same customer, even if they are not. Coca-Cola thus faced strong opposition from retailers in Japan when it started installing vending machines, but through its market research, it ultimately was able to prove that consumers used vending machines for totally different occasions and obtained different value than provided by the retailers.[24]

Multiple channels can even help one another by building **primary demand** for the product category. A classic example is the combination of a store and a direct marketing operation (e.g., catalogue, website). Potential customers encounter the brand in both channels and thus can purchase as they wish. Some retailers use this synergy to explore markets: When catalogue sales in an area reach a certain level, they take it as a sign that it is time to open a store there. The accounting methods for these combinations are necessarily approximate though, in that the supplier cannot know for certain how many customers might try on clothing in the store, go home to think about it, and then order from a website or catalogue. In response, many combination sellers represent the same owner (e.g., Victoria's Secret for lingerie, Land's End for clothing), which hires a corporate accountant to allocate costs or revenues and a human resources manager to administer compensation—that is, to reduce channel conflict. When channels are independent, it is not as easy to settle disputes, and suppliers have not paid enough attention to mechanisms for compensating the victims of excessive channel conflict.

The identification of multiple-channel conflict also requires a clear recognition of the various benefits of multiple channels to the supplier. Better coverage is an obvious benefit; other motives, usually unspoken, also are based on the idea that one channel might help the supplier manage another. For example, many suppliers serve industrial customers by sending manufacturers' representatives, but in the same market, they might reserve some customers (house accounts) to be served only by company employees. This dual distribution (vertically integrated *and* outsourced) practice is so common that it rarely creates enough conflict to harm a channel relationship, especially when the selling task is (1) ambiguous, such that it would be difficult for the supplier to determine how well an external rep is really performing (performance ambiguity problem), or (2) complex, that is putting the salesperson in a position to learn so much about a particular sales task that she or he becomes too valuable to replace (lock-in problem). These circumstances increase the supplier's dependence on a rep but make it more difficult to identify poor performers. Thus, the integrated channel provides a partial solution: From its small, in-house sales force, the supplier learns more about the task, including appropriate performance benchmarks, and develops a credible threat to terminate the rep and bring the account in-house. In short, a second channel can be useful for learning and keeping options open.[25]

Recall a similar theme in Chapter 8: Having company outlets *and* franchised outlets helps a franchisor run its entire distribution program (indeed, its entire business) better.

**MANAGING MULTIPLE CHANNELS**   When they have identified the presence of conflict and determined whether it is threatening or not, suppliers also must consider what responsibility they have to protect their multiple channels from one another. Some suppliers assume no such responsibility and thus take no action; others question what action they possibly *could* take, even if they wanted to protect their channels. Actively trying to prevent one channel from competing with another (e.g., terminating discounters) can provoke legal action (see Chapter 13) and is often futile anyway. Suppliers that try to manage the problem by devising different pricing schemes for different channels also enter legally dubious territory, creating an opportunity for arbitrage (as we discuss in relation to gray markets in a subsequent section).

More proactive options include offering more support, more service, more products, or even different products to different channel types to help them differentiate themselves. In general, suppliers gain more cooperation from their multiple channels, in terms of pricing, stocking, and display, if they can supply differentiated product lines (from the end-user's perspective) to different groups of retailers.[26] To do so, they likely need to *reserve* higher-end models for one channel and the rest of the line for another.

A variation on this theme would be to offer essentially the same product under different brand names to different channels—a common strategy in automobile and appliance markets.[27] It is effective when buyers do not know the products are virtually identical, though the channels know, and they often share that information with customers. Third-party buying guides also point out that model X of brand Y is the same as model A of brand B. The strategy thus can be futile, unless both brands possess considerable brand equity.

At the extreme, differentiation through different brands or products in different channels no longer entails a multiple-channel strategy, such as when the supplier sells a "flagship" segment of its product line through one channel and provides secondary or peripheral products only in a separate channel. For example, in high-tech settings, some firms sell their major IT through distributors and everything else over the Internet. Customers thus can access anything the supplier makes, but most of the business goes to independent resellers. The supplier contents itself with product sales that do not interest this channel anyway.

Still, some channels demand **active intervention**. For example, durable products are distinctive in that they can be rented or sold, and then later resold by various members of the channel. In the 1990s, U.S. automakers needed a reason to keep their factories running, so they sold huge volumes of cars at ridiculously low prices to rental agencies—many of which were partially owned by the automakers. Nearly as soon as they had purchased the cars, these rental agencies began reselling the fleet, filling their parking lots with barely used cars for sale at very attractive prices. Of course, this newly introduced channel hurt auto dealers, and the resulting conflict was important, intense, and frequent enough to bring the issue into the court system. To lessen the conflict, several carmakers intervened by buying the gently used cars back from rental agencies and reselling them to dealers. This interventionist shift in inventory allowed carmakers to eat their cake and have it too, for a time. They maintained production volume and avoided a war between two important channels, but to the detriment of the channels, and ultimately themselves.[28]

## Unwanted Channels: Gray Markets

One of the most pressing issues for channel managers, especially in global markets, is the existence and persistence of gray markets.[29] **Gray marketing** is the sale of authorized, branded products through unauthorized distribution channels—usually bargain/discount outlets that provide less customer service than the authorized channels do. A great variety of products gets sold through gray markets, including watches, designer clothing, and other chic apparel items. Gray marketing can be contrasted with black marketing, or **counterfeiting**, which involves selling fake goods as branded ones. Counterfeiting remains illegal in almost all world markets; in contrast, gray marketing is in many cases completely legal.[30] Who supplies these unauthorized outlets? The usual suppliers are as follows:[31]

- Authorized distributors and dealers, often from other markets
- Professional arbitragers, including the following:
  - Import/export houses
  - Professional traders, who often live near borders and who buy huge amounts in one market with low prices and then transport them to another market where prices are high
- The ultimate source and "victim," namely, the supplier itself, through either its home office or its foreign divisions

But what motivates these more-or-less clandestine sources of supply and their customers, the gray marketers? Several factors create a ripe environment for gray markets. One is **differential pricing** to different channel members: One channel over-orders and to get a discount, then sells off the excess to unauthorized channels, at a nondiscounted price. Similarly, different prices charged in different geographic markets, whether because of taxation, exchange rate differences, or simply varying price sensitivities across regions, encourages gray markets to arise. For example, foreign companies producing and selling in the People's Republic of China (PRC) sometimes must compete for sales with smugglers who sell branded products that were exported out of China and then reimported, to avoid local taxes. The product is an authorized branded product, but it also has been illegally smuggled, because it avoids import taxes on its reentry into the PRC.

When domestic products are sold through high-service, high-price channels, an opportunity also arises to introduce gray marketed goods through discount retailers. For example, gray marketers regularly attempt to buy designer fashions in Louis

Vuitton and Chanel outlets in Europe, bring the goods back to Japan (legally), and then put them on sale in Japanese stores at a price lower than the prevailing retail prices in authorized outlets in Japan. An unaware shopper may be surprised to encounter the elaborate security measures and limitations on purchase volume used by Louis Vuitton's flagship store in Paris, which exist mainly to block gray marketers.

The development of emerging markets and the worldwide liberalization of trade also favor the growth of gray markets. These **economic fundamentals** create incentives for firms to capitalize on brand equity and volume potential by offering similar products across countries. However, with this strategy, the optimal prices naturally vary across countries, due to differences in exchange rates, purchasing power, and supply-side factors (e.g., distribution, servicing, taxes). The moment price differences arise between territories, substantial gains become available through arbitrage. Gray markets need not even involve cross-border trade though; they are also common in domestic markets in which suppliers want to keep their products out of certain channels (e.g., discount chains).

Purchasers gain value from the wider availability of gray goods (due to their lower prices), but other members of the channel may suffer from them. Manufacturers complain that gray goods impair their ability to charge different prices in different markets. If the service levels provided by gray market retailers are lower than those of authorized dealers, brand equity may suffer, which also is a serious concern for manufacturers. But perhaps the strongest complaints about the escalation of gray marketing come from authorized dealers. Gray markets unequivocally erode potential volume for authorized dealers and can place severe pressure on after-sales service functions. All in all then, when it is feasible to intercept and monitor gray goods, it seems to be in a producer's interest to do so.

Yet they persist—and even are growing in many settings. Gray markets seem particularly active in developed economies, such as the United States, Canada, and the European Union, where manufacturers have both the means and the legal framework to stop them. That is, despite manufacturers' legal recourse to limit the proliferation of gray goods, they rarely do so,[32] especially in the following circumstances:

- Violations are difficult to detect or document (e.g., in distant markets, when customers are geographically dispersed).
- The potential for one channel to free ride on another is low anyway (e.g., resellers provide little service or charge separately for services rendered).
- The product is more mature.
- The distributor supplying the gray market does not carry competing brands in the focal product category.

This last item may be the most surprising, because these distributors seemingly should be far more vulnerable to pressure applied by the supplier. But suppliers appear to indulge these distributors, because they perform well and exhibit a form of loyalty that is stronger than that displayed by a diversified distributor. By granting gray market distributors some market protection, the supplier can invoke a pledge of exclusive dealing in the category. In this mutual dependence scenario, the supplier may hesitate to alienate an important distributor, even a gray market one.

It thus appears that manufacturers weigh the (often high) costs and (sometimes low) benefits of enforcement action and simply *decide to look the other way*. They are particularly forgiving of channel members that have made a powerful pledge (exclusive dealing), and they seem philosophical about gray markets for maturing products, which already are subject to greater price competition.

Some indications even imply that some manufacturers could be *positively disposed* toward gray markets, which seemingly would require other incentives to be at work. Perhaps these markets help manufacturers increase their market coverage. For suppliers of mature products, gray markets also put implicit pressure on authorized channels to compete harder, and they make the product more widely available to a price-sensitive segment. Such suppliers could profit from tolerating gray markets—all the while publicly objecting to them—as long as their authorized channels do not cut back their own purchases or support in protest.

In this sense, gray markets might allow a supplier to serve two segments, even as it proclaims it is serving only one. The segment that visits traditional market resellers cares about the shopping experience (e.g., displays, atmosphere, sales help, seller's reputation) but is less concerned about price. The segment that shops in gray markets, in contrast, will buy anywhere and from anyone, as long as the price is low. The former, price-insensitive segment is the supplier's formal target; the latter, price-sensitive segment represents a surreptitious target that the supplier serves through gray markets, even as it maintains its more highbrow image to continue appealing to its primary target.

As a result, gray markets are a major cause of channel conflict, because both upstream and downstream channel members are of two minds about them. Suppliers bemoan them in public and encourage them in private. Downstream channel members protest their "unfair" competition even as they supply these markets with goods. Even if all channel members agreed that they really wanted to stop gray marketing, the many economic incentives achieved from selling through unauthorized outlets leaves sought-after products almost invariably subject to some gray market activity, because enforcement is not easy. It thus is little wonder that gray markets remain so common and cause so much channel conflict.

## MINIMIZING THE (NEGATIVE) EFFECTS OF CHANNEL CONFLICT

A recurring theme of this chapter is that channel conflict should be managed, to ensure it is not excessive and primarily functional. To do so, channel managers need an ability to predict which circumstances tend to fuel conflict and a recognition of what they can do to stay out of the high-conflict zone.

An excellent predictor of how much channel members will dispute in the future is how much conflict they have experienced in the past. **Conflict creates conflict**. Conflict proliferates because once a relationship has experienced high levels of tension and frustration, the players find it very difficult to set their acrimonious history aside and move on. Each party questions whether the other is capable of committing to the relationship.[33] It discounts positive behaviors and accentuates negative behaviors, such that the foundations of trust get thoroughly eroded by the high levels of conflict.

Field experience indicates that strong, sustained conflict also is extremely difficult to overcome. Even if individual personnel move on, organization memory persists in sensing acrimony, such that the firm withholds its full support from the channel, in anticipation that the other party will not commit, which creates a self-fulfilling prophecy when the other side reciprocates.

## Reducing the Use of Threats

A highly effective and reliable way to *increase* channel conflict is to threaten another channel member.[34] To **threaten** means to imply that punishments, or negative sanctions, will be applied if the desired behavior or performance, or compliance, is not forthcoming. A strategy of repeated threats raises the temperature of a relationship while reducing channel members' satisfaction. Threats are perceived as coercion. Repeated **coercion** eventually moves the threatened firm into a zone of tension, frustration, and collision.

We discussed coercive power in Chapter 10, but it is worth repeating here that coercion is a tool, like a hammer, that can achieve positive purposes if used properly. Even strongly resented coercion, if handled well, can be overlooked in the short term, forgiven in the medium term, and appreciated in the long term. But just like any tool, it also can be overused. A heavy reliance on coercive tactics is dangerous, especially considering the ease with which they can escalate. Punishment (or the threat of it) provokes retaliation. Thus, the single best predictor of an automobile dealer's punitive actions against a supplier is the supplier's own punitive actions against the dealer![35] Car dealers and automakers find many ways to punish each other—being difficult to work with, cutting service, withholding information—each of which can rapidly cause damage to channel performance.

The escalation of channel conflict also results from another truism: **The better the weapon, the greater the likelihood of using it**. When a party has massive punitive capability, it tends to be far more coercive. When a supplier threatens a dealer that is capable of doing real damage, the supplier risks provoking coercion in kind, and this coercion begets ever more coercion. For example, automakers might punish dealers by failing to deliver cars on time; the dealers retaliate by withholding information from the manufacturer. Each reaction escalates the conflict—encouraging each side to seek to contain the deteriorating situation, through more coercion.

If the players perceive a short time horizon, they handle conflict by using aggressive or coercive strategies,[36] but such strategies accentuate conflict. Channel members also tend to employ punitive tactics when they have a power advantage over their counterpart,[37] so in one-sided channels, in which one party dominates, it is more likely to threaten its weaker partner, and both channel members anticipate a shorter time horizon. When power is lopsided, each channel member suspects the relationship will end sooner than if power is balanced.[38]

Yet coercion may be the best weapon, especially if it is the only weapon remaining in a critical situation. Sidebar 11-2 illustrates how the gadget manufacturer Apple faces an insurmountable problem with a grey market in Hong Kong and outrageously bold copycats in mainland China. It was time to use their coercive power in a different way.

## Intolerance of Conflict in Balanced Relationships

Industrial marketing channels in developed economies are usually good examples of **balanced power**.[39] Each side tends to be differentiated and has many alternatives to the current channel partner. Thus, upstream and downstream channel members are both powerful, so they tend to be **intolerant** of coercive tactics.

The dynamics of such balanced B2B relationships are revealing and anything but indifferent. Balanced does not mean without dispute. Disagreements abound over

## Sidebar 11-2

### Apple, Hong Kong, and parallel imports

Hong Kong is a city that seems to be obsessed with gadgets and technology. Despite that, Apple did not open its first store in Hong Kong until 2011. The new store was opened at the high-end International Financial Center Mall at an estimated cost of U.S. $20 million.

For many years, Hong Kong has had problems with grey market technology products, known locally as parallel imports. In the year before Apple opened its store, 14 housewives were caught smuggling hundreds of mobile phones and iPads into Hong Kong. Hong Kong's computer markets are known around the world, stacks of laptops, phones, and other gadgets, mainly grey market products imported from China or Japan being sold at bargain prices by resellers.

It was always easier to buy Dell or HTC than Apple as sales and shipments were tightly controlled. The newest models were always the hardest to find; older models were much more common on the grey market. The major problems for the consumers were always whether the products were genuine or whether they were counterfeit, and the fact that they did not come with a guarantee. Resellers would routinely offer restricted return policies, sometimes up to 30 days, but more often just 24 hours. Many of the devices would only work using Chinese SIM cards, or were only set up to use Japanese script.

With Hong Kong being an oasis for shoppers, especially those from mainland China, luxury brands abound. They are substantially cheaper in Hong Kong as compared to mainland China. On average, Chinese tourists spending just one night in Hong Kong spend over U.S. $1,000 on products to take home with them. It is impossible to ignore the retailing potential of the city. Around the same time as the first shop opened in Hong Kong, Apple was opening its fifth store in mainland China on Nanjing East Road in Shanghai. Clearly, since then Apple has opened a number of other stores in China.

Something else was happening in China that no one could have predicted. In the Chinese city of Kunming there were 22 Apple stores. None of them were real. They were copycat stores which the Chinese authorities swiftly ordered to be closed. Regardless, more fake Apple stores were springing up across China. Many of them were so convincing that even the employees thought they were working for Apple.

The growing demand in mainland China for branded luxury goods is growing at a terrific rate. The growth is so enormous that it has outstripped enforcement. This is particularly the case in the less developed regions of China where even a copycat store's opening is a major event. It does seem that Apple and many other global brands will need to think long and hard about how they manage their supply chains and combat the counterfeiters.

Using its enormous brand presence and reputation, together with the coercive power to forge a deal, Apple could finally announce its alliance with China Mobile toward the end of 2013 after six years of negotiation.

The results were incredible and instant. In February 2014 alone, China Mobile added 1.34 million new 4G users to their networks – the majority of them were iPhone users.

Meanwhile, the growing importance of Apple to China's economy became clear. The Chinese government initiated a crackdown on the fake stores. It seemed an obvious move in light of the fact that the majority of iPhones are manufactured in China, and this was seen as recognition of Apple's contribution to employment.

At a stroke, the deal with China Mobile seems to have turned the tide. It is estimated that the deal alone will boost shipments of iPhones by 15 million to 30 million. This will have a considerable impact given the fact that Apple shipped over 100 million iPhones globally in 2013.

**Continued**

The deal with China Mobile has massive potential. The official, non-grey market version of the iPhone will be available across China and Hong Kong via China Mobile's stores. Just as importantly, China Mobile's customers will now actually be able to use official iPhones for the first time; in the past the network's 3G technology was not compatible with the Apple handsets!

a variety of issues, including inventory policies, new account development, participation in training and sales promotion programs, and representation of competing suppliers. But much of this conflict remains latent rather than manifest.

Each side uses influence strategies (see Chapter 10), sometimes coercive but at other times noncoercive, such that the balanced partners seek to exchange information, share points of view, discuss strategies, ask for cooperation, and come to an agreement on possible payoffs. In B2B channels, *both* sides use coercive influence strategies to some degree (even if suppliers may be somewhat more fond of coercion than distributors), but both sides also tend to rely more heavily on **noncoercive strategies**, particularly when dealing with powerful counterparts. Important relationships encourage noncoercive influence, because no one wants to jeopardize these relationships with coercion attempts that create spirals of aggression and retaliation. Even more powerful parties tend to refrain from coercion.

Such self-restraint is revealing. As we noted in Chapter 10, one of the best ways to gain power is to perform a channel role exceptionally well. For example, suppliers gain power over distributors by doing a superior job of developing end-user preferences, ensuring product availability, providing quality products, offering superior technical support, and so forth. These suppliers are powerful because they offer benefits that are difficult for distributors to find elsewhere. Yet they still rely mostly on noncoercive means, such as persuasion and communication, to influence distributors, and in turn, distributors are less likely to use coercion in their dealings with the suppliers.

Of course, having read Chapter 10, you know that our message is *not* that coercion should be ruled out completely. On occasion, organizations need to raise the temperature and conflict in their relationships to improve channel performance. Coercion in a channel is not comparable to coercion in a personal relationship; there is a good time and place in business relationships for negotiating by withholding benefits or applying sanctions. Thus, threats should not be blindly disallowed but rather be used with care, because they are an extremely potent way to raise conflict. Coercion can easily be taken too far, provoking retaliation, reduced satisfaction, and the potential dissolution of the channel relationship.

### Mitigating the Effects of Conflict in Balanced Relationships

Dealers carry a limited number of product lines, supplied by a limited number of vendors. Often they sell expensive items that demand high after-sales service support, such as automobiles, garden equipment, or tires. Because they depend on a narrow range of products and suppliers, dealers are vulnerable to coercion or threats by the manufacturers whose lines they carry. Such relationship-damaging actions might include adding a mass merchandiser, adding a new dealer to the existing dealer's territory, withdrawing a product line, or imposing an outside credit agency to approve the dealer's credit applications for new customers. In an extensive study of how dealers react to such **destructive actions**,[40] five different reactions emerge:

- Passive acceptance, that is, saying or doing very little in response
- Venting by complaining vigorously without taking action
- Neglecting the supplier by relegating the line a lower priority and cutting back on resources
- Threatening to stop selling the line (even if it means closing the business)
- Engaging the supplier in constructive discussion to try to work things out and improve the situation

However, emerging research suggests that there are other possibly potential reactions and that these reactions may vary across different cultures.[41] Another potential action is for the channel member to increase their opportunistic behaviors. For example, a channel member can begin acting in a more self-interested fashion that is explicitly or implicitly prohibited, while trying to hide their behaviors through guile. In addition, constructive discussion can include either creative voice (focus on novel ideas) or considerate voice (focused on both party's point of view) or both.

So which response is a dealer likely to choose? The answer depends largely on why the dealer believes the supplier engaged in the destructive act. If dealers blame themselves, they split into two camps: constructive engagement to fix the situation or withdrawal from the relationship because the situation appears not worth salvaging. When dealers blame the supplier, they are unlikely to passively accept the situation and more likely to take some sort of action, such that the destructive act serves as a "wake-up call" that drives dealers to action. Finally, when dealers blame the environment or a changing market, they exhibit more passive acceptance. Thus, if suppliers can convince dealers they had little choice but to take the destructive action, they can mitigate resistance.

In the aftermath, relationships that started strong tend to survive, particularly if both sides depend on each other. In these relationships, the parties shrug off the disruption and move on, especially if the dealer reacts with passive acceptance. But in this case, the supplier should cushion the blow with increased communication, to reduce the chances of venting or withdrawal. Of course, even great relationships will deteriorate with repeated destructive acts.

An increasingly popular solution relies on **dealer councils**. These groups of carefully selected dealers work with the supplier to reduce the destructive impact of its actions and facilitate communication between dealers and suppliers.

## Perceived Unfairness: Aggravating the Effects of Conflicts

Research investigating the negative effects of conflict, opportunism, and unfairness indicates that **perceived unfairness** exerts the greatest negative impact on channel member cooperation and flexibility.[42] It also aggravates the negative effects of conflict and opportunism on channel performance. This "relationship poison" not only hurts the relationship directly but also amplifies the negative impacts of any background conflict.

When channel members perceive greater unfairness, they often attribute negative motives to the seller. Rather than giving their channel partner the benefit of the doubt, they assume some deliberate intention to take advantage of the situation to gain an unfair share. These channel members respond severely to conflict, often with strong negative emotions, including anger, that in turn increase the severity of their further responses. Then of course they seek retribution, and the negative spiraling of action and reaction begins.

## CONFLICT RESOLUTION STRATEGIES

How do channel members cope with conflict? We distinguish two approaches. First, they can try to keep conflict from escalating into a dysfunctional zone, by developing institutionalized mechanisms, such as arbitration boards or norms of behavior, that help diffuse disputes before they harden into hostile attitudes. Second, they might adopt patterns of behavior for resolving conflicts after they become manifest.

### Forestalling Conflict Through Institutionalization

Channel members sometimes institute policies to address conflict in early stages, or even before it arises. Such policies become **institutionalized** (i.e., part of the environment, unquestioned and taken for granted), in forms such as joint memberships in trade associations, distributor councils, and exchange-of-personnel programs. Other channels, from their very start, rely on built-in appeals to third parties, such as referrals to boards of arbitration or mediation (as is particularly popular in Europe). These policies serve subtle conflict-management functions.

**INFORMATION-INTENSIVE MECHANISMS**   Some mechanisms head off conflict by creating a better means to share information. But information-intensive mechanisms also are risky and expensive, because each side risks divulging sensitive information and must devote resources to communicating. Thus, trust and cooperation are helpful, in the sense that they keep the conflict manageable.

When channel partners agree to **joint membership in trade associations** (e.g., a committee founded by the Grocery Manufacturers of America and the Food Marketing Institute developed the Universal Product Code), they have devised a new mechanism to contain conflict through an institutionalized approach. A similar group promotes progress on efficient consumer response (ECR) efforts, as we discuss in Chapter 14 on channel logistics.[43]

**Personnel exchanges** as an institutional vehicle seek to turn channel members' focus toward devising solutions rather than engaging in conflict. The exchanges may be unilateral or bilateral, usually for a short, specified period. For example, the close connections between Wal-Mart and Procter & Gamble have been greatly facilitated by their personnel exchanges. Although such exchanges require clear guidelines, because of the likely disclosure of proprietary information, the participants return to their employers with a new, interorganizational view of their jobs, greater personal and professional involvement in the channel, and additional training. Participants also have an opportunity to meet with channel counterparts who have similar task responsibilities, professions, and interests.

Finally, **cooptation** is designed explicitly to integrate new elements into the leadership or policy-determining structure of an organization, as a means of averting threats to its stability or existence. Effective cooptation prompts ready accessibility among channel members, because it requires the establishment of routine, reliable channels for moving information, aid, and requests. It also supports effectively shared responsibility, such that various channel members likely identify with and commit to the programs developed in support of a particular product or service. However, as is the case for any information-intensive conflict resolution method, cooptation carries the risk of challenging participants' perspectives and decision-making processes. "Outsiders" participate in analyzing an existing situation, suggesting alternatives, and deliberating on the consequences. For example, when firms invite advisory councils into their decision-making processes, they often find that the councils shape the decisions, rather than just facilitating communication between upstream and downstream members.

**THIRD-PARTY MECHANISMS**    Cooptation brings together representatives of channel members. Mediation and arbitration instead bring in third parties, uninvolved with the channel. **Third-party mechanisms** seek to prevent conflict from arising or else keep manifest conflict from exploding. Two fundamental approaches differ in how much control the disputing parties have over the outcome. That is, arbitration takes away much of the control, or even all of it (binding arbitration), while mediation takes only limited control.[44]

**Mediation** is a process whereby a third party attempts to settle a dispute by persuading the parties to continue their negotiations or consider the mediator's procedural or substantive recommendations. The mediator typically offers a fresh view of the situation, which may enable it to perceive opportunities that "insiders" cannot. Mediators also help disputing parties find underlying points of agreement and promote integrative (win–win) solutions. Solutions might become acceptable simply because they have been suggested by the mediator. Mediation in business settings thus enjoys a high settlement rate (60–80 percent), even though neither party is obliged to accept the recommendations. Such success may arise because the mediator allows both parties to save face, by making concessions without appearing weak. And disputants often perceive the overall process as fair.

An alternative to mediation is **arbitration**, in which the third party actually makes the decision, and both parties state in advance that they will honor whatever decision the arbitrator makes. Arbitrators often begin with a formal fact-finding hearing that operates much like a judicial procedure, with presentations, witnesses, and cross-examinations. Arbitration may be compulsory or voluntary. In **compulsory arbitration**, the parties are required by law to submit their dispute to a third party, whose decision is final and binding. In a **voluntary arbitration** process, the parties voluntarily submit their dispute to a third party, whose decision still is final and binding, such that reneging on the decision represents a major breach of confidence. Arbitration offers all the advantages of mediation, plus the advantage that the disputants can blame the arbitrator if their constituents object to the settlement.

Some firms practice sequences of mediation and arbitration. That is, they agree upfront that if the mediator cannot settle the issue, it will pass to an arbitrator—usually the same person who served as the mediator. In an arbitration–mediation sequence, the arbitrator instead places his or her secret decision in a sealed envelope, and then the issue passes to mediation. If the parties cannot agree, they open the envelope and abide by that decision. Such sequential approaches threaten to reduce each party's decision control, which not only lowers each party's expectations (i.e., making them more reasonable) but also motivates them to negotiate cooperatively. If all else fails, the process ultimately seems more fair than simple arbitration, and the parties are more likely to comply with the ruling than they might be with simple mediation.

Institutionalizing the practice of taking disputes to third parties can also forestall conflict. Because they know they face the prospect of outside intervention, disputants work to settle their differences internally. If they cannot, the third parties provide a sort of safety net for dealing with conflict *after* it climbs too high. The input of third parties to an ongoing conflict can also contribute to the success of channel relationships, because third-party interventions prompt greater satisfaction among channel members with the financial rewards they derive from their relationship.[45]

**BUILDING RELATIONAL NORMS**  The preceding mechanisms are policies that can be proactively devised, consciously put into place, and continually maintained by management to forestall conflict or address it once it occurs. But another important class of factors can forestall or direct conflict, even though management cannot directly create or control them. That is, norms govern how channel members manage their relationship grow up over time, with the functioning of the relationship. In a channel, norms entail the expectations about behavior shared (at least partially) by all channel members. In alliance channels, common norms include the following:

- **Flexibility**: Channel members expect one another to adapt readily to changing circumstances, with a minimum of obstruction and negotiation.
- **Information exchange**: Channel members share any and all pertinent information—no matter how sensitive—freely, frequently, quickly, and thoroughly.
- **Solidarity**: Everyone works for mutual, not just one-sided, benefits.

These **relational norms** tend to come in a package: A relationship attains high levels of all these norms if it reaches a high level of any of them.[46] A channel with strong relational norms is particularly effective at forestalling conflict, because it discourages parties from pursuing their own interests at the expense of the channel. These norms also encourage various players to refrain from coercion and make an effort to work through their differences, which keep conflict within functional zones.[47]

Unfortunately, management cannot decide one day to create relational norms and then "just do it." Norms emerge from the daily interactions of the people who constitute the marketing channel. They also can be positive or negative. Thus, a channel might embrace a norm of cutthroat competition or pure self-interest seeking. Unlike policies, norms are not easy to observe, announce, publicize, or control.

## Ongoing Conflict Resolution Styles

Some conflict is a normal, and even desirable, property of channels. That means channel members need to cope with ongoing, manifest conflict. As a general rule, they seek to use this sort of conflict as a force for change, ideally through functional efforts, though in truth, their efforts frequently only make the situation worse. In this section, we thus consider various conflict resolution strategies and their consequences in terms of how

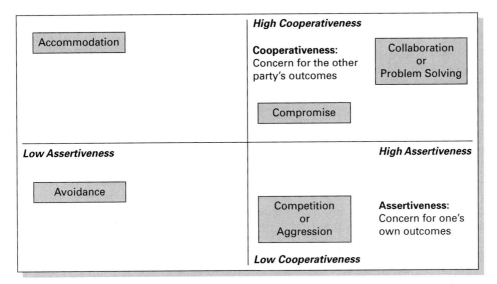

**FIGURE 11-2**  **Conflict resolution styles**

*Source:* Thomas, Kenneth W. (1976), "Conflict and Conflict Management," in M. D. Dunnette, ed., *Handbook of Industrial and Organizational Psychology* (Palo Alto, CA: Consulting Psychologists Press), pp. 889–935.

satisfied channel members are with their relationship. That is, our discussion centers not on how channel members handle a particular issue or incident but rather on the **general conflict resolution style** they employ.[48]

Figure 11-2 shows one way to conceptualize of this style, namely, by addressing the channel member's approach to bargaining. For example, in its dealings with a supplier, a retailer brings with it to the bargaining table certain levels of *assertiveness* (emphasis on achieving its own goals, such as building store traffic, increasing the uniqueness of its assortment, or increasing margins) and *cooperativeness* (concern for the other party's goals, such as building volume, creating a distinctive image, or taking share from a competitor).

A relatively passive channel member likely adopts an **avoidance** conflict resolution style, seeking to prevent any and all conflict by agreeing to pretty much anything. Avoiders typically hope to save time and head off unpleasantness, mostly by minimizing information exchanges, such that they circumvent discussions. In most channels, avoidance characterizes relationships of convenience, in which neither side feels much commitment to the other.

Another style focuses more on the other party's goals than on one's own. Unlike avoidance (which is a passive strategy), this method is more than just another way of keeping the peace. **Accommodation** is a proactive means to strengthen the relationship by cultivating the dependence of the channel partner. It also signals a genuine willingness to cooperate, which encourages reciprocation and should build trust and commitment over the longer term. But the accommodator suffers exposure to exploitation if the other side refuses to reciprocate.

A **competition** (or aggression) conflict resolution strategy involves a zero-sum game, in which the competitor pursues its own goals while ignoring the other party's and thus conceding very little. Not surprisingly, this style aggravates conflict, fosters distrust, and shortens the time horizon of the channel relationship. Channel members tend to limit their use of this style, especially in long-term relationships.

A very different style is to **compromise** repeatedly, pressing for solutions that let each side achieve its goals, but only to an intermediate degree. This centrist approach gives something to everyone, so the strategy seems fair. It is common as a solution to minor conflicts, because in this case, it is easy to get both sides to concede, leading to a faster resolution.

Finally, close, committed relationships are best served by a collaborative **problem-solving** strategy. With this ambitious style, the problem-solving channel member seeks to get it all—its own goals *and* its counterpart's, at very high levels. Many people claim to be interested in this win–win approach, perhaps because it is fashionable and contributes to a favorable self-image, as well as a favorable public presentation. But it also can be more difficult than it looks. Collaboration demands vast resources, especially in the form of information, time, and energy. The problem solver tries to get both sides to voice all their concerns and issues quickly, and then work immediately through their differences by discussing the issues directly and sharing problems with an eye to resolving them. Thus, problem solving requires creativity to devise a mutually beneficial solution. In pursuing this information-intensive strategy, negotiators must reveal substantial sensitive information, which could be used against them.

## Using Incentives to Resolve Conflict

Depending on the conflict resolution style a negotiator chooses, the best arguments for persuading its counterpart differ. However, economic incentives work well almost universally, regardless of the personalities, players, or history of the relationship. Just as reward power is a highly effective way to influence a channel member (Chapter 10), appealing to economic self-interest is a highly effective way to settle a dispute. Thus, good negotiators find ingenious ways to base their arguments on economics, and then combine them with a strong program of communications in a good interpersonal working relationship.

Consider, for example, manufacturer-sponsored promotion programs aimed at retailers. In fast-moving consumer goods industries, suppliers spend enormous sums to create point-of-purchase advertising and displays for in-store use. These programs are major sources of contention. Manufacturers accuse retailers of taking the promotion money and then not mounting the promised promotion. Retailers complain that manufacturers never pony up their fair share of promotion allowances but promise more than they can deliver. The resulting acrimony has consumed reams of pages of discussion in the grocery trade press.

But most of this acrimony could be resolved if the manufacturer would simply combine appealing economic incentives that encourage participation in a pay-for-performance system with a presentation by a salesperson who has developed a good working relationship with the retailer. The economic incentives have obvious appeal; the good relationship helps the salesperson direct the retailer's attention to the incentives. A pay-for-performance system in particular (such that the retailer pays for items sold on promotion rather than all items ordered) screens out retailers that are fundamentally uninterested in cooperating with the supplier.[49]

To function effectively though, economic incentives must do more than offer a better price or higher allowance, options that are visible and easy for competitors to match. Rather, persuasive economic arguments feature a portfolio of elements that collectively create positive financial returns for a channel partner.[50] For example, independent sales agencies strongly appreciate a product that can generate profits by the following:

• Compensating for lower volume sales with a higher commission rate, or vice versa
• Overcoming lower commission rates by being easier to sell, such that it demands less sales time (i.e., cuts costs)
• Establishing the sales agent in a growing product category, to contribute to future profits.
• Increasing overall sales synergy and spurring sales of other products in the agent's portfolio

In addition, independent agencies respond to indirect, risk-oriented arguments. A principal should try to convince its agents that sales of its products are not unpredictable but rather can be accurately forecasted. Such arguments can be conveyed far more effectively by principals that invest in vigorous, two-way communication programs within the channel.[51] Unfortunately though, economic incentives can rapidly multiply and become difficult to administer. Channel networks often have so many points of contact, across so many organizations, that the sheer task of keeping track of the channels and their incentives grows daunting.

## SUMMARY: MANAGING CHANNEL CONFLICT

Conflict, a negative trait in most human relationships, can have negative effects in many channel relationships. But it is not uniformly undesirable. A channel even can be too peaceful, such as when indifference and passivity pass for harmony, masking great differences in motivation and intention. And a contentious channel is often one engaged in functional conflict, which allows the parties to raise and work through their differences, in search of better understanding and improved performance. To adapt to environmental changes, the channel often must experience some conflict. Thus, conflict in channels should not be judged automatically as a defect or a state to be eliminated. Instead, conflict demands monitoring and management, whether to increase functional conflict or to reduce or redirect manifest conflict.

Managing conflict first means assessing it. A good way to do so is with an index that indicates, for each issue relevant to a channel, the level of frequency of disagreement, the intensity of disagreement, and the importance of the issue. If any of these is low, the issue cannot be a great source of conflict (the participants' opinions notwithstanding). The product of intensity, frequency, and importance, summed over all issues, gives a good rough approximation of actual conflict—and suggests ways to convince the parties to resolve their differences. Accordingly, more complex relationships are likely to experience more conflict.

Conflict also is a staple of marketing channels, because of their built-in differences in viewpoint and goals. Goal differences are real; curiously though, perceived differences can actually outweigh them. Different perceptions also spark dispute, because channel members see different pieces of the channel environment. A perennial source of conflict is domain clashes, such that suppliers perceive their own channels as competitors, and downstream channel members believe their suppliers are pitting them against other channel members. But the use of multiple channels has become quite common, especially as industries mature and customers make more demands. Multiple-channel conflicts require solutions based on communication, concession, creative compensation, cooperation, and product differentiation in different channels—or simple acceptance of conflict in the interest of serving customers better or more economically.

Another major source of friction, gray markets, also are growing rapidly. Both suppliers and distributors have reasons to permit them privately, even while they bemoan them publicly. For suppliers, gray markets offer higher sales, a strong means to incentivize their authorized channels, and access to different segments. Furthermore, gray markets are difficult to eliminate, so many firms join them because they can't beat them.

Conflict is self-perpetuating and self-feeding. Once it has begun, the parties often develop long memories and interpret events in a negative light. This cycle is easy to initiate with threats, which beget in-kind reactions, especially by parties that are more capable of doing harm. Reciprocation likely sends the channel into a self-destructive spiral of aggression. A good relationship instead might recover more readily from destructive acts, especially if it features balanced dependence; dealers even passively accept a supplier's destructive acts if they believe those acts were sparked by the external environment. But destructive actions cannot go on indefinitely without provoking an angry, and perhaps damaging, counter reaction.

Multiple effective methods also exist to resolve disputes. Institutionalized mechanisms seek to contain conflict early; once conflict arises, the parties' conflict resolution styles determine the future course of their dispute. The most effective style seeks to achieve the goals of *both* parties through collaboration and problem solving, but for it to work this style demands an intense commitment by both parties.

More directly, conflict can be resolved through the use of economic incentives, which are especially effective when coupled with good communication. Good incentives are less visible (and thus harder for competitors to copy) and encourage channel members to make an effort, invest, or assume some risk to collect them.

## TAKE-AWAYS

- Conflict is negative in many channel relationships, but if indifference and passivity pass for harmony, a contentious channel actually may be preferable as a means to raise and work through differences, in search of better understanding and performance.
- Channel conflict may be necessary in response to environmental changes. All conflict should be monitored and managed according to its implications.
- A good way to assess the true degree of conflict is to index the following for each relevant issue:
  - Frequency of disagreement
  - Intensity of disagreement
  - Importance of the issue

If any element is low, the issue is not a real source of conflict.

- Conflict is inevitable in marketing channels because of the following:
  - Their built-in viewpoint and goal differences
  - Their perceptual variations, which arise because channel members see different pieces of the channel environment
  - Their clashes over domains (roles, responsibilities, territories)
- Domain conflict is especially prominent in multiple-channel situations, which demand creative solutions, such as communication, concession, compensation, win–win approaches, product differentiation, or acceptance.
- Gray markets are growing rapidly, because both upstream and downstream channel members have reasons to permit them, regardless of their complaints.
- Conflict perpetuates itself through reciprocation of coercion.
- Institutionalized mechanisms to contain conflict early include information-intensive strategies and the use of third parties.
- A good relationship recovers from destructive acts by suppliers, especially if it features balanced high dependence and the destructive acts do not persist.
- The most effective, but also very challenging, conflict-resolution style is collaborating to solve the problems and achieve the goals of *both* parties.
- Conflict also can be resolved through economic incentives, which should be less visible, combine with good communication, and encourage channel members to make some investment.

## Endnotes

1. Stern, Louis W. (1996), "Relationships, Networks, and the Three Cs," in Dawn Iacobucci, ed., *Networks in Marketing* (Thousand Oaks, CA: Sage Publications), pp. 3–7.

2. Stern, Louis W. and James L. Heskett (1969), "Conflict Management in Inter-organizational Relations: A Conceptual Framework," in Louis W. Stern, ed., *Distribution Channels: Behavioral Dimensions* (Boston, MA: Houghton-Mifflin), pp. 156–175.

3. Pondy, Louis R. (1967), "Organizational Conflict: Concepts and Models," *Administrative Science Quarterly* 14, no. 1, pp. 296–320.

4. Zwick, Rami and Xiao-Ping Chen (1999), "What Price Fairness? A Bargaining Study," *Management Science* 45 (June), pp. 804–823.

5. Brown, James R. and Ralph L. Day (1981), "Measures of Manifest Conflict in Distribution Channels," *Journal of Marketing Research* 18 (August), pp. 263–274.

This article is the basis for the following discussion and examples of measuring channel conflict.

6. Dwyer, F.R., Paul H. Schurr, and Sejo Oh (1987), "Developing Buyer-Seller Relationships," *Journal of Marketing* 51 (April), pp. 11–27.

7. Anderson, James C. and James A. Narus (1984), "A Model of the Distributor's Perspective of Distributor-Manufacturer Working Relationships," *Journal of Marketing* 48 (Fall), pp. 62–74.

8. Webster, Bruce (1998), "Uses and Abuses of Co-op Advertising," *Supply House Times* 15 (March), pp. 57–64.

9. Geyskens, Inge, Jan-Benedict E.M. Steenkamp, and Nirmalya Kumar (1999), "A Meta-Analysis of Satisfaction in Marketing Channel Relationships," *Journal of Marketing Research* 36 (May), pp. 223–238.

10. Draganska, Michaela, Daniel Klapper, and Sofia B. Villas-Boas (2010), "A Larger Slice or a Larger Pie? An Empirical Investigation of Bargaining Power in the

Distribution Channel," *Marketing Science* 29 (January–February), pp. 57–74.

11. Taylor, Alex (2002), "Finally GM Is Looking Good," *Fortune* (April 1), pp. 42–46.

12. Bergen, Mark, Shantanu Dutta, and Orville C. Walker Jr. (1992), "Agency Relationships in Marketing: A Review of the Implications and Applications of Agency and Related Theories," *Journal of Marketing* 56, no. 3, pp. 1–24.

13. Magrath, Allan J. and Kenneth G. Hardy (1989), "A Strategic Paradigm for Predicting Manufacturer-Reseller Conflict," *European Journal of Marketing* 23, no. 2, pp. 94–108.

14. Ross, William T. and Diana C. Robertson (2000), "Lying: The Impact of Decision Context," *Business Ethics Quarterly* 10, no. 2, pp. 409–440.

15. John, George and Torger Reve (1982), "The Reliability and Validity of Key Informant Data from Dyadic Relationships in Marketing Channels," *Journal of Marketing Research* 19 (November), pp. 517–524.

16. Brown, James R., Robert F. Lusch, and Laurie P. Smith (1991), "Conflict and Satisfaction in an Industrial Channel of Distribution," *International Journal of Physical Distribution & Logistics Management* 21, no. 6, pp. 15–26.

17. Palmatier, Robert W., Rajiv P. Dant, and Dhruv Grewal (2007), "A Comparative Longitudinal Analysis of Theoretical Perspectives of Interorganizational Relationship Performance," *Journal of Marketing* 71 (October), pp. 172–194.

18. Johansson, Johnny K. and Ikujiro Nonaka (1987), "Market Research the Japanese Way," *Harvard Business Review* 65, no. 3, pp. 1–5.

19. LaBahn, Douglas W. and Katrin R. Harich (1997), "Sensitivity to National Business Culture: Effects on U.S.-Mexican Channel Relationship Performance," *Journal of International Marketing* 5 (December), pp. 29–51.

20. "Newsmakers: Acacia Inc.," *Sales and Marketing Management* 148 (April), p. 20.

21. Frazier, Gary L. and Tasadduq A. Shervani (1992), "Multiple Channels of Distribution and their Impact on Retailing," in Robert A. Peterson, ed., *The Future of U.S. Retailing:*

*An Agenda for the 21st Century* (Westport, CT: Quorum Books).

22. Cespedes, Frank V. and Raymond Corey (1990), "Managing Multiple Channels," *Business Horizons* 10, no. 1, pp. 67–77; Moriarty, Rowland T. and Ursula Moran (1990), "Managing Hybrid Marketing Systems," *Harvard Business Review* (November–December), pp. 146–150.

23. Sa Vinhas, Alberto, and Erin Anderson (2005), "How Potential Conflict Drives Channel Structure: Concurrent (Direct and Indirect) Channels," *Journal of Marketing Research* 42 (November).

24. Bucklin, Christine B., Pamela A. Thomas-Graham, and Elizabeth A. Webster (1997), "Channel Conflict: When Is It Dangerous?" *McKinsey Quarterly* 7, no. 3, pp. 36–43.

25. Dutta, Shantanu, Mark Bergen, Jan B. Heide, et al. (1995), "Understanding Dual Distribution: The Case of Reps and House Accounts," *Journal of Law, Economics, and Organization* 11, no. 1, pp. 189–204.

26. Villas-Boas, Miguel (1997), "Product Line Design for a Distribution Channel," *Marketing Science* 17, no. 2, pp. 156–69.

27. Sullivan, Mary W. (1998), "How Brand Names Affect the Demand for Twin Automobiles," *Journal of Marketing Research* 35 (May), pp. 154–65.

28. Purohit, Devarat (1997), "Dual Distribution Channels: The Competition between Rental Agencies and Dealers," *Marketing Science* 16 no. 3, pp. 228–245; Purohit, Devarat and Richard Staelin (1994), "Rentals, Sales, and Buybacks: Managing Secondary Distribution Channels," *Journal of Marketing Research* 31 (August), pp. 325–338.

29. This section is adapted from Coughlan, Anne T. and David A. Soberman (2005), "Strategic Segmentation Using Outlet Malls," *International Journal of Research in Marketing* 22 (March), pp. 61–86; Soberman, David A. and Anne T. Coughlan (1998), "When Is the Best Ship a Leaky One? Segmentation, Competition, and Gray Markets," INSEAD working paper 98/60/MKT; Champion, David (1998), "Marketing: The Bright Side of Gray Markets," *Harvard Business Review* 76 (September/October), pp. 19–22.

30. Weigand, Robert E. (1991), "Parallel Import Channels: Options for Preserving Territorial Integrity," *Columbia Journal of World Business* 26 (Spring), pp. 53–60; Assmus, Gert and Carsten Wiese (1995), "How to Address the Gray Market Threat Using Price Coordination," *Sloan Management Review* 36 (Spring), pp. 31–41.

31. Henricks, Mark (1997), "Harmful Diversions," *Apparel Industry Magazine* 58 (September), pp. 72–78.

32. Cespedes, Frank V., E. Raymond Corey, and V. Kasturi Rangan (1988), "Gray Markets: Causes and Cures," *Harvard Business Review* 88 (July–August), pp. 75–82; Myers, Matthew B. and David A. Griffith (1999), "Strategies for Combating Gray Market Activity," *Business Horizons* 42 (November–December), pp. 2–8; Bergen, Mark, Jan B. Heide and Shantanu Dutta (1998), "Managing Gray Markets Through Tolerance of Violations: A Transaction Cost Perspective," *Managerial and Decision Economics* 19, no. 1, pp. 157–165.

33. Anderson, Erin and Barton Weitz (1992), "The Use of Pledges to Build and Sustain Commitment in Distribution Channels," *Journal of Marketing Research* 24 (February), pp. 18–34.

34. Geyskens, Steenkamp, and Kumar (1999), op. cit.

35. Kumar, Nirmalya, Lisa K. Scheer, and Jan-Benedict E.M. Steenkamp (1998), "Interdependence, Punitive Capability, and the Reciprocation of Punitive Actions in Channel Relationships," *Journal of Marketing Research* 35 (May), pp. 225–235.

36. Ganesan, Shankar (1993), "Negotiation Strategies and the Nature of Channel Relationships," *Journal of Marketing Research* 30 (May), pp. 183–203.

37. Kumar, Scheer, and Steenkamp (1998), op. cit.

38. Anderson, Erin and Barton Weitz (1989), "Determinants of Continuity in Conventional Channel Dyads," *Marketing Science* 8 (Fall), pp. 310–323.

39. This discussion is based on Frazier, Gary L. and Raymond C. Rody (1991), "The Use of Influence Strategies in Interfirm Relationships in Industrial Product Channels," *Journal of Marketing* 55 (January), pp. 52–69.

40. Hibbard, Jonathan D., Nirmalya Kumar, and Louis W. Stern (2001), "Examining the Impact of Destructive Acts in Marketing Channel Relationships," *Journal of Marketing Research* 38, no. 1, pp. 45–61.

41. Furrer Olivier, Brian V. Tjemkes, Arzu U. Aydinlik, and Koen Adolfs (2012), "Responding to Adverse Situations within Exchange Relationships: The Cross-Cultural Validity of a Circumplex Model," *Journal of Cross-Cultural Psychology* 43 no. 6, pp. 943–966.

42. Samaha, Stephen, Robert W. Palmatier, and Rajiv P. Dant (2011), "Poisoning Relationships: Perceive Unfairness in Channels of Distribution," *Journal of Marketing* 75 (May), pp. 99–117.

43. Stern, Louis W. and Patrick J. Kaufman (1985), "Electronic Data Interchange in Selected Consumer Goods Industries," in Robert D. Buzzell, ed., *Marketing in an Electronic Age* (Boston, MA: Harvard Business School Press), pp. 52–73.

44. This section is based on Ross, William H. and Donald E. Conlon (2000), "Hybrid Forms of Third-Party Dispute Resolution: Theoretical Implications of Combining Mediation and Arbitration," *Academy of Management Review* 25, no. 2, pp. 416–427.

45. Mohr, Jakki and Robert Spekman (1994), "Characteristics of Partnership Success: Partnership Attributes, Communication Behavior, and Conflict Resolution Techniques," *Strategic Management Journal* 15, no. 1, pp. 135–152; Mohr, Jakki, and Robert Spekman (1996), "Perfecting Partnerships," *Marketing Management* 4 (Winter/Spring), pp. 34–43.

46. Heide, Jan B. and George John (1992), "Do Norms Matter in Marketing Relationships?" *Journal of Marketing* 56 (April), pp. 32–44.

47. Heide, Jan B. (1994), "Interorganizational Governance in Marketing Channels," *Journal of Marketing* 58 (April), pp. 71–85.

48. This material is based on Thomas, Kenneth W. (1976), "Conflict and Conflict Management," in M.D. Dunnette, ed., *Handbook of Industrial and Organizational Psychology*

(Palo Alto, CA: Consulting Psychologists Press), pp. 889–935; Ganesan (1993), op cit.

49. Murray, John P., Jr., and Jan B. Heide (1998), "Managing Promotion Program Participation within Manufacturer-Retailer Relationships," *Journal of Marketing* 62 (January), pp. 58–68.

50. Anderson, Erin, Leonard M. Lodish, and Barton Weitz (1987), "Resource Allocation Behavior in Conventional Channels," *Journal of Marketing Research* 24 (February), pp. 85–97.

51. Mohr, Jakki and John R. Nevin (1990), "Communication Strategies in Marketing Channels: A Theoretical Perspective," *Journal of Marketing* 54 (October), pp. 36–51.

# CHAPTER 12

# Managing Channel Relationships

**LEARNING OBJECTIVES**

**After reading this chapter, you should be able to:**

- Define and describe the hallmarks of committed relationships in marketing channels.
- Distinguish between upstream and downstream motivations for forming a relationship.
- Describe why many channel members don't want and refuse to enter committed relationships.
- Detail the performance implications of channel relationships, and explain why most firms should have a portfolio of relationships, many of which are *not* close.
- Describe how to extend the time horizon of the relationship and why doing so is critical.
- Explain why channel members deliberately increase their vulnerability and how they manage this exposure.
- Understand the role of idiosyncratic investments and give examples for any channel member.
- Outline the bases of trust.
- Describe how trust builds over time in a marketing channel.
- Explain the role of relationship velocity.
- Differentiate the five phases of a close marketing channel relationship.

## THE NATURE OF CHANNEL RELATIONSHIPS

In an effective channel relationship, two or more organizations have connections (legal, economic, and/or interpersonal) that cause them to function according to a perception that they pursue a **single interest**, shared by all the parties. A channel relationship is strategic when the connections that bind these organizations are endur-ing and substantial, cutting across aspects of each business. Membership in a channel relationship often causes each party to alter its behavior to fit the objectives of the partnership. Channel relationships go by many labels, including partnership, rela-tional governance, hybrid governance, vertical quasi-integration, and strategic alliance.

An effective channel relationship exhibits genuine commitment. **Commitment** exists when one organization desires the relationship to continue indefinitely, though it is not enough to ensure an effective channel relationship. The organization must also be willing to **sacrifice** to maintain and to grow the relationship. These sacrifices may take the form of giving up short-term profits or not pursuing other opportunities, preferring instead to devote organizational resources to the relationship. Sacrifices also are necessary, for example, to accommodate the other side's needs, more so than in an ordinary business transaction. In general, a committed party works hard to maintain and advance the relationship, even though such growth demands resources and puts a strain on it.

Yet commitment is difficult to observe. It is an attitude, intention, and expecta-tion, all wrapped into one. *True relationships encumber the parties involved, imposing on them obligations that may be very costly.* Many organizations profess commitment to each and every one of their many business relations. This façade encourages pleas-ant interactions among the members of upstream and downstream organizations, but it seldom is an accurate description of how organizations really interact. True commit-ment is revealed rather than professed; superficial commitment is disguised, presented as though it were real. Usually, that disguise is not effective. Figure 12-1 lists a cluster of

---

A committed party to a relationship (manufacturer, distributor, or other channel member) views its arrangement as a long-term relationship. Some manifestations of this outlook show up in statements such as the following, made by the committed party about its channel partner:

- We expect to be doing business with them for a long time.
- We defend them when others criticize them.
- We spend enough time with their people to work out problems and misunderstandings.
- We have a strong sense of loyalty to them.
- We are willing to grow the relationship.
- We are patient with their mistakes, even those that cause us trouble.
- We are willing to make long-term investments in them, and then to wait for the payoff to come.
- We will dedicate whatever people and resources it takes to grow the business we do with them.
- We are not continually looking for another organization as a business partner to replace or add to this one.
- If another organization offered us something better, we would not drop this organization, and we would hesitate to take on the new organization.

Clearly, these statements do not reflect normal operating procedures for two organizations. Commitment involves more than an ongoing cordial relationship. It demands confidence in the future and a willingness to invest in the partner, at the expense of other opportunities, to maintain and grow the business relationship.

---

**FIGURE 12-1   Symptoms of commitment in marketing channels**

*Source:* Anderson, Erin and Barton Weitz (1992), "The Use of Pledges to Build and Sustain Commitment in Distribution Channels," *Journal of Marketing Research* 24 (February), pp. 18–34.

behaviors and attitudes that accompany genuine commitment. No single indicator may be particularly informative, but the set taken together gives a good index of the strength of commitment an organization has toward a member of its marketing channel.

Commitment thus implies a long time horizon, *plus* an active desire to keep the relationship going, *plus* a willingness to make sacrifices to maintain and expand the relationship. A committed channel relationship is often likened to a marriage, though this analogy is misleading in one important respect: Channel organizations can and do have multiple relationships simultaneously. A better analogy is a **deep friendship**: They are difficult to build and costly to maintain, putting a natural limit on their number. And most people, like most organizations, need a portfolio of relationships, many of which are ordinary friendships or even acquaintanceships.

Of course, in some deep friendships (and marriages, sadly) one person is committed but the other is not. Such a situation of **asymmetric commitment** actually is uncommon in long-standing channel relationships. Upstream and downstream channel members tend to commit symmetrically, and their relationships persist only if both are committed.

## Upstream Motives for Building a Strong Channel Relationship

Why would an upstream channel member, such as a manufacturer, want to build a committed relationship with a downstream channel member, such as a distributor? Channel relationships begin with the manufacturer's recognition that it can profit from the many advantages a downstream channel member can offer, at least in principle. Chief among these, manufacturers tend to appreciate the ability to achieve better coverage, and to do so at lower cost (including lower overhead).

At minimum, manufacturers must **respect** downstream channel members before building a relationship with them. Yet it is surprising how often manufacturers fail to appreciate the value that channel members provide them, or else overestimate their own ability to duplicate, effectively and efficiently, another party's performance of key channel functions. For some manufacturers, their "'do it in-house technical' culture ... prevents them from understanding, respecting, and trusting intermediaries to any degree."[1] For example, their internal selling arm might view independent channel members as competition. Or companies may be staffed by people who have never worked in channels and distrust partners in general, with the assumption "they will screw things up and ... will be very expensive."[2] In contrast, a channel-centric supplier understands and respects how each independent channel member undertakes activities and converts them into meaningful service outputs, to generate effective results.

Once the building block of respect for the downstream organization exists, manufacturers seek relationships to **motivate** channel members to represent them better, in their current markets, in new markets, or with new products. Of course, there are ways to improve representation without building a strong relationship, such as exerting power (particularly reward power; see Chapter 10) and encouraging functional conflict (disputes that move the parties to align their viewpoints or agree on a course of action; see Chapter 11). But building commitment is an effective, durable way to motivate downstream channel members, particularly when the organization must assume the significant risks of performing channel functions for new products or in new markets. Sidebar 12-1 shows how South Africa's MWEB has teamed up with Spain's Fon to adapt

## Sidebar 12-1

### South Africa's MWEB goes Spanish

MWEB was founded in 1997, and with 320,000 Internet subscribers, it is the second biggest Internet provider in South Africa. Its MWEB Connect service provides Internet access and connectivity points to consumers and small- to medium-sized businesses. The MWEB Business service (founded in 1998), caters to larger businesses and organizations, and has around 11,000 subscribers.

In January 2014, MWEB entered into a partnership with the Spanish Internet giant Fon. Fon claims to have the world's largest Wi-Fi network. The primary goal behind the partnership is to grow the subscriber base in South Africa. The partnership deal was a perfect fit for MWEB – its existing customers could join a Wi-Fi community of some 12 million users that share connections around the world. The plan is to create 30,000 Wi-Fi hotspots in South Africa. One of the main focuses would be hotels, and to tackle the problem of parts of South Africa being very poorly connected. This is particularly the case in the Western Cape where the government has promised to provide free Internet access to many disadvantaged communities.

Carolyn Holgate, the general manager of MWEB Connect, pledged that it was not the company's intention to monetize the relationship with Fon, but rather to offer it as a major new benefit to existing and potential customers. In short, the intention is to use the relationship to drive up the market share that MWEB already has secured.

Although South Africa is ahead of a few other African countries in terms of the Internet and Wi-Fi, it is still way behind in terms of development in Europe, North America, and many parts of the Far East. Spiwe Chireka, of International Data Corp, a telecommunications analysis business, was confident that the MWEB deal with Fon should be considered in the longer term. The rolling out of Internet services across South Africa is reliant on a stable Wi-Fi network – this is something that the partnership will be able to deliver. Mobile phone costs in South Africa are still relatively high; the new network will drive down those costs.

MWEB's new partner, Fon, was founded in 2006. It operates on four continents. Its system is completely unlike many of its competitors. Each community member shares a part of their bandwidth as a separate Wi-Fi signal. This enables any member of the Fon community to access the Internet via one of these hotspots.

The new Fon hotspots will be set up alongside MWEB's existing network of Wi-Fi zones. At a stroke, subscribers will be able to access a far cheaper and more reliable network. MWEB had been looking at other alternatives, but the partnership with Fon offers a much quicker and more reliable means of delivering the Internet access that its customers have been waiting for. As far as Fon is concerned, the hope is that the 320,000 MWEB customers will become part of its community – this will accelerate the roll-out of Internet services across South Africa.

According to Cisco, around 26 percent of all data traffic will be transmitted over mobile networks in South Africa by 2016. This means that South Africa needs this type of investment to match the future demands of the population and the business community. In essence, the existing local fixed MWEB broadband infrastructure will operate alongside a growing community-based Fon network. Clearly, Fon sees this as the stepping-stone into Africa, and plans to roll out the networks into all of sub-Saharan Africa.

From the initial uptake of the offer, it soon became clear that this would be a highly successful partnership. From the original 30,000 hotspots, MWEB and Fon were able to announce that the figure would be closer to 160,000 within a three-year timeframe.

Fon's predictions were based on their successes in London (in partnership with British Telecom), Belgium, Brazil, and in North America. Many business analysts had been predicting that Wi-Fi needed to go "mainstream" in South Africa for some years. The infrastructure was lacking despite the importance that ISPs, network providers, major businesses, and the government had placed on it. In fact, the African National Congress had even included the widespread provision of the

## Continued

Internet across South Africa as one of the major targets in its manifesto.

Free Internet networks are essential not just across South Africa, but for the whole continent. Project Isizwe is concerned with the rollout of free Wi-Fi networks across Africa. Its CEO, Alan Knott-Craig believes that the Internet is as basic a service as water and electricity. In short, it is the key to economic development.

As of February 2014, globally Fon had created 12,375,043 hotspots. It is a new way of delivering an Internet network – essentially it is "crowd-sourced." The specialized routers work like any other device, but the portioned part of the Wi-Fi signal creates a network that any member can access for no extra cost. The community call themselves Foneros, linking back to the Spanish roots of the business. In fact, Fon is not Spanish. It is registered in the U.K., and was created by the Argentine entrepreneur, Martin Vasavsky.

Vodacom, owned by British company Vodafone, is still ranked as the largest mobile phone network provider in South Africa. They have been operating there since the early 1990s, and with 23 million subscribers, they have a 50 percent market share.

As far as Internet users are concerned, some 53 percent of South Africans use ADSL to access the Internet. Around 28 percent use mobile (cellular) networks, 17 percent use Wi-Fi, 9 percent use cell phones with WAP, and 7 percent still use dial-up.

These figures seem to be on the verge of a major change. Tablet sales are increasing at a rate of around 400 percent per year in South Africa; these gadgets are seen as one of the primary drivers in the demand for Wi-Fi hotspots.

Connection, quite literally, with consumers, is a radically new way of broadening the distribution network for Internet services. Each new customer adds to the network, and in turn, acts to attract ever more customers.

to changing buyer behavior in the highly competitive market for Internet services, by broadening its distribution and deepening its customer relationships.

A manufacturer also may seek a relationship to coordinate its marketing efforts with distributors more tightly, which would enable it to reach end-users better. It may seek greater cooperation related to the exchange of information in particular. Through their relationships, manufacturers hope to gain information about the marketplace, even though downstream channel members have economic motives to withhold that information. Distributors may withhold market information to prevent the manufacturer from using the information against them in negotiations. Or they may withhold information for a simpler reason: because it takes time to brief a principal, and that time has other, more productive uses. Downstream channel members are like a wall between the manufacturer and the final buyer, blocking the manufacturer's view and reducing its understanding of the end-user. By gaining distributor commitment, the manufacturer hopes to peek over the wall, that is, to increase information sharing. Hewlett-Packard's Imaging Division thus partners with selected European retailers, leaving the manufacturer well informed about the retail side of its business, such that 40 percent of its retailers share the immensely valuable weekly sales figures.[4]

An emerging motive to forge a relationship with downstream channel members also stems from the growing wave of **consolidation** in wholesaling. Mergers and acquisitions in many industries are transforming the wholesale level, from many smaller players (fragmentation) to a handful of giant players (consolidation). Manufacturers seek relationships because they see the pool of potential partners drying up. They fear losing distribution access, not only due to the few players left standing but also because the survivors themselves are powerful organizations that enter into more or less privileged relations with selected manufacturers. A strong relationship helps rebalance the power arrangement, while also ensuring consistent access to markets.[5]

In the longer term, the manufacturer seeks to erect **barriers to entry** against future competitors. One of the best possible barriers is a good distribution network. Unlike a price cut or a product feature, a channel is hard to duplicate. A committed channel partner in particular may refuse to carry or actively promote a new entrant's brands, as the widely and justly celebrated channel relationship between Procter & Gamble (P&G) and Wal-Mart reveals.[6] Both of these one-time adversaries are noted for using their considerable power to sway the trade. P&G's brand appeal and market expertise in hundreds of fast-moving consumer goods is so dominant it has been described as a "self-aggrandizing bully." Wal-Mart, the massive retailer, uses its volume and massive size to oblige suppliers to do business as it dictates: no intermediaries, extraordinarily low prices, extra service, preferred credit terms, investments in electronic data interchange (EDI) and radio frequency identification (RFID) technology, and so forth.

But these upstream and downstream giant bullies built a strong channel relationship, using the techniques described in this chapter. Most notably, they made investments tailored to each other. For P&G, the payoffs have come in several forms: It receives continuous data by satellite from individual Wal-Mart stores (not pooled over the entire store network), covering sales, inventory levels, and prices for each stockkeeping unit (SKU) of each brand P&G sells. Then P&G takes responsibility for reordering and shipping, often directly to the stores (a practice called **vendor-managed inventory**). The cycle is completed by electronic invoicing and electronic funds transfer. With this paperless system, P&G can manufacture to demand, cut inventories, *and* still reduce stockouts. Overall logistics costs also have declined. Furthermore, P&G does enormous business with Wal-Mart, protected from competition by the investments it has made and its intimate knowledge of Wal-Mart's needs. Finally, P&G gains an excellent source of market research, in the store-level data it garners from its partner Wal-Mart.

## Downstream Motives for Building a Strong Channel Relationship

The motives for downstream channel members to build strong relationships revolve around having an assured and stable supply of desirable products. Consolidation is a motive here again: As mergers and acquisitions concentrate market share among a few manufacturers in many industries, downstream channel members commit to the survivors to maintain product supply. Channel members also build relationships to ensure the success of their own marketing efforts. By coordinating their efforts with a supplier, channel members seek to work better together, though this is not an objective in itself. Rather, it matters because it helps the channel member serve its customer better, which in turn translates into higher volumes and higher margins.

Channel members further seek to cut costs through their strong channel relationships. For example, by coordinating logistics, the channel member can increase inventory turnover, keep lower levels of stocks, and take fewer write-downs of obsolete stock. The best of all worlds arises when stock costs get cut *and* the channel member suffers fewer out-of-stock situations.

Downstream channel members, such as distributors, build strong relationships with suppliers to **differentiate** themselves from other distributors too. By positioning themselves as the manufacturer's preferred outlets for desirable brands or selected SKUs, distributors differentiate their assortments and related service provision. By differentiating themselves, downstream channel members also discourage new competitive entries into their markets.

Distributor differentiation is often based on a strategy of offering value-added services, such as preventive or corrective maintenance, application assistance, onsite product training, engineering and design, technical expertise on call, special packaging and handling, or expedited and free telephone assistance. Distributors pursuing this strategy are more likely to work closely with their suppliers, which helps the distributor set itself apart from fierce competition, while simultaneously helping the manufacturer build a market for its products. [7]

Returning to the relationship between P&G and Wal-Mart, what benefits does the downstream retailer gain? Its inventories are lower, but without the risk of stockouts, and the chain can offer customers lower prices and greater availability of well-known brands. Wal-Mart is no longer responsible for managing its inventory (which is only a benefit if the function is done well, as it is in this case). The paperless transaction system also permits Wal-Mart to enjoy float, in that the retailer does not pay its supplier until after the consumer pays for the merchandise. This system, though difficult to build and duplicate, has given Wal-Mart a formidable competitive advantage in the saturated retail arena.

The upstream and downstream motives to forge strong relationships thus are more similar than they appear at first glance. Figure 12-2 summarizes the preceding discussion and notes the parallels between the interests of both sides. As this figure shows, upstream and downstream channel members fundamentally pursue relationships for the same reason: to attain an **enduring competitive advantage that leads to profit**. Both parties seek to improve their coordination within the channel, to serve customers better and reduce accounting and opportunity costs. Both parties seek to build stable relationships that are difficult to duplicate, which will discourage entry into their respective businesses. Fundamentally, channel relationships may resemble marriages or good friendships, but the motives of both players are calculated strategically and economically.

## Effectiveness of Strong Channel Relationships

Does building strong relationships with channel partners pay off? At first glance, the answer certainly seems to be "yes." Committed parties trust each other, and trust today enhances performance tomorrow.[8] Trusting parties do more for each other, going so far out of their way to help each other that their actions may come to resemble altruism rather than economic profit maximization. (This appearance can be deceiving.) Trusting parties find it easier to come to agreements, work out conflicts, and work with each other. In particular, trust helps the parties cope with and reverse unfavorable outcomes.[9] In this sense, trust is social capital, which organizations use to increase their effectiveness.

| Motives to Ally Strategically | The Upstream Channel Member | The Downstream Channel Member |
|---|---|---|
| Fundamentals | Motivates downstream channel members to represent it better<br>• In current markets<br>• With current products<br>• In new markets<br>• With new products | Avoids stockouts while keeping costs under control<br>• Lowers costs of all flows performed, such as lower inventory holding costs |
| Generate customer preference | Coordinates marketing efforts more tightly with downstream channel members<br>• Get closer to customers and prospects<br>• Increase<br>• Understanding of the market | Coordinates marketing efforts more tightly with upstream channel members<br>• Serve the customer better<br>• Convert prospects into customers<br>• Net effect: higher volume and margins |
| Preserve choice and flexibility of channel partners | Guarantees market access in the face of consolidation in wholesaling<br>• Keep routes to market open<br>• Rebalance power between the manufacturer and surviving channels | Assures a stable supply of desirable products, even as manufacturers consolidate<br>• In current markets<br>• Selling current products<br>• Opening to new markets<br>• With new products |
| Strategic preemption | Erects barriers to entry to other brands<br>• Induce channels to refuse access<br>• Induce channels to offer low levels of support to entrants | Differentiates itself from other downstream channel members<br>• Supplier's preferred outlet<br>• Value-added services, difficult to copy and of high value to customers |
| Superordinate goal | Seeks an enduring competitive advantage leading to profit<br>• Reduce accounting and opportunity costs | Seeks an enduring competitive advantage leading to profit<br>• Reduce accounting and opportunity costs |

**FIGURE 12-2   Motives to create and maintain strong channel relationships**

Furthermore, differentiation and commitment go together. Manufacturers whose marketing strategy aims to differentiate their offerings (rather than adopting a cost leadership strategy) are more likely to build closer relationships with channel members. These relationships enable manufacturers to implement their strategy successfully—which is particularly important in many industrial markets, where the channel, rather than advertising, has the most impact on the brand's image.[10]

And it is not just manufacturers that benefit. Some distributors have a pronounced **market orientation**. Even more than their peers, they focus on collecting, spreading, and using information about customer needs to differentiate themselves. These distributors often ally with suppliers who are also market oriented. The partnership that this market-oriented pair builds gives the market-oriented distributors a notable improvement in their financial performance.[11] This links back to a message we offered early in this book, namely, the ultimate customer is always the end-user, not the next channel member. The most successful channels are those in which all channel members realize this message and take actions to meet end-users' demands.

Because commitment today means cooperation tomorrow, the long time horizon that marks a relationship creates better strategic and economic outcomes.[12] They know they will be there to reap the benefits, so channel members are more willing to make investments that serve the end-user, reduce costs, and differentiate the channel system.

Concrete evidence also shows that channel partnerships generate higher profits. Typically, each side of a channel partnership collects more profit from its strong relationship than from its "ordinary" relationships.[13] Channel partnerships thus generate higher profits *and* share them, rather than degenerating into a situation in which any one side gets the lion's share of the benefits the partnership generates.

But this does not mean that firms should invest to build strong relationships with all channel partners. **Strong relationships are very difficult, and thus very costly, to create and maintain.**[14] And there is no guarantee that spending enough time and money will make commitment happen. Some circumstances simply do not lend themselves to the vertical, quasi-integration represented by alliances or strong relationships.[15] Even in the right circumstances, building commitment is not easy. Worst of all, we know how to *recognize* committed relationships when we see them, but we cannot specify exactly how to *create* some of the critical properties of a committed relationship.

## BUILDING CHANNEL COMMITMENT

### Need for Expectations of Continuity

A channel member who wants to build commitment in a relationship must begin by building the expectation that prospective partners will be doing business for a long time. The **expectation of continuity** is essential before any organization can cooperate and invest to build a future.[16] And continuity cannot be taken for granted. Channel members know that they will be replaced if their performance fails to satisfy.

In environments in which legal barriers to termination are low (such as the United States), channel members also fear they will be replaced even if their performance *does* satisfy! For example, principals often engage agents or resellers to represent products that are secondary or to penetrate markets they consider peripheral. If the downstream channel member makes a success of the business, it logically should fear that the manufacturer will take business away or renegotiate the terms of the arrangement, to appropriate some of the unexpected gains.[17]

What inspires confidence that a business relationship will last?[18] Continuity expectations increase in the presence of the following:

- Trust
- Two-way communication
- A reputation for fair dealing
- A long-standing, stable relationship

- Balanced power
- Combined stakes

Specifically, when downstream channel members expect to do business on behalf of a principal, they likely *trust* the manufacturers (as we discuss more in a subsequent section) and enjoy *two-way communication*, including active give and take of ideas, with that manufacturer. Trust and communication operate in a reinforcing cycle: More trust leads to more communication leads to more trust leads to more communication, and so forth. Thus, frequent, candid, detailed mutual communication is a must for a healthy channel partnership.[19] However, more than a few members of would-be channel partnerships assume they enjoy better communication and higher trust levels than they really do.

Downstream channel members also expect continuity when their manufacturer partners have a *reputation* for treating other channel members fairly, as well as when they have been doing business with their manufacturer partner for some time already. But long-standing, seemingly *stable* channel relationships also can hide problems. In particular, communication is often rather low in older relationships, as though the two parties assume they know each other so well that communication is superfluous. Older channel relationships frequently look stronger than they really are, because both sides take them for granted and permit communication to decline. Eventually, their lack of communication will damage the trust that has built up in these old, stable relationships.

Continuity expectations are higher when power is *balanced* in a relationship. Imbalanced power causes the weaker party to fear being exploited, such that it is more likely to defect. Knowing this, the stronger party discounts the potential for a future relationship, because it expects the weaker party to withdraw or go out of business. Thus, even when one party has the upper hand, it has less confidence that its relationship will last, compared with a balanced power scenario. But balanced power does not ensure a strong relationship, despite its continuity, as we noted in Chapter 10.

Finally, the *combined stakes* of the two parties also play a role: The more both sides get from the relationship, the more they expect it to continue. At least one party has too much to lose to let the relationship end without fighting to preserve it. Ideally, both parties have stakes (e.g., both derive substantial revenues from the arrangement), so both parties have an interest in avoiding a capricious end to the relationship end.

The belief among channel partners that their relationship has a future is a minimal condition for commitment. But to erect a true, strong, relational-based partnership, the next step demands that each side also *believe* that its partner is committed.

## Need for Reciprocation: Mutual Commitment

With some expectation of continuity, a strong relationship next requires the other party's commitment.[20] Earning this commitment demands that the focal party be committed itself. That is, **asymmetric commitment** is rare. Any partner to a relationship is going to do its own calculations. Why should it accept the obligations of being committed, unless it believes its counterpart is also committed and ready to assume its own obligations? Channel members that doubt the commitment of another organization may proclaim themselves partners, in the interest of preserving appearances, but they do not believe in, nor do they practice, commitment.

Deception certainly seems possible in this case, such as when one party seeks to convince its channel partner that its commitment is genuine, even when it is not. Yet most evidence suggests that this strategy rarely works. Upstream and downstream channel members are usually well informed about each other's true level of commitment. And they carefully and dynamically condition their own attitudes, depending on what they (reasonably accurately) believe about the other party's commitment. These accurate assessments are possible because organizations, unlike some people, are not very good actors. Even if every boundary spanner and point of contact were instructed to put up a façade, the counterpart ultimately can see through it. This works both ways: Truly committed firms may claim externally that they are questioning their commitment, in an attempt to conceal their dependence or vulnerability. But this projection fails too, and partners are rarely misled.

Wisely then, organizations do not gauge intentions by what their partner says but by what it *does*—and has done. The past lingers in relationships. For example, a certain level of conflict is to be expected in marketing channels, but some parties have experienced unusually high levels of manifest conflict (see Chapter 11). These relationships are difficult to salvage. Sustained conflict comes to operate like a feud, making it extremely difficult to move on and build commitment. Both upstream and downstream channel members likely discount the commitment of old adversaries, even after management changes or with assurances that "everything will be different now." Thus managers who allow conflict to remain out of control for extended periods are incurring opportunity costs that they might not recognize, because the relationship is unlikely to become a true partnership ever, even if peace ultimately is achieved.

The past lingers in a positive sense too. Once trust is established between organizations, it persists, even when individual employees move on.[21] This trait may seem surprising, because we often conceive of intangible relational states (e.g., trust, conflict, agreement on goals) as related only to people. But instead, relational states can belong to organizations, such that they outlive personnel turnover. **Organizational memory** effectively conditions what each party perceives with regard to the commitment level of its channel counterpart.

Suspicions of unbalanced commitment initiate a multistage process of change in a relationship. In the first stage, one party suspects—usually accurately—that it is more committed to the relationship than is the other party. In this uncomfortable position, the focal party feels "overcommitted" and vulnerable, fears being exploited, perceives more relationship conflict, and derives lower profits than it would if commitment levels were more balanced. Conversely, the "undercommitted" party enjoys its position of being less tied to the relationship, leaving it more satisfied with what it gains from its partnership. But the situation cannot go on indefinitely. In stage two, the overcommitted party seeks to find a way to bring the relationship back into alignment.

These stages describe a cycle of perception followed by adjustment. Two parties, such as a supplier and a distributor, reveal their levels of commitment, whether deliberately or inadvertently (or both). The resulting perceptions of commitment tend to be reasonably accurate and allow organizations to calibrate their own commitment, as an act of reciprocity. Thus, commitment tends toward alignment, often at mutually low levels. To increase commitment, one party must convince the other that its true commitment is higher and allow reciprocity to raise their mutual commitment levels.

## Strategies for Building Commitment

Imagine you are a distributor, dealing with a supplier. You gauge the supplier's commitment to you on the basis of its past behavior, focusing on two critical questions: (1) Have you had an acrimonious, conflict-laden past with this supplier? (2) What actions do you anticipate the supplier taking, to tie itself to your business?

These anticipated actions take two forms: selectivity and specialized investments. First, a higher degree of **selectivity** by the supplier gives you some degree of protection from competitors that might sell the same brand. With such high selectivity exercised by the supplier in its coverage of your market, you likely come to believe that the supplier is truly committed to a business partnership with you. At the limit, if you obtain territory exclusivity, you will regard the supplier as highly committed. Conversely, if nearly every other competitor in your market sells this brand too, you perceive little commitment from your supplier.

This question becomes somewhat more complicated when your supplier practices direct selling and maintains **house accounts** to serve some of its customers directly, in direct competition with you. Although such competition seemingly should destroy your confidence in its commitment, manufacturers often practice direct selling, even to a rather substantial degree, while still inspiring confidence in their commitment. Regardless of what you might say, you likely tolerate some direct selling, because you know some customers will only deal directly with the supplier. In that case, the supplier's direct selling does not take away any of your business. It might even relieve you of some channel duties that you do not want to perform, for specific customers with substantial demands. Other manufacturers may try to camouflage the full extent of their direct selling, but this fib is not really a major factor. Rather, the key point is your *perception* that the manufacturer is handling its direct business fairly, as opposed to being greedy and stealing business you could have earned.

Second, suppliers might seek to build assets that are dedicated to your relationship and that cannot be redeployed in connection with another distributor. These **idiosyncratic investments** are customized to your relationship; if the supplier were to replace you, it would need to write off (or at least greatly write down) this investment. To duplicate the value it has created through this investment and in its relationship with you, the supplier would need to make a new investment in a competitor that replaces you. Some notable, difficult-to-redeploy investments include the following:

- Supplier personnel and facilities dedicated to a single distributor
- A supplier's stock of learning about you—such as your methods, your people, your strengths, and your weaknesses
- Compatible reporting systems, geared to the peculiarities of your system (especially if your system is proprietary)
- Investments designed to identify your business and its business, in the minds of customer
- Investments in general training programs and other resources that help you run your business better
- A location near you but at a remove from your competitors

These assets vary in how easy they are to deploy, but all of them are costly to move. A switch in distributors means employees must be disrupted. Dedicated personnel may be reassigned, if there is other work for them, but their relationships with you become worthless. Facilities may be retrofitted, if they are still needed, but only with additional effort. Learning about you must be discarded. The supplier could offer training programs to your replacement, but doing so does not recoup the training expenses and efforts already invested in you. The supplier also could serve your competitors from a distant location, but that will incur extra costs. Worst of all for the supplier, it will be forced to explain to customers why its downstream representation has changed.

Such idiosyncratic investments are known as **credible commitments, pledges,** or **relationship-specific investments**. When manufacturers invest in you, your confidence in their commitment should soar, because they are erecting barriers to their *own* exit from their relationship with you.

Now take the perspective of the other side of the relationship: You are the supplier, gauging how committed the distributor is to its relationship with you. You likely discount pledges of commitment from partners who previously have had acrimonious relationships with you. You instead believe in the commitment of a distributor that gives you some degree of selectivity in your product category. At the limit, you will be inspired by the apparent commitment of a distributor that gives you category exclusivity (i.e., in your category, the distributor carries only your brand). And you will believe in the commitment of a distributor that invests in you in an idiosyncratic manner, such as one that

- Dedicates people and facilities to your line.
- Invests in upgrading and training the personnel serving your line.
- Seeks to learn about you and build relations with your people.
- Trains its customers in the use of your line.
- Attempts to ally its name and yours in customers' minds.
- Invests in a reporting system that is particularly compatible with yours (especially if yours is proprietary).
- Locates its facilities near you and far from your competitors.

As these parallel signals of commitment reveal, suppliers and distributors, upstream and downstream, look for similar things from their partners. A partner that makes idiosyncratic investments, offers greater selectivity, and is not stained by the lingering sense of conflict is one that is committed, which likely causes you to believe in the future of your relationship and commit yourself as well.

**HOW DOWNSTREAM CHANNEL MEMBERS COMMIT**    An exhibition of commitment inspires commitment. But other options are available for encouraging downstream channel members to commit to a supplier. At a fundamental level, a distributor enters relationships if it believes the payoffs will justify the costs. Therefore, it expects results that it cannot get through a more conventional, less committed relationship.

To achieve these results, the distributor dedicates resources to the supplier, including dedicated personnel, joint marketing, and so forth. These investments represent the distributor's efforts to expand the pie, that is, to generate exceptional results for the entire marketing channel.[22] *If* these investments are well considered, *if* the supplier works with the distributor, and *if* the distributor collects an equitable share of the pie, the distributor is motivated to invest more in the future. Over time, the accumulated investments a distributor has made become a motive to commit. The distributor works to keep its relationship going to protect its accrued investments.

In addition, two-way communication, involving the free exchange of information (even, or perhaps especially, sensitive details), close participation in the supplier's marketing efforts, allowing suppliers to see its weaknesses and strengths, and giving advice to the supplier can enhance commitment as well. Of course, no distributor will undertake these actions if the supplier expresses unwillingness. Two-way communication is a two-way street.

**HOW UPSTREAM CHANNEL MEMBERS COMMIT**    So what actions do suppliers take that commit them to their downstream channel member? Before making investments, many rigorously verify the downstream channel member's ability and motivation.[23] Once they have identified viable distributors, they can make idiosyncratic investments to expand the channel pie, such as training, mingling their brand image with the distributor's image, and so forth. Such investments both grow the pie and strengthen the relationship.

Two-way communication again plays a substantial role,[24] because it enables the manufacturer to look over the wall and see the market that the distributor serves. This transparency is somewhat dangerous for the distributor, because the supplier can use that information to exploit or compete against the downstream channel member.

Finally, it is worth highlighting that firms can create a close, committed relationship without creating a successful channel. The simple fact that two firms work together in a closely coordinated way does not ensure their success or the success of the channel. Some close, committed firms merely reinforce each other's dedication to a poor strategy.

## BUILDING CHANNEL TRUST

Another element is essential to strong relationships: trust. To some extent, trust can be created by making relationship-specific investments and communicating. But trust also is far more complex. It is a function of daily interactions, many of which are beyond top management's control. We therefore move next to the question of how to use the **concept of trust** to build stronger channel relationships.

What goes on "in the trenches" (i.e., the conduct of daily business) has an enormous impact on relationship formation, far more than pronouncements from corporate headquarters. Daily interactions between individuals in the channel lead the channel culture to improve, degrade, or stay stable. In this complex picture, the cumulative effects of daily interactions condition the relationship. In particular, daily events and one-on-one interactions determine how much trust exists, which is essential for a relationship to function and for building commitment.

**Trust**, though easy to recognize, is difficult to define.[25] Trust in a channel member is usefully conceptualized as confidence that the other party is **honest** (stands by its word, fulfills obligations, is sincere), together with assessments of the other party as **benevolent**, implying confidence that the other party is genuinely interested in one's welfare and interests, such that it will seek mutual gains rather than manipulate all the gains for itself. Overwhelming field evidence shows that in channel relationships, honesty and benevolence go together; where one is missing, so is the other. To trust a channel member is to believe in its integrity and concern for mutual well-being. To distrust is to fear deception and exploitation.

A strong relationship requires mutual commitment, and commitment cannot occur without trust. Such behavior is rational. It obviously would be a mistake to invest resources, sacrifice opportunities, and build a future with a party bent on exploitation and deception. A reasonable level of trust is necessary for *any* channel relationship to function. Distrust cannot characterize channel relationships for long; it either gets resolved, or the channel dissolves. But committed relationships exhibit higher-than-usual trust levels.

## Need for Economic Satisfaction

Channel members commit with a rational expectation of financial rewards. They will not commit without the prospect of financial returns, nor will they wait indefinitely for those rewards to materialize. Economic satisfaction plays a fundamental role in building and maintaining trust, which is necessary for committed relationships.[26]

**Economic satisfaction** is a positive, affective (emotional) response to the economic rewards generated by a channel relationship. Economic rewards are ultimately financial. So why cast them as an emotional state, rather than as utility? Why not speak in terms of money rather than affect?

The reason is that channel members simply don't compare money directly. It is difficult to put a precise accounting valuation on many outcomes (e.g., higher market share, greater store traffic). Even were a valuation to be made, it cannot be compared directly across organizations, because whereas 100,000 euros of economic returns might thrill one channel member, it could disappoint another.

Furthermore, channel members do not react to straightforward results. They react to how the results *compare* against several baselines they consider important, such as what they had expected, what they consider possible, what they consider equitable, or what they expect to gain from their next best alternative use of resources. The more the returns exceed a channel member's "reference value," the higher its likely level of satisfaction. Once an excess in returns exists, the channel member has every reason to believe that the channel can continue to generate similarly high returns.[27] Therefore, economic *satisfaction*, rather than economic *outcomes*, increases trust.

Economic satisfaction is so important that many firms agree to make risky, **generic investments** in channel members. These investments create vulnerability, because they empower the recipient to use the invested asset in the service of competitors. Yet firms that take this risk often are rewarded with higher commitment, especially if they are industry leaders and think to combine generic and idiosyncratic assets together in a package.[28] Sidebar 12-2 offers an example from the tobacco industry.

Unfortunately, we've established some circular logic here. Organizations build strong channel relationships to produce outcomes and increase economic satisfaction. Economic satisfaction increases trust and therefore builds relationships. So is economic performance a cause or an effect of committed relationships?

Well, it's both. The better the channel partnership performs financially, the more satisfied the parties are (at least roughly), and the more they trust the relationship. This trust builds commitment, which helps the parties expand their pie, which

---

## Sidebar 12-2

### Philip Morris substitutes channels for advertising

Consider an example of generic investment.[29] Philip Morris operates in France, a country with a complex set of tobacco limitations. On the one hand, cigarette advertising is totally forbidden and has been replaced by vigorous antismoking campaigns by the ministry of health. On the other hand, high tobacco taxes are a major source of revenue for the country, so government regulations oblige tobacco stores to accommodate smokers with long opening hours and a complete assortment of the 350 brands available in France. The government also seeks to ensure that rural smokers have easy access, so small tobacconists spring up all over the country, struggling to maintain the broad assortment. Jeanne Polles, the sales and marketing director for Philip Morris in France, explains, "Tobacconist shops are cluttered, not always very clean, and yet, under the new laws, it is the only place we have left to talk to our consumers."

For this supplier, the solution was training: a free half-day seminar on the importance of merchandising to any tobacco shops that wanted to join. The training, conducted by Philip Morris sales reps, offers different information than their once-a-month sales visit. The generic training actually benefits any products sold in the shops, including Philip Morris's competitors. The focus is solely to convince tobacconists of a seemingly obvious argument: Better merchandising and shelf placement boosts sales.

Philip Morris also makes no special effort to protect its generic investment from free riding, though in the process, it tries to create two idiosyncratic assets. First, the Philip Morris sales reps build good relationships with tobacconists. Second, they offer a key merchandising lesson by explaining to the tobacconists that "more people will come in if they put Marlboro in the window." This credible statement does not detract from the generic appeal of the training; it simply reflects the advantages of being a leading firm and a global brand.

---

increases satisfaction (unless the baseline comparison jumps higher than the results), which enhances trust, and so forth.

This description suggests a virtuous cycle. But the situation also can be difficult, in that we need good results to build a relationship, but we need a relationship to generate good results. This process has to start somewhere. The question is where. How do we build relationships without economic performance to establish trust?

### Strategies for Building Channel Partners' Trust

A substantial body of evidence indicates that trust is associated with several other properties, many of which involve psychological notions of noneconomic satisfaction. Because of their positive, affective (i.e., emotional) response to psychosocial aspects of the relationship,[30] satisfied channel members find interactions with their channel partners fulfilling, gratifying, and easy. They appreciate contacts and like working with their partner, who appears concerned, respectful, and willing to exchange ideas (a foundation for two-way communication).

**ROLE OF NONECONOMIC FACTORS**  Many noneconomic drivers of trust appear purely interpersonal, but they also apply to the interorganizational level, such that they get reproduced over and over, through daily interactions among people working for channel organizations. In some short-sighted channels, these positive sentiments get dismissed as "nice but not necessary," or perhaps even irrelevant or insufficiently "business-like." Yet study after study demonstrates that noneconomic satisfaction is tightly bound to trust, which is critical for building financially desirable relationships.

What produces noneconomic satisfaction? Two drivers stand out due to their absence, namely, the **absence of dysfunctional conflict**, or lingering, unresolved, intense disputes over major issues, and the **absence of coercion** by the other side. A party that perceives pressure, punishment, threats, and retribution from its partner experiences a rapid decline of positive sentiment, even if the relationship moves in a direction the channel member prefers. In contrast, the liberal use of noncoercive influence strategies, such as exchanging information, offering assistance, and making requests, effectively increases noneconomic satisfaction. These methods help resolve conflict without blunt intrusiveness. By trying to influence partners in a noncoercive way, organizations create the impression of being accommodating, responsive problem solvers.

Noneconomic satisfaction also is bound up with perceptions of fairness, on two fronts:[31] **procedural fairness**, or the sense of being treated equitably on a day-to-day basis, regardless of the rewards derived from the relationship, and **distributive fairness**, or gaining equitable rewards from the relationship, regardless of daily interaction patterns. Distributive and procedural equities reinforce noneconomic satisfaction.

**CHANNEL PARTNER SELECTION**  Organizations are poor candidates for forging committed relationships unless they possess complementary capabilities that they can exploit to create competitive advantages. With complementarity, organizations might believe they can ally through declarations, such that each corporate headquarters issues instructions: "Bonding will commence, effective immediately!" It rarely works (as demonstrated by many channel members). Trust is never awarded. It must be earned, through substantial time and effort.

Many organizations accordingly seek to build on what they already have. If parties have prior social and economic ties, they possess the invaluable asset of **social capital**, which they seek to leverage by developing their ties further. In foreign markets, for example, firms with an existing marketing arrangement with a distributor might add new products to the channel, even if that channel is not ideal for the product otherwise. As the old saying goes, familiarity breeds trust. For most firms, doing business with firms they know is the safest bet, and if they need to extend their networks, they do business with firms known to the firms they know (i.e., referrals).[32] Personal relationships and reputations in channel organizations help intensify existing relationships, increasing the social capital already embedded in them.[33]

Of course, organizations cannot always work with organizations they already know, and social capital is not necessarily related to firm size or profitability. Sometimes the best partner is a smaller account that is critical to the firm's future (e.g., because it is an innovator that influences other firms). Thus, firms often adopt elaborate **qualifying** strategies to learn about potential partner firms before doing business with them. For example, to build new forms of trust, it can be useful to identify and select new partners with similar goals. **Goal congruence** effectively dampens conflict and can lead to rapid relationship building.

In addition to goal congruence, the qualifying process for retailers seeking garment manufacturers, for example, might include assessments of their actual garment quality, manufacturing capacity, price competitiveness, general business philosophy, reputation with other apparel companies and retailers, and reputation for garment quality and on-time delivery. To conduct this sort of investigation, the retailer needs the cooperation of resellers, which is not easy to achieve. As a signal though, resellers that cooperate in the qualification phase likely are already inclined to work with the prospective supplier. Therefore, qualification tactics screen which channel members are most willing and able to partner in a trustworthy manner, leading to relationships that tend to be unusually flexible, especially in the face of uncertainty.[34]

Yet we still find firms that engage in virtually no screening, content to trust their impressions or assurances. In one notable example, a channel manager of a motorcycle manufacturer was confident in his judgment, based on his excellent track record in picking good distributors. He used his instincts to award exclusive distribution rights for Costa Rica to a seemingly impressive firm that promised a large initial order. But the partner never delivered the promised order. After some months, the manufacturer investigated, only to learn that the owner of his exclusive distributor had a brother who was also a distributor—representing a directly competing line of motorcycles![35]

Some people simply are trusting—it is part of their personality (whereas others are prone to cynicism and unlikely to trust in any circumstances). This personality trait also appears among organizations, as part of their corporate **culture**. These companies actively seek to cultivate a reputation for being trustworthy (while others seek to disguise their culture of exploitation and dishonesty). To some extent then, an organization's trustworthiness is a part of its culture.[36]

Finally, some environments are conducive to building trust. Trust increases in generous, or munificent, environments that offer resources, growth, and ample opportunity. These environments provide every incentive to work together, with rewards to be had by everyone. Trust instead declines in volatile, complex, unpredictable environments. These risky, treacherous, and difficult environments require constant monitoring and fast adaptation. Such conditions strain any relationship and create opportunities for both misunderstanding and disputes.

**DECISION-MAKING PROCESSES**    The decision making that takes place within a marketing channel is closely structured. Perhaps the most important element of that structure is how much decision making gets centralized within the upper reaches of an organization's hierarchy, whether upstream or downstream. Whatever its source, **centralization** hurts trust.[37] Concentrating decision power in the upper echelons of one organization (rather than delegating decision making to the field, across organizations) undermines participation, cooperation, and daily interactions that promote trust. Yet centralization also offers a way for an organization to marshal its own resources to get things done. That is, we cannot blindly condemn centralized decision making, but we do recognize the need to acknowledge its costs in terms of building trust.

The channel decision-making structure also consists of **formalization**, or the degree to which decision making relies on rules and explicit procedures. Formalization also tends to hinder trust, because such a mechanistic approach to interactions robs the players of their autonomy. Formalization also might signal that one party mistrusts the other, inviting reciprocal mistrust. However, evidence that is more recent suggests that the *nature* of the formalization is really what matters. That is, formalization can enhance positive attitudes and trust if it helps clarify how to perform tasks and who is responsible for them.[38] Formalization that clarifies roles thus could be helpful, rather than constraining, such that when more channel members agree about who is responsible for what (i.e., domain consensus), their level of trust rises.

In this context, we also note that the more channel members communicate, the more they cooperate on a daily basis. The more they cooperate, the more they come to trust one another. Working together on issues with mutual relevance, such as market decision making and planning, builds a basis for trust. But here again, we achieve a circular logic: Working together is both a cause (immediately) and an effect (later) of trust. This circularity, by which actions that enhance trust and commitment create further trust and commitment, helps explain why strong channel partnerships take time to build—especially when the channels are marked by distrust from the start.

**OVERCOMING CHANNEL DISTRUST**    Imagine you manage a downstream channel member and want to build a strong relationship with one of your suppliers, but the level of overall trust in the channel is low. What should you do first? Increase communication? Seek greater cooperation? Reduce conflict? Make conflict more functional? Align your organizations' goals? Reduce your efforts to influence the other party through coercion and substitute reasoned arguments and greater accommodation instead? Pay more attention to issues of fairness?

Well, yes. But here is the paradox: Even as you, the top manager, dedicate yourself to building trust, neither your employees nor the employees of your counterpart are inclined to implement your plans. Why? *Because they don't trust each other.* Even if you can induce your own employees to make the effort, your channel counterpart may block the implementation of and ignore your best efforts.

All top management can do is attempt to create a structure that is conducive to building trust and hope that employees will adjust their everyday behavior accordingly. For example, organizations might balance each other's dependence by granting selectivity and making idiosyncratic investments. In addition, they can eschew centralized decision making and use their influence over their own personnel to elicit desired behavior, hoping for reciprocity.

Ultimately though, the structures and policies instituted to implement trust only create a foundation for it. From that foundation, the daily interactions between people and the accumulation of experience are required to turn the structural opportunity into an operational reality. The bad news is that it is a slow, expensive, uncertain process. The good news is that trust encourages behaviors that reinforce trust. And if you can achieve it, a marketing channel with high levels of trust is nearly impossible to imitate.

**PREVENTING PERCEPTIONS OF UNFAIRNESS**    Relationships can be easily damaged by unresolved perceptions of unfairness.[39] Unfairness not only directly undermines channel partners' trust and commitment but also aggravates the negative effects of any unresolved conflict or perceived opportunism. Contracts are not the answer; they can enhance the negative effects of unfairness on cooperative behaviors and performance. Instead, channel members need to recognize what causes their partners to perceive unfair treatment. For example, many automobile dealers depend on manufacturers with strong brand names and invest heavily in these brands. Those investments would be difficult to salvage or reassign, so the dealership has high switching costs. The manufacturer instead has multiple candidates that want to become dealers and thus is less dependent on any one of them. As a result, the automotive industry is filled with examples of dealers that accuse their manufacturer partners of exploitation.

To avoid such accusations and the relationship deterioration that comes with them, the manufacturer needs to ensure that it exhibits **distributive fairness**, such that it determines the profits it shares with dealers by considering more than absolute rewards. Instead, both parties should compare the benefits they derive from the relationship against four baselines:

- Their own inputs, or what they put into the relationship;
- The benefits derived by comparable dealers;
- The benefits available from the next best alternative (e.g., for dealers, selling another make of car or investing capital elsewhere); and
- The other party's inputs, or what it puts into the relationship.

Low absolute rewards shared with the dealer may seem fair if

- The dealer invests little.
- Other dealers gain little.
- The dealer has no better use for it resources.
- The manufacturer invests heavily in the relationship.

Conversely, even very high absolute rewards may seem unfair or inequitable to dealers if

- The dealer invests heavily.
- Other dealers are very profitable.
- Other opportunities are appealing.
- The manufacturer invests little.

Another facet of fairness is **procedural justice**, which depends on how the stronger party treats the weaker party on a day-to-day basis (i.e., normal operating procedures). This issue is separate from the fairness of rewards. For example, auto dealers consider their supplier fairer if the manufacturer communicates both ways (listens as well as talks), appears impartial, and remains open to argument and debate. In this case, the manufacturer's personnel are critical, because procedural justice perceptions stem from how they interact with the dealer, such as whether they explain themselves clearly, act courteously, and exhibit knowledge about their channel partner's situation.

Some field evidence suggests that procedural justice actually has more impact than distributive justice on the more vulnerable party's sense that the relationship is equitable—regardless of whether the relationship achieves objective equity. A key reason is that distributive justice is not readily observable (who really knows all the factors that influence it?), whereas procedural justice is readily and regularly observable.

## THE CHANNEL RELATIONSHIP LIFE CYCLE

### The Five Stages of a Channel Relationships

A close marketing channel relationship is like a living creature, moving through its biological life cycle by proceeding through stages of development. Let's take a hypothetical supplier, Omega Industries, and a hypothetical distributor, Annecy Ltd. These two organizations may form a marketing channel through a series of ongoing transactions, each evaluated on its own merits, such that each side is ready to terminate or reduce its business dealings. This series of discrete transactions is a marketing channel, but it is not a close relationship. To develop into an ongoing, committed relationship, the channel would need to pass through five development stages,[40] as listed in Figure 12-3.

**Stage 1:  Awareness.** Omega is aware that Annecy is a feasible exchange partner, but neither party has made specific contact to explore doing business or upgrading their transactional business dealings into a stronger, more continuous relationship. (Our hypothetical example could easily go the other way, making Annecy the focal party that recognizes that Omega is a feasible supplier to upgrade to a preferred partnership level.) This stage can last a very long time, with no real progress, and it may simply dissipate if either firm decides its counterpart is not a good partnership candidate, for whatever reason. Or the arrangement could progress.

**Stage 2:  Exploration.** Omega and Annecy investigate forging a stable relationship. They likely test each other during a trial-and-evaluation period (which can be lengthy, especially for important, risky, complex channel functions). Each side forecasts and weighs the costs and benefits of creating a close marketing channel together. When the managers of each firm describe this stage, they might comment:

> You can't start out with a full-blown relationship. It's got to be incremental. You get closer as each side takes small steps.
> If it's going to be long-lasting, it doesn't happen overnight.[41] But if the players both achieve promising calculations, they engage in communication and negotiation. Norms (i.e., expected patterns of behavior) begin to form, as do mutual trust and joint satisfaction. But in this delicate stage, the relationship is just emerging from its cocoon. The behaviors adopted in this early stage have substantial impact on its future survival. In particular, each side draws inferences about the other, though without must of a basis of prior knowledge. Intangible perceptions (e.g., goal congruence) play a major role, informed largely by early interactions and outcomes. Such relationships accelerate sharply if the two sides make idiosyncratic investments.[42] In addition, each partner's use of its power determines whether both sides want to continue to evolve, and the expectations developed during this exploration phase determine whether partnership ultimately is achievable.

**Stage 3:  Expansion.** In its adolescence, the relationship starts to grow rapidly. Each side derives greater benefits, develops greater motivation, and elaborates on the relationship. If management can ensure that each side perceives the benefits are being shared equitably, trust spirals upward, and interdependence increases. In this exciting stage, morale is high, leading Annecy and Omega to cooperate and perceive that they are pursuing common goals. Interaction becomes even greater than is strictly necessary, in part

| Relationship Phase 1: Awareness | Relationship Phase 2: Exploration | Relationship Phase 3: Expansion | Relationship Phase 4: Commitment | Relationship Phase 5: Decline and Dissolution |
|---|---|---|---|---|
| • One organization sees another as a feasible exchange partner<br>• Little interaction<br>• Networks are critical: One player recommends another<br>• Physical proximity matters: Parties more likely to be aware of each other<br>• Experience with transactions in other domains (other products, markets, functions) can be used to identify parties | • Testing, probing by both sides<br>• Investigation of each other's natures and motives<br>• Interdependence grows<br>• Bargaining is intensive<br>• Selective revealing of information is initiated and must be reciprocated<br>• Great sensitivity to issues of power and justice<br>• Norms begin to emerge<br>• Role definitions become more elaborated<br>• Key feature: Each side draws inferences and tests them<br>• This stage is easily terminated by either side | • Benefits expand for both sides<br>• Interdependence expands<br>• Risk taking increases<br>• Satisfaction with results leads to greater motivation and deepening commitment<br>• Goal congruence increases<br>• Cooperation increases<br>• Communication increases<br>• Alternative partners look less attractive<br>• Key feature: Momentum must be maintained. To progress, each party must seek new areas of activity and maintain consistent efforts to create mutual payoffs | • Each party invests to build and maintain the relationship<br>• Long-time horizon<br>• Parties may be aware of alternatives but do not court them<br>• High expectations on both sides<br>• High mutual dependence<br>• High trust<br>• Partners resolve conflict and adapt to each other and to their changing environment<br>• Shared values and/or contractual mechanisms (such as shared risk) reinforce mutual dependence<br>• Key features: Loyalty, adaptability, continuity, high mutual dependence set these relationships apart | • Tends to be sparked by one side<br>• Mounting dissatisfaction leads one side to hold back investment<br>• Lack of investment provokes the other side to reciprocate<br>• Dissolution may be abrupt but is usually gradual<br>• Key feature: It takes two to build but only one to undermine.<br>• Decline often sets in without the two parties' realization |
| 1 | 2 | 3 | 4 | 5 |

**FIGURE 12-3  Relationship phases in marketing channels**

because each side's personnel like the communication, such that they might acknowledge:

> Over time, you build a history of situations, compromises, and solutions. You learn the unwritten rules and how they want to play the game, which makes it increasingly easier to do business.[43]

Managers on both sides should use this stage to deepen their interdependence, setting the stage for commitment to stabilize.

**Stage 4: Commitment.** The relationship is easily recognizable and stable—fully grown, in a sense. It has developed a substantial history, marked by investments, interdependence, and strong norms. The intangible factors (e.g., perceived goal congruence) are less important, simply because the partnership can rely instead on its rich infrastructure. Thus, both Annecy and Omega count on the relationship and invest heavily to maintain the strong partnership they have achieved. Neither side is very open to overtures by other firms; they prefer doing business with each other and may say:

> We are constantly changing things to try to improve the way we do business together. We will experiment with new ideas, test new processes, try something different. Costs are incurred on both sides but we are willing to pay them. We have learned a lot from them. They have made us a better printing company because they are demanding, innovative, and willing to try things.[44]

Yet management also must be attentive to maintaining the relationship, lest it slip into decline and dissolution. Even in the strongest relationship, strains occur.

**Stage 5: Decline to Dissolution.** When the relationship starts to die, Omega and Annecy cease to have a close partnership. They may resume their old transactional links, though they are more likely to cease doing business at all. Dissolutions are usually accompanied by acrimony, after having been initiated by one side that has grown dissatisfied with the arrangement. This side begins to withdraw and behave in a manner inconsistent with commitment. The annoyed other side reciprocates with neglectful, damaging, or destructive behavior. Decline rapidly takes a momentum of its own.

Decline and dissolution also can happen when one party takes the relationship for granted and fails to work to keep it going. Alternatively, one party might sabotage the relationship, to free itself to move on to other opportunities. But decline also can be like a cancer, a lingering process that is unapparent to the parties until it is too far advanced to be cured.

## Managing the Stages

One implication of the notion of these five stages of development is that relationships are difficult to build quickly and from the ground up. Development takes time, particularly if the targeted partners do not currently do business together. Every existing channel member is a potential asset in this respect, because extant business links, even minor ones, help the awareness and exploration phases proceed much faster and can upgrade the relationship more swiftly and surely.

But a caveat also is in order. Despite the appeal of the stages-of-development idea as a way to think about creating a relationship and keeping it going, relationship development rarely is as linear, orderly, and sequential as the five stages imply.[45] On a daily basis, relationships constitute a series of episodes or critical incidents that help the players define their common purpose, set boundaries on their relationship, create value (and claim their share of it), and evaluate their returns from the relationship. Through their repeated interactions, firms may develop sufficient critical incidents to move their relationship from a series of transactions to a real partnership, and in retrospect, managers might even remember their experiences as corresponding to stages, though they recognize those stages only after considerable development has occurred.

At the time of their development though, relationships often do not progress in an orderly way. Thus, it is difficult to say with confidence what stage a relationship is in for much of its history. However, the good news is that if a relationship seems to be regressing (e.g., moving from expansion to exploration), there is no real cause for alarm. In retrospect, the regression could be just a blip, and it does not mean the relationship is doomed to deteriorate.[46]

We thus might consider an alternative perceptive on categorizing relationships into phases, one that describes of the state of a relationship at a specific point in time by capturing **relationship velocity**, or the rate and direction of change in commitment. Relationship velocity offers a stronger predictor of performance than relationship level, due to people's propensity to use trend extrapolation as a decision heuristic.[47] For example, as shown in Figure 12-4, relationships may display the same level of commitment at two points in a relationship life cycle (dotted line), one with positive and one with negative velocity. Accounting only for their level, a channel member might predict that its customers will make similar choices at both points. Instead, and more accurately, by accounting for relationship velocity, it can include additional, behavior-relevant information. Its customers likely will make their decisions on the basis of their perceptions of the direction and rate of change in the relationship. Managers who know the velocity or trend of their relationships can better predict channel members' decisions.

## Managing Troubled Relationships

Relationships require maintenance, though they also can wear out, even if maintained properly. In a common scenario, one partner might begin to suspect that the other partner is taking advantage of the spirit of their understanding and failing to live up to its promises, actual or implied. This suspicion can poison even effectively functioning relationships, creating a self-fulfilling prophecy in which the suspicious party angrily withholds its effort and prompts the suspected party to reciprocate. The relationship then spirals downward, as performance declines.

Some kinds of relationships can better withstand the pressures of suspicion though. Research indicates that relationships bound by mutual idiosyncratic investments continue to perform even as suspicion increases.[48] Relationships with a foundation of congruent goals also continue to perform. In this case, the parties take their congruent goals for granted and forget about them when all is well, then rediscover this relationship property and use it to enhance their joint results when they face the

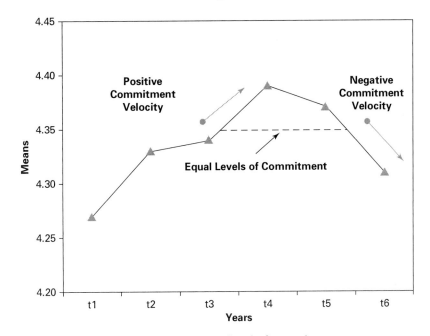

**FIGURE 12-4**   Role of relationship velocity versus level of commitment

*Notes:* Means for commitment reflect each of the first six years in 433 channel relationships.

*Source:* Adapted from Palmatier, Robert W., Mark B. Houston, Rajiv P. Dant, and Dhruv Grewal (2013), "Relationship Velocity: Toward a Theory of Relationship Dynamics," *Journal of Marketing*, 77 (January), pp. 13–30.

pressure of mounting suspicion. In contrast, dyads that rely on interpersonal trust between a key person on each side likely suffer performance decrements with greater suspicion, because the two "custodians" come under scrutiny. Other players (accountants, sales managers, finance managers) question their relationship and intervene, offsetting the beneficial effects of the trust between these key individuals.

As in this case, some of the best, most trusting relationships hold within them the seeds of their own decline.[49] Trust induces hidden costs, because at very high levels, people may not ask enough probing or difficult questions. If relationships lack enough constructive conflict, settle on agreements too easily, or become too homogeneous, they dampen creativity. Worst of all, trusted parties may exploit their partners, using their accumulated confidence to ensure that the trust or never sees what is going on.[50]

## Relationship Portfolios

So even trusting relationships can fail, and relational-based partnerships may not be worth their accounting and opportunity costs. Faced with such positive and negative assessments of close relationships, it should come as no surprise that most firms maintain a broad portfolio of channel partners, representing a wide spectrum of relationship strength levels. Ultimately, manufacturers need a portfolio of downstream relationships to cover the market and meet multiple service output demands. Downstream channel members need a portfolio of suppliers and brands to cover the assorted needs of their customers and prospects. All firms need some strong relationships with channel partners to gather information and calibrate strategy and tactics, but they can function efficiently and effectively in more conventional business interactions too.[51] Firms even might gain some unique benefits from weak ties. For example, when buying complex, information-intensive, high-risk products (e.g., IT systems), customers might prefer resellers with strong ties to IT manufacturers. Yet they also appreciate a reseller that has weak ties with multiple IT makers, because they can scan varied sources of supply to get innovative ideas and create new possibilities, without committing to any one supplier.[52]

## SUMMARY: MANAGING CHANNEL RELATIONSHIPS

Strong channel relationships, once achieved, function admirably. They generate competitive advantages, with attendant financial rewards. They are capable of outperforming a channel owned by a single organization. They function so well that the customer has no idea where one company stops and another begins. So, should every channel manager aim to build a strong relationship with all channel members?

In response, we offer a new metaphor: A relationship is more akin to truffles than to wheat. A truffle—a type of mushroom prized by gourmet cooks—cannot be produced to order or at will. No one knows exactly how to grow them. Instead, they appear randomly in nature, in *certain conditions*. And truffle hunters, despite their considerable skills, could never claim to be truffle farmers. In contrast, wheat can be grown commercially to order, according to a known formula, by any farmer who has access to the basic conditions that encourage crop growth.

The conditions that favor a strong relationship can be created, but a relationship may or may not arise. Unlike wheat, relationships cannot be produced at will, even with seemingly perfect conditions. Instead, like truffles, relationships may be best discovered by seeking them in what seem to be ideal conditions. The ability to create these conditions is limited, so relationships do not always appear where they might be expected. Many firms have tried unsuccessfully to build a strong channel relationship, perhaps without realizing that other relationships already exist, unappreciated, right under their noses. These relationships spring up, seemingly spontaneously, without top management direction, due to the (often unsuspected) efforts of field personnel.

The right conditions also depend on the firm's strategy, industry, and market. In many of these conditions, a strong relationship may not be necessary, and building one may even be counterproductive, when the costs of relationship building outweigh the benefits.[53] Instead of a truffle, the firm might wind up with a fungus—when what it really needs is a nice, "transactional" wheat crop that is not only perfectly adequate but also can generate better net results. Few firms have the resources to develop intense relationships with all the organizations with which they need to work to cover their markets. A firm must select its channel partners carefully before investing in them, because it could pick the wrong partner, or even be better off with several, mundane, but less demanding channel relationships.

That said, a relationship is appropriate in three key, simultaneous conditions, when:[54]

1. One side has special needs.
2. The other side has the capability to meet these needs.
3. Each side faces barriers to exiting the relationship.

The first two conditions create a basis for distinctive added value, which is a foundation for strategic partnerships. Parties with special needs may not find satisfaction in a traditional marketplace, using mundane transactions or regularly available channel members. A partner that can meet extraordinary needs already establishes a basis for a sophisticated exchange, to the exclusion of most other possible pairings.

The third condition prevents one side from exploiting the other. Returning to our hypothetical example, if Omega has special needs (e.g., product handling, customization) and Annecy can meet them, their fruitful exchange goes on—but not indefinitely. Annecy may make investments specific to Omega, creating vulnerability. Or it might train its customers to value Omega's brands, only to have Omega appoint a new distributor to exploit this loyal customer base. But if Omega also builds barriers to its own switching, the situation stabilizes. Ideally, both Omega and Annecy develop and recognize enduring reasons to stay with the relationship. The best reasons for doing so include relationships with strong norms or mutual dependence, which make it so difficult for the parties to disentangle themselves that they simply prefer to keep going and investing in each other and their relationship.

## TAKE-AWAYS

- A relational channel partnership exists when two or more organizations have enduring, substantial connections that cause them to function according to their perceived single, shared interest. Committed parties
  - Desire the relationship to continue indefinitely.
  - Are willing to sacrifice to maintain and grow the relationship.
- Three conditions favor a strong channel relationship:
  - The target has special needs.
  - The potential partner is able to meet these needs.
  - The potential partner can erect barriers to exit.
- Relationships serve both upstream and downstream needs to create enduring competitive advantages, leading to profits.
- Relationships require an expectation of continuity, which grows with the following:
  - Mutual communication
  - Balanced power
  - Higher combined stakes of both parties
  However, older relationships may be more fragile than they appear, because the parties may not communicate sufficiently, in the false belief they don't need so.
- No one knows how to manufacture commitment, but relationships clearly need mutual dependence and the perception of mutual commitment.
- Firms rely more heavily on actions, particularly by people at the field level, than on what top management announces. In particular, they look for the following:
  - Pledges, which are idiosyncratic investments in the partner firm that make the giver more dependent on the target by
    - Motivating the giver to support the relationship.
    - Generating real productive value that is difficult to find elsewhere.
    - Signaling commitment intent to the counterpart.

- History, both their own and that underlying the partner's reputation for fair business dealings with channel members.
- The foundation of a strong relationship is trust, which combines confidence in the other party's honesty with a sense of its genuine interest in welfare.
- Trust flourishes in response to satisfaction with noneconomic outcomes, including the absence of coercion and dysfunctional conflict. (Functional conflict and trust coexist easily.)
- Perceptions of procedural and distributive fairness support trust, also by enhancing noneconomic satisfaction.
- Economic satisfaction drives and results from relationships. As a party derives more financial rewards from the relationship, its trust increases, which strengthens the relationship, which works together more effectively, which generates more rewards and reinitiates the upward spiral of commitment.
- The search for a good partner should start with the set of familiar channel members, which usually offer some social capital that also can be enhanced.
- Relationship building is more likely to work in the following:
  - Favorable settings that offer resources, growth, and opportunity, rather than being complex, volatile, and unpredictable.
  - Decentralized decision-making settings, with a culture that cultivates trust and clarifies who is responsible for what.
  - The presence of candid, mutual, frequent communication and after the passage of time.
- Trust has a hidden downside, in that trusting partners may not generate enough constructive conflict, and each party could take advantage of the other's trust.
- A portfolio of relationships with varying degrees of closeness is desirable, because most firms need a mix of transactional and committed relationships to cover their markets and meet customer needs effectively and efficiently.

## Endnotes

1. Frazier, Gary L. (1999), "Organizing and Managing Channels of Distribution," *Journal of the Academy of Marketing Science* 2, no. 2 (Spring), pp. 226–240.
2. Hotopf, Max (2004), "The Beefs of Channel Managers," *Routes to Market* (Spring), pp. 3–4.
3. Hotopf, Max (2004), "Making A Multi-Channel Strategy Work," *Routes to Market* (Autumn), pp. 7–8.
4. Hotopf, Max (2003), "Snuggling Up to Big Retail," *Routes to Market* (Winter), pp. 13–14.
5. Fein, Adam J. and Sandy D. Jap (1999), "Manage Consolidation in the Distribution Channel," *Sloan Management Review* 41 (Fall), pp. 61–72.
6. Kumar, Nirmalya (1996), "The Power of Trust in Manufacturer-Retailer Relationships," *Harvard Business Review* 60 (November–December), pp. 92–106.
7. Kim, Keysuk (1999), "On Determinants of Joint Action in Industrial Distributor-Supplier Relationships: Beyond Economic Efficiency," *International Journal of Research in Marketing* 16 (September), pp. 217–236.
8. Palmatier, Robert W., Rajiv P. Dant, and Dhruv Grewal (2007), "A Comparative Longitudinal Analysis of Theoretical Perspectives of Interorganizational Relationship Performance," *Journal of Marketing* 71 (October), pp. 172–194.

9. Kramer, Roderick M. (1999), "Trust and Distrust in Organizations: Emerging Perspectives, Enduring Questions," *Annual Review of Psychology* 50, pp. 569–598.

10. Li, Zhan G. and Rajiv P. Dant (1999), "Effects of Manufacturers' Strategies on Channel Relationships," *Industrial Marketing Management* 28, no. 1, pp. 131–143.

11. Siguaw, Judy A., Penny M. Simpson, and Thomas L. Baker (1998), "Effects of Supplier Orientation on Distributor Market Orientation and the Channel Relationship: The Distributor Perspective," *Journal of Marketing* 62 (July), pp. 99–111; Sethuraman, Rajagopalan, James C. Anderson, and James A. Narus (1988), "Partnership Advantage and Its Determinants in Distributor and Manufacturer Working Relationships," *Journal of Business Research* 17 (December), pp. 327–347.

12. Iacobucci, Dawn and Jonathan D. Hibbard (1999), "Toward an Encompassing Theory of Business Marketing Relationships (BMRs) and Interpersonal Commercial Relationships (ICRs): An Empirical Examination," *Journal of Interactive Marketing* 13, no. 3, pp. 13–33.

13. Anderson, Erin, William T. Ross, and Barton Weitz (1998), "Commitment and its Consequences in the American Agency System of Selling Insurance," *Journal of Risk and Insurance* 65, no. 4, pp. 637–669.

14. Palmatier, Robert W., Lisa K. Scheer, Kenneth R. Evans, and Todd Arnold (2008), "Achieving Relationship Marketing Effectiveness in Business-to Business Exchanges," *Journal of the Academy of Marketing Science* 36 (June), pp. 174–190.

15. Jackson, Barbara Bund (1985), "Build Customer Relationships that Last," *Harvard Business Review* 63 (November–December), pp. 120–128.

16. Heide, Jan B. and Anne S. Miner (1992), "The Shadow of the Future: Effects of Anticipated Interaction and Frequency of Contact on Buyer-Seller Cooperation," *Academy of Management Journal* 35 (June), pp. 265–291.

17. Weiss, Allen M., Erin Anderson, and Deborah J. MacInnis (1999), "Reputation Management as a Motive for Sales Structure Decisions," *Journal of Marketing* 63 (October), pp. 74–89.

18. Anderson, Erin and Barton Weitz (1989), "Determinants of Continuity in Conventional Channel Dyads," *Marketing Science* 8 (Fall), pp. 310–323.

19. Mohr, Jakki and John R. Nevin (1990), "Communication Strategies in Marketing Channels: A Theoretical Perspective," *Journal of Marketing* 54 (October), pp. 36–51.

20. Much of this section draws on Anderson, Erin and Barton Weitz (1992), "The Use of Pledges to Build and Sustain Commitment in Distribution Channels," *Journal of Marketing Research* 24 (February), pp. 18–34.

21. Zaheer, Akbar, Bill McEvily, and Vincenzo Perrone (1998), "Does Trust Matter? Exploring the Effects of Interorganizational and Interpersonal Trust on Performance," *Organization Science* 9 (March–April), pp. 141–159.

22. Jap, Sandy D. (1999), "'Pie-Expansion' Efforts: Collaboration Processes in Buyer-Supplier Relationships," *Journal of Marketing Research* 36 (November), pp. 461–475.

23. Stump, Rodney L, and Jan B. Heide (1996), "Controlling Supplier Opportunism in Industrial Relations," *Journal of Marketing Research* 33 (November), pp. 431–441.

24. Palmatier, Robert W., Rajiv P. Dant, Dhruv Grewal, and Kenneth R. Evans (2006), "Factors Influencing the Effectiveness of Relationship Marketing: A Meta-Analysis," *Journal of Marketing* 70 (October), pp. 136–153.

25. Geyskens, Inge, Jan-Benedict E.M. Steenkamp, and Nirmalya Kumar (1998), "Generalizations About Trust in Marketing Channel Relationships Using Meta Analysis," *International Journal of Research in Marketing* 15 no. 1, pp. 223–248.

26. Ganesan, Shankar (1994), "Determinants of Long-Term Orientation in Buyer-Seller Relationships," *Journal of Marketing* 58 (April), pp. 1–19.

27. The concept of a "reference value" for a monetary cost or profit also appear in pricing literature, where a consumer's "reference price" is the price she or he expects to pay for an item; a price *lower* than that value has

a positive impact on purchase intentions. See Kalyanaram, G. and Russell, S. Winer (1995), "Empirical Generalizations from Reference Price Research," *Management Science* 14, no. 3, pp. G161–G169; Winer, R.S. (1986), "A Reference Price Model of Brand Choice for Frequently Purchased Products," *Journal of Consumer Research* 13 (September), pp. 250–256.

28. Galunic, Charles D. and Erin Anderson (2000), "From Security to Mobility: An Examination of Employee Commitment and an Emerging Psychological Contract," *Organization Science* 11 (January–February), pp. 1–20.

29. Hotopf, Max (2002), "Skilling Your Channel," *Routes to Market* (Autumn), pp. 4–7.

30. Geyskens, Inge, Jan-Benedict E.M. Steenkamp, and Nirmalya Kumar (1999), "A Meta-Analysis of Satisfaction in Marketing Channel Relationships," *Journal of Marketing Research* 36 (May), pp. 223–238.

31. Kumar, Nirmalya, Lisa K. Scheer, and Jan-Benedict E.M. Steenkamp (1995), "The Effects of Supplier Fairness on Vulnerable Resellers," *Journal of Marketing Research* 32 (February), pp. 54–65.

32. Gulati, Ranjay (1998), "Alliances and Networks," *Strategic Management Journal* 19, no. 1, pp. 293–317.

33. Weitz, Barton A. and Sandy D. Jap (1995), "Relationship Marketing and Distribution Channels," *Journal of the Academy of Marketing Science* 23, no. 4, pp. 305–320.

34. Wathne, Kenneth H. and Jan B. Heide (2004), "Relationship Governance in a Supply Chain Network," *Journal of Marketing* 68, no. 1, pp. 73–89.

35. Thomas, Andrew R. and Timothy J. Wilkonson (2005), "It's the Distribution, Stupid!" *Business Horizons* 48, no. 1, pp. 125–134.

36. Dyer, Jeffery H. and Harbir Singh (1998), "The Relational View: Cooperative Strategy and Sources of Interorganizational Competitive Advantage," *Academy of Management Review* 23, no. 4, pp. 660–679.

37. Frazier (1999), op. cit.

38. Dahlstrom, Robert and Arne Nygaard (1999), "An Empirical Investigation of Ex Post Transaction Costs in Franchised Distribution Channels," *Journal of Marketing Research* 36 (May), pp. 160–170.

39. Samaha, Stephen A., Robert W. Palmatier, and Rajiv P. Dant (2011), "Poisoning Relationships: Perceived Unfairness in Channels of Distribution," *Journal of Marketing* 75, no. 3, pp. 99–117.

40. Dwyer, F. Robert, Paul H. Schurr, and Sejo Oh (1987), "Developing Buyer-Seller Relationships," *Journal of Marketing* 51 (April), pp. 11–27.

41. Larson, Andrea (1992), "Network Dyads in Entrepreneurial Settings: A Study of the Governance of Exchange Relationships," *Administrative Science Quarterly* 37, no. 1 (March), pp. 76–104.

42. Jap, Sandy and Shankar Ganesan (2000), "Control Mechanisms and the Relationship Lifecycle: Implications for Safeguarding Specific Investments and Developing Commitment," *Journal of Marketing Research* 37 (May), pp. 227–245.

43. Larson (1992), op. cit.

44. Larson (1992), op. cit.

45. Anderson, James C. (1995), "Relationships in Business Markets: Exchange Episodes, Value Creation, and Their Empirical Assessment," *Journal of the Academy of Marketing Science* 23, no. 4, pp. 346–350.

46. Narayandas, Das and V. Kasturi Rangan (2004), "Building and Sustaining Buyer-Seller Relationships in Mature Industrial Markets," *Journal of Marketing* 68 (July), pp. 63–77.

47. Palmatier, Robert W., Mark B. Houston, Rajiv P. Dant, and Dhruv Grewal (2013), "Relationship Velocity: Toward a Theory of Relationship Dynamics," *Journal of Marketing* 77 (January), pp. 13–30.

48. Jap, Sandy and Erin Anderson (2004), "Safeguarding Interorganizational Performance and Continuity Under *Ex Post* Opportunism," *Management Science* 49, no. 12, pp. 1684–1701.

49. Anderson, Erin and Sandy D. Jap (2005), "The Dark Side of Close Relationships," *Sloan Management Review* 46 (3), pp. 75–82.

50. Selnes, Fred and James Sallis (2003), "Promoting Relationship Learning," *Journal of Marketing* 67 (July), p. 80.

51. Cannon, Joseph P. and William D. Perreault (1999), "Buyer-Seller Relationships in Business Markets," *Journal of Marketing Research* 36 (November), pp. 439–460.

52. Wuyts, Stefan, Stefan Stremersch, Christophe Van Den Bulte, and Philip Hans Franses (2004), "Vertical Marketing Systems for Complex Products: A Triadic Perspective," *Journal of Marketing Research* 41 no. 4, pp. 479–487.

53. Palmatier, Robert W., Lisa K. Scheer, Kenneth R. Evans, and Todd Arnold (2008), "Achieving Relationship Marketing Effectiveness in Business-to Business Exchanges," *Journal of the Academy of Marketing Science* 36 (June), pp. 174–190.

54. Adapted from Jackson (1985), op. cit.

# Managing Channel Policies and Legalities

**LEARNING OBJECTIVES**

**After reading this chapter, you will be able to:**

- Describe the array of channel policies available for channel management.
- Outline the types of channel activities that are subject to governmental scrutiny.
- Recognize the difference between per se and rule-of-reason criteria.
- Summarize the main U.S. legal cases that shape channel practices.
- Describe how legalities can influence marketing channel strategies.

Channel managers can use various policies to administer their distribution systems. When these policies restrain or redirect the activities of other members of channels though, they may affect the competitiveness of the overall market and thus come under antitrust scrutiny. This chapter catalogues the variety of policies available to manage channels, and the reasons each of them might be adopted, but it also clarifies when and how some of these policies might run afoul of U.S. federal antitrust laws. We focus primarily on U.S. legal stances toward these policies, but the initial discussion of the business purposes of each approach spans virtually any market in which a channel manager might operate. There are six main policies that channel managers might use:

- Market coverage
- Customer coverage
- Pricing
- Product line
- Selection and termination
- Ownership

We address each in turn, as well as the main federal antitrust laws that affect their application (as listed in Figure 13-1).

| Act | Key Provisions |
|---|---|
| Sherman Antitrust Act, 1890 | 1. Prohibits contracts, combinations, or conspiracies in restraint of inter-state or foreign commerce |
| Clayton Antitrust Act, 1914 | Where competition is, or may be, substantially lessened, it prohibits: <br> 1. Price discrimination in sales or leasing of goods <br> 2. Exclusive dealing <br> 3. Tying contracts <br> 4. Interlocking directorates among competitors <br> 5. Mergers and acquisitions. |
| Federal Trade Commission (FTC) Act, 1914 | 1. Prohibits unfair or deceptive trade practices injurious to competition or a competitor <br> 2. Sets up FTC to determine unfairness |
| Robinson-Patman Act, 1936 | 1. Discriminatory prices for goods are prohibited if they reduce competition at any point in the channel. <br> 2. Discriminatory prices can be given in good faith to meet competition. <br> 3. Brokerage allowances are allowed only if earned by an independent broker. <br> 4. Sellers must give all services and promotional allowances to all buyers on a proportionately equal basis if the buyers are in competition. The offering of alternatives may be necessary. <br> 5. Buyers are prohibited from knowingly inducing price or promotional discrimination. <br> 6. Price discrimination can be legal if it results from real cost differences in serving different customers. |
| FTC Trade Practice Rules | 1. Enforced by FTC. Defines unfair competition for individual industries. These practices are prohibited by the FTC. <br> 2. Defines rules of sound practice. These rules are not enforced by the FTC, but are recommended. |

**FIGURE 13-1**   Principal U.S. federal laws affecting marketing channel management

## MARKET COVERAGE POLICIES

Channel managers must decide how many sales outlets to establish in any given geographic area and how each outlet should participate in marketing functions to serve the needs of existing and potential customers. In Chapter 5, we discussed channel designs and management issues; from a legal perspective though, these channel intensity decisions depend on the notion of market coverage.

The question of **market coverage** creates geographical and territorial issues. When a channel structure moves from intensive toward selective coverage, it may benefit the upstream members of the channel (e.g., the distributor might gain a reputation for exclusiveness, and the lone retailer earns all the sales in that area), but end-users in the focal area suffer from diminished accessibility to the channel's products. In this sense, selective and exclusive coverage policies constitute **territorial restrictions**, according to antitrust enforcement agencies, because they limit the number of sellers in a defined territory. Yet territorial assignments remain an important and effective reward that suppliers can grant, in return for a retailer's promise to cultivate the brand's reputation and image in that area.

The supplier's objective, in instituting territorial and other so-called **vertical restraints**, is to limit the extent of intrabrand competition. Such policies also might promote interbrand competition. Whereas **intrabrand competition** occurs among wholesalers or retailers of the same brand (e.g., Coca-Cola, Chevrolet), **interbrand competition** implies competition among all the suppliers of different brands of the same product (e.g., brands of soft drinks or automobiles). By restricting intrabrand competition, the supplier protects resellers from competition among themselves, but in so doing, it also likely improves their effectiveness compared with resellers of *other* brands. For the channel, an attempt to dampen intrabrand competition and thus strengthen interbrand competition seems sensible, because the manufacturer prefers for the members of its channel compete with members in other channels, rather than among themselves.

But for antitrust regulators, efforts to confine wholesalers' or retailers' selling activities represent a restraint of trade or unfair competition, and they may be challenged under the Sherman Act (1890) or Section 5 of the Federal Trade Commission Act (1914) (see Figure 13-1). This antitrust perspective, relative to territorial restrictions, was most clearly established on June 23, 1977, when the Supreme Court handed down a decision in the *Sylvania* case, as profiled in Sidebar 13-1.[1]

## Sidebar 13-1

### Continental TV v. GTE Sylvania[2]

Prior to 1962, Sylvania, a manufacturer of television sets, sold its sets through both independent and company-owned distributors to a large number of independent retailers. RCA dominated the market at the time, holding 60 to 70 percent of national sales, and Zenith and Magnavox were major rivals. Sylvania had only 1 to 2 percent of the market. In 1962, Sylvania decided to abandon its efforts at a saturation distribution and chose instead to phase out its wholesalers and sell directly to a smaller group of franchised retailers. Sylvania retained sole discretion to determine how many retailers would operate in any geographic area; at least two retailers were franchised in every metropolitan center of more than 100,000 people. Dealers were free to sell anywhere and to any class of customers, but they agreed to operate only from locations approved by Sylvania. A critical factor was Sylvania's desire to decrease the likelihood of one retailer free-riding on the efforts of another retailer's marketing activities in the area.

Continental TV was one of Sylvania's most successful retailers in northern California. After a series of disagreements arising from Sylvania's authorization of a new outlet near one of Continental's best locations, Continental opened a new outlet in Sacramento, though its earlier request for approval for that location had been denied. Sylvania then terminated Continental's franchise. In resulting litigation, Continental counterclaimed against Sylvania. The Court sided with Sylvania, which argued that the use of its territorial allocation policy permitted its marketing channels to compete more successfully with those established by its large competitors.

In its decision, the Court favored the promotion of interbrand competition, even if intrabrand competition were restricted. It indicated that territorial restrictions encourage interbrand competition by allowing the manufacturer to achieve certain efficiencies in the distribution of its products. And, in a footnote, the Court recognized that the imposition of such restrictions is consistent with increased societal demands that manufacturers assume responsibility for the safety and quality of their products. As a result of the Court's decision, territorial restrictions, when challenged, are to be evaluated under a "rule-of-reason" doctrine, according to which proof must be established that the restrictions substantially lessen interbrand competition. Furthermore, the burden is on the plaintiff to prove that the restraints are unreasonable.

| Per se illegality: | The marketing policy is automatically unlawful, regardless of the reasons for the practice and without extended inquiry into its effects. It is only necessary for the complainant to prove the occurrence of the conduct and antitrust injury. |
|---|---|
| Modified rule of reason: | (It is also called "Quick Look.") The marketing policy is presumed to be anticompetitive if evidence of the existence and use of significant market power is found, subject to rebuttal by the defendant. |
| Rule of reason: | Before a decision is made about the legality of a marketing policy, it is necessary to undertake a broad inquiry into the nature, purpose, and effect of the policy. This requires an examination of the facts peculiar to the contested policy, its history, the reasons it was implemented, and its competitive significance. |
| Per se legality: | The marketing policy is presumed legal. |

**FIGURE 13-2**   **Legal rules used in antitrust enforcement**

As a result of the Court's decision in *Sylvania*, challenged territorial restrictions get evaluated according to a **rule-of-reason** doctrine. This doctrine places the burden of proof on the accuser to show that the restrictions substantially and unreasonably lessen interbrand competition. For definitions of the various legal rules applied in vertical restraint antitrust cases, see Figure 13-2. Briefly, an action is **per se** illegal if it is illegal in all circumstances, regardless of any explanation or implications, whereas an action is considered illegal only under a rule of reason if mitigating circumstances can permit its use.

In antitrust enforcement language, territorial restrictions might range from the absolute confinement of reseller sales, which aims to completely eliminate intra-brand competition, to lesser territorial restrictions (i.e., primary responsibility, profit pass-over arrangements, and location clauses), which simply inhibit such competition. Specifically, **absolute confinement** involves a promise by a downstream channel member that it will not sell outside its assigned territory. This promise often follows from a pledge by the supplier not to sell to anyone else in that territory (i.e., an exclusive distributorship). A territory is considered *airtight* when absolute confinement combines with exclusive distributorship.

In contrast, with a **primary responsibility** agreement, the downstream channel member agrees to exert its best efforts to ensure effective distribution of the supplier's goods in its assigned territory. If it fails to meet performance targets, it loses its preferred status, but it also remains free to sell outside its area. **Profit pass-over arrangements** require instead that a downstream channel member that sells to a customer located outside its assigned territory compensate another distributor in whose territory that customer is located. This compensation ostensibly reimburses the distributor for its efforts to stimulate demand in its territory and the cost of providing services on which the actual seller might have capitalized. Finally, a **location clause** specifies the site of a channel member's place of business and thereby spreads resellers out in a given territory, such that each has a "natural" market of customers closest to the reseller's location. However, the reseller may sell to any customer walking through its door, and end-users located closest to it may decide to purchase at more distant locations.

Manufacturers use a wide array of efficiency-related reasons to justify territorial restrictions in their channels.[3] Free-riding concerns, such as those that prompted Sylvania's decision to impose restrictions, are important. But in addition, vertical restrictions are more likely when (1) distributors have better market information than the manufacturer, (2) detecting distributor violations of the vertical restrictions is relatively easy, (3) distributors invest more in manufacturer-specific assets, (4) competition at the manufacturer level is more intense, and (5) distributors are willing to limit their sales to a single manufacturer's product. The latter two reasons could be anticompetitive, but the first three appear motivated by efficiency and thus support a rule-of-reason legal stance.

The use of territorial restrictions in the United States is widespread and, for the most part, legal. This status varies elsewhere in the world. For example, until 2000, European Union Law (first established by the Treaty of Rome) held that all territorial restriction agreements were distortions of free trade, whether vertical (i.e., between channel members at different levels of distribution) or horizontal (i.e., among competitors). Rules established by the European Commission (EC) essentially required manufacturers to supply goods to anyone who wanted to sell them. To adopt any sort of selective distribution policies, the manufacturers had to secure an exemption from the rules, by soliciting EC headquarters in Brussels.[4] For cars and electronics, manufacturers could request selective distribution on the grounds that their complex products needed substantial after-sales service. In the perfume industry, a common justification was that sales of these luxury goods depended on an aura of exclusivity, maintained by high prices, large investments in marketing, and a sophisticated sales environment.[5]

But the EC has relaxed the rules on vertical restraints and, since 2000, imposes a **single block exemption rule**. This rule states that any firm with less than 30 percent market share can engage in distribution agreements with distributors or retailers, without needing to obtain explicit permission. Restrictive business agreements involving firms with more than 30 percent market share remained prohibited.[6]

Asian regulations vary as well, but in some markets, the pattern seems to be heading toward fewer restrictions. For example, by 2015, an integration plan termed "Open Sky" will allow airlines to operate throughout the Asian region with few restrictions.[7] As these various antitrust approaches reveal, marketing channels need to check carefully into the specific regulations in each region of the world in which they sell products to avoid coming in conflict with any local or national regulations.

## CUSTOMER COVERAGE POLICIES

Rather than using territorial or geographic standards, suppliers might mandate to whom wholesalers and retailers can resell their goods and services. For example, a manufacturer might prefer to keep certain customers as house accounts, whether to maintain close relationships with valuable customers, meet requirements for technical assistance, serve key accounts more efficiently, enjoy the potential for higher expected profits, provide the price concessions needed to win certain accounts, or simply meet the demands of important channel partners (e.g., Home Depot and Wal-Mart both insist on direct sales relationships from most of their suppliers). In other cases, suppliers set customer coverage policies to ensure that the intermediaries selling their goods and services are fully capable of providing specific service outputs. In this sense, this restriction gives suppliers confidence that their products are handled only by competent resellers.

In a related motive, many manufacturers use customer coverage policies to prevent the emergence of **gray markets**, run by unauthorized resellers. Recall from Chapter 11 that gray markets represent a significant source of channel conflict. To address this concern, manufacturers write clauses into their contracts that stipulate that authorized dealers may not sell their brands to anyone but bona fide end-users. In contrast, authorized dealers are often tempted to sell off excess inventories to unauthorized dealers, including well-known discounters such as 47th Street Photo, Kmart, Syms, and so forth.

If suppliers adopt customer coverage policies to allocate different accounts to different intermediaries,[8] they likely limit intrabrand competition, because the customer finds only one seller of the firm's product. This policy can facilitate **price segmentation**, which is when the channel charges higher prices to segments of buyers that express a higher willingness to pay. The different service output demands of various segments also may require the efforts of different intermediaries, each with unique skills to provide the demanded service. From a safety point of view, specialized dealers can more effectively screen potential customers before selling controversial or potentially harmful products, as well as provide necessary information about the product's use (e.g., herbicides).

Such policies have economic rationales too. If multiple channels compete for the same customer, the threat of free riding increases, because one channel might bear the cost of providing valued service outputs while another channel closes the sale and earns the profits. In the long run, the cost-bearing channel loses both profits and economic viability, which harms the manufacturer, because the failure of this channel limits its coverage. Of course, such failures also ultimately hurt the free-riding channel, which may be unable to survive if it has to pay for all the service outputs on its own.[9]

Thus, the reasons for adopting customer coverage policies are similar to those used to justify market coverage policies. For this reason, antitrust concerns are handled similarly. However, whereas customer coverage restrictions are exercises of coercive power (e.g., prohibiting distributors from reselling to discount houses), territorial restrictions imply exercises of reward power (e.g., granting a monopoly on the sale of a brand within a defined territory). Antitrust enforcement agencies and the courts thus refer to customer coverage policies as "customer" or "resale restrictions" and consider them illegal when their effects can be shown to reduce competition substantially. Despite different terminology and elements, territorial and resale restrictions are treated identically under the law. Both are viewed as restraints of trade; both can be directly challenged under the Sherman Act. They also are both subject to the *Sylvania* decision, that is, to a rule-of-reason approach in which the acts are legal if they do not substantially lessen interbrand competition.

The presence of gray markets is not necessarily an antitrust concern, but in 1988, the U.S. Supreme Court actually upheld a Customs Service regulation permitting gray market imports (without endorsing gray markets in all conditions). Gray markets in the United States are specifically permitted when the U.S. trademark is owned by a U.S. company with its own manufacturing facility abroad or one that has established a subsidiary or affiliate abroad that is under the U.S. company's "common control."[10] For example, Duracell batteries are manufactured abroad in plants owned by Duracell, as well as in U.S. plants, all under Duracell's control. Gray marketers obtain batteries from foreign distributors that buy the products overseas, and then import them (legally) into the United States.[11] Noting the lack of protection against gray market imports established by the U.S. Customs Service, some manufacturers turn to other laws to challenge gray market imports, such as the Lanham Act, which governs trademark use.

## PRICING POLICIES

Both market and customer coverage policies aim to reduce or restrain the amount of intrabrand competition, with an indirect effect, in theory, of increasing the brand's price compared with a scenario without any such policies. Assuming a price is "reasonable," the gross margins available to resellers are sufficient to pay them for the provision of service outputs desired by end-users (according to the supplier). Restrictions on intrabrand competition result in higher prices and thus higher gross margins. Yet the price competition induced by interbrand competitors can upset this arrangement. In response, the channel might adopt two policies with direct effects on price: price maintenance and price discrimination.

### Price Maintenance

In marketing channels, suppliers and manufacturers often specify prices below or above which other channel members, such as wholesalers and retailers, may not sell their products. This price maintenance policy thus frequently uses the name **resale price maintenance (RPM)**. A minimum RPM establishes a downstream price below which the product cannot be sold; a maximum RPM specifies a downstream price above which it cannot be sold. It is also possible to specify an exact price for the product.

The argument in favor of a maximum RPM generally assumes the use of selective or exclusive distribution. Manufacturers that grant exclusivity to their dealers endow them with a local monopoly for the sale of their products, giving them a strong incentive to raise prices above competitive levels, contrary to the interests of both manufacturers and consumers. With a maximum RPM, the manufacturer can maintain a competitive price level for its products, regardless of the number of intermediaries it uses.

Several arguments favor a minimum RPM, mainly revolving around the service outputs and product that consumers obtain from a channel. End-users often prefer to gather information and services from full-service, higher-priced dealers, and then purchase from price discounters that offer few or no services. We thus encounter the problem of free riding yet again. By not offering the same pre- and post-sale service (e.g., extensive product information, demonstrations, installation, maintenance, repairs), discounters minimize their own costs, whereas the full-service dealers provide costly service without receiving compensation through the sale of the product. Their natural reaction is to reduce service levels. If the service provision is necessary to the purchase process though, the resulting service gap diminishes demand throughout the channel. By establishing a minimum RPM policy, the manufacturer limits discounting moves and thereby reduces free-riding motivations. In markets such as this, minimum RPM even might be procompetitive. Consider some variations on this argument:

- Manufacturers seek entry into appropriate retail stores, which have limited shelf and floor space. Therefore, the manufacturers purchase access by offering higher markups, advertising and brand name drawing power, advertising allowances, and other expenditures to make them more attractive than rival brands. Minimum RPM helps new manufacturers gain access, because the retailers know they will receive a specific markup, and it helps prevent loss-leader pricing (i.e., pricing items very low, sometimes even below their cost, to attract customers).[12]

- If dealers earn reasonable retail markups even with minimum RPM, channel intermediaries are more likely to engage in quality certification to help end-users minimize the risks associated with purchasing a good or service.
- Minimum RPM that ensure high enough margins may induce the intermediary to push one brand's product over others, thus increasing the brand's visibility in the market.
- For products that induce high spatial convenience demands, minimum RPM helps ensure the widespread, immediate availability of the brand.
- Because minimum RPM guarantees a reasonably high-profit margin, termination (and thus the loss of these profits) would be very costly for an intermediary. Such powerful incentives likely discourage price maintainers from becoming price discounters.[13]

Despite these reasons in support of an RPM policy, the legal status of minimum and maximum RPMs has varied over time. For years, minimum RPM were considered per se illegal, starting with the 1911 *Dr. Miles Medical Co. v. John D. Park & Sons Co.* decision. Then two legal decisions in 1984 (*Monsanto Company v. Spray-Rite Service Corporation*) and 1988 (*Business Electronics Corp. v. Sharp Electronics*) challenged this status, as profiled in Sidebars 13-2 and 13-3.

## Sidebar 13-2

### Monsanto v. Spray-Rite

In the *Monsanto Company v. Spray-Rite Service Corporation* case,[14] Spray-Rite (now defunct) sued Monsanto after Monsanto cut off its distributorship for herbicides in northern Illinois in 1968. Spray-Rite claimed that Monsanto did so because Spray-Rite would not join in an effort to fix the prices at which herbicides were sold. Spray-Rite also alleged a conspiracy between Monsanto and some of its distributors. The U.S. Supreme Court found in Spray-Rite's favor, making clear that the presence of concerted action between Monsanto and its distributors was critical to its per se ruling. The Court even explicitly stated that "a manufacturer…generally has a right to deal, or refuse to deal, with whomever it likes, as long as it does so independently." Citing the *Colgate* doctrine (discussed later in this chapter), the court went on to say that "the manufacturer can announce its resale prices in advance and refuse to deal with those who fail to comply." In other words, manufacturers may stipulate resale prices to their distributors—as long as the stipulations are unilateral. If concerted conspiratorial action occurs, a per se illegal ruling can be expected.

The *Monsanto* decision represented perhaps the first chink in the armor of the per se illegal status of resale price maintenance. The problem that it created was determining how the term "agreement" should be defined and what evidence is sufficient to support a jury verdict of a price-fixing conspiracy. The Supreme Court asserted that evidence must be presented that the distributor communicated its acquiescence regarding the manufacturer's resale pricing policy and that the acquiescence was sought by the manufacturer. The mere fact that other distributors complained about a price cut, prior to termination, was not sufficient to support a finding of agreement.

## Sidebar 13-3

### Business Electronics Corp. v. Sharp Electronics

A second major case weakened the per se illegality of maximum RPM: *Business Electronics Corp. v. Sharp Electronics*, decided in 1988. In this case, the Supreme Court ruled that a manufacturer's agreement with one dealer to stop supplying a price-cutting dealer does not necessarily violate the Sherman Act.[15] The plaintiff, Business Electronics, was the exclusive retailer of Sharp calculators in Houston from 1968 to 1972. During that period, Sharp became dissatisfied with Business Electronics' policy of selling calculators at prices lower than those suggested by Sharp. In 1972 Sharp appointed Hartwell's Office World as a second retailer of its calculators in Houston. Subsequently, Hartwell's told Sharp it would quit distributing the products unless Sharp ended its relationship with Business Electronics; in 1973, Sharp terminated Business Electronics' dealership.

The U.S. Supreme Court upheld an appeals court ruling that the agreement to terminate Business Electronics was not a per se violation of antitrust law. Such an agreement would be illegal per se only if it had been part of an agreement by the manufacturer and one or more retailers to fix prices at some level. There was no proof in this case of such a specific price-fixing agreement between Sharp and Hartwell's. Justice Antonin Scalia observed in the Court's opinion that it is sometimes legitimate and competitively useful for manufacturers to curb price competition among their dealers, and he referred to the free-rider problem as a good reason for such manufacturers' actions. If there is no specific agreement as to price between the complaining dealers and the manufacturer, the reasonableness of an agreement to terminate will be determined by the rule of reason, that is, by balancing the anticompetitive intrabrand effects against any procompetitive interbrand effects.[16]

Both the *Monsanto* and *Business Electronics* decisions stimulated manufacturers of upscale consumer goods to use unilaterally implemented minimum RPM as a central distribution policy.[17] Over time, the use of resale prices has spread widely, to include certain brands of televisions, athletic shoes, cameras, china, furniture, cosmetics, golf clubs, women's sportswear, men's suits, stereos, toys, ceiling fans, watches, appliances, skis, cookware, perfume, chocolates, luggage, and video games—just as a few examples.

Despite this prevalence though, arguments remain in opposition to minimum RPM:

1. It does not guarantee that retailers use larger gross margins to provide service; they may simply pocket the extra money.
2. Although it may foster interbrand competition, minimum RPM also inhibits competition between stores carrying the same brand.
3. If a manufacturer deems service essential, it can require that all retailers provide that service, using dealership contracts, rather than by using minimum RPM.
4. Higher prices deny goods to consumers with less money.[18]

Thus far, setting minimum resale prices remains a legal activity, as long as it is not a concerted effort, undertaken by multiple colluding parties.

The legal status of maximum RPM has taken a different route, as exemplified by the *Albrecht* and *State Oil Co. v. Khan* cases summarized in Sidebar 13-4.[19] Both cases established that minimum, maximum, or exact RPM can be implemented, if not done so in the context of an agreement to restrain trade. That is, if RPM is a manufacturer's policy, which it enacts unilaterally, by definition there can be no agreement that might be construed as an antitrust violation. According to this logic, maximum RPM agreements can be used as long as they do not harm competition, whereas minimum or exact RPM arrangements, arrived at through a legal contract or agreement, are per se illegal. These criteria suggest that control over resale prices by manufacturers is legal and possible if they:[20]

- Act unilaterally, such that all statements and actions come only from the manufacturer.
- Avoid coercion and do not make annually renewable contracts conditional on dealer adherence to the manufacturer's specified resale price.
- Vertically integrate, forming a corporate vertical marketing system.
- Avoid known discounters, by establishing screening and performance criteria that are difficult for discounters to meet.
- Announce their resale price policy upfront, when arrangements are first made with channel members, and specify that the manufacturer will refuse to deal with any dealer that is not willing to adhere to the announced terms.

As the Supreme Court noted in *Business Electronics* though, per se prohibitions on RPM do not apply "to restrictions on price to be charged by one who is in reality an agent of, not a buyer from, the manufacturer."[21] For example, restrictions could apply to a distributor that takes title to the goods it sells for a manufacturer

## Sidebar 13-4

### Albrecht v. Herald and State Oil Co. v. Khan

The *Albrecht* decision in 1968 established the per se illegality of maximum resale price maintenance.[22] Albrecht was a newspaper carrier for the Herald Company, which granted exclusive territories to its carriers. The Herald Company advertised a subscription price for home newspaper delivery and required its carriers to charge that price. Albrecht charged a higher price, leading to his termination by the Herald Company. Albrecht sued and won in the Supreme Court, which argued that when a maximum RPM policy sets prices too low, it prevents a dealer from offering services that customers need and value. This argument was challenged academically, but the per se illegality of maximum RPM remained in place until 1997.

Then the *State Oil Co. v. Khan* (1997) decision overturned *Albrecht*, with the Supreme Court ruling that maximum RPM agreements should be decided on a rule-of-reason basis (i.e., viewed as

legal unless they harmed competition).[23] In this case, Khan was a dealer of Union 76 brand gasoline. His supply contract with State Oil was, in essence, a maximum RPM contract, though this status was somewhat veiled by the specific pricing stipulations in the agreement. Khan sued, seeking the right to charge higher prices for his gasoline and pocket the difference in revenue.

In a unanimous ruling, the U.S. Supreme Court found in favor of State Oil, because the benefit to consumers, in the form of lower prices, outweighed the possible harm caused by the practices. In the previous 30 years, the Court further noted, firms had found many ways around *Albrecht*, and yet none of these actions had exerted serious negative impacts on competitiveness or welfare. Thus, a rule-of-reason criterion was deemed more appropriate for determining the legality of maximum RPM, undertaken through concerted action.

but not to an independent sales representative that never takes title to the manufacturer's goods. The Court also quoted from *U.S. v. General Electric Co.* by stating, "The owner of an article…is not violating the common law, or the Anti-Trust Law, by seeking to dispose of his article directly to the consumer and fixing the price by which his agents transfer the title from him directly to the consumer."[24] This stance also has been echoed in a 1987 lower court decision: "where the manufacturer bears the financial risks of transactions with the customers and continues to retain 'title, dominion and control over its goods,' then it is likely that the distributor is merely an agent for the manufacturer."[25]

## Price Discrimination

There are many ways channel members discriminate among their customers and suppliers, though a primary focus is price. When a seller offers a lower price to one buyer rather than another for the same product, the seller is discriminating between the buyers, with a monetary reward. Discriminating among buyers, whether using prices, service outputs, or product features, makes abundant sense. From a managerial perspective, it is foolish *not* to approach buyers with high demand elasticities differently from those with low demand elasticities. Well-conceived market segmentation schemes are discriminatory, because they recommend approaching segments dissimilarly. Without discrimination, sellers could never achieve their optimal profits. Because price sensitivity, as well as the costs to serve and intensity of competition, varies across market segments, charging different, or segmented, prices is the right economic decision.[26]

The main segmentation pricing policies enacted by channel managers revolve around reductions from the list price, promotional allowances and services, and functional discounts. The rationale and motive in each case is straightforward: increase demand, combat competitors, reward customers, and/or compensate channel partners for services rendered. Yet price discrimination, by both sellers and buyers, also may be illegal, as covered under the Robinson-Patman Act (1936).

**PRICE DISCRIMINATION BY SELLERS**   When sellers offer different prices to different buyers, the Robinson-Patman Act, Section 2(a), states:

> It shall be unlawful for any person engaged in commerce,…either directly or indirectly, to discriminate in price between different purchasers of commodities of like grade and quality, where either or any of the purchases involved in such discrimination are in commerce, where such commodities are sold for use, consumption, or resale within [any area] under the jurisdiction of the United States, and where the effect of such discrimination may be to substantially lessen competition or tend to create a monopoly in any line of commerce, or to injure, destroy or prevent competition with any person who either grants or knowingly receives the benefit of such discrimination, or with customers of either of them.

Three terms are particularly significant in this section:

* *Commodities:* The Robinson-Patman Act applies to goods and goods bundled with services if the value of the goods predominates. It does not cover the sale of

services. Some categories excluded from this legislation thus are printing, advertising, and real estate.

- *Like grade and quality:* If products contain different materials or exhibit variant workmanship, they are not considered of "like grade and quality." If the differences are minor and do not affect the basic use of the goods though, price differentials may not be allowed. For example, challenges have questioned price differences between private-label and branded goods when the product is identical (e.g., evaporated milk by Borden).[27]
- *Substantially lessen competition:* This factor is critical to all antitrust cases (including those filed under Section 2(a) of the Robinson Patman Act) that adopt the rule-of-reason doctrine. It also is increasingly difficult for plaintiffs to prove, because of the important difference between injury to competitors and injury to competition. A loss of sales by one firm and their gain by another is competition; the object of each competitor is to outsell rivals, and such injury to a competitor is not illegal. Evidence of an intent to destroy a competitor instead may indicate an injure competition as a whole in the market.

Furthermore, price discrimination among customers who do not compete is not illegal. It is perfectly legal for retailers to charge consumers different prices for identical goods and services (e.g., airline tickets, automobiles), because these end-users are not "in competition" with one another. Similarly, if one retailer does business only on the east coast of the United States and another does business only on the west coast, a vendor may charge them different prices, as long as they do not compete for the same end-users.

In contrast, price discrimination that injures any of three specific levels of competition may be prohibited by the Robinson-Patman Act:

- *Primary level.* Competition between two sellers may suffer if one of them offers discriminatory prices to some customers.
- *Secondary level.* Competition between two customers may be affected if the seller differentiates between them. By charging them different prices, the seller is aiding one buyer and harming the other in their mutual competition, which is illegal if it is sufficient to cause a substantial lessening of competition.
- *Tertiary level.* If a manufacturer discriminates in prices between two wholesalers, such that the customers of one wholesaler are favored over those of the other, this act injures competition.

Perhaps the most important case citing the Robinson-Patman Act was decided in 1993 (see Sidebar 13-5). It involved primary-level discrimination: Liggett & Myers, formerly the Brooke Group, charged Brown & Williamson with predatory pricing. In winning the case, the defendant Brown & Williamson established that predatory pricing exists only if the predator actually recovers the costs of lowering its prices to predatory levels. The case also reaffirmed the potentially positive consumer welfare implications of lower prices. That is, truly predatory pricing requires the predator to lower prices so far that they force the victim out of the market, which also harms the predator, at least in the short term. In this case, even if Brown & Williamson forced Liggett & Myers out of the market, it could not do the same to all its other competitors, so the Court found that predatory pricing could not be proven.

## Sidebar 13-5

### Liggett & Myers v. Brown & Williamson

In 1980, Liggett & Myers, which had a 2.3 percent market share, introduced a generic, unadvertised cigarette that sold for 30 percent less than the branded names. Brown & Williamson (B&W) responded by entering the market with a generic product packaged in a box identical to Liggett's and began to undercut Liggett's price. At the time, B&W had a market share of around 12 percent. In the following 18 months, B&W allegedly cut its prices substantially below average variable cost. Liggett could not sustain the below-cost pricing, and the price of generic cigarettes rose.

Liggett sued under the Robinson-Patman Act,[28] alleging that B&W's predatory price cuts were implemented with discounts given to different distributors in varying degrees—hence, price discrimination. Many aspects of this case make for interesting reading and analysis from a marketing management perspective, but the most important is the decision itself. The Court's decision rested on its assessment of whether B&W could earn back, using monopoly pricing, the costs of its predatory

actions after Liggett was driven from the market. Therefore, in addition to showing below-cost prices, Liggett, as the plaintiff, also had to demonstrate "that the competitor had a reasonable prospect...of recouping its investment in below-cost prices."[29] As the Court noted, "Recoupment is the ultimate object of an unlawful predatory scheme; it is the means by which a predator profits from predation."[30]

Through an analysis of competition in the cigarette industry, the Court came to the conclusion that B&W, despite driving Liggett from the market, lacked the power to quiet R.J. Reynolds, Philip Morris, and other competitors, so it would not be able to retrieve its investment. Finding in favor of B&W, the decision stated that without recoupment, predatory pricing would produce lower aggregate prices in the market, which enhance consumer welfare. A federal court in Texas followed the same line of reasoning shortly thereafter, when it cleared American Airlines of charges of predatory pricing waged against Northwest and Continental Airlines.[31]

**SELLERS' DEFENSES AGAINST PRICE DISCRIMINATION CHARGES**   Price discrimination is not a per se violation of the antitrust laws, especially if it has an insignificant impact on competition. In addition, discrimination may be justified when (1) carried out to dispose of perishable or obsolete goods, or under a close-out or bankruptcy sale; (2) it reflects differences in "the cost of manufacture, sale, or delivery resulting from the differing methods or quantities" in which the commodity was sold or delivered; or (3) effected "in good faith to meet an equally low price of a competitor." The first defense poses few problems; the second and third are more complex.

Starting with the second option, companies that attempt to sustain a **cost justification defense** have seldom been successful, because of the stringent standards set by the U.S. Federal Trade Commission and the courts, which require detailed documentation of full (not marginal) costs. Furthermore, this defense fails if anything less than 100 percent of the price differential results from cost differences.[32] The burden of proof is on the seller, because quantity discounts are permitted under Section 2(a) of the Robinson-Patman Act only to the extent they are justified by cost savings.

For example, the U.S. Supreme Court has ruled that quantity discounts must reflect the cost savings achieved from delivering to one place at one time, which strongly limits the use of cumulative quantity discounts. In the 1990s, pricing policies in the pharmaceutical industry attracted considerable litigation. Late in 1994, 1,346 independent pharmacies in 15 states sued the largest drug manufacturers and mail-order distributors, charging them with price discrimination. Earlier that year, four major grocery chains (Kroger, Albertson's, Safeway, and Vons) had filed a suit in Cincinnati federal court, charging 16 pharmaceutical firms and a mail-order prescription company with discriminatory and "pernicious" pricing. The suit claimed the firms' pricing policies favored institutional pharmacies, health-maintenance organizations, and mail-order prescription companies with lower prices, while charging supermarket chains more.

The **meeting competition defense** (from Section 2(b) of the Robinson-Patman Act) has proven as difficult to apply as the cost justification defense, but it is even more complex. This defense can be valid, even in the face of substantial injury to competition, if the defendant can prove its good faith, by showing the following:[33]

- The price is lawful and not produced by collusion. A seller does not have to prove the price it is meeting is lawful, but it must make some effort to find out if it is.
- The price really exists,[34] without being undercut. For example, price reductions on a "premium" version of the product to the level of the "standard" version can be a form of illegal price discrimination. But if the public is willing to pay a higher price for the premium product, their equivalent prices may be a viable form of competition.
- Competition is at the primary level. Granting a discriminatory price to some customers to enable them to meet their own competition likely is not a protected practice.[35]

According to a 1983 Supreme Court ruling, the good faith defense is applicable to efforts to gain new customers and retain existing ones. But firms are only permitted to match rival prices; they cannot undercut them.[36]

Finally, pricing differences are defensible if the seller offers a pricing policy that is equally available to all customers but is not chosen by all customers. A manufacturer can offer a discount for early invoice payments, for example. Not all customers take advantage of this discount, but they all have an equal opportunity to do so, so there is no violation.

**PRICE DISCRIMINATION BY BUYERS.**    Forcing an upstream seller to charge a discriminatory price may entail coercion by a buyer. Thus, Section 2(f) of the Robinson-Patman Act makes it unlawful for a person to induce or receive a discriminatory price knowingly. Buyers in violation of this section reasonably should be aware of the illegality of the prices they receive. The goal here is to prevent large, powerful channel members from compelling sellers to give them discriminatory lower prices. Section 5 of the Federal Trade Commission Act enforces this rule, noting that such uses of coercive power represent unfair competition.

It is also illegal for buyers to coerce favors from suppliers, such as special promotional allowances or services. Recall our discussion of **slotting allowances** from Chapter 6. These promotions are not per se illegal, but the fixed payments, made by a manufacturer to a retailer to gain access to the retailer's shelf space, could be construed as illegal in some circumstances. For example, if competing retailers agreed on the amount of slotting allowances to charge or the allocation of shelf space to manufacturers, the practice would violate antitrust regulations. They also could be challenged if used as part of a conspiracy to monopolize trade or exclude certain manufacturers from retail shelves. Finally, slotting allowances could violate the Robinson-Patman Act if it can be proven that they were used as price discrimination mechanisms.[37]

Although slotting allowances are predominant in grocery retailing, they also appear in software, music, pharmaceutical, and book selling industries.[38] Retailers insist that slotting allowances are necessary to defray the costs of stocking a new product, such as adding the new product in the store's computer system, warehouse management, and shelf placement—costs that tend to have risen with the increase in new product introductions in recent years.[39] A standard supermarket stocks about 40,000 products, but there are more than 100,000 grocery products available to the market, and thousands of new product introductions per year, which are subject to failure rates as high as 80 percent![40] In a related argument, slotting allowances could perform a beneficial signaling function, in that a manufacturer is willing to offer an upfront, fixed payment only in support of a product it believes has high market potential. Thus, retailers can use slotting allowances to screen out potentially poor products from their shelves.[41]

Considering that slotting allowances can be substantial, it is no wonder that manufacturers denigrate them as nothing more than price discrimination and extortion. Small manufacturers complain the loudest, noting that slotting allowances often prevent their simple access to store shelves. Evidence confirms that though most manufacturers selling through retailers paid some slotting allowances, the percentages are higher among companies with sales under $1 billion compared with larger firms, which likely can exert more bargaining power in the channel.[42]

Despite all these controversies, the use of slotting allowances continues, legally. As the Federal Trade Commission's (FTC) Bureau of Competition has noted, manufacturers commonly grumble about slotting allowances, but without making formal complaints. It is also hard to argue that retailers' greater channel power enables them to extract profits from manufacturers through slotting allowances, because retailers' profits have not risen appreciably as a result of slotting allowances. Consider *Augusta News Co. v. Hudson News Co.* The plaintiffs, wholesale magazine distributors that refused to pay slotting fees of up to $15,000 per store to chain store retailers, argued that these fees violated both the Sherman Act and the Robinson-Patman Act. But in ruling against them, the judge found that slotting fees, rather than being illegal brokerage payments, instead were "price reduction offers to buyers for the exclusive rights to supply a set of stores under multi-year contracts" and competitively healthy tactics.[43] Thus, both academic research and real-world examples suggest that a successful lawsuit to prevent slotting allowances as anticompetitive is unlikely.[44]

Another example of buyers' price discrimination occurs when large buyers set up dummy brokerage firms to obtain **brokerage allowances** from sellers, which permit them to receive lower prices than their competitors. This form of coercive power is illegal under Section 2(c) of the Robinson-Patman Act, which makes it unlawful to pay or accept brokerage fees or discounts, except for services rendered in connection with sales or purchases. It also prohibits brokerage fees or discounts paid to any broker who is not independent of both the buyer and the seller. Yet, as with slotting allowances, such buyer-induced price discrimination is extremely difficult to prove and therefore remains widespread in practice.

**PROMOTIONAL ALLOWANCES AND SERVICES**   To entice channel members to advertise, display, promote, or demonstrate their wares, suppliers use all sorts of monetary inducements, though the options are limited by Sections 2(d) and 2(e) of the Robinson-Patman Act. According to these sections, a seller may not grant advertising allowances;

offer other promotional assistance; or provide services, display facilities, or equipment to any buyer, unless it makes similar allowances and assistance available to all buyers. Because buyers differ in size and sales volume, the allowances equivalence obviously cannot be absolute; rather, the law stipulates that the allowances should be available to buyers on "proportionately equal terms."

These prohibitions are absolute, not dependent on injury to competition. If a plaintiff can show that discriminatory allowances exist and that the victims of this discrimination are firms in competition, the violation is illegal per se—unless the pricing action was undertaken to meet the competition. Competitive firms in this case must be in sufficient geographical proximity to compete for the same customers; for example, a manufacturer only needs to offer equivalent allowances to retailers in the same market territory, unless of course its market is national or international (e.g., mail-order, e-commerce). In addition, a time dimension is important for defining the allowance domain. Advertising allowances granted in one month do not have to be made available to other buyers five months later, because in this case, an initial allowance would determine all future allowances.[45]

According to FTC guidelines, some stipulations may be made regarding adherence to these regulations as follows:[46]

- Allowances may be made for services rendered, though they must not substantially exceed the cost of these services to the buyer or their value to the seller.
- The design of a promotional program must allow all competing buyers to implement it.
- The seller should inform all competing customers of the existence and essential features of the promotional program in ample time for them to take full advantage of it.
- If a program is not universally functionally available (i.e., suitable for and usable by), the seller must offer suitable alternatives to excluded customer. For example, sellers that market products directly to retailers and sell through wholesalers should make alternative versions of any promotional allowance offered to retailers available to wholesalers. The wholesalers then are expected to pass along the allowance to their retail customers, which compete with the direct-buying retailers.[47]
- The seller must provide customers with sufficient information to permit a clear understanding of the exact terms of the offer, including all alternatives, and the conditions for payment or services.

Thus, promotional allowances and merchandising services should be furnished in accordance with a written plan that meets these listed requirements.[48]

The FTC further recognizes two ways to measure proportional equality: purchase based or customer cost based. An equal amount of allowances or services per unit of sales is a common example of the former; support for newspaper advertisements, in connection with the resale of products, is an example of the latter. In addition, the FTC has reiterated its position that a company that grants a discriminatory promotional allowance may argue that the allowance represented a good faith response to a promotional program initiated by a competitor.[49]

**FUNCTIONAL DISCOUNTS**    In our discussion of channel functions in Chapter 3, we introduced the **equity principle**, that is, using reward power and granting discounts to individual channel members on the basis of the functions they perform. A **functional discount** implements the equity principle directly. In this case, the prices for products transferred from the manufacturer to a downstream channel member are well established, and preset discounts off the list price are available to anyone who performs certain channel flows or functions. The payments (or discounts) thus vary with the level of performance of unique channel functions. For example, a 3 percent discount off list price might be available to any buyer that makes a payment within 10 days, rather than the usual 30 days after purchase. This discount accrues to the channel member that performs a financing function in the channel, through its early payment. Another discount might be available to any distributor that promises to maintain a certain level of safety stock in its inventory warehouses and allows the manufacturer to periodically inspect the warehouses to confirm these levels. In this case, the compensation goes to the channel member bearing the costs of the physical possession and ownership functions.

In theory, functional discounts are allotted to each channel member according to its degree of participation in marketing functions that make the product or service available to end-users. In reality, functional discounts remain shrouded in controversy and confusion. Historically, these discounts were based almost exclusively on the level of distribution (e.g., wholesale vs. retail), not the exact function each member performed. In markets in which independent wholesalers sold to numerous, relatively small retail outlets, each level in the channel was distinct and could be rewarded differently (e.g., the wholesaler got a larger price discount from the manufacturer than the retailer). Each level in the channel also dealt with a specific class of customer (e.g., the wholesaler sold to retailers, retailers sold only to consumers). Wholesalers and retailers performed different functions in different markets and did not compete. The discounts thus were frequently referred to as "trade" as opposed to "functional" discounts.

Today, markets are far more complex. Distinctions in distribution systems have blurred through vertical integration. Wal-Mart performs most of its own wholesaling operations: It receives merchandise in large lots from manufacturers, breaks bulk, assorts merchandise, and reships merchandise from its warehouses to its retail stores. However, as a "retailer," it seemingly would be entitled only to the functional (trade) discounts granted to retailers (as well as quantity discounts offered by suppliers).

The problem is thus a classification issue. The Food Marketing Institute (an association whose members are mostly supermarket chains), Grocery Manufacturers of America, National Association of Chain Drug Stores, and several other wholesale and retail trade associations have urged manufacturers to avoid distinctions among competing distributor customers that are based solely on their class of trade. Instead, they should offer all downstream members access to any prices or terms of sale that have been offered to any other member. Such exhortations are necessary only if the manufacturer uses multiple channel distribution to reach the market (see Chapter 5) and offers different functional discounts to the various channels it uses.

Although the Robinson-Patman Act does not refer explicitly to functional discounts, several court decisions have established that its stipulations (and defenses) apply. As described in Sidebar 13-6, *Texaco Inc. v. Hasbrouck*[50] has left the door open to manufacturers to use functional discounts to compensate channel members for participating in specific marketing functions. When functional discounts reasonably

## Sidebar 13-6

### Texaco v. Hasbrouck

In *Texaco Inv. v. Hasbrouck*,[51] Texaco had sold gasoline directly to many independent retailers in Spokane, Washington, at its "retail tank wagon" prices; it granted more substantial discounts to two specific distributors. Those two distributors sold the gasoline to service stations that the distributors owned and operated, passing on nearly the whole discount from Texaco. The distributor-controlled retailers thereby were able to sell well below the price charged by the competing independent retailers. Between 1972 and 1981, sales at the stations supplied by the two wholesaler-distributors increased dramatically; sales at competing independents declined.

Texaco argued that its discriminatory pricing was justified by cost savings, by its good faith attempt to meet competition, and as a lawful functional discount. The Ninth Circuit Court of Appeals and the Supreme Court rejected Texaco's arguments, even while they validated the use of the cost-based and good faith defenses in lawsuits challenging functional discounts. Specifically, the Supreme Court's affirmation of the cost justification defense was significant for channel management, because it allowed functional discounts that might not be tied to classification schemes. As the Court stated:

> In general, a supplier's functional discount is said to be a discount given to a purchaser based on the purchaser's role in the supplier's distributive system, reflecting, at least in a generalized sense, the services performed by the purchaser for the supplier....[52] a legitimate functional discount constituting a reasonable reimbursement for a purchaser's actual marketing functions does not violate Section 2(a).[53]

reflect the supplier's savings or channel member's costs, they are legal. Perhaps the greatest remaining controversy thus involves the uses of a cost basis, because the channel needs to determine whether to rely on the supplier's or the reseller's costs. Discounts based on the reseller's costs will lead to different discounts granted to competing resellers, and perhaps larger discounts to less efficient buyers, which would represent a strange outcome. Yet discounts based on the seller's savings do not necessarily provide adequate or fair compensation to the reseller that performs the function.[54] Despite imperfections in both approaches, the conventional wisdom seems to favor using seller's savings.

## PRODUCT LINE POLICIES

For a wide variety of logical reasons, channel managers may wish to restrict the breadth or depth of the product lines that their channel partners sell. In this section, we look at the rationale for four policies—exclusive dealing, tying, full-line forcing, and designated product policies—as well as the antitrust concerns surrounding them.

### Exclusive Dealing

**Exclusive dealing** is the requirement by a seller or lessor that its channel intermediaries sell or lease only its products or brands, or at least no products or brands that compete directly with the seller's products. If intermediaries do not comply, the seller may invoke negative sanctions by refusing to deal with them. Such arrangements clearly reduce the freedom of choice of the intermediaries (resellers), and yet:

- Because the resellers depend on the supplier, the supplier secures the valuable benefit of being the focus of all the reseller's energies. Otherwise, especially if it has developed a strong brand image, the supplier worries that the resellers will use its brand as a loss leader, allowing other, competitive brand suppliers to free ride off the demand the reseller has stimulated by promoting the supplier's well-known brand. Such free-riding threats extend to other services too, such as the use of specialized display cases, the provision of technical training or financing, and operational assistance.
- With a long-term, exclusive relationship, sales forecasting may be easier, permitting the channel to achieve more precise and efficient production and logistics.
- Resellers receive more stable prices and more regular, frequent deliveries of the supplier's products.
- Transactions between resellers and the supplier likely are fewer in number but larger in volume.
- The channel partners can reduce administrative costs.
- Each partner may be able to secure specialized assets and long-term financing from the other.
- Resellers generally receive added promotional and other support while avoiding the higher inventory costs associated with carrying multiple brands.[55]

Requirements contracts are variants of straightforward exclusive dealing. With these contracts, buyers agree to purchase all or some of their required stock of a product from one seller, usually for a specified period and price. Such arrangements reduce the freedom of choice of the buyer, but they guarantee the buyer a source of supply at a known cost, often for a long period of time.

Exclusive dealing also lessens interbrand competition directly, because competing brands available from other suppliers get excluded from outlets. In turn, these policies are circumscribed by Section 3 of the Clayton Act, which stipulates

it shall be unlawful for any person…to lease or make a sale or contract for sale of goods, wares, merchandise, machinery, supplies or other commodities, whether patented or unpatented,…on the condition, agreement, or understanding that the lessee or purchaser thereof shall not use or deal in the goods,…of a competitor or competitors of the lessor or seller, where the effect of such lease, sale, or contract for sale or such condition, agreement or understanding may be to substantially lessen competition or tend to create a monopoly in any line of commerce.

They also may violate Section 1 of the Sherman Act and Section 5 of the FTC Act. Under the Sherman Act, exclusive contracts may be deemed unlawful restraints of trade if a dominant firm is involved and the contracts go so far beyond reasonable business needs that their necessary effect is suppressing competition.[56]

The *Tampa Electric Co. v. Nashville Coal Co.* case, decided in 1961, established the modern guidelines for assessing exclusive dealing policies from an antitrust perspective. According to the decision in this case, legality depends on the type of goods or merchandise, the geographic area of effective competition, and the substantiality of the competition being prevented. Furthermore, exclusive dealing arrangements or requirements contracts negotiated by sellers with a very small share of the relevant market have a good chance of standing up in court.[57] The critical question may be the definition of a relevant market. When shares are sufficiently high (e.g., 30–40 percent), a modified rule-of-reason standard established by *Tampa Electric* requires courts to examine the following:

- Contract duration.
- The likelihood of collusion in the industry and the degree to which other firms in the market also employ exclusive dealing.
- The height of entry barriers.
- The nature of the distribution system and distribution alternatives that remain available after exclusive dealing is taken into account.
- Other obvious anti- or procompetitive effects, such as preventing free riding or encouraging the reseller to promote the supplier's product more heavily.[58]

Although the *Tampa Electric* case was decided more than half a century ago, legal battles surrounding exclusive dealing continue. *Conwood Co. v. United States Tobacco Co.* also dealt with exclusive dealing, but in this case, the issue was category

## Sidebar 13-7

### Tampa Electric Co. v. Nashville Coal Co.

The *Tampa Electric Co. v. Nashville Coal Co.* case[59] involved a contract between Nashville Coal and Tampa Electric, a Florida public utility, to cover Tampa's expected coal requirements (i.e., not less than 500,000 tons per year) for a period of 20 years. Before any coal was delivered, Nashville declined to perform the contract, on the grounds that it was illegal under the antitrust laws because it amounted to an exclusive dealing arrangement, which foreclosed other suppliers from serving Tampa Electric. (Of course, the price of coal also had jumped, making the arrangement less profitable for Nashville Coal.) Tampa brought suit, arguing that the contract was both valid and enforceable.

To be illegal, such arrangements must have a tendency to cause a substantial, not merely remote, lessening of competition in a relevant competitive market. Justice Clark, writing for the majority, indicated that "substantiality" was to be determined by taking into account the following factors:

- The relative strength of the parties involved.
- The proportionate volume of commerce involved in relation to the total volume of commerce in the relevant market area.

- The probable immediate and future effects that preemption of that share of the market might have on effective competition within it.

The district court and the court of appeals had accepted the argument that the contract foreclosed a substantial share of the market, because Tampa's requirements equaled the total volume of coal purchased in the state of Florida before the contract's inception. The Supreme Court, in an interesting piece of economic reasoning, instead defined the relevant market as the *supply* market in an eight-state area, noting that mines in that coal-producing region were eager to sell more coal in Florida. When the market was defined as the entire multistate Appalachian coal region, the foreclosure amounted to less than 1 percent of the tonnage produced each year. The Court thus concluded that, given the nature of the market (i.e., a utility needs a stable supply at reasonable prices over a long period, the level of concentration), the small percentage of foreclosure did not actually or potentially cause a substantial reduction of competition, nor did it tend toward a monopoly.

management by category captains. **Category management** results from a collaborative agreement between a retailer and one of its major suppliers (which is designated the **category captain**) in a particular product category. The category captain, which is a supplier of one brand in the category, receives detailed information about *all* the products in the category (i.e., competitors' products and its own). With this information, it is expected to analyze the data and generate recommendations, including shelf space allocations, pricing, and targeting, to manage the entire category more effectively. The obvious risks are that the category captain's recommendations lead to competitive exclusion and that the category captain facilitates competitive collusion in the category, rather than enhancing competition.[60]

The *Conwood* case centered on allegations of the use of category management to exclude a small competitor from the market. Sales in the U.S. market for moist snuff were $1.7 billion, and the United States Tobacco Company's (USTC) products accounted for a 77 percent market share, whereas Conwood had a 13 percent market share. Conwood sued USTC, claiming that its actions as a category manager constituted unlawful monopolization of the market and led to the exclusion of competition. Conwood won the case, and a $1.05 billion award against USTC, after the court found that USTC urged retailers to carry fewer products, especially competitive ones; tried to control how many lower-priced brands were allowed into the market; and suggested that retailers carry USTC's slower-moving brands rather than better-selling competitive products. Because of these actions, retail prices for moist snuff increased, so USTC's actions harmed consumer welfare as well.[61] As this case warned, abuse of the category management process by a category captain can constitute a clear violation of antitrust laws.

## Tying

When a seller of a product or service that buyers want refuses to sell it unless they buy a second product or service, it is engaged in **tying**. A manufacturer of motion picture projectors (the tying product) might insist that only its film (the tied product) be used with the projectors, or a manufacturer of shoe machinery (the tying product) might insist that lessees of the machinery purchase service contracts (tied service) from it to maintain the machinery.

The business arguments for tying policies are similar to those for exclusive dealing, because both policies have similar aims: to lock in the purchase of a supplier-specific brand and lock out the purchase of directly competing brands. Additional reasons for tying, beyond those we discussed in relation to exclusive dealing, together with some new examples, are as follows:

- Transferring market demand already established for the tying product (e.g., can closing machines) to the tied product (cans).
- Using the tied product (paper) to meter usage of the tying product (copying machines).
- Using a low-margin tying product (razors) to sell a high-margin tied product (razor blades).
- Achieving cost savings through package sales, with the possibility of the costs of supplying and servicing channel members being lower when more products appear in the "package."
- Assuring the successful operation of the tying product (automobile) by obliging dealers to purchase tied products (repair parts) from the supplier.[62]

A tying agreement forecloses competitors from the opportunity to sell the tied commodity or service. Thus, the primary condemnation of tying, similar to exclusive dealing, is the foreclosure of interbrand competition from a marketplace. But tying contracts also invoke much more negative responses from the courts than exclusive dealing arrangements or requirements contracts. In distinguishing between a requirements contract and a tying contract in the *Standard Stations* case, the renowned Justice Felix Frankfurter asserted tying arrangements "serve hardly any purpose beyond the suppression of competition."[63] Like exclusive dealing, tying is circumscribed by the Sherman Act, the Clayton Act, and the FTC Act. Considering these negative attitudes, it is little wonder that the use of tying rarely is approved.

Yet certain types of tying contracts remain perfectly legal. If two products are made to be used jointly and one will not function properly without the other, a tying agreement is within the law. (Shoes are sold in pairs, and automobiles are sold with tires.) If a company's goodwill depends on the proper operation of equipment, a service contract may be tied to the sale or lease of the machine.[64] Ultimately, the availability and practicality of alternatives to tying arrangements appear crucial: If a firm will suffer injury unless it can protect its product, and there is no feasible alternative, the courts permit tying agreements. In addition, it is necessary to consider economic power conditions, because if the company has no leverage over a product, no tying arrangement can exist by coercion, in that the buyer can always go elsewhere to purchase. The tying product also must be successfully differentiated, and the tie must invoke substantial commerce.[65] Therefore, the legal presumption against tying arrangements is not inviolable, as a 1984 U.S. Supreme Court case involving hospital services shows (see Sidebar 13-8).

## Sidebar 13-8

### Jefferson Parish Hospital District No. 2 v. Hyde

In the *Jefferson Parish* case,[66] anesthesiologist Edwin Hyde, who had been denied admission to the staff of East Jefferson Hospital, sued the governance board of the hospital, because the hospital had an exclusive contract with a firm of anesthesiologists requiring that all anesthesiological services for the hospital's patients be performed by that firm. The Supreme Court agreed with a district court that the relevant geographic market was Jefferson Parish (i.e., metropolitan New Orleans), not the neighborhood immediately surrounding East Jefferson Hospital, reasoning that "Seventy percent of the patients residing in Jefferson Parish enter hospitals other than East Jefferson.... Thus, East Jefferson's 'dominance' over persons residing in Jefferson Parish is far from overwhelming."

The Court further explained that "the fact that the exclusive contract requires purchase of two services that would otherwise be purchased separately does not make the contract illegal. Only if patients are forced to purchase the contracting firm's services as a result of the hospital's market power would the arrangement have anticompetitive consequences." East Jefferson's market power was not significant enough to make the contract illegal.

The most important dictum in the *Jefferson Parish* decision was the following sentence, which provides the foundation for assessing other tying cases:

> The essential characteristic of an invalid tying arrangement lies in the seller's exploitation of its control over the tying product to force the buyer into the purchase of a tied product that the buyer either did not want at all, or might have preferred to purchase elsewhere on different terms.[67]

434  Part IV • Implementing Channel Strategies

Still, serious legal questions arise relative to the tying agreements, especially in a franchise setting. As we detailed in Chapter 8, an individual or group of individuals (franchisees) usually receive the license to set up outlets of a national chain, in return for their capital investment and a periodic fee paid to the parent company (franchisor). In some cases, the franchisor also requires franchisees to buy various supplies, such as meat, baked goods, or paper cups, from the central corporation or an approved supplier. In this case, the tying product is the franchise; the tied products are the supplies that the franchisee must purchase to operate the business. Franchisors argue that such requirements are necessary to maintain their service quality and reputation. Critics assert instead that the franchisees wind up purchasing supplies and raw materials at prices far above those of the competitive market.

Because the primary tying "product" is the trademark itself (e.g., "McDonald's," "Budget" Rent-A-Car, "Sheraton" Hotels), the courts have sustained tying agreements that link the trademark to supplies if the franchisors can prove that their trademarks are inseparable from their supplies and that the tied product (supplies) are essential to quality control. For example, some franchisees have contended that Baskin-Robbins ice cream products are unlawfully tied to the license of the Baskin-Robbins trademark,[68] but this claim was denied because the franchisees could not establish that the trademark was a product separate from the ice cream. In any tying cases, at least two distinct products must be involved. Thus, whereas Chock Full O'Nuts Corporation "successfully proved its affirmative defense [to tying charges] of maintaining quality control with regard to its coffee and baked goods,"[69] it could not defend its tying practices with respect to other, easily reproduced products (e.g., French fries, soft drink syrups, napkins, glasses).

For courts then, the legality of tying agreements depends on five main questions:

1. Are there two distinct products?
2. Does the seller require the buyer to purchase the tied product to obtain the tying product?
3. Does the seller have sufficient market power to force a tie-in?
4. How much commerce does the tying arrangement affect in the market for the tied product?
5. Is the tie actually necessary to fulfill a legitimate business purpose?

These "structural" criteria might not be satisfied for sellers with relatively small market shares, especially when the tying product is unpatented.[70] The Eastman Kodak case profiled in Sidebar 13-9 illustrates a successful prosecution according to these criteria.

Another successful outcome arose from the FTC's 1991 investigation of Sandoz Pharmaceuticals Corp., which it accused of violating antitrust laws by requiring buyers of Clozaril, a drug for schizophrenia, to purchase a weekly blood test from a company under contract with Sandoz.[71] Sandoz's dominant position in the drug category was obvious. The company thus agreed to settle the charges by promising not to require Clozaril purchasers to buy blood monitoring services from Sandoz or anyone designated by Sandoz.[72] European attitudes toward tying agreements are generally similar. For example, the Swedish packaging group Tetra Pak lost its case when it was determined that customer contracts that tied Tetra Pak machine users to the purchase of Tetra Pak cartons were not justified and intended instead to strengthen the company's dominant position by reinforcing its customers' economic dependence on it.[73]

## Sidebar 13-9

### Eastman Kodak Co. v. Image Technical Service, Inc.

One of the most remarkable and significant cases involving tying was decided by the U.S. Supreme Court on June 8, 1992. At that time, the Court ruled that Eastman Kodak Company would have to stand trial on a tying claim brought against it by 18 independent service organizations (ISOs).[74] The case arose out of Kodak's efforts to keep for itself the business of servicing Kodak-brand copiers. Kodak had refused to sell replacement parts to the ISOs that wanted to service Kodak copiers. In response the ISOs alleged that Kodak's conduct amounted to an illegal monopolization of the business of servicing Kodak-brand copiers and an illegal tying of the sale of servicing copiers to the sale of replacement parts.

To succeed on the tying claim, the ISOs had to prove that Kodak had "appreciable market power" in the business of selling replacement parts for Kodak-brand copiers. To succeed on the monopolization claim, the ISOs had to prove that Kodak had "monopoly power" in the sale of the replacement parts. Kodak argued that sales of its copiers represented, at most, 23 percent of the sale of copiers for all manufacturers, and the Supreme Court agreed that the 23 percent share did not amount to appreciable power in the copier sales business. But the Court also found that Kodak controlled nearly 100 percent of the market for its replacement parts—which are not interchangeable with the parts of other manufacturer's machines—and between 80 percent and 95 percent of the service market.

The Court reasoned that the relevant market for antitrust purposes is determined by the choices available to Kodak equipment owners who must use Kodak parts. Thus, Kodak's motion for summary judgment (i.e., it wanted the Supreme Court to dismiss the case because of its lack of market power in the copier market) was rejected by a 6 to 3 vote, and the case was sent back to the Federal District Court in San Francisco for trial. Kodak lost the verdicts both in that trial and in its appeal to the Ninth U.S. Circuit Court of Appeals in August 1997. Ultimately, it was ordered to pay $35 million to the plaintiffs in the case.[75]

### Full-Line Forcing

A seller's product leverage might enable it to force a buyer to purchase its whole line of goods. Such a **full-line forcing** policy is illegal if competitive sellers are unreasonably prevented from market access.[76] A common, though generally regarded as illegal, form of this policy occurs when motion picture distributors impose **block booking** on independent theater owners. That is, theaters are forced to screen many movies they do not want, to obtain the ones they do. In turn, independent movie producers are unable to sell their films to theaters whose programs have been stuffed full with the products of the major studios. Similar arrangements cover the sale of motion picture "packages" to television broadcasters. Yet such practices typically have been held to be illegal, especially when copyrighted films are used as the bait.[77]

E&J Gallo Winery, the largest seller of wine in the United States, consented to an FTC order prohibiting it from requiring its wholesalers to distribute Gallo wines so they could obtain other labels.[78] Union Carbide Corporation agreed to stop requiring its dealers to purchase their total requirements of six industrial gases (acetylene, argon, helium, hydrogen, nitrogen, and oxygen) only from it or making the purchase of these six gases a prerequisite for dealers' right to buy other gases or welding products.[79]

## Designated Product Policies

A manufacturer may want to sell some portion of its product line through a limited number of resellers, while allowing other resellers to sell a different subset of its products. Recall from Sidebar 12-1 that John Deere decided to make its entry-level tractors available for sale at Home Depot while reserving its sophisticated, high-end lawn-mowers for its authorized, service-providing dealer network. Such a policy can help preserve the manufacturer's exclusive brand and prevent brand erosion through overly broad distribution. Furthermore, it gives multiple resellers reasonable profit-making opportunities. If at least some of the products the reseller provides are exclusive to it, it can confidently invest in customer service and promotional activities, secure in the knowledge that its efforts will not fall victim to free riding.

In the United States, a manufacturer has no legal obligation to sell all of its products to all resellers that wish to do so—with two exceptions. First, if the manufacturer is a monopolist with excess capacity, because there is no other source for the product, the manufacturer is required to supply it to requesting resellers. Thus, AT&T was forced to open its long-distance lines to independent phone companies in the United States, because it was the only holder of these exchanges, so it had to grant access to its competitors, which wanted to purchase. Second, if a manufacturer has signed a contract with a reseller promising to supply all of its products, it is required to honor the contract.

Beyond these two exceptions, we also need to consider the usual antitrust restriction, that is, a refusal to deal with a reseller cannot be the result of a conspiracy or other agreement to restrain trade. An interesting instance, as presented in Sidebar 13-10, involved Toys 'R Us, such that the *retailer*, rather than a manufacturer, was accused of limiting access to various manufacturers' products at competing retailers. In a ruling, the FTC chair wrote that Toys 'R Us had "used its dominant position

## Sidebar 13-10

### U.S. Federal Trade Commission v. Toys 'R US

This case is somewhat unusual: Toys 'R Us, the *retailer*, rather than a manufacturer, was accused of limiting access to various manufacturers' products at competing retailers.[80] In May 1996, the Federal Trade Commission filed charges against Toys 'R Us, alleging that the retailer threatened not to buy any toy whose manufacturer also sold the toy through a warehouse club store chain. It thus effectively forced the suppliers into exclusive dealing with Toys 'R Us for the most popular toys in the market. In particular, Toys 'R Us sought to prevent warehouse clubs like Sam's Club, Price Club, and Costco from competing with it. Their competitive threat to Toys 'R Us was real, because the warehouse clubs had much lower cost structures than the retailer and could there-fore price compete effectively, given product supply

(e.g., Mattel's Hollywood Hair Barbie sold for $10.99 at Toys 'R Us; at warehouse clubs, it was required to come packaged with an extra dress, forcing the retail price up to $15.99 and preventing direct price comparisons). Hasbro, another toy manufacturer, refused to supply Hall of Fame G.I. Joe dolls directly to warehouse clubs; Mattel also declined to offer Fisher-Price brand pool tables to them. Toys 'R Us allegedly blocked sales of Disney's *Toy Story* movie figures to the discount chains too.

The FTC noted a substantial anticompetitive threat, because Toys 'R Us had an approximately 20 percent market share of all U.S. retail toy sales—somewhat low overall, but the relevant manufac-turers sold as much as 30 percent of their total volume through Toys 'R Us, creating significant

## Continued

dependence on the retailer, such that it could force them to participate in anticompetitive actions. After Toys 'R Us started the enforced boycott in 1993, Costco's toy sales dropped by 1.6 percent, even as its overall sales grew by 19.5 percent. Mattel's sales to warehouse clubs also fell from more than $23 million in 1991 to only $7.5 million in 1993.

Thus, on October 1, 1997, an FTC administrative judge ruled against Toys 'R Us; while awaiting review by the full FTC, New York's Attorney General also filed a lawsuit against Toys 'R Us and three of its largest suppliers (Mattel, Hasbro, and Little Tikes), alleging an illegal conspiracy to raise prices and stifle competition. On November 17, the suit was amended to add 37 additional states, Puerto Rico, and Washington, DC. Eventually 44 of the 50 states joined the lawsuit. On October 15, 1998, the FTC upheld the administrative judge's 1997 ruling, issuing a cease-and-desist order to Toys 'R Us. The FTC

chair wrote that Toys 'R Us had "used its dominant position as toy distributor to extract agreements from and among toy manufacturers to stop selling to warehouse clubs the same toys that they had sold to other toy distributors." The retailer appealed the decision, to the U.S. Circuit Court of Appeals.

But in December 1998, Hasbro settled the suit filed by the states, agreeing to pay $6 million in donations and other payments to the states and charities. In May 1999, Toys 'R Us and the other suppliers also settled. The retailer agreed to pay $40.5 million in cash and toy donations; Mattel would pay $8.2 million, and Little Tikes agreed to pay $1.3 million in cash and toys. None of the parties admitted wrongdoing though. The key to this case was twofold: the degree of harm to competition and the concerted effort made to influence multiple manufacturers, who all agreed to the restrictive dealing practices.

as toy distributor to extract agreements from and among toy manufacturers to stop selling to warehouse clubs the same toys that they had sold to other toy distributors." The key factors in this case were the degree of harm to competition and the concerted effort made to influence multiple manufacturers, all of which had agreed to the restrictive dealing practices.

## SELECTION AND TERMINATION POLICIES

A central theme throughout this text is that organizations must devote a great deal of time, attention, effort, and money to the design and management of their distribution systems. That is, to achieve success through marketing channels, channel managers must set up selection criteria and then monitor the performance of anyone they admit into the distribution system. Even with extensive distribution systems, selection procedures are necessary, because not every conceivable outlet can sell every product. (Department stores do not typically sell milk, for example.) The existence of any selection criteria imply someone does not make the cut, which means that refusing to deal with certain channel members is an unavoidable element of channel policy. The same implication stems from performance criteria, so another key element of channel policy is termination.

Sellers can both select their own distributors, according to their own criteria, and announce in advance the circumstances in which they will refuse to sell to certain intermediaries. These two commercial "freedoms" were granted by *U.S. v. Colgate & Co.* in 1919; they constitute the **Colgate doctrine**,[81] formally recognized in

Section 2(a) of the Robinson-Patman Act. Implicit in a seller's general right to select its preferred distribution system is the right to deal with certain channel members on a limited basis. General Motors, for example, is not obligated to sell Chevrolets to a Buick dealer.

The *Colgate* doctrine also contains two explicit exceptions. First, the decision not to deal must be independent or unilateral, rather than part of a concerted action. This issue was one of the problems faced by the toy manufacturers in the Toys 'R Us case we described in the previous section. It would not have been illegal for any one of these manufacturers to refuse *unilaterally* to sell a particular product to warehouse club stores. But the concerted effort, led by Toys 'R Us, made the action illegal. Second, the refusal must occur in the absence of any intent to create or maintain a monopoly. If a unilateral refusal to deal is ever illegal, it is when the refusal is undertaken by a monopolist, or an entity that hopes to become one.[82]

Refusal to deal is also an important tool that allows a channel member to exert coercive power. The right to refuse to deal thus has been narrowly confined but not prohibited completely. Suppliers may formally cut off dealers for valid business reasons, such as a failure to pay or poor performance. But suppliers cannot establish restrictive, regulated, or programmed distribution systems and then exclude dealers that have somehow stepped out of line with its edicts. A lawsuit alleging such exclusion imposes triple damages on the defendant, so the stakes are high. The courts generally ask two questions to determine if a refusal to deal violates the law:

- Was the decision to exclude certain channel members a unilateral decision by the manufacturer?
- Was there a legitimate business reason for the change in channel membership?[83]

Many of the cases brought under Sections 1 and 2 of the Sherman Act involve decisions by suppliers or franchisors to terminate an existing dealer, substitute a "new" for an "old" dealer, or vertically integrate. Thus, whereas the original *selection* of distributors or dealers for a new product seems to pose few legal problems, the *termination* of existing distributors and dealers can cause great difficulties. Any time a supplier applies exclusive dealing, customer constraints, or territorial restrictions, a dealer that has been cut off from the network may take the supplier to court, charging that the refusal to deal was based on a desire to maintain an unlawful practice.

Increasing litigation in such cases has been furthered by specific legislative decrees, such as the Automobile Dealers Franchise Act of 1956, which entitles a car dealer to sue any car manufacturer that fails to act in good faith in connection with the termination, cancellation, or nonrenewal of the dealer's franchise. However, defendants in lawsuits associated with this act have often been successful in producing evidence that the dealer has not acted in good faith, such that its own action was justified. Many other lawsuits filed every year feature franchisees in various industries who claim to have been wrongly terminated by franchisors, usually on the basis of contract and property right arguments, rather than antitrust allegations though.

Manufacturers' rights to terminate resellers vary widely across nations. Outside the United States, it often is very difficult to terminate a distributor, particularly if it has been the exclusive representative of the manufacturer's product. Here again, a manufacturer seeking to expand its distribution internationally needs to check local regulations carefully.

## OWNERSHIP POLICIES

The final policy category we address in this chapter refers back to the make-or-buy (vertical integration) question we discussed in Chapter 4 and the antitrust issues surrounding this decision. A decision to vertically integrate often puts a company in competition with independent channel intermediaries that already carry its brands, as we outlined in our discussion of dual or multichannel distribution. Recall as well that vertical integration might result from forward integration by a producer, backward integration by a retailer, or integration in either direction by a wholesaler or logistics firm. All these forms of integration can result from the creation of a new business function by existing firms (i.e., internal expansion) or the acquisition of the stock or assets of other firms (i.e., mergers).

These two integration methods differ fundamentally in their relationships to the law. **Internal expansion** is regulated by Section 2 of the Sherman Act, which prohibits monopolies and attempts to monopolize any interstate or foreign commerce. **Mergers**, or external expansions, are regulated by Section 7 of the Clayton Act, which prohibits the purchase of other firms if doing so substantially lessens competition or creates monopoly in any line of commerce in any part of the country.[84] Thus, internal expansion receives favored treatment under the law, under the theory that it expands investment and production and thus increases competition, whereas growth through mergers prompts suspicion, because it removes an entity from the market.

Either type of integration can lower costs and facilitate more effective interorganizational channel management. It also can help firms avoid many of the legal problems we have detailed in this chapter, because an integrated firm is free to control prices and allocate products to its integrated outlets without coming in conflict with any laws governing restrictive distribution policies.

### Vertical Integration by Merger

Mergers pose and antitrust danger in the same way that many of the policies we have already discussed in this chapter do: It may limit competition from foreclosing competitors' access to sources of supply or customers. Thus, when Merck (the world's largest drug company), bought Medco Containment Services (the largest distributor of discount prescription medicines in the United States), antitrust concerns arose about the potential for limited access to Medco. Another major pharmaceutical firm, Eli Lilly, had been able to purchase PCS Health Systems, another enormous managed care drug distributor, only after it agreed to restrictions imposed by the FTC that prevented it from unfairly pushing sales of Lilly brands through PCS or gaining information about the prices for competing drugs.[85] In announcing its decision to reexamine the Merck–Medco merger (and another one in the same industry), the FTC warned, "We remain concerned about the overall competitive impact of vertical integration by drug companies into the pharmacy benefits management market."[86] Although all of these "big pharma" mergers eventually were approved, the questions the FTC raised signaled why vertical mergers might draw the attention of the antitrust enforcement agencies.

In the late twentieth century, the U.S. government largely refrained from challenging vertical mergers, focusing solely on those that facilitated collusion or significantly raised barriers to new entry.[87] Yet the FTC still shows its teeth when necessary. For example, TCI and Comcast, the largest and third-largest cable television companies in the United States, agreed to form a joint venture to take ownership of QVC. At that time, QVC was one of two cable shopping ventures, with 98 percent market share; the other was Home Shopping Network, which was 79 percent controlled by TCI. Thus, the FTC investigated whether existing and potential competitors to QVC and Home Shopping Network might have trouble selling on cable TV, considering that TCI and Comcast together controlled access to about 30 percent of cable-wired homes.[88] The approval of the merger noted that the relevant market in this case was all retailing, not just home shopping by television.

Vertical mergers also have attracted attention outside the United States. For example, Grand Metropolitan, a U.K. food, beverage, and retailing conglomerate, and Elders IXL, an Australian brewer, agreed to a $5 billion pubs-for-breweries swap. Grand Met was to transfer four breweries and the Ruddles, Watneys, Truman, and Webster's beer brands to Courage, owned by Elder, and then Courage was to combine its 4,900 pubs with GrandMet's 3,570 pubs. A major challenge to the merger arose when the U.K. Monopolies and Mergers Commission issued a 500-page report concluding that the nation's large breweries were operating a "complex monopoly" to restrict competition, centered on the long-established tied-house system, which ensures most of Britain's 80,000 pubs stock the products of only the company that owns them.[89] The merger was allowed, but only after the government put into effect "guest beer orders" that explicitly allowed pubs to stock beers from suppliers other than those that owned them.[90]

On balance, mergers and similar cooperative agreements seem worthwhile, in that they can generate many advantages for firms through synergies and spillovers of knowledge, customers, innovations, and products. The threat of regulatory action also is somewhat limited, in that regulators tend to take notice only when the arrangements among competitors unduly limit competition or the supply of products to any downstream channel members.[91]

### Vertical Integration by Internal Expansion

This form of integration is limited only by laws preventing monopolies and attempts to monopolize. A firm is free to set up its own supply, distribution, and/or retailing system, unless doing so would create too much concentration in the market for its product.[92] Section 7 of the Clayton Act specifically permits a firm to set up subsidiary corporations to carry on business or extensions thereof, as long as competition is not substantially reduced.

### Dual Distribution

The term **dual distribution** describes various marketing arrangements in which manufacturers or wholesalers reach end-users by employing multiple channels for the same basic product. Although customary in many product lines (e.g., tires, personal computers), dual distribution arrangements often spark controversy, as we noted in Chapter 11. Whereas conflict appears likely among channel members in most dual distribution situations, serious legal questions arise mainly when (1) price "squeezing" is suspected or (2) horizontal combinations or conspiracies are possible among competitors.

In the former case, a seller operating at a single market level, in competition with a powerful, vertically integrated firm, might be subject to a **price squeeze**. For example, a manufacturer of fabricated aluminum might experience pressure, exerted by its raw material (ingot) supplier, to increase prices. If the ingot supplier also is a fabricator, it can use the profit gains it receives from the price increase (which means higher costs for its customer-competitor) to increase its marketing activities at the fabrication level—as was the scenario in the *Alcoa* case.[93] But an integrated supplier's attempt to eliminate a customer as a competitor by undercutting its prices and placing the customer in a price squeeze remains illegal.[94]

Similar competitive inequality marks functional discounts when different functional categories can be represented by buyers that, at least in some of their trade, compete with each other. As we mentioned in reference to the *Hasbrouck* case, oil jobbers sometimes sell at retail, and they may use the functional discounts they receive as jobbers to gain an unfair competitive advantage over retailers. Such pricing raises the possibility of violations of the Robinson-Patman Act, as well as the Sherman Act.

In the latter case, the distinction between purely vertical and **horizontal restraints** is critical for determining the legality of a marketing activity. Section 1 of the Sherman Act cannot be violated by a unilateral action by a supplier; there must be at least one other party that contracts, combines, or conspires with the supplier. Dominant manufacturers may replace distributors, but they may not enter into competition with them and destroy them. Thus, each challenge to dual distribution must be appraised according to the circumstances. If a supplier competes directly with its customers, actions that threaten the customers may be subject to antitrust scrutiny, but its intent is the crucial question. As the *Sylvania* case showed, in the United States, there must be balanced effects of a marketing policy on intrabrand and interbrand competition in situations involving vertical restraints.

## SUMMARY: MANAGING CHANNEL POLICIES AND LEGALITIES

Channel policies determine distribution strategies. Policies guide the functioning of channels and enable channel managers to achieve effective integration, coordination, and role performance throughout the channel, in the absence of outright ownership. However, established policies nearly always create the potential for conflict, because they tend to be exclusionary, elitist, or restrictive in their focus and goal, namely, to confirm that behavior within channels is not random. Limits on behavior evoke antitrust concerns—even when recent research suggests that antitrust activities actually have little effect on an economy's long-term financial performance.[95]

In this chapter, we consider six unique but interrelated channel policy types. With a market coverage policy, the channel's focus is on geographic spacing (i.e., intensive versus selective versus exclusive distribution). More intensive distribution increases short-term sales but also lowers channel members' willingness to provide costly service outputs, because of the price competition that ensues from the presence substantial intrabrand competition. Suppliers thus consider selective and exclusive distribution policies, which lower intrabrand but also interbrand competition. Following the *Sylvania* case, the legality of these policies has been determined according to the rule-of-reason doctrine.

Marketing managers also may wish to ensure that only the "right" channel members service specific kinds of customers: Company-employed salespeople call on technically savvy heavy users; distributor salespeople call on less demanding accounts; and only authorized dealers may sell the company's brand to end-users. Antitrust enforcement agencies categorize such customer coverage policies as customer or resale restrictions and govern them using the same rule-of-reason doctrine that applies to market coverage policies.

Both market and customer coverage policies have indirect effects on prices; the direct effects come from pricing policies, such as price maintenance and price discrimination. Minimum resale price maintenance is per se illegal if there is some form of agreement or concerted action between or among channel members involved in setting or policing the policy. Otherwise, it can be adopted unilaterally. Maximum resale price maintenance (if arrived at by agreement) is subject to a rule of reason; it may be implemented as long as there are no anticompetitive effects. Price discrimination is at the heart of market segmentation strategies but can run afoul of the law if it lessens competition. It includes such notable activities as promotional allowances and services and quantity and functional discounts.

The product line policies we have addressed—exclusive dealing, tying, and full-line forcing—all attempt to ensure other channel members devote undivided attention to the supplier's products. They restrict interbrand competition directly, whereas market and customer coverage policies restrict intrabrand competition. Because of their potential for foreclosing competitors, antitrust agencies tend to exhibit more concern about product line policies than about the various types of coverage policies.

To address vertical integration questions, channel managers can use ownership policies. The decision to make rather than buy leads to another choice: to expand using acquisition (or merger) or internal expansion. Internal expansion poses few problems from an antitrust perspective. Until recently, the same was true of vertical mergers, but in the wake of extensive merger and acquisition activity in the pharmaceutical and entertainment channels, regulators have reawakened to the potential competitive threat. In any case, vertical integration in combination with a multiple channel distribution strategy nearly always leads to some conflict in the channel.

Finally, this chapter has addressed primarily U.S. federal antitrust law. Yet the individual states also have become much more active; marketing executives cannot afford to make the mistake of ignoring the vast outpouring of legislation and court precedents that regulate distribution practices in each of the states in which they might sell their products. Even more broadly, antitrust and competitive laws vary widely throughout the world. It behooves channel managers to take an international perspective and gain familiarity with the variations in all the locations in which they operate.

## TAKE-AWAYS

- Many channel policies and decisions may fall under the scrutiny of antitrust authorities, including the following:
  - Market coverage policies.
  - Customer coverage policies.
  - Pricing policies.
  - Product line policies.
  - Selection and termination policies.
  - Ownership policies.
- The key laws in the United States affecting these activities are the Sherman Antitrust Act (1890), the Clayton Antitrust Act (1914), the Federal Trade Commission (FTC) Act (1914), the Robinson-Patman Act (1936), and FTC Trade Practice Rules.

- These laws
  - Prohibit conspiracies to restrain interstate or foreign trade.
  - Prohibit price discrimination, exclusive dealing, tying contracts, interlocking directorates among competitors, and mergers and acquisitions when these actions substantially lessen competition.
  - Prohibit unfair or deceptive trade practices.
  - Identify defenses to price discrimination allegations, as follows:
    - They are used in good faith to meet the competition.
    - They are backed by real differences in cost to serve different customers.
    - The lower price was available to all customers but not chosen by some.
    - The price discrimination does not harm competition (e.g., used only across different segments of final end-users, who by definition do not compete).
- Antitrust law enforcement invariably considers the impact of the business practice on intrabrand versus interbrand competition. The courts sometimes allow the restriction of intrabrand competition if it serves to enhance interbrand competition.
- An action deemed per se illegal is illegal in all circumstances, regardless of the reason for the action of any other implications of the action. An action that is illegal only under a rule of reason is one for which mitigating circumstances can permit its use.
- The legality of certain business practices, like resale price maintenance, has changed over time. Minimum RPM was per se illegal until the mid-1980s, and maximum RPM was until the late 1980s. Now both are considered under a rule of reason. To be legal, the RPM practice:
  - Cannot be undertaken as part of an agreement to restrain trade.
  - Should be undertaken unilaterally.
  - Does not use coercion.
  - Is announced upfront rather than being imposed after the fact.
- Functional discounts are useful channel tools to align the incentives of manufacturers and their channel partners; they are legal as long as they obey the laws governing price discrimination.
- Exclusive dealing is illegal if a dominant firm is involved and if the agreement serves to suppress competition in the market.
- Tying contracts are generally illegal unless it can be shown that the two products are designed to be used jointly and one will not function properly without the other.
- Under the *Colgate* doctrine, U.S. antitrust law defends the right of a seller to choose which resellers have access to its product, and to choose *not* to sell to certain intermediaries. The exception to this rule occurs when the seller is a monopolist, so denying access to the product would deny a competitor access to the market at large.
- Channel alteration through vertical integration is generally allowed unless the combined firm would monopolize the market or otherwise stifle competition. The law treats vertical integration by internal expansion more favorably than vertical integration by merger.
- The focus of this chapter is somewhat limited to U.S. law affecting channel management policies. Antitrust laws in other countries differ widely from U.S. laws.

# Endnotes

1. *Continental T.V., Inc. v. GTE Sylvania Inc.*, 433 U.S. 36 (1977).
2. Ibid.
3. Dutta, Shantanu, Jan B. Heide, and Mark Bergen (1999), "Vertical Territorial Restrictions and Public Policy: Theories and Industry Evidence," *Journal of Marketing* 63 (October), pp. 121–134.
4. Thunder, David (1991), "Key Considerations in European Distribution," *Client Communique* 3 (April), p. 1.
5. See Griffiths, John (1994), "Commission Plans Will Loosen Carmakers' Grip on Dealers," *Financial Times* October 6, p. 6; "Carved Up" (1992), *The Economist*, October 31, p. 73; de Jonquieres, Guy (1992), "Electric Suppliers Blames for EC Price Variations," August 3, p. 1; Rice, Robert (1993), "Whiff of Controversy Hangs in the Air," *Financial Times*, November 16, p. 10; Tucker, Emma and Haig Simonian (1995), "Brussels Plans to Give More Freedom to Car Dealers," *Financial Times*, May 26, p. 1.
6. Tucker, Emma (1997), "Easing the Pain of 'Vertical Restraints,' " *Financial Times*, January 22, p. 2; " 'Vertical Restraints' Eased" (1998), *Financial Times*, October 1, p. 2; "Competition: Industry Council Gives Green Light for Changes to Vertical Restraints Rules" (1999), *European Report*, May 1; "Council Formally Adopts Two Competition Regulations" (1999), *European Report*, June 16; "Competition: Commission Firms Up Single Block Exemption Rule" (1999), *European Report*, July 17.
7. Wiriyabunditkul, Payungsak (2012), "Boeing: Asean Open Skies in 2015 Will Spur Demand for Regional Air Travel," *Dow Newswires*, October 26.
8. Areeda, Phillip and Louis Kaplow (1988), *Antitrust Analysis: Problems, Text, Cases*, 4th ed. (Boston, MA: Little, Brown and Company), p. 659.
9. Posner, Richard A. (1976), *Antitrust Law: An Economic Perspective* (Chicago, IL: University of Chicago Press), p. 162.
10. *K-Mart Corporation v. Cartier, Inc.*, 56 LW 4480 (1988).
11. Ibid.; see also Wermiel, Stephen (1988), "Justices Uphold Customs Rules on Gray Market," *The Wall Street Journal*, June 1, p. 2; "A Red-Letter Day for Gray Marketeers" (1988), *BusinessWeek*, June 13, p. 30.
12. These and other reasons can be found in Ornstein, Stanley, I. (1989), "Exclusive Dealing and Antitrust," *Antitrust Bulletin* (Spring), pp. 71–74.
13. See Areeda and Kaplow, op. cit., pp. 630–635; Rubin, Paul H. (1990), *Managing Business Transactions* (New York: The Free Press), pp. 126–127.
14. *Monsanto Co. v. Spray-Rite Service Corp.*, 104 U.S. 1464 (1984).
15. *Business Electronics Corp. v. Sharp Electronics Corp.*, 99 S. Ct. 808 (1988).
16. Kaufmann, Patrick J. (1988), "Dealer Termination Agreements and Resale Price Maintenance: Implications of the Business Electronics Case and the Proposed Amendment to the Sherman Act," *Journal of Retailing* 64 (Summer), p. 120.
17. Barrett, Paul M. (1991), "Anti-Discount Policies of Manufacturers Are Penalizing Certain Cut-Price Stores," *The Wall Street Journal*, February 27, p. B1.
18. Arndt, Michael (1991), "Consumers Pay More as Price-Fixing Spreads," *Chicago Tribune*, August 18, Sec. 7, p. 5.
19. See, for example, Blair, Roger D. and Francine Lafontaine (1999), "Will *Khan* Foster or Hinder Franchising? An Economic Analysis of Maximum Resale Price Maintenance," *Journal of Public Policy & Marketing* 18, no. 1, pp. 25–36.
20. Sheffet, Mary Jane and Debra L. Scammon (1985), "Resale Price Maintenance: Is It Safe to Suggest Retail Prices?" *Journal of Marketing* 49 (Fall), pp. 89–90.
21. *Business Electronics Corp.*, 485 U.S. at 733.
22. *Albrecht v. Herald Co.*, 390 U.S. 145 (1968).
23. Blair and Lafontaine, op. cit.; Felsenthal, Edward (1997), "Manufacturers Allowed to Cap Retail Prices," *The Wall Street Journal*, November 5, p. A3; Garland, Susan B. and Mike France (1997), "You'll Charge What I Tell You to Charge," *BusinessWeek*, October 6, pp. 118–120.
24. 272 U.S. 476, 486–488 (1926).

Chapter 13 • Managing Channel Policies and Legalities **445**

25. *Ryko Manufacturing Co. v. Eden Services*, 823 F.2d 1215 at 1223 (8ᵗʰ Cir. 1987).
26. See Nagle, Thomas T. and Reed K. Holden (2002), *The Strategy and Tactics of Pricing*, 3rd ed. (Englewood Cliffs, NJ: Prentice-Hall), Chapter 9, for a discussion of segmented pricing.
27. *U.S. v. Borden Co.*, 383 U.S. 637 (1966).
28. *Brooke Group Ltd. v. Brown & Williamson Tobacco Corp.*, U.S. 114 S.Ct. 13 (1993).
29. Ibid. at 25.
30. Ibid.
31. See O'Brian, Bridget (1993), "Verdict Clears AMR on Illegal Pricing Charges," *The Wall Street Journal*, August 11, p. A3.
32. Scherer, F.M. and David Ross (1990), *Industrial Market Structure and Economic Performance*, 3rd ed. (Boston, MA: Houghton Mifflin Co.), p. 514.
33. See *Fall City Industries, Inc. v. Vanco Beverage, Inc.*, 460 U.S. 428 (1983).
34. *Standard Oil Co. v. FTC*, 340 U.S. 231 (1951).
35. *Federal Trade Commission v. Sun Oil Co.*, 371 U.S. 505 (1963).
36. *Fall City Industries v. Vanco Beverage*, op. cit.
37. Stoll, Neal R. and Shepard Goldfein (1997), "The Spring Trade Show: Explaining the Guidelines," *New York Law Journal*, Antitrust and Trade Practice Section, May 20, p. 3.
38. Gundlach, Gregory T. and Paul N. Bloom (1998), "Slotting Allowances and the Retail Sale of Alcohol Beverages," *Journal of Public Policy & Marketing* 17, no. 2, pp. 173–184.
39. Sullivan, Mary W. (1997), "Slotting Allowances and the Market for New Products," *Journal of Law and Economics* 40 (October), pp. 461–493.
40. Food Marketing Institute (2002), "Slotting Allowances in the Supermarket Industry," available at http://www.fmi.org/media/bg/slottingfees2002.pdf.
41. Chu, Wujin (1992), "Demand Signalling and Screening in Channels of Distribution," *Marketing Science* 11, pp. 327–347; Lariviere, Martin A. and V. Padmanabhan (1997), "Slotting Allowances and New Product Introductions," *Marketing Science* 16, no. 2, pp. 112–128.
42. Ibid.
43. *Augusta News Co. v. Hudson News Co.* (2001), 269 F.ed 41 (1ˢᵗ Cir.). For a description, see Balto, David (2002), "Recent Legal and Regulatory Developments in Slotting Allowances and Category Management," *Journal of Public Policy & Marketing* 21, no. 2, pp. 289–294.
44. Harps, Leslie Hansen and Warren Thayer (1997), "FTC Is Investigating 'Exclusive Dealing'," *Frozen Food Age*, May, p. 78; Sullivan, op. cit.; Cannon, Joseph P. and Paul N. Bloom (1991), "Are Slotting Allowances Legal Under the Antitrust Laws?" *Journal of Public Policy & Marketing* 10 (Spring), pp. 167–186. However, slotting allowances are prohibited for alcoholic beverages, as discussed by Gundlach and Bloom, op. cit.; Gundlach and Bloom also stress that the logic for slotting allowances varies from market to market and thus a general rule for its use should not be inferred.
45. See *Atlantic Trading Corp. v. FTC*, 258 F.2d 375 (2d Cir. 1958).
46. Federal Trade Commission, "Guides for Advertising Allowances and Other Merchandising Payments and Services," 16 C.F.R. part 240 (1983).
47. *FTC v. Fred Meyer Company, Inc.*, 390 U.S. 341 (1968).
48. Ibid., 240.6.
49. "Federal Trade Commission Adopts Changes in Robinson-Patman Act Guides" (1990), *FTC News*, August 7, pp. 1–2.
50. 496 U.S. 492 (1990).
51. 496 U.S. 492 (1990).
52. 496 U.S. 492 at 492 (1990).
53. 496 U.S. 492 at 493 (1990).
54. For an excellent discussion of this problem, see Spriggs, Mark T. and John R. Nevin (1994), "The Legal Status of Trade and Functional Price Discounts," *Journal of Public Policy & Marketing* 13 (Spring), p. 63.
55. See Ornstein, op. cit.; Areeda and Kaplow, op. cit.
56. Neale, A.D. and D.G. Goyder (1980), *The Antitrust Laws of the U.S.A.*, 3rd ed. (New York: Cambridge University Press), p. 266.
57. Scherer and Ross, op. cit., p. 563.
58. Hovenkamp, Herbert (1994), *Federal Antitrust Policy* (St. Paul, MN: West Publishing Company), p. 390.

59. 365 U.S. 320 (1961).
60. Ibid., for a detailed discussion of the issues surrounding category management and category captains.
61. Ibid.; Balto, op. cit.
62. See Areeda and Kaplow, op. cit., pp. 705–710.
63. *Standard Oil Company of California v. U.S.*, 337 U.S. 293 (1949) at 305.
64. U.S. *v. Jerrold Electronics Corp.*, 187 F. Supp. 545 (1960), affirmed per curian at 363 U.S. 567 (1961).
65. Sullivan, op. cit., p. 439.
66. *Jefferson Parish Hospital District No. 2 v. Hyde*, 104 LW 1551 (1984). See also Robert E. Taylor and Stephen Wermiel (1984), "High Court Eases Antitrust Restrictions on Accords Linking Sales of Goods, Services," *Wall Street Journal*, March 28, p. 6.
67. *Jefferson Parish Hospital District No. 2 v. Hyde*, 466 U.S. 12 (1984).
68. *Norman E. Krehl, et al. v. Baskin-Robbins Ice Cream Company, et al.*, 42 F. 2d 115 (8th Cir. 1982).
69. *In re: Chock Full O'Nuts Corp. Inc.*, 3 Trade Reg. Rep. 20, 441 (October 1973).
70. Scherer and Ross, op. cit., p. 568.
71. See Barrett, Paul M. (1991), "FTC's Hard Line on Price Fixing May Foster Discounts," *The Wall Street Journal*, January 11, p. B1.
72. *FTC News Notes* 91 (June 17, 1991), p. 1; Barrett, Paul M. (1991), "Sandoz Settles FTC Charges Over Clozaril," *The Wall Street Journal*, June 21, p. B3.
73. "Tetra Pak Appeal" (1994), *The Financial Times*, October 18, p. 10.
74. *Eastman Kodak Co. v. Image Technical Service Inc.*, U.S. 112 S.Ct. 2072 (1992).
75. Bounds, Wendy (1995), "Jury Finds Kodak Monopolized Markets in Services and Parts for Its Machines," *The Wall Street Journal*, September 19, p. A4; "Court Upholds Jury Verdict Against Kodak, Cuts Damages" (1997), *The Buffalo News*, August 27, Business Section, p. B6.
76. *U.S. v. J.I. Case Co.*, 101 F. Supp. 856 (1951).
77. *U.S. v. Paramount Pictures*, 334 U.S. 131 (1948); *U.S. v. Loew's Inc.*, 371 U.S. 45 (1962).
78. "Consent Agreement Cites E&J Gallo Winery" (1976), *FTC News Summary*, May 21, p. 1. See also "Gallo Winery Consents to FTC Rule Covering Wholesaler Dealings" (1976), *The Wall Street Journal*, May 20, p. 15.
79. "Union Carbide Settles Complaint by FTC on Industrial-Gas Sales; Airco to Fight" (1977), *The Wall Street Journal*, May 20, p. 8.
80. See Gruley, Bryan and Joseph Pereira (1996), "FTC Is to Vote Soon on Staff's Request For Antitrust Action Against Toys 'R Us," *The Wall Street Journal*, May 21, p. A3; Pereira, Joseph and Bryan Gruley (1996), "Toys 'R Us Vows It Will Challenge Any Antitrust Charges Brought by FTC," *The Wall Street Journal*, May 22, p. A3; Pereira, Joseph and Bryan Gruley (1996), "Relative Power of Toys 'R Us Is Central to Suit," *The Wall Street Journal*, May 24, p. B1; Bulkeley, William M. and John R. Wilke (1997), "Toys Loses a Warehouse-Club Ruling With Broad Marketing Implications," *The Wall Street Journal*, October 1, p. A10; "Judge Faults Toys 'R Us" (1997), *International Herald Tribune*, October 1, p. 13; Broder, John M. (1997), "Toys 'R Us Led Price Collusion, U.S. Judge Says," *The New York Times*, October 1, p. A1; Segal, David (1997), "Judge Rules Toys R Us Wasn't Playing Fair; Product Agreements Found Anti-Competitive," *Washington Post*, October 1, Financial Section, p. D10; "Action Against Toymakers Grows" (1997), *The Arizona Republic*, November 18, Business Section, p. E4; Stroud, Jerri (1997), "Missouri and Illinois Join Suit Over Toys; The FCC Concluded the Retailer Bullied Toymakers," *St. Louis Post-Dispatch*, November 19, Business Section, p. C1; Williams, Norman D., "California, 37 Other States Claim Toys 'R Us Fixed Prices" (1997), *Sacramento Bee*, November 19; Segal, David (1998), "Toys R Us Told to Change Its Tactics; FTC Says Methods Limited Manufacturers' Sales to Discounters," *Washington Post*, October 15, Financial Section, p. C12; Brinkley, Joel (1998), "F.T.C. Tells Toys 'R Us to End Anticompetitive Measures," *The New York Times*, October 15, Section C, p. 22; Chon, Gina (1998), "Hasbro Agrees to Pay $6 Million in Antitrust Settlement," *The Associated Press State & Local Wire*, December 11;Westfeldt, Amy (1999), "Toy Makers to Pay $50 Million in Cash and Toys to Settle Antitrust Suit," *The Associated Press State & Local Wire*, May 26.
81. *U.S. v. Colgate & Co.*, 250 U.S. 300 (1919).

82. See Hovenkamp, op. cit., p. 263.

83. Scammon, Debra L. and Mary Jane Sheffet (1986), "Legal Issues in Channels Modification Decisions: The Question of Refusals to Deal," *Journal of Public Policy & Marketing* 5, p. 82.

84. Under the wording of Section 7 of the Clayton Act, it is unnecessary to prove that the restraint involved has actually restrained competition. It is enough that it may tend to substantially lessen competition.

85. Burton, Thomas M. (1994), "Eli Lilly Agrees to Restrictions on Buying PCS," *The Wall Street Journal*, October 26, p. A3.

86. Novak, Viveca and Elyse Tanouye (1994), "FTC Restudies 2 Acquisitions by Drug Firms," *The Wall Street Journal*, November 15, p. A16.

87. U.S. Department of Justice (1982), *Merger Guidelines* (Washington, DC: USDOJ), pp. 22–26.

88. Novak, Viveca (1994), "TCI-Comcast Agreement to Buy QVC May Face an FTC Antitrust Challenge," *The Wall Street Journal*, September 15, p. B3.

89. Maddocks, Tom (1990), "Brewers Play the Tie-Break," *Business*, August, p. 76; Rawstorne, Philip (1990), "A Change of Pace to Restructuring," *Financial Times*, September 19, p. 17; Rawstorne, Philip (1990), "GrandMet Backed on $2.6bn Deal," *Financial Times*, November 21, p. 34.

90. Rawstorne, Philip (1991), "Reduced Importance of the Brewer's Tie," *Financial Times*, February 25, p. 20.

91. Gupta, Sudheer (2008), "Channel Structures with Knowledge Spillovers," *Marketing Science* 27, no. 2, pp. 247–261.

92. *FTC v. Consolidated Foods Corp.*, 380 U.S. 592 (1965).

93. *U.S. v. Aluminum Co. of America*, 148 F. 2d 416 (2nd Cir. 1945).

94. See, for example, *Columbia, Metal Culvert Co., Inc. v. Kaiser Aluminum & Chemical Corp.*, 579 F. 2d 20 (3rd Cir. 1978); *Coleman Motor Co. v. Chrysler Corp.*, 525 F. 2d 1338 (3d Cir. 1975); *Industrial Building Materials, Inc. v. Inter-Chemical Corp.* 437 F. 2d 1336 (19th Cir. 1970).

95. Young, Andrew Thomas and William F. Shughart (2010), "The Consequences of the US DOJ's Antitrust Activities: A Macroeconomic Perspective," *Journal of Public Choice* 142, nos. 3–4, pp. 409–422.

# CHAPTER 14

# Managing Channel Logistics

**LEARNING OBJECTIVES**

**After reading this chapter, you will be able to:**

- Define supply chain management and identify its boundaries.
- Describe the critical elements of efficient consumer response and quick response.
- Relate a brand's characteristics to the need for its supply chain to be market responsive versus physically efficient.
- Explain why channel management is needed to implement the supply chain management paradigm in an organization.
- Describe the linkages between marketing channel strategy and supply chain management.

## IMPACT OF CHANNEL LOGISTICS AND SUPPLY CHAIN MANAGEMENT

**Logistics** refers to processing and tracking factory goods during their warehousing, inventory control, transport, customs documentation, and delivery stages.[1] In the 1980s, new ideas from the consulting industry prompted a shift to a broader concept of **supply chain management (SCM)**, to include any physical input, not just finished goods, and implicate every element of the value-added chain, not just the manufacturer.[2] The premise of SCM is that routes to market (downstream) should coordinate with manufacturing processes (upstream). By looking backward, or upstream, SCM encompasses not only inventories of finished goods but also work in process and raw materials, all the way back to the suppliers of the suppliers of the suppliers. Looking forward, or downstream, SCM encompasses all channel members, down to and including customers of customers. At the extreme, SCM tells the beginning of the value-added chain what to do and when to do it, as a function of what is happening at the very end of the chain. Thus, transactions at a grocery checkout counterinitiate a backward progression of steps to determine what a farmer should plant—as well as what the tractor manufacturer should fabricate to support that farmer.

Although this extensive connectivity may seem extreme, logistics is an integral part of modern supply chain management.[3] As an organizing concept, SCM starts with **customer service**,[4] which demands the cumulative efforts of the entire channel. Customer service cannot be the sole responsibility of any single channel member. Instead, the goal must be to unify product and information flows, up and down the production and distribution chain. Such unification demands three elements: (1) a market orientation, focused on the customer; (2) effective channel management, to enable smooth transfers of products and information; and (3) effective logistics. Furthermore, the SCM paradigm establishes common values, beliefs, and tools to unite the channel members in related tasks. The notion has even grown expansive enough to introduce a new concept, in tune with environment concerns: reverse logistics, as described in Sidebar 14-1.

## Sidebar 14-1

### Reverse logistics

Forward or ordinary logistics refers to the physical distribution of products from the factory to end-users. Reverse logistics turns the process around. A reverse supply chain thus performs activities to retrieve a used product from a final customer and then dispose of or reuse it. Producers build reverse supply chains for various reasons, including as a response to pressures from environmental regulators or customers. But others see these chains as a new profit opportunity. For example, Bosch sells both new and remanufactured models of its hand tools, turning a profit on both lines while avoiding sending its bulky, long-lasting power tools to trash dumps.

Reverse supply chains comprise five key steps, in sequence:

1. Product acquisition. Perhaps the most difficult step, it typically requires cooperation with downstream channel members, such as distributors and retailers.
2. Reverse logistics. Transporting the used merchandise is also difficult, because the items are no longer in factory packaging and can be physically dispersed. Some firms outsource this stage to specialists.
3. Inspection and disposition (testing, sorting, grading). To streamline this slow, labor-intensive step, some firms turn to bar codes and sophisticated tracking. However, they still must make decisions about what to do with each item; decisions early in the process may be the key to performing this step well.
4. Reconditioning components or remanufacturing the item entirely.
5. Selling and distributing recycled components or products. This step demands substantial investments in possibly an entirely new channel to sell in an entirely different market.

When products are remanufactured, they go back to the manufacturer and get upgraded to meet the quality standards applied to new products. Alternatively, they can be used as component sources.

Regardless of the ultimate decision about what to do with the reclaimed products, an interesting question arises: Who should collect used products from the end-users and return them to the manufacturer? In the auto industry, the standard is to use third-party specialists (e.g., dismantling centers), which collect used cars and send them back to manufacturers, to be recycled in whole or in part. Consumer goods manufacturers often rely on their retailers. For example, Kodak collects disposable cameras, paying the retailer a fixed fee and transportation costs to return them. The manufacturers also could do the job themselves. Xerox collects lease-expired copiers itself, Hewlett-Packard collects computers and peripherals, and Canon collects consumer cartridges. All these methods can work, but retailers have some advantages, because of their proximity to customers, and because they can amortize their investments in the forward supply chain by building reverse supply chains.

## Continued

Compared with traditional logistics, reverse logistics are less predictable in terms of both timing and quality levels—which often means soaring costs. To contain them, the channel can build features into the forward supply chain that eventually will facilitate the reverse supply chain. New products can be designed on a platform that assumes inputs from used products, such as Bosch's inclusion of sensors in new tools that signal, when the products are returned, whether each motor is worth saving. These closed loop systems (i.e., forward activities anticipate and interlock with reverse activities) may be the key to making reverse supply chains work. They could also provide a boon to efforts to preserve the Earth's limited resources.[5]

With the expanding application of these concepts, the flow and storage of goods has become more efficient. In the 1960s, U.S. firms spent an estimated 15–30 percent of their sales dollars to pay for product flows; today, that average is around 8 percent.[6] Achieving such performance standards requires coordination, across functional silos within the firm and among the many firms in a value-added chain. Supply chain management in turn demands that every player in a channel send information to trigger behaviors by every other player in the channel. These behaviors include stockpiling and moving inventory of course, but they also refer to marketing. For example, information provided by the warehouse may tell the supplier that it should not offer a promotion this month or that it needs to adjust its price. Data from inventory management systems also might suggest the need to change the assortment to meet the express specifications of important customers.

The notion that logistics influence marketing—a key premise of SCM—actually is revolutionary for many managers. Thus, we continue to find two contrary views. Is SCM a virtuous revolution that will result in both better customer satisfaction and lower costs? Or is it a ludicrous pipe dream, because meeting customers' service output demands can never be less expensive?

Logistics (and the broader SCM concept) constitutes a vast, varied, and complex discipline, often treated as a highly technical field that fits with operations research methods. But this reputation should not deter managers from using their judgment and relying on readily available tools, such as graphs and spreadsheets, to make logistical decisions. Such formal methods are powerful tools for managers, as summarized by a wide range of logistics literature.[7] For this chapter, we focus more on the day-to-day responsibilities of logistics and supply chain managers who seek to make their channels more efficient through efficient customer response and quick response technologies. We also outline their necessary involvement in marketing channels management.

## EFFICIENT CHANNEL LOGISTICS

The roots of SCM, though attributable to consulting insights, are closely linked to applications in the retail industry. In particular, grocers innovated the notion of efficient consumer response (ECR), and fashion retailers introduced quick response (QR) systems. The retailing sector also remains the most common site to find these efficiency-oriented logistics systems.

## Efficient Consumer Response

**Efficient consumer response (ECR)** is a landmark concept for marketing channels, as well as a movement that has wrought radical changes in the U.S. grocery industry, before spreading to other sectors and countries. Yet its success still seems surprising, considering how different it is from the standard operating procedures of most channels.

The origin of ECR was fear. In 1992, the U.S. grocery store industry was feeling greatly threatened by the rapid growth of nongrocery outlets, such as drug stores.[8] These "alternative formats" (i.e., alternative to a supermarket) aggressively added food to their assortments, and consumers were responding positively. Perhaps the greatest threat came from Wal-Mart, which at that time was just beginning its move away from mass merchandising and toward a hypermarket concept (i.e., merchandise and groceries). Thus, in 1992, two grocery trade associations commissioned a study of grocery methods. The report strongly criticized existing grocery channels and proposed a radical, complex series of changes. The change program was named in accordance with its objective: to achieve efficient (as opposed to wasteful) consumer (focused on the end-user) responses (by supplying only that which they desired).

The initial proposal focused on four areas with great potential for improvement:

1. **Continuous replenishment** to end the bullwhip effect. The **bullwhip effect** refers to the systematic distortion of information as it passes through the channel, causing members to overreact to small changes in end-user demand. With a continuous replenishment program (CRP), retailers would gather end-users' purchase data using scanners, and then share that information with all upstream supply chain members. A CRP in turn requires standardized codes and methods, which could be achieved through the implementation of **electronic data interchange** (EDI). An EDI moves information over secure communication circuits, from one company's computers to another's, using a standard format and without human intervention. An EDI system can dispatch purchase orders and initiate payments automatically. But it demands large investments in proprietary systems to standardize the documentation while still protecting data security. Tens of thousands of firms use EDI; subsequently channels are adopting Internet-based alternatives, based on XML programming technology, in the hope that Web platforms will be cheaper, more flexible, but still safe from hackers.[9] The CPR initiative also encourages firms to use allocation rules to prevent "gaming" the system. For example, General Motors allocates low inventory products to dealers on the basis of their sales records.[10]

2. Identifying efficient **pricing and promotions**. The grocery industry has been plagued by poorly calibrated promotions that wreak havoc on pricing and on buyer behavior. At the consumer level, generous promotions (e.g., buy one, get one free) can create demand spikes and degrade brand equity. Insufficiently targeted promotions also encourage price comparisons and brand switching, solely in pursuit of temporary price cuts. At the wholesale level, manufacturer promotions lead to huge demand spikes that push factory production up too high, and

then drop it far too low. The production shifts in turn move inventory too high or too low, risking spoilage or stockouts.

3. Changing **product introduction** practices. Thousands of new product introductions, most of which fail, are endemic to grocery retailing. Instead, ECR would combine market research performed by various channel members to forecast new product success better, whether on a store-by-store basis or for reasonable store groupings (i.e., store clusters).

4. Changing **merchandising** practices. Again, ECR would combine market research—in this case, to find better ways to merchandise brands and categories (e.g., pet food, soups), store by store or cluster by cluster.

Over time, each of these ideas has been developed and expanded, and they continue to emerge. The umbrella term "ECR" now encompasses various means that grocers use to compete against alternative format stores, or that any channel member applies to improve its competitiveness in marketing fast-moving consumer goods (FMCG).

## Barriers to Efficient Consumer Response

The origins of ECR in the grocery industry seem nearly miraculous. When the ECR initiative was first unveiled at a trade conference in 1993, few audience members believed that grocery channels could ever set aside the adversarial relations that had long marked interactions of manufacturers and sellers. In particular, who could have guessed that the cooperation and transparency that ECR demand could be added to conflict-laden channels? Yet the near-legendary example of the arrangement between Wal-Mart and Proctor & Gamble clearly proved these doubters wrong. The irony, of course, is that Wal-Mart's entry into the food business is what drove the grocery industry to devise ECR in the first place.

Even with this successful example though, we recognize that the list of barriers to ECR is formidable.[11] At the physical level, ECR requires agreement about codes and a huge number of EDI choices (or their online equivalents). In general, ECR requires **standardization of methods**. For example, cross-docking minimizes warehousing costs related to packing the assortments of goods for a single store. But this delicate exercise also is difficult to pull off if channel members cannot agree on a massive number of issues—such as location decisions, responsibility for bulk breaking, and the use of coordinated SKUs.

Another intimidating barrier to ECR is the need to **trust other channel members**. Trust and good working relationships underlie information exchange, joint planning, and joint actions, which in turn enable the grocery channel to respond to consumers while cutting waste. Trust, as we discussed in Chapter 12, stems from equity, yet channel members have varying perceptions of what is equitable, which can undermine their coordination.[12] As a fundamental feature, ECR mandates that channel members share risk and information to produce gains for the channel, and then that they share the gains equitably. Opportunism (i.e., reneging on a promise to compensate all players fairly) is fatal to ECR.

Finally, ECR requires considerable changes to the internal operations of all channel members.[13] Jobs are lost and roles are redefined when EDI rationalizes supply chains. People representing many different functions in the organization (e.g., sales, marketing, finance, purchasing, production, shipping, warehousing, accounting) must work together in project teams. And their teamwork becomes a permanent responsibility. Rather than salespeople and purchasing agents, ECR relies on multifunctional teams on the buyer's and seller's sides, each of which needs to have a full understanding of the other's business. These are wrenching changes.

And yet, despite these challenges, ECR continues to thrive. Trade publications contain abundant discussions of ways to create ECR in specific sectors. In many cases, ECR appears almost synonymous with SCM.

## Quick Response Logistics

Rapid response, or **quick response (QR)**, methods represent another approach to efficient supply chain management.[14] They appear similar and are often compared to ECR: Both methods share a fundamental notion of allowing consumers to tell the entire channel what to make, what to ship, and when. They also commonly emphasize interfirm cooperation, data analysis, data transmission, inventory management, and waste reduction.

But in truth, QR and ECR differ notably, starting with their origins. That is, QR began, in the early 1980s, in the fashion industry, where demand is volatile and unpredictable. In contrast, for the FMCG categories sold in grocery stores, consumers know well in advance what they want, as well as what they don't want, and ECR enables them to tell the retailer and its suppliers readily. In fashion, consumers rarely know what they want until the very moment they are ready to buy it. This indecision arises because they do not know what will be fashionable or whether the latest fashions will appeal to them. In fashion retailing, consumers see and try on an item, and *then* form opinions—which they change readily. Benchmarks are difficult to find, in part due to a lack of standardization in the industry. Routinely, retailers introduce a line of clothing and only later measure consumer reactions. If its sizes tend to run bigger or smaller than normal, the retailer has the wrong size assortment. If one fabric, or color, or variation pleases more than another, retailers will find themselves with too much of one item and not enough of another. And fashion is very perishable: Consumers will not wait months to receive a restocked item, and items that sell poorly must be marked down quickly to get rid of them at all.

Historically though, store buyers still tried to forecast fashion demand well in advance and committed to orders, sometimes six seasons before the items would be sold. This is a push system (make to forecast). But consumer fashion tastes have become so difficult to forecast that many fashion retailers have adopted an opposite strategy: Try a small sample of something and see if it works. If it sells, stock more, and quickly. But how? Manufacturers need lead time. By the time a fashion is discovered, it may be too late to order more!

Hence, the impetus for quick response; its original developments are often attributed to Benetton, the Italian fashion retailer. The essence of QR is manufacturing, or more specifically, keeping manufacturing **flexible** with regard to what and how much to make. In contrast, ECR focuses more on exactly how much to make and when to put it into a warehouse. For an FMCG such as toothpaste, there is no need to keep manufacturing flexible, and there is little harm in stockpiling it for a while. The grocery retailer also can influence demand, by offering or restraining promotions, to avoid production surges. But for fashion retailers, flexibility is a critical function, so that they can get more of the latest dress or jacket, in the current season's hot colors and fabrics, and in sizes that have proven popular. Production volume must be scaled up or down dramatically, and set-ups (i.e., changing from manufacturing one item to another) should be quick. Then the items produced have to get out the factory door and to the customer rapidly.

With this focus on flexible manufacturing techniques, QR users care little about pricing and promotion—topics that are critical for ECR users. Instead, a QR system seeks to identify a fashion trend, and then charge end-users to obtain it. Mistakes are necessarily frequent, but they also need to be caught quickly and addressed with modest markdowns, followed by more drastic markdowns if required, to clear the inventory. That is, the QR system tries to minimize the use of drastic markdowns, limiting them to situations in which merchandise remains on shelves well after end-users have realized they do not want it.

Sidebar 14-2 profiles Zara, a leading QR practitioner. A notable aspect of its practices is how well Zara's marketing and channel strategies mesh with its SCM. Zara clothing also is relatively inexpensive; QR does not require premium prices. The real key is to avoid deep discounts on unwanted goods.

## Barriers to Quick Response

Just as with ECR though, QR can create some challenges. Manufacturers' QR actions can backfire and reduce the incentives for downstream channel members to exert efforts to sell that manufacturer's product—knowing that the manufacturer will move quickly to replace the inventory. This lack of incentive can lead to lower sales for the manufacturer.[15] Furthermore, considering the complexity of the production process, QR puts a great strain on the various members of a fashion channel, particularly manufacturers' subcontractors. It is difficult to maintain trusting relationships and open information transmissions across so many players. The uncertain demand environment strains the system, making it hard for any member to issue guarantees.

In response, vertical integration is becoming more common as a route to achieve QR in fashion. This sort of vertical integration is not comprehensive but rather tends to be specific to merchandise design and retailing. The design function is wholly owned, because it provides the crucial inputs for manufacturing. Retailing also is wholly owned, because the manufacturer needs stores to serve as test sites, observatories, and transmitters of fast, thorough information. (Benetton is mostly franchised but also keeps some stores under company ownership.) By owning stores, integrated providers (e.g., The Gap) can also quickly alter prices, raising them to stave off stock-outs on surprisingly popular options (and rushing more into production) or lowering them to sell out before it is obvious to consumers which items are losers. This is quick response indeed.

Just how quick does it need to be? The answer depends on how fashionable the goods are. When demand is less influenced by fashion trends, the supply chain is more conventional. For moderately priced staple clothing (e.g., basic t-shirts), it is neither necessary nor profitable to have a hyperresponsive supply chain. A good regional warehouse system can suffice to fill surprise inventory gaps, and long lead times for production and transportation can reduce costs without notable penalties.[16]

## Sidebar 14-2

### Zara, the quick response master

In the 1960s, Armancio Ortega was a salesperson in a woman's clothing store in rural Spain. His thrifty clients were unwilling to spend on fanciful indulgences. The expensive pink bathrobe in the window of the store created attention and desire but no buyers. So Ortega decided to try a novel strategy: He would copy coveted, fashionable items and sell them at very low prices. He turned his family's living room into a workshop and convinced his brother, sister, and fiancée to make inexpensive copies of fashionable clothes. The strategy worked so well that Ortega founded a manufacturing company in 1963. After 12 years of patient experimentation and system building, he vertically integrated forward into retailing, opening his first retail store in the same town as his original employer. His first choice for a name (Zorba, after the titular character in the film *Zorba the Greek*) was trademarked, so Ortega compromised and named his store Zara.

Today, Ortega is the wealthiest person in Spain. He is the majority owner of Inditex, a large, profitable, vertically integrated clothing retailer that sells under multiple brand names to target multiple segments. Zara is the flagship and accounts for three-quarters of the group's revenue, which it earns with more than 600 stores in nearly 50 countries. The secret of Zara's success is quick response (QR). Rather than being forecast driven, Zara is demand led.

Its much admired, and widely analyzed, supply chain begins in its three design centers—one each for women, men, and children. The centers turn out new products continuously, not just for each fashion season. Whereas competitors generate 2,000–4,000 new garments a year, Zara produces around 11,000 and introduces them as a steady barrage of new styles. The time required to move a design from an image in a designer's sketchbook to a product in stores is a stunningly short 15 days.

In each design center, a large staff of stylists search for design ideas, considering not just what customers are buying today but also what they might want to buy in a fortnight. The ideas can come from anywhere. Teams of trend spotters travel the world, noting what different types of people are wearing and what physical possibilities exist

(e.g., fabrics, cuts, accessories). Stylists integrate this input with information they gather from magazines focused on fashion, celebrities, entertainment, and lifestyle. Ideas to copy might come from a dress worn by the singer and designer Victoria Beckham, featured in a celebrity magazine, or from a particularly fashion-forward pedestrian on a city street. Of course, the designers also obtain information from their stores about what is currently selling.

Stylists working in teams use all this information to create prototypes. Each prototype is reviewed by three additional teams: stylists, salespeople, and fabric purchasers. All three groups must agree before a model can launch, beginning the 15-day countdown to its appearance in stores. The objective is to capture buyers' imagination, just as the expensive pink bathrobe inspired Spanish window shoppers in 1963. But Zara also makes sure its clothes are affordable, to spark impulse purchases.

The secret is its ability to avoid the twin costs of holding inventory and marking down unsold items—dominant, critical costs in fashion industries. Zara is vertically integrated backward into production; it outsources any overflow to manufacturers also located in Europe, where most of its stores appear. This colocation advantage allows Zara to move much faster than many of its competitors, which source products from Asian countries to reduce production costs. Zara thus incurs higher labor expenses, though to control production costs, it exploits the principle of postponement (i.e., converting work-in-process inventory to finished-goods inventory only at the last possible moment). Although Zara orders raw fabric early and holds it (fabric cannot be quickly manufactured), the dyeing and finishing processes occur only close to the time of sale. Its formidable manufacturing centers also sort goods according to their destination.

As the goods are moving by truck to enormous, modern warehouses at the various destinations, store managers consult their personal digital assistants (PDAs) to find photos of the soon-to-arrive new merchandise. Using their knowledge of the preferences of the clientele in their part of the city, they can quickly reject or accept each item. Accepted merchandise gets rushed, by truck or air

## Continued

freight, to the store. The rush at this stage is necessary because Zara stores have minimal storage space, which means they must be supplied just in time. Although this demand is challenging, it also allows Zara to locate its stores in prime, expensive shopping districts—space that is too valuable to use as a warehouse. Furthermore, to reduce costs and ensure it can sell inexpensive clothes out of prestigious addresses, Zara spends little on advertising.

Instead, it relies on word of mouth (WOM), which means it has to ensure customers enjoy every experience they have with the store. Specialized builders design and construct every store, integrating the store manager's reactions to elements of an existing model store. Zara thus adapts locally but still maintains a consistent look. Then, any items that do not sell are swiftly noted, removed, and rushed to another location, where they have a better chance of success. This quickly changing assortment brings browsers back; in Spain, clients visit an average clothing store three or four times a year but Zara 17 times each year. These visits create fresh WOM, which restarts the cycle: new retail sales, feedback to stylists, new prototypes, quick manufacturing with postponed work-in-progress fabric inventory, rushed finished product delivery, selling out or rushing out, and beginning again.

This exemplary QR system is agile—but it is *not* lean. Zara spends more than its competitors on transportation (all that rushing and moving inventory around), even though its production sites are in close proximity to its stores. It also spends more than its competitors on labor (European manufacturing). These costs are more than offset by inventory savings (holding, markdowns) and the ability to support a marketing strategy based on the experience created by each shop's ambiance and prime location, rather than on advertising or promotions.

Zara's success has created a sort of surrounding mythology, in which Zara is a state-of-the-art marvel, bolstered by information technology (IT). Although it certainly is heavily computerized, Zara does not use the very latest IT, and it spends much less than most retailers on IT as a percentage of sales. In particular, Zara does *not* have the following:

- An elaborate customer relationship management system.

- Sophisticated planning or scheduling software to convert demand information into production requirements.
- Logistics software to run its distribution centers.
- Extranets across factories or intranets across stores.
- Enterprise resource process software to define the whole infrastructure.
- A large IT department.
- A formal technology budget.

It doesn't even maintain personal computers in its stores! Dedicated terminals collect basic sales and inventory information, transmitted manually to headquarters daily by the store managers (not an intranet). This is not to imply that Zara shuns IT. It adopted computerization early, at the insistence by Armancio Ortega (who remains heavily involved in Zara's design and has no interest in retirement). The current CEO is a former IT manager, a testament to Zara's comfort with computerization.

But the difference is that Zara adopts IT only when internal managers call for it. For example, it was an early adopter of PDAs to replace faxes; it relies on them heavily, obliging managers to use them to place orders, rather than phoning them in. Yet Zara prefers not to automate its decision making, which remains the responsibility of field personnel, particularly store managers. These managers have much greater roles than they would in competing retailers and considerable latitude in some areas (e.g., ordering merchandise), but zero latitude in other areas (e.g., pricing).

This minimalist approach to IT works in part because the products have few components and do not need to be tracked or maintained after purchase. Zara works because of this as-needed attitude, not in spite of it. Technology aids judgments, rather than making them. Computerization is standardized and focused on areas where managers see a business case for it. Because the technology initiatives come from within Zara, they complement existing processes, rather than usurping them, as often occurs when IT instead is imposed by specialists on reluctant managers.[17]

## SUPPLY CHAIN STRATEGIES

To this point, we have described how the building blocks of SCM can be stacked in different ways to serve different environments. But a broader question might ask which strategy is better, that is, the QR philosophy (keep manufacturing design flexible, don't focus on minimizing transportation costs) or the ECR philosophy (fix design, control costs tightly). Both are pull systems, but they differ in how and where in the channel they react.

### Physical Efficiency Versus Market Responsiveness

A good starting point for this comparison is to consider the **nature of demand** for a brand.[18] A **functional brand** applies to a staple product, which people can buy in many outlets to meet their basic needs. Thus, these brands have stable, predictable demand and long life cycles, but their margins are relatively low, and they confront substantial competition. In contrast, an **innovative brand** designates a product that is both new and different, which enables it to earn higher margins. But the sales cycle of the product and brand is short and unpredictable, largely because they invoke quick imitations, which eliminates their market advantages. Fundamentally, an innovative product faces unpredictable demand that is hard to forecast and lasts for only a short life cycle. Although its margins are higher, so are its markdowns and stockout rates (due to changing tastes and forecast errors). Finally, because these products are so differentiated, they take on many variations. Figure 14-1 summarizes the contrasts between these two end points on the spectrum.

   The key to supplying functional goods therefore is to minimize three types of costs: (1) manufacturing, (2) inventory, and (3) transportation. All these costs relate to handling the good and are readily observable to accountants. Accordingly,

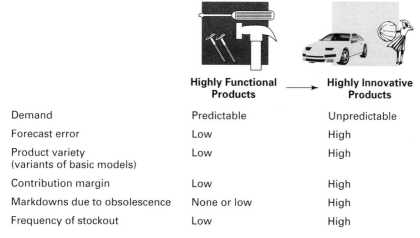

| | Highly Functional Products | Highly Innovative Products |
|---|---|---|
| Demand | Predictable | Unpredictable |
| Forecast error | Low | High |
| Product variety (variants of basic models) | Low | High |
| Contribution margin | Low | High |
| Markdowns due to obsolescence | None or low | High |
| Frequency of stockout | Low | High |

**FIGURE 14-1**  Types of goods subject to supply chain management

*Source:* Adapted from Fisher, Marshall L. (1997), "What is the Right Supply Chain for Your Product?" *Harvard Business Review* 78 (March–April), pp. 105–116.

efficient manufacturing and logistics are crucial, because the low margins available make cost consciousness important, and because predictable demand simplifies decision making. Thus ECR fits, as do other manufacturing methods that prioritize tight planning and resource management. The most important information flow is that within the chain, from retailers to manufacturers and their suppliers. The supply chains for these products must be **physically efficient**. Factories should run at high capacity; warehouses must turn inventory quickly. Product designers seek a single or stable design that does not require many updates, is easy to manufacture, and maximizes their performance. Cost and quality are the criteria used to select suppliers.

Innovative goods have opposite demands. The greatest risk is **missing the market**, by having the wrong item available at the wrong time at the wrong price. The key to their success is speed, because demand cannot be reliably estimated but instead must be addressed once it begins to surge. The point of sale represents the most critical information node. Furthermore, for innovative goods, the opportunity cost of a stockout is very high, considering their high margins. By the time the stockout is rectified, the item may have lost appeal, leaving the supplier with drastically devalued stocks. Therefore, the supply chains for innovative products need to be **market responsive**. The modular product design process should postpone final assembly as long as possible. Performance and cost can be sacrificed somewhat to achieve such modularity. Suppliers need to offer quality and flexibility, not necessarily the lowest cost, and the manufacturing system maintains a buffer stock of supplies, just in case. The obsession with reducing lead times needed to fill an order remains, even if it raises transportation and fulfillment costs.

We summarize these differences in Figure 14-2. Market responsiveness and physical efficiency represent two end points on a continuum, in which each channel can fit its own ideal supply chain philosophy.

The location of the brand on the spectrum from highly functional to highly responsive depends on its marketing strategy. The same product category can feature more innovative and more functional brands, which require different supply chains. For example, some automotive brands are very conservative and stable, appealing to buyers who resist change. Others rely on their ephemeral, faddish appeal. The more functional brands require a physically efficient supply chain and worry little about being quite so market responsive. The more innovative brands pay far more attention to the market but can afford a little less physical efficiency in their supply chains.

## Effective Supply Chain Management

On paper, supply chain management is eminently sensible. Yet for many companies, SCM is more a slogan than a reality, because the methods needed to implement pull systems are so challenging. Pull systems in channels are so different from push systems that some firms never quite make the change, hindered by ubiquitous barriers to implementation, both internal and external. To build an SCM mentality into marketing channels, prior research and real-world experience suggest two elements are critical:

| | **Physically Efficient Supply Chain (Functional Goods)** ⟶ | **Market-Responsive Supply Chain (Innovative Goods)** |
|---|---|---|
| Objective | Cut costs of manufacturing, holding inventory, transportation | Respond quickly as demand materializes. |
| Consequences of failure | Low prices and higher costs create margin squeeze | Stockouts of high-margin goods Heavy markdowns of unwanted goods |
| Manufacturing goods | Run at high capacity utilization rate | Be ready to alter production (quantity and type) swiftly Keep excess production capacity |
| Inventory | Minimize everywhere | Keep buffer stocks of parts and finished goods |
| Lead times | Can be long, as demand is predictable | Must be short |
| Supplies should be | Low cost Adequate quality | Fast, flexible Adequate quality |
| Product design | Design for ease of manufacture and to meet performance standards | Design in modules to delay final production |

**FIGURE 14-2   Two kinds of supply chains**
*Source:* Adapted from Fisher, Marshall L. (1997), "What is the Right Supply Chain for Your Product?" *Harvard Business Review* 78 (March–April), pp. 105–116.

1. An internal culture of cross-functional integration (cf. functional silos).
2. Effective channel management, to ensure trust, good working relations, good design, and the judicious exercise of power.[19] In short, the implementation of the principles described throughout this book.

The very best supply chains are "triple A" systems: agile, adaptable, and aligned.[20] **Agile** systems respond quickly to changes in volume, variety, or specifications. They can cope especially well with emergencies, such as fires or natural disasters. **Adaptable** systems change to follow major shifts in the environment, such as altered customer expectations or newly available technologies. **Aligned** systems give all parties compatible incentives, so that employees within divisions and companies across supply chains all have reasons to coordinate. Sidebar 14-3 suggests some methods to achieve these three vital properties; many of these suggestions are simply matters of good channel management.

## Sidebar 14-3

### How to build triple-A supply chains

What is the objective of a supply chain? Hau L. Lee, a prominent SCM researcher, argues that focusing on a single objective (e.g., efficiency, cost cutting, speed) is dangerous, because then people sacrifice higher objectives (product quality) to achieve these lower-level goals. Thus, a great supply chain can become an expensive, unprofitable project, unless it pursues the triple-A properties.[21]

### Agility

To ensure a quick response to any change in volume, variety, specification, or situation, Lee recommends the following:

- Forging collaborative relationships with suppliers.
- Designing for postponement, by pushing back the time at which the product must be finalized.
- Keeping buffer inventories of items that are not difficult to stock (and, more generally, keeping some slack resources in the system to respond to emergencies, such as natural disasters).
- Investing in dependable logistics systems.
- Ensuring that substantial information flows up and down the supply chain.

- Developing a fallback plan and a crisis management team to respond to emergencies.

### Adaptability

The ability to change to meet large and permanent shifts in the environment can be developed through the following methods:

- Continuously adding new suppliers and using intermediaries (e.g., consultants, trade associations) to find them.
- Evaluating the needs of ultimate customers, not just immediate consumers.
- Insisting on flexible product designs.
- Monitoring world economies to notice trends.
- Monitoring technical and product life cycles to notice changes.

### Alignment

Finally, Lee suggests that individuals and organizations have compatible incentives when they

- Exchange information freely within and across organizations.
- Give suppliers and customers clear roles, tasks, and responsibilities.
- Practice the equity principle.

## SUMMARY: MANAGING CHANNEL LOGISTICS

Logistics entails processing and tracking factory goods across the various production stages: warehousing, inventory control, transport, customs documentation, delivery to customers, and so forth. Changes in logistics can create astonishing increases in effectiveness and efficiency—if implemented appropriately. Many companies that dramatically altered their manufacturing processes reaped great rewards from so doing. Now they are turning to their marketing channels and applying similar principles (pull systems, electronic information sharing) to achieve another wave of gains. Thus, stellar examples of effective logistics are becoming more abundant, and changes in logistics are becoming more feasible.

The changes prompt notions of supply chain management, a paradigm that addresses customer service as a result of the cumulative efforts of the entire channel. That is, the channel needs to adopt a market orientation, effective management, and effective logistics practices so that all its members can unify their product and information flows up and down the production and distribution chain.

These principles appear epitomized in efficient consumer response (ECR), a philosophy that attempts to exploit the potential for improvements in continuous replenishment, pricing and promotions, product introductions, and merchandising. These improvements require channels that share information and work together to cut needless variety, redirect promotions to build brand equity, balance stocks, and eliminate bullwhip effects.

The central goals of SCM also can be achieved through a quick response (QR) system. In this case, to manage the supply chain for products whose demand is difficult to predict, QR emphasizes flexible manufacturing that can react to trends detected in point-of-sale data. To enhance information and flexibility, manufacturers in these channels often prefer to own some stores (to gain demand information) and employ designers (to reset production processes more quickly).

A spectrum, anchored by functional versus innovative products, can help channel managers determine which supply chain philosophy is most appropriate for their brand. Innovative brands (whose demand is fundamentally volatile) need supply chains that respond quickly to market signals. Functional products (whose demand is stable) need supply chains that reduce physical costs. Both types are feasible, especially as new technologies and changes in management practice facilitate their implementation. Thus we come full circle, to find that a fundamental cornerstone of good supply chain management is effective marketing channel management.

## TAKE-AWAYS

- Logistics refers to the processing and tracking of factory goods during warehousing, inventory control, transport, customs documentation, and delivery to customers.
- Marketing channels have adopted supply chain management (SCM) strategies in an attempt to unify product and information flows throughout the production and distribution chain and thus increase efficiency.
- To achieve efficient consumer response (ECR), managers focus on four areas:
  - Continuous replenishment programs (CRP) that reduce bullwhip effects.
  - Efficient pricing and promotions.
  - Changes in product introductions.
  - Changes in merchandising.
- Quick response (QR), another pull-based approach to SCM, allows consumers to tell the entire channel what to make and what to ship, then does it quickly.
- Physical efficiency and marketing responsiveness may appear to represent a trade-off between ECR and QR, but they really constitute a continuum.
- Two elements are critical to any effective supply chain system:
  - Internal culture of cross-functional integration.
  - Effective channel management, including trust, good working relations, good design, and the judicious exercise of power.

## Endnotes

1. The authors are grateful to Frédéric Dalsace, Enver Yücesan, and the late Xavier de Groote, who have been sources of instruction, guidance, and inspiration in the domain of logistics and supply chain management over the years.

2. Lambert, Douglas M. and Martha C. Cooper (2000), "Issues in Supply Chain Management," *Industrial Marketing Management* 29, no. 3, pp. 65–83.

3. Lancioni, Richard A. (2000), "New Developments in Supply Chain Management for the Millennium," *Industrial Marketing Management* 29, no. 3, pp. 1–6.

4. Sautter, Elise Truly, Arnold Maltz, and Kevin Boberg (1999), "A Customer Service Course: Bringing Marketing and Logistics Together," *Journal of Marketing Education* 21 (August), pp. 138–145.

5. Guide, Daniel R. and Luk N. Van Wassenhove (2002), "The Reverse Supply Chain," *Harvard Business Review* 80, no. 2, pp. 25–26; Savaskan, R. Canan, Shantanu Bhattacharya, and Luk N. Van Wassenhove (2004), "Closed-Loop Supply Chain Models with Product Remanufacturing," *Management Science* 50, no. 2, pp. 239–252.

6. Ballou, Ronald H., Stephen M. Gilbert, and Ashok Mukherjee (2000), "New Managerial Challenges from Supply Chain Opportunities," *Industrial Marketing Management* 29, no. 3, pp. 7–18.

7. Shankar Ganesan, Morris George, Sandy Jap, Robert W. Palmatier, and Bart Weitz (2009), "Supply Chain Management and Retailer Performance: Emerging Trends, Issues, and Implications for Research and Practice," *Journal of Retailing* 85 (March), pp. 84–94.

8. Triplett, Tim (1994), "More U.S. Grocers Turning to ECR to Cut Waste," *Marketing News* 12 (September), pp. 12–13; Anonymous (1998), "Lessons Learned from the Grocery Industry," *Oil and Gas Investor* (Second Quarter), p. 23.

9. Cooke, James (2002), "EDI: What Lies Ahead," *Modern Materials Handling* 10, no. 3, pp. 1–3.

10. Lee, Hau L., V. Padmanabhan, and Seungjin Whang (2004), "Information Distortion in a Supply Chain: The Bullwhip Effect," *Management Science* 50 (December), pp. 1875–1886.

11. O'Sullivan, Denis (1997), "ECR: Will It End In Tears?" *Logistics Focus* 5 (September), pp. 2–5; Puget, Yves (1999), "Les Quatre Niveaux de la 'Supply Chain'," *LSA* (October), p. 71.

12. Palmatier, Robert W., Mark B. Houston, Rajiv P. Dant, and Dhruv Grewal (2013), "Relationship Velocity: Toward a Theory of Relationship Dynamics," *Journal of Marketing* 77 (January), pp. 13–30.

13. Ellinger, Alexander E. (2000), "Improving Marketing/Logistics Cross-Functional Collaboration in the Supply Chain," *Industrial Marketing Management* 29, no. 3, pp. 85–96.

14. Richardson, James (1996), "Vertical Integration and Rapid Response in Fashion Apparel," *Organization Science* 7 (July–August), pp. 400–412.

15. Krishnan, Harish, Roman Kapuscinski, and David A. Butz (2010), "Quick Response and Retailer Effort," *Management Science* 56 (June), pp. 962–977.

16. van Ryzin, Garrett and Siddarth Mahajan (1999), "On the Relationship Between Inventory Costs and Variety Benefits in Retail Assortments," *Management Science* 45 (November), pp. 1496–1509; Dvorak, Robert E. and Frits van Paasschen (1996), "Retail Logistics: One Size Doesn't Fit All," *McKinsey Quarterly* 2, no. 2, pp. 120–129.

17. This Sidenote is based on a variety of sources: Bialobos, Chantal (2003), "Zara, le Marchand de Fringues le Plus Rapide de l'Europe," *Capital* 12 (December), pp. 38–42; McAfee, Andrew (2004), "Do You Have Too Much IT?" *Sloan Business Review* 46, no. 1, pp. 19–22; Anonymous (2000), "Zara

Has a Made-to-Order Plan for Success," *Fortune* (September), p. 18; Christopher, Martin (2000), "The Agile Supply Chain," *Industrial Marketing Management* 29, no. 3, pp. 37–44.

18. This section is based on Fisher, Marshall L. (1997), "What is the Right Supply Chain for Your Product?" *Harvard Business Review* 78 (March–April), pp. 105–116.

19. Palmatier, Robert W., Rajiv P. Dant, Dhruv Grewal, and Kenneth R. Evans (2006), "Factors Influencing the Effectiveness of Relationship Marketing: A Meta-Analysis," *Journal of Marketing* 70 (October), pp. 136–153.

20. Lee, Hau L. (2004), "The Triple-A Supply Chain," *Harvard Business Review* 82, no. 10, pp. 102–112.

21. Ibid.

# NAME INDEX

Note: Locators in italics indicate additional display material; "n" indicates note.

## A

Achrol, Ravi S., 118n9, 118n10
Agins, Teri, 191n17
Agrawal, Deepak, 292n21
Ahlstrom, P., 318n17, 410n38
Alfalahi, Kasim, *332, 333*
Allawadi, Kusum L., 229n31
Andel, Tom, 117n2
Anderson, Erin, 153n2, 154n16, 154n18, 154n22, 190n9, 261n7, 348n18, 348n23, 348n24, 349n41, 378n23, 379n33, 379n38, 380n50, 382, 409n13, 409nn17–18, 347n20
Anderson, James C., 261n16, 347n7, 377n7, 409n11, 410n45
Anderson, Philip, 261n7, 348n18
Ann Welsh, M., 118n9
Antia, Kersi D., 281, 348n26
Aoulou, Yves, 192n54, 292n14
Aravindakshan, Ashwin, 293n44
Areeda, Phillip, 444n8, 444n13, 445n55, 446n62
Argote, Linda, 293n50
Ariely, Dan, 191n35
Arndt, Michael, 444n18
Arnold, Todd J., 153n4, 409n14, 411n53, 462n4
Arnould, Eric J., 261n12
Assmus, Gert, 379n30
Attwood, Ed, 319n34
Aufreiter, Nora, 229n22
Aydinlik, Arzu U., 379n41
Aziz, Amal Abel, *252*

## B

Baker, Thomas L., 409n11
Balasubramanian, Sridhar, 319n20
Ball, Deborah, 191n17
Ballou, Ronald H., 462n6
Balto, David, 445n43, 446n61
Barbaro, M., 319n29
Bardy, Roland, 261n14
BarNir, Anat, 292n9
Barrett, Paul M., 470n17, 472nn71–72
Bassi, Olivia, 292n14
Bayus, Barry L., 191n30
Bechkoff, Jennifer, 153n12
Beck, Ernest, 229n33
Beckham, Victoria, 455

Bergen, Dutta, 154n30
Bergen, Mark, 153n8, 192n42, 192n53, 378n12, 378n25, 379n32, 444n3
Berner, Robert, 228n8, 228n11
Bharadwaj, Sundar G., 153n7
Bhattacharya, Shantanu, 462n5
Bialobos, Chantal, 190n3, 191n33, 462n17
Bickart, Barbara A., 191n29
Birkeland, Peter M., 292n12, 293n41
Bitner, Mary Jo., 318n12
Blair, Roger D., 444n19, 444n23
Blattberg, Robert C., 222
Bloom, Paul N., 347n9, 445n38, 445n44
Boberg, Kevin, 462n4
Boddy, D., 318n17
Bohbot, Michele, 95
Bolton, Jamie M., 153n14
Bolton, Ruth N., 318n8
Boryana, Dimitrova, 77n1
Bouillin, Arnaud, 293n36, 348n29
Bounds, Wendy, 446n75
Bouyssou, Julien, 192n55
Bowman, Douglas, 191n39
Boyle, Brett, 349n53
Bradach, Jeffrey L., 293n33
Bradford, Kevin, 153n1
Breit, William, 190n8
Brickley, James A., 292n30
Brinkley, Joel, 446n80
Broder, John M., 446n80
Brooks, Rick, 192n46
Brown, James R., 347n5, 349n36, 377n5, 378n16
Brown, Steven, 153n1
Buchanan, Lauranne, 191n25, 191n29
Bucklin, Christine B., 378n24
Bucklin, Louis P., 55n9, 78n3, 111, 118n12
Bulkeley, William M., 446n80
Burton, Thomas M., 447n85
Butaney, Gul, 191n37
Butz David, A., 462n15
Buzzell, Robert D., 379n43

## C

Cahill, Joseph B., 228n13
Cahyadi, Gundy, 318n5
Campbell, Scott, 77n2, 117n1

Cannon, Joseph P., 347n9, 411n51
Caravella, Mary, 261n23
Carmen, James M., 293n45
Carney, Mick, 292n29
Carr, Tricia, 308n27
Celly, Kirti Sawhney, 191n21
Cespedes, Frank V., 378n22, 379n32
Chabert, Patrick, 191n32
Champion, David, 378n29
Chandler, Susan, 229n19
Chang, Yu-Sang, 318n15
Chapdelaine, Sophie, 190n6
Chen, Xiao-Ping, 377n4
Chireka, Spiwe, *384*
Chon, Gina, 446n80
Chopra, Sunil, 117n4
Christopher, Martin, 463n17
Chu, Gary, *142*
Chu, Woosik, 190n2, 348n28
Chu, Wujin, 190n2, 347n9, 348n28, 445n41
Ciao, Fred C., 19, 154n16, 260n3
Coia, Anthony, 117n2
Combs, James G., 292n7
Conlon, Donald E., 379n44
Conlon, Edward, 55n2
Cooke, James, 462n9
Cooper, Martha C., 462n2
Cooper, Robin, 117n5
Copeland, Mervin, 216n12
Corey, E. Raymond, 378n22, 379n32
Cote, Joseph A., 349n54
Cottrill, Ken, 117n2
Coughlan, Anne T., 117n3, 154n26, 228n6, 229n17, 229n20, 378n29

Dahlstrom, Robert, 410n38
Dai, Yue, 347n4
Dalsace, Frédéric, 462n1
Daniels, Cora, 78n8, 190n11
Dant, Rajiv P., 55n12, 55n13, 154n21, 190n4, 191n27, 292n11, 293n35, 293n42, 293n43, 293n49, 349n39, 378n17, 379n42, 405, 408n8, 409n10, 409n24, 410n39, 410n47, 462n12, 463n19
Dark, Frederick H., 292n30
Darr, Eric D., 293n50
Day, George S., 261n24
Day, Ralph L., 377n5
de Groote, Xavier, 462n1
Deighton, John, 261n23
Dekimpe, Marnik G., 347n2

Deleersnyder, Barbara, 347n1
Desiraju, Ramarao, 229n25
Devaraj, Sarv, 55n2
Dnes, Antony W., 292n19
Donath, Bob, 348n32
Draganska, Michaela, 377n10
Drew, Stephen, 261n14
Duane Ireland, R., 319n20
Dukes, Anthony J., 190n10, 261n30, 349n45
Dunnette, M. D., 373
Dutta, Shantanu, 153n8, 191n28, 192n42, 192n53, 378n12, 378n25, 379n32, 444n3
Dvorak, Robert E., 462n16
Dwyer, F. Robert, 118n9, 153n5, 349n53, 377n6, 410n40
Dyer, Jeffery H., 410n36

**E**

El-Ansary, Adel I., 55n10
Ellinger, Alexander E., 462n13
Emerson, Richard M., 348n31
Enright, Tony, 117n2
Epple, Dennis, 293n50
Etgar, Michael, 55n11, 118n9
Evans, Kenneth R., 55n13, 191n18, 293n42, 409n14, 409n24, 411n53, 463n19

**F**

Fabricant, Ross A., 190n8
Fang, Eric, 55n6, 153n9, 154n17, 191n18, 260n3, 296, 318n7
Fang, Palmatier, 318n11, 318n13
Farris, Paul W., 166, 190n13
Fein, Adam J., 190n9, 260n1, 260n6, 261n17, 261n24, 349n47, 408n5
Felsenthal, Edward, 444n22
Ferraro, Rosellina, 192n45
Fisher, Marshall L., 457, 459, 453n18
Flint, Daniel J., 347n8
Foo, Maw-Der, 293n39
Foo, Maw-Der, 293n39
Forsyth, Donelson R., 117n6
France, Mike, 444n23
Franses, Philip Hans, 192n61, 411n52
Frazier, Gary L., 190n1, 190n9, 191n21, 281, 348n26, 348n34, 348n35, 349n50, 378n21, 379n39, 408n1
French, John R., 347n6
Fuhrman, Elizabeth, 55n3

**G**

Gallagher, Kathleen, 77n2
Galunic, Charles D., 410n28

Ganesan, Shankar, 153n1, 154n29, 192n44, 228n14, 319n40, 379n36, 380n48, 409n26, 410n42, 462n7
Garland, Susan B., 444n23
Gaski, John F., 347n12, 349n49
Gava, Marie-Jose, 192n55
Gedajlovic, Eric, 292n29
George, Morris, 154n29, 192n44, 228n14, 319n40
Getz, Gary A., 192n62
Geylani, Tansev, 190n10, 349n45
Geyskens, Inge, 347n2, 348n14, 377n9, 409n25, 410n30
Geyskens, Steenkamp, 349n51, 379n34
Gielens, Katrijn, 347n2
Gilbert, Stephen M., 462n6
Gill, James D., 348n35
Godes, David B., 229n20
Goldfein, Shepard, 445n37
Gonzalez, Victor, 327
Gooley, Toby B., 117n2
Gould, Eric D., 228n7
Goyder, D.G., 445n56
Granot, Daniel, 261n18
Grayson, Kent, 229n17
Gremler, Dwayne D., 318n12
Grewal, Dhruv, 55n13, 191n27, 293n42, 318n8, 349n39, 378n17, 408n8, 409n24, 410n47, 462n12, 463n19
Griffith, David A., 379n32
Griffiths, John, 444n5
Gruley, Bryan, 446n80
Grundahl, Marie-Pierre, 191n31
Guarino, Dave, 318n2
Guide, Daniel R., 462n5
Gulati, Ranjay, 410n32
Gundlach, Gregory T., 293n43, 347n9, 445n38
Gupta, Mahendra, 261n27
Gupta, Sudheer, 447n91

**H**

Hacker, David, 69
Hallén, Lars, 349n37
Hammond, Allen, 261n11, 348n19
Hans Franses, Philip, 192n61, 411n52
Harari, Oren, 318n19
Hardy, Kenneth G., 191n24, 358, 378n13
Harich, Katrin R., 378n19
Harlam, Bari A., 229n31
Harps, Leslie Hansen, 445n44
Hart, Paul, 348n17
He, Chuan, 153n6

Heide, Jan B., 153n13, 191n26, 191n28, 192n53, 348n27, 349n38, 349n43, 378n25, 379n32, 379nn46–47, 380n49, 409n16, 409n23, 410n34, 444n3
Heinecke, William, 272
Helliker, Kevin, 78n11
Hennart, Jean-Francois, 153n3
Henricks, Mark, 379n31
Heskett, James L., 54n11, 377n2
Hibbard, Jonathan D., 379n40, 409n12
Highlett, Mike, 117n1
Hitt, Michael A., 319n20
Holden, Reed K., 445n26
Holgate, Carolyn, *384*
Horngren, Charles T., 117n5
Hotopf, Max, 347n1, 408nn2–3, 410n29
Houston, Mark B., 375, 410n47, 462n12
Hovenkamp, Herbert, 445n58, 447n82
Hsieh, Tony, 319n35
Hughes, David, 117n2
Hult, G. Tomas M., 347n8
Hunter, Gary, 153n1
Hyde, Edwin, 433

**I**

Iacobucci, Dawn, 377n1, 409n12
Inman, J. Jeffrey, 192n45

**J**

Jackson, Barbara Bund, 409n15, 411n54
Jain, Sanjay, 78n5
James, F., 229n22
Jan-Benedict, E.M., 55n4, 153n9, 154n20, 296, 318n7, 348nn14–15, 349n42, 349n48, 377n9, 379n35, 409n25, 410nn30–31
Jap, Sandy D., 261n26, 349n47, 408n5, 409n22, 410n33, 410n49
Jarvis, Cheryl, 153n12
Jersild, Sarah, 192n60
Jeuland, Abel P., 347n3
Jindal, Rupinder, 291n1
Johanson, Jan, 349n37
Johansson, Johnny K., 378n18
John, George, 191n26, 192n53, 348n27, 349n43, 378n15, 379n46
Johnson, Jean L., 349n54
Jones, Sandra, 77n2, 78n6, 117n1
Jonquieres, Guy de, 444n5
Jordan, Miriam, 293n46

**K**

Kai, Gangshu, 347n4
Kaiser, Rob, 77n2, 117n1

Kaiser, Stefen, 118n8
Kale, Sudhir H., 374n33
Kalnins, Artur, 293n47, 293n51, 293n52
Kalra, Ajay, 191n16
Kalyanaram, G., 410n27
Kaplan, Robert S., 117n5
Kaplow, Louis, 444n8, 444n13, 445n55, 446n62
Kapuscinski, Roman, 462n15
Karabus, Antony, 319n37
Kardes, Frank R., 153n12
Karoll, Albert, 72, 75
Kasturi Rangan, V., 78n13
Kaufmann, Patrick J., 291n5, 292n25, 293n48, 348n25, 444n16
Kearney, A. T., 306, 311, 312, 319n24, 319n36
Kennedy, Tumenta F., 261n14
Ketchen, David J., 292n7
Kim, Keysuk, 408n7
Kim, Namwoon, 191n30
Klapper, Daniel, 191n34, 377n10
Klein, Benjamin, 154n24, 292n20, 292n26
Klein, Thomas A., 293n45
Kleindorfer, Paul R., 261n25
Knott-Craig, Alan, *385*
Koenig, Harold F., 347n5
Koo, Hui-Wen, 55n7, 261n15
Kramer, Roderick M., 409n9
Krauss, Clifford, 229n34
Krishnan, Harish, 462n15
Krishnan, Vish V., 319n20
Kroc, Ray, 265
Kruglanski, Arie W., 348n22
Kumar, Kavita, 154n31
Kumar, Nirmalya, 55n4, 191n20, 348n14, 348n15, 349n42, 349n48, 377n9, 379n35, 379n40, 408n6, 409n25, 410nn30–31
Kumar, V., 292n6
Kursten, Barbara, 318n5

**L**

LaBahn, Douglas W., 378n19
Lafontaine, Francine, 291n5, 292nn24–25, 292n27, 292n31, 293n52, 444n19, 444n23
Lal, Rajiv, 292n21, 292n22
Lambert, Douglas M., 462n2
Lancioni, Richard A., 462n3
Landler, M., 319n29
Lariviere, Martin A., 445n41
Larson, Andrea, 410n41, 410n43, 410n44
Lassar, Walfried M., 190n9, 191n36, 192n41
Lee, Hau L., 118n7, 460, 462n10, 463n20
Lee, Myung-Soo, 192n47

Leung, Shirley, 293n46
Levy, Michael, 228n1, 318n8
Li, Ning, 55n6
Li, Shibo, 191n16
Li, Zhan G., 409n10
Lippman, Steven, 348n30
Liu, Yunchuan, 261n30
Lo, Pei-yu, 55n7, 261n15
Lodish, Leonard M., 380n50
Love, John F., 291n5
Luhnow, David, 348n20
Lundgren, Henriette, 260n4
Lusch, Robert F., 261n29, 318n6, 318n8, 349n36, 378n16
Lusch, Robert L., 260n2
Lynch, John G., 191n35

**M**

Macbeth, D., 318n17
MacInnis, Deborah J., 409n17
Macneil, Ian R., 348n25
Maddocks, Tom, 447n89
Madhok, Anoop, 154n25
Magrath, Allan J., 191n24, 358, 378n13
Mahajan, Siddarth, 462n16
Mahi, Humaira, 347n10
Maidment, Neil, 319n25
Maier, E. P., 78n13, 190n14, 191n22
Maltz, Arnold, 462n4
Mariam Zahedi, Fatemeh, 345n38
Marklund, Johan, 153n6
Martin, Christopher, 463n17
Matta, Khalil F., 55n2
Matthew B., 379n32
Mattson-Teig, Beth, 319n30
Mayer, Kyle J., 293n51
McAfee, Andrew, 462n17
McAfee, R. Preston, 191n38
McCafferty, Dennis, 77n2, 117n1
McEvily, Bill, 409n21
McGuire, Tim, 229n22
McGuire, Timothy W., 154n19
McLaughlin, Kevin, 318n18
Menezes, Melvyn A. J., 78n13, 190n14
Mentzer, John T., 347n8
Michel, Caroline, 153n11, 292n17
Miner, Anne S., 409n16
Minkler, Alanson P., 292n13
Mohr, Jakki, 379n45, 380n51, 409n19
Moltzen, Edward, 77n2, 117n1
Moran, Francis, 78n10
Moran, Ursula, 192n52, 378n22

Moriarty, Rowland T., 192n52, 378n22
Morse, Dan, 228n10
Morton, Fiona Scott, 192n48
Moulton, Susan L., 282
Mukherjee, Ashok, 462n6
Mukherji, Biman, 319n26
Munson, Charles L., 348n13
Munson, Rosenblatt, 348n16
Murray, John P., Jr, 380n49
Murrells, Steve, *251*
Myers, Matthew B., 379n32

**N**

Naciri, Mohammad, *253*
Nagle, Thomas T., 445n26
Narasimhan, Chakravarthi, 261n27
Narayandas, Das, 191n39, 192n40, 239, 410n46
Narus, James A., 261n16, 347n7, 377n7, 409n11
Nasirwarraich, Ahmed, 261n20
Nasr, Nada I., 293n49
Neale, A. D., 445n56
Neel, Dan, 192n51
Neslin, Scott A., 222
Nevin, John R., 347n12, 349n49, 380n51, 409n19, 445n54
Niraj, Rakesh, 261n27
Nonaka, Ikujiro, 378n18
Nordin, F., 318n17
Norton, Seth W., 292n8
Novak, Viveca, 447n86, 447n88
Nygaard, Arne, 410n38

**O**

O'Brian, Bridget, 445n31
O'Brien, Matthew, 318n8
O'Brien, Timothy L., 192n43, 318n8
O'Heir, Jeff, 77n2, 117n1
O'Sullivan, Denis, 462n11
Oh, Sejo, 118n9, 153n5, 377n6
Oliver, Richard L., 154n16
Olivier, Furrer, 379n41
Onyemah, Vincent, 153n1
Onzo, Naoto, 349n54
Ornstein, Stanley I., 444n12
Ortega, Armancio, 455, 456
Osegowitsch, Thomas, 154n25

aasschen, Frits van, 462n16
dmanabhan, V., 118n7, 445n41, 462n10
almatier, Robert W., 55n6, 55nn12–13, 153n1, 153n4, 153n9, 153n12, 154n17,

154nn20–21, 154n29, 190n4, 191n18, 191n27, 192n44, 228n14, 260n2, 261n13, 293n42, 296, 318n7, 318n14, 319n40, 349n39, 378n17, 379n42, 375, 408n8, 409n14, 409n24, 410n39, 410n47, 411n53, 462n7, 462n12, 463n19
Parmar, Neil, 319n35
Parr, Ben, 319n35
Pashigian, B. Peter, 228n7
Paswan, Audehesh K., 293n35
Pauwels, Koen, 192n61
Peng, Mike W., 261n9
Pennycook, Richard, *250*
Pereira, Joseph, 446n80
Perkowski, Jack, 319n31
Perreault, William D., 411n51
Perrigot, Rozenn, 291n1
Perrone, Vincenzo, 409n21
Peterson, Robert A., 378n21
Piétralunga, Cédric, 292n5
Pirrong, Stephen Craig, 154n28
Polles, Jeanne, 396
Pondy, Louis R., 377
Posner, Richard A., 444n9
Prahalad, C. K., 261n11, 348n19
Provan, Keith G., 349n40
Puget, Yves, 462n11
Purohit, Devavrat, 378n28

**Q**

Qinghou, Zong, *142*
Quin, Stuart, 261n20

**R**

Rangan, Menezes, 191n22
Rangan, V. Kasturi, 190n14
Rao, Akshay R., 347n10
Ratchford, Brian T., 192n47
Raven, Bertram, 347n5, 348n22
Rawstorne, Philip, 447n89, 447n90
Raymond Corey, E., 378n22, 379n32
Reibstein, David J., 166, 190n13
Reinartz, Werner J., 292n6
Reisinger, Don, 319n33
Reve, Torger, 118n9, 378n15
Rezaee, Zabihollah, 261n10
Rice, Robert, 444n5
Richardson, James, 462n14
Rindfleisch, Aric, 153n13
Robertson, Diana C., 378n14
Robicheaux, Robert A., 349n53
Rody, Raymond C., 379n39

Rogers, Dale S., 117n2
Rose, Barbara, 117n1
Rosenberg, Larry J., 55n11
Rosenblatt, Meir J., 348n13
Rosenblatt, Zehava, 348n13
Rosenbloo, Bert, 77n1
Rosencher, Anne, 154n23
Ross, William H., 379n44
Ross, William T., 349n41, 378n14
Rouzies, Dominique, 153n1
Rubin, Paul H., 444n13
Rumelt, Richard R., 348n30
Ruppersberger, Gregg, 261n24

S

Sa Vinhas, Alberto, 378n23
Sailor, Matt, 78n4
Sakano, Tomoaki, 349n54
Sallis, James, 411n50
Samaha, Stephen A., 410n39
Saranow, Jennifer, 78n12
Satariano, Adam, 319n28
Saunders, Carol, 348n17
Sautter, Elise Truly, 462n4
Savaskan, R. Canan, 462n5
Sawhney, Kirti, 190n1, 191n21
Sawhney, Mohanbir, 318n8
Scammon, Debra L., 444n20, 447n83
Scheer, Lisa K., 154n20, 349n42, 349n48, 349n55,
    379n35, 400n14, 410n31, 411n53
Scherer, F. M., 445n32, 445n57, 446n70
Scherrer, Matthieu, 191n19
Schmeltzer, John, 78n2, 117n1
Schultz, Howard, 274
Schurr, Paul H., 377n6, 410n40
Schwartz, Marius, 191n38
Scott, Colin, 260n4
Segal, David, 446n80
Selnes, Fred, 411n50
Sethuraman, Rajagopalan, 409n11
Seyed-Mohamed, Nazeem, 349n37
Shane, Scott A., 292n10, 293n32, 293n39, 293n44
Shankar, Venkatesh, 192n45, 293n44
Sharma, Amol, 319n26
Shaw, Kathryn L., 292n27
Sheffet, Mary Jane, 444n20, 447n83
Shervani, Tasadduq, 190n1, 378n21
Shin, Jiwoong, 118n11
Shocker, Allan D., 191n30
Shugan, Steven M., 192n42, 347n3
Shughart, William F., 447n95

Shulman, Jeffrey, 117n3
Siguaw, Judy A., 409n11
Silva-Risso, Jorge, 192n48
Silverblatt, Howard, 318n2
Simmons, Carolyn J., 191n29
Simonian, Haig, 444n5
Simonin, Bernard L., 192n57
Simpson, James T., 349n53
Simpson, Penny M., 409n11
Singh, Harbir, 410n36
Skiera, Bernd, 319n41
Skinner, Steven J., 349n40
Smith, Laurie P., 378n16
Soberman, David A., 378n29
Song, Jaeki, 319n38
Spagat, Elliot, 192n56
Spekman, Robert, 379n45
Spencer, Jane, 117n2
Spiro, Rosann, 153n1
Spriggs, Mark T., 445n54
Spurgeon, Devon, 228n9
Srinivasan, Kannan, 190n10, 349n45
Srinivasan, Shuba, 192n61
Staelin, Richard, 154n19, 378n28
Stanek, Steve, 78n14
Steenkamp, Jan-Benedict E. M., 55n4, 153n9,
    154n20, 296, 318n7, 348nn14–15,
    349n42, 349n48, 377n9, 379n35, 409n25,
    410nn30–31
Steiner, Robert L., 190n5
Stern, Louis W., 55nn10–11, 118n9, 192n62,
    348n25, 349n55, 377nn1–2, 379n40
Stoll, Neal R., 445n37
Stremersch, Stefan, 411n52
Stroud, Jerri, 446n80
Stump, Rodney, 409n23
Stumpf, Edward, 261n20
Sturdivant, Frederick D., 192n62
Su, Xuanming, 60, 117n2
Subramani, Mani R., 349n46
Summers, John O., 349n50, 349n52
Superville, Darlene, 229n26
Sutherland, Euan, *250*
Sweeney, Daniel J., 229n30
Szymanski, David M., 153n7

T

Talukdar, Debabrata, 192n47
Tanouye, Elyse, 447n86
Taylor, Alex, 349n44, 378n11
Taylor, Robert E., 446n66

Tellis, Gerard J., 190n15
Terpstra, Vern, 192n57
Thayer, Warren, 445n44
Thomas, Andrew R., 410n35
Thomas, Kenneth W., 373, 379n48
Thomas-Graham, Pamela A., 378n24
Thompson, Paul, 260n4
Thunder, David, 444n4
Tibben-Lembke, Ronald S., 117n2
Tjemkes, Brian V., 379n41
Tomas, G., 347n8
Tomlinson, Richard, 153n10
Toosi, Nahal, 229n26
Torode, Christina, 192n49
Townsend, Matt, 318n4
Trinkle, Bob, 154n18
Triplett, Tim, 462n8
Tucker, Emma, 444nn5–6

**U**

Ulukaya, Hamdi, 143

**V**

Van Den Bulte, Christophe, 411n52
van Ryzin, Garett, 462n16
Varadarajan, P. Rajan, 153n7
Vargo, Stephen L., 318n6, 318n8
Vasquez-Nicholson, Julie, 229n29
Vasavsky, Martin, *385*
Vecchio, Leonardo Del, 148
Venkatraman, N., 349n46
Villas-Boas, Miguel, 378n26
Villas-Boas, Sofia B., 191n34, 377n10
Vinhas, Alberto Sa, 192n50, 378n23
Vogelstein, Fred, 154n27
Vossen, Thomas, 153n6

**W**

Wagner, B., 318n17
Walker, Orville C., r, 153n8, 154n30, 378n12
Washington, Ruby, 229n18
Wassenhove, Luk N. Van, 462n5
Wathne, Kenneth H., 410n34
Wattenz, Eric, 292n5
Webb, Kevin L., 319n39

Webster, Bruce, 377n8
Webster, Elizabeth A., 378n24
Wei, Yan, 153n14
Weigand, Robert E., 379n30
Weil, William, 261n20
Weiss, Allen M., 409n17
Weiss, Marc, 318n5
Weitz, Barton, 153n1, 348nn23–24, 349n41, 379n33, 379n38, 380n50, 382, 409n13, 409n18, 409n20, 410n33
Weitz, Barton A., 153n2, 228n1
Welsh, M. Ann, 118n9
Wermiel, Stephen, 444n11, 446n66
Westfeldt, Amy, 446n80
Whang, Seungjin, 118n7, 462n10
Wiese, Carsten, 379n30
Wilke, John R., 446n80
Wilkonson, Timothy J., 410n35
Williams, Norman D., 446n80
Wilson, Rick, 74
Winer, Russell S., 410n27
Wiriyabunditkul, Payungsak, 444n7
Wolk, Agnieszka, 319n41
Wortzel, Lawrence H., 191n37
Wu, D. J., 261n25
Wuyts, Stefan, 411n52

**Y**

Yang, Guang, 318n5
Yin, Shuya, 261n18
York, Anne S., 261n9, 409n16
Young, Andrew Thomas, 447n95
Yücesan, Enver, 462n1

**Z**

Zaheer, Akbar, 409n21
Zahra, Shaker, 319n20
Zarley, Craig, 78n2, 117n1
Zeithaml, Valarie A., 318n12
Zettelmeyer, Florian, 192n48
Zhang, Ran, 261n10
Zhou, Sean, 347n4
Zieger, Anne, 117n2
Zimmerman, Ann, 347n11
Zizzo, D., 260n2, 261n29
Zwick, Rami, 377n4
Zwiebach, Elliott, 229n27

# SUBJECT INDEX

Note: Locators in italics indicate additional display material; "n" indicates note.

## A

ABC. *See* Activity-based costing (ABC)
Absolute confinement, 415, 441
Accommodation, as conflict resolution style, *373*
Accumulation, marketing channel activity, 37
Acquisitions, 307, 385
Activity-based costing (ABC), 123, 136, 258
Actual profit shares, 100, 146
Adapatation techniques, retail structures
    dealing types, 223
Adaptable supply chain system, 460
Adaptive channels, 249
Advance or season dating, 232
Advertising. *See* Promotion and promotion flow
Affective conflict, 352, 355
Africa, 146
    Kenya, 338
    multiunit franchising in, 288
    Niger, wholesaling in, 245–48
    third-party logistics providers (3PL), 43, *241*
After-sales service, 57, 96, 364, 368, 416
Agency theory, 356–57
Agents, in wholesaling, 241
Aggression, as conflict resolution style, *373, 373*
Agile supply chain systems, 460
Airtight territory, 415
*Albrecht* v. *Herald Co.* (1968), *421*
Aligned supply chain system, 460
Alliances. *See also* Federations of wholesaling
    businesses
    of wholesaler-distributors, 248
Allocation, marketing channel activity, 37
Allowances. *See also* Slotting allowances
    freight, 231
    in promotions, *222*, 223–124
    and services, 426–127
Ambiguity, performance, 147, 150
American Customer Satisfaction Index (ACSI), 70
Analyzing and designing stage, marketing
    channel, 44
    benchmarking stage, 44
    implementing stage, 44–46
Anchor stores, rent in, 209
Antitrust issues. *See also individual laws*; Policy
    constraints, legal
    application, 412

customer coverage policies, 416–118
customer coverage policies, 417
enforcement agencies, 413–114, 417
enforcement, legal rules of, *415*
laws, overview of, *413*
legal rules, 415
    for territorial restrictions, 414
    for unfair competition, 414
A priori segments, 72
Arbitrage, 362, 364
Arbitration
    for conflict resolution, 370–75
Arbitration-mediation, 371
Area of primary responsibility, 415
Argentina, 226
Arm's-length market contracts, *302*
Artificial scarcity, 167
Asia, 226
Assertiveness, as conflict resolution style, *373,* 373
Assets
    intangible, power as, 333
    specific vs. general-purpose, 140, 144
    turnover in retail positioning, 206–107
Assorting, marketing channel activity, 38
Assortment and variety, 46, *66*, 69, 72, 102,
        106–107, 184, 186, 204, *205*
    assortment, defined, 69
    of CDW, *65*
    defined, 69
    demand-side retail positioning, 212–115
    gap analysis template, *112, 113*
    marketing channel development, 36–37
    music retailing, 106
    as service output, 205
    service output demand differences, *47*
    variety, defined, 69
Asymmetric commitment, 383, 390
Auctions, reverse, on-line, 257
Auditing, criteria, 84–96
    financing cost, 95–96
    information sharing, 96
    inventory holding costs, 94–95
    negotiation function, 95
    ordering cost, 96
    ownership costs, 89
    payment cost, 96

physical possession, 85
promotion function, 95
safety stock, 95
Auditing, efficiency templates, 83–96
    activity-based costing (ABC), 97
    normative profit shares, 99
Auditing, equity principle, 100–101
    radio frequency identification (RFID) function,
        100–101
*Augusta News Co.* v. *Hudson News Co.* (2001), 426
Authorized franchise system, 275, 276
Automatic replenishment (automated reordering
        system), 96
Automobile Dealers Franchise Act of 1956, 438
Avoidance, as conflict resolution style, *373, 373*
Awareness, in alliance development, 401, *402,* 404

**B**

B2B. *See* Business-to-business (B2B)
B2C. *See* Business-to-consumer (B2C)
Backward integration, 141, *149,* 439
Bait-and-switch tactics, 159, 161, 177, 188
Balanced scorecard, 240
Balance, of power, 254, 302, 315, 338
Balancing dependence, 173, 339
Banking industry
    vertical integration, *130*
Bar coding, 208, 243
Bartering, 59
Beginning-of-the-month
        (B.O.M.) inventory, 233–34
Beliefs and legitimate power, 331
Benchmarks, 44
Benefit and reward power.
        *See* Reward power
Bill-back trade deal, *222*
Bill of lading, 232
Block booking, 435
BOGO. *See* Buy one get one free (BOGO)
BOM. *See* Beginning-of-the-month (B.O.M.)
        inventory
Book and ship business class, 256
Boundary personnel, 342
Brand and brand equity
    in franchising, 268–69
    functional brands, *459*
    innovative brands, *459*
    poor coverage of, 166
    private label, 141, 185, 224–125
    pull system for building, 162
    waiting and delivery time, 210–111

Branded concepts, 269
Branded variants, 178
Brand names, in franchising, 267
Brand strategy, 167–70
    niche positioning, 169–70
    quality positioning and premium pricing,
        167–70
    premium positioning, 167–69
    scarcity, 167
    target markets and, 169
Brazil, 226, 287, 305, 311
Breadth of variety, 69
Brokers, 35, 56, 95, 108, 241, 246, 254, 256, 426
Budgeting, merchandising and, 233–35
Bulk-breaking, 79
    demand-side retail positioning, 209
    gap analysis template, 48, 111–114
    marketing channel development, 36
    service output demand differences, *47*
    service output demands, 67–70
    service output demands (SOD) template, 79–82
Bullwhip effect, 102, 451
Bundling, 257
Bureau of Competition, Federal Trade
        Commission (FTC), 426
Business-to-business (B2B). *See also* Electronic
        channels and commerce; Electronic bill
Business-to-consumer (B2C), 70, 179, *314*
*Business Electronics, Corp.* v. *Sharp Electronics*
        (1988), 419, *420*
Business format franchising, 264, 269–70.
        *See also* Franchising and franchises
Buyer-initiated channel format, 61
Buyers
    buyer-initiated channel formats, 61
    catalog shopper, 57
    power retailers and wholesalers, 258–59
    price discrimination by, 425–126
    role of, in retailing, 211
    as ultimate consumer in retail, 194
    wholesale consolidation and, 254
Buying club, 35, 57
Buying group, 61
Buying perspectives, 131
    decision making, 131
Buy one get one free (BOGO), 209, 451

**C**

Cable and pay-TV services, 62, 70, 162, 440
Canada, 364
Cannibalization, *93, 174, 179, 181, 188, 220*

Capital. *See* Financial capital; Human capital; Management

Career paths, plural form strategy in franchising and, 284–85

Carrier-rider relationships, 183–84

Cash datings, 232

Cash on delivery (C.O.D.), 232

Cash discount, 231, 232

Cash with order (C.W.O.), 232

Catalog/mail order, 57, 63, 130, 214, 217, 424–125

Catalyst firms, 254

Category captains, 432

Category exclusivity, 163

Category killer, 35, 58, *213*, *214*, 215

Category management, 432

Channel conflict, consequences, 353–55
  functional, 353–54
  management, 375–76
  manifest, 355–56
  measurement levels, 352–53
  nature of, 350–51

Channel conflict, minimizing negative effects, 365–70
  intolerance, balanced relationship, 366–68
  mitigation, balanced relationship, 368–69
  perceived unfairness, 369–70
  reducing the use of threat, 366

Channel conflict, multiple types, 359–61
  differential pricing, 363
  economic fundamentals, 364
  felt or affective, 352
  gray marketing, 363
  identification, 361–62
  latent, 351
  management, 362–63
  manifest, 352
  perceived, 351
  unwanted channels, 362–65

Channel conflict, sources
  competing goals, 356–57
  intrachannel, 359
  reality perceptions, difference, 357–59

Channel design. *See* Design, of marketing channel

Channel influence, 170–73
  creating reward power, 170–71
  investment promotion, 171–73

Channel management. *See* Supply chain management (SCM)

Channel power
  coercive, 325–126

defined, 321
double marginalization, 323
excercising, 321
expertise, 326–129
false negatives, 322
false positives, 322
grouping of sources, 333–34
influencer, 321
influence strategies, 341–45
as a tool, 322

Channel power, legitimising, 329–331
  legal, 330
  norms/values/beliefs, 331
  traditional, 330

Channel power, mirror image dependencies
  balance of power, 338–41
  bottom-up approach, 337–38
  combined analysis, 336
  defined, 334–36
  imbalance of power, 339
  measurement, 336
  negative sanctions, 325–126
  referent, 331–33
  retaliate, 326
  reward of, 325
  role performance, 337
  sales profit percentage, 337
  scarcity, 336
  sources, 324
  strategic channel alliances, 338–39
  switching cost, 337
  target of influence, 321
  utility, 336

Channels. *See* Marketing channels

Channel strategies, globalization effect, 295, 303–109
  hierarchical relationship, 314
  influencing trends, 294–95
  local knowledge and execution capability, 308
  opening of international markets, 305
  product aspects, 300–101
  revenue growth, 304
  shakeout period, 307

Channel strategies, for services, 295
  acquiring, 303
  collaboration, 301
  defensive motivations, 296
  in-house capabilities, 301–103

Channel structure, 304

Channel type decisions, 179–81. *See also* Intensity decisions

cherry-picking, 180
coverage variety, 179
Cherry-picking, 180
Chile, 305, *306*, 311, *312*
China, 133, *207*, 226, 305
Clayton Antitrust Act (1914), *413,* 442
    exclusive dealing, 430
    ownership policies, 439
    provisions, *413*
    tying, 432
    vertical integration by internal expansion, 440
Closed-loop logistics systems, *450*
Closing channel gaps, 184–87, 186. *See also* Gaps
    and gap analysis
    costs, 185–86
    environmental bounds, 186–87
    managerial bounds, 186–87
    service, 184–85
Coalitions, 339
Coercive power, 325–126, 333, 345, 426
Colgate doctrine, *419,* 437
Collaboration, as conflict resolution style,
    *373, 374*
Collaborative filtering, 244
Collusion, 425
Colombia, *306*
Commission agents, in wholesaling, 241
Commission, in multilevel direct selling
    organizations (MLDSOs), 218
Commitment
    in alliance development, 403
    asymmetric, 383
    building, 383
Company outlet stores, 282–83, 285
Company-sponsored program channel format, 62
Compensation
    in multilevel direct selling organizations
    (MLDSOs), 218
    profit pass-over arrangements, 415
Competition. *See also* Interbrand/intrabrand
    competition
    as conflict resolution style, 370, 372, *373*
    intrachannel, 359
    meeting competition defense, 425
    complacency prevention, channel competition,
    164–65
    complacency and selectivity, 164
Compromise, as conflict resolution style,
    *373, 374*
Compulsory arbitration, 371
Computer access information, 62

Computer industry, wholesaling, Internet
    expansion and, 255–56
Conflict and conflict management, 350. *See also*
    Domain conflict
    category exclusivity and, 163
    channel conflict, 351
    between channel members and
    domains, 359
    consequences of, 353–56, *354*
    costs of conflict, 356
    defined, 350
    dual distribution, 440
    goals and channel conflict, 356–57
    index of manifest conflict, 352, 353
    kinds of conflict, 351–52
    measuring conflict, 352–53
    perceptions of reality and, 357–59
    resolution strategies, 372–74
    sources of conflict, 356–65
Conflict, resolution strategies
    arbitration (compulsory and voluntary), 371
    building relation norms, 372
    cooptation, 371
    information-intensive Mechanisms, 370
    mediation, 371
Conjoint analysis, 71
Consolidation, rarity, thin markets, and, 144
Consolidation, in wholesaling, 238, 253–55.
Consortium, 248
Constant-sum scales, 73
Consumer cooperatives (co-ops), 252
Consumers and customers
    coverage policies, 416–118
    supply chain management (SCM) and, 449
Contact costs, 39
*Continental T.V. Inc. v. GTE Sylvania, Inc.*
    (1977), 414, 441
Contingent appeal, in influence strategies, 345
Continuous replenishment program (CRP), 38,
    223, 451
Contracts
    franchising, 272
    intensive distribution and, 157
    legitimate power and, 329–331
    requirements, 430
    restrictive, 169
Contract warehousing, 58
Convenience goods, 165
Convenience stores, 58, *214*
*Conwood Co. v. United States Tobacco Co,*
    431–32

Cooperation
  as conflict resolution style, 376
  in franchise relationships, 280
Cooperative advertising allowances trade deal, *222*
Cooperative relationships, 354
Cooperatives (co-ops)
  companies as shareholders, 61
  functional conflict, *354*
  in wholesaling, 61
Co-optation, 371
Cost issues
  contact costs, 39
  cost justification defense, 424
  cost-side positioning, 204–109, *205–106, 207*
  merchandise cost, 230
  retailing pricing and buying terms, 230–31
  total cost, 107–108, 120
Costs and benefits, buying perspectives
  control, 128–129
  responsibility, 128
  risks, 128
Countervailing power, 246, 338–39
Count-recount trade deal, *222*
Cross docking, 58, 452
Crossfunctional integration, 459
Cross-selling, 63
Cultural sensitivity, 359
Customer coverage policies, 416–118
  grey markets, 417
  price segmentation, 417
Customer list cross-selling, 63
Customer loyalty, 136, 238, 339
Customer relationship management (CRM), *456*
Customer service, 70, 81
  bricks-and-mortar vs. online business, 295
  CDW policy, *65, 86*
  gap analysis template, *111–114*
  as service output, 46, 70
  service output demand differences, *47*
  service output demands (SOD) template, *79*
Customized physical facilities, 141–43

**D**

Database marketing, 63
Dealer councils, 369
Dealer direct, 57
Decline and dissolution, in alliance
    development, *402,* 403
Dedicated capacity, 143
Defenses to price discrimination charges,
    424–125

Delivered sale, 231
Delivery time. *See* Waiting and delivery time
Delphi technique, 117n4
Demand-side factors
  channel overview, 36–37
Demand-side gaps. *See* Gaps and gap analysis
Demand side, retail structures, 209–112
  bulk breaking, 209
  customer service, 212
  delivery time, 210–111
  product variety, 211
  spatial convenience, 210
  waiting time, 210–111
Department store channels, 57
Dependence balancing, 173–75
  assortment choices, 173
  display choices, 173
  reassuring channel partner, 175
  territory trading for category, 173–75
Dependence and channel power
  balancing, 173–75
  imbalanced dependence, 339–41
  net dependence, 338–39
Designated product policies, 436–37
Design, of marketing channel. *See also*
      Positioning; Segmentation; Targeting
  channel structure decisions, 48
  commitment, 389
  framework for, 45
  gap analysis, 48
  implementation and, 52
  segmentation, 46–48
Design wins, 256
Differentiation and strategic alliance
    commitment, 388
Direct mailer, 59
Direct selling channel, 216–119
  distributors, role in, 218
  failure fee effects, 224
  pyramid scheme, 218
Direct selling/direct selling organizations
      (DSOs), 216–119
  channel structure, 218
  compensation plans, 218
  global retail sales through, 218
  hybrid-channel challenge to, 219–120
  legitimate, pyramid schemes versus, 218
  multilevel (MLDSO), 218
Discounts
  cash, 231
  functional, 231, 240, 427–129, 443

quantity, 231
seasonal, 231
trade, 231
Discrimination, price, 422–123
Disintermediation, 40
Display allowances trade deal, *222*
Distribution alliance, 248
Distribution capabilities, companies, 140
    brand equity, 140–41
    customized physical facilities, 141–43
    dedicated capacity, 143
    idiosyncratic knowledge, 140
    relationships, 140
    site specificity, 143–44
Distribution outsourcing, 133–36
Distribution. *See also* Consolidation, in
        wholesaling; Vertical integration;
        Wholesaling
    dual, 156, 181–84
    exclusive, 157
    intensive, 157
    master distributors, 238–40
    third-party, 136, 182
Distributive justice, 400
Distributor differentiation, 387
Distributors, retail market, 215–116
Diversity, Web purchases and prices paid
        and, 80
Diverting, 223
Dollar stores, 105, 209
Domain conflict, 52
    gray markets, 363–65
    intrachannel competition, 359
    multiple channels, 359–61
Door-to-door channel formats, 60–61
Double marginalization, 323
Downstream channel members
    bait-and-switch, 159
    benefits, 36
    free riding, 159
    general indifference, conflict management, 355
    intensive distribution, 157–61
    inter-brand price competition, 158
    intra-brand price competition, 158
    investment promotion, 171–73
    search facilitation, 36–37
    segmentation analysis, 46
    sporting, 37–38
    targeting analysis, 46
Downstream members perception, relationship
        management, 386–87

commitment building, 393–94
committed relationship, 389
competitive advantage, 387
development stages, 403–104
differentiation strategy, 387
economic satisfaction, 395
generic investment, 395–96
life cycle, 400–103
market orientation, 388
overcoming distrust, 399
portfolios, 405–106
troubles, handling, 404–105
*Dr. Miles Medical Co.* v. *John D. Park & Sons Co.*
        (1911), 419
Dual distribution, 156, 181, 440–41
    horizontal restraints, 441
    ownership policies, 440–41
    price squeeze, 440
Dual distribution decisions, 181–82
    demonstration argument, 182–83
Durables, 163, 178

**E**

East African Breweries Limited
        (EABL), 338
    third-party logistics providers (3PL), *326*
*Eastman Kodak Co.* v. *Image Technical Service,*
        *Inc.* (1992), *435*
E-commerce, channel strategies, 309–114
    creative pricing, 313
    free-riding, 313
    lack of immediacy, 311
    new markets, 311
Economic issues
    noneconomic satisfaction, 397
    satisfaction and strategic alliances, 395–96
    survival, downstream distribution and
        outsourcing, 134
Economic order quantity (EOQ), 95
Economies of scale
    downstream distribution and
        outsourcing, 134
    in franchising, 268, 269
    picking, in wholesaling, 242
Economies of scope, *302*
Efficiency template, 96, 97, 119–124
Efficient consumer response (ECR), 451–53
    information-intensive conflict resolution
        and, 370
Electronic bill presentment and payment
        (EBPP), 107

Electronic channels and commerce. *See also*
        Internet
    allowances and services, 427
    online sales, 216
    as percentage of 2009 sales, *217*
    wholesaling and, 255–56
Electronic data interchange (EDI), 208
    automatic purchase orders/payments through,
        451
    benefits of, 326
    coercive power and, 325
    forward buying problem and, 223
    Wal-Mart and, 325
Electronic exchanges, 256
Electronic funds transfers (EFTs), 386
Electronic order systems, 243
Electronics industry, wholesaling and Internet
        expansion and, 255–56
Emerging channel structure. *See* Channel
        strategies; e-commerce
Emerging markets, 364
End-of-month dating, 232
End-of-month inventory, 230
End-users. *See also* Consumers and customers
    defined, in marketing channel, 36
    geographic distribution of, 118n9
    segmentation and channel preferences
        examples, 46–48
    speculation by, 110
End-users, channel functions. *See also* Auditing
    company outlets, Franchising strategies,
        282–83
    as downstream channel members, 36
    franchisee exploitation, 285
    ownership redirection, 285
    plural forms, 283
    segmentation analysis, 46–48
    targeting analysis, 46
Enforcement, of franchise contracts. *See*
        Franchising and franchises
Entrepreneurial spirit and franchising, 272–74
Environmental bounds, 103–105
Environmental issues, uncertainty and vertical
        integration, 145–46
Equity Principle, 48, *86*, *88*, 100–101, 116
Europe, 37, 131, 224
European Commission, 276, 416
European Union (EU), franchising defined by, 276
European Union Law, 416
*Ex ante/ex post* competitive markets, 137
Exclusive dealing, 163, 429–432

Exclusive distribution, 157
Exclusivity and distribution intensity, 157, 163
Expansion, as part of alliance development, 401
Expert power, 326–129
Exploitation, 246
Exploration, in alliance development, 401
Export distribution channels, 259
Export intermediary, *245*
External expansion, vertical integration by, 439
Extra dating, 232
Extreme specialists/generalists, 254, 260

**F**

Failure fees, 224
Farm cooperatives (co-ops), 251
Fashion industry
    quick response (QR) and, 453–54
Fast-moving consumer goods (FMCG), 162, 165,
        178, 452–53
Federal Trade Commission (FTC) Act (1914),
        413, 424, 426
    exclusive dealing, 429–430
    full-line forcing, 435
    market coverage policies, 413
    price discrimination by buyers, 425–126
    promotional allowances and services, 426–127
    provisions, *413*
    slotting allowances, 425
    tying, 432
    vertical integration by merger, 439
Federations of wholesaling businesses, 248, 260
Fee for service, in wholesaling, 257
Felt conflict, 352
Financial capital, for franchises, 270
Financial service providers, 60
Financing flow
    efficiency template and, 121–124
Flexibility, relational norm building (conflict
        management), 372
Flows, marketing channel. *See also* Financing
        flow; Negotiation and negotiation
        flow; Ownership and ownership flow;
        Promotion and promotion flow; Risk and
        risking flow
    efficiency template and, 96–103
Focus groups, 72
Food Marketing Institute, 370, 428
Food retailers, 57. *See also* Farm cooperatives
        (co-ops); Grocery stores and
        supermarkets
Forecasting, in fashion industry, 453–54, *455–56*

Foreign markets
  export distribution channels and, 244–45, *245*
  successful entry into, 226
Forward buying effects, 223
  continous replenishment
      programs (CRP), 223
  diverting issues, 223
Forward integration, 439
Forward logistics, *92–93*
Forward vertical integration. *See* Vertical
      integration
Fragmentation, 254
France
  backward integration example in, *149*
  franchise operations, 274–75
  hypermarkets, *195–96*
  McDonald's franchises in, *265–66*
  retailing figures, 194
      substitution of channels foradvertising, *396*
Franchising and franchises
  advantages, 264
  after-sales service support, 57
  authorized system, 275, 276
  benefits to, 264, *265–66*
  ceding of power, 263
  company outlets
      plural form, 283–85
      redirection of ownership, 285
      temporary situations, 283
      variation in situations, 283
  conflict with franchisors, 268–69
  as consultants, 268
  contracts, 272
      care and responsibilities
          of parties to, 276–77
      enforcement of, 280
      landlord/real estate relationship, 279
      payment system, 277–79
      safeguards outside, 280–81
      subjects addressed in, *282*
      termination of, 277, 279
  defined, 262–64, 276
  distinguished from other channels, 276
  drawbacks for, 264
  leasing feature, 265
  McDonald's, *265–66, 273, 278, 279, 280*
  ongoing benefits, 268
  power and, 274
  redirection of ownership, 285
  retailer-based channel formats, 57
  right-of-first-refusal clause, 280

start-up package, 267
  subsidiaries versus, 263
  vertical integration, 276
Franchising strategies
  adaptation trends, 286
  business format, 276
  contract consistency, 280
  contract enforcement, 280
  contracting, 276–77
Franchising structure
  benefits, 264–67
  branded concept, 269
  brand name, 267
  business format, 263
  competitive advantages, 268
  consolidators, 269
  consultant, 272
  defined, 262
  deliberate loss of separate identity, 263
  financial capital, 270–71
  franchisees, 262
  franchisor benefits, 269–70
  free riding, 269
  human capital, 272
  managerial capital, 270–71
  negative elements, 274–75
  ongoing benefits, 268
  personnel shortage, 271
  residual claimants, 272
  start-up package, 267
  system, 262
Franchisor
  benefits/services provided by, 264
  defined, 262–64
  ongoing challenges for
      conflict, 287
      cooperative atmosphere, 286–87
      survival, 286
Free on board (F.O.B.), 231
Free goods trade deal, *222*
Free riding, 106, 159, 171, 219, 269, 313
  customer coverage policies, 416–118
  in franchising, 269, 289
Freight allowances, 231
French and Raven approach, to indexing
      power, 324
FTC Trade Practice Rules, 413
FTE. *See* Full-time equivalent (FTE)
Fulfillment houses, 130
Full-line forcing, product line policies, 435, *436*
Full-time equivalent (FTE), 208

Functional brands/goods, 457, 458
Functional conflict, 353–55, *354*
Functional discounts, 231, 427–129, *429*, 441
Functional substitutability, 118n12
Furniture industry
   restrictive contracts and, 169
   taxonomy implications, 213
   waiting and delivery time and, 210
Future datings, 232

## G

Gap-analysis, auditing, 103
   closing of, 184–86
   combining, 108–111
   cost, 105–108
   evaluation, 111
   service, 105–106
   sources, 103–105
   templates for, 111–115
Gaps and gap analysis
   channel design and, 103–115
   closing gaps, 184, 186
   combined channel gaps, 108–111
   environmental bounds, 104
   gap analysis template, 111–115
   managerial bounds, 104
   sources of gaps, 103–105
   types of gaps, 109
Geographic issues. *See* Market coverage policies
Gift market, 62
Global issues
   resale price maintenance (RPM), 162
   retailing, 225–126
   wholesaler-distributor expansion, 255–59
Globalization effects, retail market, 225–126
   in BRIC nations, 226
   Internet retail channels, 219–120
   virtuous cycle, 226
GMROI. *See* Gross margin return on inventory
   investment (GMROI)
GMROL. *See* Gross margin per full-time
   equivalent employee (GMROL)
GMROS. *See* Gross margin per square foot
   (GMROS)
Goal conflict, 52, 287
Gray markets, 223, 363–65, 417
Grocery Manufacturers of America (GMA),
   370, 428
Grocery stores and supermarkets
   backward integration example, *149*
   coercive power and, 325

   efficient consumer response (ECR) and,
      451, 452
   expertise power and, 329
   food retailers, 57
   forward buying problem and, 223
   pricing policies, 418–122
   private label programs in, 141, 224
   service outputs and, 185
   waiting and delivery time strategy, 210
Gross margin percentage, 230
Gross margin per full-time equivalent employee
   (GMROL), 208
Gross margin per square foot (GMROS), 208
Gross margin of profit, 230
Gross margin return on inventory investment
   (GMROI), 207, 230

## H

Health care industry, pricing policies, 425
High-service retailing systems, 204
Home parties, 60
Home shopping technologies, 63, 215, 440
Human capital, in franchising, 272
Hybrid shopping, 215, 219–120
Hypermarket, 58

## I

Idiosyncrasies, 137
Idiosyncratic investments, 138, 140, 392–94
Idiosyncratic knowledge, 140, 172
Imbalanced dependence, 339–41
Implementation of marketing channel
   framework for, 45
   power source identification, 333
Imports, gray markets and, 417–118
Independence from a single
   manufacturer, 136
Index of manifest conflict, 353
India, 226, *327*
Individual on-site sales, 60
Indonesia, *306*
Industrial marketing channels in developed
   economies, 366
Influencers/specifiers, 60
Influence strategies, power and, 341–45
Infomediary, 180
Information exchange influence strategy, 342–44
Information exchange, relational norm building
   and, 372
Information-intensive conflict resolution
   mechanism, 371

Information provision, 110, 219
  gap analysis template, *112–113*
  service output demand differences, *47*
Information technology (IT)
  minimalist example, *456*
  in wholesaling, 237
Infrastructural dimensions of the market, 118n10
Initial markup or mark-on, 230
Innovative brands/goods, 457
Integration, crossfunctional, 459. *See also* Vertical
      integration
Integration of truck and rail (intermodal), 59
Integrative (win-win) solutions, to conflict, 371
Intensity decisions
  brand strategy, 167
  channel influencing, 170
  competition prevention, 164
  dependence balancing, 173
  downstream member's perspectives, 157
  exclusive distribution, 157
  local monopoly, 157
  manufacturer's other strategies, 177
  opportunity cost, 175
  product category, 165
  saturation, 157
  transaction cost, 176
  upstream member' s perspectives, 161
Intensive distribution, 157–63
  downstream channel members' perspectives,
      157–61
  upstream channel members' perspectives,
      161–64
Interbrand/intrabrand competition, 414, 420,
      430, 433, 441–42, 443
Intermediaries. *See also* Wholesaling
  bulk-breaking function, 79
  defined, in marketing channel, 35–36
  for electronic bill presentment and payment,
      107
  export, *245*
  in marketing channel, 37–38
  reduction in number of producer contacts
      through, 38–42
  as search facilitators, 36–37
  sorting function of, 35–36
Internal expansion, vertical integration by, 440
International issues. *See* Global issues
Internet
  as cannibalistic channel, 181
  retail channels, hybrid, 219–120
  as retail outlet, 215–120

wholesaling and, 255–56
Intrabrand competition. *See* Interbrand/
      intrabrand competition
Intrachannel competition, 359
Inventory. *See also* Wholesaling
  beginning-of-the-month (B.O.M.), 233
  holding costs, 94, 108, 110, 211
  turnover goals, 204, 233
Italy, 36

**J**

Japan
  multiple channels, 289
  retailing figures, 194
  wholesaling in, 241, 251, 258
*Jefferson Parish Hospital District No. 2* v. *Hyde*
      (1984), *433*
Jobbers, 237, 441
Just-in-time shipments, 208

**K**

Kenya, 338
Kiosks, 62, 156, 188
Kitting, 58, 244, 256, 258, 303
Korea, 307

**L**

Landlords of bricks-and-mortar retailing stores,
      209
  franchisors as, 276, 279
Lanham Act, 418
Latent conflict, 351
Latent power, 341
Leasing, 279
  location, 279
  market differences, 282
  termination threats, 279
Leasing and franchising, 279
Legal issues. *See* Environmental bounds;
        Legitimate power; Policy constraints, legal
Legalistic influence strategy, 342
Legitimate power, 329–331
Licenses/licensing, 56
  business format franchising and, 263, 267
  for franchises, 267
Location clause, 415
Locker stock, 56
Lock-in problem, 362
Logistic management
  consumer response, 451–52
  consumer response, barriers, 452–53
  customer service, 449

Logistic management (*Continued*)
  quick response logistics, 453–54
  quick response logistics, barriers to, 454–56
  supply chain management (SCM), 448
Logistics. *See also* Supply chain management
      (SCM)
  closed-loop systems, *450*
  defined, 448
  forward/ordinary, *449*
  overview, 448–50
  reverse, 84, 90–94, 205, *449*
Loss-leader pricing, 419
Low-margin/high-turnover model, 204,
      *205, 207*
Low-price retailing systems, 204

# M

Magazine wholesalers, 253
Mail order/catalog, 57
Making perspectives, 136
  company specific capabilities, 137–38
  zero salvage value, 139
Malaysia, *306,* 311
Management, in franchising, 288
Managerial bounds, 103–105, 186
Manifest conflict, 352, 353, 355–56
Manufacturer-led initiatives, in wholesaling, 249
  decentralized solution, 249
Manufacturer-owned full service wholesaler-
      distributor, 56
Manufacturer's other strategies, 177–79
  brand building, 177–78
  branded variants, 178
  coverage selection, 178–79
  new product instructions, 178
Manufacturers. *See also* Vertical integration
  coercive power of, 325
  customer coverage policies, 416
  defined, in marketing channel, 34
  manufacturer-based channel formats, 56
  outlets, 56
  resale price maintenance (RPM), 162, 188, 418
  respect for downstream channel members,
      383–86
Manufacturing
  quick response (QR) in, 453–54
  retailer domination of, 220–126
  trade deals to retailers, *222*
  wholesaling and, 237, 240
Margin, 204, *205–106*
Margin management, 207

Markdown percentage, 230
Markdowns, 230, 234–35, 454, *456*
Market coverage policies, 413–116
  absolute confinement, 415
  interband competition, 414
  intraband competition, 414
  location clause, 415
  primary responsibility, 415
  profit pass-over arrangements, 415
  rule-of-reason, 415
  vertical restraints, 414
Marketing channels. *See also* Design, of
      marketing channel; Flows, marketing
      channel; Implementation of marketing
      channel
  alternative formats, 56–63
  defined, 33
  framework for analysis, 44–54
  members of, 34–42
  reasons for existence and change, 36–42
  work of, 42
Marketing channels, key functions, 42–44
  auditing, 48–49
  make-or buy, 49
  need for, 36
  ownership. *See* physical possession
  physical possession, 43
Marketing channels, participants
  combinations, 36
  end-users, 36
  intermediaries, 35
  manufacturers, 34
Marketing channel strategies
  benchmarking, 51
  defined, 33
  designing, 49–51
  implementation of, 52–53
  importance of, 31
Markets, infrastructural dimensions of, 118n10
Markup (mark-on), 230
Mass merchandiser, 35, 58, 179, 212, *214,*
      220–121, 369
Master distributors, 238–40
Mediated power, 333
Mediation, for conflict resolution, 370
Meeting competition defense, 425
Membership, channel, 84
Merchandise cost, 230
Merchandising efficient consumer response
      (ECR) and, 452
  planning and control, 233–35

point-of-consumption formats, 62
service merchandising/rack jobbing, 61
Merchants, 237
Mergers, 439
Mexico, 68, *306*
Middle East, 288
Middlemen. *See* Intermediaries
Modified rule of reason, *415*
*Monsanto Company* v. *Spray-Rite Service Corporation* (1984), 419
Moral hazard problem, 224
Motion picture distributions, block booking by, 435
Motivation. *See also* Entrepreneurial spirit and franchising
  downstream, 386–87
  intrinsic, 344
  upstream, 383–86
Multichannel, 215–116
Multichannel shopping experience
  direct selling, 216–119
  hybrid shopping, 219–120
  Internet as retail outlet, 215–116
Multilevel marketing organizations, 61
Multinational corporations (MNCs), environmental uncertainty and, 146
Multiple channels, 215–120, 359–61
Multiple types of channels, 359–61
Multiunit franchising, 288–89
  payment systems, 277–79
  power of contiguity, 289
  product name, 275–76
  self-enforcing agreements, 281–82
Music retailing
  speculation and postponement, 110
Mutuality, 331
Mutual strategy, 284
Mystery shoppers, *328*

**N**

National Association of Chain Drug Stores, 428
National Association of Wholesaler-Distributors (NAW), 237
Nature, relationship management
  assymetric commitment, 382–83
  deep friendship, 383
  sacrifice, 382
  single interest, 381
Negative reward power, 325
Negotiation and negotiation flow
  efficiency template and, 121–124

product returns and, 95
Net dependence and channel power, 338–39
New-to-the-world categories, 166
Niche markets, 169
Niger, 246–48
Noncoercive power, 333
Noncompliance, in franchising, 290
Noncontingent appeal, in influence strategies, 344–45
Nondurable goods, trade deals for, *222*
Noneconomic satisfaction and strategic alliances, 396–97
Normative channel, 122
Normative profit shares, 99–100
Norms, 331, 372

**O**

Off invoice trade deal, *222*
Off-retail, 230
One-on-one exploratory interviews, 394
Ongoing styles, Conflict, resolution strategies
  accomodation, 373
  avoidance, 373
  competition, 373
  compromising, 374
  general approach, 373
  personnel exchanges, 370
  profits generation, 375
  third-party mechanism, 371
  through institutionalization, 370
  using incentives, 374
Online bill payment system, 89, 104, 186
Online exchanges, 256–57
Online retailing. *See* Electronic channels and commerce
Online reverse auctions, 257
Open-to-buy, 234
Operating profit, 235
Opportunism, 138, 452
Opportunity cost, 175–76
  competitive intensity, 175
  market area, importance of, 175
  reassuring channel partner, 175–76
Ordinary dating, 232
Ordinary logistics, *449*
Original equipment manufacturers (OEMs), 31
Original retail, 230
Outlet stores
  company, 182, 274, 282–83
  franchising, 282–83

Outsource distribution
  buying perspectives, 132
  economies of scale, 134
  heavier market coverage, 135
  independence from single manufacturer, 136
  market discipline, 133
  motivation, 133–34
  specialization, 134
  survival of the economic fittest, 134
Outsourcing
  service provider–based channel format, 58
  third-party, for returned products, *91–92*
  vertical integration, 126
Ownership and ownership flow
  ownership policies, legal constraints on, 439
  physical possession flow distinguished from, 85
Ownership policies, 439–41
  internal expansion, 439
  vertical integration by internal expansion, 440
  vertical integration by merger, 439–40

**P**

Partners, in strategic alliances, 322, 382
Payment options, 129
  moral hazard, 131
  pricing determination, 129–131
Payment system, in franchise contracts, 277–79
Pay-for-performance system, 374
Pay-per-serving point of dispensing, 62
People's Republic of China. *See* China
Perceived conflict, 351
Perceptions of reality and channel conflict, 356, 357
Performance and performance flow
  ambiguity and vertical integration, 147
Per se illegality, *415, 420, 421*
Per se legality, *415*
Pharmaceutical industry
  expertise power and, *327*
  vertical integration by merger, 439
Physical efficiency, 457–58
Picking, in wholesaling, 242
Piggybacking channels, 183
Plumbing and heating supplies, functional
      conflict in, *354*
Plural form, in franchising, 283–85
Point-of-consumption merchandising formats, 62
Point-of-purchase (POP), 374
Point-of-sale (POS), *461*
Policy constraints, legal
  customer coverage, 416–118
  market coverage, 413–116

ownership, 439
pricing policies, 418–129
product line, 429–437
selection and termination, 437–38
Positioning
  brand strategy and, 167–70
  demand-side, 209–112
  financial and cost-side, 204–109
  retail strategy and, 204
  taxonomy implications, 212–115
Postponement, principle of, 109–111
Power
  authorized franchise system and, 275, 276
  balance of, 338
  channel, nature and sources of, *334*
  coercive, 325–126
  defined, 321–122, 332
  exercised, 321
  expert, 326–129
  influence strategies, 326–129
  legitimate, 329–331, 345
  mediated and unmediated, 333
  nature of, 320–124
  necessity of, 323–124
  noncoercive, 333
  referent, 331–32
  reward, 170–71
  separating the five power sources, 333
  sources of, 324–334
  views of, 323
Power retailing, 258
Predatory pricing, 423
Presentment, 186
Presentment and payment (EBPP); Outsourcing
  catalogs, 63
  channel conflict example, *314*
  channel formats, 62
  power relationships in, 366, 368
Price
  brand strategy and, 167
Price squeeze, dual distribution, 440–41
Pricing policies, 418–129
  discrimination by buyers, 425–126
  discrimination by sellers, 422–124
  efficient consumer response (ECR) and, 451
  functional discounts, 427–129
  meeting competition, 425
  price discrimination, 422–126
  price maintenance, 418–122
  promotional allowances, 426–127
  resale price maintenance (RPM), 418–122

self-defenses against discrimination, 424–125
Private branding, 224–125
Private labels, 34, 224–125.
Problem solving, as conflict resolution style, *373, 374*
Procedural justice, 400
Product category, 165–66
 convenience goods, 165
 selective distribution, 166
 shopping goods, 165
 specialty goods, 165
Product line policies
 designation, distributors, 435–37
 exclusive dealing, 429–432
 full-line forcing, 435
 legal constraints on, 429–437
 tying, 432–35
Product promotion mailing with normal correspondence, 63
Product returns, *90–94*
Products, classification of, 210
Profits
 profit pass-over arrangements, 415
Promise influence strategy, 343
Promotion and promotion flow
 advertising, plumbing and heating supplies (functional conflict), *354*
 allowances and services, 426–127
Proximo dating, 232
Proxy indicators, 337
Psychic income, 272
Pull system, 457, 458, 460
Punishment and coercive power, 366
Push system, 453, 458
Pyramid schemes, 218–119

**Q**

QR. *See* Quick response (QR)
Qualitative focus groups, 72
Quantity discounts, 231
Quasi monopoly, 164
Quasi-vertical integration, *127–128*
Quick delivery, 68, 69, *205*
Quick response (QR), 450, 453–56, 461

**R**

Rack jobbing, 61
Rapid response, in supply chain management, 453
Rarity vs. specificity, in vertical integration, 144
Real estate, in franchise contracts, 277

Receipt of goods (R.O.G.), 232
Reciprocity, 131, 157, 391
Recommendation influence strategy, 341–45
Referent power, 331–33
Relational governance, 127
Relational norm building and conflict resolution, 372
Relationship management
 asymmetric commitment, 390
 commitment building, 389–94
 credibility, 393
 expectation of continuity, 389–90
 house accounts, 392
 idiosyncratic investments, 392
 organizational memory, 391
 pledges, 393
 relationship-specific investment, 393
 selctivity criteria, 392
Request influence strategy, 342
Requirements contracts, 430
Resale price maintenance (RPM), 418–122
Resellers
 authorized/unauthorized, 417
 conflict viewpoint of, *358*
 designated product policies, 436–37
 exclusive dealing, 429–430
 functional conflict example, *354*
 market coverage policies and, 413–116
 selection and termination policies, 437–38
Residual claimant, in franchising, 272
Restraint, in Clayton Act, 447n84
Restraint of trade, 414
Retailer cooperative, 276
Retailer-sponsored cooperatives
 consumer cooperative, 252
 farm cooperative, 249–53, 251
Retailing, strategic issues in
 direct selling, 216–119
 failure fees, 224
 forward buying on deals, 223
 globalization, 225–126
 hybrid shopping, 219–120
 Internet as retail outlet, 215–116
 multichannel shopping experience, 215–120
 power retailing, in wholesaling, 258
 private branding, 224–125
 retailer power, 220–126
 slotting allowances, 223–124
Retailing. *See also* Electronic channels and commerce
 defined, 194
 demand-side positioning, 209–112

Retailing (*Continued*)
   expertise power over suppliers, *327*
   financial and cost-side positioning, 204–109
   positioning strategy, 204–115
   pricing and buying terms, 230–32
   product returns (reverse logistics), *90–94*
   retailer-based channel formats, 57–58
   search facilitation, 36
   taxonomy of retailer types, 212–115
   top 100 retailers, *195–103*
   types of, *214*
   wholesaling distinguished from, 194
Retail structures
   buyers, role in, 211
   globalization, role in, 194
   retail sale, 194
   whole sale, 194
Retail structures, positioning strategies
   cost-side, 204–109
   gross margin per full-time equivalent
       employee (GMROL), 208
   gross margin per square foot (GMROS), 208
   gross margin return on inventory investment
       (GMROI), 207
   strategic profit model (SPM), 206
Retaliation, coercive power and, 326, 366, 368
Return on investment (ROI), criteria, 128, 132
   direct cost, 132
   net effectiveness, 132
   overhead, 132
   specific capabilities, companies, 137
Returns, reverse logistics of, *90–94*
Reverse auctions, online, 257
Reverse logistics, 84, *90–94*, *449–50*
Reverse supply chain, *449–50*
Reward power, 170–71, 325, 345
Right-of-first-refusal clause, 280
Risk and risking flow
   product returns and, *90–94*
Road railers, 59
Robinson-Patman Act, 413
   Colgate doctrine, 437
   functional discounts and, 427–129
   overview, *413*
   price discrimination, 422–129
   price squeeze, 440
   promotional allowances and services, 426–127
   provisions, *413*
Role integrity, 331
Roller freight, 59
Route, 60

Royalty on sales, in franchising, 277
RPM. *See* Resale price maintenance (RPM)
Rule of reason, *414–115*
Russia, 226, *306*, 311

**S**

Sale retail, 230
Sales drives trade deal, *222*
Sales, General amd Administrative (SG&A), 212
Sales-to-inventory ratio, 230
Sales issues
   direct sales organizations (DSOs), 216–119
   e-commerce 2012, 215–116
   hybrid shopping, 219–120
   merchandise planning and control, 233–35
   multilevel direct selling organizations
       (MLDSOs), 218
   sales drives trade deal, *222*
   sales, general, and administrative (SG&A)
       expenses, 212
Sales royalties, in franchising, 278
Sales, tied, 278
Saturation distribution, *414*
Scalia, Antonin, *420*
Scanning, 243
Scarcity, 167, 335
Scheduled trains, 59
SCM. *See* Supply chain management (SCM)
S.D.–G.L. (sight draft–bill of lading), 232
Seasonal discounts, 231
Season dating, 232
Segmentation, 46, 106. 112. *See also* Service
       outputs
   end-user channel preferences, 72–76, 156
   service output demands (SOD) template, 79–82
   service output needs, 72
Segmentation analysis
   bulk breaking, 67–68
   customer service, 70
   importance of, 65–66
   information sharing, 71
   product, variety and assortment, 69–70
   service output, 67, 72
       process perspectives, 72–74
   spatial convenience, 68
   targeting, 75–76
   waiting time, 68–69
Selection policies
   colgate doctrine, 437
   designation, distributors, 437–39
Selection and termination policies, 437–38

Selectivity, 157, 161, 163, 165, 172, 176, 392
Sellers, price discrimination by, 422–123
Service channel, key characteristics
  coproduction, 299
  heterogeneity, 298
  intangibility, 298
  offensive motivations, 296
  perishability of inventory, 299
  servicee, defined, 298
  service ratio, 297–100
  shifting, impact on, 295–57
  transition strategy, 298, 303
Service merchandising/rack jobbing, 61
Service outputs, 46, 65, 67–74, 79–82, 171.
     *See also* Assortment and variety; Bulk-
     breaking; Spatial convenience; Waiting
     and delivery time
  demand differences, *47*
  price and, 71
  production of, 71
  product variety, 69
  service output demand analysis in marketing
    channel design, 75–76
  service output demands (SOD) template, 79–82
Service provider-based channel formats, 58–60
Sherman Antitrust Act (1890), *413*
  exclusive dealing, 429–432
  market coverage policies, 417
  ownership policies, 439
  price squeeze, 440
  provisions, *413*
  resale restrictions, 417
  selection and termination policies, 437–38
  slotting allowances, 425
  tying, 432
  vertical/horizontal restraints and, 440
Shirking, 138, 269
Shopping carts, as customer service, 212
Shopping malls, 209
Site specificity and vertical integration, 143–44
SKUs. *See* Stock-keeping units (SKUs)
Slotting allowances, *222*, 223–124, 426
Software, collaborative filtering, 244
Solidarity, relational norm building and, 331
Solutions retailing, 71
Sorting, marketing channel activity, 37
South Africa, 254
South America, 226
Spain, *205*
Spatial convenience, 68, 72, 79
  demand-side retail positioning, 210

gap analysis template, 48, *112–114*
Internet shopping and, 215–116
retailer types and, *214*
service output demand differences, *47*
service output demands, 72–74
service output demands (SOD) template,
    79–82
Specialization, 134
Specialty catalogs, 63
Specialty discounters, 58
Specialty products, 108, 210
Specialty stores, 58, *213*
Specificity vs. rarity, in
    vertical integration, 144
Specifiers/influencers, 60
Speculation and postponement,
    principle of, 109
Speed, quick delivery and, 68
SPM. *See* Strategic profit model (SPM)
Stack trains, 59
*State Oil Co.* v. *Khan* (1997), 420, *421*
Stock-keeping units (SKUs), 242
Stockouts, 102
Stockturn, 233
Store brands (private labels), 224–125
Storing strategies
  benchmarks, 284
  career paths, 284–85
  competition, 284
  consultants, 284
  district managers, 284
  laboratories, 285
  mutual strategies, 284
Strategic channel decisions
  channel intensity, 156
  channel types, 156
  dual distribution, 156
Strategic profit model (SPM), 206
Street money trade deal, *222*
Subprocessors, 58
Substitutions, functional substitutability, 118n12
Suppliers. *See also* Alliances; Conflict and
    conflict management
  functional conflict example, *354*
  retailers' expertise power over, *327*
Supply chain management (SCM). *See also*
    Logistics
  defined, 448
  efficient consumer response (ECR), 451–53
  overview, 448–49
  player behavior, 450

Supply chain management (*Continued*)
quick response (QR), 453–54
requirements for, 457–59
types of goods for, *457*
Supply chain management strategies, 458–59
adaptable systems, 459
agile systems, 459
aligned systems, 459
physical efficiency vs market responsiveness,
457–58
Supply chain, other participants, 240–41
agents, 241
brokers, 241
commission agents, 241
customers, 241
manufacturers' sales branches, 240
third-party logistic providers, 241
Supply chains market-responsive (innovative
goods), 458, *459*
physical efficiency (functional goods), 457–58
reverse, *449*
Triple-A system (agility, adaptability,
alignment), *460*
Supply-side gaps. *See* Gaps and gap analysis
Survival trends, franchising, 275–86
cannibalization, 287
cooperative atmosphere, 286
goal incongruity, 287
source of conflict, 287
termination, 279–80
trade name, 275–76
trust and fairness levels, 287
Switching costs, vertical integration, 337
Switzerland, *198, 199, 201*
Sylvania case. *See Continental T.V. Inc. v. GTE
Sylvania, Inc.* (1977)
Symmetric dependence, 338

**T**

Taiwan, *41*
*Tampa Electric Co. v. Nashville Coal Co.* (1961),
430, *431*
Tangible goods and wholesaling, 236
Targeting
In customer service, 70
online bill payment system, 89, 104, 186
service outputs, 67–71
Technology. *See also* Electronic data
interchange (EDI); Internet; Multiple
channelselectronic bill presentment and
payment (EBPP), 107

Taxonomy, retail positioning strategies, 212–115
category killer, 215
speciality store, 215
Technology-aided market channels, 63
Television home shopping/satellite networks, 63
Temporary franchises and company stores, 282
Termination issues
in franchising, 277, 279–80
policies, 437–38
Termination policies, 437–38
Terms or inventory financing trade deal, *222*
Territorial issues, 413
*Texaco v. Hasbrouck* (1990), *429*
Thailand, 272
Thin markets, vertical integration and, 144
Third-party issues
catalog services, 63
conflict resolution mechanism, 371–72
distributors, 182
influencer formats, 62
mystery shoppers, *328*
product returns (reverse logistics), *90–94*
reverse logistics provider, 94
Third-party logistics providers (3PL), 241
Threat influence strategy, 341
Threats
coercive power and, 325
in conflict situations, 365
Total cost, 230
Trade deals for consumer nondurable
goods, *222*
Trade discount, 231
Trade liberalization, 226
Trade name or product franchising, 275
Trade-offs, 127
Trade shows, 63
Trading partners, 175
Trains, scheduled, 59
Transaction cost, 176–77
selectivity criteria, 177
Transaction-specific asset, 139, 141
Transportation costs, 231
Treaty of Rome, 416
Triple-A supply chains, *460*
Trust
efficient consumer response (ECR) and, 452
in federations of wholesalers, 248
quick response (QR) and, 453–54
Trust-building, relationship management
absence of coersion, 397
absence of dysfunctional conflict, 397

decision-making, 398–99
goal concruence, 397
noneconomic factors, 396–97
partner selection, 397
prevention, unfairness perception, 399–100
procedural justice, 400
qualifying aspects, 397
social capital, 397
Turkey, *207*
Turnover, 204
Tying
full-line forcing, 435
product line policies, 432–35

**U**

Uncertainty, environmental issues and vertical
integration, 145–46
United Kingdom
franchise contracts in, 280
private label programs in, 224–125
retailing figures, 195
Universal Product Code (UPC), 370
Unmediated power, 333
Upstream channel members, intensive
distribution, 161–64
category exclusivity, 163
channel conflict, 351
integration by selectivity, 149–50, 163
pull strategy, 162
resale price maintenance (RPM), 162
Upstream members perception, relationship
management, 383–86
barriers to entry, 386
commitment building, 394
consolidation, 383
motivation, 383
respect, 383
vendor-managed inventory, 386
*U.S. Federal Trade Commission* v. *Toys "R" Us*
(1998), *436*
*U.S.* v. *Colgate & Co.* (1919), *437*
*U.S.* v. *General Electric Co.* (1926), 422

**V**

Valence, in influence strategies, 344
Value added
in supply chain management (SCM), 448, 449
Value-added functions, in wholesaling, 243–44
absorb risk, 244
efficient infrastructure, 243
filter, 244

time and place utility, 243
transformation, goods, 244
Value-added orders, 256
Value-added reseller (VAR), 59, 182, 332,
359, 360
Value model, 258
Variety, 66. *See also* Assortment and variety
Vending merchandising format, 62
Vendor-managed inventory initiatives, 386
Vertical integration
backward integration, *149*
brand equity, 140–41
company-specific, 140–41
consolidation effects, 144
costs and benefits, 128–129
customized physical facilities, 141, 144
decision framework, 150–51
dedicated capacity, 143
degrees of, 127–128
environmental uncertainty, 145–47
by external expansion, 439
forward, 131, 141
idiosyncratic knowledge, 140
by internal expansion, 439, 440
learning from customers, 148
by merger, 439–40
outsourcing decisions versus (make-or-buy),
128
ownership policies, 439
performance ambiguity, reduction of, 147
quick response (QR) and, 454
rarity versus specificity, 144
relational governance, 127–128
relationships, 140
site specificity, 143–44
thin markets, effects of, 144
trade-offs, 127
Vertical restraints, 414, 416
Virtuous cycle, 226, 396
Voluntary arbitration, 371

**W**

Waiting and delivery time, 46, 214. *See also*
Service outputs
demand-side retail positioning, 209–112
gap analysis template, *112–114*
service output demand differences, *47*
service output demands, 72–74
service output demands (SOD) template, 80
Warehouse clubs, 57, *214*
Warehouse stores, 209

Web agent, 181
Web channels. *See* Electronic channels and commerce
Web distribution, 181
Wholesaler-distributors, 236–38
Wholesaler-distributor. *See also* Wholesaling
  defined, 237
  importance of, 237–38
Wholesaling
  in an emerging economy (Niger example), 246–48
  B2B e-online exchanges, 256–57
  challenges of, 242
  consolidation and, 253–55
  cooperatives (co-ops), 249–52
  defined, 236
  distributing versus, 238
  electronic commerce and, 255–56
  essential tasks, 240
  export distribution channels and, 245
  federations of, 248
  future of, 244, 259
  international expansion, 255
  manufacturer-owned full service wholesaler-distributor, 56
  master distributors, 238–40
  merchant wholesalers, 35
  online reverse auctions, 257
  overview, 236–41
  pharmaceuticals in, 242
  profitability, 257
  supply chain and, 238, 240
  value added, 243–44
  vertical integration and, 258–59
  voluntary groups, 249–50
  wholesale clubs, 57
Wholesaling strategies, alliance-based, 248
  attractiveness, 254

consolidation techniques, Wholesaling strategies, 253–55
consortium, 248
fragmentation, 254
holding company, 249
vertically integrating forward, 254
wholesaler-led initiatives, 248
winners, identification of, 254
Wholesaling strategies, historical perspectives, 242
  challenges in, 242
  in emerging economies, 245–48
  in foriegn markets, 244–45
  picking, 242
Wholesaling structure. *See also* supply chain, other participants, 240–41
  manufacturers, vertical integration of, 258–59
  master distributors, 238–40
Wholesaling trends
  activity-based costing (ABC), 258
  B2B online exchanges, 256–57
  bidding by reverse auctions, 257
  electronic commerce, 255–56
  international expansion, 255
  service fee, 257
WIP. *See* Work in process (WIP)
Word of mouth (WOM), *456*
Work in process (WIP), 448, *455*

## Z

Zero-based channel, 101–103
  gap analysis and, 103–112
Zero-based concept, auditing
  bullwhip effect, 102
  environmental bounds, 104
  managerial bounds, 104
  new channel, guidelines for, 103
Zero-sum game, 373

# COMPANY INDEX

Note: Locators in italics indicate additional display material; "n" indicates note.

## A

ADA (car rental), *275*
AEON, *196*
Affiliated Distributors, 248
Ahold, *197*
Albertson's, 425
Albrecht, 420, *421*, 444n22
Aldi Einkauf, *195*
Allianz, *130*
Allstate, 34
Amazon.com, 141, 215, 219, 244, 313, 314
AMC, 61
American Airlines, *424*
Amway, 61, 218, 229n15
Anheuser-Busch, 34
Annecy, 400, 401, 403, 407
Ann Taylor, 212, *213*
A&P, 224, 225
A Pea in the Pod, 170
Apple iTunes, *203*, 212
ARA, 59
Arrow Electronics, 256, 303
Atlas Electronics, 137
AT&T, 182, 436
Auchan, 58, *196*
Audi, 174
Augusta News Co., 426, 445n43
Autobytel.com, 181
Avis, 278, 279
Avon, 218, 220

## B

Baby Mine Store, Inc., *90*
Baccarat, 182
Bandai, 184
Barnes & Noble, 219
Baskin-Robbins, 434
Bass Pro Shops, 63
Benetton, *206*, 224, 453, 454
Best Buy, *90*, 165, 179, *196*, *213*, *214*, 215
Big Boys Toys, 159, *160*
Bisou Bisou, 69
Black & Decker, 179
BLE, 249
Bloomingdale's, 326

BMW, *328*
Boots, *201*
Bosch, *449–50*
Bright Dairy, *142*
Brooke Group, 423
Brown & Williamson (B&W), 423, *424*
Budget Rent-A-Car, 267, 434
Burger King, 288
Business Electronics, 419, *420*, 421

## C

Cabasse, 167, 169
Cabela's, 70
Calvin Klein, 162
Campbell Soup Co., 223
Canon, *449*
Carrefour, 226
    global expansion of, 194
    as hypermarket, 36, 58, 194
    low-margin/high-turnover model, 204
    size of, 194
Cartier, 167, *168*
Caterpillar, *58*
Caterpillar Logistics Services, 58
CDW, 111, *113–114*
    channel flow and Equity Principle, *86–89*
    commission rate incentives, 100
    gap analysis and, *65–66*
    gap analysis template, 111, *113–114*
    government market and, 95, 65, 104
    as intermediary for small/medium business buyers, 65, *65–66*, 67
    low waiting time, 68
    managerial bounds and, 105
    promotional flow and
        supply-side gaps, 106
Cendant, 136
Chanel, 364
Channel Velocity, 89, *91*, *93*
Chevrolet, 414, 438
Chico's, 212, *213*
Chock Full O'NutsCisco Systems Premier (CSP), *87*, *88*
Chobani, *143*
Corporation, 434
Cisco, *87*, *88*

Clark Material Handling, 43
Clorox, 220
Cobweb Designs, 37
Coca-Cola, *308*
  branded manufacturing, 34
  brand equity, 162
  buyer-induced price discrimination, 426
  fast moving consumer goods, 178
  multiple channels, 360
  as retailer promotion, 221
Colgate, 220, *419*, 437, 438, 443
Comcast, 439, 440
CompuAdd, 63
CompUSA, *90*
Computer Discount Warehouse. *See* CDW
Continental Airlines, *424*
Continental TV, *414*
Conwood, 431, 432
Cooperative     Association     Yokohama
  Merchandising Center (MDC), 251
Coop Italia, *199*
Coop Switzerland, *199*
Costco, 36, 57, 204, 209, 211, 212, *213,* 226,
  *436, 437*
Cost Cutter [Kroger], 224
Cotter & Co., 224
CTI, *302*
Cutco Cutlery, 148
CyberGuard, 182

**D**

Daiei, *203*
Damart, 63
Damas, *168*
Danone, 141, *142, 143*
Dayton Hudson Corp., 57
Delhaize Group, *198*
Dell (USA), *201*
Dell Computer, *66,* 68, *302*
Depot's Business Solutions Group, 35
Dillard's, *213*
Direct Selling Association (DSA), 230–31
DirecTV, 70
Disney, *436*
Distribution America, 61
Dixons, *201,* 307
Dollar General, *201*
Dollar Stores, 105, 209
Dove International, 183
Dr. Atkins' Nutritionals, 34
Dresdner, *130*
Drug Emporium, 58

Dry Storage, 58
Dunkin' Donuts, 269, 285
Duracell, 417, 418

**E**

E&J Gallo Winery, 435
East African Breweries Limited (EABL), 338
East Jefferson Hospital, *433*
Eastman Kodak, 434, *435*
eBay, *91, 93,* 95
Eddie Bauer, 63
Edy's, 183, 192n58
E. Leclerc, *197*
Elders IXL, 440
Electrolux, 60
Eli Lilly, 439
El-Tod Agricultural Community Development
  Farmers' Association, *252*
Empire/Sobey's, *199*
England, Inc., 210
Ericsson, *332, 333*

**F**

F&M Distributors, 58
FAGE Total, *143*
fandango.com, 76
Farmacias Similares, *327*
Fast Retailing, 274
FedEx, 51, 249, *302,* 303
Federated Department Stores, 57
Fingerhut, 57, 259
Fisher-Price, *436*
Florsheim, 63
Fon, *384, 385*
Foot Locker, 357
47th Street Photo, 417
Fred Meyer, 221
Frito-Lay, 258
Fujitsu, *302,* 303
Fuller Brush, 60
Future Shop, 165

**G**

Galeries Lafayette, 174
Gap, 33, 58, 70, 103, *109,* 111, 116, 117n2, *200,*
  *206, 212, 213, 214,* 224, 454
GCH Retail, *335*
General Electric, 129, 179, 296, 422
General Mills, *142, 143*
General Motors (GM), 340, 356, 438, 451
Georgia-Pacific, 240
GESCO, 56
Gillette, 258

GJ's Wholesale Club, 57, *202*
Global, 63
Grand Metropolitan, 440
G. R. Kinney Company, 58
Guy Degrenne, 182
Gymboree, 211

**H**

H&M, 204, *206, 207*, 210
H&R Block, 34
Hamburger University, *265*
Hangzhou Wahaha Group, *142*
Harley-Davidson, 167, 332
Hartwell's Office World, *420*
Hasbro, *436, 437*
Hasbrouck, 428, *429, 441*
H. E. Butt, *199*
Herald Company, *421*
Herbalife, 218
Hewlett-Packard, *66*, 71, 102, 322, 385, *449*
Home Depot, 204
    customer coverage policies, 416
    customer service, 212
    sales, general, and administrative (SG&A)
        expenses, *213*
    solutions retailing, 65
    as top retailer, *195*
Home Shopping Network, 63, 440
Honda, 133
Hot Topic, 69
Hudson News Co., 426, 445n43
Hypermarket USA, 58

**I**

IBM, 56, 129, 296, 300
IKEA, *197*
Image Technical Service, Inc., *435*, 446n74
Inditex, *199, 455*
Ingersoll-Rand International
        Bobcat, 42
Intel, 296
Intercore Resources, Inc., 248
Intermarché, *149*

**J**

Janie and Jack, 211
J. C. Penney, 34, 57, 69, *199*, 212, *213*, 224
J. E. Ekornes, 169
J. M. Jones Co., 224
John Deere, 315, 436
John Lewis, *202*
Johanson, 159, 160, 171, 172
John D. Park & Sons Co., 419

J. Sainsbury, *197*
Jupiter, 137, 138, 139

**K**

Kenco, 134
Kenmore and Craftsman [Sears], 224
Kentucky Fried Chicken (KFC), 57, 289
Kesko, *203*
Kingfisher, *200*
Kinney Shoes, 58
Kmart, 58, 224, 417
    designer-exclusive program, 224
    gross margin per full-time equivalent employee
        (GMROL), 208
    net dependence and, 338, *224–125*
    size of, *201*
Kodak, 434, *435*
Kohl's, 69, *199, 213*
Kraft Foodservice, 56
Krispy Kreme, 286
Kroger, 194, *195*, 221, 224, 425

**L**

Land O'Lakes, 251
Lands' End, *94*
    cost and service output demands, 313
    cost and reverse logistics,*93, 94*
    mail order/catalog channel, 57, *214*
Legend, 133
Levi Strauss, 40, 56
Liggett & Myers, 423, *424*
Limited, 58, *213*
Limited Brands, *203*
Little Tikes, *437*
Loblaw, 141, *198*, 224, *225*
Lotte, *202*
Louis Delhaize, *200*
Louis Vuitton Moet Hennessey (LVMH), 173, 174
Lowe's
    customer service, 212
    sales, general, and administrative (SG&A)
        expenses, *213*
    size of, *200*
Luxottica, 148

**M**

M&M/Mars, 183
Macy's, *198*
Magnavox, *414*
Manoukian, *130*
Market Day, 62
Marks & Spencer, *199*, 225, 226
Mars, 183

Martha Stewart [Kmart], 224
Mary Kay, 218, 229n15
Masthead Broker Association, 254
Mattel, 56, 162, 183, 184, *436, 437*
May Merchandising, 61
McCormick Harvesting Machine Company, 263
McDonald's, 57, 434
   countries, *198*
   criticisms of, *266*
   franchise operations, *265–66,* 267, 272, 279, 284, 285, 287, 288
   sales, *198*
McKesson Corp., *91*
Medco Containment Services, 439
Media Center PCs, 71
Meijer, *199*
Mercadona, *198*
Mercedes-Benz, 34, 167
Merck, 439
Mervins, 57
Metro, *195, 202*
Michaels Craft Stores, Inc., 208
Microsoft, 71
Migros Genossenschaft, *198*
Dr. Miles Medical Co., 419
Millennium Development Goal, *252*
Miller Beer, 338
Misr el Kheir Foundation, *253*
Mitsukoshi, *200*, 332
Monsanto, 238, *419,* 420
Montgomery Ward, 224
Moore Business Forms, 63
Multibar Foods, Inc., 34
Musicland Group, 58
MWEB, *384*

**N**
NAPA, 224
Nashville Coal Co., 430, *431*
Neiman Marcus, 220, 305
Nestlé USA, 221
Nike, 357
Nordstrom, 212, *213*
NuSkin, 61

**O**
Ocean Spray, 251
Office Depot, 35, 194
Office Max, 58
Okuma, 249
Old Mutual, 254
Omega, 400, 401, 403, 407

Optic, *328*
Orbitz, 136
Otra N.V., 249
Otto Versand, *201*

**P**
Pace, 57
Pao de Azucar, 226
PCS Health Systems, 439
Philip Morris, *396*
Pizza Hut, 272
Price Club, 57, *436*
Price/Costco, 36, 57, 204, 209, 211, 212, *213,* 226, *436, 437*
Printemps, 174
Procter & Gamble, 38
   cooperatives (co-ops), *354*
   efficient consumer response (ECR) and, 370
   strategic alliances, 386, 387
Publix, 57

**Q**
Quaker Oats Co., 34
QVC, 439, 440

**R**
Ralph Lauren, 162, 332
RCA, *414*
RCI, 238
Revlon, 56
Rewe, *196*
R. H. Macy & Co., *198*
R. J. Reynolds, *424*
R. R. Donnelly, 59

**S**
SABMiller Brewing, 339
Safeway (UK), 57
Safeway, Inc. (USA), *197*
Sainsbury, *197*
Saks Fifth Avenue, 326
Sam's Club, 36, 57, 204, 209, *214, 436*
Samsung, *332, 333*
Sandoz Pharmaceuticals Corp., 434
Schwarz Group, *195*
Sealy, 178
Sears, *211*
   brand name identity program, 224
   brand selection expansion, 224
   net dependence and, *224–125*

hybrid shopping, 215
  size of, *200*
  waiting and delivery time, 210–111
ServiceMaster, 59
7-Eleven, 58, *214*
Shaklee, 61
Sharp, *328*
Sheraton hotels, 434
Snap-On Tools, 60
Sony, 34
  brand equity, 287
  sales to women, 182
Souq.com, 309, *310*
Spicer Division of Dana Corporation, 43
Spiegel, 57
Spray-Rite Service Corporation, *419*
Staples, *200*
Starbucks, 274, 275, 287
State Farm, 34
State Oil Co., 420, *421*
Sunkist, 251
Super Kmart Centers, 58
Super Valu Stores Inc., 224
SuperTarget, 210
SuperValu, *197*
Swatch, 182
Sylvania, *414, 415
Syms, 417

**T**

Tampa Electric Co., 430, *431*
Target, 211
  celebrity-endorsed lines, 224
  as mass merchandiser, 58
  product variety of, 69
  return policy, *90*
  sales, general, and administrative (SG&A)
    expenses, *213*
  size of, 194, *195, 203*
  supercenter format, 210, 221
  as third-party retailer, 40
TCI, 439, 440
Tesco, 304, 307, 308
Tetra Pak, 434
Texaco Inc., 428
3M, 178
The Gap, 34, 58, 116, *206, 212, 213,* 224, 454
Tiffany's, 50, 226
TJX Cos., 198
TMI, 258
Topco, 61
Tower Records, 300

Toyota, 358
Toys "R" Us, 58
Trader Joe's, 185, 224
Travelocity, 136
True-Value, 224
Tru-Test [Cotter & Co.], 224
Tupperware, 60, 179, *180,* 192n46, 218
Tweeter, 211, 215

**U**

Uniglo, 274
Union Carbide Corporation, 435
United States Tobacco Company (USTC), 432
Uny, *201*
U.S. Direct Selling Organization, 216
USF Processors, Inc., *91*

**V**

VARs, 60, 77n2, *114,* 117n1, 182
VF Corporation, *206*
Victoria's Secret, 361
Vivendi Universal, 186
Volkswagen, 174
Volvo GM, 249
Volvo Trucks North America, Inc., 249
Vons, 425

**W**

Walgreens, 194, *195,* 210, 212, *213*
Wal-Mart, 38, 70, 258, 304, 452
  coercive power of, 325
  customer coverage policies, 416
  efficient consumer response (ECR) and,
    451, 452
  electronics returns policy, 179
  Equity Principle and, 100
  exclusive dealing, 430
  globalization of, 226
  gross margin per full-time equivalent employee
    (GMROL), 208
  low-margin/high-turnover/customer service,
    204
  as mass merchandiser, 58, 212, *214*
  music retailing, 106
  power retailing by, 258
  product variety of, 69
  quick delivery time, 210
  ratio of 2003 sales to global retail sales, 231
  retail apparel sales, 35
  sales, general, and administrative (SG&A)
    expenses, 212, *213*
  sales figures, 194, *195*
  strategic alliances, 386, 387

Wal-Mart (*Continued*)
  supercenter format, 221
  as third-party retailer, 40
  as wholesaler, *389*, 428
Walt Disney, 56
Warnaco, 162
Wesco, 244
Whirlpool, 134
White Hen Pantry, 58
Williams Sonoma, 63
Wm. Morrison, *198*
Woolworths, *196*
World's Finest Chocolate, 62
W. W. Grainger, *94*

**X**
Xerox, *449*
**Y**
Yamada Denki, *198*
Yoki Alimentos, *142*
Yoplait, 141, *142*, *143*
**Z**
Zannier, 285
zappos.com, 313
Zara, 204, *205–106*, *207*,
  454, *455–56*
Zenith, *414*